A History of Advertising

A History of Advertising

The First 300,000 Years

JEF I. RICHARDS

ROWMAN & LITTLEFIELD
Lanham • Boulder • New York • London

In memory of the most remarkable person I've ever known:
my father, James I. Richards.

Published by Rowman & Littlefield
An imprint of The Rowman & Littlefield Publishing Group, Inc.
4501 Forbes Boulevard, Suite 200, Lanham, Maryland 20706
www.rowman.com

86-90 Paul Street, London EC2A 4NE

British Library Cataloguing in Publication Information Available

Library of Congress Cataloging-in-Publication Data

Names: Richards, Jef I., author.
Title: A history of advertising : the first 300,000 years / Jef I.
  Richards.
Description: Lanham : Rowman & Littlefield, [2022] | Includes
  bibliographical references and index. | Summary: "This full-color book
  offers a sweeping history of advertising. It places developments in the
  advertising and marketing industries within a framework of major
  cultural events to help readers understand the conditions under which
  advertising developed. Timelines of historical and advertising industry
  events begin each chronological section"— Provided by publisher.
Identifiers: LCCN 2021038849 (print) | LCCN 2021038850 (ebook) | ISBN
  9781538141212 (cloth ; alk. paper) | ISBN 9781538141229 (epub)
Subjects: LCSH: Advertising—History.
Classification: LCC HF5811 .R53 2022 (print) | LCC HF5811 (ebook) | DDC
  659.1—dc23
LC record available at https://lccn.loc.gov/2021038849
LC ebook record available at https://lccn.loc.gov/2021038850

♾️™ The paper used in this publication meets the minimum requirements of
American National Standard for Information Sciences—Permanence of Paper
for Printed Library Materials, ANSI/NISO Z39.48-1992.

Contents

Introduction

This is a history, though probably one most historians won't like. They, properly, want to paint a picture that allows the reader to slip into a time and experience it. My purpose is different.

I've taught advertising for decades, and I was bothered by how little advertising practitioners know about their profession's past. Advertising professors don't always know that much, either. When I talk about history in class, I get teaching evaluations suggesting that I'm stuck in the past, talking about things irrelevant to today's environment. I beg to differ! The irony is that when I was young, I hated studying history. Like my students, I saw no relevance. But as I edge closer and closer to becoming history, I can't get enough of it.

Edmund Burke, a member of the British Parliament in the eighteenth century, is remembered as saying, "Those who don't know history are destined to repeat it." This statement warns us against forgetting a lesson already learned. But history offers even more. We might gain insights that allow us to learn something entirely new—for example, historical trends giving us predictive visions. Or we might grasp realities only visible from a distance. We also can find humor, or entertainment of other sorts, or even the beauty of art through the lens of history. But most of all, I think we bear a responsibility to recognize and honor the many people on whose shoulders we stand. We do, of course, hope that those after us will appreciate *our* contributions. Not since Adam, though, can anyone truly lay claim entirely to their own success.

Most advertising history books focus on some narrow time period, or they explore only a narrow range of activity within the profession. My purpose is to provide a forty-thousand-foot view, covering more topics than most of the history books, but to control size, those topics will not be exhaustively described. Frankly, most books state facts without reference to where those facts were gathered. And some of those facts are of questionable validity! There is little worse than learning historical facts only to spout those facts to someone who points out their fallacy. I try to provide photos to substantiate many of the facts, and citations for others. Anything I get wrong, you should be able to figure out where I screwed up! I think you will find several differences between this advertising history and others.

Think of this volume as a "portable museum of advertising." You walk through a museum, see an artifact, and read a card describing it. That's the approach here. Flip through the pages, look at the artifacts, and read the surrounding text. It is organized by topics in rough chronological order. The timing necessarily overlaps, but rest assured that what happened in the third chapter is almost entirely prior to content from the seventh chapter. Almost. You can read this book from front to back, but because it is arranged by topic, you also have the option of just reading a topic that grabs your fancy. Most are mercifully short. Ideally you'll find this a little more reader-friendly than the average history book. Or you can think of it as a reference book.

Many advertising histories talk incessantly about people—how they looked, how they dressed, and what they said. People are important, but they are covered well elsewhere, so I see no need to repeat them. I do name several people and their major contributions, but you can read those other books for more details. Here you will find more detail on technologies and media used to reach audiences across time. If you have read another history of advertising, hopefully this book will provide a different perspective.

I tried hard to document sources, to avoid mistakes, but I'm human. There *will* be errors, and I've undoubtedly missed some facts that some may believe are gross oversights. What I consider important is not everyone's opinion. I hope, though, that the holes are small.

ANCIENT TIMES THROUGH THE DARK AGES

GENERAL HISTORY	ADVERTISING HISTORY
65,000,000 BCE Dinosaur extinction	
2,500,000 BCE Beginning of Old Stone Age	
1,900,000 BCE Peking Man (*Homo erectus*)	
400,000 BCE Neanderthals begin	
300,000 BCE *Homo sapiens* (modern humans) begin	
70,000 BCE *Homo erectus* extinction	
58,000 BCE Ostrich eggshell fragments with marks	
38,800 BCE Earliest cave paintings	
30,000 BCE Neanderthals die out	
18,000 BCE Clay pottery first produced	
	15,000 BCE Possible bison branding (France)
10,000 BCE Old Stone Age ends; Middle Stone Age begins	
6000 BCE New Stone Age starts	

GENERAL HISTORY

5800 BCE
Noah's Great Flood

4000 BCE
Glass, door lock, and eye makeup are invented

3500 BCE
Wheel and plow invented

3400 BCE
Nail invented (bronze)

3200 BCE
Cuneiform and hieroglyphic writing invented

3100 BCE
Narmer becomes the first pharaoh of Egypt

3000 BCE
Stone Age ends; Bronze Age begins

2700 BCE
Silk invented

2600 BCE
Papyrus invented

2560 BCE
Great Pyramid of Giza completed

2532 BCE
The Great Sphinx is completed

1806 BCE
Sobekneferu becomes first queen
to serve as pharaoh of Egypt

1754 BCE
Code of Hammurabi

1600 BCE
Modern alphabet invented

1573 BCE
Jericho destroyed

1523 BCE
Ahmose I unifies Upper and Lower Egypt

1500 BCE
Moses ascends Mount Sinai

ADVERTISING HISTORY

Potters' marks are the potters' brand

Egyptian stelae promote government messages

Hanging tag on a bottle of oil

Cattle branding (Egypt)

2615 BCE
Pharaoh Huni's cartouche is his logo

Earliest evidence of deceptive sales practices

1700 BCE
Indus Valley seals used as trademarks*

GENERAL HISTORY

ADVERTISING HISTORY

1450 BCE
Dholavira sign*

1353 BCE
Nefertiti becomes queen of Egypt

1333 BCE
Tutankhamun rules Egypt

1300 BCE
Approximate start of the Trojan War

1274 BCE
Battle of Kadesh (history's largest chariot battle)

1152 BCE
Workers' strike during Ramses III
necropolis construction

Ramses III's mortuary temple is
one-thousand-foot billboard

1000 BCE
The compass invented in China

800 BCE
End of Bronze Age; start of Iron Age

800 BCE
Homer writes *The Illiad* and *The Odyssey*

776 BCE
First Olympic Games

750 BCE
Shop signs (Rome)

750 BCE
Sonic logos

735 BCE
Sewers invented

660 BCE
Japan founded

600 BCE
First coins struck

563 BCE
Gautama Buddha born

551 BCE
Confucius (Kong Qiu) is born

520 BCE
Vase with "Buy me and you'll get a bargain"
on it

509 BCE
Roman Republic begins

GENERAL HISTORY

ADVERTISING HISTORY

500 BCE
Yo-yo invented

Egyptian tablets along roadways

Stamped bricks

Town criers (Carthage)

483 BCE
Gautama Buddha dies

479 BCE
Confucius dies

470 BCE
Socrates born

430 BCE
Plague of Athens kills as many as one hundred thousand

427 BCE
Plato born

399 BCE
Socrates swallows hemlock

384 BCE
Aristotle born

347 BCE
Plato dies

332 BCE
Alexander the Great conquers Egypt

322 BCE
Aristotle dies of indigestion

250 BCE
First known electric battery

Wine banners (China)

214 BCE
Great Wall of China construction begins

196 BCE
Rosetta Stone created

174 BCE
Circus Maximus seats 150,000 spectators

150 BCE
Parchment invented

131 BCE
Newspaper invented (Romans)

100 BCE
Concrete invented

GENERAL HISTORY **ADVERTISING HISTORY**

100 BCE
Julius Caesar born

73 BCE
Spartacus leads Roman revolt

51 BCE
Cleopatra VII becomes ruler of Egypt

45 BCE
Town criers in Heraclea (Italy)

44 BCE
Julius Caesar assassinated by
several Roman senators

30 BCE
Cleopatra VII, the final Egyptian pharaoh, dies

27 BCE
Roman Empire established by Augustus Caesar

4 BCE
Jesus Christ born

1 CE
First bound books

29 CE
Jesus Christ crucified

41 CE
Roman Emperor Caligula is assassinated by his
guards

42 CE
Christian Church founded by St. Peter

64 CE
Great Fire of Rome (as Nero fiddles?) Brothel sign in Ephesus (Turkey)

79 CE
Mount Vesuvius buries Pompeii Political and other signs in Pompeii
and Herculaneum (Italy) and Herculaneum

First true advertising professionals: wall painters

80 CE
Roman Colosseum opens,
seating seventy thousand

105 CE
First modern paper produced

125 CE
Hanging gourds are doctors' signs (China)

140 CE
Chariot racing team signs (Roman Empire)

GENERAL HISTORY   ADVERTISING HISTORY

165 CE
Antonine Plague kills over
five million in the Roman Empire

230 CE
First known ruler of Japan is Emperor Sujin

336 CE
First Christ's Mass (to become Christmas)

410 CE
Fall of Rome

476 CE
Fall of Western Roman Empire

496 CE
St. Valentine's Day begins on February 14

536 CE
Dust storms cause an eighteen-
month winter in Europe

541 CE
Bubonic plague of Justinian kills
10 percent of world population

565 CE
Loch Ness Monster first sighted

571 CE
Mohammad born

600 CE
Pope Gregory begins "God bless you"
as response to sneeze

632 CE
Mohammad dies from Medinan fever

861 CE
Vikings discover Iceland

925 CE
First coat of arms, a family logo

960 CE
Deceptive tea naming (China)

982 CE
Greenland deceptively named

1057 CE
Lady Godiva rides nude through Coventry

1066 CE
Norman Conquest of England   Occupational surnames begin
by William the Conqueror   Town criers in England

GENERAL HISTORY

ADVERTISING HISTORY

1086 CE
Domesday Survey

1088 CE
First university established in Bologna, Italy

1095 CE
Beginning of the Crusades (lasted until 1291)

1178 CE
Tower of Pisa begins to lean

Free wine samples by town criers

1200 CE
Earliest known advertising character

1206 CE
Genghis Khan begins conquest of Asia

1215 CE
Magna Carta signed

1247 CE
Robin Hood died (maybe)

1250 CE
Streets are first given names

1258 CE
Town criers allowed to "cry the wine" (France)

1266 CE
Bakers Marking Law (England)

1280 CE
Gunpowder invented by Roger Bacon

1294 CE
Pope Celestine V abdicates

*may be older

1

Advertising Archaeology

Where to Begin?

Now the serpent was more crafty than any other beast of the field that the Lord God had made. He said to the woman, "Did God actually say, 'You shall not eat of any tree in the garden'?" And the woman said to the serpent, "We may eat of the fruit of the trees in the garden, but God said, 'You shall not eat of the fruit of the tree that is in the midst of the garden, neither shall you touch it, lest you die.'" But the serpent said to the woman, "You will not surely die. For God knows that when you eat of it your eyes will be opened, and you will be like God, knowing good and evil."

—*Holy Bible, English Standard Version, Genesis 3:1–5*

If we assumed this biblical account were literally and historically accurate, I might start this book arguing that the serpent was the first advertiser, and this was the very first instance of deceptive advertising. Setting aside that some people would challenge this description's historical accuracy, others likely would argue that it isn't advertising—it's direct selling! Or perhaps it's public relations. Does that really make a difference? Of course, if the serpent was the first adman, that makes me a professional descendant of the serpent.

To tell the story of the history of anything, we must start by describing the boundaries of that thing. So how is "advertising" defined? While everyone seems to know what you mean when you say "advertising," there is no agreed-upon definition. Richards & Curran (2002) used a panel of experts to compose a definition:

> Advertising is a paid, mediated form of communication from an identifiable source, designed to persuade the receiver to take some action, now or in the future.

But that definition hasn't been universally adopted.

Advertising is constantly changing. The definition above already is outmoded because of those changes. Kerr & Richards (2020), using a similar method, propose a slightly different definition.

While we need to define the "thing" for which this history applies, it is an exercise in folly to apply a definition that changes so quickly. We could use this year's definition, or last year's, or from one thousand years ago, with none being more legitimate than the others.

Also, events that fall outside a current definition might still be important. An author writing a history of medicine might be reluctant to talk of leeches as a legitimate part of "medicine," but medical practitioners in the past did use leeches, and it affected that field.

Therefore, it makes sense not to define advertising narrowly, but rather to mow a broader path that sweeps in practices that affect where advertising is now. The definition I use here is simple:

> An advertisement is any communication with the intent and/or effect of promoting a product, service, idea/concept, brand, or other entity (real or imagined).

I'm defining ads as simply "promotional communication." And "promoting" is another way of saying "persuading" because, let's face it, advertising is about persuasion. As I think of it, the serpent in that Bible story did one heck of a job persuading Eve.

There are several subtle, yet important, assumptions underlying this definition. A couple of them are especially worth mentioning. First, if someone intends it to be an ad, it is an ad regardless of whether it works or is even used. Second, something can be an ad even if it was not intended to be one. A Picasso signature on a painting certainly promotes that painting, despite it just being his name. Third, while we think of an advertisement as appearing in a medium of some type (e.g., television or newspaper), that's not required. One person talking to another can be advertising. Finally, advertising generally is considered a positive message about the product, service, and so on, but it also can be negative, such as when an ad spokesperson gets into legal trouble, changing the meaning of the ad.

An early book on direct advertising (Anonymous 1914) says this:

> [S]trictly speaking, any method used to attract the public or a section of it for the user's own purpose is advertising. Robinson Crusoe used an advertisement when he wanted a ship—he put a shirt on a pole. The butcher or fishmonger who stands outside his shop and shouts, "Buy, buy, buy!" or "Fine fresh fish!" is advertising.

I agree with that statement, and that is how I am approaching this challenging task.

I also use the terms "branding" or "brand," because branding and brand identity are core objectives of advertising. It is nearly impossible to disentangle the concepts, and there's no need for us to pull them apart. Simply, branding is establishing a specific personality for a product or service in people's minds. Advertising generally is the tool of choice to do that. So if you think Cadillac is "high quality," that's part of the brand's image. If you think it is "prestigious," that's another part. So a brand is whatever consumers think it is, often—at least in part—thanks to advertising.

In addition to all that, because the surrounding culture helps us understand why something happens, I will try to note some external events leading to advertising developments, as well as some sociocultural occurrences that temporally coincide with those developments. The remainder of this chapter will be dedicated to presenting a series of possible starting points for this history, beyond the serpent, and I'll leave it up to you to decide where the story begins.

PRIMORDIAL SOUP, UNDERGROUND ART, AND UNCERTAINTY

For around 170 million years, dinosaurs ruled the planet, ending around 65 million years ago. I think it's safe to ignore their contributions to this field. They weren't big communicators. So advertising, in that grand scheme of things, is relatively new.

The earliest fossils of man's ancestor (*Homo erectus*) were discovered in Africa, from around 1.9 million years ago, 63 million years after dinosaurs died. The Neanderthal entered around 400,000 years ago. Then modern man (*Homo sapiens*) arrived around 100,000 years later (Dvorsky 2018). So advertising couldn't be more than about 300,000 years old[1] (unless we include the serpent's salesmanship to Eve).

OF EGGS AND CAVES

The earliest evidence of recorded communication dates back sixty thousand years. Some 270 ostrich egg shell fragments were discovered in 1997, in Diepkloof, South Africa, that were intentionally marked by someone (Texier et al. 2010). The marks seemed to be a system of symbolic representation (i.e., written communication), and the shells appeared to serve as cups or bottles for liquid (Figure 1.1).[2] A limited number of symbols were used, and their meaning is unknown. Di Palma (2015) suggests the marks might denote ownership, making them precursors of trademarks that advertise their owner. At this time, though, we don't know the marks' purpose.

FIGURE 1.1.   A sixty-thousand-year-old ostrich egg discovered in the Diepkloof Rock Shelter shows intentional marking.
COURTESY OF PIERRE-JEAN TEXIER

Another early recorded form of communication dates to at least 40,800 years ago (Amos 2012). It was just a red disk shape (one of several) painted inside a cave in Spain. We don't know whether it was painted by humans or Neanderthals. The cave has more than one hundred images, including stencils of hands, but the disk appears to be the oldest. Was this an advertisement? Probably not, but without knowing its purpose or effect we can't say for certain. If that red disk was painted to say, for example, "Brunhilde was here," then it was promoting Brunhilde's brand image within cave man (and cave woman) circles, putting it within advertising's domain.

Another cave in Spain has charcoal and painted images dating back about 35,500 years (Pike et al. 2012), and one in France has some going back about 32,000 years (Hammer 2015), but we can't know whether they were advertising. Available evidence, then, tells us that advertising is something less than 41,000 years old, and perhaps quite a bit less, but there is at least a possibility some bit of caveman artistry was the work of an early advertising art director.

Recently, in a South African cave, a tiny flake of stone about the size of two thumbnails was discovered with six near-parallel straight lines on it, crossed by three slightly curved lines, all in red ocher (Henshilwood et al. 2018). This may be an even earlier, seventy-three-thousand-year-old drawing by *Homo sapiens*. For all we know, maybe it was a tiny piece of an ad by Brunhilde's great-great-great- . . . grandmother!

As one historian of signs observes:

> The history of Signs dates back to the earliest forms of "Picture Writing" and hieroglyphics of the Egyptians and that of their contemporary primitive neighbors, who left posterity records of their living and habits on tablets of clay and stone. Signs or symbols used by them were developed from "Picture Writing" found in caves of Paleolithic times and formed the basis of written alphabets which now serve our modern requirements. (Wagner 1954)

But when he wrote that, we still were blissfully ignorant of the power of ostrich eggs.

BUFFALO BUTTS

While some suggest that ancient cave paintings in Lascaux, France, depicting marks on the flanks of bison, the earliest examples of owners branding livestock (e.g., Montgomery 2014), date back seventeen thousand years, others place the date at closer to seven thousand years ago (e.g., Rivkin & Sutherland 2004; O'Connor 2012). And again, the meaning of those marks is no more than a guess.

Seen through the lens of modernity, it makes sense that marking an animal was staking an ownership claim. Our concept of "branding" comes from using a hot branding iron to mark cattle as a rancher's property, but that doesn't mean this was the practice in antiquity. The cave artist might have been depicting the animal's injuries, or maybe the marks were mistakes and erasers hadn't yet been invented. Or maybe they were indicators of magic, aimed at giving the hunter dominion over the animals (Villeneuve 2008). The guess about branding might be off the mark. Much later, Wheeler (1946, p. 84) claims that by 2,700 BCE ("Before Common Era" means the same thing as BC), cattle branding appeared in Egypt as a mark of ownership.

FUNERALS AS ADVERTISING

Funerals have been around for a long time, as have the rituals accompanying them. Exploration of an Italian cave found evidence of such rituals from 5500 to 5200 BCE. It included scraping the flesh off dead peoples' bones. Not exactly pleasant. So what does this have to do with advertising? In an article describing that discovery, authors make this declaration:

> [D]eath rituals can be about many things: advertising the status of the deceased, forging political relations, fending off the vengeful dead, and many other social tasks. A fundamental job, however, is to accomplish the social act of dying—to transform someone from a living being with one set of capabilities and social relations into a new entity with a new kind of existence, be it an active, socially present spirit or only a well-observed memory. (Robb et al. 2015)

Though most people wouldn't think of funerals as advertising, these archaeologists make a good point. Today we embalm rather than scrape, but we continue to have ritual and ceremony around someone's passing. The reasons are multiple, but one is to actively communicate—to promote—the end of life. Today we might call this public relations, but as you will see below, there are rituals associated with funerals that do seem advertising-like.

ADVERTISING POT—THE EARLY YEARS

Around 5000–4000 BCE, pottery in the Near East began including "potters' marks." The earliest were very simple lines, triangles, and so forth. Were these marks a form of promotion? As professor of Ancient Near Eastern Archaeology at New York University, Daniel Thomas Potts (2018) states, "A big question is their function." He believes these early pots and vases were for personal use, not for sale. Yes, that's really his name.

In an earlier piece Potts (1981) states, "The hand-made vessels, perhaps manufactured at home by individuals for their families, may have been fired in communal kilns, of which we have no evidence, and thus required some kind of distinguishing mark so that families could retrieve their own vessels from the kiln after firing, being sure that they had in their possession the pot or pots which they had in fact themselves made." In a village with just one kiln, a potter might need a unique mark on his pots just to be sure his aren't confused with someone else's. Potts goes on to say, "Another obvious alternative would be that the signs represent not owner's or maker's marks, but rather goods which might be contained in the fired pot, but this alternative is, I think, less likely than the one just discussed."

Ahmed (2014), talking about more recent marks, around 3600–2500 BCE, has a similar take:

> These "potter marks" may have been trademarks, or signs of personal prosperity, or they may have indicated place or person of manufacture. Perhaps they even have had an amuletic value. The marks may also have constituted a purely functional device for assigning a particular pot or group of vessels to their place inside the pottery kiln, thereby acting as a sure identification of the owner of that particular pottery.

He concedes a possible advertising-type purpose, but, like Potts, he sees other possibilities. And, as with the cave drawings, one option includes magic.

Potts is more confident that the early marks were related in some way to ownership. When asked whether he thought these marks might represent a form of advertising or branding, Potts (2018) responded, "So, branding in the sense of cattle branding, to identify one's property, yes, probably, but not in the sense of a distinguishing mark which consumers in a market place could recognize." By this point in history, it seems, we are more closely approaching what we can comfortably declare to be some early form of advertising.

As time progressed, those marks more likely filled an advertising role. Di Palma (2015) says potters' marks might have started out as mere identification, then over time some potters came to barter with their neighbors, and the marks came to represent those potters' work in the marketplace. No matter their original purpose, potters' marks evolved into something more like an ad for the potter, as commerce in those societies developed.

The wheel was invented around 3500 BCE, which is in the time period Ahmed was discussing. The metal nail (bronze) was invented around 3400 BCE, and writing developed about 3200 BCE (cuneiform). The "New Stone Age" lasted until almost 3000 BCE, followed by the Bronze Age. So if Potts, Ahmed, and Di Palma are correct, advertising's roots may genuinely extend back to the Stone Age!

LABELING FOR THE RICH AND POWERFUL

Petrie (1900) reports discovery of an interesting item found in a royal tomb at Abydos, Egypt, dating to around 3000 BCE. Wengrow (2008) declares this particular item, a piece of wood about eight centimeters wide, was likely a label bearing some resemblance to a modern wine label. Its design was similar to a hang tag found on products today. The information on both the wooden tag and a modern wine label is fairly similar. An inscription, in hieroglyphics, describes apparent contents as a quantity of "finest oil of Tjehenu" (Figure 1.2), an area now a part of Libya.

FIGURE 1.2.   Drawing of the wood label referring to the "finest oil of Tjehenu" in the lower left corner (Wengrow 2008).

Wengrow argues that early hieroglyphic script was used to provide basic information like names, places, and so on, with no attention to niceties like grammar. On this item were the names of a king (Horus-Den) and an administrator (Hemaka). Those same names were impressed into clay stoppers for wine jars in the tomb. Both the wood piece and the clay stoppers appear to be product packaging with information easily construed as branding. This is the earliest and clearest example of promotional packaging/product labeling, fitting my operating definition of advertising.

STELE! STELE!!!

A stele (or stela) is a slab of wood or stone. It usually is taller than it is wide. These were common in ancient Egypt, and still are. Think tombstones. That was one common use of them in old Egypt. Stelae have been found dating to about 3100 BCE, carved with early hieroglyphs. Clearly, stelae were not for use by the average citizen. They generally represented announcements or dedications by government or religion, including funerals (Figure 1.3). An obelisk is a tall and tapered form of stele.

The question, then, is whether this fits our meaning of advertising. Is a pharaoh's decree, carved in stone, an ad published by the government? Is a grave marker an ad to promote the reputation—or at least the fact of having existed—of the deceased?

Is a modern carved stone declaring "Jesus Saves!" an advertisement? I would argue the answer is "yes." We see such signs, not usually in stone, but frequently as paid placements on billboards. This pretty clearly is intended to promote a religious idea, fitting my definition. It also is arguable that the answer to the other two questions is the same. These stelae from as far back as five thousand years ago might be advertisements.

FIGURE 1.3. This four thousand-year-old Egyptian stele makes reference to Pharaoh Montuhotep receiving offerings. He was considered divine, so offerings were brought to him. Was this an ad to reinforce that god-like image?

It makes sense that these rock or wood slabs served as ads. Stelae were the billboards of their time, used for one-way mass communication. They could be impressively large, though transportation of heavy rocks would have been problematic, and the fact that so many have been discovered is a testament to their longevity. Few ads today will last so long.

The Rosetta Stone was a stele, though created in 196 BCE (Figure 1.4). It is believed that the Stone was created to promote a series of royal decrees that, themselves, were to promote King Ptolemy V as a deity. It was, in part, about gaining the favor of the high priests during a time of political turmoil. It was a sales pitch, so we know that stelae were used, by then, as promotional tools.

This also raises the question of whether the pyramids and Sphinx of Egypt might likewise be ads. The Great Pyramid and Sphinx of Giza were completed around 2560 BCE. Starčević (2015) suggests these were powerful symbols as part of a pharaoh's brand. As he argues, "[A]ll the symbols, figures and reliefs were focused on creating the image of a ruler as a god, in order to achieve an impact on people." Call it "self-branding." Clearly these enormous structures promoted the pharaohs' lives, and later became part of "Brand Egypt." They certainly are ads for that country today.

FIGURE 1.4. The Rosetta Stone, now in the British Museum, could be seen as an advertisement, as it was created to promote King Ptolemy V.

WHAT'S IN A CARTOUCHE?

FIGURE 1.5. Two cartouches of Pharaoh Ramses II, who ruled from 1279 to 1213 BCE. This is roughly interpreted as "Amun's beloved Ramses." In this way, Ramses tied his reputation to Amun, one of Egypt's most powerful gods.

FIGURE 1.6. A cartouche (logo) of Pharaoh Thutmose III, who ruled Egypt from 1479 to 1425 BCE.

Around that same time, the cartouche (or "shenu") was born, continuing in use for over two millennia. A cartouche is an oval with a line at one end and hieroglyphs inside (Figures 1.5 and 1.6). A single cartouche can be found repeatedly throughout a tomb in the area of Thebes (Luxor), often measuring multiple feet in length. They can be either vertical or horizontal. The relevance is clear.

The first pharaoh to put his name into a cartouche was Huni, around 2615 BCE. Initially the cartouche was reserved for pharaohs, and glyphs inside spelled out that pharaoh's name. Later, high officials and others were permitted its use. It was a pharaoh's (or official's) "mark," like a trademark. In essence, the cartouche was a logo symbolizing its owner's power and character. It was a device used mostly on a tomb or sarcophagus, so it mainly promoted the pharaoh's (or whoever's) reputation after death.

In other words, these were ads used to secure a form of immortality. Indeed, the cartouche has been invaluable to Egyptologists for identifying tombs. That we know so much about those pharaohs and high officials thousands of years later is due, in large part, to the cartouche. Those ads made them immortal.

WHEN IS AN AD BORN?

A further complication to identifying the start of advertising is identifying the origin of a specific advertisement. Let me put it this way: Just because something is an ad and it's 4,500 years old, does that necessarily make it a 4,500-year-old ad?

The Sphinx and pyramids are part of Egypt's brand today. They've appeared on Egyptian

FIGURE 1.7. This sample of Egyptian currency illustrates how a 4,500-year-old man-made construction, the Sphinx, can be integral to a country's brand.

money (Figure 1.7). Even if you don't believe they're pharaoh advertising, at some point they absolutely became part of Egypt's advertising. I would argue that anything used to support, enhance, or extend a brand is *de facto* advertising. But did they become advertising when built or later, when they evolved into part of the country's brand? If the latter, was that when one person recognized it as part of the brand, or one hundred, or one thousand, or what? I suspect you can see the problem.

Though only a fraction as old as those pyramids, Machu Picchu was constructed around 1450 and is a major part of Peru's brand today. But it was a lost city until discovered in 1911. It is pretty certain the city was not constructed with any promotional aims, but, like those pyramids, at some point it became a symbol used extensively to promote tourism for a country. Part of the signature image of Machu Picchu is the city, and part is the mountains around it. So the next question becomes: Is it a five-hundred-plus-year-old ad, or a one-hundred-plus-year-old ad? Or, since the mountains are millions of years old, does that make this literally an ad "as old as the hills"?

SEALED WITH AN OX

Moore and Reid (2008) argue that all brands carry information about two aspects of the branded item: (1) quality, and (2) origin. They find evidence of branding in the ancient Harappan civilization of the Indus Valley, where northwest India meets Pakistan, during the Bronze Age.

Harappa was a center of trade and commerce. Moore and Reid state, "There are hundreds of square seals with animal figures, used as trademarks, found at Mohenjo-daro, Harappa, and Lothal." Ahmed (2014) says as many as four thousand still exist. The seals were used much like we would stamp melted wax onto an envelope to seal it a century ago. Seals generally were made of soapstone (Figure 1.8). Calling these trademarks, again, seems a jump to conclusions, but there is ample evidence the seals were used in trade, sealing jars and being stamped onto crates.

These seals typically depicted an animal with some accompanying text, but the language is still unknown, so we don't know what they say. Evidence suggests they indicate origin, and probably quality, fitting them within Moore and Reid's branding concept. Wolpert (2000) declares that the images and text were "probably made for merchants who used them to 'brand' their wares." These seals date from around 2300 to 1700 BCE, or about four thousand

FIGURE 1.8. Seals similar to this one—only about 1¼ by 1½ inches in size—have been discovered throughout the Indus Valley. A four-thousand-year-old ad?

years ago. What we know about them seems to point toward them being advertising.

A SIGN OF ADVERTISING

The Indus Valley appears to be a key location in advertising's history, or perhaps just an area where more of that history is preserved. In that area, between Ahmedabad, India, and Karachi, Pakistan, is the village of Dholavira. Just north of that village is a major archaeological site that was occupied around 2650–2100 BCE, abandoned, and then reoccupied until around 1450 BCE. Site excavation began in 1990 and has revealed much about the Harappan

FIGURE 1.9.   A reproduction of the Signboard of Dholavira. Do we need to know what this ten-foot sign says to call it an ad?

civilization. One discovery is important here: a signboard, about ten feet long and fourteen and a half inches tall.

The board was made of wood, which rotted away, but characters or "lettering" on the sign were made of gypsum, preserving them. Ten characters were on the sign (Figure 1.9). Again, the Harappan language has yet to be deciphered.

The sign's date would be 1450 BCE at the latest, but it seems older. It was found at a gate to the town. R. S. Bisht, who discovered the board in 1991, says, "It is believed that the stone signboard was hung on a wooden plank in front of the gate. This could be the oldest signboard known to us" (Sharma 2004). The fact that this was a large sign, publicly located, almost certainly makes it advertising. This would be so even if it were only the town name, just as we would likely consider the "Welcome to Las Vegas, Nevada" sign an ad for that city.

CODE OF HAMMURABI

Around 1754 BCE, King Hammurabi of Mesopotamia created a group of laws, now called the Code of Hammurabi. It's one of the oldest pieces of text of significant length yet to be translated, containing 282 rules for Mesopotamia's citizens to follow. It appears on a black stone stele. It's one of the oldest legal codes still in existence. Some of it was brutal, such as penalties requiring violators to lose hands or eyes, but parts were quite advanced, such as establishing a minimum wage law. One piece of it deserves special attention.

The Code's Article 265 says, "If a herdsman, to whose care cattle or sheep have been entrusted, be guilty of fraud and make false returns of the natural increase, or sell them for money, then shall he be convicted and pay the owner ten times the loss." So cattle thieves were not unknown. It turns out Mesopotamia marked animals with different colors, representing different owners, allowing for the rightful owner to be identified (Finet 1983; Blancou 2001). So while we are not certain whether cattle branding occurred in caveman times, we do know it was common in the eighteenth century BCE. It promoted (advertised) an owner's claim to the livestock.

DECEPTIVE MARKETING'S LONG ROOTS

A clay tablet from 1,750 BCE was discovered around ancient Babylon. Translated by Leo Oppenheim (1967), it is the oldest evidence we have (other than perhaps that biblical serpent) of deceptive sales practices. It was a consumer complaint about deception by a copper merchant. The consumer, Nanni, wrote this complaint to a merchant named Ea-nasir:

Tell Ea-nasir: Nanni sends the following message:

When you came, you said to me as follows: "I will give Gimil-Sin (when he comes) fine quality copper ingots." You left then but you did not do what you promised me. You put ingots which were not good before my messenger (Sit-Sin) and said: "If you want to take them, take them; if you do not want to take them, go away!"

What do you take me for, that you treat somebody like me with such contempt? I have sent as messengers gentlemen like ourselves to collect the bag with my money (deposited with you) but you have treated me with contempt by sending them back to me empty-handed several times, and that through enemy territory. Is there anyone among the merchants who trade with Telmun who has treated me in this way? You alone treat my messenger with contempt! On account of that one (trifling) mina of silver which I owe(?) you, you feel free to speak in such a way, while I have given to the palace on your behalf 1,080 pounds of copper, and umi-abum has likewise given 1,080 pounds of copper, apart from what we both have had written on a sealed tablet to be kept in the temple of Samas.

How have you treated me for that copper? You have withheld my money bag from me in enemy territory; it is now up to you to restore (my money) to me in full.

Take cognizance that (from now on) I will not accept here any copper from you that is not of fine quality. I shall (from now on) select and take the ingots individually in my own yard, and I shall exercise against you my right of rejection because you have treated me with contempt. (Oppenheim 1967, pp. 82–83)

This was written in clay, remaining legible for thirty-seven centuries. So imagine how much has been lost from that time. Yet here we have details of a commercial transaction gone awry. Ea-nasir's claim was, by today's standards, personal selling rather than advertising; it certainly was promotional communication. This seems to fit my advertising definition. Even if you can't accept that theory, this tablet suggests a remarkably well-developed system of commerce, so it requires no enormous leap of faith to believe that some advertising-like promotion existed at that time to connect a consumer and a merchant.

All of this was a couple of hundred years before Moses reportedly received the Ten Commandments (circa 1500 BCE). That, too, was written on a tablet. And it promoted certain rules. Perhaps that tablet was an ad from a higher advertiser.

A REPUTATION CARVED IN STONE

Ramses III ruled Egypt for about thirty-one years, dying in 1155 BCE. His mortuary was enormous. Its outer facing was described by *Popular Science* magazine (Anonymous 1935) as "a temple wall nearly a third of a mile long. . . . The 1,600-foot 'billboard' . . . used by Rameses III . . . to advertise his prowess in war." That was an exaggeration. Current estimates put it at only about one thousand feet, or closer to one fifth of a mile (Figure 1.10). It's still impressive and covered with a message.

FIGURE 1.10. The face of the Medinet Habu temple is one thousand feet wide and covered in hieroglyphs.

The inscriptions are described in some detail by Sales (2012). This is like the stelae and Sphinx mentioned earlier. Both promoted reputations after death. It most certainly was promotional, and if you think of this as a billboard, it is one of the largest ever constructed.

COINS AND FACES

Aside from stone, wood, and ceramics, metal was a medium before the current era (BCE). Metallurgy was born at least as far back as the Copper Age (4000–3000 BCE), but an important use of metals came much later: coins.

Part of Turkey once formed the Kingdom of Lydia, where coins first appeared around 600 BCE. They were made from electrum, a blend of gold and silver. Some were inscribed with names like Kalil and Walwet, though to whom those refer is unknown. When Lydia was conquered in 546 BCE, coins became a staple in Persia.

FIGURE 1.11. Alexander the Great drachm coin, circa 325 BCE, depicting the face of Heracles.

An early coin displayed a crouching lion, but they soon depicted gods and kings. For kings, clearly ego played a role in creating coins with their likeness. Antiochus IV ordered new coins with his image almost immediately after seizing the throne in 175 BCE (Lowinger 2017). The National Bank of Belgium's museum website[3] states, "In 305 BC, Ptolemy I of Egypt was the first to depict his own portrait on his currency, both as a legitimisation of his power and as a propaganda instrument."

Alexander the Great ruled Macedonia from 336 to 323 BCE. His coins continued to be used in trade for centuries (Figure 1.11). They tended to portray the demigod

Heracles or the goddess Athena, with the full figure of a god or goddess on the other side (Troxell 1997).

Was Alexander trying to create an association between himself and Heracles? It requires no stretch of the imagination to see these kings using the coinage to advertise their greatness. Coins allowed rulers to put their message in the pockets of nearly every citizen.

Augustus Caesar ruled in Rome from 27 BCE to 14 CE. Coins were minted throughout his reign, frequently depicting this ruler (e.g., Figure 1.12). That choice might have been decided by Augustus himself, but also might have been decided by some subordinate trying to make points with his superior. Wallace-Hadrill (1986) argues that such coinage very probably had a persuasive, rather than informative, intent. People already knew he captured Egypt, but coins were used to convince people that he kept evil at bay.

FIGURE 1.12. Augustus Caesar denar coin, minted 19 BCE.

Persuasion and symbolism connote advertising. If coins had only economic functions, there would be no need to change the images on them, ever. But throughout history almost every new ruler was followed by new coins with new imagery. Unlike most forms of currency, coins have longevity, which is why I can show them to you.

Society moved from the Bronze Age to the Iron Age around 800 BCE. Iron was used to make tools, but most coins were made of other metals, though iron was used to cast coins in Sparta, Greece, during the fifth century BCE.

WHERE IN THE WORLD IS SHEM?

In the time periods discussed so far, there was no such thing as paper. However, papyrus was a writing medium from about 2600 BCE, so it makes sense some evidence of advertising using that medium should exist. One papyrus has been mentioned in previous histories as perhaps the earliest advertisement:

> The man-slave, Shem, having run away from his good master, Hapu the Weaver, all good citizens of Thebes are enjoyed to help return him. He is Hittite, 5.2 tall, of ruddy complexion and brown eyes. For news of his whereabouts, half a gold coin is offered. And for his return to the shop of Hapu the Weaver, where the best cloth is woven to your desires, a whole gold coin is offered. (Wood 1958)

James Playsted Wood reports that text as being found on a three-thousand-year-old papyrus in the ruins of Thebes. Though they might have relied on Wood, many other sources repeat that claim (Foster 1967, p. 23; Mogel 1993, p. 4; Barrés-Baker 2006, p. 6; Dynel 2011, p. 356, etc.), but a less specific mention can be found as far back as Sampson (1874, p. 34).

Schuwer (1966, p. 9) presents it as dating to 3000 BCE, which would make it far older. This would be an issue if there weren't an even bigger problem: this papyrus might not exist.

Most accounts point to the British Museum as its location. Dr. Adrienn Almásy, curator in that institution's Department of Ancient Egypt and Sudan, finds no evidence that it ever was in that collection.[4] In addition, Dr. Almásy notes that 3000 BCE is impossible, since the oldest papyrus ever discovered isn't that old. Also, the Hittite Empire, where it supposedly originated, flourished only between 1600 and 1150 BCE. And a photo that has been shown as being the papyrus has Greek text on it, meaning 300 BCE is about the earliest date possible, and Greek text would not mention a Hittite. She is not convinced it ever existed. This might be a case of one author copying another who then is copied by another. It is too bad, since this would have been a very clear example of advertising.

TABLET FOLLIES

Another story that seems to merit debunking, for now, suggests a discovered ancient Babylonian clay tablet, circa 3000 BCE, was an ad for an ointment dealer, a scribe, and a shoemaker. Presbrey (1929) tells this story in his otherwise wonderful advertising history. The story was repeated many times (e.g., Trout 2008; Kazmi & Batra 2009; Lasker & Worstell 2014). But, like Shem's papyrus, this clay tablet might not exist.

Admittedly, the story of this tablet is less specific, making it harder to trace. Such a clay tablet, given that age and location, almost certainly would have been written with cuneiform, a writing system developed by the Sumerians. And many cuneiform samples have been preserved. The British Museum alone has 130,000-plus samples, and many other museums hold large collections. Even several university museums hold tens of thousands. So if this tablet exists, it simply may be the proverbial needle in a haystack or, more accurately, clay stack.

A POTPOURRI OF OTHERS

There are several other mentions of promotions that probably deserve comment as contenders for some of the earliest advertising. For example, in 753 BCE Rome there apparently was a large marketplace or bazaar full of *tabernae* (shops), with shop signs (Bourbon 2004). Around this same time in ancient Greece, by some accounts, some *pornnai* (prostitutes) wore sandals that left the advertising message "Follow Me" (ΑΚΟΛΟΥΘΕΙ AKOLOUTHEI) in the dirt as they walked through the city (Chrystal 2016).

There are more that are difficult to substantiate, like the claim that some prostitutes around 750 BCE hammered nails into their shoe soles to create a distinctive sound—a "sonic logo"—promoting their services. And supposedly Egyptians around 500 BCE put tablets alongside roadways offering goods for sale. The first road signs! In the Roman Empire, some say (Bouchoux 2009), there were bricks that had a "trademark" of sorts stamped on them. But it turns out that the earliest stamped bricks were in Egypt, and have been found dating only to the fourth century BCE (Bodel 1983). Any of these might be early ancestors of the ad profession.

THERE'S NO PROFIT IN THIS

As you can see, there are many possible starting points for advertising history, depending what we decide is sufficiently advertising-like. It would help if we knew more about the purposes and effects of those communications at the time of their use, and perhaps someday we will know more thanks to the work of archaeologists, anthropologists, and others. But we do know enough to safely conclude that some or even most of these are, at a minimum, precursors or foundations of today's advertising field.

To most people, the word "advertising" is about making money. It is worth noting that few of the artifacts above are about monetary profit, except those related to prostitution. This might be one reason why it is difficult to point at one and say, "This is where advertising began." Focus on profit, though, ignores many reasons for advertising, like drawing attention to an event, building a reputation, informing the public about some new development, and so forth. The many uses for advertising are why there is so much ambiguity regarding its genesis.

FIGURE 1.13.   Dave Coverly's cartoon makes the point, cleverly, that as much as we might like to think we are so much more advanced than cultures of four or five thousand years ago, perhaps the differences are less immense than we'd like to believe.
REPRINTED WITH PERMISSION

Nor should we forget that many ad media might not have withstood the passage of time. Papyrus and silk were invented around 3000–2600 BCE and used for writing and art, but most have since become dust.

In the next chapter, there still will be communicative uncertainties. However, as you will see, there are also a few more certainties regarding historical artifacts that fit even a modern concept of advertising.

From Late BCE to Early CE

L et me make a brief statement about terminology. Just as BCE means "Before Common Era," CE means "Common Era." It corresponds to what we called AD ("Anno Domini"). I'm using CE because AD means something quite different in the context of this book! But there is a bit more of the story in BCE before we get to CE.

A BARGAIN VASE

I already mentioned "potters' marks" on ceramic pieces like vases. Once writing developed, potters began putting written text on their works. For Greek settlements this happened around the tenth century BCE.

If early potters' marks identified the potter, it makes sense they would begin putting their names on products. This, too, might be about the creator's brand. But sometimes those signatures were more crude (e.g., Figure 2.1) than others, which likely didn't help their brand. Figure 2.2 shows a vase where the potter did a nicer job writing his name. But the text wasn't always the creator's name.

Potters, and sometimes separate painters of the pots, used a variety of messages to decorate these items. Figure 2.3 is the same vase as in Figure 2.2, but it shows that the potter actually named the characters depicted. Here, one figure is Heracles (Hercules), which is clearly printed on the work (in ancient Greek). Called "talking vases," some have inscriptions reciting a poem or song, or a descriptive remark about an image on the vase, such as "the boy is beautiful" (Boardman 2003).

FIGURE 2.1. The potter, Gamedes, signed his work, but in a less refined fashion than many vases of that time.

THE LOUVRE MUSEUM

FIGURE 2.2. The potter, Euphronios, worked his name into the aesthetic design of this vase.
THE LOUVRE MUSEUM

FIGURE 2.3. The name Heracles is clearly printed on this vase.
THE LOUVRE MUSEUM

One such example is, for our purposes, "the" vase (Figure 2.4). It is a lekythos, a vase for holding oil. It is classified as a "black figure" object, indicating the visual design method. This special vase dates to about 520 BCE, a time when both Confucius and Gautama Buddha were alive.

What makes it unique is what is written on it. A composite of images is shown in Figure 2.5, revealing the entire message wrapping around the vase. In ancient Greek it says, "ΟΝΙΣΘΕ ΜΕ ΚΑΙ ΕΝΕΠΟΛΕΣΕΙ ΚΑΛΟΣ." Translated: ΟΝΙΣΘΕ ΜΕ ("buy me"), ΚΑΙ ("and"), ΕΝΕΠΟΛΕΣΕΙ ΚΑΛΟΣ ("you'll get a bargain"). Put together, it says, "Buy me and you'll get a bargain." Can anyone argue this *isn't* a sales pitch?[1]

About forty years after Aesop's death, this is the clearest early commercial advertisement with an obvious sales pitch still existing today, and a very early example of point-of-purchase advertising.

This seems to fit even today's narrowest advertising definition. The concept of a written sales pitch clearly was understood back then. At least it was by this potter!

FIGURE 2.5. "Buy me and you'll get a bargain."

CRYING FOR A LIVING

Before printing presses, with literacy being rare, a form of word-of-mouth advertising arose: criers. These professional loudmouths would stand in public venues and yell about events and products, promoting them. Early evidence of criers comes from the writings of Polybius

FIGURE 2.4. The bargain vase.
THE LOUVRE MUSEUM

(c. 130 BCE), who mentions them in ancient Carthage as far back as 500 BCE (Church 1886). Jones (1955) mentions that Carthaginians added a twist by dressing criers in shirts emblazoned with lettering on front and back, creating what would later be known as "sandwich men," with the man sandwiched between two ads. This might well be the first example of advertising that appealed to two senses simultaneously. It certainly was an early example of word-of-mouth advertising.

Another account of public criers, much later, is found on a tablet discovered near Heraclea, in southern Italy. This tablet, the "tabula Heracleensis," circa 45 BCE, not only talks about criers (*praecones*) but also announces their ineligibility for public office (Bond 2016). Apparently, like advertising practitioners today, criers were not held in high regard.

BANNER ADVERTISING IN CHINA

In the mid-third century BCE, a man named Han Fei Tzu authored a series of influential Chinese essays (Watson 1964). He was a political activist, though he was a member of a royal family in north-central China, and he fought corruption in government. Many policies he advocated were, in fact, adopted by the Chinese Empire after 221 BCE. But one story he told catches our attention:

> Once there was a Sung man selling wine. His measures were very fair. His reception of customers was very courteous. The wine he made was excellent. He hoisted his banner in an imposing manner. Yet he had no business and the wine would become sour. Wondering at the cause, he asked his acquaintance, an elder of the village, named Yang Ching. "It is because your dog is fierce," replied Ching. "If my dog is fierce, why does my wine not sell well?" "Because customers are afraid of it. When people send out children with money and pots or jars to buy wine from you, your dog would jump at them and sometimes bite them. This is the reason why your wine does not sell well and becomes sour." Indeed, the state has dogs, too. Thus experts in statecraft, bearing the right tact in mind, want to enlighten the sovereign of ten thousand chariots, whereas ministers like the fierce dog of the wine merchant would jump at them and bite them. This is the reason why the lord of men is deluded and experts in statecraft are not taken into service. (Liao 1959)

The mention of the man hoisting his banner is salient here.[2] It appears this was an advertising banner/flag promoting the sale of wine. The dogs apparently were metaphors for manipulative government officials. Was the banner cloth, or silk? After all, the Chinese invented silk around 2700 to 3000 BCE. Did it have writing or a symbol on it? We don't know. But it does appear that some type of advertisement helped people find wine around 250 BCE.

MOLTEN MEMORIES

Centuries after the bargain vase, we might expect advertising to have advanced. By the time another major religious figure was alive—Jesus of Nazareth—advertising in the Roman Empire does seem more advanced. Just forty-nine years after his death, in 79 CE, a wealth of

FIGURE 2.6.   Sign in Pompeii that indicates the location of a brothel, strongly suggestive of a body part.

FIGURE 2.7.   Political promotions on the front of a building on the main street.

FIGURE 2.8.   A sign for two politicians: Trebius and Marcus Cerrinius Vatia.
NATIONAL ARCHAELOGICAL MUSEUM OF NAPLES

FIGURE 2.9.   A political sign painted on a building in Peru, as seen in 2018, not unlike the signs in ancient Pompeii.

culture was preserved when Mount Vesuvius erupted and blanketed both Pompeii and Herculaneum with lava and ash (Cooley & Cooley 2004). With this tragedy, a lot of advertising was preserved from the elements.

Viewing the art found in Pompeii's ruins, it's clear those people seemed somewhat fixated on sex (Johnson 2017). Much of the art would make a sailor blush. There even is public signage promoting a brothel district. In Figure 2.6, a molded image of a penis on the outside wall of a building can be seen.

But that is not the only advertising that was preserved. Indeed, political advertising is the largest category found there. As the city was unearthed, archaeologists found house after house with writing on their exterior walls. Already, about two thousand political inscriptions have been discovered, and even more are being discovered (Marchini 2018). About 40 percent were on the nicest houses in town. Perhaps politicians pursued wealthy citizens' houses for influential endorsements (Pappas 2013). A building on Pompeii's main street (Figure 2.7) is nearly covered with red political texts. Some display just a name, but others show something like a slogan.

Figure 2.8 shows a segment from a building where the names are relatively clear, but scholars have interpreted this piece as displaying "Vote for Trebius, an honest man, for aedile" on top and "Vote for Marcus Cerrinius Vatia for aedile, who is worthy of public office. Iarinus (recommends him)" on the bottom.[3] Notice that these slogans bear a haunting resemblance to today's.

Some characterize these as "graffiti," since they are hand-lettered on buildings. Yet they might more properly be characterized as grassroots political advertising, which exists today. Driving through southern Peru, you might witness similar signage painted on houses and stores, as seen in Figure 2.9. And, like in Pompeii, red paint is common.

Political signage wasn't the only variety to use a hand-printed approach. In the city Herculaneum, not far from Pompeii, a wine shop sign is visible (Figure 2.10). It could have been painted by the same people.

An image of Cupid holding shoes was found in Herculaneum, too. It apparently was a cobbler's shop sign (Wagner 1954). The "love" of shoes is nothing new, apparently.

Rokicki (1987) notes that *scriptores* were sign painters of that time. Walls were an ideal medium. Simple whitewash could make any wall infinitely reusable. These painters might be the first true advertising professionals, having a specialty dedicated to creating ads.

FIGURE 2.10.   The sign of a wine shop in Herculaneum, with wine jugs visible.

Not all signs in Pompeii were hand-painted. A marble slab sign advertising a commercial bathhouse also was discovered. The all-text sign, circa 50 CE (Figure 2.11), declares, "Thermae / M(arci) Crassi Frugi / aqua marina et baln(eum) / aqua dulci Ianuarius l(ibertus)," interpreted as "The hot baths of Marcus Crassus Frugi; sea water available and a bath with fresh water. The freedman Januarius" (Keppie 1991).[4] The emperor Nero had that bathhouse owner put to death two years before Vesuvius erupted.

FIGURE 2.11.   Sign promoting a commercial bathhouse, from Pompeii.

NATIONAL ARCHAELOGICAL MUSEUM OF NAPLES

Yet another carved stone sign can be found, promoting a coppersmith's shop. Figure 2.12 is wholly pictographic, with no text, but it clearly portrays activities found inside the merchant's shop: weighing metal (left), pounding it to shape (center), and the fine finishing (right). It even includes the coppersmith's dog (upper right).

Advertising, closely resembling today's, is plentiful from Pompeii and Herculaneum. I mention only a few examples. But most ads in this treasure trove promote just one profession: politics and prostitution. Nearly all of this field's historians have pointed to these examples (e.g., Tungate 2007; Nevett 1982; Wood 1958; Presbrey 1929; Larwood & Hotten 1875; Sampson 1874). They all agree these are ads!

FIGURE 2.12.   A carved stone sign from a coppersmith's shop, found in Pompeii.

NATIONAL ARCHAELOGICAL MUSEUM OF NAPLES

PUTTING HER LEFT FOOT FORWARD

The Turkish were not so different from the Romans of Pompeii. Amid the ruins of Ephesus, Turkey, resides a marble walkway engraved with what is believed to be a crude, graffiti-like sign directing customers to a nearby brothel. The impression of a foot, a cross, a woman's head, and a heart are found on the walk, along with what appears to be a coin hole. Some opine that the foot size represents customers' age limit, the cross refers to a crossroad (it's a left foot, meaning to turn left at that crossroad), the coin hole suggests price, and the woman is the product. There was, in fact, a brothel to the left at the crossroad. This practice dates back to the first century CE. If done today, we probably would call this guerilla advertising.

RACING FOR SESTERCES

Sports were big then, as today. This preceded basketball or football, but racing was huge in the Roman Empire. Like automobile racing today, chariot racing had its teams and heroes. Struck (2010) claims the best-paid athlete in history was a man named Gaius Appuleius Diocles, who earned 35,863,120 sesterces in prize money over twenty-four years of competing. In 2010, that amount would be $15 billion. Upon retirement (146 CE), a monument was erected to him. He earned that much, obviously, because of the sport's popularity.

FIGURE 2.13. A mosaic sign promoting the Blue Team. This one is from the early third century, found in Villa dei Severi at Baccano.

Teams were by color: Red, White, Blue, and Green. Gaius drove for the White Team; then he moved to the Green and later to Red. We are more sophisticated today, as we have the Cincinnati Reds, the White Sox, the Blue Devils, and the Green Bay Packers! Our chariots do have more horsepower.

Not unlike sport teams today, fans backed teams, and advertisements for teams were common. Mosaic "posters" appeared outside Roman stadiums showing, for example, a charioteer in a blue jersey with a horse, representing the Blue Team (Figure 2.13). Fans even had lead "curse amulets" representing an opposing team, punctured with nails, like voodoo dolls (Struck 2010). These, too, might be ads: competitive advertising, or a form of sports merchandising.

THE FRUITS OF ADVERTISING

In the fourth and fifth centuries, two authors, Ge Hong (317–318) and Fan Ye (c. 445), provide historical accounts of China. Hong (also known as Zhichuan), a collector of Daoist materials, provides insight into religious life, particularly for Daoists, in early medieval China.[5] Ye (also known as Weizong), a historian and politician, describes the formation of the Kushan empire, drawing largely from a report to the Chinese emperor by General Ban Yong around 125 CE.

FIGURE 2.14. The modern medical symbol, Caduceus.

Both authors mention "gourd hanging." Chinese doctors and pharmacists would hang a gourd outside their house to advertise their profession, like the "Caduceus" (Figure 2.14) used to represent medicine today. A bottle gourd was iconic of Douist "immortals." It symbolized immortality and also served as a medicine bottle (Flaws 1994). In parts of China this practice continues today, making it an advertising practice over 1,700 years old! The Caduceus wasn't used for medicine until around 1500 CE, and it was adopted as an official American medical symbol in 1902.

THIS IS ADVERTISING

In this chapter you have seen some clearer examples of advertising. Some is text, some pictures, some symbolism, and some a combination—used in point-of-purchase advertising, political advertising, audio or word-of-mouth advertising, banners, guerilla methods, medical advertising, and sports marketing, with a lot of sex trade promotions. There is little doubt that two millennia ago, advertising already was well established and valued in trade.

This doesn't mean, however, that advertising techniques have expanded and improved continuously since that time. It turns out that advertising had yet to go through the Dark Ages.

3

The Dark Ages of Advertising

It is pretty obvious that advertising was used in many ways throughout the Roman Empire. But the Empire fell in 476 CE when Romulus Augustulus was deposed. This began a time known alternately as the Dark Ages and as medieval times. The Roman Empire was an advanced and structured society. When it dissolved, those qualities faded. One result was the loss of literacy.

ADVERTISING FOR THE ILLITERATE

Hieroglyphics (Lazzaro 2017) and cuneiform (Editors 2016) were the oldest systems of writing, emerging around 3200 BCE. Symbols from the Harappan society, mentioned earlier, were part of another system, likely just a few hundred years younger (Kak 1989).

But arrival of written language didn't mean everyone suddenly understood it. Even in 2018, about 15 percent of adults were illiterate, according to the World Literacy Foundation. They couldn't even read this book!

Greek poet Homer composed the *Iliad* and *Odyssey* sometime between 700 and 1100 BCE. Initially they probably were oral compositions (Sherefkin 2012). Inscriptions from about 600 BCE, however, suggest literacy was already spreading in Judah (Falk 2012). The Roman Empire's rise began about 27 BCE. By that time some degree of literacy had been established.

Citizens of the Empire learned reading and writing at a much higher rate than most people, though still low by today's standards. Eckardt (2018) estimates Roman literacy at 15 percent before the collapse. Much of that was thanks to the Greeks. After the Empire's fall, the flow of learning from Greece subsided. The breakdown in trade and military structure, and a population drop between 400 and 700 CE, led to a largely illiterate population. Feudalism prevailed and society fragmented, creating centuries of illiteracy.

What this means is that even within the Empire, 85 percent of people couldn't read, and it dropped afterward. Any ads with written appeals could reach only the well educated, mostly the wealthy. Ads for the masses needed to be visual for about the next millennium. So by

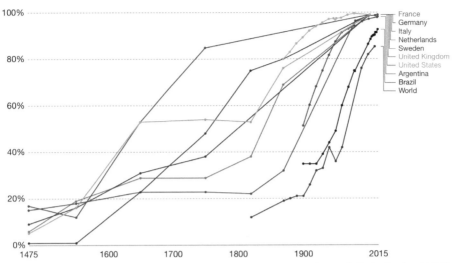

FIGURE 3.1.   Literacy rates from 1475 to 2015, as presented by Roser & Ortiz-Ospina (2018).

comparing text vs. visual in any ad at that time, we can estimate whether the ad targeted the elite or the masses.

While medieval literacy was low, Roser & Ortiz-Ospina (2018) composed a graph (Figure 3.1) displaying literacy more recently, from 1475 to 2015. Before 1800 CE, mass advertising leaned toward the visual.

So the Dark Ages saw fewer hand-lettered signs (Presbrey 1929) and a rise in visual imagery (Seidel, Kelly, & Lowery 1958). This helps explain the increasing use of criers.

HARK, THE HERALDRY!

The first "logo" may have been an Indus Valley seal, or a potters' mark, or a cartouche of a pharaoh. Probably it was one of those. But by the Dark Ages businesses were commonly using distinctive marks.

Pongsapitaksanti (2010) mentions merchant shops in Japan's Heian period (794–1185 CE) being depicted on scrolls as having cloth curtains at the entrances with the shop's name or logo. Petty (2016) notes similar symbolic branding occurred in China in the tenth century, about the same time.

Marks representing family brands, such as a "coat of arms," arose under Emperor Henry the Fowler (Henry I), 919–936 CE (Jenkins 1886). By around 1244 CE, Mathew Paris had created a list of seventy-five coats of arms (Cartwright 2018). Armor frequently bore distinctive coats of arms in battle or in tournaments. This was known as "heraldry." Originally the purpose was to distinguish friend from foe (Lant & Morr 2017). A superior warrior's symbol (logo) might engender fear, and even retreat. Most combatants likely were not literate, so the heraldry tended to be graphic elements only.

But as Presbrey (1929) observes, heraldry did not stay confined to family branding. Taverns and inns even used coats of arms. The idea, he believes, "had its origin in the use of some baronial establishments as inns while their owners were away for long periods, as during the crusades."

Cartwright (2018) argues that today's company logos are *de facto* descendants of ancient heraldry. They are still intended to promote superiority and, of course, identity. They also are related to nation branding. *Encyclopedia Britannica* claims many flag designs are based on coats of arms. So the Union Jack, the Stars & Stripes, and so forth also appear to be advertisements!

MEDIEVAL DECEPTIONS

No doubt deceptive advertising began long before the Dark Ages. Remember the serpent in the garden? So perhaps deception is as old as advertising. But we know Chinese merchants during the Northern Song Dynasty (960–1127 CE) used deceptive techniques to fool buyers into thinking low-grade "garden tea" was actually high-grade "hill tea." They did this by using names like "Misty Mountain Tea," "Cloudy Mountain Tea," and "Garden in the Sky Tea" (Evans 1992).

But probably the boldest and most well-documented deceptive promotion in that period belongs to Erik Thorvaldsson (aka Erik the Red). He founded a settlement on an island 80 percent covered with ice in 982 CE. He named it "Greenland" intentionally, to attract settlers (Evans 2016). We still use that name more than a thousand years later, and some might yet be deceived.

VERY PERSONAL BRANDING

For most of history people didn't use surnames. It was only around the eleventh and twelfth centuries that they came into use. Some people began adopting occupational surnames, indicative of what they did or sold for a living (Foster 1967). Their name advertised their trade!

In some places, like Turkey, use of surnames spread slowly. Turkey didn't even require them until 1934, and even then many occupational surnames were adopted (Gersuny 1974). Adoption of surnames and occupational surnames occurred simultaneously, no matter where or when that took place.

Neither signs nor literacy, nor business cards, were needed when a person's name told consumers about the business. Gormley (1987) suggests the Domesday survey completed in 1086, an enormous tax assessment effort throughout England and Wales, was one catalyst for this development.

Initially, these names only became hereditary when a son followed his father into the same trade. "Miller" is a good example. In an agrarian society, mills were important to grind grains and corn. According to SurnameDB.com, Reginald Miller's name was on the rolls in 1327. Tinker was another. A tinker fixed things. They still do. Robert le Tinker's name was recorded in 1243.

A weaver weaved fibers into cloth. The spelling was different, but the name Wevre dates to 1086, and Carpenter (spelled "Carpentier") appeared in 1066. Baker was found in the name of William le Bakere, circa 1177.

This was a powerful, practical, and inexpensive mode of advertising. By the 1300s, the English town of Bristol alone listed ninety-two occupational surnames (Britnell 2001). This was an important advertising tool of medieval society. But when descendants rejected their fathers' trades, this advertising largely fell apart. Eventually it was more common for businesses to be named after their owner than for owners to be named after their business.

NEEDLES OF THE WHITE RABBIT

The National Museum of China holds an important advertising artifact: a bronze printing plate from around 1127–1279 CE (Figure 3.2). The ad is for "Quality Needle Shop of Jinan Liu's Family," in the Shandong province. On the plate's side it says, "Use the white rabbit that is in front of the door as recognition." The rabbit image appears on the plate. Eckhardt & Bengtsson (2010) note that rabbits were important cultural symbols representing feminine energy, and the target likely was women with limited literacy. This rabbit is the earliest known (non-humanoid) advertising character.

FIGURE 3.2.   Bronze printing plate for Jinan Liu's shop.
NATIONAL MUSEUM OF CHINA

Not only is this one of the earliest existing examples of advertising for print on paper, but it also appears to be the oldest example of plate-printed advertising and an early example of a business logo. It reveals a clear branding strategy, though the art of copywriting remains crude.

SHOP SIGNS BY THE MOTHER OF INVENTION

Throughout medieval times, many towns expanded. Until about the twelfth century, there were no street names. Even after names were used, there were no building numbers, making it hard to tell people your business address. When towns were still small, you could simply describe the building (or point to it).

Over time cities grew too big for such simple navigation. Foster (1967) explains:

Hitherto, a person wishing to have a set of silver spoons made inquired for the shop of Jack Silversmith, and the answer might have been: "Down St. Stephens Alley a way." But as St. Stephens Alley grew to half a mile in length and had no street numbers, finding Jack Silversmith might require some exploring, so Jack Silversmith did something which was a big step in advertising. He hung out a sign. It could have been a large wooden spoon painted silver, with Jack Silversmith's name over it. But the sign wasn't there to attract customers or claim that Jack Silversmith made the best spoons in London, nor was it there to suggest silver spoons as a status symbol. It was there only to help people who wanted spoons to find Jack Silversmith. Advertising had not progressed beyond its most basic function—helping people find what they needed. It was still only informative, not persuasive.

Numbering buildings did not generally arise until the 1700s (Yagos 2017). William Penn is said to have introduced the idea to America as early as 1682 (Mencken 1948). Building numbers in England first appeared in 1708, and in both Paris and Prague it started around 1727 (Tantner 2009). Until then, business signs were important finding aids (e.g., "across the street from the sign . . .").

EARLY SIGNS OF BEER AND BUSH

In 1389, England's King Richard II created a law requiring beer breweries to hang a sign indicating that fact. Otherwise, the beer could be confiscated! Drinking water often was polluted, as sewage systems weren't used, so brewed beer was safer. The sign dictate was a safety measure (Casey 2013).

Taverns began a sort of competition with signs, distinguishing their pub from others. Lant & Morr (2017) explain, "One pub would become The Green Dragon, another the Two Cocks. And these images turned to names, allowing patrons to develop a sense of brand loyalty to their favorite brewer."

Some signs in England dated back to the Romans. In Rome the *tabernae*—small indoor markets—that sold wine hung vine leaves outside to signal that fact (Johnson, n.d.). England wasn't really the climate for grapes, so the British hung small ivy bushes. Initially, the bush indicated wine. Shops selling beer hung long poles or "ale stakes" of the type used to stir ale. Some put a bush on a pole, indicating they sold both. Over time the "bush" became a sign of a public house (pub) selling alcohol in any form. Even as names and designs changed, the bush continued to be used. Live bushes gave way to wood or iron representations of a bush, sometimes as part of the bracket holding a fancier sign (Figure 3.3). For centuries, bushes advertised alcohol.

FIGURE 3.3. A sign from 1777, where the "bush" is of the Roman style that uses grapes but is made of iron.

BEER WITH ROOTS

"Branding" wasn't a concept in 1366, but one of today's brands has roots extending back that far, when a brewery named Den Hoorn was founded in Leuven, Belgium. It was bought in 1717 by Sabastian Artois, the company's master brewer, and he put his name on it. After

FIGURE 3.4. A brand and logo that has roots reaching back to 1366 CE.

another 209 years, it brewed a beer called Christmas Star. The Latin word for star is *stella*, so Stella Artois was born. This is a really old beer! Part of its logo, the horn, even originated with Den Hoorn (Figure 3.4). That horn is the oldest and longest-lasting ad element/brand connection still existing.

A SOUND FORM OF ADVERTISING

It's said town criers first came to England in 1066 CE when William the Conqueror invaded. Criers were sent from town to town to remind people that Harold Godwynson was King Edward's rightful successor. Sheasby (2014) argues this is myth, because a scene from

the Bayeux Tapestry, depicting Edward's funeral, several months before William invaded, clearly shows two criers (aka "bell-men" and "skelligmen") below the coffin. If true (Figure 3.5), criers existed in England earlier than thought. Walker (2001) is one who claims criers came with William, but he notes this conflict.

FIGURE 3.5. Part of the Bayeux Tapestry, showing Edward in his coffin and two town criers below.

Back then criers patrolled streets, detained troublemakers, and literally put out fires, in addition to their crying duties. They largely served the royalty. They would read (yell) announcements from the government and then post the written notice in a prominent place.

By 1141 CE, criers in France, using the Latin title *praeco*, were sufficiently organized that twelve of them formed a company and obtained an official charter from King Louis the Younger. Five were paid by taverns to loudly promote wines and provide samples (Presbrey 1929), so they were becoming more trade oriented.

In 1258, France's King Philip Augustus decreed that criers in Paris could go to any tavern and "cry the wine," charging the tavern a fee, even without the owner's permission. Criers also had some exclusive legal right to announce auctions (Presbrey 1929).

A typical sort of cry, though at least a couple of centuries later, is provided by Nelson (1941):

Here are oranges, fine ripe oranges,
Of golden color to the eye,
And fragrant perfume they're dispensing,
Sweeter than roses; come then and buy.

Criers were the advertising *medium*, and crying often was considered "publication" of an event. Criers in England and France used horns to get attention (Sampson 1874). While not called that, these were some of the earliest ad jingles.

Not all claims about criers are as well documented as those above, but some are intriguing. Nevett (1982) tells of a cosmetics dealer in Greece, named Aesclyptoe, who had a catchy script for criers:

> For eyes that are shining, for cheeks like the dawn,
> For beauty that lasts after girlhood has gone,
> For prices in reason the woman who knows
> Will buy her cosmetics of Aesclyptoe.

Others have told that story (e.g., Fletcher 2008), but I have doubts. It was a Greek merchant, and yet it rhymes in English! This story would, however, suggest copywriting was finally being taken seriously. Schuwer (1966) claims that in thirteenth-century France there were cries that would pass as slogans, such as "Fuller's earth! Fuller's earth! Freshly dug to clean your wool. Come and buy, my sacks are full!"

By the mid-fourteenth century, shops in England were packed tightly along narrow streets. There was little to call attention to a single shop. One solution was to use a crier to attract passersby. From a baker's shop you might hear something in Middle English like "Hote pyes hote!" (Wood 1958).

Criers arrived in Australia and New Zealand in the late 1800s. The first in Australia was a convict. Today that profession still exists in those countries and is governed by the Ancient and Honourable Guild of Australian Town Criers (AHGATC) and the Honourable Guild of Town Criers in New Zealand (HGTCNZ).

FIGURE 3.6.   A modern town crier in vintage attire, Tony Appleton.
REPRINTED WITH PERMISSION

Town criers still exist. When Prince William and Kate Middleton had their third child in 2018, an unofficial crier named Tony Appleton announced the birth (McCluskey 2018). He stays true to criers of old, wearing nineteenth-century garb (Figure 3.6). Today's "carnival barker" is another descendant of this noisy profession. This word-of-mouth advertising method has proved itself over the millennia.

BLOODY AWFUL BARBER ADVERTISING

Where Chinese medical professionals hung gourds, hair cutters also had a promotional symbol. Bloodletting was a medical practice extending back at least three thousand years to ancient Egypt. A person's vein was cut to let blood drain, supposedly correcting an imbalance in the patient's health (Greenstone 2010). During the medieval period, clergy did some doctoring and let blood. Physicians saw it as beneath their dignity.

In 1163, Pope Alexander III stopped priests from bloodletting. Barbers took over. They also pulled teeth, set bones, treated wounds, and even did amputations, acting as early surgeons (Cohen 2012).

FIGURE 3.7. The barber pole has become so important an image that today, even when it doesn't hang outside a barber shop, it often is found as part of the barber's logo.

It turns out that barbers began "advertising" this practice by putting bowls of clients' blood in their windows to announce this service. Not surprisingly, some passersby weren't thrilled, and in 1307 a law was passed that "no barbers shall be so bold or so hardy as to put blood in their windows." Barbers still needed to promote their services, so the barber pole was born shortly thereafter. Fitzharris (2013) explains that the red-and-white stripes on the pole represented the bloody bandages hung to dry outside a shop, and it spiraled to represent the bandages twisting in the wind.

In 1540, a law required surgeons and barbers to distinguish their services by their pole's colors. Barbers became blue and white, while surgeons took red and white (Fitzharris 2013). For a time during slavery in the United States, black-and-white poles indicated barbers who served African Americans. Today lighted, rotating red, white, and blue poles are common (Figure 3.7). It was barbers, not public relations, who first learned to put a spin on their business.

THE BEGINNINGS OF WRAP

You find the darnedest things in tombs. Chinese archaeologists found the oldest existing packaging with a promotional message on it, used as a funerary object around 1300 CE. It was two pieces of wrapping paper about ten by thirteen inches, with images of lotuses and clouds and seventy Chinese characters. The text described oil paint, apparently wrapped in the paper: "Compared with other oil paints, the tint of our product is unique." It even included the store's address. One mark might even have been a trademark, according to Cao Yannong (Anonymous 2001). The package description sounds like something found in a twenty-first-century store. I can't say whether you would find it in a twenty-first-century tomb.

By contrast, the first printed promotional product wrapping in Britain was in 1660 CE, for Buckworth's Cough Lozenges. Apparently, Buckworth's were of questionable effectiveness (Curth 2006).

POSTERS OF PYES AND MORE

Histories of advertising, and of posters (aka "broadsides"), mention William Caxton as producer of the first printed poster in England (e.g., Sampson 1874; Rickards 1971; Nevett 1982; Halldin 2013). Caxton owned London's first printing press (1476 CE). The ad was about three by five and one-quarter inches, but clearly intended to be "posted," saying, "Supplico stet cedula." Very loosely, this means "Pray do not pull down this advertisement" (Nevett 1982). This was circa 1472–1477 CE and is an ad for a set of instructions for clergy, known as the Pyes of Salisbury (Figure 3.8). It apparently was posted on the doors of the Westminster almonry.

While undoubtedly true that Caxton's is the oldest poster printed on a printing press, an older poster exists, in pieces. Van Dijk (1956) details a hand-lettered poster from around 1340 CE that he discovered in an Oxford library (Figure 3.9).[1] Four fragments were mixed in with liturgical manuscripts. He recognized them as not belonging there, even though they were liturgical. It was a poster advertising the services of a "writing master," though it happens that he wasn't much of a master. The writing was clear, but of poor quality and little expertise. Van Dijk concludes:

> Once it hung in the open air outside the workshop, near the entrance of a church, on the market or some other public place where it attracted the attention of the passers-by, showing some examples of the master's writing and musical notation.

Van Dijk's discovery, from about the time the Black Plague began, likely is the oldest advertising poster of which anything remains. Both of these posters were text-based, unlike the predominant use of imagery at that time, but both were targeted at clergy, among the most educated classes of people.

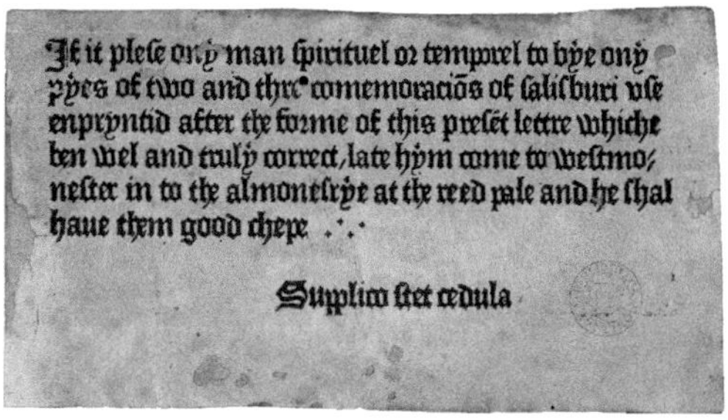

FIGURE 3.8.   Advertisement for the Pyes of Salisbury, circa 1477 CE.

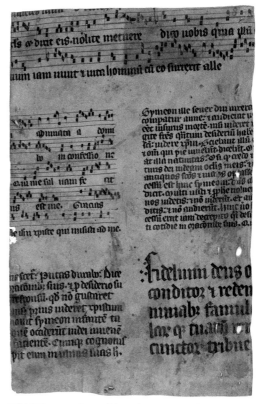

FIGURE 3.9.   One of four fragments of an advertising poster promoting a writing master, circa 1340 CE.

FREE STUFF

The poem "Piers Plowman," written in Middle English 1370–1390, has a line deserving our attention. Line 228 says, "Tauerners 'a tast for nouht' tolden the same" (Robertson & Uebel 2004, p. 182). In modern English, it means "Innkeepers said the same thing, 'A taste for free!'" It suggests that by the late fourteenth century advertising via "sampling," giving away free or cheap samples of a product, already had begun. And if you look back to my earlier description of criers, you should note that it is believed some of them were handing out samples as early as the 1100s.

Everyone loves getting something for free, so this advertising technique still lives (and is especially common in grocery stores).

CONCLUSION

As the world emerged from the Dark Ages, advertising had blossomed into a smorgasbord of methods, and was a commonplace tool for business, government, and the pulpit. Presbrey (1929) reaches the conclusion, "When it came to pulling Europe out of the Dark Ages it was business men, the class of men who today are advertising, who did it." Literacy rates continued to be abysmal, so visual imagery continued to rule.

Part II

THE RENAISSANCE THROUGH THE VICTORIAN AGE

GENERAL HISTORY

ADVERTISING HISTORY

1300
Renaissance begins

Product wrap bearing promotional message (China)

1307
The end of barbers using bowls of blood as ads

1311
Lincoln Cathedral becomes the tallest building in the world

1337
Hundred Years' War (ends 1453)

1340
Oldest existing hand-lettered poster (England)

1345
Tenochtitlan, the Aztec capital, founded

1346
Black Death blankets Europe and Asia, killing more than seventy-five million

1366
Stella Artois brand is born as Den Hoorn brewery

1380
Free product sampling by innkeepers

1384
King of Poland is a woman, Jadwiga

1387
The Canterbury Tales written by Geoffrey Chaucer

GENERAL HISTORY

ADVERTISING HISTORY

1389
Breweries must hang signs, by law (England)

1420
Forbidden City in China is completed

1431
Joan of Arc is burned at the
stake in Rouen, France

1436
Vlad Dracul becomes Voivode of Wallachia

1439
Kissing is banned in England

1450
Johannes Gutenberg creates a printing press

1455
War of the Roses starts (ends in 1485)

1475
Printers' marks introduced

1476
First printed poster in England

1483
Richard III seizes the throne of England

1491
Earliest illustrated advertising handbill

1492
Christopher Columbus arrives in America

1498
First catalog, promotes fifteen books

1506
Leonardo da Vinci completes the *Mona Lisa*

1509
Peter Henlein invents the watch

1517
Martin Luther begins the Reformation,
starting Protestant Christianity

1519
Hernán Cortés begins conquest of Mexico

1525
First printed news booklet (England)

1526
First slaves in American colony
(to become South Carolina)

GENERAL HISTORY

ADVERTISING HISTORY

1533
The Inca Empire ends with
execution of Emperor Atahualpa

1534
Reward for identifying a billsticker and
execution for withholding a name (France)

1535
First printing press in America (Mexico City)

1536
Anne Boleyn, queen of England,
is beheaded by King Henry VIII

1543
Copernicus publishes theory that the
Earth revolves around the Sun

1545
Cocoliztli epidemic kills fifteen million
in Mexico and Central America

1564
William Shakespeare is born

1567
First lottery advertisement (England)

1577
Innkeepers required by law to post signs
(France)

1587
Mary, Queen of Scots, is beheaded for
plotting to murder Queen Elizabeth

1590
The Roanoke Island colony of
115 people vanishes

1591
First ad in a newsbook (Germany)

1596
Flush toilet invented

1598
Rio Grande is the first theater
performance in America

1600
The Renaissance ends

1609
First printed newspaper (Germany)

GENERAL HISTORY

ADVERTISING HISTORY

1610
Sir Arthur Gorges and Sir Walter Cope run
the public register for commerce (Britain)

1612
First ads in a newspaper (France)

1617
The "cigar store Indian" becomes an ad
for tobacconists

1618
Thirty Years' War begins (ends 1648) in Europe

1619
Official beginning of slavery in America

1620
Pilgrims arrive in North America, at
Plymouth Rock, aboard the *Mayflower*

1622
First newspaper in Britain, the *Weekly Newes*

First newspaper ad in Britain

Tradesman's cards begin

1624
New Amsterdam is founded by the Dutch,
to become New York City

1626
Peter Minuit buys Manhattan
for cloth and brass buttons

First paid ad placement (Netherlands)

1630
Theophraste Renaudot establishes the
Bureau d'Addresse et de Rencontres (France)

1631
Colonel Robert Gibbon Johnson publicly eats a
tomato (proving they weren't poisonous)

1636
Cambridge College is established,
to become Harvard in 1639

1638
First printing press in North America (Boston)

1641
First public relations pamphlets created
by Harvard College

1642
English Civil War begins, ending in 1649

1643
Typhus epidemic in England

GENERAL HISTORY

ADVERTISING HISTORY

1644
Ming Dynasty in China ends

Newsbook uses handbills to promote itself

1645
British soldiers first called "red coats"

1647
First "witch" convicted in America,
Alse Young of Connecticut

1648
Trade tokens first created (Britain)

1649
King Charles I of England executed

1651
Longest war in history begins between the Isles
of Scilly and the Netherlands (ends in 1986)

1652
Cape Town (South Africa)
is founded by the Dutch

Earliest illustrated advertisement
in an English newspaper

Editorial condemning patent
medicine advertising

1653
First Scottish newspaper

1657
First advertising-only newspaper,
The Publick Advertiser

1660
Restoration of the British monarchy

First promotional product wrap in Britain

1665
Great Plague of London kills
about one hundred thousand

First magazine is published in Paris
(*Journal des Scavans*)

First English-language magazine
(*Philosophical Transactions*)

1666
First separate advertising supplement
for a newspaper

1667
A seed catalog is published

1681
William Penn promotes Pennsylvania
with direct advertising booklet

1682
House and building numbering begins

GENERAL HISTORY

1687
Isaac Newton gets a bump on his head,
causing him to launch the field of physics

1690
First paper money in America

First American newspaper

1692
Salem witch trials in Massachusetts

1693
First woman's magazine (*The Ladies' Mercury*)

William and Mary College is second
college chartered in America

1700
April Fools' Day begins

1704
The Boston News-Letter is the
first successful American newspaper

1714
Typewriter is patented
(but first practical one is 1808)

1720
Great Plague of Marseille kills as
many as one hundred thousand

1741
First magazine in American colonies

ADVERTISING HISTORY

Tavernkeepers required by law to post signs
(France)

First advertising playing cards

First newspaper ads in America

First slavery-related newspaper ads in America

1710
First newspaper editorial entirely about
advertising (Britain)

1712
Newpaper and advertising duties begin (Britain)

1730
First regular newapaper with "Advertiser" in title
(*The Daily Advertiser*)

1740
First hoarding in London

First paid mgazine advertisement in America

1743
First half-page newspaper advertisement

1744
Benjamin Franklin publishes mail-order catalog
of books with a satisfaction guarantee

GENERAL HISTORY

ADVERTISING HISTORY

1749
Folding paper fans used as promotional devices
A wager on the effectiveness of advertising

1759
Essay about advertising by Dr. Samuel Johnson in *The Idler*

1760
Industrial Revolution begins

New York Gazette runs ads across its front page

1761
Legal limits on sign sizes; must not hang over street (France)

1762
Street number addresses first used in England

Signs must not hang over street, by law (Britain)

1765
Lloyds of London established
American Revolution begins (ends in 1783)

Wedgwood pottery claims a royal endorsement

1766
First full-page newspaper advertisement

1769
Daniel Boone explores what will become Kentucky

1770
Russian plague kills as many as one hundred thousand

1773
Boston Tea Party   First American circus advertising

1774
Ben Franklin fired as deputy postmaster of Northern District of American Continent

Rhode Island is first American colony to forbid importing slaves

1775
Ben Franklin appointed first postmaster general

Patrick Henry proclaims, "Give me liberty or give me death"

American Revolutionary War begins

United Colonies changes name to United States

1776
American Declaration of Independence signed

1781
John Hanson becomes first president of the United States in Congress Assembled

GENERAL HISTORY

ADVERTISING HISTORY

1783
All North American states ban
import of African slaves

1784
First successful American *daily* newspaper

1785
Kingdom of Hawai'i
established by Kamehameha

1786
First general advertising agency established
by William Tayler (Britain)

1787
US Constitution signed in Philadelphia

Trade tokens reemerge as a promotional tool

1789
George Washington is first elected US president

First political advertising buttons in
United States

French Revolution begins (ends 1799)

Modern posters emerge

1791
US Bill of Rights ratified

1793
Eli Whitney invents the cotton gin

1794
Earliest known lawyer advertising

1799
Rosetta Stone discovered

1800
US White House is completed

First professional ad copywriter: Charles Lamb

1803
Napoleonic Wars (end 1815)

First newspaper in Australia

Louisiana is purchased by the
United States from France

1804
First locomotive operates

World population hits one billion

1805
Explorers Lewis and Clark
reach the Pacific Ocean

1806
Andrew Jackson kills a man in a duel

1808
Beethoven's Fifth Symphony performed

GENERAL HISTORY

ADVERTISING HISTORY

1809
Dr. Ephraim McDowell in Danville, Kentucky, performs first successful abdominal surgery

1812
War of 1812, between the United States and Britain, begins (ends 1815)

1813
Gas street lighting begins

1814
US White House burned down by the British

New Zealand colonized by missionaries

1815
Napoleon Bonaparte is defeated at the Battle of Waterloo by the British and Prussians

1816
Mary Shelley writes *Frankenstein, or The Modern Prometheus* at age eighteen

1817
Bicycle invented

1820
Coin counterstamping begins (Britain)

First woman to lead an ad agency

Johnny Walker trade character created

1822
First computer invented (sort of) by Charles Babbage

1824
First political opinion poll conducted

1825
Erie Canal is opened in New York

1826
First photograph

1827
First African American newspaper

1829
Curierul Romanesc is the first newspaper in Romania

First mass-transit advertising (Britain)

1830
Joseph Smith publishes Book of Mormon

First public railways opened (England and United States)

First nationally advertised household product (Britain)

GENERAL HISTORY

ADVERTISING HISTORY

1831
Edgar Allan Poe kicked out of
West Point Military Academy

1835
First commercial billboard in the United States

1836
Battle of the Alamo

Sam Houston elected president
of the Republic of Texas

1837
Charles Dickens publishes *Oliver Twist*

Chromolithography makes
full-color printing possible

1838
Samuel Morse demonstrates
his telegraph system

Three-dimensional images invented

1839
"O.K." is first adopted, when used
in the *Boston Morning Post*

The Opium Wars between
China and Britain begin

First company formed to rent hoardings

1840
First gas-lighted advertising sign

1841
US President William Henry Harrison
dies after thirty-one days in office

Volney Palmer opens the first agency
in the United States

1842
The bobblehead is created

1843
Alexander Bain invents the fax machine

First advertisement with a photograph

1844
Mormon leader Joseph Smith assassinated

Telegraph invented

1845
Bangkok Recorder is the
first newspaper in Thailand

1846
Anesthesia first used

Samuel Colt manufactures the first pistol

1848
First Women's Rights Convention
in Seneca Falls, New York

First postcard advertising (United States)

GENERAL HISTORY

ADVERTISING HISTORY

1849
For one day, the United States had no president
Harriet Tubman escapes slavery
Antonio Meucci invents the first telephone

1850
Taiping Rebellion in China begins (ends 1864), twenty-five million deaths

First sandwich-board ad in Britain

1851
San Francisco fire destroys most of city
Soap first sold in bar form

Agence Havas is the first ad agency in France
Soap packaged in branded wrappers

1852
Public education begins in Massachusetts (United States)

Smith Brothers Cough Candy first advertised

1853
London Hackney Carriage Act to regulate transit ads

1854
First poster with a photograph

1855
First color newspaper photograph

First book about advertising published

1856
Full-page newspaper ads start again

1857
First comprehensive trademark protection laws created (France)

1858
Pencil with attached eraser patented

1859
Charles Darwin presents his theory of evolution

1860
First known audio recording

Butter is branded with butter presses
Abraham Lincoln is first to use photographs on campaign buttons
First 3D advertisement created
American Agriculturist periodical rejects deceptive advertisements

1861
US Civil War begins (ends 1865)
First transcontinental telegram sent

GENERAL HISTORY

ADVERTISING HISTORY

1862
Private Die Proprietary Revenue Stamps
(United States)

Civil War "store cards" begin

UK Billposters' Association founded

1863
Abraham Lincoln issues the Emancipation
Proclamation, abolishing slavery

Thomas Crapper patents a
pedestal flushing toilet

Bear River Massacre of Native Americans

1864
Abraham Lincoln's son, Robert, is saved
from death by Edwin Booth
(brother of John Wilkes Booth)

Carlton & Smith agency opens,
later to be renamed J. Walter Thompson

First documented spam

1865
Abraham Lincoln assassinated
by John Wilkes Booth

George P. Rowell & Company opens

1866
First book on the history of advertising published

1867
United States buys Alaska from Russia

Gordon & Gotch, in Australia, becomes
the first international ad agency

Rowell publishes *Advertiser's Gazette*,
the first advertising trade journal

1868
US President Andrew Johnson impeached

Underwood Devil trade character created

1869
Transcontinental railroad opens

N. W. Ayer & Son agency opens

Rowell's American Newspaper Directory
published

1870
First nationwide sign-painting service
in the United States

1871
P. T. Barnum opens "the Greatest Show on
Earth"

Henry Morton Stanley finds Dr. David
Livingstone

The Great Chicago Fire starts in Mrs. O'Leary's
barn

First poster advertisement with a
nude woman on it

1872
Montgomery Ward catalog created

International Bill Posters' Association
of North America founded

GENERAL HISTORY

ADVERTISING HISTORY

1873
Blue jeans invented

First convention of advertising agents held in New York City

Louis Prang creates full-color advertising trade card

1876
Alexander Graham Bell's telephone invented

N. W. Ayer & Son creates the "open contract"

1877
Thomas Lipton issues "Lipton Pounds"

First ad agency founded by a woman

1878
First telephone directory
Thomas Edison patents the phonograph

First telephone directory advertising

1879
Thomas Edison patents the electric light bulb

First advertising survey

1880
Wabash, Indiana, is the first town illuminated by electric lights

Romania's first agency, the David Adania Agency, opens

Japan's first agency, Kukido-Kumi, opens

Enameled sheet-iron signs first offered

John E. Powers, the first full-time copywriter, is hired by John Wanamaker

Farm Journal of Philadelphia guarantees its advertisers are reputable

1881
Shootout at the OK Corral in Tombstone, Arizona (United States)

President James A. Garfield assassinated by Charles J. Guiteau

Lord & Thomas agency opens

First electric advertising sign

1882
First actor endorsement in an ad

1883
New York World is first newspaper to tie ad rates to circulation

1884
Mark Twain publishes
The Adventures of Huckleberry Finn

1886
Sigmund Freud sets up his neurology practice
The Statue of Liberty is dedicated in New York
Karl Benz patents the first automobile

Burlap book bags used as promotional products

GENERAL HISTORY

ADVERTISING HISTORY

1887

Sir Arthur Conan Doyle publishes *A Study in Scarlet*, his first Sherlock Holmes story

Pears' Soap uses famous artist's painting, *Bubbles*, in ads

American Newspaper Publishers' Association changes rules for advertising commissions

Postage and revenue stamp underprinting with advertising (Britain)

1888

Eastman Kodak introduces the box camera

Vincent van Gogh cuts off part of his ear

Sears catalog begins as R. W. Sears Watch Company

Rowell publishes *Printers' Ink*, the first national advertising trade journal

Association of General Newspaper Agents formed

Asa Candler gives out coupons to promote his Coca-Cola drink

1889

The Eiffel Tower opens

Matchbooks used as promotional products

British Indecent Advertisements Act

Westinghouse Electric Co. creates a department to handle public relations

1890

Clément Ader is the first to fly a self-propelled airplane, but just 8 inches above the ground

Adolphus Busch creates branded corkscrews for promotions

Trading stamps are first issued

1891

Thomas Edison patents the motion picture camera

George Batten opens first full-service agency, later to become part of BBDO

First electric "spectacular" sign (United States)

1892

A collapsible 14.5-foot boat called *Sapolio* crosses the Atlantic to promote soap

Ladies' Home Journal magazine prohibits patent medicine ads

Carbolic Smoke Ball lawsuit

National Society for Checking the Abuse of Public Advertising formed

1893

Coca-Cola registered as a trademark

First full-page full-color magazine advertisement

Munsey's Magazine drops price from 25¢ to 10¢

Ads projected on clouds

First advertising picture postcards

Heinz pickle charms distributed at Chicago World Columbian Exposition

Postage and revenue stamp underprinting with advertising (New Zealand)

Aunt Jemima trade character created

First university course to include advertising as a topic

GENERAL HISTORY

1894
John Harvey Kellogg makes corn flakes

1896
Guglielmo Marconi invents wireless radio

The Olympic Games are revived
after 1,500 years

The Anglo-Zanzibar War lasts less
than forty-five minutes

1897
The *New York Sun* newspaper runs an editorial
stating, "Yes, Virginia there is a Santa Claus"

Dracula by Bram Stoker is published

1898
Spanish-American War begins and ends

1899
First death by automobile, in London

ADVERTISING HISTORY

Billboard Advertising magazine published,
later to become *Billboard*

1895
First psychological studies of advertising

Ads shot from guns

US Postal Service begins Rural Free Delivery

Association of Advertising Agents begins

Earliest product placement in a movie

First motion picture advertisement

First automobile advertisement

Association of American Advertisers created

Earliest version of telemarketing (Budapest)

4

Emerging from the Dark

The concept of advertising was radically changed by the advent of the printing press, and has changed relatively little since then.

—*Jack Myers (1993)*

The medieval period is said to have ended during the 1400s. Next came the start of Early Modern History and the middle of the Renaissance. The English language also changed, so I will begin with language.

AD-YMOLOGY

Some advertising etymology deserves mention. Words are important. The beginning of advertising is hard to pinpoint in part because the word "advertising" didn't exist. A word's development reflects a growing use of the thing it describes, and a need to distinguish its meaning from other meanings.

I am writing in English, so that's my focus.[1] According to Britannica.com, before 1100 CE "Old English" was the language of England, replaced by Middle English until around 1500, and then Modern English. This change affects spelling, pronunciation, and word use.

The oldest common term in this field appears to be "market," beginning in the twelfth century. It meant "people assembled for purpose of trade," which differs from the meaning of "marketing" today. It really meant a selling place, derived from the word *markat* ("marketplace"), and/or from *mercari* ("to trade") or *mercmerx* ("merchandise"), among others.

The 1200s brought the word "sign," meaning both gestures ("a sign") and signatures ("to sign"). It evolved from the Middle English *signe* and from the Latin *signum*.

The next century introduced "promote" and "advertise." Promote comes from the Latin *promotus*, derived from *promovēre* ("to move forward"). Advertise came from the Middle English *advertisen* or *avertysen* ("to pay attention to" or "inform, notify"). It seems to have a joint British-French origin. "Barker" also arose at this time, meaning a person who advertises by verbally announcing at the entrance to a show.

"Advertisement," the noun, didn't materialize until the fifteenth century. It derived from the Anglo-French *avertisement* or *advertissement*. The British derivative "advert" (as a verb) probably started at this time, as did "market" as a verb ("to sell"). And "bill," meaning a notice (or ad), also developed in the 1400s.

Another term used then, though no longer common, is the Latin *Si Quis* ("if anybody," used to mean "announcement"). This was a notice, but used mostly for ecclesiastical declarations. The 1472 William Caxton poster described earlier was called a Si Quis (Sampson 1874).

Starčević (2015) claims "brand" came from the Nordic *brandr*, meaning "burn down," referring to use of a hot iron to stamp a symbol on an animal. The Vikings brought it to England, where it was adopted around 1552.

Other relevant words of note include slogan (1513), town crier (1560), marketing (1561), signboard (1632), advertising (1717), handbill (1718), puffery (1731), patent medicine (1770), broadside (1786), marketer (1787), journalism (1791), propaganda, used as promotion of a questionable nature (early 1800s), advert, as a noun (1814), poster, as a placard for posting (1818), hoarding (1823), billboard (1843), sandwich man (1864), subliminal (1883), sandwich board (1897), public relations (1898), copywriter (1911), branding (1913), advertorial (1917), brand name (1922), commercial, used for broadcast advertisement (1935), point-of-purchase (1939), telemarketing (1963), account planning (1968), infomercial (1981), virtual reality (1987), spam, used to mean unsolicited commercial messages (1990), augmented reality (1992), e-commerce (1993), and m-commerce (1997). The order and timing of these terms speaks volumes about how advertising evolved.

THE MOVING TYPE OF ADVERTISING

Advertising's next historical phase undoubtedly started with Gutenberg's printing press with movable type, around 1450 (e.g., Sampson 1874), although the Chinese had used movable type for nearly four centuries and Koreans had introduced metal movable type in the 1200s (Febvre & Martin 1976). Gutenberg's true contribution was the easily moldable metal alloy he used for type (Foster 1967) and the printing process he pioneered. His type, approach, and press design made printing consistent, practical, and relatively fast. "Mass communication" reached greater masses.

Printing didn't take off as quickly as it might have, because governments immediately censored and licensed printing to control it. In England, the Worshipful Company of Stationers (the "Stationers' Company"), a printers' guild, became the government's regulator. And in 1586 it was declared that all printing was to be done at Oxford and Cambridge Universities, and by the City of London (Rickards 1971). The Stationers even had power to search houses and seize illicit materials (Mendle 1995).

Concern quickly arose regarding the power of printing (Rickards 1971). Pope Alexander VI even issued a papal bull against unlicensed book printing in 1501 CE (Beare 2012). Those restrictions, and literacy limited to the wealthy and clergy, confined most printing to government and religious purposes.

It also was confined principally to Europe. The first printing press reached the Americas (Mexico City) in 1535. The second landed in Lima, Peru, in 1585. Both were limited mostly to government announcements. The first press to reach the future United States was in 1638 at Harvard University, long after Gutenberg (Presbrey 1929).

MARKS IN PRINT

Egyptian pharaohs left cartouches as their identifiers. Potters left their marks on ceramics with the same general purpose. As the printing press took off, professional printers began using their own "printers' marks" (Smith 1923).

William Caxton was a prestigious printer and had his own mark (Figure 4.1). Aldus Manutius, Caxton's contemporary, also used a mark (Figure 4.2). These were their logos, to advertise their business, even if the only media they used were their own printed products.

FIGURE 4.1. The printer's mark of William Caxton from around 1475 identified him as the producer of a book or other printed material.

Protecting That Mark

Competition led less skilled printers to palm off their printed books as coming from more respected printers. In Bologna, Italy, in 1478 a printer named Benedict Hector gave this advice in his publication, *Justinus et Floras* (translated by Larwood & Hotten 1875):

> Purchaser, be aware when you wish to buy books issued from my printing-office. Look at my sign, which is represented on the title-page, and you can never be mistaken. For some evil-disposed printers have affixed my name to their uncorrected and faulty works, in order to secure a better sale for them.

Hector's sign was his trademark. Signs passed from father to son (Larwood & Hotten 1875).

Petty (2016) provides an example from the early 1700s,

FIGURE 4.2. The mark of Aldus Manutius from the 1400s.

where a London cutlery maker advertised his guild mark, telling people to avoid counterfeits. Marks had meaning, probably advertising high quality and certainly distinguishing sellers.

That value also began gaining legal traction. Like England's Stationers' Company, in Milan, Italy, the Milanese Printers Guild regulated printers. Trademark infringement became so important the guild announced, "No printer or dealer must use for his sign a token identical with or closely similar to that already in use with an authorized printer or dealer" (Putnam 1898).

But the earliest English law affecting marks probably was the Bakers Marking Law of 1266 CE, regulating marks stamped on bread (Johnson 2005). The first known case in Anglo-American law involving trademark infringement wasn't until 1618, 140 years after Benedict Hector's warning. That case involved a cloth maker stealing another cloth maker's mark, much like Hector's warning (Stolte 1997).

A trademark is a part—often a major part—of a brand. Sometimes the terms are virtually synonymous, and the mark almost always is a big part of the brand's value. By the sixteenth century we see legal attention given to protecting brands by regulating their trademarks. These are some early forms of advertising law.

MAGIC ROCKS

Another bit of advertising law came as a warranty law case from 1603 England: *Chandler v. Lopus*. Preston (1975) notes this was a significant early legal case at a time when there was very little to protect consumers from untrustworthy sellers. The promotional claim here was verbal.

Chandler sold Lopus a rock. It wasn't a diamond; it was just a rock. But Chandler claimed it was a "bezar stone," a supposed cure-all. Lopus bought the rock and rubbed it on whatever body part needed healing, but he wasn't cured. Lopus sued Chandler for violation of warranty, because it obviously wasn't a real bezar. The judge decided Chandler had made a "mere affirmation of fact" and not a warranty; he only *said* it was a bezar—he didn't *promise*.

So for the next couple of hundred years, courts decided that merely making a claim about a product created no warranty. To create a warranty, one of three words must be used: warranty, promise, or guarantee. This undoubtedly slowed the expansion of consumer protection laws until the 1800s, all because of a magic rock.

BIRTH OF NEWSPAPERS

Newspapers didn't begin with Gutenberg. News reports were published before that, but were produced in small batches. In China they had Tipao (or Dibao), government announcements, back in 202 BCE. By the 1500s, Venice had handwritten weekly newssheets called *Gazzettes* (Barrés-Baker 2006). Given the prevailing illiteracy, mass production wasn't needed, which probably helps explain the delay in adopting this technology.

Richard Fawkes (Faques), the king's printer, published a news booklet (a "black letter tract") in 1513 about a battle (King & Simpkin 2012). Called *Trewe Encountre*, it detailed the Battle of Flodden Field between England and Scotland, and was published within a month of the event. This is the earliest known printed news publication.

The first publication one might call a news*paper* is believed to be the *Avisa Relation oder Zeitung*, printed in Strasbourg in 1609, followed closely by the *Journal General d'Affiches* ("General Journal of Posters"), beginning in 1612 and funded by King Louis VIII of France. There is some debate about what was the first newspaper. The line between newspaper and newsbook is fine. The 1605 *Relation aller Fürnemmen und gedenckwürdigen Historien* ("Account of All Distinguished and Commemorable News"), from Strasbourg, is another candidate. The evolution from newsbook to newspaper was barely a century.

Advertising was a part of these almost from the start, although the actual date is hard to pin down. The earliest newsbook in Germany was from around 1525, and Presbrey (1929, p. 39) reports that it contained an ad for a book about a medicinal herb. Its last line makes the advertising nature clear: "Let whoever does not know the meaning of this buy the book at once and read it with all zeal." But elsewhere Presbrey (p. 289) claims, "The first 'puff,' which appeared in a German newsbook in 1591, announced the discovery of a mysterious and wonderful curative herb." This latter remark seems taken from Sampson (1874, p. 63). Other writers make reference to 1591 (Tipper & Hotchkiss 1914; Rivers 1929), but all might come from Sampson. Regardless, it seems the first ad was for a book.

Some accounts suggest the first English language advertisement was in 1625 (but see below) for the book *Epithalamium Gallo-Britannicum*, appearing on the back of a newspaper called *A continuation of the weekely newes* (Presbrey 1929). As Russell (1937) notes, "All the earliest advertisements we find in the pages of the newspapers of the sixteenth century are of books and pamphlets."

Printers often owned the news publications and printed books, so it makes sense that much of the newspaper/newsbook advertising pitched books. This also makes it impossible to know when the first *paid* ad space occurred.

Sampson (1874) suggests the *Journal General d'Affiches* actually was the first true newspaper to carry advertisements, circa 1612. Those might also be book ads. We do know Nathaniel Butter's *Weekly Newes*,[2] Britain's first newspaper, carried an advertisement in 1622, as follows:

> If any gentleman, or other accustomed to buy cite weekly relations of newes, be desirous to continue the same, let them know that the writer or transcriber rather, of this newes, hath published two former Newes, the one dated the second and the other the thirteenth of August, all of which doe carry a like title, with the arms of the King of Bohemia on the other side of the title-page, and have dependence one upon another: which manner of writing and printing he doth propose to continue weekly, by God's assistance, from the best and most certain intelligence.
>   Farewell; this twenty three of August 1622. (Ainsworth 1856)

Like the books, this one was publisher self-interest and likely not a paid placement.

Sampson (1874) suggests the first such ad for something other than a book or self-promotion, maybe the first *paid* newspaper ad placement, was in a Dutch paper on November 21, 1626. It was an auction ad for the sale of sugar, pepper, ivory, and more.

Coffeehouses were key to newspaper distribution in the late 1600s in England. Coffee had been recently introduced, and its popularity grew quickly. It was considered a health drink (Elliott 1962). Literacy remained low, so this was a way to find the widely dispersed readers. At this point there still were no house addresses, so home delivery wasn't practical.

Britain's *Weekly Newes* opened in 1622 (Shaaber 1932), and Scotland's first newspaper in 1653 (Russell 1937). The *London Gazette* was established in 1665, becoming England's first regularly published newspaper (Foster 1967). It is still published today!

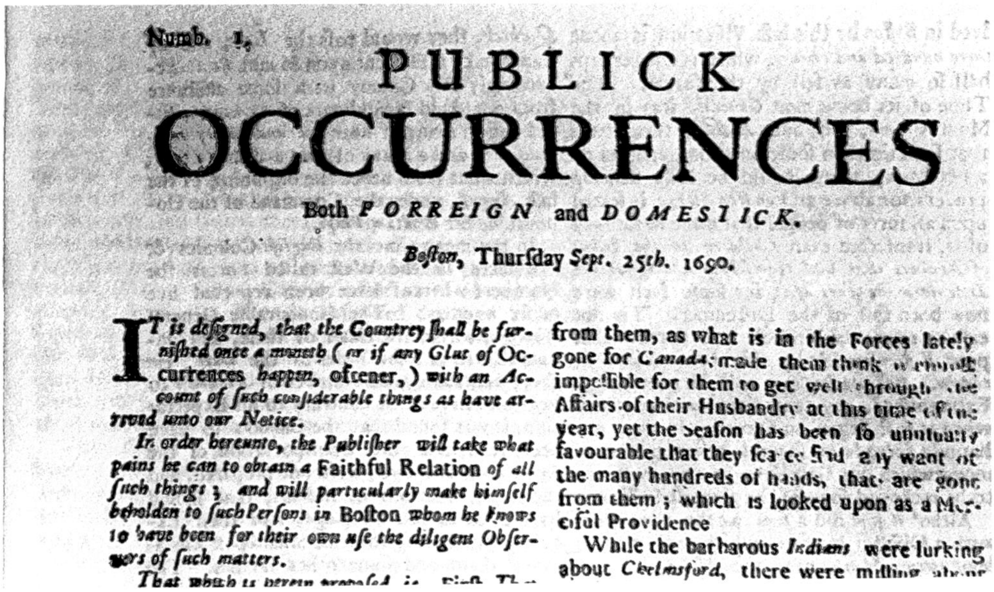

FIGURE 4.3. The first newspaper published in what would become the United States, *Publick Occurrences* had just one issue, in 1690.

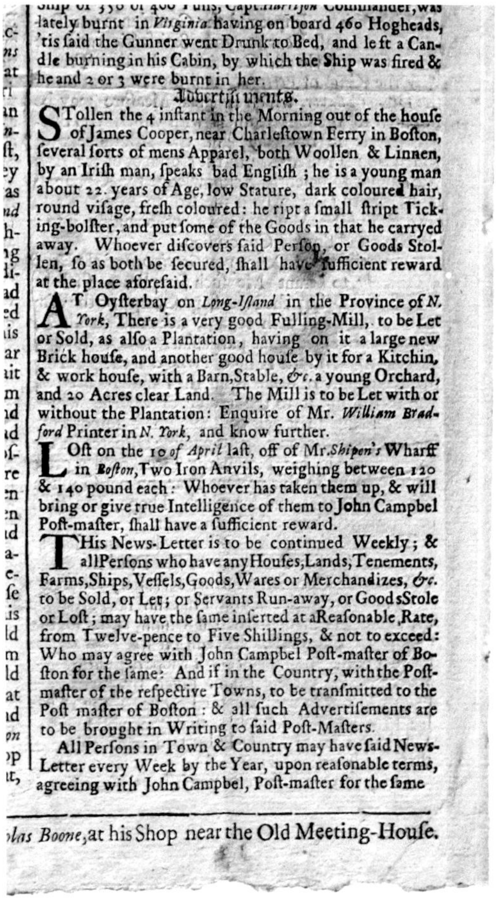

The first American newspaper lasted just one issue: *Publick Occurrences, Both Forrein and Domestick* in 1690 (Figure 4.3). It was published by Benjamin Harris in Boston, but the governor banned it (Editors of Advertising Age 1976). It contained no advertising.

The first successful newspaper in the United States, lasting several years, began in 1704: the *Boston News-Letter*. The first two issues had no real advertising, other than one promoting the *News-Letter* as an advertising venue (Applegate 1998). The third issue had three advertisements (and self-promotion), the first newspaper ads in America. Two ads sought the return of stolen/lost items, and one was selling real estate in Oyster Bay, Long Island (Figure 4.4).

Another important event was when Benjamin Franklin, in 1729, bought a

FIGURE 4.4. The third issue of the *Boston News-Letter*, dated May 1 to May 8, 1704, contained these advertisements, with first letters spelling out SALT.

newspaper, *Universal Instructor in All the Arts and Sciences and Pennsylvania Gazette*. It was about a year old. Franklin renamed it the *Pennsylvania Gazette* (Presbrey 1929). He had some experience working for his brother and quickly proved he knew how to succeed as a publisher (Applegate 1998). He put his stamp on both journalism and advertising.

At the end of the 1700s, only about 10 percent of people in the United States lived in cities, and only city dwellers had access to newspapers (Foster 1967). Literacy still was low, but this situation was changing.

Among the literate in cities, newspapers were being devoured. Most were no more than four pages, so they were read cover to cover, including every ad (Editors of Advertising Age 1976). But not every country had newspapers. Australia had no newspaper until 1803, the *Sydney Gazette* (Crawford 2008).

This is the first medium I've discussed that became financially supported by advertising. While advertising had previously served the person paying for the ad, it now was beginning to serve an additional master: the medium. *It was this marriage of newspapers and advertising that invented new avenues for the advertising industry to prosper.*

THE MARRIAGE OF NEWSPAPERS AND ADVERTISING

In 1692, in London, the *City Mercury* was created to be free, with its only purpose being advertising distribution. A thousand copies per week were placed in coffeehouses, bookstores, and bars. It survived for two years, until its publishers decided combining news and advertisements worked better (Russell 1937). This was the advent of the "free shopper" (Beard 2017).

That was the first *free* advertising-focused newspaper, but the first ad-only newspaper was the *Publick Advertiser*, beginning in 1657 CE. It cost a penny (Nevett 1982). In 1666, the *London Gazette* declared that while a "Paper of Intelligence" would never include advertising, it would publish a separate "Paper of Advertisements," thus creating the first advertising *supplement* (Wood 1958). This revealed the ongoing news/advertising tension, helping explain why advertising's growth in newspapers was not speedier.

There also was tension between newspapers and coffeehouses. Coffeehouses became the *de facto* distribution channel for newspapers, but those shops' owners were unhappy about it. The "coffee-men" wanted papers to be news only, while many were as much as half advertising. Those shop owners felt they were being used to profit others, which they most certainly were (Turner 1953). But they fought a losing battle.

Established in 1730, the *Daily Advertiser* might qualify as the first true newspaper, not an advertising "shopper," with "advertiser" in its title (Figure 4.5).[3] It was a major London newspaper throughout the eighteenth century (Kahl 1961), but it was not the only newspaper to use "advertiser" in its title, suggesting the importance of advertising to the news industry (Wood 1958).

FIGURE 4.5.   A December 1772 issue of the *Daily Advertiser*.

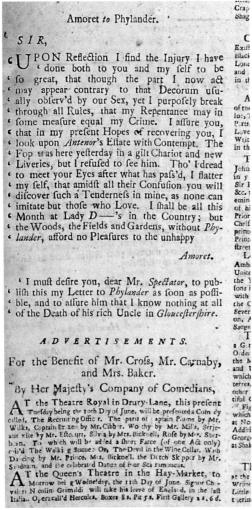

FIGURE 4.6.   Advertisements as they appear on the back side of the June 10, 1712, issue of the *Spectator* newspaper.

In the seventeenth and eighteenth centuries, advertising occupied a tiny fraction of the available space in most papers. The range of advertised goods and services was quite limited, and the ads tended to be all text in the same font as the news text around them, or smaller (e.g., Figure 4.6). And it took time for publishers to recognize the revenue potential. But that gradually changed. On July 18, 1743, the first half-page advertisement appeared in an American newspaper, the *New York Weekly Journal,* for a music box where figurines rang bells and a barber came out to shave the bell ringers. This ad was a radical change, both because of the size and due to the fact that it cut across two columns! It was well ahead of its time (Presbrey 1929).

On October 30, 1760, another standard of newsprint dissolved when the *New York Gazette* ran advertisements across its entire front page (Applegate 1998). Advertising was now so important that old rules were being sacrificed. This likely reflects realization of advertising's potential as a serious revenue source.

Publishers who embraced advertising found their purses bulging. With growing competition for readers, reducing subscription prices by increasing advertising income became a consideration, but it remained a gamble. Sampson (1874) believes London's *General Advertiser,* circa 1745, was the first real newspaper (not an ad-only paper) conceived from the start to be advertising supported. Russell (1937) concludes, "It was not till *The General Advertiser* proved that the financial foundation of every successful paper was to be found in its advertising columns that the periodical press began to flourish and to increase in numbers and importance."

An interesting thing happened with the increase in advertisements. It turns out that by the 1760s ads were as popular as news articles (Presbrey 1929). In part, this resulted from the limited amount of available reading material, and a paper shortage during the American Revolutionary War made it worse (Foster 1967). In addition, advertising became a popular source of information about commerce in towns too big for word-of-mouth methods.

Another milestone arose on November 22, 1766, when the first full-page newspaper advertisement appeared in the *Providence Gazette*. The ad, for Joseph and William Russell, promoted a variety of goods just imported from England (Figure 4.7).

The first successful American *daily* newspaper appeared in 1784. The *Pennsylvania Packet and General Advertiser* was a weekly when established in 1771 but was later converted to the *Pennsylvania Packet & Daily Advertiser* (Figure 4.8). It wasn't the first daily in America, but it was the first to last for any period of time, in large part because of advertising (Applegate 1998). It had so much advertising that either more pages or more issues were needed, and the selected option was to do both. The first issue under this new moniker, September 21, 1784, had sixteen columns total, of which ten were filled with advertising (Schuwer 1966). As the 1800s approached, it was clear advertising had a solid foothold in the newspaper industry.

FIGURE 4.7. The first full-page newspaper advertisement as it appeared in the *Providence Gazette*, November 22, 1766.
COURTESY OF AMERICAN ANTIQUARIAN SOCIETY

FIGURE 4.8. The *Pennsylvania Packet & Daily Advertiser* was an influential newspaper of its time.

GROWTH OF ADVERTISING

The seventeenth and eighteenth centuries saw rapid growth in advertising acceptance by merchants. Initially, the idea of advertising in newspapers was foreign. But even the *London Gazette*, which so maligned newspapers publishing ads in 1666, was itself accepting advertising by 1669. Until around 1688, newspapers included no more than about three or four ads, but after England's King James II was overthrown, the numbers increased dramatically (Russell 1937).

Over the next century, newspaper advertising grew dramatically. Britain's *Newcastle Courant* in 1711 ran 238 advertisements, but by 1761 it was 1,878 (Gardner 2016). In 1801, it reached 4,211. Similarly, the *Salisbury Journal* of 1737 published 200 ads; in 1752 it was over 1,000, in 1761 it reached 2,000, and in 1768 it was up to 3,000.

During most of that time, Britain levied duties (taxes) on both newspapers and the ads in them. Also, newspapers charged advertisers more for larger ads, but the government taxed a flat rate per ad, creating an incentive to encourage bigger ads. Ad space expanded immensely (Gardner 2016). By 1750, up to three-quarters of a newspaper's space was advertising (Beard 2017).

Newspapers were expanding in America, too. In 1765, there were 25 newspapers in the colonies (Presbrey 1929). By 1775, there were between 37 and 48 (Applegate 1998). That number rose to 106 by 1790, and 532 by 1820 (Editors of Advertising Age 1976). This was during a severe paper shortage! And nearly every newspaper carried advertising by then. An English newspaper in 1795 declared there were four daily papers in New York City, and a single paper might carry 350 ads (Sampson 1874). In 1818, there were seven newspapers in New York City, with only 125,000 people (Presbrey 1929).

The first US census, in 1790, counted 3,172,000 White residents and 600,000 Blacks. Only about 10 percent lived in cities, so most never saw a newspaper, let alone a newspaper ad. Even if they did, most advertised goods were far from where they lived (Foster 1967). So there remained limiting factors in the spread of advertising, but it had come a long way since 1704.

THE PAPAS

Publishers of the *Pennsylvania Packet & Daily Advertiser*, John Dunlap and David C. Claypoole, helped position advertising as fundamental for newspaper success. They were true advertising innovators. But a couple of men, earlier, were perhaps the real founders of modern advertising.

A former druggist named John Houghton (circa 1680 CE) has been dubbed the "Father of Advertising" (Turner 1953) or "Father of Publication Advertising" (Presbrey 1929). Houghton was a salesman's salesman who put his creativity into sales. A newspaper he published had the catchy name *A Collection for the Improvement of Husbandry and Trade* (Figure 4.9). As an early visionary, he played a serious role in advertising's evolution.

FIGURE 4.9.   John Houghton's *A Collection for the Improvement of Husbandry and Trade*, October 20, 1693.

Initially promoting just books and patent medicines, like other newspapers, Houghton saw potential for a broader range of advertisers: lotteries, employment, matrimonial opportunities, and more. An 1897 magazine article remarks, "Early newspaper advertising owes more to one John Houghton than to any other individual, since it was he who first impressed on the public mind the fact that advertising is a universal medium for bringing buyer and seller together and can be applied to any trade or profession" (Herzberg 1897).

Houghton also transitioned advertising from a publication's announcement to a more direct connection between buyer and seller, simply by including the advertiser's name and address in the ad, changing the newspaper's role. This also made it clearer that the advertiser paid for this insertion, as opposed to being news (MacRury 2009). That set the stage for product branding by identifying the source, though branding came later.

Another ad innovator came a bit later. Ben Franklin, upon acquiring the *Pennsylvania Gazette* in 1729, made layout and design changes to advertisements that affected newspapers everywhere. He made headlines larger and used ornamental borders and illustrations. One review suggested:

He opened up soggy columns by separating each advertisement from its neighbors above and below with several lines of white space. A 14-point heading for each advertisement was another innovation. At first the heading constituted the first line of the advertisement. Later it was shortened and centered, making a real heading. (Editors of Advertising Age 1976)

Franklin is remembered as the first US postmaster general, a founding father of the United States, an inventor, a scientist, author of *Poor Richard's Almanack*, US ambassador to France, and a publisher. But few people know he was a "Father of the Field of Advertising." Both men helped shape the field, and both helped make newspapers profitable.

THE ROLE OF NEWSPAPER LAWS

European countries published newsbooks and newspapers long before America, but their growth in the New World quickly outpaced Europe. This was almost entirely the result of laws that slowed journalistic growth, especially in England.

As mentioned earlier, the government restricted who could run a press. But there were few presses in the sixteenth century, so it was in the seventeenth century that legal restrictions really picked up.

One early attempt at press censorship was via the Star Chamber, an English court that operated from 1487 to 1641 CE. Near the end, in 1632, it forbade publishing foreign news. This was a reaction to complaints from Spanish diplomats who were unhappy about war coverage (Raymond 1996).

Then, in 1643, Parliament created a press licensing board even more restrictive than the Star Chamber, immediately followed by a law declaring that women (called "mercuries") found selling certain newssheets must be whipped (Elliott 1962), all in an effort to keep the press in check. This was intended "to avoid heresy, scandal (i.e., diminution of the reputation of the king and nobility), division, and sedition" (Mendle 1995).

Licensing became even more structured with the Licensing of the Press Act of 1662, aimed at "seditious treasonable and unlicensed Bookes and Pamphlets and for regulating of Printing and Printing Presses." Ironically, the following year, Sir Roger L'Estrange became Surveyor of the Imprimery (i.e., chief censor), while he, himself, published newspapers (Nevett 1982). He licensed publications *and* charged fees to businesses that posted handbills (Barrés-Baker 2006). He also aggressively pursued printers publishing what he considered anti-government propaganda. Apparently his conflicts of interest were not a huge concern.

Censorship aside, licensing fees were an obstacle to newspapers flourishing, since they increased operating costs. This barrier was raised higher in 1712 when England imposed "stamp duties" on both newspapers and advertisements, effective 1713 (Sampson 1874). Publishers paid duty on every copy of their newspaper and, additionally, on every advertisement in their newspaper. Although amounts changed, duties continued for nearly a century and a half. The ad tax finally was abolished in 1853, and the newspaper tax ended in 1855 (Nevett 1982). An example of a stamp to show the duty had been paid can be viewed in Figure 4.10.

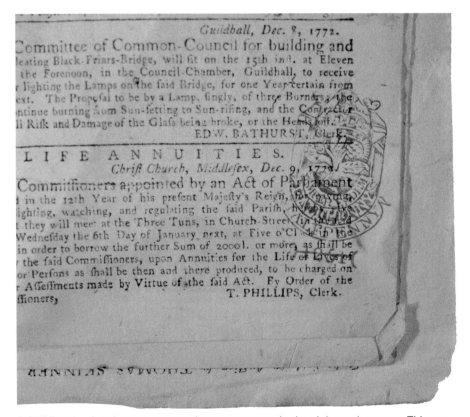

FIGURE 4.10.   A red stamp appeared on newspapers in the eighteenth century. This one is from December 1772, on the *Daily Advertiser*.

These taxes put some publications out of business, as apparently intended. The taxes were aimed at stifling press criticism of government (Wood 1958). It also discouraged both widespread circulation of newspapers and acceptance of advertisements. It effectively put the brakes on newsprint growth in England. When the ad duty was doubled in 1757, ad sales dropped. Book advertisements in the *London Evening Post* dropped by half between 1745 and 1765 (Gardner 2016).

British colonies in America were subject to those duties, for a time. Massachusetts had such a tax from 1755 to 1757, and even in that short time it damaged the newspaper industry there. In 1765, Britain attempted to apply both duties to all the colonies (Presbrey 1929). When word reached the colonies, "Sons of Liberty" groups formed to fight it. In other words, *this was one of the triggers of the Revolutionary War.* We might never have celebrated the Fourth of July—US Independence Day—if not for an unfair tax on advertising!

In fact, US founding father Sam Adams even used advertising as a tool in the fight, urging people to boycott British goods. One such ad read:

WILLIAM JACKSON, an IMPORTER. . . . It is desired that the SONS and DAUGHTERS of LIBERTY, would not buy any one thing of him, for in so doing they will bring Disgrace upon themselves, and their Posterity, for ever and ever, AMEN. (Mierau 2000)

And George Washington used advertising to call for men to join him in the fight (Mierau 2000). So advertising played multiple roles in transforming the United Colonies into the United States of America. *Without the British war on advertising, the USA might never have happened!*

ADVERTISING MONKEYSHINES

Advertising also was key to another important law affecting newspapers: libel. In fact, one case is still cited by lawyers today.

The *New York Weekly Journal* was established in 1733 as a political organ. Soon the *Journal* ran a mock classified advertisement searching for a runaway monkey, clearly alluding to Governor William Cosby (yes, Bill Cosby). Another ad referred to a lost dog. The governor was not amused. Since the ads' author(s) couldn't be identified, its printer, John Peter Zenger, was arrested on libel charges in late 1734.

He was found not guilty because the ad was based on fact. This established a legal principle that truth is an absolute defense to libel. This law provided newspapers with new legal protection, giving the American press additional ammunition for expansion. As Magnet (2010) suggests, this too was revolutionary!

BEYOND NEWSPAPERS: MAGAZINES

Magazines probably began with *Erbauliche Monaths Unterredungen* ("Edifying Monthly Discussions") published by a German theologian in 1663. In 1665, Paris had its first magazine,

Journal des Scavans, translated as "Journal of Learned Men." The first English-language magazine was *Philosophical Transactions*, also in 1665 (Haveman 2015). None of these resembled *Good Housekeeping* or *Sports Illustrated*, nor were they likely to be big advertising draws.

The world's first woman's magazine, the *Ladies' Mercury*, came in 1693. It lasted only four issues. It was a sister publication to *Athenian Mercury* and some other short-lived *Mercuries*. The publisher was open to advertising, since the *Ladies' Mercury* was first announced through an ad in the *Athenian Mercury* (Stearns 1930). Stearns (1930) hypothesizes that the *Ladies' Mercury* was an experiment to learn just who readers were.

A few years later, newspapers took direct aim at women as prospective readers. *The Tatler* (1709–1711)[4] and *The Spectator* (1711–1714) (Figure 4.11), both published by Richard Steele and Joseph Addison, broke that new ground (Turner 1953). Both were newspapers, but their content resembled magazine articles of the future.

There was another publication directed at women, taking advantage of *The Tatler*'s popularity, called the *Female Tatler*, in 1709–1710. It was published "by Mrs. Crackenthorpe, a Lady that knows every thing."

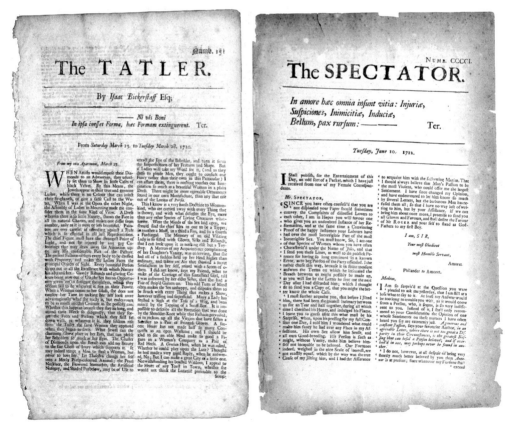

FIGURE 4.11. Two newspapers that changed the tone and approach of newspapers, and set the stage for modern magazines, *The Tatler* and *The Spectator*.

In 1704, Daniel Defoe, author of *Robinson Crusoe*, introduced *A Review of the Affairs of France and of all Europe* (Haveman 2015). This was a political magazine of likely broader appeal, with content closer to *The Tatler* and *The Spectator*. It soon included advertisements.

Edward Cave, in 1731, was first to use the word "magazine" in the *Gentleman's Magazine: or, Monthly Intelligencer* in London (Williamson 2016). It is believed he took the word from the Arabic *makhzin*, meaning "storehouse."

The first magazines in the American colonies were in 1741. Andrew Bradford published *American Magazine, or A Monthly View of the Political State of the British Colonies* on February 13 of that year. Three days later, Ben Franklin published the *General Magazine, and Historical Chronicle for all the British Plantations in America*. Short titles, evidently, were not fashionable.

The reason Bradford beat Franklin likely was because Franklin had telegraphed his move in November 1740, with ads promoting his coming magazine (Willard et al. 1938). Neither magazine lasted long. Bradford published three issues and Franklin six (Applegate 1998). Franklin's magazine did, though, publish the first paid magazine advertisement in America in 1741 (Figure 4.12).[5]

THE is a FERRY kept over Potomack (by the Subscriber) being the Post Road and much the nighest way from Annapolis to Williamsburg, where all Gentlemen may depend on a ready Passage in a good new Boat with able Hands Richard Brett, Deputy-Post-Master at Potomack.

FIGURE 4.12. According to Oswald (1917), this is the first advertisement to appear in an American magazine, Ben Franklin's *General Magazine, and Historical Chronicle for all the British Plantations in America*.

ILLUSTRATED PRINT

If advertising existed before written language, it was an illustration of some variety (e.g., a handprint), so it is impossible to identify the very first illustrated advertisement. But afterward, use of illustrations seemed to disappear. Early print advertisements were almost entirely text. Even fancy fonts didn't exist. Once illustrations came, they were not quickly adopted. Some of the earliest illustrated advertisements probably were found in Pompeii and Herculaneum, but they were less common after the fall of Rome.

The first known illustrated advertising handbill (or broadside or poster) was for the *History of the Beautiful Melusina*,[6] a mythological romance tale by Jean d'Arras, printed in Antwerp in 1491. This was a carved illustration—a woodcut—of a bathing woman-serpent, making it also an early example of sex in advertising (Figure 4.13).

FIGURE 4.13. Melusina, as depicted in 1491.

Around 1,500 small, standardized block engravings became part of the options printers could pull out of their type trays (Rickards 1971). These were similar to today's icons and dingbats (Figure 4.14). Many might not truly qualify as "illustrations," but rather as ornaments or decorations.

FIGURE 4.14. Illustrations of this sort became a part of printers' regular arsenal, this one from the *Post Boy*, June 13, 1719.

The earliest known illustrated advertisement to appear in an English newspaper was in 1652, published in the *Faithfull Scout*, of London (Barrés-Baker 2006). It depicted two stolen jewels. The ad was placed by a goldsmith who asked that friends of the thieves rat them out (Sale 2002). One of the oldest illustrated posters was in 1705, for the Bållhuset Theater in Stockholm (Halldin 2013).

When Ben Franklin took over the *Pennsylvania Gazette* in 1729, he began using illustrations in ads, particularly those small icon types. He used symbols like horses to illustrate horses for sale, and books for book sellers. And he created ornamental borders for certain advertisers (Editors of Advertising Age 1976). He expanded advertising in the newspaper significantly.

The seventeenth-century illustrations frequently were carved into wood blocks. However, by the late eighteenth century many of them were engraved into copper (Presbrey 1929). And with the invention of lithographic printing in 1793, woodcuts began disappearing.

TRADESMAN'S CARDS

Some more elaborate illustrations were used in forms of advertising other than newspapers. Beginning in the 1600s, tradesman's cards (or shop cards or tradesmen's bills or shopkeepers' bills) weren't cards at all but paper handbills about the size of a book page used to promote a business (Wood 1958). They were the business cards of the day (Figure 4.15).

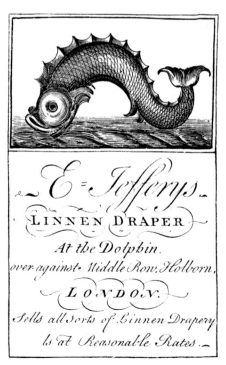

FIGURE 4.15. Two tradesman's cards from the 1700s.

This method is believed to have first appeared in 1622 (Beard 2017). Six copies were discovered bound into a book published in 1630. The card read as follows:

> Whosoever shall desire to purchase, or put to Sale, to take in Lease, or let to Farme, to Grant, Assigne, Exchange, or otherwise to Contract, or Deale, with or for any Lands, Lease, Rents, Annuities, Mansion-houses, Offices Saleable, or other Estates of what yearly value soever, or to save any such from danger of Forfeiture, through the want of present money : May eyther in their owne names, or in the name of any other trusted by them, have secure meanes with all privacy requisite : for the speedy effecting what shall be desired, in any the Cases aforesayd, or the like : At the Porcht House against St. Andrewe's Church in Holborne, LONDON.
> God save our gracious King Charles.

This form of advertising really came into its own in the eighteenth century, with few remaining earlier examples. Heal (1968) argues these cards are of great archaeological value, as a clear everyday record of trade. One might say that of all advertising. Many had no address, since street address numbering only began in the early part of that century. They did, however, collectively represent an advance in advertising aesthetics showcasing the potential of printing. Not all were so impressive. Many were simply paper representations of the sign hanging outside a business.

SIGNS OF ROYALTY AND REBUS

Business signs date back at least to Pompeii and Herculaneum (79 CE), but by the 1300s they were common, and even more so by the 1400s. By then Paris had more than three thousand signs (Schuwer 1966). The population of Paris in 1400 was around 280,000.

Back then, signs were almost entirely unregulated. Some pushed the boundaries of good taste. Many hung from iron brackets, swinging with every wind gust, sticking out over the streets (Figure 4.16). They were mostly painted wood, and certain images were in common use then. In England, the first such image was the Crown, circa 1467. Walter Walters, the apparent owner of that establishment, is said to have made a pun about making his son heir to the Crown. The pun wasn't so funny to King Edward IV, who ordered Walters put to death for treason (Larwood & Hotten 1875). Even so, the Crown continued as a popular symbol on business signs.

FIGURE 4.16. A drawing of the "General Wayne" inn in Baltimore, as seen in *Scribner's Monthly* (1879).

Other images joined the Crown. Some vendors used portraits of famous people, like a king or William Shakespeare. All manner of animals were popular: pigs, dogs, lions, and more (Gardner 1899b). The same was true in the New World. But businesses also used visual elements that fit their trade, like a boot to indicate a shoemaker.

Puns were used in these early days of signs, particularly visual puns, given the low literacy. The "rebus" ("Rebus de Picardie") was a visual pun used in many signs. The name

FIGURE 4.17. An example of a "rebus," or visual pun, from the early nineteenth century.

Hancock could be represented by an image of a hand and an image of a rooster (i.e., a "cock") (Elliott 1962). An example can be seen in Figure 4.17.

Earlier I mentioned using heraldic symbols, particularly coats of arms, as advertising. Inns often evolved from large houses of nobility, so their signs frequently used that family's coat of arms. The inns, then, might take their name from the most noticeable part of the coat of arms—for example, the Gold Fox or the Red Crown (Wood 1958). Joseph Addison wrote in *The Spectator* of April 2, 1711, "Our streets are filled with blue Boars, black Swans and red Lions, not to mention flying pigs and hogs in Armour, with many other creatures more extraordinary than any in the Desarts of Africk."

Something happened with signage, then, not found in modern advertising. Signs were affixed to buildings, and there was cost in changing them. Some signs became well known as major landmarks, before street numbers. So when one business moved out and another moved in, they sometimes kept the sign, even for a different business. This resulted in total absurdities. A blacksmith might logically use an anvil on his sign, but then the shop is bought by a baker and the anvil sign continues to be used. Presbrey (1929) suggests the baker might add the image of a bun, so his address becomes "At the Sign of the Anvil and the Bun." If the baker served very hard rolls, this might be an apt sign, but many combinations made no sense at all.

This appeared in the *British Apollo* newspaper in 1710 (Rivers 1929):

I am amazed at the Signs
As I pass thru the Town
To see the odd Mixture,
A Magpie and Crown,
The Whale and the Crow,
The Razor and Hen,
The Leg and Seven Stars,
The Ax and the Bottle,

The Tun and the Lute,
The Eagle and Child,
The Shovel and Boot.

Other regulation of signage developed over time. In 1577 France, innkeepers were ordered to post a sign on the most conspicuous part of their inn. In 1693, tavernkeepers were forced to do the same: "Nobody shall be allowed to open a tavern in the said city and its suburbs without having a sign and a bush" (Larwood & Hotten 1875). The bush, as mentioned earlier, was literally that: an image of a bush, originally symbolizing a wine shop.

While those laws required signs, in the mid-1600s England also put limits on signs. The signs hanging from buildings had become larger and larger as merchants competed for attention, to the point that signs from opposite sides of a street would touch. The danger of signs falling and injuring someone likewise increased. Like billboards today, they were seen by some as visual pollution. King Charles II finally declared, "No signs shall be hung across the streets shutting out the air and light of the heavens" (Wood 1958). Even after that, however, there were incidents when the fronts of buildings collapsed from the weight of a sign and even when passersby were killed (Gardner 1899a).

In 1761, things started to change when merchants in France faced mandated restrictions on sign size and placement (Casey 2013). Signs could no longer extend more than four inches from a building's face (Larwood & Hotten 1875). In 1762, England followed France's lead, ordering that signs be flat against the building face (Gardner 1899b; Elliott 1962). Heal (1968) says, "The last streets to keep their signs hanging were Wood Street and Whitecross Street, where they remained till 1773."

FIGURE 4.18.   The golden grasshopper from 1563.

Some older hanging signs still exist. A golden grasshopper from 1563 still hangs on Lombard Street in London (Figure 4.18). That sign was hung by Sir Thomas Gresham. At some point Gresham added the grasshopper to his family's coat of arms. Other vintage signs from London are rare, thanks to the Great Fire of London in 1666.

Another sign believed to be from before the fire continues to hang in London. It is the "Three Squirrels" sign from the Goslings and Sharpe bank on Fleet Street, circa 1660 (Figure 4.19). Fleet Street was long, so many old signs from London began there (Price 1895).[7]

Restrictions on hanging signs forced merchants to rethink their approach to advertising. The law in London said that "no sign posts shall hang cross, but the signs shall be fixed against the balconies, or some other convenient part of the side of the house." So signs built flat into the brick or other masonry of a building front appeared. One of these was the "Three Kings" sign from 1667, sup-

FIGURE 4.19.   The Three Squirrels sign from around 1660.

FIGURE 4.20. The Three Kings tavern sign of 1667.

posedly for a tavern (Figure 4.20). It is said that this sign might actually have been for an inn, with the kings as the patron saints of travelers. Norman (1893) devotes an entire book chapter to this sign.

Another, from 1688, can be found just outside the St. Paul's tube station in London (Figure 4.21). The figure on the sign is known as Panyer Boy (or Boy and Panyer), which had appeared on the east side of Panyer Alley between Paternoster Row and Newgate Street (Norman 1893).

Moving forward into the nineteenth century, more signs are preserved. For example, the Bull and Mouth Inn sign dates back at least to 1829 (Figure 4.22). This was a "coaching inn," like a motel back then, and its name might be a sort of rebus, with the original name being Boulogne Mouth (Norman 1893).

FIGURE 4.21. The Panyer Boy sign. It states, cryptically, "When y Have SoughT the Citty Round Yet Still Ths is the HighT Ground, August 27, 1688."

FIGURE 4.22. Sign for the Bull and Mouth Inn, from 1829 or earlier. Note that the sign depicts a large face, with a bull sitting in its mouth.

Over time, hanging signs returned and are common in today's London (Figure 4.23), but with more regulatory oversight. Laws tend to follow both dangers and power, and signs can be powerful. In 1743, the Bauer family supposedly honored their father, who used a sign with a red shield, by changing their surname to Rothschild, taken from a German term for "red shield" (Wagner 1954). The next year, Mayer Amschel Rothschild started what would become a banking empire, with that sign playing a historical role.

One thing of note in all these signs is the dependence on the visual. Poor literacy again came into play.

Signs made of wood, metal, or stone weren't the only advertising hanging from or affixed to walls. Paper was now being used for more than just tradesman's cards. Paper signs could be posted almost anywhere.

POST NO BILLS!

Earlier I mentioned posters of the fourteenth and fifteenth centuries. This was the start of what Presbrey (1929) called "the beginnings of tackup advertisements in England." Thanks to Gutenberg, paper ads found promising possibilities.

Posters rapidly achieved popularity. At that time, posters were simple text on paper, closer to today's fliers or handbills. The term "posters" hadn't been adopted yet; they were called "bills."

Bills were being stuck on every available surface, using brushes with pots of glue (Figure 4.24), becoming perhaps the first truly annoying form of media placement. Some were seriously annoyed. In 1534, town criers in France were required to announce rewards for revealing billstickers' (those sticking ads everywhere) names, and anyone withholding a name would be "publicly burnt in the town." This might be the genesis of the phrase, "Post No Bills!" Yet five years later the government ordered its own notices be prominently posted, making it illegal to remove them (Rickards 1971).

Adoption of posters was not restricted to Europe. One Japanese dry goods store in 1638 is believed to have published five hundred thousand to six hundred thousand advertising posters (Pongsapitaksanti 2010).

Poster popularity was evident in 1644 when a Dutch newsbook, *Le Mercure Anglois*, used them to promote itself. This might be the first example of a newspaper using another medium for self-promotion (Barrés-Baker 2006).

Posted bills were popular with the patent medicine crowd. Daniel Defoe's novel, *A Journal of the Plague Year* (1722), details quack medicine sales coming in the wake of the Great Plague. He describes how houses and street corners were "plaster'd over with Doctor Bills, and Papers of ignorant Fellows; quacking and tamperin in Physick, and inviting the People to come to them for Remedies."

These bills were not favored by some, especially those in government. Billstickers in Paris in 1652 were threatened with flogging and, soon, printing bills without the King's approval could result in execution (Rickards 1971). In 1721, the Corporation des Colleurs (Society of Billstickers) was legally limited to forty practitioners within Paris.

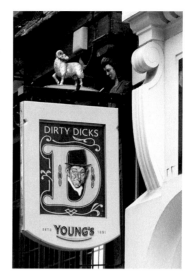

FIGURE 4.23. Some hanging signs of today resemble those signs of the eighteenth century, though the brackets clearly differ. This sign hangs in front of Dirty Dick's tavern, in London, which was established in 1745. It undoubtedly bore one of those old-style signs in the distant past.
COURTESY OF JOE VIDEAN

FIGURE 4.24. Billstickers continue the practice in 2018, though now it's done from motorcycles. This one, in Naples, Italy, still uses a brush and a pot of glue.

When Britain imposed duties on newspapers and ads, advertising rates increased, providing incentive to use alternative media like bills. By the late eighteenth and early nineteenth centuries, it was a horribly competitive trade. One day bills would be pasted everywhere, and that night a competitor would cover them with his own bills. Sampson (1874) called this *predatory* billsticking. Eventually prime locations erected boards ("hoardings") on

which to post ads, selling exclusive rights to billposters. These "advertisement stations" didn't eliminate predation, but did reduce it.

The first hoarding was in 1740 when a London clothing seller asked a crier whether he could post his handbill beside a government announcement, which caused the city to establish a fee for posting on its boards (Presbrey 1929). The first company to rent hoardings was formed in 1839. That was the real birth of the "billboard"—a term coined no more than four years later.

FIGURE 4.25.   Artist John Orlando Parry captured a London street scene circa 1834.

Billsticking became so prevalent in cities (Figure 4.25) that it became the topic of conversations, articles, and at least one song:

> I'm Sammy Slap the billsticker, and you must all agree, sirs,
> I sticks to business like a trump while business sticks to me, sirs.
> There's some folks calls me plasterer, but they deserve a banging,
> Cause yer see, genteelly speaking, that my trade is paperhanging.
> With my paste, paste, paste!
> All the world is-puffing,
> So I'll paste, paste, paste! (Sampson 1874)

Two industries involved in posting bills were lotteries and, later, circuses. Both applied this medium with vigor in the late 1700s. Other outdoor advertising, though, included painting directly on rocks, walls, and fences. By then, in the United States, eighteen-inch thin-paper handbills known as "broadsides" were in use (Hendon & Muhs 1985).

Handbills and posters were generally synonymous, but today's concept of posters developed during the French Revolution, beginning in 1789 (Gallo 1972). Posters were used in commerce, but also for war propaganda. Some included color and aesthetic design (Figure 4.26).

As bills and posters spread, some began including multiple products. It is no stretch to imagine multi-page advertisements being printed. And so along came catalogs.

FIGURE 4.26.   A poster from the French Revolution, circa 1793.

CATALOGS

Recall that the first newspaper ads were for books. Well, the first known catalog was little more than a list of fifteen books from Aldus Pius Manutius, Venice, in 1498 (Fryxell 2012). Manutius was the inventor of paperback books. That catalog was published to promote them.

In 1595, another book catalog was published. As a complete bibliography of English books over 150 years or more, it was 123 pages long: Andrew Maunsell's *The First Part of the Catalogue of English printed Bookes: which concerneth such Matters of Divinite as have bin either written in oure Tongue or translated out of some other Language, and have bin published to the Glory of God and Edification of the Church of Christ in England.*[8]

In 1667, a gardener named William Lucas published *A Catalogue of Seeds, Plants, etc.* with prices (Fryxell 2012). And in 1744, Benjamin Franklin published *A Catalogue of Choice and Valuable Books, Consisting of Near 600 Volumes, in most Faculties and Sciences*, another list of books for sale. Franklin did something new in his sixteen-page catalog: He offered what might be the first "customer satisfaction" guarantee. This catalog also introduced the first mail-order business! That same year Franklin published a pamphlet promoting the Franklin Stove: *An Account of the New Invented Pennsylvania Fire-Places*. Another sales catalog, it is preserved in the US National Archives.[9]

These catalogs were paper, like newspapers and posters, but ad media at that time were not confined to paper. While most were about money, some were more about money than others.

ADVERTISING COMES INTO MONEY

In the mid-1600s, advertisers found a new opportunity in England. Poor citizens needed smaller coins than wealthier people, resulting in minting copper or brass farthings (one-quarter of a penny), but during the English civil war (1642–1651) minting ceased, causing a shortage of small change. Several merchants began issuing coins of their own. These "trade tokens" could be exchanged for goods at those businesses, much like today's coupons.

The Crown minted coins in gold and silver, but anything less than a penny was too small for precious metals. Minting in lesser metals was too expensive, so the government turned a blind eye to merchants who filled this gap. They were, after all, only of "token" value. Frequently cast in copper or brass, or even lead, pewter, and leather, they served as farthings or halfpennies[10] and were stamped with a business name or shop sign replica (Elliott 1962).

The first copper alloy trade tokens were struck in 1648, during the English civil war. They became valuable advertising media. Merchants, and even towns, issued tokens from 1648 to 1672 (Figure 4.27), until Charles II introduced royal copper halfpennies and farthings, demonetizing the tokens. Some tokens made their way to the Americas after being devalued in Britain, becoming part of the American money system at that time.

FIGURE 4.27. A 1665 trade token for John Quick in High Street, Aldgate, though note that Aldgate is spelled Algate (Akerman 1849).

FIGURE 4.28. A 1793 trade token for Goldsmith and Sons, in Sudbury. Note that "Payable at" and the merchant's name appear on the coin's edge.

A coin shortage happened again in the late 1700s. The minting machines were antiquated by this time and couldn't keep up with demand. There also was no good coin distribution system to ensure broad availability (Whiting 1971). And there was a counterfeiting problem, opening the door to privately minted coins carrying local trust.

This revival was even more popular for advertisers, because new methods of minting made it better than in the past (Figures 4.28 and 4.29). A waterwheel-driven pressing and cutting system made the coins in higher volume and greater uniformity than before. These tokens began production in high volumes in 1787 (Whiting 1971).

FIGURE 4.29. A 1795 trade token that reads, "Payable by J. Smyth at Padsole Paper Mill."

The coins were called Conder tokens or Provincial tokens, and usually were larger than their predecessors. They advertised businesses, and occasionally advertised *issues* ("causes"). From 1790 until 1863, private industries sometimes also issued their own paper money. Advertising was a true money maker.

PROMOTIONAL PRODUCTS AND MORE

The techniques listed above aren't an exhaustive inventory of advertisers' tools back then—and a few more need mention.

When William Penn founded Pennsylvania, he needed to promote the land. In 1681, he published perhaps the first American direct advertising booklet. Its title: "Some account of the province of Pennsylvania, lately granted by the King, under the great seal of England to William Penn and his heirs and assigns."[11] This is reminiscent of Erik the Red's naming a frozen landmass Greenland in 982 CE, except Erik's description was wholly misleading.

In 1700 in London, Thomas Tuttle published playing cards with his tradesman's card on the back. These were the first advertising playing cards, but they also might be the very first promotional product! Each card depicted either a tradesman (e.g., carpenter, bricklayer, etc.) at work or a particular instrument or tool (e.g., a compass). Tuttle had been appointed "Instrument Maker to the King."[12] In a way, the deck of cards also was a catalog of his products. It was inventive advertising for its time.

Those cards might be the first functional product distributed as advertisements; the paper fan might be second. The War of Austrian Succession ended in April 1748, with the treaty signed in October. In April 1749, a celebration was held. Handel wrote music for the event, and a souvenir fan was produced for it (Figure 4.30).

A similar souvenir was produced in 1788, when the King's Theater at London's Haymarket had fans printed with the opera house layout, so attendees could see where the prince and others were seated. This helped promote ticket sales.

That same year, another fan depicted Warren Hastings' impeachment trial from his position of first governor-general to Bengal. It was a commemorative fan, since the trial began in 1788 but didn't end until 1795. It was another form of promotional fan. Fans obviously were a hot form of advertising, promoting memories of major events.

FIGURE 4.30. This souvenir fan was produced to commemorate the Aix-la-Chapelle celebration in London's Green Park on April 27, 1749.

On April 30, 1789, George Washington was inaugurated as the first president of the United States. This event led to another commemorative promotional product: the political button. There was no need for a "campaign" button, since Washington ran unopposed. But the inauguration of the first president of this nation was an event of historical significance, and vendors saw an opportunity. These were positioned as "patriotic" buttons. They had no pin back, but were actual coat buttons. About twenty-six different buttons were sold over the next several years. Some were simple, with just "GW" stamped on them, while others were far more complex. Several had "Long Live the President" on them (Figure 4.31). These were the first political advertising buttons in the United States.

FIGURE 4.31. This commemorative button celebrating George Washington's inauguration was produced by Crumpton & Company.

THE BIRTH OF PUBLIC RELATIONS

Like advertising, identifying the genesis of public relations (PR) depends on how it is defined. Basically, it is about relationships of a represented entity to one or more "publics." It is viewed by many as shining the most positive light on something.

Sir Walter Raleigh wanted to settle Roanoke Island in 1584. Captain Barlowe told Raleigh, "[T]he soile is the most plentiful, sweete, fruitful, and wholesome of all the worlde . . . they have those Okes that we have, but farre greater and better . . . the highest and reddest Cedars of the world and a great abundance of Pine or Pitch Trees." He depicted Native Americans as "most gentle, loving, and faithful, void of all guile or treason" (Cutlip & Baker 2012). Barlowe shined a positive light on Roanoke, enhancing the potential for funding a second voyage. He is remembered for this bit of "propaganda," and perhaps as an early PR professional.

This resembles William Penn promoting Pennsylvania. But Penn's intent was property sales, while Barlowe's was support for exploration. But there has always been a fuzzy line between advertising and public relations, which is why PR is included here. Another example came half a century later.

Harvard College, established September 1636, became the first institution of higher education in the colonies. The first fund-raising initiative for higher education came five years later, when Harvard sent three preachers to England on a "begging mission" (Cutlip & Baker 2012). They realized they needed some written material promoting the school. This led to publishing a forty-seven-page document called "New England's First Fruits" in 1643, partly about converting Native Americans to Christianity and partly about "the Colledge, and the proceedings of Learning therein." From our perspective, it was an early public relations pamphlet.

A major push for PR came from the South Sea Trading Company, formed in 1711 by the British Parliament. It had a monopoly representing England in trading with Spanish colonies in the West Indies and South America (Reed 1999). The company sold stock with a guaranteed return on investment, so it sold well. In a very early version of a Ponzi scheme, the company ended up defrauding investors. It now is known as the South Sea Bubble of 1720 (Walsh 2014). Many people lost fortunes. Sir Isaac Newton lost what today would be several million American dollars. Leading up to that "bubble," this company pioneered use of several PR tools, including the press release and the press conference.

Later, there is ample evidence of PR leading into the US Revolutionary War. Between 1763 and 1776 the publicity used to build the patriots' resistance was impressive. Samuel Adams was a leader in this, and has been dubbed a propagandist by some (e.g., Miller 1936). He wrote forty-plus articles for the *Boston Gazette* from 1770 to 1772, to educate people about the need for independence from the British. He also moved men who agreed with him into positions of influence. As Mierau (2000) remarks, "With handbills, posters, speeches, and newspaper ads, Adams urged people to boycott (refuse to buy) English goods."

Adams was not alone engaging in publicity at that time. The Boston Tea Party (1773) was all about public relations. This probably wasn't the first war where media helped sway opinion, but it likely was the first to approach this in such a strategic manner. And in its aftermath, similar techniques were employed to secure ratification of the US Constitution (Cutlip & Baker 2012).

The success of these campaigns laid a foundation for future public relations practice. PR might have roots extending farther back into history, but the field made major advances in the seventeenth and eighteenth centuries. And it proved that mass media could work to the benefit of an important cause, beyond just selling products.

CONCLUSION

The number of options for promoting a product, service, business, or idea post-Gutenberg far outstripped anything seen in previous centuries. And the content of advertising was beginning to evolve. The next chapter will focus on that content.

5

Some Seventeenth- and Eighteenth-Century Advertisements

In the pages of old magazines and newspapers, half-filled with patent-medicine advertisements, it is a melancholy picture that unfolds. The women had Falling Wombs, the men had Failing Powers; their children were afflicted with Worms.

—*Jean Burton, as quoted in Rowsome (1959)*

It is one thing to talk about the ad process, but quite another to look at the outcome. Most examples come from newspapers of the time. It seems worthwhile to look at a few.

ADS OF NOTE

Not all ads were for products. Many were for the government. In Figure 5.1, you can see what appears to be a tax notice from 1669, via advertising.

It should be clear that advertising in the seventeenth and eighteenth centuries was different from today's. Yet some content wasn't all that different.

From the *Mercurius Politicus* newspaper, 1660 CE, this might be the very first toothpaste ad (Sampson 1874):

> MOST Excellent and Approved Dentifrices to scour and cleanse the Teeth, making them white as Ivory, preserves from the Toothach; so that, being constantly used, the parties using it are never troubled with the Toothach; it fastens the Teeth, sweetens the Breath, and preserves the mouth and gums from Cankers and Imposthumes. Made by Robert Turner, Gentleman; and the right are onely to be had at Thomas Rookes, Stationer, at the Holy Lamb at the East end of St Pauls Church, near the School, in sealed papers, at 12d. the paper. The Reader is desired to beware of counterfeits.

This pitch is amazingly familiar. The "beware of counterfeits" line is similar to what we saw with printers' marks.

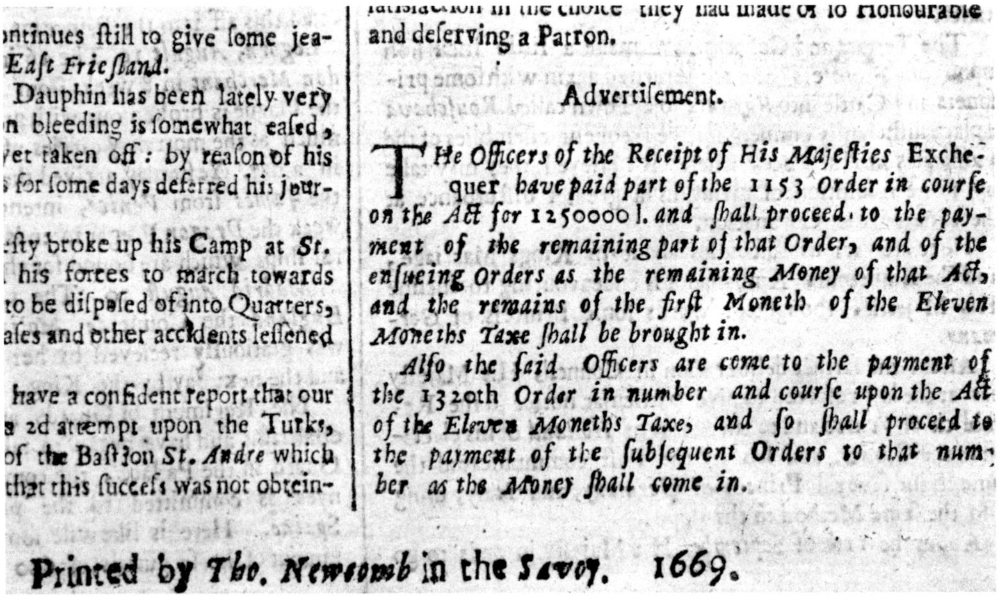

ntinues still to give some jea-
East Friesland.
Dauphin has been lately very
n bleeding is somewhat eased,
yet taken off: by reason of his
s for some days deferred his jour-

sty broke up his Camp at St.
his forces to march towards
to be dispsed of into Quarters,
ases and other accidents lessened

have a confident report that our
a 2d attempt upon the Turks,
of the Bastion St. Andre which
that this success was not obtein-

and deserving a Patron.

Advertisement.

THe Officers of the Receipt of His Majesties Exchequer have paid part of the 1153 Order in course on the Act for 1250000 l. and shall proceed to the payment of the remaining part of that Order, and of the ensueing Orders as the remaining Money of that Act, and the remains of the first Moneth of the Eleven Moneths Taxe shall be brought in.

Also the said Officers are come to the payment of the 1320th Order in number and course upon the Act of the Eleven Moneths Taxe, and so shall proceed to the payment of the subsequent Orders to that number as the Money shall come in.

Printed by Tho. Newcomb in the Savoy. 1669.

FIGURE 5.1. An advertisement from the *London Gazette* in 1669.

That same year, in that same newspaper, was an ad for a lost dog (Sampson 1874). This one was placed by King James II:

> A Smooth Black DOG, less than a Grey-hound, with white under his breast, belonging to the Kings Majesty, was taken from White-hall, the eighteenth day of this instant June, or thereabouts. If anyone can give notice to John Ellis, one of his Majesties servants, or to his Majesties Back-Stairs, shall be well rewarded for their labour.

Perhaps the first newspaper beverage advertisement, for coffee, was in the the *Publick Advertiser* in 1657 (Nevett 1982). This helped usher the coffee habit into England:

> In Bartholomew Lane on the back side of the Old Exchange, the drink called Coffee (which is a very wholsom and physical drink, having many excellent vertues, closes the Orifice of the Stomack, fortifies the heat within, helpeth Digestion, quickneth the Spirits, maketh the heart lighten, is good against Eye-sores, Coughs, or Colds, Rhumes, Consumption, Head-ach, Dropsie, Gout, Scurvy, Kings Evil, and many others) is to be sold both in the morning and at three o'clock in the afternoon.

Notice the health claims!

I qualified that as the first "newspaper" ad for coffee, because a coffee handbill preceded it by about five years (Ukers 1922), shown in Figure 5.2. Coffee first arrived in England in 1637, and the first coffeehouse opened in 1650. It is possible this handbill wasn't the first coffee ad.

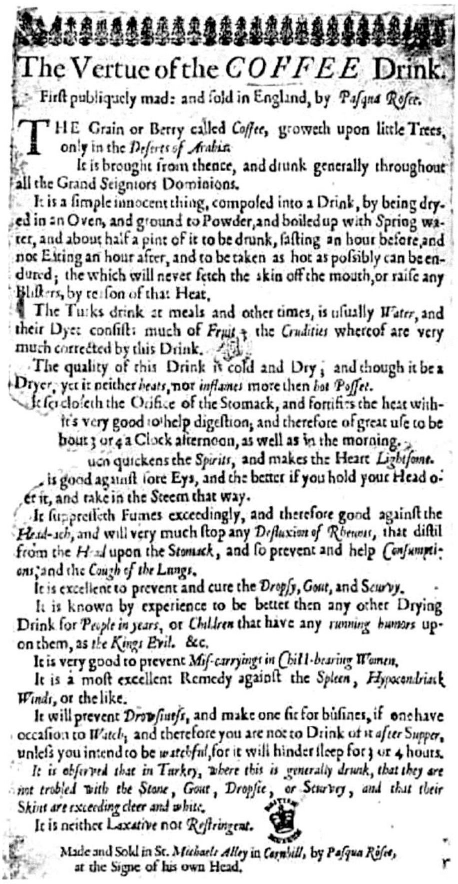

Shortly afterward, in 1658, *Mercurius Politicus* ran an ad for tea (Nevett 1982):

That Excellent and by all Physitians approved China Drink called by the Chineans Tcha, by other Nations Tay, alias Tee, is sold at the Sultaness Head, a Cophee House, in Sweeting's Rents, by the Royal Exchange, London.

This might be what started the British addiction to tea!

The probable first exterminator ad, with some creative copywriting, appeared in 1740 in the *London Daily Post and General Advertiser* (Sampson 1874):

MARY SOUTHALL
Successor to John Southall, the first and only person that ever found out the nature of BUGGS, Author of the Treatise of those nauseous venomous Insects, published with the Approbation (and for which he had the honour to receive the unanimous Thanks) of the Royal Society,
GIVES NOTICE,
THAT since his decease she hath followed the same business, and lives at the house of Mrs Mary Roundhall, in Bearlane,

FIGURE 5.2.   A handbill promoting coffee, circa 1652.

Christ Church Parish, Southwaik. Such quality and gentry as are troubled with buggs, and are desirous to be kept free from those vermin, may know, on sending their commands to her lodgings aforesaid, when she will agree with them on easy terms, and at the first sight will justly tell them which of their beds are infested, &c, and which are free, and what is the expense of clearing the infested ones, never putting any one to more expense than necessary. Persons who cannot afford to pay her price, and is willing to destroy them themselves, may by sending notice to her place of abode afore- said, be furnished with the NON PAREIL LIQUOR, &C. &C.

Ouch!

In 1768, the *Boston Gazette* ran an ad by Paul Revere, selling false teeth (Editors of Advertising Age 1976):

Whereas many persons are so unfortunate as to lose their fore-teeth by accident, and otherways to their great detriment, not only in looks, but speaking both in public and private:—this is to inform all such that they may have them replaced with artificial ones that looks as well as the natural, and answers the end of speaking to all intents, by PAUL REVERE, Goldsmith, near the head of Dr. Clark's Wharf, Boston.

Revere used advertising frequently throughout his life. And in 1773, in the *Maryland Advocate & Commercial Advertiser*, George Washington placed an ad to lease some of his land (Editors of Advertising Age 1976).

These advertisements provide insight into the sorts of things being promoted, and the advertisers creating them. But a couple of categories hold special, though not flattering, places in advertising history. First was a very dark chapter: slavery.

ADVERTISING ENABLES SLAVERY

Stories of American slavery generally begin with arrival of the *White Lion* ship in 1619 carrying twenty or so Africans, but American slavery began earlier. African slaves were brought by the Spanish in 1526 (Guasco 2017). It ended in 1865. Throughout, advertising was used to buy, sell, and capture slaves. Thousands of ads were used. But we often forget slavery also occurred in Europe.

One British ad, in 1659 in the *Mercurius Politicus*, said:

A Negro-boy, about nine years of age, in a gray Searge suit, his hair cut close to his head, was lost on Tuesday last, August 9, at night, in St Nicholas Lane, London. If any one can give notice of him to Mr Tho. Barker, at the Sugar Loaf, in that Lane, they shall be well rewarded for their pains.

Sampson (1874) notes the boy is advertised as "lost," like a runaway dog. An ad in the *London Daily Journal* in 1728 read:

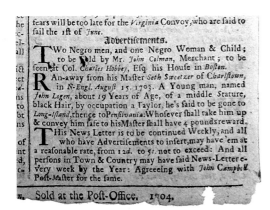

FIGURE 5.3. Two slavery-related advertisements appeared in the *Boston News-Letter*'s May 29–June 5, 1704, issue.

To be sold, a Negro boy, aged eleven years. Enquire of the Virginia Coffeehouse in Threadneedle street, behind the Royal Exchange.

Fewer ads appeared in America that early, since newspapers were rare. But the very first slavery-related newspaper advertisements in America appeared in the seventh issue of America's first newspaper, the *Boston News-Letter* (Figure 5.3).

Over a few days in 1734, the *New York Gazette* ran ads about "a Negro man," "an Indian man," "an English man," and "a Welch man" (Turner 1953). Slavery wasn't confined to Africans. A particularly unflattering example from the *New York Gazette* in 1770 declared:

> Run away from the Subscriber, living at the White plains, in the Manor of Cortlandt, the twenty-fourth of November last, a Mustee Wench, Servant to John Underhill, named Lucey; she is very well set and pretty fat: Had on when she went away, a long Gown with ruffled Cuffs, and several striped Pettycoats, and a black Hat. Whoever takes up the said Wench, and brings her to the Subscriber, shall receive Forty Shillings Reward, and all reasonable Charges, paid by John Underhill. (Hagist 2016)

A "runaway" ad for a Dutch slave is from the *New York Journal* in 1775:

> Six Dollars Reward. A Dutch servant girl, named Christiana Beryon, had liberty on the 12th instant to go to Philadelphia, under pretence of getting a kinsman to purchase her time, and is not returned; she took with her change of apparel, and appears well dressed in the German manner (except her cap and bonnet, which are country made); she is about 28 years of age, heavy made, in height rather above the middle size, has lost most of her single teeth, speaks broken English. Whoever takes up and secures the said servant, so that her master may get her again, shall receive the above reward, paid by David Cooper. (Hagist 2016)

Some ads were for neither the sale of slaves nor the return of runaway slaves, instead aiming at "keeping them in line," such as this one from 1772 in *Purdie & Dixon's Virginia Gazette*:

> There are two old Negroes lurking about my Plantation, one a Man, named Cuffy, the other a woman, named Grace; they are outlandish Negroes, and speak very bad, although ty have been in the Country a Number of Years; they are cloathed in Negro cotton; the Man is bald, and has a remarkable large Navel. The Owner is desired to come and take them away. Francis Peters. (Hagist 2016)

Rhode Island, in 1774, was the first colony to ban importing slaves, and all northern states followed in 1783. But southern states continued bringing in slaves for another century (Figures 5.4 and 5.5).

Unfortunately, slavery advertising wasn't the only horrific advertising tradition. Patent medicines were another.

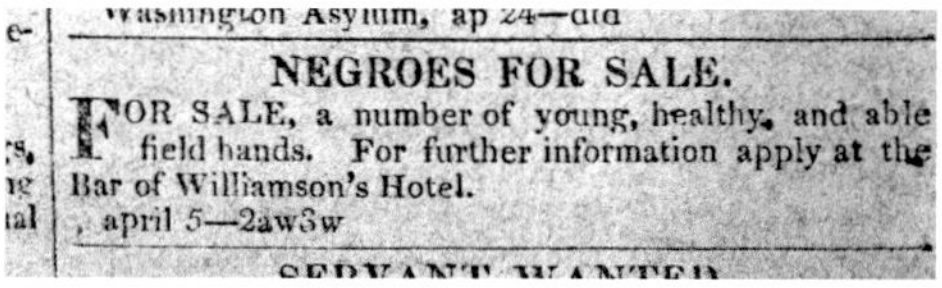

NEGROES FOR SALE.

FOR SALE, a number of young, healthy, and able field hands. For further information apply at the Bar of Williamson's Hotel.

april 5—2aw3w

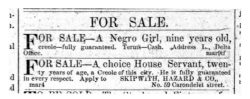

FIGURE 5.4. An ad that appeared in the *Daily National Intelligencer*, April 25, 1826.

FOR SALE.

FOR SALE—A Negro Girl, nine years old, creole—fully guaranteed. Terms—Cash. Address L., Delta Office. mar9tf

FOR SALE—A choice House Servant, twenty years of age, a Creole of this city. He is fully guaranteed in every respect. Apply to SKIPWITH, HAZARD & CO., No. 59 Carondelet street. mar4

FIGURE 5.5. An ad from the *Daily Delta*, March 11, 1859.

DUCKS DON'T MAKE THE ONLY QUACKS

Early print advertising was mostly book promotions, but once space was sold to others, barely a heartbeat passed before patent medicine ads were everywhere (Russell 1937). Most of those products were pure hokum—"quack" medicine. In 1652, Samuel Sheppard, in *Mercurius Mastix*, condemned newsbooks for enabling patent medicines (Elliott 1962):

> Besides all Iterations, Petitions, Epistles, News at home and abroad rayling and praying in one breath (two grand helps which they never want) they have now found out another quaint device in their trading. There is never a mountebank who either by professing of Chymistry, or any other Art drains money from the people of the nation, but these arch-cheats have a share in the booty, and besides filling-up of his paper (which he knew not how to do otherwise) he must have a feeling to authorise the Charlatan, forsooth, by putting him in the News-book. There he gives you a Bill of his Cures, and because the fellow cannot lye sufficiently himself, he gets one of these to do't for him and then to be sure it passes for currant, just like those who being about to sell a diseased or stolen horse in Smithheld, are fain to get a voucher who will say or swear anything they please for sixpence. But why should we be angry with them for this? For it is commonly truer than the rest of their news. Nay they have taken the Cryers trade from them, for all stolen goods must be inserted in these pamphlets—the fittest place for them, all theirs being stolen they do so filch from one another. I dare be bold to say they confer notes, and then judge you whether this be not fine cozenage, when we have that in ten or twelve pamphlets, which would hardly fill up a page in one?

When a 1643 typhus epidemic hit England, all manner of "costly powders" were sold as cures (Barrés-Baker 2006). The Great Plague of London in 1665 offered another opening for "conjurors and witches and all sorts of deceivers," in Daniel Defoe's words, to push pills and potions (Keltie 1870).

Joseph Addison, in *The Tatler* (1710), mentions quack medicine ads in coffee houses:

> The walls of the Coffee-houses were hung round with gilt frames containing the bills of "Golden Elixers", "Popular Pills", "Beautifying Waters", "Drops and Lozenges", all as infallible as the Pope. The Rainbow, in particular I should have taken for a Quacks Hall or the parlour of some eminent mountebank.[1]

Ads from that time are shown in Figures 5.6 and 5.7. Quack medicines continued into the twenty-first century, so we'll visit this again later.

On a lighter note, there is one advertisement story that is interesting. It was a bet.

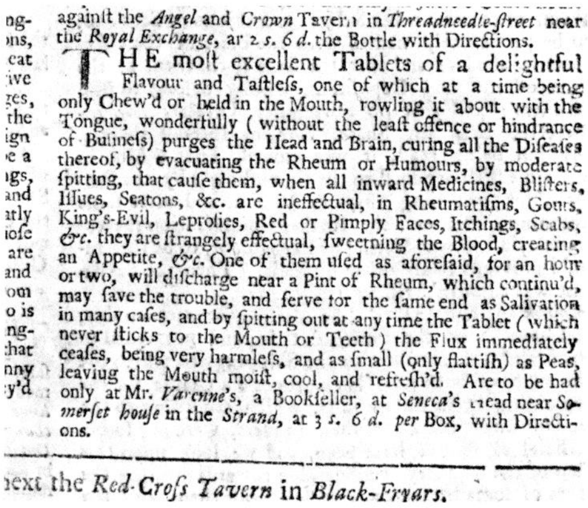

against the *Angel* and *Crown* Tavern in *Threadneedle-street* near the *Royal Exchange*, ar 2 s. 6 d. the Bottle with Directions.

THE most excellent Tablets of a delightful Flavour and Tasteless, one of which at a time being only Chew'd or held in the Mouth, rowling it about with the Tongue, wonderfully (without the least offence or hindrance of Business) purges the Head and Brain, curing all the Diseases thereof, by evacuating the Rheum or Humours, by moderate spitting, that cause them, when all inward Medicines, Blisters, Issues, Seatons, &c. are ineffectual, in Rheumatisms, Gouts, King's-Evil, Leprosies, Red or Pimply Faces, Itchings, Scabs, &c. they are strangely effectual, sweetning the Blood, creating an Appetite, &c. One of them used as aforesaid, for an hour or two, will discharge near a Pint of Rheum, which continu'd, may save the trouble, and serve for the same end as Salivation in many cases, and by spitting out at any time the Tablet (which never sticks to the Mouth or Teeth) the Flux immediately ceases, being very harmless, and as small (only flattish) as Peas, leaving the Mouth moist, cool, and refresh'd. Are to be had only at Mr. *Varenne's*, a Bookseller, at *Seneca's* Head near *Somerset house* in the *Strand*, at 3 s. 6 d. per Box, with Directions.

next the *Red-Cross Tavern* in *Black-Fryars.*

FIGURE 5.6. An ad from the *Post Boy*, November 28, 1706.

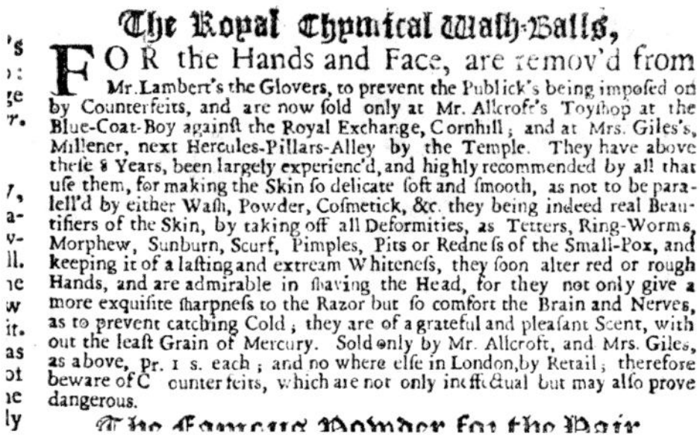

The Royal Chymical Wash-Balls,

FOR the Hands and Face, are remov'd from Mr. Lambert's the Glovers, to prevent the Publick's being imposed on by Counterfeits, and are now sold only at Mr. Allcroft's Toyshop at the Blue-Coat-Boy against the Royal Exchange, Cornhill, and at Mrs. Giles's, Millener, next Hercules-Pillars-Alley by the Temple. They have above three 8 Years, been largely experienc'd, and highly recommended by all that use them, for making the Skin so delicate soft and smooth, as not to be parallel'd by either Wash, Powder, Cosmetick, &c. they being indeed real Beautifiers of the Skin, by taking off all Deformities, as Tetters, Ring-Worms, Morphew, Sunburn, Scurf, Pimples, Pits or Redness of the Small-Pox, and keeping it of a lasting and extream Whiteness, they soon alter red or rough Hands, and are admirable in shaving the Head, for they not only give a more exquisite sharpness to the Razor but so comfort the Brain and Nerves, as to prevent catching Cold; they are of a grateful and pleasant Scent, with out the least Grain of Mercury. Sold only by Mr. Allcroft, and Mrs. Giles, as above, Pr. 1 s. each; and no where else in London, by Retail; therefore beware of Counterfeits, which are not only ineffectual but may also prove dangerous.

The Famous Powder for the Hair

FIGURE 5.7. An ad from the *Post Boy*, May 31, 1715.

AN EXPERIMENT AND WAGER

Around the start of 1749, the 2nd Duke of Montagu, the 4th Earl of Chesterfield, and others were embroiled in a discussion about the public's gullibility. Word has it that Montagu was the ringleader in what would become a famous tale of an outrageous advertisement. Montagu reportedly argued that advertising "the most impossible thing in the world, he would find fools enough in London to fill a playhouse who would think him earnest."

The ad ran on January 16 in the *Daily Advertiser*:

AT the New Theatre in the Hay market, on Monday next, the 12th instant, is to be seen a person who performs the several most surprising things following, viz. —First, he takes a common walking cane from any of the spectators, and thereon plays the music of every Instrument now in use, and likewise sings to surprising perfection. —Secondly, he presents you with a common Wine Bottle, which any of the spectators may first examine; this Bottle is placed on a Table in the middle of the Stage, and he (without any equivocation) goes into it, in the sight of all the Spectators, and sings in it; during his stay in the bottle, any Person may handle it, and see plainly that it does not exceed a common Tavern Bottle.—Those on the Stage, or in the Boxes, may come in masked habits (if agreeable to them); and the Performer, if desired, will inform them who they are. Stage, 7s. 6d. Boxes, 5s. Pit, 3s. Gallery, 2s. Tickets to be had at the Theatre. To begin at half an hour after six o'clock. The performance continues about two hours and a half.

Monday, the theater was packed with dukes, duchesses, and other dignitaries. But it resulted in a riot when no performer appeared, and the theater was virtually destroyed when someone threw a lighted candle onto the stage and others began tearing up the benches (Chamberlain 1770). Montagu won his bet.

While this was a test of gullibility, it likely also was the first experiment evaluating advertising efficacy! It did prove the famous quote attributed to P. T. Barnum—namely, that a sucker is born every minute.

This wasn't the first meeting of gambling and advertising. One dominant advertising category then involved gambling: lotteries.

ADVERTISING WINS THE LOTTERY

The first lottery advertisement was for the first British National Lottery, held in 1567 and created by Queen Elizabeth I (Figure 5.8). Tickets were ten shillings and the top prize was £5,000. Lotteries had existed before, but this was the first Royal Lottery. It lasted just two years, after which lotteries became local.

In 1694, an English "Million Lottery" began, but a law restricting lotteries was soon enacted. Lotteries returned again in 1710, but laws again cut them back. Finally, from 1769 to 1826, regular state lotteries were held in Britain (Ewen 1932).

Those involved in advertising for those later lotteries prospered. By 1775, a "lottery mania" had arrived, and an average of £13,000 was spent advertising each lottery (Gardner 2016). By 1790, the leading contractor was Thomas Bish. Bish used newspaper ads, posters, pamphlets, and more to promote lotteries, unlike his competitors. He even hired copywriters, putting himself ahead of most advertisers, of anything, at that time. Lottery ads spearheaded changes in advertising style. They used satire, which other advertisers soon adopted (Gardner 2016). For the first time, lottery advertising actually entertained.

Another vice achieved popularity as a hot advertising topic.

FIGURE 5.8.   The first British lottery advertisement, 1567.

SMOKING HOT ADS

Jean Nicot introduced tobacco to the civilized world in 1560, describing it as an American herb with wondrous healing powers. It quickly proved to have its detractors. King James I of England described it as "a custome lothsome to the Eye, hateful to the Nose, harmful to the Braine, dangerous to the Lungs" (Richards 1987).

A rare ad not for books in 1626 promoted the sale of bulk goods, including tobacco. So tobacco was among the very first products advertised in a newspaper. But newspapers weren't the first advertising medium for this product.

Carved wood statues once stood in front of tobacco shops everywhere. They advertised tobacco, particularly cigars. This was an early "trade character."

The earliest record of this "cigar store Indian" was in a book, *The Smoaking Age, or The Life and Death of Tobacco*, in 1617 (Sessions 1996/97). That original statue was a small countertop figurine resembling an African man in a feathered skirt. At the time, such figures were called "black boys," "blackamoors," or "Virginie Men."

These figures grew to life size around 1840, while evolving into Native Americans. In the early 1800s, sculptors who carved ornaments for sailing ships (e.g., a mermaid) expanded into carving cigar store figures (Figure 5.9). By then, they considered themselves in "the image business." Perhaps this had dual meaning, as they carved images of people while simultaneously contributing to the brand images of businesses. These figures were plentiful until the late nineteenth century, when they fell into disuse, perceived as old fashioned (Sessions 1996/97).

The ad in Figure 5.10 ran in New York City in May 1789 (Wood 1958). In 1935, Lorillard ran advertising claiming that was "[t]he world's first Tobacco advertisement," which is untrue, though it's the oldest advertisement from any of today's tobacco companies. Note that it, too, depicts a Native American.

FIGURE 5.9.   A "cigar store Indian" wood figure. This is one version of many that appeared in front of tobacco stores throughout the eighteenth and nineteenth centuries.

Tobacco & Snuff of the beſt quality & flavor,
At the Manufactory, No. 4. Chatham ſtreet, near the Gaol
By Peter and George Lorillard,
Where may be had as follows :

Cut tobacco,	Prig or carrot do.
Common kitefoot do.	Maccuba ſnuff,
Common ſmoaking do.	Rappee do.
Segars do.	Straſburgh do.
Ladies twiſt do.	Common rappee do.
Pigtail do. in ſmall rolls,	Scented rappee do. of different kinds,
Plug do.	
Hogtail do.	Scotch do.

The above Tobacco and Snuff will be ſold reaſonable, and warranted as good as any on the continent. If not found to prove good, any part of it may be returned, if not damaged.

N. B. Proper allowance will be made to thoſe that purchaſe a quantity.   May 27—tm.

FIGURE 5.10.   Lorillard tobacco advertisement from May 27, 1789.

HOW ADVERTISING WAS SEEN BACK THEN

Advertising is frequently criticized, and it was in the past, too. By 1652, there were so many ads in newsbooks that some readers objected to both the number and the content (Presbrey 1929), even though the numbers were small. That year Samuel Sheppard published his editorial in the *Mercurius Mastix* denouncing so many newsbooks for promoting patent medicine "cures." This was the first ever newsbook/newspaper editorial about advertising, though it was more about newsbooks than advertising. Ironically, Sheppard's newsbook lasted only one issue.

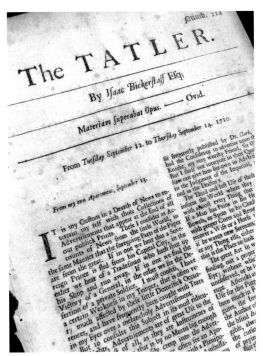

FIGURE 5.11.   This September 12–14, 1710, issue of *The Tatler* was dedicated to Addison's essay regarding advertising.

The next editorial about advertising appeared in *The Tatler* in 1710. This was the first editorial entirely about advertising (Figure 5.11). Joseph Addison, its author, applauds the copywriting of one ad (perfume) and blasts the decency of another: Carminative Wind-expelling Pills. Addison seems to support advertising in general, while pointing out that it's not perfect.

Responding to that essay, in his *nom de plume* as Isaac Bickerstaff, Addison received what likely is the first ever job application from an aspiring advertising copywriter:

Mr. BICKERSTAFF,

I AM going to set up for a scrivener, and have thought of a project which may turns both to your account and mine. It came into my head, upon reading that learned and useful paper of yours concerning advertisements. You must understand, I have made myself master in the whole art of advertising, both as to the style and the letter. Now if you and I could so manage it that no body should write advertisements besides myself, or print them any where but in your paper, we might both of us get estates in a little time. For this end, I would likewise propose, that you should enlarge the design of advertisements and have sent you two or three samples of my work in this kind, which I have made for particular friends, and intend to open shop with. The first is for a gentleman, who would willingly marry, if he could find a wife to his liking; the second is for a poor whig, who is lately turned out of his post; and the third for a person of a contrary party, who is willing to get into one.[2]

Not everyone of that time was offended by ads! Yet advertising continued to be attacked, even gaining a nickname.

In 1740, Henry Fielding published some satire about advertising in *The Champion* newspaper, using a derogatory term for ads—*puffs*:

Whereas many Persons, Novices in the Art of Puffing, have rashly undertaken, though greatly to their own Detriment, to puff their own Wares, Writings, Projects, Merits and Accomplishments; This is to certify, for the Good of the Public, that I Gustavus Puffendorf first Student under the great Professor of Rose-Street, Covent-Garden. . . . This is to certify, I say, that Puffs, secundum Artem, of all Degrees and Magnitudes, for all Arts, Mysteries and Professions are to be had of me, if properly bespoke, at my House, the Sign of the Powder-Puff, in Blow-Bladder-Street, and no where else in the Three Kingdoms.

N.B. I am promised a P[aten]t to be Puff-Master General of Great Britain. After the passing of which, let any Adventurer presume to puff for himself or Friends, either directly or indirectly, at his peril.

Second N.B. There is another Person has had the Assurance to set up the Sign of the Powder-Puff. But beware of Counterfeits.

This began more than a year of rants about puffing.

The *Weekly Register* defined it in 1732: "Puff is become a cant Word to signify the Applause that Writers or Booksellers give to what they write or publish, in Order to increase its Reputation and Sale" (Mason 2013). Remember, most early advertising was to sell books. The *Grub-Street Journal* in 1735 said puffs "are frequently exploded from the posteriors or back-side of a News-paper; and in that they give the book-seller some ease under the pains occasioned by flatulent compositions, which are very apt to afflict him with the spleen, or a hypochondriacal and windy melancholy." This statement was flattering of neither books nor book advertising.

Mason (2013) further describes puffery as (1) an exaggeration and (2) an ad disguised as a news story or opinion piece. However, the terms "puff" and "puffing" were quickly adopted as synonyms for advertisements and advertising.

By 1779, puffing had become the subject of a play, *The Critic*, by Richard Brinsley Sheridan (Elliott 1962). A starring role is "Mr. Puff," introduced as a newspaper writer who praises anyone or anything for a price. He was depicted as a PR man with monetized ethics, suggesting advertising and PR were seen as conjoined.

A famous advertising essay was written in 1759. Dr. Samuel Johnson published an influential dictionary of the English language, long before the Oxford dictionary, but he was recognized as a critic of English literature. He published essays in *The Idler*, the fortieth of which was about the art of advertising. Some famous quotes from that essay persist today:

Whatever is common is despised. Advertisements are now so numerous that they are very negligently perused, and it is, therefore, become necessary to gain attention by magnificence of promises, and by eloquence sometimes sublime and sometimes pathetick.

Promise, large promise, is the soul of an advertisement.

The trade of advertising is now so near to perfection, that it is not easy to propose any improvement.

This essayist is defending advertising while simultaneously cautioning advertisers to use care.

In 1789, another influential person gave us insight into his attitude toward advertising, simply by writing a letter responding to an ad. A week before he was officially elected the first president of the United States (February 4), George Washington wrote this letter:

Mount Vernon,
January 29th, 1789

MY DEAR SIR:

Having learnt from an Advertisement in the New York Daily Advertiser, that there were superfine American Broad Cloths to be sold at No. 44 in Water Street; I have ventured to trouble you with the Commission of purchasing enough to make me a suit of cloaths. As to the colour, I shall leave it altogether to your taste; only observing that if the dye should [166] not appear to be well fixed & clear, or if the cloth should not really be very fine, then (in my judgment) some colour mixed in grain might be preferable to an indifferent (stained) dye. I shall have occasion to trouble you for nothing but the cloth & twist to make the button holes.

IF these articles can be procured and forwarded, in a package by the stage in any short time your attention will be gratefully acknowledged. Mrs. Washington would be equally thankful to you for purchasing for her use as much of what is called (in the Advertisement) London Smoke as will make her a riding habit. If the choice of these cloths should have been disposed of in New York where could they be had from Hartford in Connecticut where I perceive a Manufactory of them is established? With every sentiment of sincere friendship

I am always, Affectionately Yrs.,
[Signed] G. WASHINGTON

Perhaps an ad led to General Washington being properly attired for his inauguration. Clearly ads did carry enough respect to influence the first US president!

Over these two centuries, advertising affected society in many ways. That resulted both from changes in advertising and from changes in society.

SOCIETAL CHANGES

The world changed following the Middle Ages. In the 1500s, London grew from about seventy-five thousand people to two hundred thousand. Paris was about twice that by 1600 CE. Cities reached sizes that made word-of-mouth impractical (Nevett 1982). Over the next century, those populations reached about six hundred thousand for both cities. Advertising was necessary.

Before 1690, America was made of small communities with small general stores. But between 1690 and 1720, some of those communities (Boston, New York, Philadelphia,

Charleston) grew enough to support specialty shops (Applegate 2012). With one, or even a few, general merchandise stores, the need for advertising was nearly nonexistent. It was one-stop shopping. But with specialties, customers with a special need must be attracted, since customers wouldn't be shopping there for other goods.

Traveling salesmen, or "Yankee peddlers," who roamed the countryside selling wares, also arrived. They were direct competitors to established merchants, so this increased demand for advertising (Applegate 2012). Society's complexity increased, helping advertising flourish.

As advertising proved its worth for one merchant, another would see the value and advertise, leading to exponential adoption of advertising as a tool. A consequence was that advertising became a conduit for technological information (Nevett 1982). Not only could inventors inform the public, but they also helped others become inventors. And revenue flowed.

This situation set the stage for the birth of the Industrial Revolution, circa 1760, which mechanized society and fostered a culture of invention. That, in turn, further increased the need for advertising. The Industrial Revolution might never have happened, or never reached such momentum, but for the catalyst of advertising.

Advertising's expansion at the birth of the Industrial Revolution wasn't entirely coincidental. But it was the right tool at the right time. Every new invention needed a way to spread the word. Advertising was the facilitator of innovation. In the brief time between the formation of the United States in 1776 and the census of 1800, the country's population more than doubled (2.5 to 5.3 million, including slaves but not Native Americans). While it began in Europe, the United States was the center of this revolution after around 1808.

The early years of the Industrial Revolution coincided with the French Revolution (1789–1799). This revolution was about human rights, and it had wide-ranging effects. One important consequence was bolstering individual rights of intellectual property ownership (Di Palma 2015) while introducing capitalistic thinking, dovetailing perfectly with the Industrial Revolution. A worldwide climate of innovation was nurtured, increasing the need for advertising even more.

One invention coming out of France during the Industrial Revolution was a process for making soda ash out of salt in 1790. This revolutionized the soap industry, making soap inexpensive (Sivulka 2001). And soap, it turns out, was a major driver of consumer advertising in the next century. Advertising in the nineteenth century really cleaned up!

CONCLUSION

Not only were these two centuries the real beginnings of newspapers and newspaper advertising, but they also are the first centuries from which so many ads still are available. The paper back then had high cotton content, helping preserve it, so many are still viewable. Therefore, we have a much better grasp of what advertising was like then. Thankfully, we have even more artifacts from the 1800s, since that is when this field coalesced as a profession.

The Result of Revolutions

The industrial revolution is usually studied from the point of view of the producer, how machines made things. But the real revolution was in how things were distributed, how advertising made things worth buying.

—*James B. Twitchell (1996)*

The American Revolution, French Revolution, and Industrial Revolution coincided at the eighteenth century's close. For advertising as an industry, this period was an incubator. Each revolution added fertilizer, with near immediate impact. And the next century saw advertising's *evolution*, playing against the background of society's coterminous evolution.

INDUSTRIAL REVOLUTION, UNDER STEAM

The globe shifted on its axis in the 1800s, powered by the Industrial Revolution. Inventions occurred throughout history, but innovations born from the late 1700s through the late 1800s probably exceeded the previous twenty centuries combined!

Eli Whitney's 1793 cotton gin frequently is hailed as an early catalyst. But Henry Fourdrinier's paper-making machine in 1801 might be even more important.

The typewriter, invented by William Austin Burt in 1829, introduced a Gutenberg press for the masses. Corrugated paper, which revolutionized packaging, came in 1856. The graphite pencil was invented in 1795, and in 1858 it was improved by attaching an *eraser*.

Gas lighting arrived in England in the 1790s, reaching the United States in 1816

Paul Revere, famous for his "The British are coming!" word-of-mouth advertising, clearly believed in the power of ads. This is one he ran for his foundry business in the early 1800s.

and Paris in 1820. Suddenly streets and factories could be lighted after dark. This meant factories and stores could operate beyond sunset.

The McCormick Reaper, beginning in 1831, was a horse-drawn reaping machine that replaced hand-cutting crops. This machine drastically increased the speed of harvesting.

Alexander Bain's timely invention of the electric clock in 1840, the Samuel Colt revolver pistol in 1846, the first synthetic plastic (celluloid) in 1856—each changed the world. The first artificial infant food created by Henri Nestle in 1867, oleomargarine (now called "margarine") in 1869, blue jeans in 1873, the first phonograph in 1877, and the first mechanical dishwasher in 1886 are just a few more examples of the thousands of important inventions from that time.

Each promising new product needed to be advertised, adding to the field's groundswell. A single innovation could spur an entire chain of events. Mechanized production led to cheaper production of, for example, furniture, so more furniture was made, all needing promotion. Each piece of furniture wasn't necessarily an invention but was the child of inventions. I do want to call out a few specific inventions because of their ultimate significance to advertising's evolution.

LET'S TALK "DIRTY"

American society was widely dispersed and rural, but cities were growing. A similar (though less extreme) pattern was occurring worldwide. Increased population density, even overcrowding, spread disease. This was before antibiotics. Sanitation and hygiene weren't that well developed (Sivulka 2001).

Bathing was something done a few times a month, not daily, making matters worse. While the flush toilet was invented around 1596, it was Thomas Crapper's improvements, circa 1880, that eventually helped replace outhouses (Sivulka 2001). There wasn't even toilet paper until 1857. Unsanitary conditions contributed to disease, making people easy targets for patent medicine sellers.

Historically, soap was unpleasant to make at home and expensive to buy, so was used sparingly. But in 1791, a new process was invented to produce soap more cheaply (Sivulka 2001). This and other advances made soap more accessible. Cleanliness still was not a habit, at least not in America. Historian Jack Larsen reflects, "Early nineteenth-century Americans lived in a world of dirt . . . and pungent smells. . . . Men's and women's working clothes alike were often stiff with dirt and dried sweat" (Mierau 2000).

Soap became one of the first mass-produced consumer products. Initially grocers stocked soap in huge slabs, with no brand name. Customers bought chunks wrapped in plain paper. Benjamin T. Babbitt, in 1851, was first to sell soap in bar form—Babbitt's Best Soap (Figure 6.1)—and first to package it in branded wrappers (Foster 1967). Babbitt also invented a way to stimulate purchase, by giving wrappers value. Users were encouraged to exchange wrappers for premiums like lithographs, rings, and other items (Sivulka 2001). This was an early use of premiums to promote sales.

A competitive industry quickly developed. Soap was one of the first products advertised nationwide in the United States. Soap manufacturers were "the first to make advertising a regular part of business policy for marketing a staple household article" (Printers' Ink 1938). Detergent powders, too, were introduced. Cleanliness became important to society. Babbitt and others really cleaned up.

FIGURE 6.1.   Babbitt's was a leading soap company in the late 1800s.

Neither the story of soap nor the history of human health could be told without embracing advertising's role. If "cleanliness is next to godliness," I'd argue advertising was a stairway to heaven.

ADVERTISING IN MOTION

Horses or boats were the only transportation options circa 1800, but even horses offered advertising opportunities (Figure 6.2). Of course, boats were limited to water routes. Towns often formed next to water. Transport of goods inland could be costly or virtually impossible. This impeded population dispersion across America. Steam power for boats began in the late 1700s, significantly increasing speeds and reducing the costs of shipping. In 1825, the United States opened the Erie Canal, reducing freight costs between New York and the Great Lakes, creating opportunities for towns along the canal, and making New York even more important for commerce.

FIGURE 6.2.   A horse-based ad for the final English lottery in 1826.

Transatlantic shipping became realistic with the introduction of steamships. The SS *Savanah* was the first steam-powered ship to cross the Atlantic in 1819, opening channels for international trade, making it reasonably fast and cheap. Now excess crops, textiles, and more could be sold to a previously inaccessible market. Goods flowed more freely between Europe and America, along with advertising.

Then came the railroad. While a crude rail system had been formed earlier, the first steam locomotive was introduced in 1804. It went through revisions, but a public railway opened in England in September 1830, four months after the first section of the Baltimore and Ohio

FIGURE 6.3.   A train station as depicted in the 1870s.

Railroad in the United States. The South Carolina Canal and Railroad Company began operating that same year.

Suddenly goods could be transported anywhere tracks could be laid. By the 1850s, the US government was giving rights to lay track across government-owned lands, effectively extending the railroad to every corner of the country. In 1869, a transcontinental railroad began operations. Now raw materials could easily and cheaply be moved from all corners of the nation, facilitating manufacturing, and personal travel was faster and more comfortable, making migration easier. Railroads changed everything.

Of course, transit advertising, as a medium, reaped benefits. Advertising handbills were strung from the ceilings of train cars, and signs were pasted on the outside. Over time, frames appeared, into which "car card" advertisements were placed. By the 1880s, this was widespread (Clarke 1970). Train stations, too, became blanketed in ads (Figure 6.3).

Railways also enabled national product distribution, which necessitated national advertising. Sellers now could reach larger markets than ever before.

And this wasn't the only new transportation method. The earliest real ancestor of the bicycle came in 1817, followed by tricycles and quadracycles. The version that kicked off bicycle-mania was Henry Lawson's "safety" bicycle in 1876. It allowed riders' feet to reach the ground. In 1885, John Kemp Starley produced his "Rover" safety bicycle, with rear-wheel drive, which gained popularity. Another rear-drive Starley model, the "Psycho," appears in Figure 6.4. I suppose naming strategies were not well developed back then. For short-range transportation, bicycles began replacing horses, reducing the need for horse stables, feed, saddles, and so forth.

FIGURE 6.4.   A Starley bicycle ad from March 1887.

FIGURE 6.5.   The first automobile ad, from *Scientific American* in 1898.

Then there was the automobile. Some earlier manifestations of the car existed, but it was Karl Benz's gasoline-powered automobile in 1885 that started the world down a new road. And advertising would never be the same. The first automobile advertisement appeared in *Scientific American* magazine in 1898 (Figure 6.5).

SHOCKING DEVELOPMENTS

Ben Franklin's electricity experiments date to the mid-1700s, but it was the early 1800s before major advancements in electricity's use and application were realized. By 1832 electricity could be generated, by 1835 electrical power could be sent over long distances, and by 1837 we had electric motors.

Thomas Edison's electric lightbulb finally arrived in 1879, and he began wiring towns in 1882, though Wabash, Indiana, received electric lighting in 1880. Most homes didn't have electricity until well into the twentieth century. The first electric passenger train arrived in 1879, and electric streetcars came in 1884. By then electricity was becoming more useful, and new products began popping up using this technology (Figure 6.6).

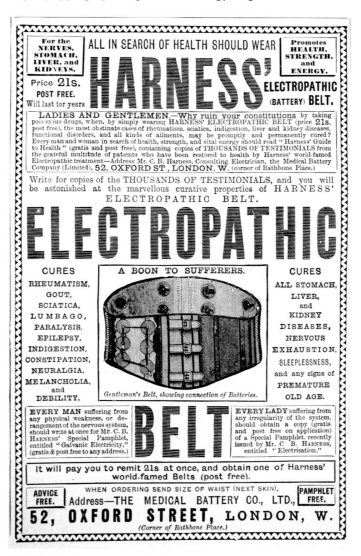

FIGURE 6.6. The patent medicine industry was an early adopter of electricity, offering battery-operated devices to perform medical miracles. This one is from 1887.

One important use of electricity arose well before the Civil War. The telegraph was invented in 1844 by Samuel Morse. He connected Baltimore to Washington, DC, for instantaneous communication. By 1851, the Morse system was used in Europe. Now, instead of sending couriers over long distances, messages could be sent and responses returned almost instantly. Like railroads and electricity, this profoundly changed the world. It was the first step in long-distance communication. The next step was sending voice.

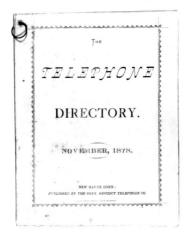

The first basic telephone was invented by Antonio Meucci in 1849, but Alexander Graham Bell generally gets credit for his version in 1876. By the early 1880s, thousands of phones were in use. In 1896, Guglielmo Marconi created the first crude wireless radio.

Advertisers now could conduct business over great distances. The real promise for the advertising field, however, was yet to be realized.

One immediate impact, though, was the first telephone directory, in 1878. It had just 50 names, more of a sheet, but a few months later the first real telephone "book" had 391 names and addresses (Figure 6.7). In addition, there were advertisements in the back of the book!

FIGURE 6.7. The first telephone "book" ever published also had the first telephone directory advertising.

An important new advertising medium, this introduced telephone directory advertising. The first British directory came two years later.

BRANDING: IT'S NOT JUST FOR CATTLE ANYMORE

The concept of a legally protectable identity goes back centuries, but in the nineteenth century it really took root. France lobbed the first shot over the bow, passing the Factory, Manufacture and Workplace Act in 1803, making it illegal to present someone else's mark as your own. In 1857, France created a comprehensive trademark system. Spain created a trademark system in 1850 (Petty 2016). England did so in 1875, and Portugal in 1883. The United States, in the early 1800s, had courts dealing with suits involving "trade names" of products. But the first US national trademark law arrived in 1870. These laws allowed vendors to protect a name, a design, and sometimes even more.

Trademark systems allowed a mark to be registered with the government as a way of proving ownership, allowing lawsuits against anyone using a mark they don't own. The timing was fortuitous, because these laws arrived just as true "branding" began. We often think of branding as burning a hot "branding iron" onto the rump of a cow to prove which rancher owns it. The idea is the same for any product: put an identifiable mark on your property proving it's yours.

Before the Industrial Revolution, most goods were sold locally. Those transported over a distance were sold in bulk. You would go to a store and ask the grocer for a pound of flour and a slab of butter. With no brands, the competition between manufacturers was minimal. Manufacturing was labor-intensive, so production quantities were small. There was little need to advertise.

Mechanization changed that, increasing production scale. Suddenly there was more competition. The railroad system enabled selling over great geographical areas, so one producer could compete with producers hundreds of miles away. A store now had the option to stock butter or flour from multiple suppliers, meaning those manufacturers needed to put their mark on their products. Branding became essential. Trademark laws protected brands, making branding more attractive (Sivulka 2001). Eventually, even bulk items like flour and butter appeared with brands attached (Figure 6.8).

FIGURE 6.8.   Beginning around 1860, butter was branded using a butter press like this one for Polar Creamery, pressing the brand into the butter.

In 1850, about 10 percent of bread in the United States was commercially baked, but by 1900 it was 25 percent, and by 1930 it was 60 percent (Pope 1983). The marketplace changed rapidly. Advertising helped drive much of this change.

The ability for national advertising through media like magazines increased in the late 1800s, just as branding became popular. But in some countries it began even earlier. Warren's Blacking (shoe polish) is thought to be the first nationally advertised household product in Britain, in 1830, solidly establishing that brand (Strachan 2007). And patent medicines jumped on branding early. Beecham's Pills, a laxative advertised as a cure-all, started in 1842.

I mentioned Babbitt's Soap's branded wrappers in 1851. Packaging became important to branding. Another early brand, Studebaker wagons (later automobiles), formed in 1852. That brand continued until 1966.

Several brands still recognizable today started in that century. The first ad for Smith's Brothers Cough Candy appeared in 1852. Cute fact: The two brothers used to illustrate that brand were originally named "Trade" and "Mark." Other familiar brands from back then included Cadbury (1824), Quaker Oats (1878), Ivory Soap (1879), Listerine (1879), and Kodak (1888).

Emergence of trade characters is another aspect of branding that came out of that time. Using real humans or human-like drawings, like the Smith Brothers, was common. The Gold Dust Twins (1892) are another example (Figure 6.9). But cartoon-type characters also gained popularity.[1] The Underwood Devil was created in 1868, before US trademark law, so it wasn't registered until 1905. RCA's "Nipper" dog character was created in 1895.

Let the GOLD DUST TWINS do your work'

GOLD DUST

Wash day is Work Day unless you use Gold Dust. It's the all but never ending bending, rubbing and scrubbing that makes tired backs and weary bodies.

GOLD DUST

will do the heavy work and do it better than anything else. Whiter clothes, quicker results and greater economy is what the use of Gold Dust offers you.

| OTHER GENERAL USES FOR GOLD DUST | Scrubbing floors, washing clothes and dishes, cleaning woodwork, oilcloth, silverware and tinware, polishing brass work, cleansing bath room, pipes, etc., and making the finest soft soap. |

Made by THE N. K. FAIRBANK COMPANY, Chicago—Makers of FAIRY SOAP.

GOLD DUST makes hard water soft

FIGURE 6.9.   The Gold Dust twins were early trade characters that today generally are viewed as racially biased.

Charles E. Hires deserves credit for advancing the promotion of individual brands. In what we would call a "push" strategy, in 1893 Hires went directly to retailers with a sales pitch on why they should carry his root beer extract rather than unknown brands. He followed that with regular circulars offering retailers ideas on how to increase profits (Printers' Ink 1938). Other advertisers implored consumers to demand stores carry their brands, to "pull" the brands into stores.

The rise of brands, buttressed by the trademark laws to protect them, altered the relationships between consumers, retailers, and suppliers. It also affected the relationship between consumers and the products they bought. Brands brought meaning to products.

READIN', WRITIN' & 'RITHMETIC

Again, literacy soared in the eighteenth and nineteenth centuries. In the past education and literacy had belonged to the rich, civic leaders, and the clergy. Others, like merchants, were finding a need to be literate. Books became more common, giving even common citizens a reason to learn how to read. Perceptions of literacy changed. So there was another revolution I haven't yet mentioned: the Educational Revolution.

By the mid-1800s literacy was perceived as a key to fighting crime, allowing the teaching of morals and enabling a more enlightened populace (Sherefkin 2012). Some steps toward compulsory education had been taken earlier, but the first US state to establish mandatory public education was Massachusetts in 1852. In the coming decades, the other states followed. This occurred in other countries as well. France passed a law in 1882 making primary schooling mandatory and free.

As the century began, the idea of "common schools" arose, aimed at educating everyone (Reese 2000). They meant everyone who was male and White. But this is one reason why illiteracy dropped rapidly.

Valuing education also trickled up to a desire for higher education by those that previously had no access to it. Higher education had been aimed at training clergy and civic leaders, and the truth is, in America even grade schools and high schools were not for everyone. Free public schools were rare. Even in England, government-funded public schools didn't happen until 1870. But the American Revolution further altered thinking about education's function (Lucas 1994).

Even until the American Civil War in the 1860s, there was pushback against anything perceived as "vocational" higher education. Only literature, writing, arithmetic, and other "liberal arts" were deemed acceptable. It was okay to train doctors and lawyers, but not engineers or scientists, as those seemed too remote from the classics. And no advertising course would have been considered, since it would be a skills course. By the end of the century, more skills courses were being taught at schools. Two events helped move society in that direction.

First, the "Yale Report" of 1828 was an effort to fight teaching "technical" courses (Lucas 1994). The report's position eventually lost. Going into the American Revolution, the colonies boasted 9 colleges, but as the country entered the Civil War it had 250 colleges, several of which were technical institutes teaching technical subjects alongside liberal arts.

The second event was Congress passing the Morrill Federal Land Grant Act of 1862, creating "land grant" universities aimed at educating most everyone (Curran-Kelly & Workman 2007). This Act established higher education for the masses, instead of just the wealthy. This new breed of university embraced sciences and "professional" courses shunned by the Yale Report, setting the stage for teaching journalism, psychology, and business, all of which led to university-level advertising education (Ross & Richards 2008).

Really, there was a third factor, though its impact was more complicated. Women had begun seeking higher education by the late 1800s. Some women, principally in Europe, had achieved higher education earlier, but it still was rare as the 1800s began. A Bethlehem Female Seminary opened in the United States in 1742, but Oberlin College was the first co-educational college, admitting women in 1837. That same year, Mount Holyoke Female Seminary opened, becoming the first of the "7 Sisters"—seven prominent women's colleges, also called the "women's ivy league." Over the next few decades, several schools for women arose (Gallo 1972). This changed higher education significantly, affecting educational priorities regarding the courses offered. The original mission of these colleges was to prepare women to be wives, teachers, and social benefactors, again focused on the wealthy.

I also should note that the first college for African Americans was created in 1837. And two more African American colleges came in 1854. Education was changing.

Advertising education really began in the 1890s, with practitioners like Nathaniel C. Fowler Jr. starting the Fowler School of Advertising, and E. St. Elmo Lewis offering private training (Figure 6.10). These admen taught in their spare time. But larger numbers of students were reached by correspondence schools. Edward T. Page and Samuel T. Davis created one in 1896. It was a leading ad program for a time (Figure 6.11).

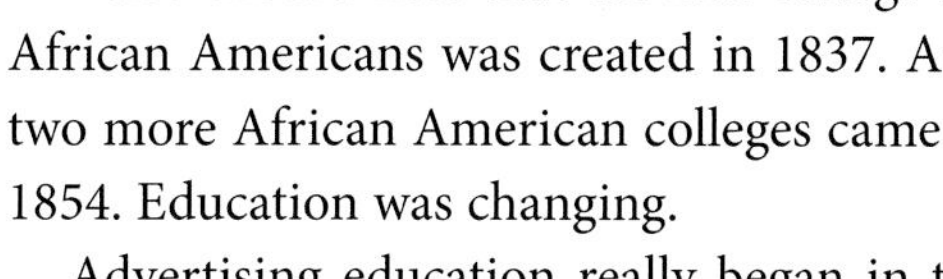

PERSONAL instruction in advertising, writing and management course covers fifty-two topics as follows: Adwriting, printing and display; designing and engraving, office systems, follow-up systems, and advertising management. I do not take more than 50 students. E. ST. ELMO LEWIS, 518 Walnut St., Phila.

FIGURE 6.10. A classified ad by famed adman E. St. Elmo Lewis.

FIGURE 6.11. The Page-Davis correspondence school was an early leader in ad education.

It was the twentieth century before advertising was taught at universities, but the public general education level had increased tremendously by then. Businesses were growing and the economy was flourishing, in part because society was embracing better education.

FOURTH ESTATE, NINETEENTH-CENTURY STYLE

Entering the 1800s, newspapers were relatively mature, nearly resembling what we see today, except the lack of photos and color. But as literacy flourished, so did the newspaper industry.

Britain by 1829 had one newspaper for every thirty-six people. Pennsylvania had one for every four (Turner 1953). That seems absurd, but many newspapers were very small and on a shoestring budget. Literate people were hungry for reading material. Newspapers relied less on home circulation. Most people accessed papers in public gathering places, where they might read multiple papers. This was before television and radio, so reading was an important source of entertainment. And those relying on advertising revenues benefited from the lack of mechanism for checking advertising circulation numbers. Advertisers didn't know who read their ads.

In 1830 America, fifty-plus years after the United States was born, a literal handful of papers had jumped to about one thousand, with around one hundred magazines. In the next twenty-four years the number swelled to four thousand (Presbrey 1929). By 1900, there were about twenty thousand newspapers published in America!

Readership/circulation likewise exploded (Nevett 1982). One reason was the creation of a "penny" newspaper—*The Sun*—in 1833. While other newspapers cost five to six cents, this one emphasized affordability. Within about four years it became the world's largest circulation newspaper, at about 130,000. Others joined the penny press approach, including New York City's *The Herald* in 1835 and the *New York Tribune* in 1841 (Thompson 2004).

These penny dailies reached far larger audiences, opening the door to nationally distributed products (Nevett 1982). The *Tribune* reached a circulation of 200,000 by the 1850s, and the *New York Herald* reached about 84,000 in 1861. The *New York Ledger* distinguished itself by being the first weekly publication to reach 400,000, in 1855 (Fox 1984).

The *Boston News-Letter* in 1719 had a circulation of about 300. The *New York Gazatteer* in 1774 was printing 3,600 copies. Prior to 1800 the *Columbian Centinel* probably held the record at 4,000 copies per issue. Clearly, the 1800s were one giant leap for newspapers.

One factor slowing newspaper growth elsewhere was the newspaper and advertising taxes/duties. Thanks to such duties, newspapers were not growing in England at a rate even close to that of the United States. American newspapers and advertisements had no such yoke.

In 1829, the four hundred newspapers in Britain contained less advertising than just twelve American papers (Schuwer 1966). By the 1830s, the United States had twice as many papers as Great Britain. The English advertising duty finally was reduced in 1833, and the stamp duty followed suit in 1836, leading to some growth in newspaper circulation (Nevett 1982).

A Newspaper Society was created to push for complete abolition of the advertising duty, and that happened in 1853. Two years later, the newspaper stamp duty also ended. A significant increase in the number of newspapers over the next several years resulted (Tungate 2007).

While newspaper numbers were exploding in America and Britain, the first modern newspaper didn't appear in Japan until 1861. And it was an English-language publication: the *Nagasaki Shipping List and Advertiser* (Pongsapitaksanti 2010). That same year in America, the *New York Times* added a Sunday edition, thanks to demand for American Civil War news (Presbrey 1929).

Magazines, too, gained traction as a major information medium. They became an important advertising medium after 1860, with the greatest growth even later. *Harper's* magazine averaged about seven pages of advertising in its October issues by the early 1880s, but a decade later the magazine averaged eighty-five pages (Stole 2006)! In 1889, a magazine circulation of 100,000 was incredible, but six years later *Ladies' Home Journal* had nearly 750,000, *Youth's Companion* was more than 570,000, and several others were far past 100,000 (Printers' Ink 1938).

Specialization also changed the media landscape. Religious periodicals had a robust following by 1870. There were about two hundred with a combined circulation near five million (Presbrey 1929). Between 1830 and 1890, farm journals, women's periodicals, and others were "targeting" narrower populations with focused content. That appealed to advertisers who sold to specific consumer groups (Foster 1967). The 1800s was the "century of print media," with it becoming a major social force. Advertising was both a catalyst and a beneficiary.

A single advertisement now could reach enormous numbers of people, more geographically dispersed than ever. And the numbers of ads in any one issue meant this reach, and influence, included more and more products and brands. A brand once reaching a few thousand now could reach millions, given sufficient budget.

PRESSING ISSUES, AT LEAST ON PAPER

Major factors in these changes are traceable to technological advances in printing, also because of the Industrial Revolution. Little changed between 1450 and 1790, but a complete reinvention of the printing trade occurred in the next century.

Throughout the 1700s, the newspaper industry was hamstrung by severe paper shortages. Paper making was labor-intense, and paper at that time was made from rags, which were not always in great surplus. In American colonies, rags were used for patching and cleaning and more. The production process also suffered from the inability to purify water, and dirty water would deposit dirt, insects, and other impurities on the finished paper, affecting both appearance and readability. This paper shortage was a problem in the buildup to the American Revolution, given the growing public demand for news (Foster 1967).

Two game-changing inventions came in the late 1700s. First was a better printing process: lithography. A Bavarian playwright and actor, Alois Senefelder, invented it in 1796 to publish theatrical materials. Two years later, Nicolas-Louis Robert of France introduced a machine to produce paper in continuous sheets, automating paper production. Paper and ink quality, however, continued as barriers to fine details in illustrations (Presbrey 1929).

Soon another invention made an even bigger impression. In 1801, the Fourdrinier Machine arrived, and by 1807 it was improved. This invention became the new standard in automated paper making. It sped up the process tremendously, virtually ending hand production. This didn't, however, end paper shortages. Paper still required cloth rags. Then, in 1838, Charles Fenerty created a method to make paper from wood pulp. Paper supplies suddenly were more abundant, though shortages occasionally occurred in later years as demand continued increasing.

Paper prices dropped drastically, cutting publishing costs for newspapers and magazines, though some publishers used the cost reduction to increase their newspaper's size. This cost reduction, though, helped make the "penny" newspapers possible.

Lithography wasn't the only improvement in press technology. Before 1800, newspapers were printed on wooden hand-operated presses, capable of printing about 250 sheets per hour. Printing tens of thousands of newspapers was unimaginable at that rate. But Lord Charles Stanhope, around 1800, invented the first wholly iron printing press. Its design was more efficient. About three years later, Friedrich Koenig improved it by adding steam power. *The Times* newspaper was being published on Koenig's press by 1814, putting out 1,100 sheets per hour. By 1828, a four-cylinder press increased the rate to 4,000 sheets per hour, and the 1833 creation of rotary presses achieved rates of 20,000 sheets per hour, which publishers at the start of the century could never have imagined.

Other printing improvements include a machine to set type using a keyboard, circa 1822. Typesetting always had been done by printers pulling one letter at a time out of boxes and spelling out word after word for an entire page. This machine had flaws and never was a success, but it nudged industry thinking forward.

In 1837, Godefroy Engelmann, an Alsatian printer, gave lithography new possibilities by introducing chromolithography: full-color printing (i.e., not just printing with a single color of ink). There were several other advancements, but one must-mention is the halftone process. This method made it practical to print photographs in periodicals. No single inventor or date can be credited, but the first halftone photograph, of Steinway Hall on 14th Street in New York City, was published in the *New York Daily Graphic* on December 2, 1873. A process called photogravure improved on that in 1878.

The last advancement I'll mention is linotype, developed by Ottmar Mergenthaler in 1886. Instead of loose letters of type, linotype put whole lines of type into a single cast. This sped up the process and eliminated an assembly line of people, making periodicals and books even cheaper. This invention dominated the industry for the next eight decades.

By 1900, the ability to quickly produce a printed product, in enormous numbers, with color and photographs, made the printing and publishing fields barely resemble a century earlier. This also meant that advertising had passed through its own revolution.

LESS POVERTY, MORE CONSUMERS

Other social adjustments developed, including a notable drop in poverty, a significant improvement in health, and fewer food shortages (Gallo 1972). Technological advancements combined with an increased focus on cleanliness led to those improvements.

Some innovations also spurred increases in productivity (Applegate 1998), affecting prices and, therefore, what people could afford. Lifestyles changed faster than ever experienced in history.

Advertising lubricated these changes by informing the public of new possibilities, and by stimulating demand for products people didn't even know they needed. But there also were shifts in population distribution across the United States at this time. People were moving to settle the West, or moving from the country to the city (Norris 1990). The former meant advertising would need to reach farther than before, while the latter meant cities were becoming larger and more complex and advertising was essential for all the new businesses springing up.

Besides shifts within the country came shifts between countries. Immigration was enormous, with millions moving to America. US Census statistics in the first half of the century didn't gather country of birth information, but the 1850 Census found 2.25 million people were immigrants. By the 1900 Census, that number grew to 10.3 million.

Also, birthrates dropped in the nineteenth century, but were still high. In 1800, the average woman bore more than seven live children. By 1900, that number had dropped to just over half that number (Haines 1994). So between immigration and birthrates, the US population grew from 5.3 million in 1800 to 76.2 million in 1900. To put this into perspective, the entire world population during that time went from 978 million to 1.65 billion.

The result was expanding numbers of consumers for all the new products and services being brought to market, meaning an ever-growing need for more advertising. Other countries were growing, but by far less, helping explain why US advertising soon took a leadership position internationally.

Another important change during that century was freeing African Americans from slavery after the Civil War. Before the war, slavery provided a low-cost workforce, dramatically affecting the American economy. After President Lincoln signed the Emancipation Proclamation in 1863 (a similar development happened in 1833 for Britain), freed slaves suddenly became prospective customers. Of course, racial prejudice and poverty kept them from playing a big role as consumers during those first decades of freedom (Bosarge 2015).

One other change was brought about by the women's suffrage movement, born in July 1848 at a women's rights conference. Unlike the African American populace, women cut across all socioeconomic classes and did much of the shopping for their families, so they became a focus for the advertising industry very quickly.

CONCLUSION

The number of moving parts in this tapestry was nothing short of amazing in such a relatively short period of time. That was the true "revolution" springing from the Industrial Revolution.

Think about the coincidence of those moving parts. A rapidly growing population, suddenly able to communicate and travel quickly over great distances, with more education and higher literacy than ever, innovating every industry like never before, able to produce products in greater numbers, able to communicate cheaper and in drastically greater numbers, able to reach consumers across greater geographic markets, with greater competition than ever, and so on, combined to form an unimaginable *need* and *capability* for advertising. Not only was advertising required far more than ever, but it now could reach more people than ever.

So many changes were happening that it is difficult to summarize what the nineteenth century meant to the advertising industry. All of the influential factors taken together might be summarized, on one level, as a "century of competition." That competition fed, and was fed by, advertising.

Understanding this backdrop is essential to appreciating what was happening *in* the advertising industry during this century.

Nineteenth-Century Methods and Media

In the beginning was the word. (Pictures came later.) And the word became spoken, and printed, juxtapositioned against images or deftly placed atop musical notes. And the words (no matter how original) were called "copy." And those who crafted them were called "copywriters," the poets of commerce, the highest calling in advertising.

—Keith Reinhard, copywriter

While it is clear advertising began thousands of years ago, some observers believe advertising as an industry really found its start in the 1800s. The best argument to support this theory is an advance in the field's sophistication and organization by the introduction of general advertising agents and agencies.

THE ADVENT OF AD AGENCIES

Ad agencies didn't suddenly arrive from nowhere; the idea actually took a couple of centuries to mature. In 1594, Michel Eyquem de Montaigne, a French Renaissance philosopher, published an essay titled "Of a Defect in our Policies." An English translation of the part relevant to us is:

> My father had this idea: he was a man of some experience and sound natural judgment, which always stood him in good stead, and he said that once, the idea came to him that in every town there ought to be some sort of place where people could go if they had any particular need or query and where they could register their requirements with an official specially appointed to deal with such matters. For instance, they might go and say "I want to sell some pearls," or "I want some pearls to sell." Or "I want someone to travel to Paris with me." Or "I want a particular type of servant." Or a master. Or perhaps someone needs a workman to do some job or other—everyone's requirements would be different. And it does seem that it would indeed be advantageous to everyone if we could make our needs known in this way, for many are the times when our needs go unnoticed and unfulfilled for want of opportunity to satisfy them. (Schuwer 1966)

He was suggesting a clearinghouse for commerce. I doubt Montaigne or his readers ever suspected this paragraph would give birth to the *idea* of advertising agencies. It did.

In 1610 England, King James I appointed Sir Arthur Gorges and Sir Walter Cope to work for the Crown. They might be considered the first advertising agents, and for a king! King James approved an office called "The Publique Register, for generall commerce." It was that clearinghouse, letting sellers post notice of goods for sale, and buyers post notice about goods they sought. While Gorges and Cope were charged with providing that information clearinghouse, beginning in 1611 the law let users decide how much to pay these agents. It wasn't terribly profitable and closed in less than a year. Another man, Captain Robert Innes, later received a similar "patent" (King's approval) to do the same, but, given the same limitation, his office appears never to have opened (Presbrey 1929).

Theophraste Renaudot, King Louis VIII's personal doctor, latched onto a variation of the idea. He established the *Bureau d'Addresse et de Rencontres* in 1630, which was a recruitment office and place to post job notices. Then, to obtain more reach for those notices, in 1631 he started the first French newspaper: *La Gazette* (Tungate 2007). He became not only the first French newspaper publisher and journalist but also the inventor of the personal ad. In a way, he became what could be considered an advertising agent, though one who specialized in recruitment advertising.

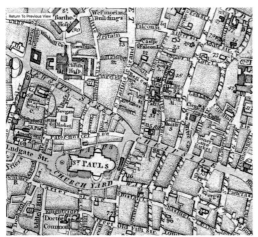

FIGURE 7.1. The birthplace of modern advertising agencies, the office of William Tayler, 5 Warwick Court, London, barely a block away from St. Paul's Cathedral. Today that area is called Warwick Square.

The first general (i.e., not specialized) advertising agency was that of William Tayler, in England.[1] He opened his office in 1786. There are conflicting reports about where it sat. Most reports say it was in London's Warwick Square, others say Warwick Lane, but an ad Tayler placed says Warwick Court.[2] Figure 7.1 is a map from 1795 showing Warwick Court, a city block from St. Paul's Cathedral, making it presumably ground zero as the genesis of all modern advertising agencies. In 1803, Tayler took Thomas Newton in as partner, and the agency became Tayler & Newton (Gardner 2016).

Tayler basically sold ad space for several newspapers. As the major go-between, he held great sway with both newspaper publishers and advertisers. He was a mover and shaker in London, even playing an important role when the government sought to increase the newspaper stamp duty (Gardner 2016).

The second ad agency probably was R. F. White & Son, opened by James "Jem" White in 1800. Some information suggests White might have worked for Tayler before that, especially since White's first office also was in Warwick Court (Gardner 2016). Tayler offered only newspaper ad space to clients, but White offered more: copywriting. He helped businesses by crafting the ad's wording. The writer Charles Lamb is known to have done some copywriting for White. It seems likely that either White or Lamb was the first professional advertising copywriter. Soon other agencies began appearing. Samuel and Thomas Deacon set up shop, as did James Lawson and Charles Barker, both in 1812 (Gardner 2016). But it appears copywriting was unique to White's agency.

The first US agency didn't arrive until 1841, when Volney B. Palmer opened one at the northwest corner of Third and Chestnut Streets in Philadelphia (Applegate 1998). Like Tayler, Palmer's services were strictly newspaper space brokering. He cleverly created a near-monopoly, buying large blocks of newspaper space at discounted rates, then reselling space to advertisers. He called himself an "agent for country newspapers." By 1849, he boasted being sole representative for 1,300 newspapers (Applegate 1998). Palmer later struggled with serious mental illness (Wood 1958). Whether that was cause or consequence of his chosen field, we can only conjecture.

Palmer eventually opened a New York office, but it appears he was beat to that market by John L. Hooper (Presbrey 1929). Hooper had worked for the *New York Tribune* before creating his agency. He assumed full responsibility for his clients' debts to the publications, so newspapers got paid even when Hooper's client stiffed them.

The earliest agency with a name still in use, though not originally an ad agency, is Havas. On the heels of "freedom of the press" being declared in France in 1830, Charles-Louis Havas established Bureau Havas in 1832. It was renamed Agence Havas in 1835. It was a news agency but evolved into both today's Agence-France-Presse (AFP) and Havas Worldwide. The latter, an ad agency, was the consequence of Agence Havas creating France's first publicity agency in 1851.

Edmund Charles Mather started the Mather advertising agency in 1850, which later became Mather & Crowther and, much later, Ogilvy & Mather (now just Ogilvy).

In 1855, Gordon & Gotch opened in Melbourne, Australia, launched by a dentist and a newspaper salesman. Selling ads in Australia must've been like pulling teeth. This firm was the first international agency, establishing an office in London in 1867, followed by offices in South Africa and New Zealand (Waller 2012).

Carlton & Smith was founded in 1864. Four years later, a bookkeeper named James Walter Thompson was hired. He became an ad salesman, and in 1878 he bought the agency. In 1896, the agency was renamed J. Walter Thompson, shortened to JWT in 2005, then expanded again in 2014, and in 2018 combined with a digital network to become Wunderman Thompson.

Thompson brought an innovation to his agency. He noticed that magazines stay around longer than newspapers, making them a better investment, and yet very few magazines accepted advertising (Tungate 2007). He convinced magazine publishers to accept ads. His agency became known as the magazine advertising agency. By 1900, Thompson controlled most space in both general and women's magazines, so even other agencies could not put ads in those magazines without buying space from him (Wood 1958). J. Walter Thompson also was the first American ad agency to open an office in London, in 1899, likely making it America's first international ad agency.

In 1869, Francis Wayland Ayer opened an agency in New York named after his father, N.W. Ayer & Son (Editors of Advertising Age 1976). It began selling space for religious newspapers. In 1877, it acquired Volney Palmer's agency, giving it bragging rights as the oldest American agency, and boosting Ayer's reputation.

In 1876, Ayer made a move that changed agencies forever—introducing the "open contract." It was a contract that left many terms unspecified (open), giving the agency authority to represent an advertiser for an indefinite time period (Riggs 2015). The agent promised to negotiate the lowest cost for newspaper space, billing the advertiser that cost plus a specified percentage (Foster 1967). This shifted agents' loyalty from newspapers to advertisers! By the 1890s, this agency had grown to be America's largest (Pope 1983).

The year 1873 brought the start of another of today's largest agencies, when Daniel Lord opened his agency in Chicago. In 1881, he was joined by Ambrose Thomas, their agency becoming Lord & Thomas, one of the earliest in America to do more than just broker newspaper space, by 1884 claiming to write and illustrate ads. Today it is FCB Global.

George Batten opened the George Batten Company in 1891. Batten was a staunch advocate of truth in advertising. After merging with another agency, today this is BBDO Worldwide.

As a profession, advertising now was global. Romania's first advertising agency began in 1880, the David Adania Agency. Japan's first agency, Kukido-Kumi, opened that same year, though the oldest Japanese agency still operating is Kokokusha, founded in 1888.

I'll mention one more: Charles Austin Bates created the Bates Agency in 1893. Bates was an advertising copywriter and critic who influenced the field greatly. He also gave another copywriter, Earnest Elmo Calkins, a start in 1897. Calkins, too, became a legend.

WHAT ARE AD AGENCIES?

The industry really began advancing as a profession following the Civil War. The turning point likely was 1873, with the first convention of advertising agents, at the Astor House in Manhattan. George P. Rowell was the convention's "master spirit," and Samuel M. Pettengill ran it. Principal topics were (1) commissions being collected from newspapers, and (2) the relationship of agents to advertisers. The meeting's resolutions referred to agents as "Newspaper Advertising Agents." This was how they saw themselves, but this also was before J. Walter Thompson began his assault on magazines.

Jem White's agency aside, throughout the 1800s ad agencies were almost exclusively newspaper space brokers. Clients created their own advertisements, and agencies bought them ad space. There was debate about whether the agents' master was the advertiser (client) or the newspaper (Miracle 1977). N.W. Ayer & Son drove its stake in the ground, positioning itself as the *advertiser's* agent, unlike most agencies.

Ralph M. Hower identified four phases of agency development (Applegate 1998). The first stage was acting as an agent for publishers, selling space, and working in-house at newspapers. The second was "space-jobbing," where agents had their own agencies but still sold space. Third, "space-wholesaling" was when agents bought up space and resold it at a profit. George Rowell is credited with that innovation circa 1865, though Volney Palmer is believed to have already done that.

The fourth stage, the "advertising concession agency," began with the Carlton & Smith agency buying most of the space in a publication for a specific time period, taking sole responsibility for that space. In this stage the agency takes on liability for deadbeat advertisers. Each stage (or model) paints a different picture regarding where agents' loyalty resided.

By the 1880s, the largest agencies were helping advertisers create ads, though some advertisers were reluctant to cede control. N.W. Ayer and J. Walter Thompson were among those offering clients a broader range of services. And the entire industry was experiencing that shift in agents' loyalty to the advertisers' interests (Turner 1953).

In 1897, N.W. Ayer still billed itself as "newspaper advertising agents," but changes began in 1899 when it created an outdoor advertising department (Wood 1958). Ayer worked for the National Biscuit Company, which included significant market analysis, and Ayer is credited with creating the "Uneeda Biscuit" brand (Clarke 1970).

It is hard to envision advertising agencies before 1900: no telephones or computers or televisions. They usually were small, one-room operations that might have a boss, someone to quote rates, a bookkeeper, a clerk, and an office boy, crowded into that room. Only the largest would have more (Fox 1984). Even small agencies today are larger and more complex. It's hard to imagine, too, what was accomplished in such meager surroundings. One person who began reforming all that was George P. Rowell (see Figure 7.2).

FIGURE 7.2.   By 1869, this was just one part of the offices of the George P. Rowell & Co. advertising agency.

ADVERTISING ON A ROWELL

Presbrey (1929) claims that "George P. Rowell did perhaps more than any other man to develop advertising in the 19th century and bring it to the point from which the expansion of the last 30 years has taken place." He did change the world of advertising.

Rowell opened his agency in Boston in 1865, after working in bill collections and ad sales for the *Boston Post*. His agency office was "a room about 15 feet square with two windows looking out on a court, and contained no closet or any additional space or conveniences" (Rowell 1906). He quickly outgrew it.

Rowell secured space in about one hundred newspapers and contracted that space to his clients. Unlike other agents, he bought large blocks of space and then sold it in small pieces, essentially buying wholesale and selling retail (Applegate 1998). He negotiated deep discounts with newspapers by promising a long-term relationship.

He established the *Advertisers' Gazette* in 1867, renamed the *American Newspaper Reporter* in 1871, offering ad-related advice to clients and newspapers. This probably was the first advertising trade journal.

Like other agents Rowell kept a list of newspapers where he could buy ad space, but unlike most, in 1869 he published his list: *Rowell's American Newspaper Directory*. It identified 5,778 newspapers and was the first complete list of American newspapers, including their estimated circulations. This was more information than other agents collected, so it became "the" authoritative source of information on the publishing industry.

In 1888, he founded the first national advertising trade journal, *Printers' Ink* (Figure 7.3.). This journal facilitated a way in which advertising knowledge could be shared, beyond word-of-mouth. It was advertising's main journal for decades.

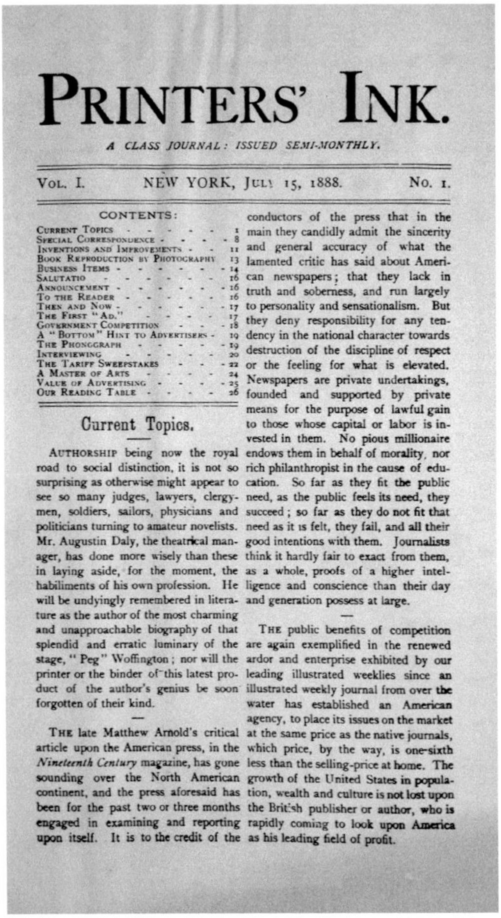

PRINTERS' INK.

A CLASS JOURNAL: ISSUED SEMI-MONTHLY.

VOL. I. NEW YORK, JULY 15, 1888. NO. 1.

CONTENTS:

Current Topics.

AUTHORSHIP being now the royal road to social distinction, it is not so surprising as otherwise might appear to see so many judges, lawyers, clergymen, soldiers, sailors, physicians and politicians turning to amateur novelists. Mr. Augustin Daly, the theatrical manager, has done more wisely than these in laying aside, for the moment, the habiliments of his own profession. He will be undyingly remembered in literature as the author of the most charming and unapproachable biography of that splendid and erratic luminary of the stage, "Peg" Woffington; nor will the printer or the binder of this latest product of the author's genius be soon forgotten of their kind.

—

THE late Matthew Arnold's critical article upon the American press, in the *Nineteenth Century* magazine, has gone sounding over the North American continent, and the press aforesaid has been for the past two or three months engaged in examining and reporting upon itself. It is to the credit of the conductors of the press that in the main they candidly admit the sincerity and general accuracy of what the lamented critic has said about American newspapers; that they lack in truth and soberness, and run largely to personality and sensationalism. But they deny responsibility for any tendency in the national character towards destruction of the discipline of respect or the feeling for what is elevated. Newspapers are private undertakings, founded and supported by private means for the purpose of lawful gain to those whose capital or labor is invested in them. No pious millionaire endows them in behalf of morality, nor rich philanthropist in the cause of education. So far as they fit the public need, as the public feels its need, they succeed; so far as they do not fit that need as it is felt, they fail, and all their good intentions with them. Journalists think it hardly fair to exact from them, as a whole, proofs of a higher intelligence and conscience than their day and generation possess at large.

—

THE public benefits of competition are again exemplified in the renewed ardor and enterprise exhibited by our leading illustrated weeklies since an illustrated weekly journal from over the water has established an American agency, to place its issues on the market at the same price as the native journals, which price, by the way, is one-sixth less than the selling-price at home. The growth of the United States in population, wealth and culture is not lost upon the British publisher or author, who is rapidly coming to look upon America as his leading field of profit.

FIGURE 7.3. Volume 1, Number 1, of *Printers' Ink*, July 15, 1888.

He also promoted ethics in advertising, believing it was good business. In 1971, he wrote:

> Honesty is by all odds the very strongest point which can be crowded into an advertisement. Come right down with the facts, boldly, firmly, unflinchingly. Say directly what it is, what it has done, what it will do. Leave out all ifs. Do not claim too much, but what you do claim must be claimed without the smallest shadow of weakness. Do not say "we are convinced that," "we believe that," or "ours is among the best," or "equal to any" or "surpassed by none." Say flatly "the best," or say nothing. Do not refer to rivals. Ignore every person, place or thing except yourself, your address and your article. Be serious and dignified, but active and lively. Leave wit, however good it may be, entirely aside.

Not all his advice was great, as seen in that last line. He also believed advertisers, not agencies, should write ads, and he rejected making advertising more of a science. But his advice was particularly influential.

Rowell published his advice through *Printers' Ink*, opening an office in the *New York Times* building in Manhattan. He served as president of the Sphinx Club (later called the Advertising Club of New York).

Rowell's influence on the industry is hard to overstate. But ad content, too, was changing at that time, thanks to the move toward copywriting that Rowell denounced.

TO WRITE'S NOT WRONG

Writing an advertisement is a talent not perfected overnight. A few noted copywriters made reputations before the twentieth century. Earlier I mentioned a prospective "scrivener" who asked for a job at *The Tatler* in 1710, and might have been the world's first professional advertising copywriter. But even before him some town criers displayed deftness with wording their auditory appeals.

When advertisers wrote their own ads, they were copywriters. But the earliest confirmed "professional" copywriter was Charles Lamb, who worked for Jem White circa 1800. It is arguable that others should be considered for that honor.

Thomas Bish was the biggest promoter of the English state lottery, around 1790, and his ads were pervasive and influential. Hicks (2012) suggests he hired "talented people like the songwriter Robert Houlton, the wit and journalist Theodore Hook, the comic poet Thomas Hood and even Charles Lamb, to compose their lottery jingles" (e.g., Sam Snob in Figure 7.4). The exact dates of those hires are unknown. Bish worked decades into the next century.

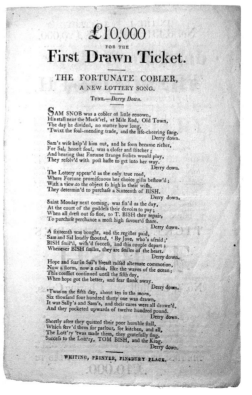

FIGURE 7.4.   An 1804 broadside by Thomas Bish promoting the lottery (showing front and back).

Lamb apparently worked for both White and Bish, so I'll give him the title until better evidence emerges. In his essay "On the Danger of Confounding Moral with Personal Deformity," Lamb (1879) actually opines about how to write better advertisements.

Bish deserves credit for advancing the craft of copywriting. The sample broadside shown here illustrates how, through creative copy about Sam Snob, ads not only informed but also entertained. This wasn't common before Bish.

Others employed poets as copywriters by the early to mid-1800s. Still, most advertisements were written by advertisers, and it showed. Professional writing, though, was beginning to show.

Another leader in professional copywriting was S. M. Pettengill. He had worked for Volney Palmer as a clerk and solicitor, but left in 1849 to form his own agency in 1852, S. M. Pettengill & Co (Pettengill & Co. 1897). Like Jem White, earlier, Pettengill offered copywriting to his clients (Editors of Advertising Age 1976). He had many patent medicine accounts, and the writing talent showed in many of those ads.

By the 1860s, copy was taken more seriously, with humor and "jingles" being used (Presbrey 1929). Then freelance writers began offering their services, and by 1884 there were hundreds of them (Printers' Ink 1938). Pettengill was on the leading edge.

A decade later a true copywriting legend began working for Lord & Taylor, and in May 1880 he was hired by John Wanamaker, owner of the leading Philadelphia department store. His name was John E. Powers. One of his first successes was convincing his boss to change the store's name from Grand Depot to Wanamaker's (Fox 1984). Powers eventually was called the "father of honest advertising" and the "father of creative advertising." The "Powers Style" used simple language and consumer insights, avoiding hyperbole, to provide straightforward appeals. Powers is considered the first *full-time* advertising copywriter.

Other legendary copywriters followed Powers. Charles Austin Bates and Earnest Elmo Calkins both were important, but Calkins was unique. He was deaf as a result of childhood measles. Bates hired him because he had won a copywriting competition Bates judged. Calkins locked horns with Bates' art department, one of the earliest; he didn't think the design did his copy justice. Calkins took evening design classes (Tungate 2007). He joined with Ralph Holden and formed Calkins & Holden in 1902, one of the earliest full-service agencies, offering copy, art, and media planning and buying.

Rowell's agency hired a young writer named John Irving Romer in the 1880s. Like Rowell, Romer advocated truth in advertising. His fame was not his copywriting, though—it was his later role as editor of the *Printers' Ink* journal from 1908 to 1933 and his role in a truth-in-advertising movement.

Also in the 1880s, the J. H. Bates agency hired a copywriter named Joseph Addison Richards. He wrote the advertising for Pears' Soap, a leading soap brand (Printers' Ink 1938). Jarvis A. Wood was hired by N.W. Ayer in 1888. He wasn't hired as a copywriter, but he became one (Laird 2001). By 1889, London's Thomas Smith Agency claimed it had an "Ad-writing and Designing Department" (Robertson 2011).

The 1880s represented a clear shift to agencies adding copywriting services. Most copywriters hired then were part-time, but that changed, too. N.W. Ayer hired its first full-time writer in 1892.

Nathaniel C. Fowler Jr., known as the "publicity laureate," opened a Boston agency and founded the Fowler School of Advertising in the 1890s (Fox 1984). They say he wrote ten-thousand-plus advertisements and several books, including his best known: *Fowler's Publicity*. Known for copywriting Columbia Bicycles ads, he also pushed the idea that women make most household purchasing decisions, so ads should be directed at them.

Another nineteenth-century copywriter of note was Artemas Ward. Ward was principal copywriter for Sapolio Soap, beginning in 1885. Working directly with Sapolio and through his agency, Ward & Gow, he was "an acknowledged genius in advertising" (Anonymous 1909). Ward's writing gained him a reputation, but he also is known for a great publicity stunt. In 1892, he sent Captain William Albert Andrews across the Atlantic in a fourteen-and-a-half-foot folding boat named *Sapolio*, on the four-hundred-year anniversary of Christopher Columbus' crossing. This was the smallest craft ever to cross the ocean. The boat was displayed at the great Chicago Exposition in 1893.

SLOGANS, THEY'RE GRRRREAT!

Soon these men began writing slogans. In advertising we often refer to a prominent slogan as a "tagline." We don't know where these began, partly because defining "slogan" is nearly impossible. But ads prior to the mid-1800s generally didn't use anything approximating a slogan. In the latter half of the century, as copywriting became ascendant, slogans gained popularity. Lines like "Beecham's Pills. Worth a Guinea a Box," and Kodak's "You Press the Button, We Do the Rest," were frequently repeated, which is the very essence of a slogan.

It seems politicians were among the earliest adopters. Abe Lincoln, in his 1860 campaign for president, used two slogans: (1) "Free land, free speech and free men," and (2) "Vote Yourself a Farm." Slogans gained traction in the 1890s. Ivory Soap's "It Floats" was created in 1891 and lasted decades.

By the century's end, professional writing was well established. That wasn't the only expansion of agency services, though. Copy was one part of composing ads. The other part was visual design.

THE ART OF ADVERTISING

Illustrations were not unusual in advertising. Visual communication was found on ads in Pompeii and Herculaneum in 79 CE, and throughout medieval times signs were visual. Tradesman's cards of the seventeenth and eighteenth centuries frequently were beautifully illustrated. But newspaper and magazine production didn't easily lend itself to the visual. Paper costs and ink quality also were barriers to illustration. However, like copy, visuals found a place in print advertising as the 1800s progressed.

THE CAT AND THE BOOT;
OR, AN IMPROVEMENT UPON MIRRORS.

As I one morning shaving sat,
  For dinner time preparing,
A dreadful howling from the cat
  Set all the room a staring!
Sudden I turn'd—beheld a scene
  I could not but delight in,
For in my boot, so bright and clean,
  The cat her face was fighting.
Bright was the boot—its surface fair,
  In lustre nothing lacking;
I never saw one half so clear,
  Except by Warren's Blacking.
(Warren! that name shall last as long
  As beaus and belles shall dash on,
Immortalized in every song
  That chants the praise of fashion :
For, oh! without his *Blacking*, all
  Attempts we may abolish,
To raise upon our boots at all
  The least of jet or polish.)
Surpris'd its brilliancy I view'd
  With silent admiration ;
The glass that on the table stood
  Waxed dimly on its station.
I took the boot, the glass displac'd,
  For soon I was aware,
The latter only was disgrac'd
  Whene'er the boot was near.
And quickly found that I could shave,
  Much better by its bloom,
Than any mirror that I have
  Within my drawing-room.
And since that time; I've often smil'd
  To think how puss was frighten'd,
When at the boot she tugg'd and toil'd
  By Warren's *Blacking* brighten'd.

A Shilling of Warren's Paste Blacking is equal to
four Shilling Bottles of *Liquid Blacking*; prepared by

Robert Warren

30, STRAND, London ;
and sold by most Venders of *Blacking* in every Town in
the Kingdom, in Pots, 6d. 12d. and 18d. each.
☞ Ask for WARREN'S Blacking.

FIGURE 7.5. Warren's Blacking ad, circa 1820.

Perhaps the earliest illustrated periodical advertisement to gain any notoriety occurred in 1820. An ad for Warren's Blacking shoe polish was illustrated by the renowned caricaturist, George Cruikshank. The picture was of a cat hissing at its own reflection in a boot. It became a famous ad in its time (Figure 7.5).

That wasn't the first illustrated ad. Earlier ads simply didn't have the eye-catching quality of Cruikshank's work (Figure 7.6).

Visual elements did have setbacks. James Gordon Bennett, founder of the *New York Herald*, around 1848 dictated restrictions on advertisements in his newspaper. No ad could appear for longer than two weeks, and illustrations were banned, to ensure no advertiser had an advantage in drawing attention (Editors of Advertising Age 1976). "Penny papers" nearly abandoned ad illustrations back then (Presbrey 1929).

By the 1860s, illustrations were more welcome. Most magazines didn't accept advertising, but they did accept illustrations. A few heavily illustrated publications, like *Frank Leslie's Illustrated Newspaper* and *Harper's Weekly*, accepted advertisements with illustrations. Other periodicals experienced pressure to do the same. Photography, too, was gaining use, and by the 1860s it appeared in some ads.

In the 1880s, art moved to the forefront. Trade cards—smaller than tradesman's cards a century earlier—were popular by then and often used color. By then art and design were putting prior ads to shame.

Then, in 1886, renowned artist Sir John Everett Millais painted *A Child's World*, initially sold to Sir William Ingram but purchased in 1887 by Thomas J. Barratt, managing director of A. & F. Pears. Barratt used the image in advertising for Pears' Soap. He enhanced Pears' Soap's brand image by associating it with this established work of art.

It depicted a young boy blowing bubbles, with one bubble hanging above his head. Much to the chagrin of Millais, Pears added a bar of its soap at the boy's feet (Figure 7.7).

HUDSON RIVER
STEAM BOATS.
The PARAGON, Capt. Wiswall.
The CAR OF NEPTUNE, Capt. Roorbach,
The RICHMOND, Capt. Bartholomew.

IN order to accommodate the public, these vessels will make four trips in each week during the season of 1815, in the following order, viz.
  A Boat will leave New-York every Monday, Wednesday, Friday and Saturday, at 5 o'clock in the afternoon—and leave Albany on the same days at 9 o'clock in the morning.
  N. B. The Car of Neptune will commence the season by leaving N. York on Saturday 18th inst
March 14   tf

FIGURE 7.6. An ad from the *New York Evening Post*, August 2, 1815.

The painting was renamed *Bubbles*. This was the first time a bona fide work of "fine art," not originally created for advertising, was used in an advertisement. It also represented an early "image" advertisement, as it didn't focus on the product's function.

Promotional use of *Bubbles* ignited debate, including criticism of Millais allowing it. But the Pears' ad attracted lots of attention, helping the brand. One art magazine editor remarked, "[A]rtistic advertising is in the words of Prof. Richman, 'a forceful weapon for disseminating good art in the most public manner possible'" (Presbrey 1929). Pears' Soap used it for decades.

It seems natural other advertisers would follow suit. Although the first full-color advertisement appeared in 1880 in an insert in *Frank Leslie's Popular Monthly* magazine, in 1893 the first *full-page* full-color advertisement was the back cover of *Youth's Companion*. Like the Pears' ad, this was another piece of fine art, *The Awakening of Love* by Leon-Jean-Basile Perrault. It advertised Mellin's Food (Figure 7.8).

By the mid-1890s, Mather and Crowther (London) and Charles Austin Bates (New York) had created art departments in their agencies. N.W. Ayer in 1898 hired its first art director and created an ad design and composition department. But Robertson (2011) claims George Batten Co., in 1891, was the first full-service agency, as Batten only accepted clients who let him control the entire process, including ad creation.

So agencies evolved from simply "middlemen" arranging ad placement in newspapers to specialists offering advertisers a whole menu of services. Advertising had matured into a genuine profession.

FIGURE 7.7.   *Bubbles* (previously *A Child's World*) by Sir John Everett Millais, as used to promote Pears' Soap.

FIGURE 7.8.   An ad for Mellin's Food using *The Awakening of Love* by Leon-Jean-Basile Perrault.

THE 3 C'S: CIRCULATION, COMMISSIONS, AND CONTRACTS

Like William Tayler and George Rowell, several ad agents collected lists of newspapers they could use for clients' ads. But accurate circulation (number of copies of XYZ newspaper circulating on a given day) and readership (number of people reading this day's issue of XYZ newspaper) figures for newspapers were nonexistent. Initially, readership was more important, since most of the readers were doing so in public places like coffee shops.

But publishers routinely lied about circulation (Fox 1984). They inflated readership and circulation figures because larger numbers attracted more advertisers, and they could charge more per ad. Except when numbers were small enough to hand count, numbers couldn't be validated. Some publishers were more honest than others, so even relative numbers (i.e., A claims more readers than B) were misleading. It was a mess.

During Britain's stamp duty period, there was a real measure of circulation: duties paid. It didn't measure readership, though, since one paper could be read by dozens of people in a coffee shop. That would grossly undercount the number of eyes seeing ads. And stamp duty ended in 1855, leaving no substitute measure. Publishers often claimed the number printed, not the number sold. And publishers could print as many newspapers as they wanted.

This problem wasn't just in the United States and Britain. Australia had similar chaos. Publishers would charge by the amount of space (measured in column inches) used for an ad, and agents sold as much space as possible to advertisers without considering circulation (Crawford 2008). Apparently advertising ethics weren't yet invented.

Some agents, too, were more honest than others, and some more perceptive at recognizing inflated figures. But agents made money by taking a percentage of funds spent buying space, so big numbers led to big profits for agents. Merchants tended to know only whether money spent on advertising seemed to bring enough customers to be profitable. Nobody was policing circulation, let alone readership, of ads.

Lots of debate and adjustment to fees occurred throughout the century. The earliest ad agent, Tayler, charged a 5 percent commission on what he spent buying ad space for clients (Gardner 2016). Five decades later, the first US ad agent, Palmer, charged 25 percent (Editors of Advertising Age 1976). Tayler was making it up as he went, with no peers or history on which to base his fee. Palmer had Tayler's experience as history, and he had no competition at the start, so he could charge whatever clients would pay.

The first ad agent convention, in 1873, addressed commissions. The other topic was relationships of advertisers and agents. N.W. Ayer shook up the industry when it introduced its "open contract" approach, affecting both.

Ayer's contract stated: (1) Ayer was the advertiser's agent, (2) how much money would be spent, (3) the time period covered, and (4) a commission of 10 percent (Editors of Advertising Age 1976). It was "open" because specific space purchases weren't detailed but were left up to the agent. This approach locked in terms for an extended time period, so agents wouldn't be competing for an advertiser every week. The relationship between agent and advertiser changed, because the agent no longer sold newspaper space *to* advertisers; he bought it *for* advertisers, while negotiating low rates. He was now an advertiser's agent. Soon that 10 percent commission became 12.5 percent, and then 15 percent, all within five years.

Adding to the commissions turmoil, the American Newspaper Publishers' Association in 1887 introduced an enormous change. Most agencies were buying blocks of newspaper space and reselling to advertisers at a profit. Now newspapers would build commission into their prices and pay that portion to the agency (Foster 1967). This shifted some control back to the newspapers while protecting agencies, since advertisers not hiring agents still paid full price ("gross rate"). Merchants could not save money by foregoing agencies.

This led to new arguments. Established agencies wanted commissions paid only to certain authorized agencies, forcing less qualified agencies to pay gross rate without kickbacks (Pope 1983). Agencies also wanted control over commission size. Frank Munsey, publisher of *Munsey's Magazine*, in 1898 criticized this system as bribes for agents to convince clients to advertise in newspapers (Norris 1990). Still, this system continued through the next century.

In 1892, Australia, newspapers rebelled against paying commissions to agencies. They were paying 10 percent at that time. Some newspapers wouldn't deal with agents (Waller 2012).

Joseph Pulitzer's *New York World* was the first newspaper to link advertising rates to circulation, in 1883.[3] Accurate figures continued to be elusive, though.

By century's end, publishers' numbers were coming closer to reality (Presbrey 1929). In 1899, the Association of American Advertisers attempted verifying circulation figures. And in 1896 the US Postal Service began Rural Free Delivery (RFD), helping increase circulation numbers for many publications. People in rural areas often had to travel miles to pick up mail, but RFD delivered mail, including periodicals, to homes!

So by 1900 periodical circulation had fewer obstacles for advertisers to reach anywhere in the country cost-effectively. Concerns regarding circulation figures, though, weren't entirely quashed.

ADVERTISING'S BIG FOOTPRINT

Newspaper and magazine advertisements tended to be small and mostly text. But art was creeping in, and images gobbled space. So ads started consuming more space. With the advent of agencies, too, we were seeing the birth of the "advertising professional." Before the late 1800s, the only full-time ad people probably were sign painters, but now an entire industry was rising around promoting products and services, and full-time professionals were essential. As a result, and because of the Industrial Revolution, more innovation began spreading through the field. New technologies allowed for new forms of ad. And since more merchants were advertising, competition for consumers' attention grew. All this paved the road to more, and sometimes better, advertisements.

Simultaneously, the field was reaching more people, though slowly. The first newspaper ad in Romania appeared in *Curierul Romanesc* (the *Romanian Courier*) in 1829 (Pop 2018). The first newspaper ad in Thailand wasn't until 1845, in the *Bangkok Recorder* (Pongsapitaksanti 2010).

By the 1830s, advertisers sought methods to make their ads stand out. James Gordon Bennett, editor and publisher of the *New York Herald*, briefly allowed advertisers to experiment with ads that were two columns wide. After a time he stopped it, concerned that larger advertisers could overshadow smaller ones (Turner 1953). Double-column ads didn't return until 1867, when it's believed the Lord & Taylor department store was first to again cross the line between columns. And there were other size restrictions, like a ban on large typefaces.

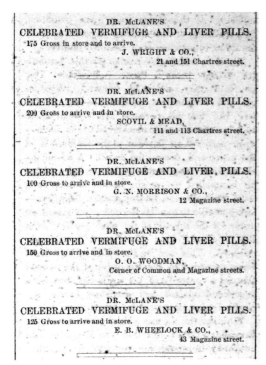

Other publishers likewise placed limits on ad and type size.

In late 1847, Bennett announced he would no longer allow ads to run more than one day (Wood 1958). But the *Herald* continued to be in high demand by advertisers. The field had reached the point that publishers and merchants fought for control of ad space.

Typefaces were in transition. Roman type, from previous centuries, was being replaced with styles like Baskerville and Bodoni. With this came innovations such as using two or three words in capital letters to start a sentence (Presbrey 1929). By the 1840s, shadow and relief typefaces were being used for emphasis by some publications.

The 1850s found advertisers using workarounds to publishers' rules. Where ads were size limited, with illustrations or large type prohibited, advertisers might run the same ad multiple times on a page (Figure 7.9). In 1856, ads for the *New York Ledger*

FIGURE 7.9.   An example of an advertiser running the same ad multiple times, in this case with different retailer names, from the *Daily Delta*, March 11, 1859.

could be found repeated so often they filled entire pages in other newspapers. And limited typeface size was overcome by creating large letters out of multiple small letters. By the next decade they added other tricks, like printing their company name over and over in the ad:

McCLATCHY AND SMITH
McCLATCHY AND SMITH
McCLATCHY AND SMITH
McCLATCHY AND SMITH
McCLATCHY AND SMITH

With that technique, 12-point type could have an effect similar to 60-point type. It was the Age of Repetition. By the 1870s, strict limits on advertising layouts were easing.

While the first full-page newspaper ad appeared in 1766, that approach wasn't copied. The next advertiser to use it might have been theatrical agent George Lea, who supposedly ran the "first" full-page ad in the *New York Herald* in 1856 (Anonymous 1901). But some credit Robert Bonner as running the first full-page ad in the *New York Ledger* in 1856 (e.g., Doyle 2011), and others give John Wanamaker's store credit in 1879 (e.g., Kenner 1936). Regardless, full-page advertising clearly was rare until the late 1800s, when large ads became common. Merchants apparently decided that size matters!

Many newspapers had become addicted to revenues from advertising, so even front pages became dominated by advertising. But as news became more important during the Civil War, news moved to the front (Presbrey 1929).

Magazines resisted advertising for ages. *Harper's* magazine refused ads—other than ads for its publisher's books—until July 1864. *The Atlantic* began accepting ads in February 1860 (Presbrey 1929). Once those prestigious magazines relented, others followed. With a later nudge by J. Walter Thompson, the conversion was complete. And magazines accepted more and larger illustrations in ads than were found in newspapers.

Along with size, volume also continued to expand. The *New York Herald*, in its April 13, 1869, issue, had eight columns of editorial material, thirty-eight columns of news, and fifty columns of advertising (Wood 1958). A turning point for magazines was the 1890s. *McClure's Magazine* began selling at a bargain price: fifteen cents. *Cosmopolitan* then dropped to twelve and a half cents. Frank A. Munsey then pushed the envelope, dropping *Munsey's Magazine* from twenty-five cents to ten cents (Figure 7.10). The next month *Munsey's* reported, "Munsey's at ten cents has made a larger percentage of increase in circulation on the October issue at this rock bottom price than any magazine in the world ever made in a like time." This put magazines in reach of the middle class, further increasing circulation, with ads reaching more consumers.

FIGURE 7.10. The price of *Munsey's Magazine* was dropped from twenty-five to ten cents in October 1893.

The Postal Act of 1879 also helped spread magazine advertising. It gave magazines low-cost mailing options (Clarke 1970), so heavier magazines could be sent to subscribers without extra postage.

Many other changes, such as the growth of "big stores," likewise helped (Turner 1953). Even the largest stores in 1800 weren't so big, but advertising helped stores grow by increasing store traffic. Big stores competed for shoppers, inflating pressure to get noticed. The century's last three decades or so became the era of big—big stores and big advertising.

SHINING A LIGHT ON ADVERTISING

Efforts to stand out weren't confined to newspaper and magazine ads, though. Merchants found new opportunities. Although electric lighting was years away, it turns out that the first lighted advertising sign—using gas—was used in 1840. It was P. T. Barnum who lighted the sign in front of his museum (Wagner 1954).

FIGURE 7.11.   A P. T. Barnum poster was hard to ignore, as seen in this 1882 example.

FIGURE 7.12.   The very first electric "spectacular," in 1891, was built where today's Flatiron Building is located.

Barnum also enlarged pictures on posters in the 1840s. He wanted his own face four times larger than ever before. The illustration, cut from a pine block, definitely was noticed. An illustrated poster craze for traveling circuses followed (Hendon & Muhs 1985). Soon posters, like gas lighting, created brighter forms of advertising. Barnum's posters for his museum, menagerie, and circus used bright color schemes, just as his advertising claims became more brilliant (Figure 7.11). He knew how to shine a spotlight on featured acts.

The first electric sign appeared in London, spelling EDISON with incandescent bulbs at the 1882 International Electrical Exposition. In 1891, the first electric "spectacular"—an enormous lighted sign—appeared in New York City, at Broadway and Fifth (Anonymous 2016). It contained 1,457 bulbs and touted, "Buy Homes on Long Island" (Figure 7.12). Thus began the street's nickname, "Great White Way."

The next lighting innovation was in 1898, when neon, krypton, and xenon were discovered, leading to new lighting tubes, eventually unveiled at the Paris Motor Show in 1910. It was 1912 when the first neon sign was sold to a barbershop on Boulevard Monmartre in Paris. This century truly made advertising shine.

MOTION PROMOTION

The notion of motion also came to promotion. Hind (1958) suggests a card tacked up inside a river steamboat was the original transit advertising. We know in 1829 that George Shillibeer founded the first regular bus system, the Omnibus, in London: horse-drawn carriages carrying sixteen to eighteen people. From the start those buses were covered in ads (Figure 7.13). This marked one of the earliest mass-transit advertising forms. I say "mass" transit because there already were horses with ads hung across them, and undoubtedly some wagons. Those prior versions tended to be advertiser-owned vehicles, while the Omnibus was owned by someone else.

Surprisingly, it found a way to annoy people! Ads covered bus windows on hot days, preventing air flow. The London Hackney Carriage Act of 1853 was aimed at regulating that issue (Nevett 1982). Over time, ads appeared not only outside but also inside the buses, where "car cards" were displayed.

Bus owners soon realized ads could reach both passersby *and* riders (Clarke 1970). And while British newspapers and their ads were taxed, transit ads were not.

By the 1840s, horses definitely were pulling carts festooned with ads. *Punch* magazine said:

FIGURE 7.13. London Omnibus from the end of the 1800s.

> Go where you will, you are stopped by a monster cart running over with advertisements, or are nearly knocked down by an advertising house put upon wheels, which calls upon you, when too late, not to forget "Number One." (Nevett 1982)

Horses also pulled streetcars on rails by mid-century. Streetcar conductors were advertising salespeople, contracting for space in and on their cars (Hind 1958). The Lord & Taylor department store and B. T. Babbitt soap were some of the earliest to advertise this way. Presbrey (1929) describes the ads inside the streetcars:

> In some cars this panel seems to have been a narrow frame placed inside on either side of the door, in others an oblong affair containing three or four sections and fastened more or less loosely over the windows, where it added to other rattle produced by the bouncing of the car over the tracks.

Eventually buckboards and surreys, too, bore ads while wandering through the countryside. Sloops had ads emblazoned on sails (Printers' Ink 1938). Sleighs in the snow and even umbrellas perched on farm wagons hawked wares (Wood 1958). And with trains, the attractiveness of this advertising opportunity grew exponentially. Advertising was no longer a stationary art. It was moving up . . . even into the sky.

WHEN ADVERTISING WAS UP IN THE AIR

Aerial advertising was born in the 1890s, before the Wright brothers. Box kites flew dragging advertising banners, likely the first flying ads.

A "cloud projector," by L. K. Rogers, shined ads on clouds in 1893. From the Manufacturers Building's roof at the World Columbian Exposition in Chicago, the projector displayed

FIGURE 7.14.   This cartoon about cloud projector advertising appeared in *Funny Folks* magazine on April 9, 1892.

on the clouds the number of people attending that day's event. The device had been revealed in a military display a year earlier.

When the exposition ended, the cloud projector moved to the Pulitzer Building roof in New York, becoming an advertising medium (see Figure 7.14). When there were no clouds, exploding rockets created them (Turner 1953). Famous brand names were projected by "light cannons" on trees, buildings, and steam clouds. No bats. The method quickly was adopted, and advertising was projected on almost any surface available, including Niagra Falls (Huhtamo 2010).

In 1896, a new ad method dropped. Recalls a Royal Academician:

> I was in my garden and I heard sudden reports of artillery. Presently from the sky fell masses of green and red paper advertising a tooth powder. These fell all over my garden and I am not exaggerating when I tell you that these were spread over two acres at least. It took my gardener a week to collect all these pieces of paper which were blown out of guns into my garden. (Turner 1953)

This is the earliest record of advertisements being shot from a gun or cannon.

Balloons, too, began around that time. An account at the end of the century says:

> [An] extraordinary balloon . . . shaped like a scent-bottle, whereon a perfumer's name was writ very large indeed. A car, capable of holding thirty persons, was attached and the bottle used to float all over Paris. Each trip cost some £400, but a far more effective advertisement was secured than if the money had been spent in the ordinary humdrum way. (Vivian 1902)

A steam-powered airship capable of being steered was invented in 1852. Count Ferdinand von Zeppelin patented another airship in 1895. A seventy-five-foot balloon airship from 1902 is shown in Figure 7.15. To buy this, the owner, Stanley Spencer, signed a sponsorship deal with Mellin and

FIGURE 7.15.   A 1902 balloon airship used to advertise Mellin's Food.

Company, a baby food maker. He promised to make twenty-five flights with "Mellin's Food" in gigantic print on the side. He test-flew it over London in 1901, catching the imaginations of people in the streets.

. . . AND MUSIC IN THE AIR

As ads grew in size, we had to step back to take them in. As they rose into the air we had to look up. Vision was critical to message delivery. How an ad strikes our senses is important, but vision is just one sense. Sound played a big role long before it was recorded or broadcast.

Town criers offered auditory pitches from at least the eleventh century, rhyming or singing about products for sale. And the nineteenth century brought means to spread rhymes, jingles, or songs more broadly than ever before.

In fact, most were jingles. Many claim the first jingle occurred in the twentieth century, but in Figure 7.16 you can see proof that such notions are in error.

McLaren & Prelinger (1998) suggest a "jingle craze" began with the De Long Hook and Eye Company in 1891, and their popularity stemmed from their memorability. But Dictionary.com suggests "jingle," as applied to a "catchy array of words in prose or verse," dates to the 1640s. Perhaps criers' promotional rhymes were called jingles long before the 1890s. Recall that criers also were called *bell*men, so it makes sense that they might jingle.

FIGURE 7.16.   A book of jingles to promote Bell-cap-sic medicinal and surgical plasters, published in 1898.

There were songs or jingles promoting products, but some also were about advertising. Here is a song titled "Advertisements," circa 1890:

> He skipped the leading articles and scorned the latest news.
> But every bold advertisement with rapture he'd peruse.
> He read, he talked of nothing else; the thing became a bore.
> You got quite sick of Eno's Salt and Rowland's Kalydor. (Nevett 1982)

Word-of-mouth advertising, likely the oldest promotional method, has always been common. It sometimes was called "collateral advertising" (Russell 1937), though that term has another meaning today. The point of jingles was to drive consumers to help spread the sales pitch.

Songs and jingles, then, were distributed mostly through printed text. Consumers converted them to sound. Sound technologies, though, began arriving at century's end. More on that later.

NEITHER SNOW NOR RAIN NOR HEAT NOR GLOOM OF NIGHT[4]

Postal services go back to pharaohs' couriers in Egypt, around 2400 BCE. The first postal system was in Persia around 550 BCE. In China it began around 220 BCE, while Europe goes only to around Augustus Caesar, 62 BCE to 14 CE. The US postal system began in 1775. Advertising could have used any of these, but 1848 was the beginning of advertising mail in America.

The term "circularize" was coined then, meaning "to send circulars" (i.e., handbills). Ben Franklin's early catalogs aside, this was the birth of direct mail advertising. The US postal rate was a penny in 1850, making mail relatively affordable. It took off. By 1855, it gained traction in England, and in 1870 the English rate dropped to a halfpenny, making mail advertising soar (Presbrey 1929).

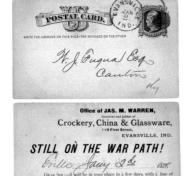

The first postcard was in 1840 in the United Kingdom; the first postcard in the United States dates to 1848 (Willoughby 1992). Believe it or not, that first card contained printed advertising! It wasn't an "official" postcard, just a handmade card sent by mail. The term "mailed cards" was adopted. Some creative advertisers were able to foresee more possibilities in mail as an ad delivery mechanism.

With an act of Congress, real US postcards began in 1861. In that first year the postcard became a regular advertising medium (Kern-Foxworth 1994). Initially the postcard ads used only text, with the message on the card's back, not the face (Figure 7.17).

FIGURE 7.17. A fairly typical advertising postcard from 1878, front and back.

The first advertising picture postcards in the United States commemorated the World Columbian Exposition of 1893 (Figure 7.18). These were government productions. Commercial businesses weren't allowed to print postcards until 1898, when the Private Mailing Card Act was passed. Thereafter, businesses could publish postcards, if labeled "Private Mailing Card."

Direct mail advertising became nearly synonymous with mail order sales in 1869, when E. C. Allen began selling recipes for washing compounds. He established the *People's Literary Companion*. Disguised as a magazine, it was a catalog advertising mail order products. By 1870, Allen's circulation was five hundred thousand (Browne & Kreiser 2003). This likely was the first mail order catalog for a broad range of products (not just books or seeds).

Direct mail was pushed up another notch when Aaron Montgomery Ward sent out the Montgomery Ward catalog in 1872. Ward realized that the new transcontinental railroad made nationwide sales possible.

FIGURE 7.18. One of several picture postcards used to advertise the World Columbian Exposition of 1893.

Ward's first catalog was a single sheet—a circular—but quickly expanded (Printers' Ink 1938). By 1887, it was 540 pages.

Then a telegraph operator for the Great Northern Railroad, Richard W. Sears, encountered a jeweler who refused to accept a shipment of watches in 1884, sticking the railroad with them. Sears decided to try selling them by mail, sending a direct mail piece in 1888 as "The R.W. Sears Watch Co." By 1894, his was a full catalog. Only twenty-four years old, Sears had $100,000, making him a very wealthy man. He recognized that American farm families were an untapped market, so he catered to them (Mierau 2000).

He soon sold an amazing variety of products by mail. Between 1908 and 1940 Sears sold more than seventy thousand houses in kit form. Those houses ultimately became ads for Sears, encouraging neighbors to buy kits, and to see the Sears catalog as "The Wish Book."

Interestingly, at this time (beginning in 1913), it was legal to ship children by mail. The first, a baby boy under eleven pounds, was mailed to his grandmother for fifteen cents, insured for fifty dollars.[5] It probably is good that advertising professionals, including Sears, never latched onto this possibility. It was a time when "anything goes" was almost literally true for advertising.

At first, both Ward and Sears charged fees for catalogs (fifteen cents and ten cents, respectively). After a couple of decades, they became free, and demand increased significantly (Printers' Ink 1938).

MAKING ADVERTISING THAT STICKS

The postage stamp was another notable development for advertising mail. James Chalmers invented the adhesive postage stamp around 1837, though Lovrenc Kosir of Austria-Hungary proposed "artifically affixed postal tax stamps" in 1835. The United Kingdom's first stamp was in 1840, and the United States followed in 1847.

FIGURE 7.19. The 1887 1/2d Vermilion stamp used by Pears' Soap for advertising.

In 1887, stamps actually became an advertising medium. In Great Britain, the 1887 1/2d Vermilion postal and revenue stamp was "underprinted" by Pears' Soap, where "Pears' Soap" was printed on the gummed side of stamps (Figure 7.19).[6] Pears' originally sought to have this done officially, but when the postmaster rejected it, Pears' printed the message on its own, on top of the gum. Anyone licking these stamps would likely notice the message.

A few years later, in 1893, New Zealand awarded a contract to Truebridge, Miller & Reich, an advertising agency, to sell the backs of stamps to advertisers. The experiment didn't last long. There was concern about licking ink, and the ad couldn't be seen after the stamp was on the envelope. But the agency apparently believed in its product (Figure 7.20).

FIGURE 7.20. The reverse side of an 1894 stamp promoting stamp advertising.

Another stamp advertisement approach needs mention—*revenue* stamps. The US Revenue Act of 1862 required stamps be attached to many products: books, medicines, playing

FIGURE 7.21. A revenue stamp for a patent medicine, from 1864.

cards, and more. This is how products were taxed. The Act allowed private companies to design and print the stamps, even offering them a discount on taxes if they did so. The ad tended to pay for itself. Figure 7.21 is one of these "Private Die Proprietary Revenue Stamps."

Postcards, postage stamps, and revenue stamps were advertising opportunities created by government and given government's "stamp" of approval. Consumers might assume these companies were government endorsed. Another government medium, as in the past, was money.

WE'RE IN THE MONEY . . . AGAIN . . . AND AGAIN

A British law in 1817 ended minting trade tokens, which were more popular than ever. There were, though, some exceptions (Whiting 1971). The tokens never completely disappeared, though most lost their legal tender status.

There were special cases like the East India Company (EIC). England created the EIC in 1600 to manage trade with India and Pacific Rim countries. It was a private company with stockholders but frequently acted like an arm of the British government. Eventually it became something of a government itself, forming an army and ruling over portions of India. In 1784, the British passed a law to subsume the company.

Acting as an Indian government, EIC issued its own coinage. It still was technically a private company, and the company name was on the coins (Figure 7.22) until Britain required all its territories have uniform coinage via the Coinage Act of 1835. This was a unique example of legal currency advertising a private company.

As early as around 1790, insurance companies, factories, railroads, and more issued their own paper money in the United States. Between 1837 and 1863 was the

FIGURE 7.22. An 1835 coin, ¼ Anna, from the East India Company.

Free Banking Era, during which almost anyone could become a bank and issue bank notes. This was the "wild west" of banking, and helped force banking system changes. Until then, private issue bank notes promoted a variety of companies (Figure 7.23). This was a paper version of the trade tokens from prior centuries.

FIGURE 7.23. A private issue bank note, sometimes called "merchant script," promoting the White & Hill company.

Then came the American Civil War in the spring of 1861. By 1862, there was a precious metals shortage as people hoarded anything that might retain value. Coins disappeared from circulation, so paper money was issued for amounts below a dollar. By that fall, governmentally unsanctioned coins were being issued. This continued for a couple of years, then the government put a stop to it. Perhaps twenty-five million coins were produced in that short time.

These tokens came in three versions: patriotic tokens, sutler tokens, and store cards. The patriotic tokens bore patriotic slogans, and the sutler ones displayed military information. The "store cards" held the name (and more) of a business (Figure 7.24), similar to the old Conder tokens.

FIGURE 7.24. A Civil War store card from 1863 declaring it is "Not One Cent" and promoting the C. Doscher business in New York.

Advertisers were not limited to minting new coins; some used existing coins. Between 1820 and 1880 was a phenomenon called "counterstamping." It wasn't limited to advertising, but certainly was popular in advertising. A merchant would take an old coin, stamp his brand on it, and put the coin back into circulation. Everyone who handled the coin would see the brand.

One company using this technique was, unsurprisingly, Pears' Soap (Figure 7.25). The example here is a French coin. It was illegal in Britain to deface a coin portraying a British monarch, so Pears' imported French coins (Taylor 2006). French coins weren't unusual in Britain.

This practice died in the late 1800s as more advertising options arose. Elongated or stretched coins also were used for advertising, starting with the 1893 World Columbian Exposition. Those elongated coins, another form of stamped coins, are still popular today as tourist souvenirs.

FIGURE 7.25. An 1857 French coin stamped with the Pears' Soap name is a typical example of coin counterstamping.

Finally, there were British bills known as "Lipton Pounds" or "Lipton Notes" around 1877. Thomas Lipton, later of Lipton Tea fame, opened a grocery in 1871 and eventually issued notes that appeared, at a glance, to be regular one pound notes, with £1 printed at the top. On closer inspection, it was a promotional ploy. On them was printed, "I promise to give on demand in any of my establishments HAM, BUT-TER, and EGGS as given elsewhere to the value of one pound for fifteen shillings." Some people mistook these for genuine currency, and at least one was jailed for trying to pass them off as legal currency. Lipton was sued by someone who received it as change from a vendor (Waugh 1950).

By today's standards, putting a product name on a coin or paper bill might seem like a trivial advertising form, since the name can appear on key fobs, baseball hats, shoes, and thousands of other items, but those weren't options back then. Choices were limited. And no promotional product comes with a government endorsement.

PRODUCTS THAT PROMOTE

Promotional products are items that have use on their own but double as advertising media. They also are called advertising specialties, swag, or, more pejoratively, tchotchkes or even "trinkets and trash." I already mentioned the folding fans used for advertising in the previous century.

FIGURE 7.26.   Ketterlinus continued to publish calendars for many years. This 1879 version was its own advertisement.

Calendars as advertising were one of the oldest promotional products, introduced in the 1850s. Ketterlinus Lithographic Producing Company of Philadelphia was one of the first printers to create them. They became exceedingly popular (Figure 7.26) and were common by the 1880s. It is believed Thomas Dowler Murphy and Edmund Burke Osborne were the first to add artwork to advertising calendars (Barklow 1922). It turns out a picture of George Washington was less successful as calendar art than the first calendar girl, named Cosette. Imagine that. The popularity of calendars soared in the 1900s with the introduction of "pin-up girls."

While almanacs date to 1457, they were popular as advertising matter in the mid- to late 1800s. Even before the 1850s the patent medicine industry had discovered the potential of this promotional product (Figure 7.27).

In late nineteenth-century China the most popular advertising device was the pictorial calendar (O'Barr 2007). These frequently were found on the walls of Chinese homes.

Punch magazine, circa 1850s, was critical of advertising and at one point "sarcastically observed that people would be advertising on umbrellas next." Soon, umbrellas were the newest promotional product.

Paper bags, too, became promotional products. The Union Paper Bag Machine Company in 1852 patented a device to make paper bags. Almost overnight, those bags were imprinted with brand names and logos (Mierau 2000).

Ignoring those, some authors suggest the first real promotional product was created by Jasper Freemont Meek, of Coshocton, Ohio, in 1886. Meek needed to keep his newspaper's printing press from being idle, so he printed "Buy Cantwell's Shoes" on burlap book bags for a friend who owned a shoe business. Afterward, he began printing ads on horse blankets and more. Saying Meek *invented* promotional products seems a stretch, but clearly he spearheaded creating a promotional products industry.

Meek's innovation opened eyes to the possibilities of turning commonplace items into advertising media. Consequently, he's been called the "father of specialty advertising," as it once was known (Herpel & Slack 1983).

By 1889, matchbooks were used to advertise the Mendelson Opera Company. Two hundred of those actually were hand-printed by the opera company's manager.

Beer brewer Adolphus Busch, in the 1890s, created branded corkscrews for salesmen to

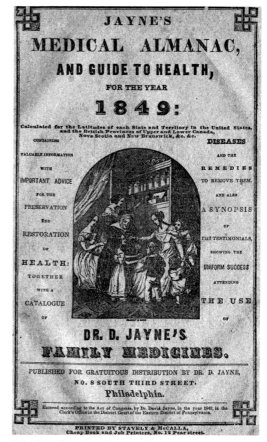

FIGURE 7.27. An almanac from 1849, promoting Dr. Jayne's patent medicines.

FIGURE 7.28. This corkscrew was produced for Anheuser Busch in the 1890s.

give to customers (Figure 7.28). Prior promotions had put brand names on various products; Busch might be the first to have a custom-designed product to hold the brand name.

Back to Jasper Meek's home in Coshocton, Ohio, a fellow citizen named H. D. Beach developed a way to produce imprinted wooden yardsticks, paint mixers, flyswatters, and file dividers. It led to competition with Meek, and some cooperation, turning Coshocton into the home of the promotional products industry (Herpel & Slack 1983). But it wasn't the only important location.

At the Chicago World Colombian Exposition in 1893, Henry John Heinz offered a custom giveaway. He hired boys to distribute handbills, promising "a novel watch charm" to anyone visiting his booth. It was a one-and-a-quarter-inch-long green plastic pickle with "Heinz" on it. Hundreds of thousands claimed the prize, helping make

Heinz a household name. I can't help but wonder whether Heinz had enough charms made, or if this volume left him in a pickle.

One promotional product led to ideas for others. In the twentieth century, this industry spread like a virus. Catalogs of tchotchkes eventually offered thousands of products to showcase a brand. But one exceedingly popular advertising medium in the late 1800s also might be categorized as a promotional product: trade cards.

TRADE, TRADESMAN, OR TRADING?

Trade cards of that time were a variation on the tradesman's cards of previous centuries. Sometimes called "trading" cards—they were, indeed, traded—these were collected like baseball cards in more recent years. They became a product category in their own right, making them promotional products. And these cards often had national distribution, so they were nationwide advertising when most media were local.

FIGURE 7.29.   Louis Prang's own trade card.

Louis Prang of Boston gets much of the credit for this craze. Prang, a printer, began publishing advertising trade cards in the 1850s. In 1873, he created a full-color trade card for the Vienna International Exposition, and it won a prize. Color made the difference. It appears Prang might have been the first to publish color trade cards, and he began printing them for many advertisers (Figure 7.29).

That fad took off in the 1880s, lasting a couple of decades. Shoppers might come home from a store with a handful of cards and paste them into a scrapbook (Crane n.d.). The cards generally had a color picture on one side, with or without an advertising message, and more of an ad pitch on the back (Figure 7.30). Some were fancier, being cut in distinctive shapes. And some, called mechanical cards, even had movable parts (Figure 7.31).

Trade cards gained traction mainly because of technological advances. Another medium that benefited from technology is the advertising button.

FIGURE 7.30. Trade cards were popular with patent medicine brands. Here you can see both the front and the back of one.

FIGURE 7.31. Clark's is an example of a mechanical card. The image on the bottom shows how this one could be folded to change the picture.

BUTTON, BUTTON . . .

FIGURE 7.32.   An Abraham Lincoln presidential campaign button from 1860, using a photograph.

Buttons in the 1700s were buttons used on clothing, like the George Washington button shown earlier. These continued to be important for political campaigns. One advance, though, was the use of photos. The first campaign buttons to include photographs were for Abraham Lincoln in 1860 (Figure 7.32). Other advertisers soon adopted this promotional tool.

FIGURE 7.33.   A Whitehead & Hoag advertising button, for Davis Baking Powder, from 1896.

Yet another advance was in 1896, when Whitehead & Hoag received a patent for the "badge pin." This was the metal pin used for a pin-back button (Figure 7.33).

ADS WITH DEPTH

The ability to print color meant profound changes to advertising. And we had come so far from the old, crude, wood-block printing of small icons in ads. But a couple of other inventions additionally helped change the picture.

Capturing and freezing a moment in time became possible in 1826 when Joseph Nicephore Niepce took the first photograph. It took a few years, but by the 1840s photography was becoming an industry. It is believed the first advertisement with a photograph was in 1843, in the *Philadelphia Public Ledger*, thanks to photographer Robert Cornelius. He owned a photographic studio, and the ad probably was for his business.[7] Cornelius also is known for taking the first selfie!

Contrary to claims about Cornelius, Robertson (2011) believes the earliest photographically illustrated ad—though not in a newspaper—was a real estate poster for lots outside Paris, with a landscape photo by Bisson Freres, displayed in railroad ticket offices in 1854. He also claims the first US photo ad was a poster in Augusta, Georgia, in 1863. That ad was by rice planter Louis Manigault, depicting his slave, Dolly, who had run away.[8]

The Cornelius ad would have preceded the first newspaper story photo, published in 1848 in *L'Illustration* in Paris. And it wasn't long before color came to photos. On Christmas Day 1855, the *Illustrated London News* supposedly printed the first color photos in an English newspaper. If true, they were hand-colored, because that was the year an idea for creating color photos was first suggested. The first color photos based on that idea appeared in 1861.

Almost simultaneously, in 1838 the first stereoscope—a way of using two slightly different images, side by side, to create a three-dimensional (3D) image—was invented by Sir Charles

Wheatstone. In 1849, Sir David Brewster created a more practical stereoscope. It was an early version of something you've probably used: the View-Master.

Combining the Brewster Stereoscope with photography made stereo imagery incredibly popular. Oliver Wendell Holmes, father of the US Supreme Court justice by that name, in 1861 invented a more portable handheld stereoscope that quickly replaced heavy desktop models, making "stereoviews" more consumer-friendly.

In 1860, Eli Whitney Blake Jr., a scientist *and* great-nephew of the Eli Whitney of cotton gin fame, wrote this in the *American Journal of Science and Arts*:

> Prof. H. W. Dove, to whom we are indebted for so many beautiful stereoscopic experiments, in his *Optische Studien*, gives a specimen of stereoscopic printing to illustrate the double refraction of Iceland Spar, as seen in binocular vision.
>
> This effect is produced by printing for the left eye, lines in the ordinary manner, while for the right eye, the alternate lines are slightly advanced. Upon combining the two by means of the stereoscope, the printing appears to be in two planes, more or less distant from each other.
>
> Should the "spacing" of the two not correspond exactly, single words will rise toward or fall back from the eye; thus by varying the spaces between the words even in the slightest degree, a marked effect is produced. In this age of advertising it might be worth the while of enterprising individuals to print their advertisements in a stereoscopic form. It would certainly gain for them a more general and careful study than this class of literature can generally command. I annex, as an example of this mode of printing, a stereoscopic advertisement of this Journal, which may be observed by simply placing the instrument over it. (Blake 1860)

Although unsophisticated, not a stereo photograph, and presented only as an ad concept for the *Journal*, Blake's example is almost certainly the first ever 3D advertisement (Figure 7.34).

Blake's ad made the 3D image the ad's essence. Ads using stereoviews soon followed. Initially the 3D images weren't of products for sale; rather, they were landscapes and so forth, with a business name and sales pitch printed on the edge or back.

FIGURE 7.34. A speculative advertisement created by Eli Whitney Blake Jr. for the *American Journal of Science and Arts*, demonstrating the potential for 3D advertising.

The only exception seemed to be photographers or stereoscope image sellers who used one stereoview to sell others (e.g., Figure 7.35).

Stereoscope imaging was the genesis of virtual reality (VR). Back then it offered what some have called "virtual tourism," allowing people to see distant places with more realism than ever before. Soon advertisers, such as tobacco companies, were tapping into the public's fascination with 3D images as a way of showcasing brands.

FIGURE 7.35.   A stereoview image from the 1860s (front and back) published by Richard Walzl, with an advertising message promoting other images.

Another technology was introduced by W. Rollmann in 1853, called the "anaglyph" 3D. Much later it became an important method, and it is still used today. Different-colored filters were placed in front of each eye, to view slightly different images to create the 3D effect.

Thomas Edison patented an "optical phonograph" in 1888, which was the earliest movie making. William Friese-Green then created the first 3D anaglyphic motion pictures in 1889. That technique is still used for 3D motion pictures 130 years later. It laid the foundation for anaglyphic 3D advertisements, too.

The first motion picture advertisements occurred in 1897, thanks to Edison. The ad, for Admiral Cigarettes, shows the brand name behind four people: Uncle Sam, a clergyman, a Native American, and a businessman. A young woman comes out of a box, crosses the

FIGURE 7.36. A screenshot from the first motion picture advertisement for Admiral Cigarettes.

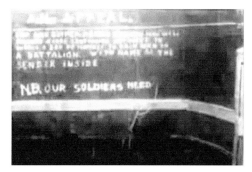

FIGURE 7.37. "Matches an Appeal," the first animated advertising commercial.

stage, and hands out four cigarettes. A banner unfurls saying, "We All Smoke" (Figure 7.36). Around this same time there were films advertising Haig Whisky, Pabst's Milwaukee Beer, and Maillard's Chocolate (Robertson 2011).

Two years later came the first animated advertising film (Figure 7.37). Called "Matches an Appeal," it was created by Arthur Melbourne-Cooper, showing a matchstick man writing on a blackboard. It might be the earliest animated film of any type.

Afterward, photography would be central to much—if not most—advertising. All of this represents the start of both virtual and augmented reality methods.

AD POLLUTION

Outdoor advertising was pretty primitive in 1800. Children were given token pay to post bills on walls and fences. Many citizens couldn't afford newspaper subscriptions, but literacy had improved, so posted bills worked as advertising. And in Britain, unlike newspaper ads, bills weren't taxed. They also weren't subject to restrictions imposed by newspapers.

Bills often were pasted over competitors' bills, thwarting advertisers' efforts (Seidel, Kelly, & Lowery 1958). Bills were everywhere. In Britain, this was sometimes called "placarding the streets." It spread not only through the cities but into the countryside as well. Dedicated boards, or "hoardings," were erected for bills—hence, "bill boards"—offering some control over what was posted, circa 1839. Hoardings soon appeared everywhere.

This billposting virus in England led to laws. The 1817 Metropolitan Paving Act required that hoardings be licensed, though this was frequently ignored, resulting in arrests of bill posters (Hicks 2012). When it reached the point that homeowners would find posters covering their front doors, the Metropolitan Police Act of 1839 prohibited posting on properties without the owners' consent (Turner 1953).

The first commercial billboard in the United States was erected by Jared Bell in 1835. Bell was printing circus posters, and built a board fifty square feet on which to post them.

But outdoor advertising didn't get its start in Sydney, Australia, until 1854, when Isaac & Joseph Roff produced the first bills. And it wasn't until the late 1870s that another company, Hollander & Govett, set up hoardings for clients' posters (Crawford 2008).

Over time billboard construction quality improved and sizes increased. The new printing technologies allowed creation of larger bills and posters. And by 1851 some ads were being created by using dozens of sheets of paper (Presbrey 1929).

By the 1860s, the controlled boards (aka "advertising stations" or "bill stations") were replacing bills being stuck everywhere. More bills were being neatly hung and protected from predatory bill posters. The industry had reached a new level of professionalism. The US Civil War stimulated government spending on war recruitment posters, which added legitimacy to this medium.

Until the 1860s, a "poster" generally was synonymous with a "bill." It was an ad printed on paper to be posted. What we consider a poster today tends to be large, in color,

FIGURE 7.38. An advertising poster by Jules Cheret, from 1869.

and on stiff paper or cardboard. Color lithography really enabled the modern poster. In 1866, Jules Cheret created lithographed posters that he hung across Paris. Henri de Toulouse-Lautrec followed by creating posters that continue to be valued today (Halldin 2013). Advertising adopted these new forms of poster almost immediately. Both Cheret and Toulouse-Lautrec became major contributors to advertising (Figure 7.38).

In 1871, Pearl Tobacco got attention by being probably the first to use a nude woman in an advertising poster (Figure 7.39). Sex in advertising is not new. This also was an early example of an "image" ad. The line between art and advertising was quite blurred in posters, boosting the bill posting industry's image.

Posters were all the rage. There were poster exhibitions, poster clubs, poster galleries, and even poster magazines (Rickards 1971).

While bill posting achieved more professionalism, bills also were being hand-delivered to houses! These "handbills" were common as early as the 1820s (Nevett 1982).

Meanwhile, signs were being painted on boards, rocks, walls, and barn roofs (Wood 1958). The Bradbury and Houghteling sign painting company was formed in 1870 as the first nationwide paint service in the United States. One founder, Sam Houghteling, boasted, "I've painted on rocks while standing up to my neck in water" and "put the name of 'Vitality Bitters' on Lookout Mountain" (Gudis 2004).

FIGURE 7.39. This Pearl Tobacco poster from 1871 likely was the first advertising poster to display a nude woman.

Enameled metal was introduced in 1857, and in 1880 England the Patent Enamel Company began offering enameled sheet iron signs, hailed as "The plate that outlasts all others" (Baglee & Morley 1988). This was the beginning of sheet metal (often called "tin") signs. The relative permanence of metal signs added longevity that could be found in only a few other, less-colorful advertising media (e.g., coins, stone).

By the close of the Victorian Era, there were few places in the developed world where consumers could escape posters, bills, or signs. Advertising's presence in these media had expanded beyond anything citizens at the start of the Era would have conceived. Even walking away from a sign didn't always work, since some would follow you.

AD ON A SANDWICH

In part because of posted bills being regulated, the ad industry invented moving billboards. Wood (1958) notes, "Inspired advertisers hired troops of derelicts, dressed them in uniforms, and marched a seedy burlesque of the Guards or a company of foot through the streets as an advertising scheme."

A common practice was to tie two boards together, draping them over a boy or man hired to walk the streets sandwiched between boards so an ad was displayed on both his back and his front. This is why they were called "sandwich men." Some believe Charles Dickens invented the term when he used "sandwich" to describe a boy wearing such boards.[9] They were walking billboards.

In New York, these men are said to have appeared in the 1820s, though they arrived in London around 1850 (Figure 7.40). The boards also could be stood on a sidewalk, leaning against each other as an inverted "V" without anyone between. This earned the name "sandwich board."

Sandwich boards and sandwich men were all the rage. And the latter not only wore the ads but also typically passed out handbills. Since many were unemployed, it was a cost-effective advertising technique.

As competition escalated, advertisers sought ways to distinguish their mobile ads. A man wearing an ad while riding a horse might get more attention, and travel farther, than merely walking. A dog wearing an ad hanging from its collar might grab attention unattainable by men. Sometimes a man's front board would be a teaser, with the clincher hanging on his back (Wood 1958).

FIGURE 7.40. This 1880 drawing depicts "sandwich men" of the day.

A sandwich man's life wasn't terribly prestigious. Nevett (1982) reflects:

Advertisers paid two shillings per day for his services, from which the contractor who hired him out took a commission of 25%. For this he was subjected to humiliation at the hands of small boys, who flung mud at him and tickled him with straws. He was kicked and knocked over by the conductors of passing omnibuses. He was pushed into the gutter by police, whipped by coachmen, and sprayed with dirt by passing traffic. In short, as Smith commented, "Few men who earn their living in the streets are better abused and more persistently jeered at than the unfortunate individuals who let themselves out for hire as walking advertisements."

Yet these methods are still common, even after all this time.

BANNER LADIES

One of the stranger ideas in advertising arose in the 1870s and continued through the rest of the century. Capturing a promotion in a photo was now common, but this entailed a photo of women dressed in the products, holding a banner with the advertiser's name. And the products generally weren't clothing. These ladies were photographed adorned in kitchenware, pretzels, lightbulbs, and most anything imaginable. A woman dressed in spoons, among other things (a pitcher? a clock?), can be seen in Figure 7.41.

As seen here, some of these women had the most unusual hats. These "banner ladies" have been called human billboards or walking advertisements. The photos usually were distributed as "cabinet cards" (around 4¼ × 6½ inches).

FIGURE 7.41. A "banner lady" dressed in spoons and other items, with a banner at her side.

FIGURE 7.42. A spin on the banner ladies was the baby-as-ad, as seen clearly in this Atlas Flour cabinet card of the same era.

While not quite as flamboyant, some advertisers used children wearing a brand name. Both Atlas Flour and Laurel Flour seemed fond of this approach (Figure 7.42).

IS THIS FOR REAL?

The first general book of advertising history was authored by Henry Sampson (1874).[10] He tells of a gravestone used as an ad by the deceased's widow. The gravestone, he claims, said:

Sacred to the Memory of
JOHN ROBERTS,
Stonemason and Tombcutter,
Who died on Saturday, October the 8th, 1800.
N.B.—The business carried on by the Widow at No* 1, Freshfield place.

Interestingly, Nevett (1982) provides a nearly identical account, but the stone's text is different (Figure 7.43):

Here lyes Jeremy Jobbins
An affectionate husband and
a tender parent
His disconsolate widow
In hope of a better meating
Continues to carry on
The long established
TRIPE and TROTTER
business
At the same place
as
Before her lamented
bereavement
Reader, Pause & Notice the address

FIGURE 7.43. Nevett provides this illustration of a supposed grave marker.

I've not managed to confirm either account, and both might be fanciful, but it doesn't stretch the imagination to accept them as real. In the advertising field, the term "tombstone advertising" actually has a different meaning.

TOGETHERNESS

During this century, the advertising industry really became an industry, becoming more organized. And organization leads to organizations. The first real advertising associations are found in the nineteenth century.

Edward Sheldon established the United Kingdom's Billposters' Association in 1862. This organization didn't represent the entire ad industry, but was the first ad organization. A decade later, in St. Louis, came the International Bill Posters' Association of North America, the first US advertising organization, though it only lasted a dozen years. The seed had been planted. In 1891, a more permanent organization was founded: the Associated Bill Posters' Association of the United States and Canada (Hendon & Muhs 1985). These bill poster associations might today be outdoor or out-of-home associations.

While the national organizations were beginning, bill posters within states also started to move in that direction. The first US state outdoor advertising association was formed in Michigan in 1875.

Not far behind bill posters, ad agents started to organize. The Association of General Newspaper Agents was born in 1888. Recall that nearly all advertising agents then saw themselves as newspaper agents. This association sprang from the need for conflict resolution and to improve business between advertisers, agents, and publishers. Before the century's end, two other such organizations were formed: the Association of Advertising Agents (1896) and the Association of American Advertisers (1899). The latter eventually became the

Association of National Advertisers. And I'll go ahead and mention the American Advertising Agents Association, created in 1900.

The next group to follow suit were copywriters. In 1890 in Detroit, they formed the Business Writers Association. The National Association of Window Trimmers, people who created window displays for stores, formed in 1898.

At the local level, organizations formed to represent a broader swath of advertising people: advertisers, agents, publishers, bill posters, printers, and more. Two of the largest were the Agate Club, in 1894 Chicago, and the Sphinx Club, in 1896 New York City. The Sphinx Club was soon re-branded as the Advertising Men's League. And in 1915 it became the Advertising Club of New York. The Agate Club used that name until it changed to the Chicago Media Association late in the next century.

Associations form out of a desire for coordination and information sharing, and a need for education. The fact that so many popped up in just two decades implies that the field finally reached a point where these needs dictated such organization. Another benefit of greater organization is greater public attention, which at that time manifested itself in articles and books allowing the public to learn about advertising.

ALL ABOUT ADS

I've already mentioned some early articles about advertising, including from 1652, 1710, and 1759. But the 1800s brought more, and they went beyond earlier critical essays. For example, in 1836, *Tait's Edinburgh Magazine* ran an article called, "Advertising in Scotland." And a piece in the *Edinburgh Review, or Critical Journal* in 1843 was titled "The Advertising System; the breadth of advertising, with examples from newspapers, etc.," detailing the advertising process of that time. Both early pieces provide a broader picture of how advertising was practiced at the time.

This century also brought the first advertising books. Given the pejorative term "puffing" in use at the time, it might come as no surprise that—not counting those lists of newspapers—the very first book about advertising was titled *Puffs and Mysteries; or, The Romance of Advertising*, as it appeared in 1855. This was followed in 1866 by *The History of Signboards, From the Earliest Times to the Present Day*, and in 1874 by *A History of Advertising from the Earliest Times*. By 1900, many more books about advertising were in print.

CONCLUSION

The industry (or industries) of advertising found a footing in the 1800s. Advertising grew from toddler to young adult. But more important, its size exploded, as did its complexity. Notice how many firsts there were in this and the previous chapter. Not only was it the end of the Industrial Revolution, but it was also the advent of an advertising revolution. There is a bit more to tell, though, before jumping to the next one hundred years.

8

Appeals and Social Implications via Nineteenth-Century Advertising

A lot was happening in the 1800s, with the ad industry's maturation on top of that. But advertising and society were interacting in new ways. Gender is a good example. While advertising was very much an industry of men, women did have a presence.

ADVERTISING'S FEMININE SIDE

I mentioned James "Jem" White as maybe the second agency head ever, in 1800. He died at age forty-five, so in 1820 his wife, Margaret (Faulder) White, became the first woman to head an ad agency. Margaret then married Richard Barker, who helped manage the agency.

The next woman-owned agency came in 1877 Stockholm, Sweden. Sofia Gumaelius, a newspaper publisher's daughter, founded the agency Gumaelius Annonsbyrå. It became the first agency founded by a woman, and it still operates today.

In 1880, a German immigrant to the United States, Mathilde C. Weil, opened the M.C. Weil agency in New York. Weil started in advertising by buying and selling ad space for a German newspaper. Some claim this was the first woman-owned agency, missing both White and Gumaelius (e.g., Krismann 2005). But *Printers' Ink* magazine (1896, vol. 16)—referring to New York—declared:

> Two of the city advertising agencies are owned and controlled by women. These are both located in the Times Building, and each controls an important line of local advertising, besides considerable general business. The first one to go into the business was Miss M. Volkman, a German lady of good business ability, just now abroad; the other is Miss M. C. Weil, who is also German. The business handled by these two ladies is almost exclusively of English firms of the best standing.

Reference to an earlier agency by M. Volkman is unclear, but appears to refer to Meta Volkman, whose brother owned the newspaper where Weil worked. She was a close friend of Weil. Clearly both were influential in advertising.

Women took other roles in advertising, too. J. Walter Thompson hired its first woman space buyer in 1885: Alice Stoddard. And the 1897 book, *Occupations for Women*, included a chapter titled "Women in Advertising," suggesting that women pursue advertising jobs (Willard, Winslow, & White 1897).

Women gained ground as an important consumer segment, too. In 1800, they had relatively little impact, since they bought mostly necessities and there was no brand competition.

FIGURE 8.1. The first edition of *Godey's Lady's Book*, from 1830.

But when the Industrial Revolution brought new opportunities, like sewing machines and washing machines, their consumer roles changed (Jones 1955). In 1830, a magazine targeting women began: *Godey's Lady's Book* (Figure 8.1). If you recall, the first women's magazine was the *Ladies' Mercury*, in 1693, though it was short lived. *Godey's* became a serious entrée into the women's market.

By mid-century, women were on the rise in society. Some claim the women's suffrage movement began in 1903, but it really began at an 1848 women's rights convention in Seneca Falls, New York. After that convention (circa 1851), Susan B. Anthony and Elizabeth Cady Stanton were circulating petitions for a constitutional amendment to guarantee women's rights.

By the Civil War's end, technologies were making women's household workloads more manageable. Bicycles gave them easier mobility. Even gas lighting meant no carrying coal or wood to lengthen their day (Gallo 1972). And colleges for women were becoming accessible. They now had some tools to help liberate them. Suffrage wasn't limited to the United States; in New Zealand women received voting rights in 1893.

By late century women were appearing in ads, because they were both readers and shoppers. Newspaper publishers and advertisers were paying more attention to women. And women weren't the only ones finding new paths in society. African American roles, too, shifted.

SLAVE IN A BOX

When the century began, African Americans' place in the ad industry was almost exclusively in ads seeking the sale or retrieval of slaves. That continued for decades.

Harriet Tubman escaped slavery with her brothers, Ben and Henry ("Harry"), in 1849. The *Cambridge Democrat* ran an ad by her owner, calling Harriet "Minty," her birth name:

THREE HUNDRED DOLLARS REWARD. RAN AWAY from the subscriber on Monday the 17th ult., three negroes, named as follows: HARRY, aged about 19 years, has on one side of his neck a wen, just under the ear, he is of a dark chestnut color, about 5 feet 8 or 9 inches hight; BEN, aged about 25 years, is very quick to speak when spoken to, he is of a chestnut color, about six feet high; MINTY, aged about 27 years, is of a chestnut color, fine looking and about 5 feet high. One hundred dollars reward will be given for each of the above named negroes, if taken out of the state, and $50 each if taken in the State. They must be lodged in Baltimore, Easton or Cambridge Jail, in Maryland. ELIZA ANN BRODESS Near Bucktown, Dorchester county, Md. Oct. 3d, 1849.

Harriet led perhaps three hundred slaves to freedom via the "underground railroad," and slave owners ran ads offering a $40,000 bounty for her death or capture (Kern-Foxworth 1994).

Even before slavery ended, in 1827 John Russwurm and Samuel Cornish founded *Freedom's Journal*, the first African American newspaper in the United States. It provided much more positive images of African Americans in its ads than seen previously (Moss 2003).

US slavery ended in 1865. By the 1870s, African Americans appeared regularly in advertisements, particularly on trade cards. Kern-Foxworth (1994) suggests, "The first large-scale use of blacks in advertising actually came with the introduction of trade cards" (Figure 8.2). Those cards led to African American characters in other advertising. Characters like the Gold Dust Twins, Aunt Jemima (Figure 8.3), and Rastus the Cream of Wheat chef, introduced in 1892,

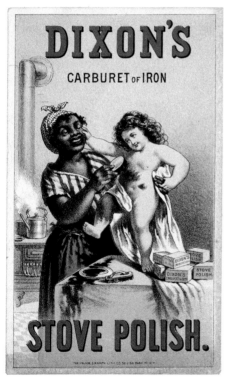

FIGURE 8.2.   African Americans frequently were shown on trade cards in slave-type roles, as on this Dixon's card from 1880.

FIGURE 8.3.   Aunt Jemima, as she appeared early in her career as an ad spokes-character.

1893, and 1895, respectively, became fixtures in American advertising. Each offered White people a "slave in a box" (Bosarge 2015), as the product would do much of the work.

The food industry made good use of this because of stereotypes that African Americans were good cooks (Moss 2003). They frequently were portrayed as entertainers, and their facial characteristics typically were exaggerated and unflattering. But those ads were about selling to White people, not to African Americans.

While both Blacks and women were playing bigger roles, some things stayed the same. Some of the biggest advertisers were the same as the previous century. As before, lotteries were dominant.

SHIFTING LEADERSHIP

Lotteries were leading advertisers in Britain for the first quarter century, until they were banned. American states started banning lotteries in 1833, and all but Louisiana followed suit by 1860 (Presbrey 1929). Unfortunately, lotteries didn't help advertising's reputation, as most people lost money on them.

As lotteries diminished, circuses grew. The first American circus advertising was in 1793. It was straightforward advertising for John Bill Rickett's Circus, which performed with George and Martha Washington in the audience that year (Foster 1967). But circuses were leading outdoor advertisers by 1800, using broadsides (Hendon & Muhs 1985).

Their greatest influence began in 1835, with Phineas T. Barnum. On July 15 he ran an ad in the *Philadelphia Inquirer* promising anyone visiting the local Masonic Hall would experience "one of the greatest natural curiosities every witnessed": Joice Heth, an African American woman he claimed was 161 years old and had been a slave of George Washington's father. This was one of his earliest outrageous ad claims. He bought Ms. Heth for $1,000 and ended up making $1,500 *per week* from this show.

Barnum learned selling by working as a clerk at his father's grocery. He was a genius at selling lottery tickets! For that purpose, he experimented with advertising (Presbrey 1929). By the 1840s, he already had a reputation for being more flamboyant than his competitors. Recall that he was the first to build an illuminated sign in 1840, and he put his face on posters larger than life. M. R. Werner claimed, "Barnum was one of the first men in the United States to realize the power of the paid adjective in advertising theatrical attractions" (Applegate 1998). Even his newspaper ads were hard to miss (Figure 8.4). As he transitioned from museum owner to circus owner, his advertising became even more colorful, literally and figuratively. Other circuses followed (Hendon & Muhs 1985).

Barnum also was king of publicity stunts. One time he sent a man around placing bricks on several street corners. The man returned, replacing the brick he'd put there with a different one. He said nothing. On the hour, he presented a ticket and entered Barnum's museum. Supposedly, five hundred people followed him and bought a ticket in the very first hour, hoping to find out what was happening. The police eventually stopped him, but news reporters wrote about it for weeks (Applegate 1998).

Another time Barnum's ads announced he had a preserved mermaid. And after he created "The Greatest Show on Earth" in 1871, he featured Jumbo the "giant" African elephant. Some called him "The Prince of Humbug" (Cutlip & Baker 2012). While excess and questionable ethics were his hallmark, P. T. Barnum was one of the most influential figures in nineteenth-century advertising. The lessons learned by others, however, often were that truth is of questionable value. Nowhere was that more obvious than with patent medicines.

SCAM MEDICINES, CONTINUED

In 1800, New York City consisted of 60,000 people. By 1900, the population was 3.8 million. London, already large in 1800, went from 950,000 residents to 6 million during that time. Besides being crowded into confined spaces, the rapid growth was complicated by issues like water treatment and health care delivery (Sivulka 2001). Disease flourished, creating more opportunities for medical scam artists. Not all patent medicines were frauds, but most were (Figure 8.5).

These fraudsters actually advanced the advertising field as they innovated their sales methods. They were among the largest and most effective advertisers. Of course, that efficacy was often thanks to fraudulent claims, but they also created groundbreaking ad designs and appeals, and reached for a national market before most advertisers saw that potential.

Thomas Holloway sold an "Ointment and Universal Pill," and in a few years he made a fortune advertising them (Elliott 1962). Turner (1953) concludes:

> It has been said that in the second half of the nineteenth century anyone with £10,000 to spend on pushing a patent medicine could not fail to make [a] large fortune. Whether or not the medicine had any virtue was of small consequence.

FIGURE 8.4. An 1872 newspaper ad for P. T. Barnum's museum.

Publishers tended to know many meds were fake, and put those ads at the bottom of their pages, with more respectable ads above them (Nevett 1982). Some began rejecting ads that

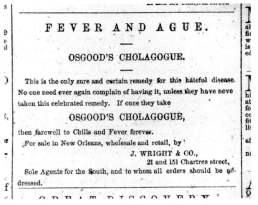

FIGURE 8.5.   An 1859 ad hailing a "certain remedy" for a malaria-type disease.

were beyond the fraudulent. The *New York Tribune* in the 1840s rejected ads for venereal disease "cures" and abortionists. In 1865, the *New York Herald* forbade medicine ads its publisher found offensive (Pope 1983). The general disrepute of patent medicine ads, pervading every advertising medium, unfortunately infected public perceptions of advertising.

A pushback against patent medicines began in a big way around 1860. *The Lancet*, a British medical journal, began denouncing harmful "cures." This made the issue more public, attracting newspapers' attention and leading to Britain's Pharmacy and Poisons Act of 1868 (Presbrey 1929). This didn't solve the problem, but it helped.

Before the US Civil War, annual sales of patent medicines in the United States was $3.5 million (Fox 1984). By 1900, that figure swelled to $75 million. These ads accounted for something like half of all advertising after the war (Petty 2016).

Presbrey (1929) credits the war with kicking the patent medicine industry into overdrive, as men returned with illnesses and infirmities, giving potion sellers new ailments to fix. He called it the "great patent-medicine craze," and I think he meant both in ad volume and in outrageousness (Figure 8.6). The rise of medical gadgets coincided, with electricity as catalyst.

The *Ladies' Home Journal* (*LHJ*), published by Cyrus H. K. Curtis, fired the shot heard around the advertising world in 1892, by announcing it would no longer accept patent medicine advertising. This was shocking news, because most magazines were making fortunes from that industry. *LHJ* was putting principles in front of income. Like *The Lancet*, it was a publication—not the ad industry—taking a stand against advertising fraud.

A major legal case in England also came in 1892. One patent med manufacturer, the Carbolic Smoke Ball Company, claimed its smoke ball could cure various ailments, including flu. It ran ads promising to pay a £100 reward to anyone who, after using its product, contracted influenza, colds, or associated diseases (Figure 8.7).

Mrs. Louisa Elizabeth Carlill used the smoke ball and then got the flu. She asked for the reward. Refusing to pay, the company claimed Mrs. Carlill shouldn't have believed the ad. A court awarded her the £100, plus costs. By the way, the active ingredient in the smoke ball, carbolic acid, is a poison (Simpson 1985).

The court in this decision declared that the contents of the ad created a contract with anyone who met the company's offer. The ad was a contract, and thus enforceable. It was not, said the court, mere *puffery*. Mrs. Carlill lived until 1942, when she died of old age . . . and influenza (Simpson 1985).

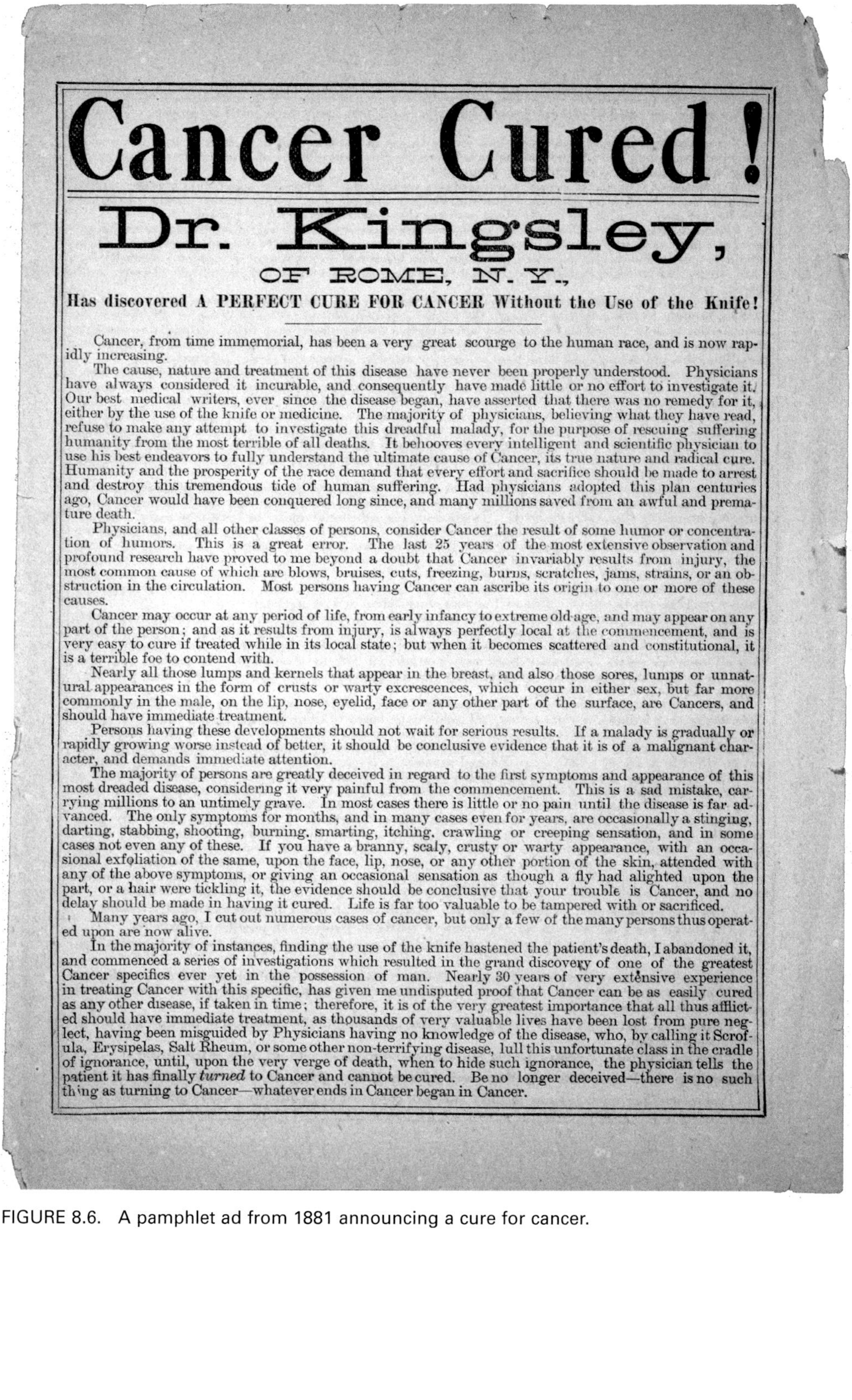

Cancer Cured!

Dr. Kingsley,

OF ROME, N. Y.,

Has discovered A PERFECT CURE FOR CANCER Without the Use of the Knife!

Cancer, from time immemorial, has been a very great scourge to the human race, and is now rapidly increasing.

The cause, nature and treatment of this disease have never been properly understood. Physicians have always considered it incurable, and consequently have made little or no effort to investigate it. Our best medical writers, ever since the disease began, have asserted that there was no remedy for it, either by the use of the knife or medicine. The majority of physicians, believing what they have read, refuse to make any attempt to investigate this dreadful malady, for the purpose of rescuing suffering humanity from the most terrible of all deaths. It behooves every intelligent and scientific physician to use his best endeavors to fully understand the ultimate cause of Cancer, its true nature and radical cure. Humanity and the prosperity of the race demand that every effort and sacrifice should be made to arrest and destroy this tremendous tide of human suffering. Had physicians adopted this plan centuries ago, Cancer would have been conquered long since, and many millions saved from an awful and premature death.

Physicians, and all other classes of persons, consider Cancer the result of some humor or concentration of humors. This is a great error. The last 25 years of the most extensive observation and profound research have proved to me beyond a doubt that Cancer invariably results from injury, the most common cause of which are blows, bruises, cuts, freezing, burns, scratches, jams, strains, or an obstruction in the circulation. Most persons having Cancer can ascribe its origin to one or more of these causes.

Cancer may occur at any period of life, from early infancy to extreme old age, and may appear on any part of the person; and as it results from injury, is always perfectly local at the commencement, and is very easy to cure if treated while in its local state; but when it becomes scattered and constitutional, it is a terrible foe to contend with.

Nearly all those lumps and kernels that appear in the breast, and also those sores, lumps or unnatural appearances in the form of crusts or warty excrescences, which occur in either sex, but far more commonly in the male, on the lip, nose, eyelid, face or any other part of the surface, are Cancers, and should have immediate treatment.

Persons having these developments should not wait for serious results. If a malady is gradually or rapidly growing worse instead of better, it should be conclusive evidence that it is of a malignant character, and demands immediate attention.

The majority of persons are greatly deceived in regard to the first symptoms and appearance of this most dreaded disease, considering it very painful from the commencement. This is a sad mistake, carrying millions to an untimely grave. In most cases there is little or no pain until the disease is far advanced. The only symptoms for months, and in many cases even for years, are occasionally a stinging, darting, stabbing, shooting, burning, smarting, itching, crawling or creeping sensation, and in some cases not even any of these. If you have a branny, scaly, crusty or warty appearance, with an occasional exfoliation of the same, upon the face, lip, nose, or any other portion of the skin, attended with any of the above symptoms, or giving an occasional sensation as though a fly had alighted upon the part, or a hair were tickling it, the evidence should be conclusive that your trouble is Cancer, and no delay should be made in having it cured. Life is far too valuable to be tampered with or sacrificed.

Many years ago, I cut out numerous cases of cancer, but only a few of the many persons thus operated upon are now alive.

In the majority of instances, finding the use of the knife hastened the patient's death, I abandoned it, and commenced a series of investigations which resulted in the grand discovery of one of the greatest Cancer specifics ever yet in the possession of man. Nearly 30 years of very extensive experience in treating Cancer with this specific, has given me undisputed proof that Cancer can be as easily cured as any other disease, if taken in time; therefore, it is of the very greatest importance that all thus afflicted should have immediate treatment, as thousands of very valuable lives have been lost from pure neglect, having been misguided by Physicians having no knowledge of the disease, who, by calling it Scrofula, Erysipelas, Salt Rheum, or some other non-terrifying disease, lull this unfortunate class in the cradle of ignorance, until, upon the very verge of death, when to hide such ignorance, the physician tells the patient it has finally *turned* to Cancer and cannot be cured. Be no longer deceived—there is no such thing as turning to Cancer—whatever ends in Cancer began in Cancer.

FIGURE 8.6. A pamphlet ad from 1881 announcing a cure for cancer.

FIGURE 8.7. An ad similar to this ran on November 13, 1891, in the *Pall Mall Gazette*, and was at the center of the *Carlill v. Carbolic Smoke Ball Company* lawsuit in 1892.

Of course, advertising deception wasn't confined to potion sellers. It was adopted by a broad cross section of merchants of that day.

NO FOOLING

Tolerance for advertising fraud diminished as time progressed, though little was done to address it until late in the 1800s. It wasn't initially addressed through law or action of ad agents, but by publishers drawing a line in the sand.

The *Ladies' Home Journal* wasn't the first publication to stand against deceptive advertising, though likely the one with the largest circulation, exceeding half a million. *The Lancet* also tried, but both were focused only on patent medicines.

In 1859, Orange Judd, publisher of *American Agriculturist*, ran a full-page story about advertising fraud, and in 1860 he announced he wouldn't accept *any* deceptive ads in his periodical. He promised to "exclude deceptive advertisements, also those persons who are reported not to perform what they promise." When an advertiser did run a fraudulent fertilizer ad, Judd offered a refund to anyone who was cheated. That policy was followed for thirty years, until Judd retired (Lewis 1909).

The *Farm Journal* of Philadelphia in 1880 took a stand and offered a "Fair Play Notice," guaranteeing that only reputable companies could advertise there. This notice appeared in every issue, for years:

> FAIR PLAY. We believe, through careful inquiry, that all the advertisements in this paper are signed by trustworthy persons, and to prove our faith by works, we will make good to subscribers any loss sustained by trusting advertisers who prove to be deliberate swindlers. Rogues shall not ply their trade at the expense of our readers, who are our friends, through the medium of these columns. Let this be understood by everybody now and henceforth. (Kenner 1936)

Another farm journal, the *Rural New Yorker*, included a "Square Deal" notice beginning in 1890. And by the early twentieth century, many other farm publications followed suit. Lewis (1909) notes that by the time of his article there were sixteen leading farm papers with this policy. So the farm publications really spearheaded the fight against advertising fraud.

Other publications also jumped aboard, particularly after the *LHJ* announcement. And while slower, newspapers joined in, too (Pope 1983).

At least one attempt to regulate advertising didn't involve fraud. The British Indecent Advertisements Act, in 1889, prohibited "any picture or printed or written matter which is of an indecent or obscene nature." Indecent matter meant "[a]ny advertisement relating to syphilis, gonorrhœa, nervous debility, or other complaint or infirmity arising from or relating to sexual intercourse." Soon after the law was passed, a handbill was alleged of violation. While one judge thought it indecent, another disagreed. American advertising continued to be accused of lacking decency and propriety by the British (Sampson 1874), which might be why that law was written.

New York State passed a law against misleading advertising in 1898, private lawsuits regarding fraudulent misrepresentation occurred, and the US Postmaster General controlled fraudulent schemes that used mail. So a few regulatory options existed, but there was little consumer protection.

The advertising industry finally joined the fight. In 1890, the London Bill-Posters Association and the United Bill-Posters Association established a Joint Censorship Committee (Nevett 1982). Any billposter receiving a questionable bill to post could submit it to the committee for evaluation. In 1892, a National Society for Checking the Abuse of Public Advertising (SCAPA) was created "to check the abuses of Public Advertising, the spoliation of rural scenery, and architecture." It was aimed at limiting the spread of bills and posters, though some extremists felt all billboards were bad (Turner 1953).

The US laws most important for advertising weren't about advertising. They were about business trusts.

HOW BIG DO WE TRUST?

This century was all about the creation and growth of businesses, and nowhere was this more true than in America. The Industrial Revolution was the main catalyst, of course. Some industries, like transportation (railroads) and communication (telegraph), aided growth of other companies, allowing reach beyond anything previously known. Some companies became behemoths.

The Civil War played another role. War leads to war contracts, for munitions, footwear, uniforms, food, and so on. Some companies won contracts, and some didn't. Winners often were those already equipped to handle the demand. Where uniform goods were essential, winners needed to be fully mechanized, ensuring consistency, meaning larger companies tended to win contracts. Contracts gave them resources to grow larger. Open immigration policies added endless, inexpensive labor. And tax laws at that time encouraged growth through vertical integration. Those enormous companies could buy their suppliers, making them even bigger.

Some industries became dominated by one company, or a small handful, and abuse followed. Railroad owners were early abusers. They held power and used it, discriminating against customers they didn't like and helping legislators who provided them help in return (Applegate 2012). They had monopolies, since the government gave them rights-of-way across land. Deciding in which towns to stop and how much to charge for freight gave them absolute power, which corrupts.

So state lawmakers stepped in to limit them. Some companies found a trick to escape state regulations, by creating "trusts." A company in, for example, Kentucky faced with state laws might join with a company from Tennessee and one from Virginia, creating a massive company holding all three in trust, making the trust's home office somewhere else, like Delaware. As a Delaware corporation, the company was mostly out of reach of laws in those other three states. This led to the creation of a whiskey trust, a sugar trust, an oil trust, and more. Trusts became so powerful that their abuses sometimes eclipsed those of the railroads.

States tried to regulate the railroads, but the US Supreme Court stopped that in 1886, declaring those laws unconstitutional. Congress finally took action, passing the Interstate Commerce Act of 1887, which included restrictions on railroads' powers. That didn't help with abuses by the trusts, but in 1890 Congress enacted the Sherman Antitrust Act, prohibiting trusts and other "combinations in restraint of trade."

Government finally recognized that businesses, left wholly unchecked, would abuse that freedom given the powers accompanying great size. While these laws had no direct impact on advertising, they set the stage for public policies yet to come.

The advertising industry also harbored concerns about these trusts, not knowing how they might affect advertising. Some ad professionals feared that this trust-mania might lead to abolishing the need for advertising in some industries, since too much concentration could eliminate competition, making advertising seem unnecessary (Presbrey 1929).

CONCLUSION

In describing advertising agents of the last part of the century, Wood (1958) notes that their success was undeniable, but their profession thrived under a cloud. Advertising was seen as "a bastard form of journalism and an illegitimate offspring of business."

For most of the century, advertising's reputation was poor, but it was starting to be appreciated as a valuable tool for merchants. Fox (1984) argues:

> By slow degrees the advertising business reformed itself. The steps toward respectability included the extraction of honest circulation statements from publishers, the writing of contracts for truthful relations between agents and advertisers, the launching of successful major campaigns by national advertisers other than patent medicines, and the spreading popularity of an advertising style associated with a copywriter of undoubted integrity. Taken together, these developments allowed advertising people—not for the last time—to congratulate themselves on putting to rest the bad old days and ascending to a higher moral plane.

I would add to this an awakening, the need to create a more honest advertising environment. But that part of the story is yet to come.

Part III

THE TWENTIETH CENTURY AND BEYOND

GENERAL HISTORY		ADVERTISING HISTORY
		1900
	●	First public relations agency formed
		Billboard sizes are standardized (United States)
1901	●	
US President William McKinley is shot by Leon Czolgosz In Buffalo, New York		Japanese agency Dentsu is founded
Gustave Whitehead is the first to make a controlled self-powered aircraft flight		
1902	●	
Teddy bear is invented		Advertising on an airship
		Good Housekeeping promises to guarantee every ad it publishes
		Second public relations agency formed
1903	●	
Wilbur and Orville Wright fly a powered airplane at Kitty Hawk, North Carolina		Consumer information is first collected for direct mail lists
First Tour de France bicycle race		
1904	●	
"Winner" of Olympics marathon ran most of the race in a car		First university course dedicated to advertising as a topic
		John E. Kennedy defines advertising as "Salesmanship in Print"
		National Federation of Advertising Clubs of America established

GENERAL HISTORY

1905
Albert Einstein publishes his theory
of special relativity

Upton Sinclair publishes *The Jungle*

1907
Harry Houdini escapes after being chained and
submerged in water

A ball drops, for the first time, in New York City's
Times Square at midnight
on New Year's Eve

Ivan Pavlov publishes "Conditioned Reflexes"
in Russia

Bakelite (the first synthetic plastic)
is invented by Leo Baekeland

1908
First animated cartoon, *Fantasmagorie*,
is created

An enormous blast near the Podkamennaya
Tunguska river in Siberia, believed to be
a meteor strike

Henry Ford introduces the
Model T automobile

1911
The Indianapolis 500 Mile Sweepstakes Race
is first run

Roald Amundsen reaches the South Pole

1912
RMS *Titanic* passenger liner strikes an iceberg
and sinks, killing more than 1,500 people

ADVERTISING HISTORY

Collier's magazine publishes exposé on patent
medicines

Ivy Lee offers "Declaration of Principles"
for public relations

First direct mail advertising agency

The song "In My Merry Oldsmobile" becomes
a hit

1906
US Pure Food and Drug Act

Advertisements Regulation Acts regulates
outdoor advertising (Britain)

First female copywriter at J. Walter Thompson

First university professor of advertising

Imprinted wooden pencils become promotional
devices

American Bar Association prohibits lawyers
from advertising

1909
Good Housekeeping Seal of Approval announced

First breakfast cereal advertising premium

1910
Curtis Advertising Code published

First university degree in advertising

Association of Advertising Women founded

Professional athletes now endorse products
in ads

Truth-in-advertising movement begins
(United States)

First neon sign (France)

GENERAL HISTORY

ADVERTISING HISTORY

1913
Bureau of Verified Circulations and the Advertising Audit Association are formed

The Suchard chocolatiers' blimp was the first non-rigid airship with advertising on it

First movie trailer

1914
World War I begins when Archduke Franz Ferdinand is assassinated by Gavrilo Princip (ends 1918)

First commercial passenger airplane flight

Federal Trade Commission Act becomes law (United States)

First university advertising course in Japan

1916
John D. Rockefeller becomes world's first billionaire

Stanley Resor & Associates buy J. Walter Thompson

1917
Vladimir Lenin starts the Bolshevik Revolution in Russia

US Committee on Public Information, Division of Pictorial Publicity, creates posters for the war effort

Direct Mail Advertising Association created

1918
British women over thirty win right to vote

Influenza pandemic (the Spanish flu) kills between seventeen and one hundred million

1919
Dutch women win right to vote

Edward L. Bernays opens the eighth public relations agency

N. W. Ayer is first agency to open a PR department

The first photograph to appear on a billboard

First commercial movie about advertising

1920
Prohibition begins in United States (ends 1933)

Women win right to vote in United States

Art Directors Club of New York begins

Famous psychologist joins J. Walter Thompson

1921
Tulsa Race Riot kills hundreds of African Americans

The National Better Business Bureau of the Associated Advertising Clubs of the World is founded

Art Directors Club creates the first advertising art competition

First radio commercial

1922
The Union of Soviet Socialist Republics (aka the Soviet Union) is founded

Howard Carter and Lord Carnarvon open the tomb of Tutankhamun

First paid radio commercial (possibly 1923)

First Department of Advertising at a university

Advertising skywriting introduced

GENERAL HISTORY

1923

The first radio network, the Red Network, founded

Jockey Frank Hayes wins a horse race at Belmont Park, New York, after his death

1925

The Abominable Snowman is first sighted in the Himalayas

Tennessee law bans teaching evolution in schools, resulting in the Scopes Trial (United States)

1926

John Logie Baird demonstrates the first working television system

1927

First talking movie, *The Jazz Singer*

World population reaches two billion

Charles Lindbergh flies solo across the Atlantic Ocean

1929

Stock market crash of 1929

First mass-marketed sunglasses

Arctic explorer Peter Freuchen digs his way out of an avalanche using his own frozen feces

St. Valentine's Day Massacre

1930

First radio soap opera, *Painted Dreams*

Automotive radios introduced

ADVERTISING HISTORY

Better Business Bureau of Australia is established

Young & Rubicam is founded

International Advertising Conference in London

A. C. Nielsen market research company formed

Daniel Starch and Staff (research company) formed

1924

National Vigilance Committee founded in Britain

First university advertising course in China

Harvard University Advertising Awards begin

AAAA creative code announced (United States)

US presidential candidates advertise on radio

The Eiffel Tower becomes the world's largest advertisement

Burma-Shave places serial signs along highways

First Goodyear blimp flies

Publicis is created (France)

First cigarette advertisement targeted at women

Consumer's Club created (to become Consumers' Research, Inc. in 1929)

1928

Merger creates BBDO

Rudolph Guenther-Russell Law agency goes public

Boxtop coupons are introduced

First advertising "talkie" produced

Agency merger creates McCann-Erickson

Advertising Age magazine published

Airplanes pull advertising banners for the first time

First television commercial

GENERAL HISTORY

ADVERTISING HISTORY

1931

Mobster Al Capone is convicted of tax evasion

Audit Bureau of Circulations created (Britain)

1932

Some radio programs offer promotional premiums

1933

Adolph Hitler becomes chancellor of Germany

Albert Einstein moves from Germany to the United States

US Traffic Audit Bureau established

Booklets of comics become promotional tools

1934

National Broadcasting Company publishes a Radio Code restricting advertising

First Black-owned public relations agency in the United States

1935

Monopoly board game goes on sale

Consumers' Union is formed

Leo Burnett Agency opens

Columbia Broadcasting System publishes a Radio Code

1936

Oscar Mayer creates the Weinermobile

The first programmable computer is invented by Konrad Zuse

Advertising Research Foundation created

US liquor industry voluntarily abstains from radio advertising

A. C. Nielsen creates its Radio Index

1937

Adman Bruce Barton becomes a US congressman

International Code of Standards developed

Washington Daily News publishes the first perfumed advertising page

1938

Invention of the chocolate chip cookie, by Ruth Graves Wakefield and Sue Brides

Federal Food, Drug and Cosmetic Act (United States)

Wheeler-Lea Amendment to the FTC Act

1939

RCA introduces all-electronic television

The first nationally broadcast commercial jingle

1940

Igor Sikorsky invents the helicopter

1941

United States enters World War II after Pearl Harbor is attacked

First *legal* television commercial

First animated television commercial

GENERAL HISTORY

ADVERTISING HISTORY

1942
War Advertising Council created to support war effort

Alex Osborn introduces the world to "brainstorming"

Outdoor Advertising Association of America creates OBIE Awards

Valentine v. Chrestensen is first US Supreme Court case involving advertising

1943
Lord & Thomas becomes Foote, Cone, & Belding

A cigarette company billboard in Times Square, New York, puffs smoke

1944
Brand Names Research Foundation created

1945
World War II ends with United States dropping atomic bombs on Hiroshima and Nagasaki

First ballpoint pen is "the Reynolds"

First US city to flouridate its water is Grand Rapids, Michigan

1946
The microwave oven is patented by Percy Spencer

Eniac, the first general-purpose digital computer, is introduced

Fleishman-Hillard PR agency opens

First bumper sticker created

1947
Holography is invented by Dennis Gabor

UFO crash in Roswell, New Mexico

First computer bug discovered was a moth

Public Relations Society of America founded

1948
Hindu leader Mohandas Gandhi assassinated by Nathuram Godse

Emerson Foote is forced out of Foote, Cone, & Belding

Ogilvy & Mather agency is founded

Advertising Hall of Fame established

US liquor industry voluntarily abstains from television advertising

First television commercial with an all-Black cast

First television tie-in promotional product

1949
Communist China founded

Soviet Union joins the atomic club

Doyle Dane Bernbach is created

First television infomercial

1950
Korean War begins (ends 1953)

Japan Advertising Agencies Association created

GENERAL HISTORY

ADVERTISING HISTORY

1951
Ronald Reagan is a model for Chesterfield cigarettes

First color television commercial

1952
Passenger jet travel begins

United Kingdom joins the atomic club

United States tests first hydrogen bomb

Edelman PR agency is founded

First national direct mail political campaign

1953
Edmund Hillary and Tenzing Norgay are first to reach top of Mt. Everest

Burson-Marsteller public relations opens

1954
US Supreme Court ends school segregation

Pocket radios become available

International Advertising Film Festival begins in Venice, later moves to Cannes

1955
Ronald Reagan hosts CBS's *General Electric Theater*

Disneyland opened in Anaheim, California

Vietnam War begins (ends 1975)

First television commercial in the United Kingdom

First Spanish-language commercials in the United States

1956
An interstate highway system opens in the United States

Jonas Salk's polio vaccine becomes publicly available

US Justice Department accuses AAAA of price fixing

First television commercial in Australia

Promotion makes a book a *New York Times* bestseller, but it doesn't exist

First video recorded television commercial

First full-service Black-owned agency

1957
First space satellite, *Sputnik 1*, launched by the Soviet Union

Asian flu kills an estimated 1.1 million

James Vicary claims he can subliminally advertise to consumers

1958
United States loses a hydrogen bomb off the coast of Savannah, Georgia

1959
The Barbie Doll is introduced by Mattel

Alaska becomes the forty-ninth state in the United States

Hawaii becomes the fiftieth state in the United States

Pepsi company trades with Soviet Union for military equipment, to have the sixth largest military in the world

The silicon chip is invented

The Creative Revolution begins

Clio Awards start

Payola scandal for radio and television

GENERAL HISTORY

ADVERTISING HISTORY

1960

Birth-control pill is made available to women

The first laser is created

France joins the nuclear club

World population reaches three billion

Emerson Foote becomes president of McCann-Erickson

Interpublic Group is formed

Ogilvy & Mather agrees to a fee-based pay system, rather than commission-based

ADDY Awards are born

Creative Hall of Fame starts

1961

Major Yuri Alexeyevich Gagarin, riding *Vostok 1*, becomes the first person to orbit the Earth

Alan Shepard, aboard *Freedom 7*, becomes the first American in space

1962

The Cuban Missile Crisis

The Beatles fail an audition for a recording contract

Royal College of Physicians proclaims smoking is linked to health problems

President John F. Kennedy presents his Consumer Bill of Rights

Papert Koenig Lois is second agency to go public

Advertising Standards Authority established (Britain)

First Latino agency in the United States

1963

"Instant replay" is first used in TV sports

US President John F. Kennedy is assassinated by Lee Harvey Oswald (later shot by Jack Ruby)

The hula-hoop is patented

Valentina Tereshkova, in *Vostok 6*, becomes the first woman in space

The US Postal Service introduces zip codes

Civil rights leader Medgar Evers assassinated by White supremacist Byron De La Beckwith

D&AD Awards founded

1964

The US Surgeon General announces cigarette smoking is hazardous to health

China joins the nuclear club

The G.I. Joe action figure is introduced

ADMAP magazine published

New York Times v. Sullivan provides protection for "editorial advertising"

First television commercial in Russia

First lenticular 3D magazine advertisement

1965

Civil rights activist Malcolm X assassinated

Crispin Advertising is created

"Account Planning" concept is born

US Federal Trade Commission requires cigarette ads and packages carry a health warning

Tobacco advertising banned from UK television

Highway Beautification Act regulates outdoor advertising (United States)

The term "psychographics" first used

GENERAL HISTORY

ADVERTISING HISTORY

1966

Star Trek, the TV series, begins

Wells Rich Greene is founded

A court finds an advertising agency guilty
of fraud on behalf of client

1967

Three American astronauts die during training

The first AFL-NFL World Championship
(American football) game is held,
later to be called Super Bowl I

First heart transplant

AT&T begins using toll-free 1-800 numbers

1968

The first dot-matrix printer, the EP-101,
introduced by Epson

Martin Luther King assassinated
by James Earl Ray

Robert F. Kennedy, US presidential candidate,
assassinated by Sirhan Sirhan

Start of the Effie Awards

"Shared mail" coupons begin with Valpak

1969

The first video telephone is introduced

The Beatles hold their final public performance
on the roof of Apple Records

First manned lunar landing, with Neil Armstrong
and Buzz Aldrin

Advanced Research Projects Agency Network
(ARPANET) begins

Communication Arts magazine published

Tobacco advertising banned from Canadian
television and radio

The Nader Report and an ABA Commission
both criticize the FTC

1970

Apollo 13 transmits "Houston,
we've got a problem!"

Paul McCartney sues to dissolve the Beatles

1971

First e-mail message is sent on the ARPANET

Soviet *Mars 2* lander is first manmade
object to reach Mars

Soyuz 11 crew dies after undocking
from space station

Coca-Cola "Hilltop" commercial

Burrell McBain agency opens

DMA's Mail Preference Service helps consumers
to opt-out of mail lists (United States)

National Advertising Review Board is formed
(United States)

1972

First scientific handheld calculator,
the HP-35, introduced

Saatchi & Saatchi agency begins takeover of
several other agencies

The free-standing insert (FSI) in newspapers
is introduced

GENERAL HISTORY

1973
First true handheld mobile phone created by Motorola

US Supreme Court decision in *Roe v. Wade*

1974
First cordless pager, the Motorola Pageboy, is sold

India joins the nuclear club

The Universal Product Code (UPC) is first used

World Trade Center (then world's tallest building) opens in New York City

US President Richard Nixon resigns

1975
Arthur Ashe is first Black Wimbledon champion

Digital camera invented at Eastman Kodak

Betamax videotape introduced by Sony

1976
Apple Computer Company incorporated by Steven Jobs and Stephen Wozniak on April Fools' Day

First commercial laser printer, the IBM 3800

VHS videotape introduced by JVC

1977
First *Star Wars* movie opens

"King of Rock and Roll" Elvis Presley dies of heart failure

1978
First test tube baby

Velcro introduced to consumer market

Openly gay politician Harvey Milk assassinated by Dan White

918 members of the Peoples Temple cult, led by Jim Jones, commit suicide in Guyana

1979
The Walkman portable cassette player introduced by Sony

Three Mile Island Nuclear Generating Station Accident

Margaret Thatcher becomes the first woman prime minister of England

ADVERTISING HISTORY

The One Show begins

Subliminal Seduction is published

First in-game advertisement

First television commercial created with a computer

Children's Advertising Review Unit of the Better Business Bureaus is formed (United States)

Blow-in cards, inserted in magazines, begin

Japan Advertising Review Organization created

Nestlé Infant Formula scandal

First condom commercial (United States)

"Two-all-beef-patties-special-sauce-lettuce-cheese-pickles-onions, on a sesame seed bun": McDonald's commercial

Virginia Pharmacy Supreme Court decision finally protects most advertising

Advertising Council of Nigeria established

Bates v. State Bar of Arizona allows lawyers to advertise

Direct Marketing News published

First television commercial in India

First email spam

Values Attitudes and Lifestyles (VALS) model introduced

Adweek magazine published

First foreign television commerical broadcast in China

GENERAL HISTORY

ADVERTISING HISTORY

1980

Sony presents the first consumer video camera

Compact discs are first demonstrated

John Lennon, former Beatle, is shot to death by Mark David Chapman

Ronald Reagan, a former actor, elected US president

Sosa and Associates agency is founded

Supreme Court's *Central Hudson Gas* decision creates a test for protection of advertising

Brazilian National Council for Self-Regulation created

1981

MTV begins

The DeLorean DMC-12 automobile begins production

President Reagan is shot in the chest by John Hinckley Jr.

IBM introduces the IBM Personal Computer, model 5150

Egyptian President Anwar Sadat assassinated

First PhD in advertising

Korea Broadcasting Advertising Corporation is formed

First presecription drug ad aimed at consumers

Metromedia, Inc. v. City of San Diego found protecting commercial signs more than noncommercial was unconstitutional

Absolut Vodka advertises in a gay magazine

1982

USA Today launched as first general readership national newspaper in United States

Sony launches first consumer compact disc player, the CDP-101

Seiko launches first LCD TV wristwatch

Wieden & Kennedy opens

"The Big Bang" of agency mergers creates Omnicom

Chiat/Day brings "Account Planning" to the United States

E.T. the Extra-Terrestrial includes placement of Reese's Pieces candy

1983

The ARPANET becomes the internet

Pioneer 10 space probe is the first manmade object to leave the solar system

Goodby, Berlin & Silverstein founded

First television commercial for a prescription drug

Mail Preference Service helps consumers to opt out of mail lists (Britain and France)

First advergame

1984

Indira Gandhi, first female prime minister of India, assassinated by Satwant Singh and Beant Singh

Apple Macintosh computer introduced

Apple Computer's "1984" commercial plays once, during the Super Bowl

Fast food commercial is highlighted in US presidential campaign

1985

Mafia boss Paul Castellano assassinated by rival crime gang

World's first .com domain name, symbolics.com, is registered

Martin Sorrell buys Wire and Plastic Products (WPP) and begins series of takeovers

GENERAL HISTORY

ADVERTISING HISTORY

1986
Challenger space shuttle explodes seventy-three seconds after liftoff

Ukrainian Chernobyl nuclear plant disaster

First condom commercial (United Kingdom)

1987
First television commercial showing a model in a bra (United States)

1988
Photoshop software created

Shockvertising gets its start

First English commercial in the Soviet Union

First holographic ad on a magazine cover

1989
Tiananmen Square massacre in Beijing

Berlin Wall torn down by citizens

Young & Rubicam indicted for bribery of a foreign agent

First magazine ad to include sound

1990
World Wide Web is created by Tim Berners-Lee

Hubble Space Telescope launched

Volvo's deceptive "monster truck rally" advertising

First advertising in space

Computer-generated coupons begin

1991
Internet opened to commercial use

Kentucky Fried Chicken is renamed "KFC"

Rajiv Gandhi, former prime minister of India, assassinated by Thenmozhi Rajaratnam

Soviet Union dissolves

Persian Gulf War is led by the United States in Kuwait and Saudi Arabia

Basketball star Magic Johnson announces he is HIV positive

European Advertising Standards Alliance begins

Frequent shopper cards arrive

First true bus wrap

1992
Bozell Worldwide spins off media function, creating BJK&E Media

Soldier of Fortune magazine found liable for running a murder-for-hire ad

1993
David Koresh leads the Branch Davidian cult during the Waco siege by law enforcement officials

Publicis begins series of takeovers

First clickable web ad

1994
Computer "cookies" invented

Former political prisoner Nelson Mandela inaugurated president of South Africa

The Quick Response (QR) code is introduced

The computer cookie is invented

First university advertising course in Russia

City of Ladue v. Gilleo declared citizens have a right to put signs in their yards and windows

Advertising spokesman O. J. Simpson is charged with murder

First banner ad

GENERAL HISTORY

1995
Bombing in Oklahoma City kills 168

Israeli Prime Minister Yitzhak Rabin assassinated by Yigal Amir

1996
United States begins converting television to HDTV

1997
Britain returns Hong Kong to China after 155 years

Diana, Princess of Wales, killed in automobile crash after chase by paparazzi

1998
Google founded

Pakistan joins the nuclear club

1999
First digital video recorder, ReplayTV, is announced

Oldsmobiles stop production

Dr. Jack Kevorkian is found guilty of murder for assisted suicide

Twelve students and one teacher killed in shooting at Columbine High School in Littleton, Colorado

2001
The dot-com bubble bursts, causing loss of trillions $USD in stock by 2002

Terrorist attack fells the World Trade Center in New York (aka 9/11)

Wikipedia begins

Apple iPod introduced

Satellite radios become reality

ADVERTISING HISTORY

First university course dedicated to internet advertising

First advertising blog

Internet ad space brokering starts

CMYK magazine published

44 Liquormart v. Rhode Island decision provides more protection for advertising

US liquor industry begins television commercials after sixty years

First animated banner ad

Catholic Church's Handbook on Ethics in Advertising published

First advertisement filmed in space

First pop-up ad

PRWeek magazine published

one, a magazine published

Master Settlement Agreement between tobacco companies and forty-six US states

Tobacco advertising in the United States no longer appears on billboards

2000
First advertising via social media

Google introduces AdWords

First mobile text messaging advertisement

GENERAL HISTORY

ADVERTISING HISTORY

2003

Columbia space shuttle broke apart during return to Earth

Second Gulf War begins (ends 2011)

Former president of Iraq, Saddam Hussein, captured by US forces in Tikrit

Controlling the Assault of Non-Solicited Pornography and Marketing (CAN-SPAM) Act regulates e-mail (United States)

Do-Not-Call Implementation Act helps consumers opt out of phone lists (United States)

The first online advertising exchange is created

2004

Facebook founded

The Lance Armstrong Foundation issues silicone bracelets that raise millions of dollars

Record $33 million spent on a television commercial

2005

YouTube founded

Major ad agency president sent to jail for fraud

Digital billboards begin

2006

North Korea joins the nuclear club

US Vice President Dick Cheney accidentally shoots his friend, Harry Whittington, in the face

First gay rights demonstration in Moscow

Twitter founded

Droga5 agency opens

2007

Apple iPhone introduced

Thirty-two people are shot and killed at the Virginia Tech university in Blacksburg, Virginia

Mobile coupons become a reality

First user-generated commercial to run on the Super Bowl

2008

Barack Obama elected first non-White US president

Pinterest founded

First advertising-focused high school

First "Peel 'n' Taste" strips put in magazine ads

First augmented-reality magazine advertisement

2009

"King of Pop" Michael Jackson dies of heart failure at age fifty

2010

Apple introduces the iPad

Instagram founded

The Advertising Option Icon is introduced

Institute for Advertising Ethics formed

First talking newspaper advertisement

First scented billboard

Geo-fencing becomes an advertising tool

2011

Fukushima nuclear reactor melts down after flooding

Militant leader Osama bin Laden is killed by US military

Snapchat founded

The term "Native Advertising" enters the industry's lexicon

GENERAL HISTORY

ADVERTISING HISTORY

2012

Skydiver Felix Baumgartner jumps from helium balloon at height of twenty-four miles

Newsweek discontinues print edition, going entirely digital

Facebook passes one billion users

Twenty children and six adults killed in shooting at Sandy Hook Elementry School in Newtown, Connecticut

First video in a magazine advertisement

2013

Seven-time Tour de France winner Lance Armstrong admits using drugs to win

First fully edible magazine advertisement

2014

The earliest use of a chumbox

2015

US Supreme Court requires all states to permit same-sex marriages

Reed v. Town of Gilbert said government can't regulate signs based on their content

Advertising spokesman Jared Fogle is convicted of child porn and soliciting minors for sex

2016

Chicago Cubs win the World Series for the first time since 1908

Forty-nine people are shot and killed at the Pulse gay nightclub in Orlando, Florida

2017

Fifty-eight people are shot and killed at Mandalay Bay Resort and Casino in Las Vegas, Nevada

Twenty-six people are shot and killed at a church in Sutherland Springs, Texas

Fearless Girl sculpture appears in New York City's financial district

A "Braille billboard" is displayed

2018

Private company, SpaceX, puts a car in space and uses it for advertising

Longest commercial in history, to date

2019

US President Donald Trump is impeached

Japan's Emperor Akihito abdicates his throne

UK Prime Minister Theresa May resigns over failure to negotiate withdrawal from the European Union (Brexit)

Notre Dame Cathedral in Paris burns, destroying the roof and spire

China is the first country to land a probe on the dark side of the moon

World's first musical about advertising

2020

Coronavirus (COVID-19) pandemic shuts down commerce worldwide

The Twentieth-Century Advertising Explosion and Beyond

Historians of the future will not have to rely on the meagre collections of museums, will not have to pore over obscure documents and ancient prints, to reconstruct a faithful picture of 1926. Day by day a picture of our time is recorded completely and vividly in the advertising in American newspapers and magazines. Were all other sources of information on the life of today to fail, the advertising would reproduce for future times, as it does for our own, the action, color, variety, dignity, and aspirations of the American Scene.

—*N.W. Ayer & Son advertising agency, 1926*

Just as nineteenth-century advertising was dramatically affected by what was happening outside the field, twentieth-century advertising was both a cause and a consequence of outside events. Those events interacted with advertising developments, creating a whole new world.

AND ADVERTISING SHALL LEAD THEM

The late nineteenth and early twentieth centuries saw shifts in society, particularly in America (Sivulka 2001). Industrialization resulted in a major increase in factories. With new branding competition, gas and electrical lighting, and events like the US Civil War, many factories grew and grew. All this led to job opportunities in urban areas. And as people took those jobs they needed groceries, and clothes, and hardware, so other people moved to those areas to open stores. Those stores, of course, needed advertising.

Between 1870 and 1920, the US population expanded by ten million. That meant more consumers for advertisers to reach. This expanding society, in concert with national mass advertising of popular products like bicycles and pianos, resulted in a homogeneity of leisure activities across America (Norris 1990). Advertising created social trends.

Department stores, the first big-box stores, got their start. Sears Roebuck, Montgomery Ward, and Wanamaker's were just a few of them. Chain stores also were new. The Great Atlantic & Pacific Tea Company (aka A&P) and Woolworth's were two early leaders. Not only were manufacturers ballooning in size, but so were many retailers. Thus national

Electric Motors Solve the Sewing Problem

Every woman realizes that it is hard work to run a sewing-machine. No matter what make your machine is, how easy it runs or how well you like to sew, after a while the foot-work becomes tiresome and then drudgery.

Save Work

By furnishing *all* the power necessary to run the machine, the electric sewing-machine motor abolishes the hard work connected with sewing and enables the operator to devote her whole attention to her needle-craft.

Easily Attached

With a screw-driver any handy man—and most women—can attach this motor to any sewing-machine. Screw the plug into any convenient electric-light socket and the sewing-machine is ready for work.

Perfect Control

A slight pressure of one foot on the treadle starts the machine, which runs fast or slow at the will of the operator. Lifting the foot from the

treadle stops the machine. It is as safe and simple as the electric flat-iron and just as reliable.

Half a Cent an Hour

As this little motor requires less current than an ordinary incandescent lamp, its cost of operation is therefore less than half a cent an hour.

The Modern Method

Use this sewing-machine motor for one season's sewing and you will never go back to the old foot-power, back-tiring method of running a sewing-machine.

Made To Last

This small motor is made by the largest electrical manufacturer in the world, which insures that it is just as carefully designed and built as its "bigger brothers" that turn the great wheels of modern factories.

See the General Electric Company's Sewing Machine Motor in actual operation in the display rooms of lighting companies, electrical supply dealers and contractors.

Meanwhile write for an illustrated booklet, "How to Solve the Sewing Problem."

General Electric Company

Dept. 39-C   Schenectady, N. Y.

Sales Agencies in 1500 Cities and Towns in the United States.

The guarantee on page 12 is important to every reader

FIGURE 9.1. A 1911 advertisement for an electric sewing machine, as electricity was reaching into private homes.

advertising was not limited to manufacturers. These developments helped establish more standardized retailing methods, changing the very nature of advertising (Printers' Ink 1938).

Today we talk about "the commercialization of Christmas" and "the commercialization of amateur sports," and such. But in the first few years of the twentieth century, "commercialization" was in its infancy. Corporate influence on consumer culture was still new, and yet it was being felt (Stole 2006). Advertising was the face of that influence.

Society was being overwhelmed by the repercussions of the Industrial Revolution. By 1900, thousands of passenger cars already were in use, as were 600,000 phones, jumping to 2.2 million by 1905. In New York (and London, Paris, and Berlin), subways were under construction. New York's first line opened in 1904. And by 1911 scads of new electrical household products were entering homes (Figure 9.1), especially vacuum cleaners (Printers' Ink 1938). New inventions tapped advertising to help sales, while some (e.g., telephones and subways) also became advertising media.

These developments set the stage for a very different century. But like that previous century, defining events included wars.

READY, AIM, ADVERTISE!

There were several wars in the 1800s, and the 1900s were no different. But the world wars are uniquely critical to understanding the ad industry of that time. Unlike previous wars, these were the first wars using advertising and public relations (PR) as part of the military arsenal, not just as a recruitment tool.

A World at War

For World War I (WWI), like during the Civil War, ads recruited soldiers. Starting in 1914 in England, a committee of advertising creatives oversaw production of both newspaper ads and signs (Wood 1958). Recruitment was its central effort, as its name suggested: the Parliamentary Recruitment Committee. London soon was plastered with recruitment posters.

The United States joined the war in 1917, and President Woodrow Wilson created a Committee on Public Information (CPI), also called the Creel Commission, to corral public opinion behind US entrance into WWI. Within CPI was a Division of Pictorial Publicity, where three hundred *volunteer* artists produced 1,484 ad designs in just nineteen months. They created posters, banners, and other materials to steer public opinion. An enormous menu of ad and PR talent gained intensive experience in persuasive messaging.

A 1914 British ad depicted its minister of war pointing his finger, commanding men to "join your country's army" (Figure 9.2), but CPI artist James Montgomery Flagg is credited with inventing the Uncle Sam character in 1917, pointing and saying, "I want YOU for U.S. Army!"

FIGURE 9.2. A 1914 recruitment advertisement from Britain, featuring Lord Kitchener, the minister of war.

(Figure 9.3). Flagg was a prolific commercial artist who designed many magazine covers. His Uncle Sam poster was considered one of the war's most successful designs (Rickards 1971), though the US Navy had a pretty good contender (Figure 9.4). Flagg recalled, "A number of us who were too old or too scared to fight, prostituted our talents by making posters inciting a large mob of young men who had never done anything to us, to hop over and get shot at. . . . We sold the war to youth" (Fox 1984).

FIGURE 9.3. A famous 1917 army recruitment poster by James Montgomery Flagg.

But the ads weren't only for recruitment. They were strategic weapons. Many encouraged citizens back home to conserve resources so as to supply the military. Others urged people to buy bonds to fund the war, and still others encouraged them to work harder supplying military resources (Figure 9.5). And the war moved many women into the workforce, replacing men who went to war. Advertising really was a resource management tool.

FIGURE 9.4. This poster was created by Howard Chandler Christy, also in 1917.

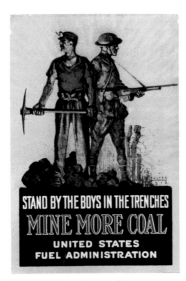

FIGURE 9.5.   Many of the war
posters focused on encouraging
"those at home" to work harder.

There were restrictions on advertising during the war. Sign makers had trouble getting materials to create signs. Many advertisers altered their advertising by both reducing volume and adjusting messages to support (or capitalize on) the war effort (Figure 9.6). Advertisers also helped underwrite the military's newspaper, *Stars and Stripes*. But, overall, institutions other than businesses learned that advertising could do more than sell products, leading to "institutional" advertising. It's arguable that advertising helped shorten the war and save millions of lives (Presbrey 1929).

Wood (1958) concludes:

Advertising came triumphantly out of World War I. It was better, it was bigger, it was reputable. It had proved its ability to sway peoples' opinions and govern their actions. It had sold ideas and regulated human conduct. It had been used effectively by governments.

The ad industry proved itself, fighting alongside the soldiers.

A World at War . . . Again!

Unfortunately, after just a few years the next world war began. Again, America wasn't first to join, but it jumped in when in late 1941 Japan attacked Pearl Harbor. The War Advertising Council (WAC) was created in 1942 to do what CPI's Division of Pictorial Publicity had done. This time the industry pushed it. This time *both* sides used advertising and public relations, making it a "war of rival propagandas" (Gallo 1972). The ability to send radio broadcasts across enemy lines, a medium not existing during WWI, opened doors to new PR opportunities.

Radio's value as an ad medium also soared as the public turned to it for war news. This showcased the power of PR in a way no peacetime activities ever could.

FIGURE 9.6.   In 1916, Lucky Strike cigarettes
adopted a campaign tying its product to the
war effort.

It wasn't just the Allies using it. The Japanese used Tokyo Rose, and the Germans promoted Axis Sally.

The US Office of War Information acted as the official war information conduit. Over five hundred US magazines worked to create a campaign in 1942 promoting US war bonds. The ad industry created more ads during World War II (WWII) than in the years leading up to the war, because Congress had approved a tax deduction for war-themed ads. So advertisers incorporated war themes in their ads, and some encouraged conservation rather than purchase.

Posters were still important, but war-related ads came in many forms. Though US involvement in this war lasted more than twice as long as during WWI, the WAC produced *hundreds* of times as much free advertising in just its first year as CPI did in all of WWI (Wood 1958).

When WAC received a request to help fight inflation, a dozen agencies delivered a series of seventy-two full-page print ads, picked a dozen, and talked 492 magazines into running them. Total circulation of those magazines was ninety-one million (Wood 1958).

American soldiers stationed in other countries complained that special editions of magazines were sent to them without advertising. They felt ads told them more about what was happening at home than articles did. They wanted to know what friends and family were buying and wearing. When they did see the ads depicting war scenes, soldiers often found them absurd (Wood 1958).

FIGURE 9.7. An ad from 1943 demonizing the enemy to encourage worker care.

While advertising played positive roles in the war, not all was positive. To marshal public opinion to support the war effort, some ads dehumanized or even demonized the enemy. By today's standards, these often crossed the line into the grossly offensive category (Figure 9.7).

As in WWI, rationing ensured that adequate resources were directed to the war front. Some restrictions were problematic for advertisers, so in 1944 the Brand Names Research Foundation was created to push back against government limits. It fought critics of advertising and trademarks, even after the war. A public "battle against brand marketing" had festered during the war (Petty 2018), and the foundation played defense.

There was one fascinating effort by the Allies involving tactically applied deceptive advertising: the *war magicians*. Jasper Maskelyne, an illusionist, joined Britain's Royal Engineers early in the war. He created an illusion of a German ship on the River Thames to convince superiors that illusions could help win the war.

Maskelyne ended up supervising fourteen people known as the "Magic Gang," who developed a series of illusions, using materials like canvas and plywood, to create the appearance of entire armored divisions to make the enemy believe they were up against larger forces than were actually available. Perhaps the most notable illusion was hiding the city of Alexandria *and* the Suez Canal, so German bombers couldn't strike them (Fisher 1983).

German advertising was entirely under its government's control, under the Reich Minister of Propaganda, Joseph Goebbels. This is what tarnished the term "propaganda."

Enter the Atomic Age

The war ended in July 1945, with the first use of atomic weapons. By 1949, the War Advertising Council became the Advertising Council. Between the war and the Great Depression, people everywhere had lived sparsely for many years. The war's end also marked the end of that pent-up demand and the beginning of a long-awaited prosperity (Mierau 2000). The advertising industry adapted quickly to the resulting opportunities.

Both the Atomic Age and a "cold war" started. Nuclear power and bombs were at the forefront of everyone's minds. People built fallout shelters and schoolchildren were taught to "duck and cover" should nuclear war happen. Nuclear power plants were constructed. The ever-present threat of atomic disaster had some impact on advertising as well (Figures 9.8 and 9.9).

FIGURE 9.8.   A Seagram's Canadian Whisky ad from 1947, promoting atomic power.

FIGURE 9.9.   Atomic themes were not just for ads; they also fostered a number of new products.

Ads at War with War

Other wars followed. For the United States that included the Korean and Vietnam Wars. But advertising played only minor roles. By the Persian Gulf War, in late 1990, however, advertising's role in war had completely changed. Television networks and cable news stations offered extensive coverage. Advertisers concerned about associating their brands with death and destruction pulled ads from those stations. Times had changed.

READING AND DEPRESSION CHANGE THE WORLD

Following WWI, incomes rose significantly. Women filled jobs when men went to war, and many stayed in the workplace afterward (Gallo 1972). Also, consumer credit expanded, enabling purchase of all manner of consumer goods, including automobiles. This fostered new opportunities for advertising.

And literacy grew. US literacy in 1870 had reached 80 percent, but by 1920 it was 94 percent. African Americans experienced the most substantial change, going from 20 percent to nearly 80 percent (Norris 1990).

The traveling salesman, a big part of the nineteenth century, began to disappear. And frozen food appeared, thanks to Clarence Birdseye's quick-freeze machine, in 1925 (Printers' Ink 1938). Shopping, consumption, and advertising patterns were all dramatically altered.

The Great Depression, beginning with the stock market crash in 1929, tore apart the economy. Products still needed to sell, so advertising was required. But there was a mad rush to cancel ads after the crash (Wood 1958). People were jobless, and many blamed the Depression on big business, making it tough for advertising. As the face of industry, advertising became a frequent target. The Lord & Thomas agency cut salaries by 25 percent, eventually firing fifty employees. BBDO, to its credit, carried employees through the downturn but found itself overstaffed (Tungate 2007). Total advertising volume dropped from $3.4 billion in 1929 to $2.6 billion in 1930 to $2.3 billion in 1931 (Fox 1984). It took the ad industry seventeen years to recover (Editors of Advertising Age 1976).

In 1933, General Hugh S. Johnson, of the National Recovery Administration, wrote to major US advertisers encouraging them to aggressively advertise. He announced the public was beginning to shop again, looking to replace worn-out products, and that they anxiously look to advertising for news (Wood 1958).

That same year, the National Association of Manufacturers (NAM) created a public relations campaign. Those running NAM felt that negative attitudes toward business stemmed largely from misunderstandings. This campaign was mounted to correct those misimpressions (Stole 2006). Companies added their advertising to impress people with their contributions to the economy. Advertising and public relations were viewed as tools to dig out from under the public distaste that grew during the Depression.

But to understand the advertising climate at that time, it's important to grasp both the Truth-in-Advertising movement and the consumer movement(s). Advertising's reputation was in the balance.

TRUTH-IN-ADVERTISING

Patent medicines were a scourge of the advertising industry's reputation for centuries. They dominated (and financed) newspapers and magazines everywhere, and during the Civil War they were so common that drug addiction was known as "the Army disease" (Carson 1961).

A Movement Is Born

When the *Ladies' Home Journal* (*LHJ*) announced in 1892 that it no longer would accept patent medicine advertisements, it was unbelievable. The idea of a publication divorcing itself from its largest group of advertisers was shocking.

Not only did *LHJ* stop running those ads, but it also campaigned against them. Edward Bok, its editor, made this his pet cause. In 1904, he wrote editorials like "The Patent-Medicine Curse," warning the public about alcohol in those medicines. He explained that patent medicine sellers had no legal obligation to list ingredients, and talked about dirty marketing tactics being used. He also told readers that catarrh "cures" were actually cocaine. In truth, most of these drugs were useless or even dangerous.

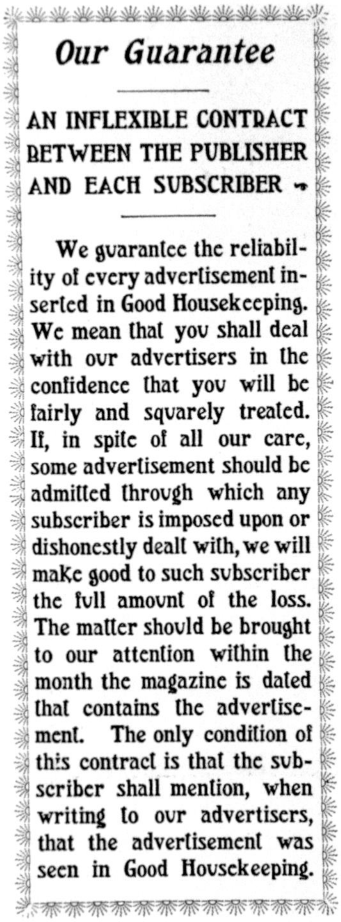

LHJ probably was the genesis of the Truth-in-Advertising movement. Patent medicines were not the only factor, but there really was no legal barrier to outlandish claims back then. Publishers argued that they couldn't act as censors of ads in their pages, because it was too big a job and might affect readers' trust of other advertisers (Nevett 1982).

In 1902, *Good Housekeeping* entered the fray, announcing it would guarantee the reliability of every ad in its pages, testing them in its Experiment Station (Figure 9.10). Recall that decades earlier farm journals made guarantees, but *Good Housekeeping* was the first general readership magazine to do it. In 1909, it announced a "Seal of Approval," which would appear in advertisements for products it had tested (Figure 9.11).

In 1903, newspapers joined the cause. The Scripps-McRae League of Newspapers appointed a censor of all advertising in the chain, while the *Chicago Tribune*, the *Philadelphia North American*, and others began a full-out attack on patent medicines and other fraud (Wood 1958). The *New York Times* published a list of claims it would not accept, in its "Advertising Index Expurgatorious" (Kenner 1936). *Delineator* magazine's advertising manager, John Adams Thayer, loudly denounced fraudulent advertising.

Our Guarantee

AN INFLEXIBLE CONTRACT BETWEEN THE PUBLISHER AND EACH SUBSCRIBER →

We guarantee the reliability of every advertisement inserted in Good Housekeeping. We mean that you shall deal with our advertisers in the confidence that you will be fairly and squarely treated. If, in spite of all our care, some advertisement should be admitted through which any subscriber is imposed upon or dishonestly dealt with, we will make good to such subscriber the full amount of the loss. The matter should be brought to our attention within the month the magazine is dated that contains the advertisement. The only condition of this contract is that the subscriber shall mention, when writing to our advertisers, that the advertisement was seen in Good Housekeeping.

FIGURE 9.10. *Good Housekeeping* magazine printed this guarantee in its pages beginning in 1902.

Then 1905 was a busy year. First, *Collier's* magazine jumped in, in a big way. Samuel Hopkins Adams, who did some serious research into patent medicines, wrote a tome about fraud. He took it to *LHJ*, hoping to have it published. *LHJ* found the writing a bit too heavy for its readers, so Adams took it to *Collier's*, which ended up publishing a series of articles titled "The Great American Fraud" (Figure 9.12).

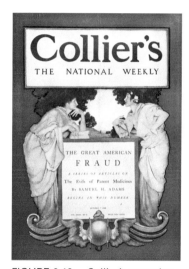

FIGURE 9.11. The *Good Housekeeping* "Seal of Approval" from 1909.

The Ad Industry Steps Up

An advertising agency finally stepped up, refusing patent medicine accounts: N.W. Ayer & Sons (Norris 1990). In fairness, it had dropped some of those accounts in the 1890s, but it didn't abandon the rest until 1905.

Upton Sinclair published *The Jungle* in 1905, exposing unsafe, unsanitary conditions in the meat packing industry. This is relevant mainly because Sinclair's book and Adams' articles, together, helped push Congress to finally pass the Pure Food and Drug Act, regulating both food and drugs. In part, it forbade falsely labeling a drug, which was all about truth-in-advertising.

That year George Rowell also published several articles in his journal, *Printers' Ink*, accusing advertisers using false promises of doing immense damage to the advertising industry. He made the point that false advertising is bad business. Simultaneous with passage of the food

FIGURE 9.12. *Collier's* magazine in 1905 published several articles about fraudulent patent medicine advertisements.

and drug law, in 1906 the American Medical Association created a propaganda department aimed at fighting quackery.

W. N. Aubuchon, national president of the Advertising Clubs of America, in 1907 wrote many essays on advertising, pushing a state law prohibiting false advertising. The British Parliament that same year passed the Advertisements Regulation Act, to curb hoardings. And another newspaper, the *St. Louis Post Dispatch*, announced that it reserved the right to reject advertisement that was objectionable "either in its subject matter or phraseaology" (Kenner 1936). The tide was building.

Then, in 1910, Cyrus H. K. Curtis, publisher of both *LHJ* and the *Saturday Evening Post*, presented a self-regulatory code his magazines would follow: the Curtis Advertising Code. Its purpose was "to protect both our advertisers and our readers from all copy that is fraudulent or deceptive," and it began by saying, "We exclude all advertising that in any way tends to deceive, defraud, or injure our readers." This "code" became a prototype for advertising clearance policies by other publications.

The Ten Commandments . . . of Advertising

The industry's first "Truth Conference" was in Boston in 1911, during the 7th Associated Advertising Clubs of America conference. Attendance was triple the previous year's conference, at 2,260 attendees. One retired ad executive, Joseph H. Appel, presented his "Ten Commandments of Advertising":

1. Thou shalt have no other gods in advertising but Truth.
2. Thou shalt not make any graven image of wealth, or power, or station, and thou shalt not bow down thyself to them nor serve them except with honor.
3. Thou shalt not use the power of advertising in an unworthy cause or in behalf of unworthy goods.
4. Remember the working day to keep it holy.
5. Honor thy business and thy advertising, that they may honor thee, and thy days of usefulness may be long upon the land.
6. Thou shalt not kill fair competition from without, nor ambition from within thine organization.
7. Thou shalt not lie, misstate, exaggerate, misrepresent nor conceal; thou shalt not bear false witness to the public, but thou shalt be fair to thy merchandise.
8. Thou shalt not steal by false pretense in statements, spoken, written or printed.
9. Thou shalt not permit adulteration or substitution in advertised goods.
10. Thou shalt not covet, nor imitate, nor run down thy neighbor's business; thou shalt not covet, nor imitate, nor run down thy neighbor's name, nor his fame, nor his wares, nor his trade, nor anything that is thy neighbors. (Kenner 1936)

Printers' Ink editor John Irving Romer was unimpressed. He felt the conference was all talk and no action. There was no clear way to stop deceptive advertising. Only two states, New York and Massachusetts, had laws prohibiting deceptive advertising, and they weren't adequate. That same year *Printers' Ink* proposed a model law to regulate advertising: the *Printers' Ink* Model Statute. It was intended to make deceptive advertising illegal, with states encouraged to adopt it. It eventually was adopted by about half the United States.

This also was when the Associated Advertising Clubs of the World (AACW) adopted the slogan "Truth in Advertising" (Figure 9.13). Romer suggested establishing "vigilance committees" throughout the country to create and enforce codes of conduct.

FIGURE 9.13. The Associated Advertising Clubs of the World integrated "TRUTH" into its logo, as seen in this 1915 advertisement.

Vigilance and the BBB

Advertising clubs across the United States began doing just that. The Advertising Men's League in New York was first out of the gate in 1912. Other cities followed. The AACW created its own National Vigilance Committee, which looked for more generalized solutions. One idea was to create Better Business Bureaus (BBB). *Printers' Ink* (1938) later argued, "The [*Printers' Ink*] Model Statute was the chief factor in bringing the Better Business Bureau into existence and it became the principal weapon of the Bureaus in their ceaseless efforts in behalf of honest advertising." In 1921, the National Vigilance Committee was renamed the National Better Business Bureau of the Associated Advertising Clubs of the World. By then it already had investigated 6,815 complaints (Pope 1983). The national BBB became international by creating its Canadian bureau in 1928, though a third country wasn't until 1959 when Mexico was added.

The Truth-in-Advertising movement hit Australia in 1920. It was the motto of that country's annual advertising convention. The convention included this topic, but its real purpose was a "quest for legitimacy" as an industry (Waller 2012). That also was an impetus in the United States. While that legitimacy existed in businesspeople's minds, it was lacking in the general public. Developing an Australian Better Business Bureau also was discussed at that convention, becoming a reality in 1923 (Waller 2012).

The United Kingdom initiated a National Vigilance Committee in 1924. It became the Advertising Investigation Department of the Advertising Association in 1928.

The Better Business Bureaus seemed to end much of the vocal concerns about truth in advertising. Apparently, the industry felt it now had a mechanism to police advertising. But in 1924 the American Association of Advertising Agencies announced its Standards of Practice, a code of ethics; and in 1937 the International Chamber of Commerce adopted an International Code of Standards for advertising.

A movement that was started by magazines, joined by newspapers, and finally embraced by the ad industry, culminated in the birth of Better Business Bureaus. That became a clearinghouse for consumer complaints about businesses. While this tool to aid consumers was getting started, another movement was beginning.

CONSUMER RIGHTS . . . AND WRONGS

The notion of protecting consumers from advertising fraud reaches back to 1859, but the movement took off in 1916, when the National Consumers' League was founded. The league reviewed manufacturer labor policies and published lists of those it approved. An influential book, *Your Money's Worth: A Study in the Waste of the Consumer's Dollars*, by Stuart Chase and Frederick J. Schlink, was published in 1927. It exposed, among other things, advertising fraud.

Consumer's Club

The Consumer's Club began in New York City in 1927, evolving to Consumers' Research, Inc. (CR) in 1929, with that same Schlink as its president. CR was an aggressive advocate for consumers, seeking to provide them with more and better product information (Stole 2006). It published the *Consumers' Research Bulletin*, offering marketplace advice. CR has been described as a "militant left-wing group" (Leighton 1973).

During the Depression, in 1932, Schlink and CR secretary Arthur Kallet published a more influential book: *100,000,000 Guinea Pigs: Dangers in Everyday Foods, Drugs, and Cosmetics*. It was a best-selling attack on food and drug advertising (Wood 1958). But it used old examples without telling readers, implying that improper ad claims were more recent and frequent than was true. Some forty-one employees at CR went on strike, protesting, and some board members resigned.

Consumers' Union

Unhappy with CR leadership, in 1935 a group of its employees started the Consumers' Union (CU). Billing itself as "A Nonprofit Testing Organization for Consumers," CU published advice in regular *Consumers' Union Reports* and a *Consumers' Union Buying Guide*. Colston E. Warne, an economist, was president.

Both organizations tried undermining the ad industry. Ironically, both relied on consumer support to survive, and advertising was used to recruit members.

Also during the Depression, the Agricultural Adjustment Administration, which replaced the Federal Farm Board during Roosevelt's "New Deal," created consumer councils. Its original plan was to create councils in more than three thousand counties.

The National Recovery Administration had a Consumers' Advisory Board, the National Emergency Council had a Consumers' Division, and the National Bituminous Coal Commission had a Consumers' Council (Leighton 1973). The Roosevelt administration, without question, aimed at consumer input. All were part of the growing consumer movements. I say "movements," plural, because there really were several.

So during the Depression, advertising was attacked from all sides. Consumer organizations found a ready audience for advertising criticisms. For an ad industry trying to recover from serious financial losses, the timing could not have been worse (Stole 2006). But to these critics advertising was wasteful, often fraudulent, and frequently offensive. This push manifested itself in efforts to pass laws controlling advertising.

Congress and Education

A 1933 law was rushed through Congress to regulate one type of advertising. The Securities Act put responsibility on those issuing or underwriting securities for advertising claims. The nation was wary of the stock market following its crash, so this law's approval was unquestioned.

US Senator Royal S. Copeland, also in 1933, introduced in Congress "[a] BILL to prevent the manufacture, shipment, and sale of adulterated or misbranded food, drugs, and cosmetics, and to regulate traffic therein; to prevent the false advertisement of food, drugs, and cosmetics, and for other purposes." It was drafted by Assistant Secretary of Agriculture Rexford Tugwell, and became known as the Tugwell Bill.

Original wording would have moved food, drug, and cosmetic advertising authority from the Federal Trade Commission to the Food and Drug Administration (Fox 1984). Tugwell felt there was too little protection for consumers and no punishment for advertisers. Both advertising and drug industries fought the Tugwell wording, which created criminal penalties and gave broad discretion regarding what constituted false advertising. The ad industry had powerful connections with media, which proved tremendously beneficial (Stole 2006).

The Tugwell Bill was defeated, and a subsequent version toned down anti-advertising provisions. Finally, in 1938 a significantly modified version—the Federal Food, Drug and Cosmetic Act (aka the Copeland Bill)—was passed. The Copeland Bill was silent regarding advertising.

As Congress wrestled with language, in 1937 the American Association of Advertising Agencies (AAAA) set up a Committee on Consumer Relations to collect data and conduct research about advertising economics, to devise a defense for the industry. Stephens College (Missouri), the same year, founded an Institute for Consumer Education to better educate consumers, while creating the Annual National Conference on Consumer Education (Stole 2006). The following year, the AAAA introduced a Consumer's Advertising Council to educate consumers about advertising's value. But these are just a few of the more notable consumer organizations invented during the 1930s. *Business Week* magazine conducted a survey in early 1939 that found twenty-two national consumer groups operating (Fox 1984).

By the late 1930s, principles pushed by CR, CU, and other consumer groups, including anti-advertising sentiments, found their way into university classrooms. Economics textbooks integrated material from consumer movements, too. Although "home economics" classes had been taught at universities since the nineteenth century, consumer groups' interests dovetailed nicely with those programs.

In response, advertisers began providing "educational" classroom materials, like booklets and free samples, reaching pre-college students (Stole 2006). These were the first real efforts for most of these advertisers to reach adolescents.

In a way, World War II was the best thing that could have happened for the advertising industry, diverting attention away from consumer movements. The industry, again helping the war cause, gained credibility and respect it had lost during the Depression. But once war ended, the consumer movements found new traction. In 1947, a National Association of Consumers was established to resume lobbying on behalf of consumers, though it died after about a decade (Petty 2018).

Consumer Bill of Rights

In March 1962, consumer movements experienced perhaps their biggest win. President John F. Kennedy presented his "Consumer Bill of Rights," which included:

1. The Right to Safety. In other words, products should not harm users.
2. The Right to be Informed. Consumers deserve complete, appropriate, and truthful information.
3. The Right to Choose. Consumers deserve options in the marketplace.
4. The Right to be Heard. They have the right to voice their complaints about products.

This turned out to be one of Kennedy's long-lasting legacies. In 1985, the principles were adopted and expanded by the United Nations as the "United Nations Guidelines for Consumer Protection." It added four more rights:

5. The Right to Satisfaction of Basic Needs. This refers to things like food and shelter.
6. The Right to Redress. Consumers deserve reimbursement for poor products and deceptive advertising, for example.
7. The Right to Consumer Education. This fits with #2, above.
8. The Right to a Healthy Environment. This deals with workplace conditions, but also with safe conditions at home.

A book was published in 1965, taking on one particular consumer interest: automotive safety. Ralph Nader's book, *Unsafe at Any Speed*, accused automobile manufacturers of undermining safety provisions mandated by government. The book's first sentence accused, "For over half a century the automobile has brought death, injury and the most inestimable sorrow and deprivation to millions of people." This book imploded the auto industry, much like *The Jungle* did to meat packing. It also changed the US government, making it more pro-consumer. Nader became the face of the consumer movements. The focus, though, was on manufacturing rather than advertising.

That changed when Nader wrote another book: *"The Nader Report" on the Federal Trade Commission*. This 1969 report condemned the FTC for failure to adequately restrain advertisers who misled consumers. In 1971, Nader invented a watchdog group called "Public Citizen" to lobby for consumer interests. For the rest of the century, Nader was at the forefront of consumer activism.

THE NEWSPAPER BLUES

Through the 1900s newspapers were healthy, and most of their revenue came from advertising. Readers purchased subscriptions, but that income was a minor part of the business model. Up to 80 percent of newsprint funds came from advertising. In 2015, subscription revenue passed advertising, worldwide, a watershed that further inflated concerns about print media's future (World Assn. of News Publishers 2015).

What changed, of course, was the internet. By the mid-1990s, newsprint was awakening to shifts in media use. Readers looked to the internet for information, and newspapers were paying the price. By 2000, it was serious. Between 2000 and 2018, employment in US newspapers dropped 55 percent, with no end in sight. From 2004 through 2018, more than two thousand US newspapers died.

The Pew Research Center states that total US circulation[1] drop began almost simultaneously with internet commercialization in 1990. It continued to slowly drop, but by 2013 total daily circulation dropped below levels since 1940, when the United States had less than half the population. Real drops in revenue began around 2006. In 2005, total revenue was over $60 billion. A decade later it was about half that, including both print and digital revenue. Newspaper advertising lost much of its appeal.

However, some would argue it was advertising's popularity that kept newspapers from sinking faster. So-called preprint advertising, or free-standing inserts (FSIs), contained coupons and sales announcements that kept bargain shoppers subscribing to newspapers. This might explain why, around 1990, subscriptions to Sunday editions surpassed weekday subscriptions. The Sunday paper tended to hold the most preprint ads. That Sunday edition preference continued every year after 1990.

But preprints soon migrated online, and coupons became accessible through websites and mobile apps. Newspapers no longer had a monopoly on those ads. And classified advertisements, "want ads," likewise migrated online. The earliest newspaper ads really were more like classified ads than like display ads, so the oldest type of newspaper ads also were abandoning newspapers.

That actually began with Craigslist, a website created by Craig Newmark in 1995, which became an online venue for buying and selling personal property, services, and more in the San Francisco area. Like classified ads, it was local and more person to person. In the twenty-first century's first years, Craigslist rapidly expanded city to city. By 2012, it covered seven hundred cities in seventy countries. Some former subscribers found they no longer needed newspapers.

News-like material became available on the internet. Citizens were dedicating larger portions of their media time to online sources, pulling time away from print. They also found their news needs being satisfied online. By the century's second decade, newspapers were struggling to survive.

This describes the industry as a whole. There were exceptions, most notable of which was the *New York Times*. It, too, experienced a drastic drop in print subscriptions. In 2008, it delivered about a million copies on an average weekday, but by 2018 it was down to 487,000. Unlike most newspapers, however, it pursued a successful online subscription strategy. In 2014, it achieved an online paid circulation of 799,000, to buttress its print circulation. By 2018, it reached 2.86 million. Its total circulation more than tripled since 2008. It also published apps. By the close of 2019, the newspaper claimed a total 5,251,000 paid subscriptions, a figure formerly unimaginable for newspapers. Unfortunately, its advertising continued to decline, so the company's revenue was more and more dependent on subscriptions (Tracy 2020a). The COVID-19 crisis brought an explosion of digital subscribers, so by May 2020 subscriptions passed 6 million. But advertisers didn't follow (Tracy 2020b).

With more media options for consumers, including hundreds of television channels—a single medium—where there were three or four channels in the mid-twentieth century, it shouldn't surprise anyone that newspapers no longer rule. There is another implication, though. The *New York Times* gained subscriptions by *national* reach, while the dying newspapers tended to be local. So newspapers were becoming more of a national advertising forum than ever before.

CONCLUSION

The twentieth century was a time of war and activism, with advertising in the midst. It had major impacts on the industry, but the industry also had effects on those events. There was, of course, more than is detailed here.

Industry People, Agencies, and Changes

That gentleman will call the Joint Chiefs of Staff. I think they're scared of him. They're merely professional killers; he's in advertising!

—*Robert Ludlum, in the novel* The Road to Gandolfino

AD EDUCATION GROWS UP

Advertising education, beyond how to paint or carve a sign, really started as advertising agencies began to grow, beginning with one advertising professional training an assistant. We believe William Tayler, the first ad agent, trained Jem White, the second.

Most nineteenth-century advertising was for newspapers and magazines, so when universities finally offered ad classes, they usually were in journalism programs. The first journalism program was established in 1869 by General Robert E. Lee, who was president of Washington College after the Civil War. But no university course including advertising was taught until 1893, by Joseph French Johnson at the University of Pennsylvania. Advertising was only part of that course.

Private advertising schools popped up before universities embraced it. The earliest (beyond practitioners offering private lessons) was a correspondence program by Edward T. Page and Samuel T. Davis. Page had given lectures at Chicago's Orchestra Hall in 1896 and turned them into mail-order lessons (Coolsen 1947). Witt K. Cochrane organized a Chicago College of Advertising in 1902 (Sandage 1998), and by 1904 the International Correspondence Schools offered advertising lessons (Figure 10.1).

FIGURE 10.1. The International Correspondence Schools offered classes in advertisement writing, as seen in this ad from 1904.

By then, in-house instruction was becoming more organized. Lord & Thomas began its own copywriting school within the agency. Originally, the agency's top writer was to teach it, but unfortunately the new chief copywriter, John E. Kennedy, was a brilliant writer but a not-so-brilliant teacher.

Earnest Elmo Calkins wrote in 1905 that "the profession of an advertising man steadily rose until now it aspires to rank with that of the three 'black graces'—law, medicine and divinity. Some day the advertising man . . . expects to be recognized as a member in one of the professions." The industry, hungry for respect, aspired to be a profession. One avenue to that goal seemed to be for advertising—like those black graces—to be taught in universities.

In 1901, Walter Dill Scott, a psychology professor at Northwestern University, was asked to speak at Chicago's advertising club: the Agate Club. He lectured at its annual banquet (Ross & Richards 2008), where he was a hit, and continued his involvement in advertising. He subsequently conducted research on advertising psychology and wrote the first book on that topic. The first university course with advertising as its central topic actually was created by Dr. Scott at Northwestern in 1904, in psychology.

The first advertising textbook (not correspondence lessons) appeared in 1905: *Modern Advertising* by Earnest Elmo Calkins and Ralph Holden. That same year New York University offered the first course that had "advertising" in its title, taught by George E. Allen and William R. Hotchkin (Ross & Richards 2008).

The first advertising course taught in journalism was by John B. Powell at the University of Missouri in 1908. That program also was the first to offer a university advertising degree, in 1910. In addition, in 1913 the University of Missouri hosted two advertising "fraternities." Alpha Delta Sigma (ADS) was a men's fraternity, and Gamma Alpha Chi (GAC) was for women. In 1969, GAC merged with ADS, becoming co-educational, and was absorbed by the American Advertising Federation in 1973.

As advertising education expanded, demand for textbook options rose. *Modern Advertising* had the basics, but had been created more for self-instruction, not for universities. The first textbook clearly crafted for university instruction in advertising was by Daniel Starch at the University of Wisconsin, who later became a top advertising researcher. Published in 1914, it was called *Advertising—Its Principles, Practice, and Technique*. Some suggest Paul T. Cherington's 1913 book, *Advertising as a Business Force*, was first, but it wasn't designed for university instruction but for use by advertising clubs. Cherington was a marketing professor at Harvard.

Advertising developed in journalism programs, while marketing was in business schools. The first university marketing course was at the University of Michigan in 1902, taught by Edward David Jones. The first overt crossover of advertising and marketing was in 1915, when George Burton Hotchkiss at New York University spearheaded creation of a Department of Advertising and Marketing.

Hotchkiss, too, founded the National Association of Teachers of Advertising in 1915. In 1933, it changed its name to the National Association of Marketing Teachers, and in 1937 it merged with the American Marketing Society to become the American Marketing Association.

In 1922, the University of Oklahoma created the first Department of Advertising. Jumping ahead, in 1958 Michigan State University hired a former advertising executive, John Crawford, to chair a new Department of Advertising. The next year, Charles Sandage formed one at the University of Illinois. All three of these departments were in journalism or, more broadly, communication schools. Other programs became separate departments over the next several decades.

In 1959, two organizations, the Ford Foundation and the Carnegie Foundation, published reports that criticized business schools for having become too "applied." One consequence was that many business programs across the United States jettisoned advertising classes. By then it was being taught in both business and journalism, so many universities moved advertising entirely into journalism. Some business schools didn't remove advertising, instead simply reducing its presence. Nationwide most ad education was now journalism-based.

Advertising education isn't confined to this country. Japan was early to follow what was occurring in the United States, with Waseda University teaching advertising in 1914. But "advertising" wasn't used in its course titles until 1953 (Richards & Ross 2014). China began teaching advertising in 1924, at Yanching University in Peking. American University in Cairo offered Egypt's first ad course in 1937–1938, and Italy did so at the School of Milan in 1952–1953. In 1960, it came to Lebanon, at Lebanese University, and in 1963 it started in the Philippines at the Philippine College of Commerce. Hong Kong Baptist University was first in Hong Kong, in 1968. Spain added it in 1971, Malaysia in 1972, South Korea in 1974, and Russia in 1994. Australia's first separate advertising degree was at Queensland University of Technology in 1974. This certainly isn't an exhaustive list.

Public relations education also was spreading. The first university PR program in Turkey was at Ankara University in 1966, and Singapore added full degree programs in *both* advertising and public relations in 1992 at Nanyang Technological University.

There was some resistance to higher education as background for advertising work, let alone collegiate advertising courses. In the early 1920s, Claude Hopkins famously argued that advertising had no place for a "college man," while Stanley Resor boasted about the number of college graduates—even doctorates—working in his agency (Fox 1984). Among those with degrees, a 1928 study found more ad men graduated from the University of Michigan than any other university, though English was the most popular major (Pope 1983). By that decade's end, nearly every state had schools teaching advertising (Presbrey 1929).

A few other milestones are worth mention. The first "PhD in Advertising" was conferred by the University of Texas Department of Advertising in 1981. That department also created the first "Internet Advertising" university course, in 1995. Michigan State University's Department of Advertising and Public Relations in 2017 was the first program to offer separate baccalaureate degrees in advertising management (BS) and creative advertising (BA). And beyond university education, the High School for Innovation in Advertising and Media opened in 2008 in Brooklyn, New York, making it the first advertising-oriented high school.

WHO'S WHO OF ADVERTISING

The number of people involved with advertising in the twentieth century is immense, and even just the major influencers wouldn't fit in this book. The names below are those I believe, at a bare minimum, must be recognized. This isn't a business of machines, in advertising the entire value resides in people and their ideas.

Some greats from the previous century were still playing big roles as this century began, including Earnest Elmo Calkins, George Rowell, J. Walter Thompson, and Charles Austin Bates. Another dominant player was Albert D. Lasker.

Lasker has been hailed as the "father of modern advertising" (e.g., Tungate 2007). He transitioned from newspaper reporter to working for Lord & Thomas, and within fourteen years, at age thirty-two, he bought the agency.

Even before that, Lasker made a mark on the ad industry by recognizing talent in both John E. Kennedy and Claude C. Hopkins. Both became copywriting legends. Thanks to them, Lord & Thomas gained a reputation for wordsmithing, eventually employing more copywriters than any other agency. It became one of the world's largest agencies, second only to J. Walter Thompson (JWT). This helped elevate copywriting as an essential part of advertising (Wood 1958).

In 1918, Lasker met former president Theodore Roosevelt, who remarked, "They tell me you are America's greatest advertising man." Lasker's retort was "No man can claim that distinction so long as you live."

John E. Kennedy appears in advertising history for more than copywriting—it was the way he ended up being hired by Lasker in 1904 that made him a star. Kennedy knew of Lasker and one afternoon sent this note up to him:

> I am in the saloon downstairs, and I can tell you what advertising is. I know that you don't know.
> . . . If you wish to know what advertising is, send the word "Yes" down by messenger.

Intrigued, Lasker agreed. Kennedy told him the answer was three words: "salesmanship in print." This became the Lord & Thomas approach over the next decades and was known as "reason-why" advertising. An advertising trade journal, *Advertising & Selling*, announced, "[H]is is a great idea. . . . His style is now the foundation stone of successful advertising" (Fox 1984).

Cyrus H. K. Curtis, publisher of *Ladies' Home Journal*, met Lasker on a train. Curtis commented that he was going to order a beer because of an ad . . . for Schlitz Beer. He told Lasker that he should hire whoever wrote that ad. Lasker knew Curtis was "a near-teetotaler," so he was convinced and hired Claude C. Hopkins (Cruikshank & Schultz 2010). It's said he was hired at the unbelievable salary of $185,000 per year, in 1907! Some believe him the greatest copywriter in advertising history.

Hopkins was the rare creative who believed in research! He probably is best remembered for his book, *Scientific Advertising* (1923), which pushed research as the foundation of advertising claims and advocated advertising as a science. Hopkins later became president and chairman of Lord & Thomas.

Stanley Resor, a Yale graduate, in 1907 worked at a small Cincinnati agency. As agencies like Lord & Thomas were revealing the need for copywriters, Resor found himself trying to hire one. He called Helen Lansdowne, across the river in Kentucky. She eventually was hired. The next year JWT tried to hire Resor to run its Chicago office. He opened its Cincinnati office instead and took Lansdowne with him, making her the first female copywriter at JWT.

Resor moved to JWT's main office in New York in 1912, taking Lansdowne along. He replaced her in Cincinnati with James Webb Young, who became another famous figure in ad history.

In 1916, Resor and a group of associates bought JWT from its founder, and the next year he married Lansdowne. He also co-founded the American Association of Advertising Agencies that year. He was president of JWT from 1916 to 1955, and chairman from 1955 to 1961. Stanley Resor and Helen Lansdowne Resor, with help from James Webb Young, made JWT the world's largest agency. Stanley was the first college graduate to run a major advertising agency. He, too, was a believer in advertising as science, and that laws of human behavior were subject to scientific discovery. He worked to elevate advertising to a profession.

Theodore F. MacManus, another copywriter, worked for General Motors crafting car ads. In 1927, he formed his own agency, MacManus, Inc. His most famous pitch was for Cadillac in 1915, "The Penalty of Leadership," telling consumers that owning a Cadillac came with responsibilities (Figure 10.2). Decades later, Elvis Presley hung the ad in his mansion.

Unlike Hopkins and Resor, MacManus wasn't a devotee of research. He wrote copy based on what he, as a consumer, would want to know. An outspoken critic of "reason-why" advertising, he argued it treated people as fools, while his approach gave them more respect (Fox 1984). His solution, seen in the Cadillac ad, was what we might call "image" advertising. MacManus

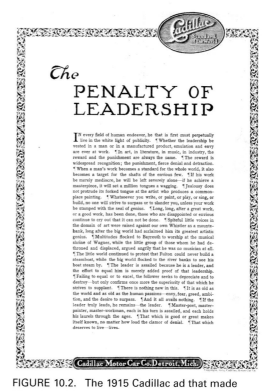

FIGURE 10.2. The 1915 Cadillac ad that made Theodore F. MacManus famous ran in the *Saturday Evening Post* that January 2.

also is remembered as a leader in advertising ethics. Ironically, this man, with a career built on automobiles, never learned to drive.

George Batten also deserves mention. His agency, George Batten Company, began in 1891 and within fifteen years had fifty employees. That was a large agency, then. It was the first ad agency to offer in-house printing, circa 1894, which was quite an innovation (Tungate 2007). His greatest fame probably came after his demise, when his agency merged with the BDO agency, forming BBDO.

BDO was created in 1919 by Bruce Barton, Roy Durstine, and Alex Osborn. Those three hired a man named John Caples, who also made a place in ad history.

Bruce Fairchild Barton published a book, *The Man Nobody Knows*, in which he presented Jesus of Nazareth as the world's greatest business executive, creating a world-altering movement with just twelve men. His book also represented advertising as a positive force for humanity. The book was controversial but propelled Barton to literary and business fame. In 1937, he was elected a US congressman.

Roy Sarles Durstine had made a name for himself in 1912 working as public relations director for Theodore Roosevelt's presidential campaign. Then he worked for Calkins & Holden, before going out on his own. In 1936, he became president of BBDO; then, in 1939, he left to found another agency. Durstine won the very first annual award for radio advertising, in 1936. His advertising approach stressed sincerity.

Alex Faickney Osborn was the creative, but he also was behind the merger with the Batten Company, creating Batten, Barton, Durstine & Osborn. Osborn is best known for introducing "brainstorming" in his 1942 book, *How to "Think Up"*. Brainstorming became a hallmark of BBDO.

John Caples, another copywriter, is remembered for composing a US School of Music's mail-order piano lessons ad in 1925: "They Laughed When I Sat Down at the Piano, But When I Started to Play!" (Figure 10.3). He became creative director for BBDO. But Caples also is known for being an advocate of testing the effectiveness of creative work, like Claude Hopkins, nudging science into advertising.

John Orr Young and Raymond Rubicam worked at N.W. Ayer, sharing an office. Young was an account man, and Rubicam a copywriter. In 1923, they took a walk, talked, and decided to start an agency. Young & Rubicam (Y&R) started in 1923. One early client, Postum, was happy with their work and promised them more business—if they'd move from Philadelphia to New York. That happened in 1926, onto Madison Avenue.

Earlier, Young had experience in newspaper space sales, and then he worked under Claude Hopkins as a copywriter at Lord & Thomas. As Fox (1984) explains it, Young quickened his leaving L&T by sending around a mock letterhead:

                                                            LOUD & PROMISE
                                                              Badvertising

A.D. Rascal, President   Cable Address: Predatory
Fraud Hopkins, V.P.

After nine years with Y&R, Young was squeezed out.

FIGURE 10.3. John Caples' most famous ad, from 1925.

Rubicam was a talented copywriter. His work included Steinway's "The Instrument of the Immortals." And Rubicam was another copywriter who believed in research. He worked with Dr. George Gallup to invent new approaches to advertising research. He had a reputation for attracting the best creative talent. During the Great Depression his agency grew while others failed, and during WWII his agency donated significant resources to the War Advertising Council.

On a sadder note, J. Stirling Getchell opened an agency in 1931, during the Depression. He had enormous impact on advertising styles, but died in 1940 at age forty-one. Before going out on his own, his first big agency job was at Lord & Thomas as a copywriter, then he cut his art direction teeth at the George Batten Company. His work was attention-getting. He used photos and a layout resembling tabloid newspapers, and is credited for making Plymouth automobiles a household name, and for coining the term "ad-maker."

Then there was Leo Noble Burnett, who opened the Leo Burnett Agency in Chicago in 1935. Known for apples at his reception desk and using Alpha 245 pencils, Burnett was another copywriter and built his agency around creatives. He believed writers should find the drama in a product and tell the story inherent in it. Research took a back seat. His agency was known for, among other things, creating advertising characters, from Tony the Tiger to the Marlboro Man. Burnett brought character to the ad business.

One copywriter who worked for Burnett must be mentioned, if only because his name was inspiration for the lead character on the television series *Mad Men*. The show's star was named Don Draper. The real adman was Draper Daniels, a character not all that unlike his TV namesake. Daniels was creative director at Burnett's agency and is credited with creating the Marlboro Man (Stein 2009).

At the end of 1942, Albert Lasker retired from Lord & Thomas. He cashed out for $10 million, passing the agency to three of his most trusted people: Emerson Foote, Fairfax Cone, and Don Belding. The agency immediately became Foote, Cone & Belding (FCB). Foote became president, even as the youngest of the three at age thirty-eight.

Emerson Foote entered advertising in 1931 as copywriter at a small San Francisco agency, but within four years he had his own agency, Yeomans & Foote. He then moved to J. Stirling Getchell, Inc., and in 1938 to Lord & Thomas, where he was account executive for Lucky Strike cigarettes.

Foote is a fascinating story. Early in life he stuttered badly, but later he was a frequent keynote speaker. As he got older, it also became clear he had bipolar disorder. He was hospitalized at one point. Soon afterward, in 1948, he was forced out of FCB after quitting the agency's largest client, American Tobacco, costing the agency 20 percent of its revenue.

But that didn't end his career. Marion Harper, chairman of McCann Erickson, hired Foote as vice president in 1952. He became president in 1960, then chairman in 1962. He'd run two of the largest agencies in the world! From 1964 to 1976, he was chair of the National Inter-Agency Council on Smoking and Health (Foote 2014).

Fairfax Mastick Cone also began in San Francisco working at a newspaper advertising desk but then became a copywriter at Lord & Thomas. Cone invented L.S./M.F.T. ("Lucky Strike Means Fine Tobacco"), which appeared in Lucky Strike ads for years (Figure 10.4). Cone believed copywriters should "[t]ell your story straight and directly to your logical audience." He was critical of the ad industry. *Time* magazine labeled him "the most respected scold of the industry." He served as president and chairman of FCB (Cone 1969).

Don Belding joined Lord & Thomas as an office boy. He, too, was a copywriter and an account manager. Belding helped organize the War Advertising Council, and later served as the company's chairman.

David Ogilvy took a circuitous route to legend status. Born in England, he started in advertising by writing an instruction manual for AGA cooking stoves. He sold stoves door to door in Scotland. His brother worked at the agency Mather & Crowther, and showed the instruction manual to his boss, leading to David's first agency job as an account executive. David eventually talked the agency into sending him to the United States for experience at George Gallup's Audience Research Institute, where he learned research. Then, during WWII, he worked for British Intelligence, where he learned propaganda. After the war he lived with the Amish in Pennsylvania.

By 1948, Ogilvy wanted back into advertising, deciding the only way into a US agency was to open his own (Tungate 2007). Having just $6,000, he convinced Mather & Crowther to help. His brother was now managing director of the agency, so it lent him money and the agency's name.

He opened Hewitt, Ogilvy, Benson & Mather on Madison Avenue in New York City. Ogilvy was vice president of research (Fox 1984). In 1953, the Hewitt name was dropped, and Benson was jettisoned in 1964, leaving Ogilvy & Mather. In 2018, it was shortened to Ogilvy.

David gained fame on several fronts, including copywriting. The watershed event was his creative concept for Hathaway shirts. A mustached Russian model was chosen for an ad. On the drive to the photo shoot, Ogilvy stopped and bought an eye patch, which he insisted the model wear for some photos. He wanted to make the man look more interesting. A photo with the patch was used for "The Man in the Hathaway Shirt" in 1951 (Figure 10.5), and demand for the shirts soared (Fox 1984). More of "The Man" ads followed. Ogilvy's fame was secure.

His work on Rolls-Royce also gained attention, including a headline he wrote: "At 60 miles an hour the loudest noise in the New Rolls-Royce comes from the electric clock." *Time* magazine in 1962 labeled him "the most sought-after wizard in today's advertising industry." By

FIGURE 10.4.   Fairfax Cone created L.S./M.F.T., as seen in this ad from 1945.

The man in the Hathaway shirt

AMERICAN MEN are beginning to realize that it is ridiculous to buy good suits and then spoil the effect by wearing an ordinary, mass-produced shirt. Hence the growing popularity of HATHAWAY shirts, which are in a class by themselves.

HATHAWAY shirts wear infinitely longer—a matter of years. They make you look younger and more distinguished, because of the subtle way HATHAWAY cut collars. The whole shirt is tailored more generously, and is therefore more comfortable. The tails are longer, and stay in your

trousers. The buttons are mother-of-pearl. Even the stitching has an antebellum elegance about it.

Above all, HATHAWAY make their shirts of remarkable fabrics, collected from the four corners of the earth—Viyella and Aertex from England, woolen taffeta from Scotland, Sea Island cotton from the West Indies, hand-woven madras from India, broadcloth from Manchester, linen batiste from Paris, hand-blocked silks from England, exclusive cottons from the best weavers in America. You will get a

great deal of quiet satisfaction out of wearing shirts which are in such impeccable taste.

HATHAWAY shirts are made by a small company of dedicated craftsmen in the little town of Waterville, Maine. They have been at it, man and boy, for one hundred and fifteen years.

At better stores everywhere, or write C. F. HATHAWAY, Waterville, Maine, for the name of your nearest store. In New York, telephone MU 9-4157. Prices from $5.50 to $25.00.

FIGURE 10.5. The 1951 ad that made David Ogilvy a legend.

his death, Ogilvy also was the most quoted advertising professional of all time.

Another copywriter, Rosser Reeves, reached fame in a very different way. He dropped out of college to work in a bank, and ended up handling the bank's advertising, then moving into an agency. His reputation was as a sales theoretician. He moved through several agencies, landing at Ted Bates Inc. in 1940, which became his professional home. He eventually served as agency chairman.

Reeves' biggest claim to fame was his idea that ads should offer a "Unique Selling Proposition" (USP), which he explained in his 1961 book, *Reality in Advertising*. He believed in logical consumers who were overwhelmed with product pitches. The advertiser's challenge was to make a simple, clear, and memorable statement setting the brand apart from others, with a benefit consumers want. He felt that once a USP is determined for a brand, the copy almost writes itself.

He once explained, "Our problem is, a client comes into my office and throws two newly minted half-dollars onto my desk and says, 'Mine is the one on the left. You prove it's better.'" The USP was his answer. This put the focus on advertising efficacy, rather than creativity. His work seldom was presented as a sample of creative excellence, but his success is undeniable.

For M&M candies, his USP was "They melt in your mouth, not in your hand." This differentiated it from other chocolate candies, offering a unique benefit. For Bic pens, it was "It writes the first time, every time." Again, this was a simple and clear benefit that differentiated the brand from the experience most consumers had with other pens. His approach built Ted Bates into a major agency.

Next on the must-know list is Bill Bernbach. In 1949, he opened an agency on Madison Avenue in New York with Ned Doyle and Maxwell Dane, joined by Bob Gage and Phyllis Robinson: Doyle Dane Bernbach (DDB). Bernbach was a copywriter who also did some art direction, but within a decade he inspired advertising's "Creative Revolution."

He was another creative who didn't embrace research, cautioning, "I warn you against believing that advertising is a science." He felt advertising was more art than science, and that too many agencies relied on science to their clients' detriment. His work for Volkswagen was what started this revolution.

It was a time of big cars with fins, but Volkswagen sold little cars called "Beetles." Bernbach, rather than downplay size, shined a light on it. In 1959, he began using headlines like "Think small" and "Lemon," showing the car had benefits (Figure 10.6). Art director Helmut Krone helped bring his vision to life. The ad industry had never seen anything like it.

Bernbach wasn't alone at DDB. Earlier in life, James E. "Ned" Doyle, a law student selling magazine ad space to pay tuition, realized he earned more money selling space than he would as a lawyer, so he dropped out. In 1936, he became the first advertising director for *Look* magazine, where he met Maxwell Dane. Doyle moved to *Good Housekeeping* just before WWII. He served in the Marines, but after the war he joined Grey Advertising, where he met the agency's creative director, Bill Bernbach. In 1949, he and Bernbach—now vice presidents at Grey—went out on their own and invited Dane to join them.

Maxwell "Mac" Dane owned an agency, Maxwell Dane Inc., when Doyle and Bernbach approached him. Dane became the business side of DDB, though his experi-

Think small.

FIGURE 10.6. This ad clearly illustrated the "weakness" of a Volkswagen Beetle, while proving it to be an asset, kicking off the "Creative Revolution" in 1959.

ence was broader. He started his career selling newspaper space, moved to a department store, then a newspaper, and finally to an ad agency, where he served as both account executive and copywriter. He moved to *Look* as advertising/promotion manager, then to a radio station, before opening his own agency in 1944. Dane holds the distinction of being among the twenty names on President Nixon's enemies list.

Howard Luck Gossage was a "copywriter who influenced ad-makers worldwide" and a self-described iconoclast, which is an understatement. He was quirky but made his career in advertising. He's been described as an adman who hated advertising. He built an agency—Freeman, Mander & Gossage—in a repurposed firehouse in San Francisco's old Barbary Shore area. He was famous for long-copy ads for Fina Oil and Chemical Company, Qantas Airlines, and Heileman Brewing Company. One Fina ad was all headline, in *pink* all caps, saying, "IF YOU'RE DRIVING DOWN THE ROAD AND YOU SEE A FINA STATION AND IT'S ON YOUR SIDE SO YOU DON'T HAVE TO MAKE A U-TURN THROUGH TRAFFIC AND THERE AREN'T SIX CARS WAITING AND YOU NEED GAS OR SOMETHING ** PLEASE STOP IN."

Some of his most interesting work was outside the commercial world. He promoted the Sierra Club and helped found Friends of the Earth. This was his "persuasion for the better." And he played a key role in the Anguillan Revolution, which I'll describe later.

Hosting characters like John Steinbeck, Tom Wolfe, Marshall McLuhan, and Buckminster Fuller at his firehouse "Salon," he was known for off-beat ideas. He even created fads. To help a local classical radio station, he connected it with Rainier Ale. The beer company was a paying client, while the radio station had little money. So he combined efforts, creating Beethoven, Brahms, and Bach sweatshirts and an ad campaign encouraging people to proudly display their snobbiness. "Be the first highbrow in your neighborhood to own a Beethoven, Brahms, or Bach sweatshirt," screamed the headline. And the shirts sold!

Called the "Socrates of San Francisco," Gossage was an "advertising is art" advocate. He once said, "The object of your advertising should not be to communicate with your consumers or your prospects at all, but to terrorize your competition's copywriters."

Then there's George Lois, who spent about a year with Bernbach at DDB, winning multiple awards for art direction while there. In 1960, Fred Papert, an account guy, and Julian Koenig, a copywriter, asked Lois to join them to create an agency: Papert Koenig Lois (PKL). It was built on the same model as DDB, with creative work as its centerpiece, and was just the second agency ever to go public on the US Stock Exchange. Lois wasn't a big believer in research, either. PKL became a major player in the Creative Revolution, and Lois was a major figure.

Lois did an ad for Xerox (the Haloid Company at that time, though George says PKL convinced the company to change its name), showing how easy it was to use its copiers. Previously, copying was messy and complicated. Lois made a commercial showing a little girl visiting her dad's office and making a copy for him on the Xerox copier. The main Xerox competitor, A.B. Dick, complained to the FTC, saying this was fraud—no kid could run such a complex machine. The FTC ordered them to stop running it. Lois re-shot the commercial. This time he invited FTC investigators. Instead of a little girl, a chimpanzee made the copy (Figure 10.7). The chimp succeeded. Both commercials were shown on a CBS news show, getting immense publicity.

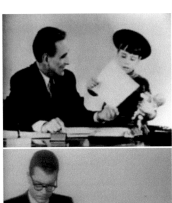

FIGURE 10.7. The top image is a frame from Lois' original commercial for Xerox, and the bottom is from the remake using the chimp.

Lois' fame was for both his talent and his personality. Over time he was inducted into the One Club Creative Hall of Fame, the American Advertising Federation's Hall of Fame, and the Art Directors Hall of Fame. He received Lifetime Achievement Awards from the American Institute of Graphic Arts and the Society of Publication Designers.

He is known for designing ninety-two different covers for *Esquire* magazine, from 1962 to 1972, but also did extraordinary advertising for clients that included Robert F. Kennedy, MTV, Tommy Hilfiger, *USA Today*, and more. In 1968, he left PKL to form Lois Holland Callaway, leaving there a decade later for other positions, then created another agency, Lois/USA, in 1991.

The focus so far has been on men. It had been an extremely male-dominated profession, so the biggest names were male. The Creative Revolution, though, also made it possible for women to get notice. Mary Wells, later known as Mary Wells Lawrence, was a huge part of the revolution.

Wells was a copywriter for department stores, then moved to McCann Erickson, and later to DDB. Then she jumped to Jack Tinker & Partners, where she completely reworked Braniff International Airways' image, even repainting their aircrafts and creating new crew uniforms. That campaign was noticed.

In 1966, she founded Wells Rich Greene, serving as its president. That agency created iconic commercials of the 1960s and 1970s, including Alka-Seltzer's "Plop, plop, fizz, fizz, oh what a relief it is" and its "I can't believe I ate the whole thing" campaigns, as well as "Trust the Midas touch" for Midas Mufflers, "Flick your Bic" for Bic pens, and I♥NY. Fox (1984) claims, "[S]he was the richest, most celebrated woman in the history of the business."

William Montague "Bill" Backer was the mind behind one of the most famous television commercials ever, the Coca-Cola "Hilltop" commercial featuring "I'd like to teach the world to sing." Backer worked for McCann Erickson at that time. He'd started in the mailroom in 1953, but soon started writing jingles. By the early 1970s, he turned out some of the most memorable jingles in the business, including Coca-Cola's "It's the Real Thing," and "If you've got the time, we've got the beer" for Miller High Life. The "Hilltop" commercial was in 1971, and it made him a true star. He was elevated to creative director of McCann in 1972, and in 1978 to vice chairman.

In 1979, Backer joined Carl Spielvogel to create Backer & Spielvogel. It later merged with Ted Bates to became Backer Spielvogel Bates, for which he served as vice chairman and worldwide creative director. But it was Backer who taught the ad world to sing.

Keith Reinhard was yet another copywriter and the creative mind behind McDonald's restaurants' "You Deserve a Break Today" campaign, the McDonaldland characters, and my personal favorite (circa 1974), "Two-all-beef-patties-special-sauce-lettuce-cheese-pickles-onions on a sesame seed bun." He's also responsible for the State Farm insurance company's "Like a Good Neighbor, State Farm is There." His creative work alone would put him on any "legends of advertising" list.

On top of that, Reinhard rose to lead the Needham Harper agency. In that role he engineered creation of a leading advertising conglomerate: Omnicom. He later led the DDB Worldwide, and then was chairman emeritus of the DDB Worldwide Communications Group. Amazingly, this "king of TV advertising" grew up in a Mennonite community, where he couldn't watch television.

Oliviero Toscani is a unique figure in advertising history. He had a strong reputation as a fashion photographer, doing work for stand-out brands like Chanel and Esprit. But those

accomplishments wouldn't rank him among the ad elite. His work as art director for Benetton, which hired him in 1982, makes him worth listing here (Tungate 2007). His early work for Benetton was unremarkable, but over time he broke the molds for fashion brands, creating a series of provocative, even offensive, ads (e.g., Figure 10.8).

His work was controversial but effective at propelling Benetton to the forefront of public awareness. Toscani's work was the virtual definition of "shockvertising," using shocking content to gain attention (Parry et al. 2013).

FIGURE 10.8. In 1992, this Benetton ad, by Oliviero Toscani, became a topic of debate around the world.

Toscani worked there until 2000, but he returned to Benetton in 2017. But thanks to an offensive remark he made in a radio interview, regarding a bridge collapse that killed forty-three people, he was fired in 2020.

No list of advertising legends should omit Lee Clow. He had been inspired by the Creative Revolution and Bernbach. He became an art director at N.W. Ayer's West Coast office. But

Clow's personal style was more California beach sandals than New York pinstripe suit. In 1973, he joined a California agency called Chiat/Day, which fit his style. A few years into that job, he reached the advertising stratosphere with the "1984" commercial for Apple Computer (Figure 10.9). It broke all previous molds.

Clow did more exceptional work for Apple over the years, including the "Think Different" campaign, as well as for brands like Taco Bell and Adidas. He retired in 2019, publishing a Valentine's Day "love letter" to the advertising industry, part of which read, "The years I spent doing this thing called advertising have been fun, chal-

FIGURE 10.9. Apple Computer's 1984 commercial, the brainchild of Lee Clow, Steve Hayden, and Brent Thomas, introduced the Macintosh computer.

lenging, rewarding, maddening, sometimes painful, but mostly joyful. And I wouldn't trade a day of it for anything else."

One more copywriter, Dan Wieden, deserves note, though I should tip my hat to his art director partner, David Kennedy, too. They formed the Wieden & Kennedy agency on April Fools' Day in 1982. Wieden is probably best known for Nike's "Just Do It" in 1988. He wrote this after hearing that a double-murderer named Gary Gilmore, facing a firing squad, said, "Let's do it." *Campaign* magazine called it "arguably the best tagline of the 20th Century." By the 1990s, Wieden & Kennedy was one of the hottest firms in the United States. It grew from 4 people to more than 1,400, and was named National Agency of the Year in both 1991 and 1996. Wieden's reputation was one of "rule breaking."

There are so many other names I'd love to include, like Armando Testa ("father of Italian advertising"), but space is limited. There are others I discuss under other headings. Note that almost every name here was a copywriter. It's not that account people, researchers, and others weren't influential, but creativity is at the center of the ad industry, and the 1900s were when creativity truly shined. And speaking of creativity . . .

DOING ADVERTISING WRITE

Ad copywriting styles have evolved, and devolved, over time. If you look at ads before the mid-nineteenth century, it is a study in boring. Most ads told *what* was for sale and little more. There were exceptions, but most of those were deceptive. And there were a few true innovators like Thomas Bish's lottery ads. But there was almost no competition, since that was before the era of branding. In the late 1800s, consumers encountered brand choices, which is when writing really became important.

John E. Powers is credited as the first copywriter with a distinctive style, circa 1880. Called the "Powers Style," his approach was heavy in facts and honesty, avoiding exaggeration. He wrote in ordinary, not flowery, language. Powers saw advertising as a form of news. Working for Wanamaker's department store, Powers once said:

> Print the news of the store. No "catchy headings," no catches, no headings, no smartness, no brag, no "fine writing," no fooling, no foolery, no attempt at advertising, no anxiety to sell, no mercenary admiration; hang up the goods in the papers, one at a time, a few today, tomorrow the same or others.

The next step in the evolution of copy was John E. Kennedy, circa 1905. Recall Kennedy is remembered for saying advertising is "salesmanship in print." He focused on facts, but his facts were about providing a specific reason to buy, which came to be known as "reason-why" advertising. This quickly became the field's dominant style.

Beard (2005) does a wonderful job of tracing these styles and the role of humor in these various incarnations. He points out that humor was largely shunned in both the Powers and the Kennedy approaches.

Theodore MacManus was the anti-Kennedy, focusing on impressionistic, image-oriented methods. This was the "soft-sell," while reason-why ads were more "hard-sell." His ads appealed to emotion, not reason. Neither embraced humor, but by the 1920s advertisers were becoming more accepting of humor and entertainment in ads. There still were many who rejected it. Lord & Thomas was even running ads warning advertisers not to rely on "cleverness," or even novelty, in ads (Beard 2005).

Rosser Reeves' Unique Selling Proposition (USP) in the 1940s was a refinement of the reason-why approach. It said that an advertiser should identify a reason why that is unique to its brand, and promote that. Reeves found a lot of devotees.

By the 1950s and 1960s, David Ogilvy was gaining fame, relying on both the hard-sell and the soft-sell styles, while Leo Burnett leaned heavily on soft-sell. Ogilvy shunned humor; Burnett capitalized on it (Beard 2005). Bill Bernbach was another one not afraid of humor.

The tension between reason-why (or USP) and image styles continued into the twenty-first century, as did humor versus serious appeals. Popular entertainment like television shows, tabloids, and video games affected society's acceptance of humor and entertainment, so both became more common. But events like the terrorist attacks on the World Trade Center in 2001 put limits, for a time, on the use of humor (Beard 2005).

Advertising "creatives," when talking about a campaign's creative concept, often use the term "Big Idea," referring to the story told in the ad, including whether it is to be funny or serious or something else entirely. The Big Idea makes this ad different from, and hopefully better than, ads by competitors.

George Lois (with Bill Pitts, 1991) wrote a book about the Big Idea. Some say it was Lois who coined this phrase, and others claim it came from David Ogilvy. But the earliest printed mention of the Big Idea was by Daniel Starch in 1914: "Such work is largely evolution—it cannot be developed in a moment nor created out of a session of thinking with the purpose of finding a 'big idea' around which to operate." Bernbach's creating a VW ad with "Lemon" as the headline was built on the Big Idea of using what appear to be critical remarks as irony. That tapped both humor and surprise to deliver the claim. There actually was a USP in the Lemon ad, but it contained so much more than just that.

University of Oregon professor Dr. Deborah Morrison claims an advertisement must both "work and reward." To her, an ad must be strategically driven *and* make a genuine audience connection. The reason-why and USP are both about the strategy of what the advertiser wants to communicate, and image advertising is about a longer-term strategy. But the reward is where humor fits. It is a reason for the consumer to pay attention to the ad.

In the late 1900s and beyond, more rewards were developed, beyond humor. "Activations" (discussed later) are forms of reward that get consumers *actively* involved with a brand. Promoting a camera by having consumers take a picture with it is one example of activation. Not all activations involve copywriting, but not all ads involve copy, either. While the soft- and hard-sell methods continued, the rewards seem to embody some of the biggest changes since the 1960s, following the Creative Revolution.

THE REVOLUTION WITHIN

Advertising was undergoing lots of changes, including the appearance of ads. From around 1880 to 1920, illustrations became far more common (Pope 1983). The 1920s saw a rise of art deco styles in advertising and architecture (Mierau 2000). And illustrations evolved from drawings to paintings to photography (Pollay 1985).

But the most talked-about change was the Creative Revolution, beginning in 1959. Even more than sixty years later, it remains a topic of discussion.

This Revolution certainly was about the quality and innovation of creative work, but that was a symptom not a cause. George Lois worked for Bernbach at the kickoff and almost immediately helped push this Revolution (it deserves a capital R). I asked George what really happened. His response:

> What set the Advertising Creative Revolution of the 1960s apart from anything before it was Bill Bernbach. It was Bill who first put a copywriter and art director in the same room and locked the door (figuratively of course) and let them create together.
>
> This was a transformative concept. From that point on advertising changed. Time honored rules were broken and creativity flowed in advertising. Also the talent at DDB at the time was remarkable. Bob Gage, Bill Taubin, Helmut Krone, Phylis Lambert, Paul Rand, and me, all helped to move advertising in a new and distinctly different direction.
>
> When I left and started the second creative ad agency in the world, Papert Koenig Lois, that was the second phase of the revolution. Then, some of the people who worked with me, Mary Wells, Sam Scali, Len Sirowitz went out on their own. This opened the flood gates, and advertising was never the same.
>
> Also, before the Creative Revolution, the "creative" people sat in a room with their thumbs up their ass waiting for the marketing people to give them some facts and usually a terrible advertising idea to work from.
>
> Then came the Creative Revolution where two people went into a room and locked the door, and didn't come out until the art director and the copywriter came out with a great ad campaign.

The team concept, then, was central to this Revolution. It empowered ad creatives.

Reviewing ads of the 1930s, 1940s, and 1950s, you can imagine corporate executives rejecting creative ideas, saying, "We're a highly regarded business, and that's not business-like. It's just not professional!" And this also was during the growth of research, which was seeking better ways to *persuade* consumers (Fox 1984). Almost without exception those ads were simple and straightforward, conveying product facts and features. Even when it veered into telling a story, the story would be unimaginative. Samuel (2012) notes:

> Pre-Bernbach, a copywriter would deliver his or her copy . . . to an art director who would then add a complementary visual. . . . Although a copywriter himself, Bernbach recognized the synergies to be created by abandoning this assembly-line approach for one that took full advantage of the talents of each member of the team.

Once the Revolution began, more and more ads used humor, metaphor, irony, surprise, and even absurdity to engage consumers. This might be an outcome of the "group think" team approach, but the VW campaign alone showed other businesses it was possible to take themselves a little less seriously. It revealed the power of genuinely creative advertising, so others gave it a try. It snowballed, and suddenly it was "in vogue" for agencies to push creativity boundaries. Creative competition between agencies exploded, forcing even more conservative firms to reach beyond their comfort zones.

This happened simultaneously with the 1960s *social* revolution, which pushed all of society outside its previous limits. In the 1950s, men wore hats, dark ties, and white shirts to work. A decade later, much of that was gone. The creativity unleashed in advertising found expression in music, art, and elsewhere. Bernbach had the right idea at the right time.

Legendary adman John Hegarty recalled:

> What [Bernbach's work] did was create an entire generation who actually wanted to work advertising. Before us, advertising people still secretly yearned to be artists and novelists. But we wanted to be part of that whole sixties revolution in music, fashion and design—and we felt we could do that through advertising. (Tungate 2007)

Some of history's most memorable advertising came out of that. Other admen, like David Ogilvy, were not directly influenced by Bernbach but absolutely were part of the revolution. It seems fair to say the next sixty-plus years echoed the lessons from that time.

AGENCY BIRTHDAYS AND GROWTH

Agencies born into twentieth-century advertising are too numerous to cover. And even older agencies were changing. N.W. Ayer, in just the year 1900, added both copy and business-getting departments. This was the age of "service agencies," in which agents offered a range of services to clients. But several agencies and developments need mention here.

Agencies began popping up in other countries. A major Japanese agency, Dentsu, got its start in 1901 when a journalist, Hoshiro Mitsunaga, created Telegraph Service Company, a news agency. It became an advertising agency only because newspapers bought stories from Mitsunaga but paid with advertising space instead of cash. He created a subsidiary, Japan Advertising, to sell that space. In 1907, it was consolidated under the name Nippon Denpo-Tsushin Sha, later shortened to Dentsu (Tungate 2007). In 1974, *Advertising Age* magazine named it the world's largest agency. Dentsu's main Japanese competitor was Hakuhodo, founded in 1895.

In Australia, Thomas A. Miller established an agency around 1902, quickly followed by Harry J. Weston's agency. In 1905, the first Indian agency, B. Dattaram and Company, was formed. And the first Ottoman Empire agency, Ilancilik Kollektif Sirketi, was opened in 1909.

Agencies of note since 1900 are shown in Table 10.1.

This list isn't exhaustive. Before the Civil War, there were about 30 US agencies; by one estimate in 2020, more than 120,000 existed. Across the planet there are perhaps half a million. Whether or not that's accurate, the numbers are big. But most memorable ads from your childhood likely originated with one of the agencies on this list.

One change in agencies over that time was their international reach. In 1937, just four American agencies were international, but by 1960 there were thirty-six, with 281 offices globally (Nevett 1982). They were even more aggressive after that. Few American agencies

Table 10.1. Major Agencies by Date of Creation

Year	Agency	Location
1901	Dentsu	Japan (Tokyo)
1902	Miller Agency	*Australia (Sydney)
1902	Weston Company	Australia (Sydney)
1905	B. Dattaram and Company	*India (Mumbai)
1906	D'Arcy Advertising (later D'Arcy MacManus)	USA (St. Louis, MO)
1909	Ilancilik Kollektif Sirketi	*Ottoman Empire
1911	Campbell Ewald	USA (Detroit, MI)
1911	H. K. McCann	USA (New York, NY)
1914	Escritorio Tecnico de Publicidade	*Portugal (Lisbon)
1917	Grey Studios (later called Grey Advertising)	USA (New York, NY)
1918	BDO (Barton, Durstine & Osborn)	USA (New York, NY)
1918	Carl Crow agency	China (Shanghai)
1919	Rudolph Guenther-Russell Law (later The Gate Worldwide)	USA (Chicago, IL)
1921	Bozell & Jacobs (later Bozell Worldwide)	USA (Omaha, NE)
1923	Young & Rubicam	USA (Philadelphia, PA)
1923	Blackett & Sample (Dancer Fitzgerald Sample)	USA (Chicago, IL)
1925	Maurice H. Needham Co. (later Needham Harper Steers)	USA (Chicago, IL)
1928	BBDO (via merger)	USA (New York, NY)
1928	West African Publicity, Ltd.	*Nigeria (Lagos)
1926	Publicis	France (Paris)
1929	Benton & Bowles	USA (New York, NY)
1930	McCann Erickson (via merger)	USA (New York, NY)
1935	Leo Burnett Company	USA (Chicago, IL)
1937	W. B. Doner & Co. (later Doner Company)	USA (Baltimore, MD)
1937	Compton Advertising (formerly Blackman Adv.)	USA (New York, NY)
1940	Ted Bates, Inc.	USA (New York, NY)
1943	Foote Cone & Belding (formerly Lord & Thomas)	USA (Chicago, IL)
1946	Sullivan, Stauffer, Colwell & Bayles	USA (New York, NY)
1948	Hewitt, Ogilvy, Benson & Mather (later Ogilvy)	USA (New York, NY)
1949	Doyle Dane Bernbach	USA (New York, NY)
1956	Studio Armando Testa	Italy (Turin)
1956	Vince Cullers Advertising	USA (Chicago, IL)
1959	GGK	Switzerland (Basel)
1960	Papert Koenig Lois	USA (New York, NY)
1960	Collett Dickenson Pearce & Partners	England (London)
1962	Carmichael Lynch	USA (Minneapolis, MN)
1965	Crispin Advertising (later Crispin Porter + Bogusky)	USA (Miami, FL)
1965	Martin & Woltz (later the Martin Agency)	USA (Richmond, VA)
1966	Wells, Rich, Greene	USA (New York, NY)
1967	Della Femina Travisano & Partners	USA (New York, NY)
1967	Scali McCabe Sloves	USA (New York, NY)
1968	Chiat/Day/Hoefer (via merger)	USA (Los Angeles, CA)
1969	David Deutsch Assoc. (later Deutsch Inc.)	USA (New York, NY)
1969	UniWorld	USA (New York, NY)
1970	Saatchi & Saatchi	England (London)
1970	TBWA	France (Paris)
1971	Burrell McBain (later Burrell Communications)	USA (Chicago, IL)
1971	Wire & Plastic Products (later WPP)	England (London)
1971	GSD&M	USA (Austin, TX)
1973	Ammirati Puris AvRutick (later Ammirati Puris Lintas)	USA (New York, NY)
1973	Cheil Communications (later Cheil Worldwide)	South Korea (Seoul)
1977	Abbott Mead Vickers	England (London)

(continued)

Table 10.1. *Continued*

Year	Agency	Location
1979	Mojo	Australia (Sydney)
1980	Sosa and Assoc. (later Bromley Communications)	USA (San Antonio, TX)
1980	Eastern Exclusives (later Digitas)	USA (Boston, MA)
1981	Fallon McElligott Rice	USA (Minneapolis, MN)
1982	Wieden & Kennedy	USA (Portland, OR)
1982	Scanad (later Scangroup)	Kenya (Nairobi)
1982	Bartle Bogle Hegarty	England (London)
1983	Goodby, Berlin & Silverstein	USA (San Francisco, CA)
1983	Fred/Alan, Inc.	USA (New York, NY)
1983	Hunt Lascaris	South Africa (Johannesburg)
1986	Omnicom (via merger)	USA (New York, NY)
1990	John Knowles Richie	England (London)
1994	Razorfish	USA (New York, NY)
1994	AKQA	England (London)
1995	M&C Saatchi	England (London)
1996	Mother	England (London)
2002	McGarryBowen	USA (New York, NY)
2006	Droga5	USA (New York, NY)
2011	CJ Worx	Thailand (Bangkok)
2011	Digital Jungle	China (Beijing)

*First agency in that geographic area

were in the Netherlands as of 1960, but by 1980 there was "a true American invasion" (Roling 2011). Though American agencies were dominant, by the 1980s British agencies were catching up, particularly in creative excellence (Clark 1988).

In 1992, there was another challenge. Michael Ovitz owned a talent agency called Creative Artists Associates, in Beverly Hills. CAA shocked the ad industry by stealing the Coca-Cola account away from ad agencies, though it did work together with McCann Erickson. Other major advertisers soon negotiated with CAA. But most never signed, and Coke ended its affiliation with CAA after three years (Elliott 2000).

CAA ultimately failed, but it put advertising agencies on notice that they were vulnerable. But another vulnerability already had been exposed. Several agencies had gone public.

AGENCIES GO PUBLIC

In 1929, ten days before the stock market crash that started the Great Depression, the Rudolph Guenther-Russell Law agency sold a small amount of agency stock to the public. This was the first agency to go public. It ended up buying back its stock.

The next agency to go public was Papert Koenig Lois in 1962, followed by Foote, Cone & Belding in 1963 (Figure 10.10) and Doyle Dane Bernbach in 1964 (Appel 2017b). Grey Advertising followed in 1965, with Ogilvy & Mather in 1966 and Wells Rich Greene in 1968. In 1969, the world's largest agency, J. Walter Thompson, joined in. Five of those seven were among the world's ten largest agencies (Fox 1984).

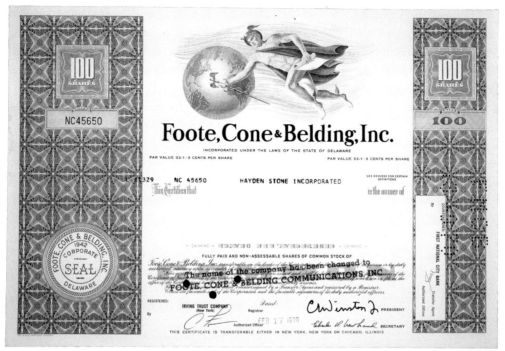

FIGURE 10.10. Stock certificate of Foote, Cone & Belding, one of the earliest of the big agencies to go public.

Both Grey and Wells bought back their shares five years later. But others, including Young & Rubicam in 1998, went public. But the bigger picture is the story of the industry's "merger mania," which created major public offerings.

AGENCY MARRIAGES

Around 1900, Lord & Thomas was America's largest agency (Turner 1953). Its annual billings were under $1 million. By 1912, billings were $6 million, reaching $18.8 million in 1926. Its name changed to Foote, Cone & Belding, and its 1991 billings exceeded $5 billion. That's one agency! Agencies became big business and were attractive for takeover.

One agency subsuming another has happened since the mid-1800s. But the dominoes of acquisition really began with a company called Interpublic, thanks to McCann Erickson.

McCann Erickson (ME) itself was the result of a merger: H. K. McCann Company and Erickson Company in 1930. But under the direction of Marion Harper, in 1960 ME created the Interpublic Group (IPG). It was a holding company, and ME was now a subsidiary. IPG acquired the Pritchard Wood agency in 1961 and passed J. Walter Thompson to become the world's biggest advertising company (Tungate 2007). This was only the start of IPG collecting agencies; for example, it picked up Erwin, Wasey, Ruthrauff & Ryan in 1963. IPG slowed for a while but in the 1970s made some notable acquisitions, including Campbell-Ewald in

1973 and Sullivan, Stauffer, Colwell & Bayles (SSC&B) in 1979. A later important acquisition was the Lowe Group in 1990. IPG became a mega-agency, or conglomeration of agencies.

Others were merging, too. But the Saatchi brothers, Maurice and Charles, really kicked off the industry's merger mania in 1972. Their British agency, Saatchi & Saatchi (S&S), took over a few companies between 1972 and 1975. But they then managed a clever "reverse takeover" of London-based Garland Compton. Through this, they went public overnight and got the funding needed for the purchase. Over the next dozen years they swallowed about thirty-five companies, most being ad agencies, including major firms like Compton Advertising, Dorland Advertising, Ted Bates, Backer & Spielvogel, and Dancer Fitzgerald Sample. It also included market research firms, including Yankelovich Skelly & White.

In 1982, the foundation was laid for "the big bang" in advertising. Keith Reinhard took the reins at Needham Harper Steers and called a staff meeting, announcing:

> Look, we have to do something. We're the number 16 agency in the world. It seems clear to me that the advertising industry is going to become a two-tiered business. There will always be vitality in the bottom tier, the boutique agencies. And then there will be a top tier of maybe six or seven giants. There will be no middle. Unfortunately, we're in the middle. And we better find a way out. (Tungate 2007)

Reinhard's vision was prescient.

He tried to seduce Doyle Dane Bernbach (DDB), without success, then worked on Allen Rosenshine at BBDO. Reinhard and Rosenshine, together, worked on key figures at DDB. Eventually the three agencies—three of the top twenty—merged, staggering the entire industry in 1986. This new king-of-the-hill was named Omnicom and was the *world's largest agency*. Combined annual billings were about $5 billion. A few conflicts of interest were created, costing about $250 million in billings, but that was a small consequence.

The Saatchi brothers had tried to take over DDB but were undercut by Reinhard and Rosenshine. So S&S went after, and won, Ted Bates in 1988, reaching annual billings of $7.5 billion and making it the *world's largest agency*. Unfortunately, a 1987 stock market crash created problems. By 1989's close, S&S had laid off seven thousand employees, and in 1994 Maurice was removed as chairman. His brother soon followed.

Martin Sorrell worked for the Saatchi brothers from 1977 to 1984 and directed many takeovers. He then bought a British shopping basket maker, Wire and Plastic Products (WPP), in 1985. Over the next three years he acquired eighteen advertising-related companies. One, in 1987, caught the ad world's attention in a big way: J. Walter Thompson. Hill & Knowlton public relations also was subsumed at that time. Sorrell then engineered a hostile takeover of Ogilvy & Mather, in 1989, and Young & Rubicam (Y&R) and Grey Advertising, both major global networks. The Y&R deal in 2000 was the largest advertising takeover ever, making WPP the *biggest agency in the world*. It continued to dominate, but Sorrell left WPP under a cloud in 2018, forming S4 Capital.

Then there is Publicis, a leading agency in France for decades. In 1972, its headquarters burned, two years after going public. It would have lost all its records if not for Maurice Lévy, who saved its computer data. He later became the agency's president.

Publicis had been around since 1926 and had acquired other firms, but its move toward superpower status began in 1988 after buying 20 percent of Foote, Cone, & Belding (FCB). In 1993, it acquired the Feldman, Calleux et Associés (FCA) advertising network. By 1996, it had swallowed other agencies and found that most of its revenue was from outside France. In 1998, it acquired Hal Riney & Partners, and the next year it took a 49 percent interest in Burrell Communications. In 2000, it took over Fallon McElligott, and then in 2001 it secured Saatchi & Saatchi. All told, Publicis has acquired seventy organizations, including some major takeovers.

Dentsu is a different story. Founded in 1901, for decades it was the dominant advertising force in Japan. Owning a news service, it influenced media in ways Western agencies didn't, though it suffered after the Japanese government opened a news service in 1936. In the 1950s, Dentsu invested in radio and television networks, making it a media owner, and consequently a very powerful agency, able to negotiate advertising rates and placements others never could.

Dentsu also hired influential people's relatives, building an unprecedented network of influence and creating a monopoly over major Japanese companies, even direct competitors like Datsun (Nissan) and Honda. Conflicts of interest were sidestepped by physically separating the account groups. The company grew and grew, especially as the Japanese economy exploded in the 1960s and 1970s.

Dentsu formed alliances with some Western agencies, such as McCann Erickson in 1960, J. Walter Thompson in 1974, Young & Rubicam in 1981, and Eurocom France in 1987. Those connections, particularly Y&R, leveraged its presence in other countries. But Dentsu also was one of the first outside agencies to open an office in China, in 1981. In the early 1990s, though, Dentsu began its takeover streak.

In 2013, Omnicom and Publicis announced a merger. It fell through, though, after a struggle for control between Publicis' Maurice Levy and Omnicom's John Wren (Davies, Kim, & Abboud 2014).

By 2018, the world's top five agencies were:

Agency	Location	Worldwide Revenue (billions)
WPP Group	London	$19
Omnicom Group	New York	$15.3
Publicis Groupe	Paris	$9.6
Interpublic Group	New York	$7.5
Dentsu	Tokyo	$6

Source: WorldAtlas

All were products of merger and acquisition.

It is difficult to track all of their properties, but as of 2014 these major holding companies included a wide variety of brands. Below is a list of major holdings of each from that year.

WPP

Young & Rubicam Group
Ogilvy & Mather
J. Walter Thompson Company
Grey Group
WPP Digital
United Network
GroupM
TenthAvenue
Hill & Knowlton Strategies PR
Others
Omnicom Group
DDB Worldwide Communications Group
BBDO Worldwide
TBWA Worldwide
Goodby, Silverstein & Partners
GSD&M
MarketStar

Omnicom Media Group

CDM Group
Medical Specialist Communications
LLNS
FleishmanHillard PR
Ketchum PR
Porter Novelli PR
Marina Maher Communications PR
Others

Publicis Groupe

Publicis Worldwide
Leo Burnett Worldwide
DigitasLBI
Saatchi & Saatchi
Bartle Bogle Hegarty
Bromley Communications
Fallon
Razorfish
Rosetta
Starcom Mediavest Group
ZenithOptimedia
Publicis Healthcare Comm. Group
MLS Group PR
Others

Interpublic Group

McCann Worldgroup
FCB
Lowe & Partners Worldwide
Carmichael Lynch
Deutsch
Hill Holliday
GolinHarris PR
IPG Mediabrands
Others
Dentsu Inc.
Dentsu
Dentsu Aegis Network

You can see that each holding company absorbed some of history's most influential agencies. This provides a fair overview of the five companies controlling much (most?) of the world's advertising business.

Merger mania changed everything. Of the one hundred biggest agencies of the 1980s, two-thirds were taken over by the 1990s. But in spite of this frenzy, some agencies also were *dividing*, creating spin-offs.

SPIN-OFFS

Around 1990, media functions within agencies were spotlighted. Some agencies created dedicated media units and others spun-off media operations (Appel 2017a). In 1992, Bozell

Worldwide created BJK&E Media, and Grey Advertising established Media Connections. N.W. Ayer in 1994 founded Media Edge, WPP created MindShare, McCann Erickson made Universal McCann, and Omnicom launched OMD (Roling 2011). In 1995, Saatchi & Saatchi opened Zenith Media in the United States, and in 1997 Leo Burnett converted its media department into Starcom. This trend, pulling media out of agencies and making them separate companies, was pervasive. One ad exec argued, "Separating media from creative was the worst mistake the industry ever made" (Tungate 2007).

Separate media companies helped small and boutique agencies with no dedicated media personnel. But the media function controlled the money, historically. Commissions were based on a percent of media purchased, so moving that function outside meant surrendering control over the money. But the timing was good, with the spread of the internet, since it undermined the entire commission structure.

COMMISSIONS (AGAIN) AND COMPENSATION

Commissions were born with agencies. When agencies did nothing but buy and resell media, commissions were a perfect revenue solution. As services like creative production were added, however, there was no direct connection between the amount of media purchased and the amount of service being provided. Initially the size of the commission was adjusted to be large enough to fund those services, but then research was added, and package design, and more "ancillary" services. The more services offered, the more clients wanted . . . all for the same commission (Fox 1984).

Commissions weren't just a problem for agencies, but also for clients. There was no incentive for agencies to pinch pennies when buying media. The more they spent, the more money they made. Few agencies would confess, but television advertising became popular partly because it cost more than other media, and agencies got a percentage.

National media didn't care much for the commission system, because it was a kickback to agencies, and advertisers who avoided agencies still paid the higher (gross) rate. Media profited more from them, so preferred not to pay agency commissions.

Recall that commissions, since 1887, were set by the American Newspaper Publishers' Association, forcing newspapers, rather than advertisers, to pay agencies. It leveled out at 15 percent of media buys. Other media (magazines, radio, TV) later adopted that approach. In 1919, the Curtis Publishing Company, a dominant player in magazines, announced it would pay recognized agencies a 15 percent commission, with the qualifier that any agency rebating any of the commission to an advertiser would be cut off (Wood 1958). This innovation helped stabilize commissions at 15 percent across all paid media.

The US Justice Department in 1956 accused the American Association of Advertising Agencies (AAAA) of price fixing, declaring this system disadvantaged advertisers wanting to avoid agencies. The basic approach didn't end, but it created opportunities for other approaches.

Four years later, in 1960, David Ogilvy began undermining the commission system. He stole the Shell Oil account from J. Walter Thompson by proposing a fee-based system rather than a commission. He believed a fee system was morally superior, because profit didn't depend on clients' spending level. Many competitors disagreed, and Thompson's president argued Ogilvy would destroy the agency system. But Ogilvy's agency nearly doubled in size (Roman 2009). This did, though, slam wide the door to Pandora's box.

In 1990, IBM hired consultants to review its ad agency compensations, resulting in IBM moving to a performance-based method. This action might have been why other companies did the same. And fee-based compensation schemes already were becoming more popular.

Fees worked well for advertisers buying their own media, since they now could choose whether to hire agencies. It also worked well for agencies handling business-to-business clients, as they frequently spent less on media (Spake et al. 1999).

The internet, commercialized in the 1990s, altered the advertising world in multiple ways. Now clients demanded their agencies create internet ads, and even websites, but the cost of that service could not be absorbed by commissions. The media cost was negligible, but the work was enormous.

Also, clients pressured agencies to reduce commissions. In 1987, the $150 million Nissan account was up for review, but it offered only 8 percent of billings as compensation. Ogilvy and Mather pulled out of competition for the account. Its US chairman stated, "If you pay peanuts, you get monkeys" (Jones 1999). Studies by the Association of National Advertisers (ANA) found that in 1992 less than half of agencies were paid reduced rates (less than 15 percent), but by 1995 it was over three-quarters (Spake et al. 1999).

This was fertile ground for fee-based approaches. Some agencies tried incentive-based systems, where compensation would escalate by meeting established performance benchmarks. By 2000, the 15 percent commission method was largely history, though it was used as a benchmark for judging other methods (Albarda 2018).

Coca-Cola pushed a "value-based" compensation in 2009, which would guarantee agencies nothing but out-of-pocket costs for underperformance of key performance indicators. But overperformance could mean up to 30 percent profit. Earlier, Coke had experimented with flat-fee hourly compensation in some locations (Mullman & Zmuda 2009).

The ANA conducted a study in 2013 to understand compensation approaches. It found labor-based or project-based fees were most common, accounting for 75 percent of one thousand agreements researched. But 61 percent of survey respondents indicated they also use performance-based arrangements. The system dominating a century earlier now accounted for about 5 percent of agreements (Neff 2013).

ADVERTISING HAS STANDARDS

In 1900, there was little uniformity in the ad industry, including how print advertising space was measured. Space was bought in blocks or squares, often a column wide by a column high (Pope 1983). But sizes varied greatly from publication to publication, especially as publications experimented with typefaces, and each publication's pricing depended on things like product type, column headings, and position in the publication.

Complicated pricing, along with being inevitably negotiable, created opportunities for agents to overcharge advertisers. There was no transparency, so it was a fertile field for fraud.

Consequently, advertisers couldn't know whether they were getting their money's worth. As Pope (1983) says, "Thus, until well into the new century, agents and advertisers bought literally billions of dollars of advertising space—worrying all the while—without a reliable idea of how many copies of the publications they were using actually were printed or reached customers."

The Advertisers' Protection Society formed in 1900, with a mission that included demanding publications provide clear circulation numbers (Elliott 1962). This also was when one form of standardization occurred in the United States: standard billboard sizes. This provided assurance that an ad would fit on boards across the country.

Finally, in 1912 the US Congress passed a law requiring periodicals to publish sworn circulation statements twice a year. There still was no way to verify numbers (Pope 1983). The Bureau of Verified Circulations began in 1913, almost simultaneously with the Advertising Audit Association. These were started by a mix of newspaper publishers, advertising agents, advertisers, and others.

The next year they merged, forming the Audit Bureau of Circulations (ABC). Publications, advertisers, and ad agents were members. Any periodical misrepresenting its circulation could be expelled from the ABC, and ad agents could stop dealing with that publication (Myers 1960).

This organization pushed the advertising industry far ahead. The ABC was renamed in 2012: the Alliance for Audited Media (AAM). The media environment necessitated this change, since digital media didn't use "circulations" but still required auditing. ABC began auditing internet sites back in 1995. This name conveyed that the organization was "platform and channel agnostic" (Elliott 2012).

Australia considered a similar ABC as early as 1920, but it didn't create its bureau until 1932. A Swiss Audit Bureau of Circulations happened in 1925, and a British version followed in 1931. Many countries continued having no ability to audit their periodicals' circulation.

In the United States, a Traffic Audit Bureau (TAB) was added in 1933 to authenticate outdoor advertising traffic counts (Taylor, Claus, & Claus 2005). Its system studied traffic patterns and measured the "circulation and space position value" of billboards. Decades later the out-of-home advertising industry added another standardization called the Outdoor Visibility Rating System (OVRS), essentially replacing the less sophisticated "space position value" approach, in 1989.

Recall George Rowell published a directory of newspaper information, including purported circulation figures. It merged with a directory published by N.W. Ayer in 1908. Rowell had added advertising rates to his directory, though accuracy was questionable. Given Rowell's success, copycat directories appeared over the years. Following creation of ABC, standardization of circulation figures resulted in some rate standardization. In 1919, a standardized directory of media information was published: Standard Rate & Data Service (SRDS). This new directory's content was similar to previous directories, with the benefit of better verifiability (Myers 1960). This became the industry standard.

Finally, much concern over unethical space pricing had been addressed. These steps, along with the Truth-in-Advertising movement and creation of the new Federal Trade Commission (see Chapter 12), did much to clean up the industry.

PUBLIC RELATIONS ORGANIZES

Public relations began millennia ago, perhaps even with the serpent in the garden. In 1600 CE, William Kempe, an actor in some Shakespeare plays, promoted himself by dancing one hundred miles, from London to Norwich, over nine days. In the 1600s, the Catholic Church established a college of propaganda to "help propagate the faith." Propaganda, then, meant informing the public (Seitel 2004).

Certain historical events, like the Boston Tea Party in 1773, were publicity mechanisms that were *de facto* public relations events (Guth & Marsh 2003). And if the legend of Lady Godiva's nude horse ride has any truth to it, that was definitely a publicity gambit from the eleventh century. But just as the advertising industry emerged from the dark when agencies were created, the same could be said of public relations when it was professionalized as a recognized specialty, which began in the mid- to late nineteenth century.

Phineas T. Barnum (aka P. T. Barnum) might be the start of *professionalizing* public relations. His career was built on using advertising and publicity to promote his businesses. Even calling his circus "The Greatest Show on Earth," circa 1875, was a masterwork of "positioning." His approach to everything generated press coverage as never done before.

George Westinghouse, too, played a big role when he created a public relations department at Westinghouse Electric Company in 1889, though it wasn't called that. Journalist E. H. Heinrichs was department head (Ziaukas 2007). Westinghouse was busy battling with Thomas Edison over electricity's future, and publicity was a key weapon in that battle. This had led some to call Heinrichs "America's First Press Agent." He was shockingly important in that fight!

Also in 1889, Jeremiah Rusk was named Secretary of Agriculture by President Benjamin Harrison. Agriculture was probably the most important industry then, and that industry was rapidly evolving. Rusk wanted more information, more quickly, reaching the public, so he published farm bulletins. His successor "Tama" Jim Wilson expanded that effort (Cutlip & Baker 2012). Public relations, then, established an important foothold in government.

At this point public relations' legitimacy was being recognized, and in 1897 General Electric also created a publicity department. The University of Michigan in 1897 started a publicity office (Guth & Marsh 2003). And Citizens' Union in 1903 hired a "press representative" for a political candidate. That representative was Ivy Ledbetter Lee, former *New York Times* journalist, launching Ivy Lee's public relations career, making him a founder of modern PR.

The first public relations agency was the Publicity Bureau, founded by George V. S. Michaelis, Herbert Small, and Thomas Marvin in 1900. They likewise came from the newspaper industry. Their first client was Harvard University! The bureau later represented several major companies, including American Telephone & Telegraph. Two years later, William Wolf Smith opened a second agency, and after two more years Ivy Lee joined with George F. Parker to form the third agency, Parker and Lee. Lee left in 1908 to work for the Pennsylvania Railroad as its first publicity director.

It wasn't an easy job. PR practitioners fought resistance from newspapers, though much was self-inflicted, resulting from practitioners who used something less than truth to promote clients. But they also were breaking new ground and needed to convince the press of their worth.

In 1905, Lee articulated a "Declaration of Principles" to define the public relations field:

> This is not a secret press bureau. All our work is done in the open. We aim to supply news. This is not an advertising agency; if you think any of our matter ought properly to go to your business office, do not use it. Our matter is accurate. Further details on any subject treated will be supplied promptly, and any editor will be assisted most cheerfully in verifying directly any statement of fact. Upon inquiry, full information will be given to any editor concerning those on whose behalf an article is sent out. In brief, our plan is, frankly and openly, on behalf of business concerns and public institutions, to supply to the press and public of the United States prompt and accurate information concerning subjects which it is of value and interest to the public to know about. Corporations and public institutions give out much information in which the news point is lost to view. Nevertheless, it is quite as important to the public to have this news as it is to the establishments themselves to give it currency. I send out only matter every detail of which I am willing to assist any editor in verifying for himself. I am always at your service for the purpose of enabling you to obtain more complete information concerning any of the subjects brought forward in my copy. (Russell & Bishop 2009)

With this, Lee did PR for the PR industry, while challenging others in the field to live by a set of ethical principles. Some consider this the point at which modern public relations began.

President Woodrow Wilson created the Committee on Public Information (CPI, aka Creel Commission), in 1917 to mold public opinion toward supporting US entry into WWI. This combined advertising, journalism, and public relations to develop posters and billboards while maintaining a foreign press bureau. CPI was a tremendous success, contributing to the reputation of PR. Two practitioners in CPI's press bureau were Ivy Lee and a young fellow named Edward L. Bernays, a nephew of Sigmund Freud, who would become a PR legend.

In 1919, Bernays opened America's eighth PR agency. He advocated using scientific approaches to shaping public opinion (Kuenstler 2012). He applied psychology, perhaps influenced by his famous uncle. He put little faith in public judgment, and believed strongly that PR could influence public thinking. While Ivy Lee helped pioneer the "publicity function" of PR, *informing* the public, Bernays moved PR toward *molding* public opinion (Stole 2006). In 1923, Bernays published a groundbreaking book, *Crystallizing Public Opinion*. Like Ivy Lee, Bernays explained that PR is not about deception, but rather two-way communication between client and public. Bernays preferred the term "public relations" over the more common "propaganda."

Late in life, unfortunately, Ivy Lee worked for the Nazis in Germany, which may be why Bernays, rather than Lee, is considered the "father of public relations." But Bernays also used his PR skills to promote himself in that role (Guth & Marsh 2003).

The field was gaining acceptance as WWI ended. N.W. Ayer became the first advertising agency to add a publicity department, in 1919 (Cutlip & Baker 2012). And in 1930 the National Association of Manufacturers was the first industry trade association to form a PR department.

Two other major influences happened in 1927. First was when John W. Hill opened his agency. Six years later Hill hired Don Knowlton. The agency became Hill & Knowlton, a name familiar decades later.

The other influence was AT&T hiring Arthur W. Page as vice president of PR, a career change for Page. Over time he was considered the "father of corporate public relations." Page also served as an unpaid consultant to multiple US presidents.

Page established his own set of principles: (1) tell the truth, (2) prove it with action, (3) listen to stakeholders, (4) manage for tomorrow, (5) conduct public relations as if the whole enterprise depends on it, (6) realize that an enterprise's true character is expressed by its people, and (7) remain calm, patient, and good-humored. His legacy includes the Arthur W. Page Society, an association for senior PR and corporate communication professionals, and the Arthur W. Page Center for Integrity in Public Communication.

World War II brought another round of opportunities for PR people. The WWI effort was so successful, even more resources were put behind it this time. About one hundred thousand "information" people worked for the government during the war (Cutlip & Baker 2012). Adolph Hitler's use of information, and Joseph Goebbels as Reich Minister of Public Enlightenment and Propaganda, didn't help people's trust of public relations, and probably explains later negative connotations around the word "propaganda."

Another significant firm started in 1946. Alfred Fleishman and Bob Hillard formed the Fleishman-Hillard PR agency. Their timing was good. This was the start of the field's biggest expansion period, 1945 to 1980 (Cutlip and Baker 2012). The Edelman agency began in 1952, and Burson-Marsteller opened the next year. Both rode that wave to become tremendous forces in PR. As an aside, the first PR agency in China started in 1985, as a joint venture between Burson-Marsteller and the Xinhua news agency. PR was now global.

With the internet, after 1990, Bernays' vision of two-way communication was fully realized. PR became real time, where monitoring and responding to public opinion needs to happen instantly. It also means that crises can spread in a blink, making PR practitioners more essential than ever. Research, too, came with electronic communications.

MAD MEN ON MAD AVE.

"Madison Avenue" (New York City) became synonymous with "advertising" in the twentieth century. The popular television series *Mad Men* (2007–2015) was based on that, as were the books *Madison Avenue, USA*, and *Mad Women: The Other Side of Life on Madison Avenue in the '60s and Beyond*.

The term began at least by 1923 (Marchand 1985). But we know the American Association of Advertising Agencies (AAAA) moved to the corner of 23rd and Madison Avenue in 1917, and seven AAAA member agencies already were on Madison Avenue. Some of the most influential agencies had offices there at one time or another, including J. Walter Thompson, H. K. McCann, George Batten Company, BBDO, Young & Rubicam, and more (Appel 2017c).

By 1937, twenty-two of the AAAA's sixty New York member agencies (37 percent) were on Madison. Around twenty-five others were within walking distance. Even as late as the 1970s, about 25 percent of AAAA members were on Madison, but numbers dropped quickly after that, thanks to increasing rents and decreasing profits (Rothenberg 1989). Some agencies moved to less desirable neighborhoods or to Brooklyn. In 2017, only 12 percent of

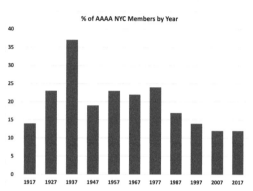

% of AAAA NYC Members by Year

FIGURE 10.11. Percent of New York City agency members of the American Association of Advertising Agencies, by year (data from Appel 2017c).

New York AAAA members—about one-third of the 1937 numbers and even a bit less than in 1917—were on Madison (Figure 10.11). Still, "Madison Avenue" means advertising.

AWARDS, AWARDS, EVERYWHERE

The advertising industry in the twenty-first century is known as the fount of many awards. But that phenomenon began in the 1900s. The first advertising art competition was created by the Art Directors Club. The club was founded in 1920, and in 1921 Earnest Elmo Calkins created a competitive exhibition. The work was judged on visual aesthetics alone.

The first more general advertising awards were created at Harvard University School of Business in 1923. Edward W. Bok, former editor of *Ladies' Home Journal*, invented and funded them to raise the standards of advertising in US and Canadian publications. Winners were selected by a jury of experts. Bok presented it as an "experiment," with the first awards in 1924.

The awards died along with Bok in 1930, but while they lasted Barton, Durstine, and Osborn (BDO) won more of them than any other agency (Fox 1984). In that first year the Distinguished Service to Advertising Award went to the National Vigilance Committee of the Associated Advertising Clubs of the World (Presbrey 1929). Ray Rubicam won an award in 1925 and used that to springboard launching the Young & Rubicam agency (Fox 1984).

The next major award was in 1942, by the Outdoor Advertising Association of America (OAAA): the OBIE Awards for excellence in outdoor advertising. The name was derived from the ancient Egyptian obelisk (a tall, tapered stele), an early outdoor advertising form. Coca-Cola won the first Best of Show Award. The OAAA changed its name to the Out-of-Home Advertising Association of America in 2019.

The New York Ad Club suggested to the Advertising Federation of America (AFA) creating an Advertising Hall of Fame, to honor service that "added materially to the social and economic values of advertising." Founded in 1948, it became a post-career award for a lifetime of service and high ethical standards. The AFA merged with the Advertising Association of the West (AAW) in 1967, becoming the American Advertising Federation, which continued administering the Hall of Fame.

In 1954, the International Advertising Film Festival was born in Venice, Italy. In 1955, it was in Monte Carlo, Monaco, and in 1956 in Cannes, France. Then it alternated between Cannes and Venice until 1984, landing permanently in Cannes and becoming the Cannes International Advertising Festival. It evolved from judging only television and film advertising to encompassing all manner of ads. In 2011, it became the Cannes Lions Festival of Creativity. The Cannes awards are, in fact, about creativity. The "Lions" refer to the trophy shape, inspired by the winged lion of the Piazza San Marcos in Venice.

The Clio awards began in 1959 as advertising "creative excellence" awards. They were the ad industry's equivalent to the motion picture industry's Oscars. These were a premier advertising award, but in 1991 a Clio award show was memorable for the wrong reasons. Around three hundred-plus people attended. The event started late, and a caterer ended up coming onto the stage and handing out some awards, because the emcee never arrived! The caterer ran out of script to tell who won awards, so the lights came up. People stormed the stage, stealing awards. It was an embarrassing mess (Elliott 1991). Predictions followed that this might have ended the Clio awards. Fortunately, it did not.

The ADDY awards began in 1960, but it was geographically limited. In 1962, it expanded to cover all ad clubs in AFA District 4. It became national in 1966, and in 1967 AFA merged with AAW, which brought its own "Best of the West" awards that were merged into the ADDYs. In 2013, the American Advertising Federation renamed the ADDYs as the American Advertising Awards, though ADDY continued in popular use.

Also in 1960, the Creative Hall of Fame emerged, later becoming the One Club Creative Hall of Fame. The first inductees, one per year, were Leo Burnett, George Gribbin, David Ogilvy, and Bill Bernbach. A Copy Hall of Fame followed in 1961. Those same legends were the first four writers honored. The Copy Hall of Fame was folded into the Creative Hall of Fame during the late 1970s.

Effie awards are a bit different. The New York American Marketing Association established them in 1968. While the other awards looked at factors like aesthetics and *perceived* success, the Effies were about *demonstrated* effectiveness.

The One Show was a joint venture between the Art Directors' Club and the Copy Club of New York, in 1973. Originally, the Advertising Club of New York (ANDY awards) also was involved. The idea was to combine those three sets of awards into The One Show, as the preeminent advertising creativity competition. This would cut down on the proliferation of awards and the multiple entry fees (Sloane 1972). In 1977, the Copy Club took sole ownership of The One Show, and in 1979 it became The One Club.

Countless awards were birthed over the coming years, some of which are listed in Table 10.2. There are many more, such as the Rx Club Show and Manny awards for healthcare advertising, and the Midas awards for financial advertising.

The Top Advertising Contest of Thailand (TACT) awards deserve mention here. This one is a bit different, begun by two marketing professors in the National Institute of Development Administration (NIDA) Graduate School of Business, along with the Faculty of

Table 10.2. Major Advertising Awards

Awards/Recognitions	Dates	Administered by
ADC Awards	1921–	Art Directors Club
Harvard Awards	1923–1930	Harvard Business School
ECHO Awards	1929	Direct Mail Marketing Assn.
OBIE Awards	1942–	Out-of-Home Advertising Ass'n of America
Advertising Creative Circle of Great Britain	1945–	[unknown]
Advertising Hall of Fame	1948–	American Advertising Federation
Cannes Lions	1956–	Ascential Events
Clio Awards	1959–	Clio Awards, LLC
American Advertising (ADDY) Awards	1960–	American Advertising Federation
The One Club Creative Hall of Fame	1960–	The One Club
Copy Hall of Fame	1961–1970s	Copy Club of New York
D&AD Awards	1963–	British Design & Art Direction
Galaxy Awards	1963–	Japan Council for Better Radio & Television
International ANDY Awards	1964–	Advertising Club of New York
Effie Awards	1968–	Effie Worldwide
Art Directors' Club Hall of Fame	1971–	Art Directors Club
Mobius Awards	1971–	US International Film & Video Festival
The One Show	1973–	The One Club
National Student Advertising Competition	1973–	American Advertising Federation
D&AD Student Awards	1976–	British Design & Art Direction
British Arrows (British Television Advert. Awards)	1976–	British Arrows, London
Top Advertising Contest of Thailand (TACT)	1976/77–2005	NIDA Business School, Thammasat Business School, and Silpakorn University
The Loeries	1978–	The Loerie Awards Company NPC
Caples Awards	1978	Andi Emerson
BAD Award	1985–	Bangkok Art Director Association
London International Awards	1986–	LIA
Eurobest Awards	1988–	Ascential Events
Golden Award of Montreux	1989–	Golden Award Montreux Festival
Cresta International Advertising Awards	1993–	Creative Standards International Ltd.
Summit International Awards	1994–	SIA
Cannes Young Creatives Competition	1995–	Ascential Events
Webby Awards	1996–	Int'l Academy of Digital Arts & Sciences
Internet Advertising Competition	1999–	Web Marketing Association
Cristal Festival	2001–	Cristal Festival, Saint-Bon-Tarentaise, France
YoungGuns International Awards	2001–	YoungGuns, Sydney
Digital Media Advertising Creative Showcase	2006–2010	[unknown]
Intercontinental Advertising Cup	2007	[unknown]
A' Advertising Awards	2010–	A'Design Award
Business-to-Business Hall of Fame	2016	Association of National Advertisers

Commerce and Accountancy at Thammasat University, in order to elevate the quality of advertising in Thailand. The Faculty of Decorative Arts at Silpakorn University joined later. According to Dr. Boonchai Hongcharu of the NIDA Business School, it was run by universities to remove it from industry control, creating an "unbiased" contest. Unfortunately, the competition ended.

Awards were a twentieth-century invention for advertising, but are still running strong into the twenty-first. There have been some within the industry who criticize these events, but it is impossible to imagine an ad industry without awards.

ADVERTISING TRADE PUBLICATIONS

Trade periodicals—for any field—were largely unknown until the late 1800s. George Rowell's *Advertisers' Gazette* was advertising's first, in 1867. There was an earlier periodical, *Typographic Advertiser*, in 1855, but the term "advertiser" was used the same way it was on newspaper titles of the time, meaning it contained advertising. It was a typesetter's trade publication.

A list of the most common advertising trade periodicals is in Table 10.3.

Table 10.3. Advertising Trade Publications

Publication	Date	Notes
Advertisers' Gazette	1867–1871	publisher: George Rowell
American Newspaper Reporter	1871	fka Advertisers' Gazette
Printers' Ink	1888–1967	publisher: George Rowell
Advertisers' Gazette	1889	appears to be different from Rowell's
Advertising & Selling	1891	
Profitable Advertising	1891–1909	publisher: C.F. David agency
Advertising	1891	publisher: Thomas Smith agency
Fame	1892	publisher: Artemas Ward
Advertising World	1894	publisher: Charles S. Anderson
Billboard Advertising	1894	publishers: William Donaldson and James Hennegan
Practical Advertising	1895	publisher: Mather & Crowther agency
Advertiser's Review	1896*	
Art in Advertising	1896*	
National Advertiser	1896*	
Harman's Journal of Window Dressing and Decorating	1896*	
American Advertiser	1896*	
The Bill Poster	1896	
Current Advertising	1896	publisher: Charles Austin Bates
The Billboard	1897	fka Billboard Advertising
The Poster	1898	
Judicious Advertising & Advertising Experience	1902	publisher: Lord & Thomas agency
Mahin's Magazine	1902	publisher: John L. Mahin (absorbed by Judicious Advertising in 1904)
Advertising-Selling	1909	publisher: Advertising & Selling Company (absorbed both Profitable Advertising and Selling Magazine)
Associated Advertising	1910	publisher: Assoc. Adv. Clubs of America
Advertiser's Weekly	1913	publishers: George Edgar & J. C. Akerman

Publication	Date	Notes
De Bedrijfsreklame	1916	Netherlands
Advertising Age	1930	publisher: G. D. Crain Jr.
Modern Advertising	1935	publisher: Nat'l Publications, Inc.
Journal of Marketing	1936	publisher: Nat'l Assn. of Marketing Teachers
CA, The Journal of Commercial Art	1959	publishers: Richard Coyne & Robert Blanchard
Journal of Advertising Research	1960	publisher: Advertising Research Foundation
ADMAP	1964	publisher: Roger Cook
Campaign	1968	publisher: British Printing Corporation
Communication Arts	1969	fka CA, The Journal of Commercial Art
Journal of Advertising	1972	publisher: American Academy of Advertising
Journal of Current Issues and Research in Advertising	1978	publishers: Claude R. Martin & James H. Leigh
Direct Marketing News	1978	
Adweek	1979	publisher: Adweek
Telemarketing	1982	
Lürzer's Archive	1984	publisher: Luerzer's Archive USA, Inc.
Brandweek	1986–2011	publisher: Adweek
Creativity	1986	publisher: Crain Communications
Adbusters	1989	publishers: Kalle Lasn & Bill Schmalz (this takes a critical view of advertising)
Mediaweek	1991–2011	publisher: Adweek
CMYK	1996	publisher: Aroune-Freigen Publishing
Telemarketing & Call Center Solutions	1996	fka Telemarketing
Call Center Solutions	1998	fka Telemarketing & Call Center Solutions
PRWeek	1998	publisher: Haymarket Publishing
one. a magazine	1998	publisher: The One Club
Call Center CRM Solutions	2000	fka Call Center Solutions
Customer Interaction Solutions	2000	fka Call Center CRM Solutions
Journal of Interactive Advertising	2000	publishers: University of Texas & Michigan State University
Advertising & Society Review	2000	publisher: Advertising Educational Foundation
DMN	2016	fka Direct Marketing News
Advertising & Society Quarterly	2017	fka Advertising & Society Review

*Known to exist in 1896, but actual first year of publication is unknown

An interesting note in this is the 1894 publication of *Billboard Advertising*. This magazine evolved over the decades into, first, *The Billboard*, then *Billboard Music Week* (1961), and then just *Billboard* (1963). It also changed its focus from advertising to entertainment and music.

Throughout the twentieth century and beyond, only a few of these publications have dominated. The first few decades were, beyond doubt, following the lead of *Printers' Ink*, at least in the United States. By the mid-twentieth century, though, *Advertising Age* (aka *Ad Age*) took command. And while that one continued to be the major player, by the 1980s *Adweek* was making inroads. While *Ad Age* was a national publication, *Adweek* offered regionally tailored versions. This gave the latter a different appeal, helping it grow. In Europe, however, *ADMAP* became the big dog. Of course, within given niches, like direct marketing, other publications led.

ASSOCIATIONS

No history of advertising would be complete without addressing the organizations representing the profession's members. There are too many to discuss at length, so a simple list is shown in Table 10.4.

Table 10.4. Advertising Associations

Organization	Date	Country	Notes
United Kingdom's Billposters' Association	1862	Britain	
International Bill Posters' Association of North America	1872	USA	
Association of General Newspaper Agents	1888	USA	
Business Writers Association	1890	USA	First copywriters' association
Associated Bill Posters' Association of the United States and Canada	1891	USA/Canada	
Agate Club	1894	USA/Chicago	Local
Association of Advertising Agents	1896	USA	
Sphinx Club	1896	USA/New York	Local
Society for Checking Abuses of Public Advertising	1898	Britain	Consumer protection group
National Association of Window Trimmers	1898	USA	
Association of American Advertisers	1899	USA	
Advertisers' Protection Society	1900	Britain	To get accurate circulation #
American Advertising Agents Association	1900	USA	
Advertising Men's Club of Kansas City	1902	USA/Kansas City	Local
Advertising Association of the West	1903	USA	
St. Louis Advertising Men's League	1903	USA/St. Louis	Local
National Federation of Advertising Clubs of America	1904	USA	
Advertising Novelty Manufacturers' Association	1904	USA	
Advertising Manufacturers Association	1904	USA	
Advertising Federation of America	1905	USA	
Chicago Advertising Association	1905	USA/Chicago	Local
Canadian Institute of Communication Agencies	1905	Canada	
Incorporated Society of Advertising Agents	1905	Britain	
Advertising Clubs of America	1905	USA	fka Nat'l Fed. of Adv. Clubs of America
Press Advertisement Managers Association	1906	USA	
Associated Bill Posters and Distributors of the United States and Canada	1906	USA/Canada	Merger of former organizations
Painted Outdoor Advertising Association	1909	USA	
Association of National Advertising Managers	1910	USA	fka Assn. of American Advertisers
Association of Advertising Women	1910	Britain	
Admen's Club of Atlanta	1911	USA/Atlanta	Local
New York City Association of Advertising Agencies	1911	USA/New York	Local
Women's Publicity Club of Boston	1911	USA/Boston	Local
Associated Advertising Clubs of America	1912	USA	fka Adv. Clubs of America
National Association of Advertising Specialty Manufacturers	1912	USA	fka Adv. Novelty Mfr's Assn.
League of Advertising Women of New York	1912	USA	

Organization	Date	Country	Notes
National Advertising and General Benefit and Benevolent Society	1913	Canada	
The Publicity Club of London	1913	Britain	
Associated Advertising Clubs of the World	1914	USA	fka Assoc. Adv. Clubs of America
Audit Bureau of Circulations	1914	USA	
British Association of Advertising	1914	Britain	
Advertising Club of New York	1915	USA/New York	fka Sphinx Club
National Association of Teachers of Advertising	1915	USA	
National Outdoor Advertising Bureau	1915	USA	
Women's Advertising Club of St. Louis	1916	USA/St. Louis	Local
Financial Advertisers Association	1916	USA	
Association of British Advertising Agents	1917	Britain	
American Association of Advertising Agencies	1917	USA	
Direct Mail Advertising Association	1917	USA	
New South Wales Ad Men's Institute	1917	Australia	
Women's Advertising Club of Chicago	1917	USA/Chicago	Local
Art Directors Club of New York	1920	USA/New York	Local
Incorporated Society of British Advertisers	1920	Britain	fka Advertisers Protection Society
Advertising Association of Australia & New Zealand	1921	Australia/New Zealand	
Women's Advertising Club of London	1923	Britain/London	Local
Advertising Association	1924	Britain	
Screen Advertising Association	1924	USA	
Outdoor Advertising Association of America	1925	USA	Combined Poster Adv. Assn. & Painted Outdoor Adv. Assn.
Swiss Audit Bureau of Circulations	1925	Switzerland	
Advertising Association	1926	Britain	fka British Assn. of Advertising
Institute of Incorporated Practitioners in Advertising	1927	Britain	fka Assn. of British Adv. Agents
British Direct Mail Advertising Association	1927	Britain	
Australian Association of National Advertisers	1928	Australia	
American Marketing Society	1931	USA	
British Audit Bureau of Circulations	1931	Britain	
Traffic Audit Bureau	1931	USA	
Audit Bureau of Circulation	1932	Australia	
National Association of Teachers of Marketing	1933	USA	fka Nat'l Assn. of Teachers of Advertising
Advertising Women of New York	1934	USA	fka League of Adv. Women of New York
Advertising Research Foundation	1936	USA	
National Association of Accredited Publicity Directors	1936	USA	
American Marketing Association	1937	USA	Merger of American Marketing Society & Nat'l Assn. of Teachers of Marketing
Expert Advertising Association	1938	USA	
Consumer's Advertising Council	1938	USA	
American Council on Public Relations	1939	USA	
American Public Relations Association	1944	USA	

(*continued*)

Table 10.4. *Continued*

Organization	Date	Country	Notes
National Association of Public Relations Counsel	1944	USA	
Associated Third Class Mail Users Association	1947	USA	
Public Relations Society of America	1947	USA	
National Associations of Consumers	1947	USA	
Advertising & Design Club of Canada	1948	Canada	
Advertising Specialty Institute	1950	USA	
Japan Advertising Agencies Association	1950	Japan	
El Instituto de la Publicidad	1950	Spain	
Radio Bureau of Advertising	1950	USA	
Malaysian Advertising Association	1952	Malaysia	
International Advertising Association	1953	USA	fka Export Adv. Assn.
Institute of Practitioners of Advertising	1954	Britain	fka Institute of Incorporated Practitioners of Advertising
International Public Relations Association	1955	Britain	
American Academy of Advertising	1958	USA	
Philippine Association of National Advertisers	1958	Philippines	
Korean Public Relations Institute	1958	South Korea	
Advertising Writers Association of New York	1961	USA/New York	Local
Designers & Art Directors Association of London	1963	Britain/London	
Specialty Advertising Association	1964	USA	
Business Advertising Association of Thailand	1965	Thailand	
National Advertising Benevolent Society	1966	Canada	fka Nat'l Adv. and General Benefit and Benevolent Society
American Advertising Federation	1967	USA	Combined Adv. Federation of America & Adv. Assn. of the West
Nikkei Advertising Research Institute	1967	Japan	
Public Relations Student Society of America	1967	USA	
Copy Club	1969	USA	fka Adv. Writers Assn.
Japan Academy of Advertising	1969	Japan	
Art Directors Club Netherlands	1969	Netherlands	
Specialty Advertising Association International	1971	USA	fka Specialty Adv. Assn.
Association of Advertising Practitioners of Nigeria	1973	Nigeria	
Direct Mail Marketing Association	1973	USA	fka Direct Mail Adv. Assn.
British Direct Mail Marketing Association	1975	Britain	fka British Direct Mail Adv. Assn.
Advertising Practitioners Council of Nigeria	1988	Nigeria	
Advertising Agency Association of British Columbia	1975	Canada/BC	
China Advertising Association for Foreign Trade and Economic Cooperation	1981	China	
Korean Broadcast Advertising Corporation	1981	South Korea	
Direct Marketing Association	1983	USA	fka Direct Mail Marketing Assn.
Association of Quebec Advertising Agencies	1988	Canada/Quebec	
Advertising Practitioners Council of Nigeria	1988	Nigeria	
Korean Advertising Society	1989	South Korea	
Korea Audit Bureau of Circulations	1989	South Korea	

Organization	Date	Country	Notes
Advertising Educators' Association of Canada	1990	Canada	
National Advertisers' Association of Nigeria	1992	Nigeria	
Promotional Products Association International	1993	USA	fka Specialty Adv. Assn.
Association of Hispanic Advertising Agencies	1996	USA	
Interactive Advertising Bureau	1996	USA	
Future of Advertising Stakeholders	1998	USA	Digital only
China Advertising Education Society	1999	China	
Branded Content Marketing Association	2003	Britain	
Outdoor Media Centre	2010	Britain	fka Outdoor Adv. Assn.
Digital Advertising Association of Thailand	2012	Thailand	
Coalition for Better Ads	2016	USA	
Data & Marketing Association	2016	USA	fka Direct Marketing Assn.
She Runs It	2016	USA	fka Adv. Women of New York
Out of Home Advertising Association of America	2019	USA	fka Outdoor Adv. Assn. of America

Within various specialty areas (online, out-of-home, direct), the governing associations vary. But within advertising more generally, three organizations came to lead in the United States. Representing *agencies* is the American Association of Advertising Agencies. The merchants buying advertising fall under the Association of National Advertisers. And individuals working anywhere in the industry, often belonging to local advertising clubs, are represented by the American Advertising Federation.

HONEY, I SHRUNK THE PLANET

The world became smaller when the steamship and railroads enabled global transportation. And new transportation technologies continued to make distances shrink.

The Advertising Clubs of the America was established in 1905, but in 1914 it became the Associated Advertising Clubs of the World (AACW), one of the industry's earliest steps toward globalization. That was followed in 1923 by an international advertising conference in London, sponsored by the AACW, with 4,850 attendees. It wasn't the first international advertising conference, where a handful of people attended from a nearby country;[1] this was the first truly multinational advertising conference. The keynote speaker was Winston Churchill.

The first Australian ad conference was in 1918, and Brazil's first was in 1938. Japan formed a Japan Advertising Agencies Association in 1950, the year Spain set up its El Instituto de la Publicidad (National Advertising Institute). Japan's Nikkei Advertising Research Institute followed in 1967. In Nigeria in 1973, the Association of Advertising Practitioners of Nigeria arose, and an Advertising Practitioners Council followed in 1988. The Korean Broadcast Advertising Corporation (KOBACO) began in 1981. Oh, and an International Public Relations Association began in 1955 in London. Evidence of the industry's maturation in these countries could be found in these symbols of organization.

China, by contrast, had advertising early in the century, but ads virtually disappeared in 1949 when the Communist Party took over. Under the rule of Deng Xiaoping, in 1978 the

Communist Party entered a new phase focused on economic reforms, allowing a return of advertising (Li 2017). This marked the end of the Cultural Revolution, and opening the world's most populous country to advertising was momentous.

In 1979, Shanghai TV ran an ad for a Swiss Rado wristwatch, the first foreign television commercial in China. Its citizens wanted to buy the watch, but it was not available there until 1983 (Li 2017). The China Advertising Association for Foreign Trade and Economic Cooperation (CAAFTEC) opened in 1981, becoming China's first national advertising organization, later called the China Advertising Association of Commerce.

By 2000, advertising could be found nearly everywhere on the planet. And as the world's citizens found the internet, ads from every country could now be accessed. As of 2017, there were 7.53 billion people in the world, and 3.9 billion (52 percent) were internet users. The world now was only as big as a computer screen.

ADVERTISING SPENDING

Ad spending has changed tremendously, even since 1900. Looking just at the United States, total ad spending as of 1776 was *estimated* at a mere $200,000, hitting $1 million by 1800. By 1900, it reached $450 million, and by 1909 a full $1 billion! But these are estimates. There is no easy way to measure ad spend, especially since everyone who attempts measuring it probably defines advertising differently.

If Nike purchases shirts with its logo on them as employee uniforms, should the cost of the shirt be counted, or just the cost of embroidering that logo? And when an architect designs a building with a special place for a company's sign, do we include just the sign's cost or also the building and design costs in creating that space?

From 1948 to 2009, an industry forecaster named Robert J. Coen, at Universal McCann, published annual reports on advertising spending. Before him L. D. H. Weld, also of McCann, had compiled data. Data was collected and published for 1935 to 2007. Coen's, at least, used a consistent approach to deriving those annual figures. Since 2007, the most readily available source of data comes from the Statista company. Its data likely is internally consistent but differs from Coen's. Statista, for example, estimates total US ad spend for 2019—its highest ever—at $242.54 billion. Coen estimated the United States hit $245.48 billion in 2003. Statista's data doesn't reach before 2000, so my figures are based on Coen's. I estimated amounts beyond 2007 based on the percentage increase in ad spending each subsequent year, as estimated by Statista.

Figure 10.12 shows three lines. The bottom, orange line is based on the estimated ad spending in 1915, $1.1 billion, adjusted for inflation up until 2019, equaling $28 billion. The middle, blue line indicates estimated dollars spent 1900–2020, beginning at $450 million and ending at $448 billion, per Coen's figures. The top, gray line represents 3 percent of the Gross Domestic Product (GDP) over that period. Three percent was used because advertising expenditures have topped out at 2.8 percent of GDP (1915–1925) and bottomed at 1.2 percent (1945). Most years it hovers around 2 percent of GDP, as seen in the chart.

Looking at total global expenditures, Coen found in 1950 that the United States accounted for 77 percent of global spending, dropping to 57 percent by 1970 and 47 percent by 2007.

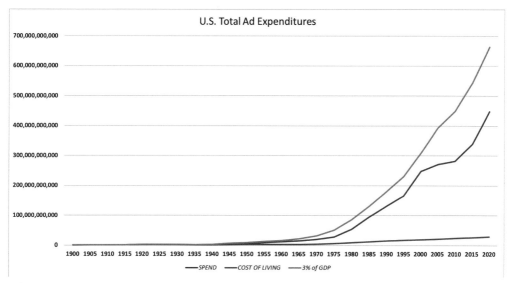

FIGURE 10.12. Advertising expenditures in the United States, 1900–2020, compared to normal inflation and GDP.

Still, of about two hundred countries, just one commanded nearly half of all advertising. Statista estimates in 2019 that the United States accounted for 43 percent of global spending. As of 2019, Statista shows China as second at 17 percent and Japan third at 8 percent, with the United Kingdom and Germany tied at 5 percent (Figure 10.13).

Distribution of those investments changed. Ad spending by medium, from 1935 to 2005, using Coen's data, is seen in Figure 10.14. By 2020, online (including mobile) accounted for

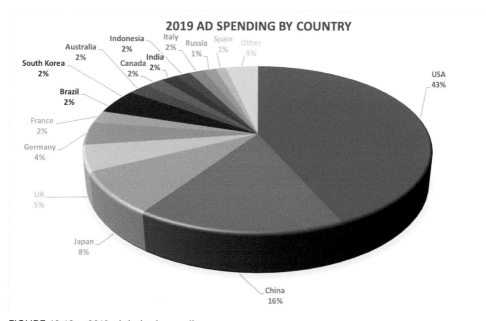

FIGURE 10.13. 2019 global ad spending.

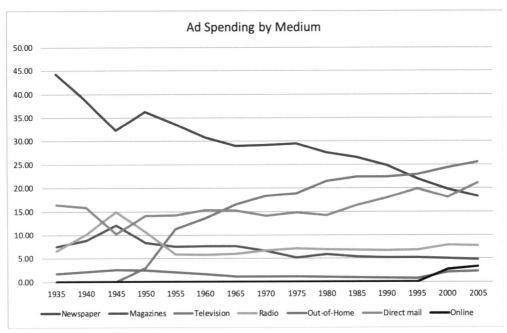

FIGURE 10.14.   US ad spending by medium, 1935–2005, based on percent of total.

32.4 percent, direct mail 22.3 percent, television only 19.5 percent, newspaper down to 9.2 percent, out-of-home at 5.4 percent, and magazines at 1.1 percent of total ad spending, according to Statista. Note that figures for promotional products, events, and more aren't included.

Ad spending continues to rise over the years, but the medium of choice constantly changes. Radio and television were king in the twentieth century, but that dominance has dropped.

LET'S COOPERATE!

Cooperative advertising—cost sharing between two or more businesses—arose around 1900. It frequently is where a retailer splits the cost of ads with a manufacturer. This is "vertical" cooperative advertising, and the money provided to the retailer is an advertising allowance (US Senate 1963). Where a *group* of producers or retailers join to run ads, that is "horizontal" cooperative advertising.

This began in England between 1900 and 1905, using horizontal ads for tea, apples, and currants (Presbrey 1929). It almost spread to the United States in 1901, when prune growers tried using it, but they didn't reach an agreement (Printers' Ink 1938). In 1907, the California Fruit Growers joined forces to share ad costs to move an overproduction of oranges. That group came to use the brand "Sunkist," thanks to the Lord & Thomas advertising agency. This was the first cooperative advertising in the United States.

This strategy became a norm in advertising. The initial purpose was to help smaller businesses advertise. All parties benefit, which is why it found popularity (US Senate 1963). The horizontal approach became common in several agricultural product categories (milk, beef, avocados, bananas, etc.), and the vertical form allowed national advertisers to do local advertising at reduced costs. The rise of franchises contributed to it reaching normative status, since franchise agreements generally include cooperative advertising requirements. Even the spread of shopping malls, beginning with Italy's Galleria Vittorio in 1877, created new opportunities for cooperative ads.

In 2015, cooperative advertising accounted for something like $36 billion in North America. That is a notable part of total ad spend. Survey data that year suggests the typical local advertiser used four co-op ad programs, receiving $25,000 in allowances (Borrell Associates 2015).

ADVERTISER, HEAL THYSELF

Common sayings like "a shoemaker's children go barefoot" are truisms. For advertising we might say, "Ad people don't toot their own horns." Ad agencies don't sign their work. Few of them have even taken out ads, beyond telephone directories and websites. The industry really has done almost nothing to promote itself.

In 1926, it got help from the *New York Evening Post*. At the suggestion of leading industry figures (Earnest Elmo Calkins, Cyrus H. K. Curtis, Edward W. Bok), an advertising news column began. Nothing previously promoted the ad industry to the general public, even though it was by then a $2 billion business (Editors of Advertising Age 1976).

Not until the twenty-first century did the industry decide it needed publicity. Advertising Week NYC was born in 2004 (Figure 10.15), to make the public aware of the economic impact advertising had on New York City. It included a parade of "America's Favorite Ad Icons," like Tony the Tiger, the Pillsbury Doughboy, and more, from Times Square to Madison Avenue. There were meetings, parties, and more. The AAAA held its creative conference in conjunction with the event, and the city's mayor even spoke at a reception (Elliott 2004).

FIGURE 10.15. Ad for the inaugural Advertising Week in New York, 2004.

With sixty thousand attendees, this became a regular event. It eventually evolved into an industry-centered rather than publicity event, but continued to offer at least one outward-facing activity, the parade, renamed the "Madison Avenue Walk of Fame."

Advertising Week Europe, which was similar, began in 2013 in London. Advertising Week Asia arrived in Tokyo in 2016, along with Advertising Week Havana. In 2017, Advertising

Week LATAM started in Mexico City. Advertising Week APAC (Asia-Pacific) was in Sydney, Australia, in 2018, followed by Advertising Week Africa in Johannesburg in 2019. The event now existed all around the world, but without that original promotional purpose as its focus.

CONCLUSION

The advertising business became a *bona fide* industry in the 1800s, but it became a major driver of the GDP in the 1900s. In the last quarter of that century, business realities struck and profit margins evaporated. But the industry had evolved to something more like a science than probably ever was imagined a century earlier.

11

The Science of Advertising

The science of advertising is in its infancy. It is growing in importance and efficiency every day. It used to be a speculative venture. Now it is a scientific certainty.

—*Charles Austin Bates (1898)*

Today's world seems entirely data driven, including advertising. Data is the essence of advertising science. Research and data probably are the most pronounced changes in advertising since 1900.

SHRINKING ADVERTISING

Desires morphing advertising into a science began in the mid-nineteenth century. The first real strides began at century's end, as advertising caught the attention of some psychologists.

Psychology as a rudimentary field had been around for hundreds of years but wasn't much of a science. It was more philosophy than science. But late in that century, the experimental study of psychology began converting it to science. Coincidentally, psychology and advertising matured nearly simultaneously.

The two fields first met in 1895 when Harlow Gale at the University of Minnesota performed the world's first psychological studies of advertising, mailing questionnaires to businessmen to get their opinions about advertising. He later conducted experiments, using advertising, regarding involuntary attention (Coolsen 1947).

In 1895, too, *Printers' Ink* magazine first mentioned psychology, predicting, "Probably, when we are a little more enlightened, the advertisement writer, like the teacher, will study psychology. For, however diverse their occupations may at first sight appear, the advertising writer and the teacher have one great object in common—to influence the human mind."

Early psychological models of advertising got a start then, but not from a psychologist. E. St. Elmo Lewis, a copywriter, set down his principles of good ad copy, stating that it should (1) attract attention, (2) awaken interest, and (3) create conviction. This three-step model was expanded to four by Dukesmith et al. (1904): attention, interest, desire, and conviction.

Later, that evolved to attention, interest, desire, and action (AIDA), proposed by C. P. Russell (1921). In 1961, Robert J. Lavidge and Gary A. Steiner improved it with their Hierarchy of Effects model: awareness, knowledge, liking, preference, conviction, and purchase. And in 1984 Ivan L. Preston and Esther Thorson presented a twenty-nine-step version: the Association Model. As psychological approaches took hold, advertising was becoming a science.

Walter Dill Scott, a psychologist at Northwestern University, was the main driver of applying psychology to advertising. Chicago's admen asked him, in 1901, to speak at the Agate Club about ad psychology. His speech, "The Psychology of Involuntary Attention as Applied to Advertising," led him to begin publishing articles about it in *Mahin's Magazine*, which he then compiled into a 1903 book, *The Theory of Advertising*. He taught the first university course about advertising in 1904 and published another book, *The Psychology of Advertising*, in 1908. He became the world's first professor of advertising at Northwestern's School of Commerce in 1909.

Scott argued that "man is a creature that rarely reasons at all" and suggested ads should tap emotions, not logic, contrary to the popular "reason-why" approach. His university colleagues denigrated his work, which they considered too "applied." One leading psychologist wrote to Scott, warning him to stop publishing material about advertising (Coolsen 1947). But Scott became president of the American Psychological Association and president of Northwestern.

In 1913, John Broadus Watson published the article "Psychology as the Behaviorist Views It," laying the foundation for a new psychological paradigm: behaviorism. With it, Watson argued for a more scientific approach, including experimentation, asserting:

> To be a science, psychology must use the same material that all other sciences use. Its facts must be capable of verification by other capable investigators everywhere. Its methods must be the methods of science in general (Kreshel 1990).

Previously, psychologists relied on "introspection," looking within themselves to ponder how minds work. Watson's ideas took hold and he became famous. In 1915, he was president of the American Psychological Association.

J. B. Watson was the first psychologist working in an ad agency when he joined J. Walter Thompson in 1920. His peers didn't uniformly embrace this move (Kreshel 1990). In his sixteen years at Thompson, Watson had a major impact on advertising. From there he moved to another agency, William Esty.

By 1943, McCann Erickson was hiring psychologists, bringing Drs. Herta Herzog and Hans Zeisel in and creating a psychological research staff (Tungate 2007). Psychology was fully infused into the field, though not without some criticism.

BELOW THE THRESHOLD

Vance Packard in 1957 published a book called *The Hidden Persuaders*, all about advertising psychology. It contended the ad industry uses psychology to reach into consumers' minds, manipulating them with appeals they don't notice. It was a top-selling conspiracy theory.

Around this same time, James Vicary, a market researcher, held a press conference announcing he had created a device to project "subliminal" (below the threshold of awareness) messages. He claimed that in a movie theater he flashed—too fast for conscious recognition—"Drink Coca-Cola" and "Hungry? Eat Popcorn" onto the screen while the film *Picnic* was being viewed. He claimed Coke sales jumped 57.5 percent and popcorn sales were up 18.1 percent (Richards & Zakia 1981).

A couple of weeks later, the *Saturday Review* published an editorial suggesting Vicary's invention be placed at the center of the next nuclear explosive test. A US senator complained about it to the Federal Communications Commission (FCC), and two congressmen submitted bills in Congress to regulate Vicary's technique (Richards & Zakia 1981).

Another company, Precon, jumped in offering to both create subliminal messages and sell the projection device. Some movie directors actually used it in films.

Britain passed a law prohibiting subliminal methods in advertising "or otherwise," and the US FCC put broadcasters on notice that subliminal messaging was contrary to the public interest (Richards & Zakia 1981). New Zealand, though, determined that subliminal appeals didn't work (Clark 1988).

After a while, this idea was largely forgotten, until renewed by Wilson Bryan Key's 1973 book, *Subliminal Seduction*, another best seller about an evil ad industry engaging in mind control. In 1974, the United Nations Human Rights Commission expressed concern about subliminals being used to indoctrinate people (Richards & Zakia 1981).

Public response was similar to Vicary's announcement, but also led to college textbooks in psychology, advertising, and marketing all adding subliminal advertising discussions. Key published three more books on the same topic.

A British psychology professor, Norman Dixon, in 1971 published a serious book on this topic, *Subliminal Perception: The Nature of a Controversy*. His research found subliminal effects were so small as to be almost nonexistent, but his book got no noticeable public attention. He published another one a decade later, with essentially identical results.

DATA ON DATA COLLECTION

Politics might be the root of all evil, but it also seems to be the start of many things. The first known political opinion poll, in 1824, was conducted by the *Harrisburg Pennsylvanian* newspaper in Wilmington, Delaware. It found Andrew Jackson leading John Quincy Adams in the presidential campaign, 335 votes to 169. Henry Clay had 19 and William H. Crawford had 9. Jackson won a plurality of electoral votes, but the House of Representatives chose Adams as the winner. This marked the beginning of survey research.

The first use of survey research in advertising wasn't until 1879. The N.W. Ayer and George P. Rowell agencies were competing for a mechanical threshing machine account. Ayer presented the client the first market survey, asking state and local officials about grain production estimates, and asking publishers about circulation figures in farming communities (West 1999). Ayer won the account.

As some practitioners pushed to make advertising more systematized and scientific, surveys became a tool to make that happen. Britain in 1903 recognized US advertising as more effective because of market surveys (Presbrey 1929). By around 1910, surveys research gained sufficient repute to be a true specialty (Editors of Advertising Age 1976).

Charles Coolidge Parlin was hired by Curtis Publishing, describing his work as "commercial research." He conducted a survey of the agriculture market for *Country Gentleman* magazine. He established a commercial research department at Curtis, using research to drive advertising sales. In the 1920s, Parlin founded the first commercial research company, creating a whole new industry.

Research methods soon expanded beyond surveys. By the 1920s, agencies were copy testing to assess ad effectiveness. Analysis techniques also improved (e.g., Miracle 1977).

Stanley Resor and associates bought J. Walter Thompson in 1916 and immediately established a market research department. Three years later, JWT had both planning and statistical investigation departments (Pope 1983). In 1922, Paul Cherington became JWT's director of research. He now is considered a true pioneer in both advertising research and election polling.

In 1923, University of Wisconsin marketing professor Daniel Starch set up a market research company, Daniel Starch and Staff, and researched ad recognition. Later he was research director for the AAAA. He developed a method, the "Starch test," to measure ad recognition levels.

John O'Toole (1981) suggests ad research began with Albert Lasker at the Lord & Thomas agency, as told by market researcher George Gallup:

> George Gallup once told me that market research really began in the 1920s when Lord & Thomas was handling a canned evaporated milk account. The product was introduced in a test market in Indiana where the sell-in to retail stores was successful and displays of the product were in evidence everywhere as the advertising was launched. Sales were excellent in the initial weeks, then dropped to almost nothing. Obviously something about the product was discouraging repurchase. Lasker dispatched a goodly proportion of his staff to that Indiana town to knock on doors, talk to housewives and find out what it was (it turned out to be a slight almond taste that was easily corrected). And so another industry was born.

In 1922, Herbert Hoover, then secretary of commerce, reorganized the Bureau of Foreign and Domestic Commerce to disseminate market information. To facilitate this process, a series of market studies were conducted (Printers' Ink 1938).

George H. Gallup, a journalism and advertising professor, was invited to New York by Ray Rubicam in 1932. He opened a research department for the Young & Rubicam agency and developed a copy-testing technique. But his passion was public opinion surveys. Tungate (2007) suggests, "He discovered that while the largest percentage of ads focused on the economy and efficiency of products, those that pushed the right buttons with readers concerned quality, vanity and sex-appeal."

Gallup later founded the American Institute of Public Opinion and the British Institute of Public Opinion, and created an advertising and marketing research company: Gallup & Robinson, Inc. His name became synonymous with public opinion research. While at Y&R, he helped build the agency's reputation around "science," increasing its revenue even during the Depression.

Arthur C. Nielsen founded the A.C. Nielsen Company in 1923. He created the concept of "market share" in 1935, and in 1936 introduced the Audimeter, a device to electrically survey radio use. His contributions to advertising include the concepts "cost per thousand" and "designated market area," But his rating system, assessing listeners, became the ad industry for determining radio programs' values (Mierau 2000). For decades Nielsen had people around the United States keep diaries of their television viewing, but in 1987 his company introduced a new "People Meter" to replace diaries. That technology was far more accurate.

Earnest Dichter came from Vienna in 1939, offering services as a psychologist and researcher, immediately taking on an advertising agency client. Most research prior to Dichter was "quantitative," which includes surveys. Dichter, though, was more "qualitative," seeking insights rather than numbers. He conducted in-depth interviews, used projective techniques, and applied observational methods. He unearthed facts about products and consumers that probably would have been missed by surveys. Dichter is called the "father of motivational research."

By the 1950s, more and more consumer goods companies were adding research departments, reducing their reliance on agencies. Some agencies shed their research programs in response, spinning them into independent research companies (Tungate 2007).

Not everyone in advertising was a fan of research. Some creatives, in particular, reacted even viscerally to it. One famous copywriter, Walter Weir, said, "Merchandising men and research men are statistic-ing the creative man to death. No one yet has succeeded in making an advertisement by setting in type a research report" (Fox 1984).

STRATEGIC OR ACCOUNT?

A fundamental shift in agencies' approach to research came in 1965, at a British agency, Pritchard Wood & Partners (PWP). The brainchild of Stanley Pollitt, it soon was known as "account planning."

Pollitt recognized weaknesses in the way research was conducted. People developing a campaign asked questions, sending them to the research department for answers. But they could be the wrong questions, or even questions designed to support decisions already made.

He proposed creating a consumer "expert" who, through in-depth understanding of consumers, could determine what questions needed to be answered. Qualitative research now took a central place in advertising.

In 1967, J. Walter Thompson's London office renamed its marketing department the account planning department. Stephen King is credited by some, alongside Pollitt, as co-originator of account planning. King and Pollitt genuinely were exploring this simultaneously, without knowing it. Tony Stead, of JWT, coined the term "account planning" (Tungate 2007).

In 1968, Pollitt, with Gabe Massimi and Martin Boase, left PWP to form Boase Massimi Pollitt (BMP). This firm was designed for advertising through account planning (Feldwick 2015).

Account planning caught traction in England by 1973, when other agencies followed BMP's lead; it took longer elsewhere. In 1979, the Account Planning Group, an association for account planners, began. By 1985, eighteen of the top twenty UK agencies had account planning departments.

McCann Erickson London in 1988 dissolved its planning department at the insistence of its creative director. But it was brought back after a time.

It reached the United States in 1982, when Jane Newman joined the Chiat/Day agency. Newman had learned planning at BMP. Other US agencies, though, clung to the old research model. In 1990, a US Account Planning Group was formed.

In the early 1990s, big US agencies adopted account planning. One changed, and then it cascaded so most changed over just four or five years. Initially, many of them merely renamed research departments, not really adopting the account planning philosophy. No one in the United States was training planners, so agencies hired nearly anyone with a British accent claiming account planning expertise. Over time it became fully integrated into American agency culture.

Many agencies resisted the term "account planning" because they didn't invent it. To avoid becoming "account planning" lemmings, they instead followed one another in adopting "strategic planning." Later, some matured into using "strategic account planning."

No matter the name, all were digging through consumer information searching for a "consumer insight" to drive sales. The timing was good, because those piles were just beginning to reach enormous proportions, thanks to the internet and advances in data collection.

SOPHISTICATED ADVERTISING HAS SOPHISTICATED PROBLEMS

Better understanding of consumers' wants and needs was only part of advertising "science." Media planning and new technologies propelled the field forward, but steps forward often required steps back.

The environment grew more dense with promotions, making it harder to get noticed, since more ads competed for consumer attention. Advertisers often responded by increasing advertising to improve their "share of voice," but this only made the clutter worse. Audiences rebelled against more of their media space or time being occupied by advertising. For example, when television gave more time to advertising, it cut time for the programs people wanted to watch.

This made it possible to charge viewers to subscribe to advertising-free media. First, for television, remote controls enabled channel switching when advertising occurred. This "zapping" was followed by "zipping," home recording machines that allowed a program to be recorded, then fast-forwarded through commercials.

HBO, Cinemax, and Showtime (and others) built programming off this clutter problem, offering programs uninterrupted by commercials. Netflix and Hulu then offered hundreds of viewing options on demand, making some consumers discontinue watching ad-supported broadcast programming. Television no longer reached the immense audiences it once did.

US television was popular in the 1950s through the mid-1970s but had only a few channels. Typical viewers might watch one of three national networks (CBS, NBC, ABC) and perhaps an "independent" local station. Reliance on antennas to receive those stations could mean one or more channels had poor reception, further limiting choices.

As cable television (CATV) became more common in the late 1970s, options exploded. Instead of four channels, viewers might have dozens of options, and by 2000 it was hundreds. Before cable, advertisers could run their commercials on three networks simultaneously (called a "roadblock"), being certain to reach almost everyone watching any television station at that time. When options were in the hundreds, that wasn't even imaginable.

These exposure-limiting problems weren't limited to television. Radio was affected as cassette tape players were installed in automobiles, followed by satellite radio giving listeners many options. Print media, too, had these problems. Billboards allowed an ad to be on display 24/7 for weeks or months (or years), but electronic billboards meant an ad might appear only a few seconds at a time, rotating with other ads. Competition had increased.

What happened, really, was that power shifted from advertiser to consumer. Back when TV roadblocks reached most consumers, those ads were mostly waste. Advertisers were reaching thousands, or millions, of people who had no interest in the advertised product. Expansion to hundreds of television options means advertisers selling yarn might advertise on an "all knitting channel," reaching only real potential users of the product. Most waste is eliminated. And it's cheaper to advertise on one specialty station than on three major networks.

Maximizing this efficiency isn't always so simple. If you sell orange juice, you're unlikely to find an all-juice channel. That's just part of the puzzle. Big problems need big solutions. Advertisers decided that the big solution comes from big data.

BIGGISH, BIG, AND BIGGER DATA

Mary Gardiner Jones, former FTC commissioner, mentioned in 1991 that American Express held 410 pieces of information about each of its customers, updated weekly (Jones 1991). The commercialized internet was just beginning, and the only type of advertising collecting such data was direct marketing. Most of the industry had no concept of the true value of data.

In days of old, ad agencies conducted studies that generated data. After a while, that information pile deepened, especially with prolific researchers. Researchers in the 1950s looked to computers for data analysis (Barnes 2013). But that analysis found connections in existing data, thereby creating more data. The internet, circa 1990s, opened the floodgates. That's when Big Data really began in the advertising field. We collected data from every click and search. And then people *really* started using the internet in ways that enabled data generation, like online shopping.

By 2013, IBM estimated that each and every day 2.5 quintillion bytes of information are generated (Yakbuksi 2013). And that was years ago. As data (or anything else) goes, that is *big*!

Any data pile too big to calculate simple statistics on a hand calculator in an hour or two probably qualifies as Big Data. But Nate Silver has said, "[M]ost of the data is just noise, as most of the universe is filled with empty space" (Barnes 2013). Tools were developed to help sift through all that data. Today we can "scrape" data with available tools, collecting and analyzing only what we value, avoiding that "noise."

One tool that enabled more practical data use was the relational database, allowing one piece of data to be connected to another. This first arrived in 1969–1970, opening the door to computer use by more than computer scientists. Almost simultaneously, the computer spreadsheet was introduced, further helping to democratize data handling. Computers were expensive and big, so only businesses owned them. Some basic knowledge of programming (or knowledge of Basic programming[1]) tended to be a requirement.

Introduction of the IBM PC in 1981 made computer ownership possible even to very small businesses and a few individuals. This also spurred development of all manner of new software, as the computer market rapidly expanded.

By the mid-1990s the internet was commercialized and data storage costs were dropping like a rock. The ability to collect and store data was greatly enhanced.

The term "Big Data" was coined by Steve Bryson et al. (1999). Those authors note:

> Interactively browsing a data set is less difficult when the data resides in physical memory. But many data sets are larger than the physical memory of a particular computer, and some data sets are much larger than any computer's memory.

That was the essence of Big Data, as initially defined.

That also was when "Internet of Things" was coined by Kevin Ashton, meaning almost everything we own or use could feed data onto the internet, from automobiles to refrigerators to room lights and door locks. All that data could be captured and analyzed. That was the platform from which the twenty-first century was launched, and the Internet of Things became reality.

The ad industry began embracing data in the 1990s, seeing the potential for more efficient consumer targeting. Data helped match the right product or service with the right appeal to fit the right medium that would reach the right consumer at the right moment. Consumers were leaving data droppings everywhere, if only they could be collected and interpreted.

So superstores like Walmart and Target became data collectors. So did new online retailers like Amazon and Facebook, and search engines like Google were especially well positioned to gather those droppings. Even smaller retailers and chains were capturing data through devices like loyalty programs (Figure 11.1).

A whole industry of data aggregators and brokers was born, like Epsilon and Acxiom and others. These companies took databases from multiple sources, combining them into even bigger databases. Acxiom claimed to have data on about seven hundred million people, averaging around 1,500 facts on each of them. Data had immense value to advertisers. In 2018, the Interpublic Group bought Acxiom for $2.3 billion USD. In 2019, the Publicis Groupe, another advertising agency holding company, bought Epsilon for $4.4 billion USD. Publicis immediately leveraged that purchase to win its biggest account of the year: Disney (Hsu 2019).

FIGURE 11.1. Loyalty/rewards cards became so popular that customers often found themselves carrying a large collection in their wallet or purse.

Besides targeting, data created opportunities for better, faster, and more efficient advertising media buying. Computers could make many decisions, taking advantage of opportunities before they disappeared, thereby optimizing the buys. This was called "programmatic buying." But that led to even more sophisticated computer-based approaches.

As 2020 approached, the industry used terms like "data-enabled advertising" and "bespoke advertising solutions," referring to an electronically connected advertising ecosystem where ads not seen by a consumer on one medium (e.g., TV) would "know" to reach that consumer on another medium (e.g., smartphone). They also talked about "contextual intelligence," with advertising "knowing" the context in which it was displayed (e.g., drama programming, comedy, etc.). This promised to take advertising beyond a fixed, dumb targeting to more dynamic and adaptive means of reaching the right consumers at the right moments (Moulding 2019).

Data makes advertising into a more scientific (read: data-driven) endeavor. But it also raises the specter of privacy violations.

NO NEED FOR ARTIFICIAL STUPIDITY

In striving to become a science, the industry has been infused with increasingly more technology. It became more sophisticated, but also more complex, necessitating more knowledge to deal with it.

It still is too early to say much about the role of artificial intelligence (AI) in advertising. Advertisers and agencies already rely on AI to help mine big piles of data (Kietzmann et al. 2018). It's also used to predict whether consumers will click on a particular ad, and even to create ads.

Kaput (2020) says, "Artificial intelligence is taking over the world of advertising." The volume of data being compiled on consumers presents a problem: How do we discover all the useful insights buried there? AI holds promise for dealing with it in ways not possible by humans. It also can make complex decisions faster than humans. What we call "programmatic advertising" illustrates how a well-crafted AI algorithm can achieve what no mortal could hope to do.

A program called Albert, designed for the ad industry, uses AI to outpace people. RedBalloon used Albert to test 6,500 versions of a Google text ad in a single day, learning as it went. The program ballooned the company's return on investment in advertising, while cutting its marketing costs.

This is just one AI application. Artificial "intelligence" still is rudimentary. But over the next few years it will become truly exciting, and predominant.

WHAT'S IN *YOUR* UNDERWEAR DRAWER?

Data has great benefits, but it also can be misused. The primary misuse is in the collecting process. Too often collected data was not intended for collection, and certainly wasn't to be used in any way you please. People don't necessarily want everyone to know what medicines they take or whether they wear boxers or briefs . . . in pink.

Privacy, as a legal right, was invented in 1890. The US Constitution said nothing explicit about it, but two lawyers argued that right was implied (Curran & Richards 2004). In 1965, the US Supreme Court decided married couples had such a right, constitutionally protected (*Griswold v. Connecticut* 1965). No one applied it to advertising, though.

After that, privacy laws were created, though not until the Privacy Act of 1974. The laws multiplied as computers invaded our lives. But legislators are always behind the technological curve, and the laws dealt with one problem at a time, such as health data. Result: a Swiss cheese patchwork of laws. The European Union (EU) adopted directives protecting privacy, which were more aggressive at dealing with the problems (Curran & Richards 2004). But problems persisted, regardless of jurisdiction, thanks to the shifting sands of technological advancement.

As advertisers gathered more data, pressure followed for the US FTC to set boundaries. For a long time it did nothing, so some organizations began proposing self-regulations to deal with excesses. Finally, in 1999, the FTC endorsed self-regulations written by the Network Advertising Initiative (NAI). A decade later the FTC dropped that and proposed a "Do Not Track" law, permitting consumers to "opt out" of having their information collected. In 2013, it abandoned that push. As legal authorities sat on their thumbs, private industry sought solutions, hoping the law would again endorse what industry proposed.

A study was conducted to find a symbol to put on online ads for catching consumers' attention. Consumers could click that symbol and be taken to a page of information about their right to "opt out" of data collection by that advertiser.

Note that rather than requiring advertisers gather personal information only if consumers "opt in" (obtain permission), the industry chose an "opt-out" approach allowing advertisers to gather consumers' data until consumers take affirmative action to stop them.

The Future of Privacy Forum in 2010 announced the new symbol: the "Power I" icon. Another symbol—the "Asterisk Man"—actually was more effective (Hastak & Culnan 2010),

but industry liked the Power I, so ignored the study results. Nine months later, pretending that never happened,
a new "Advertising Option Icon" was announced, accom-
panied by the term "AdChoices" (Figure 11.2).

FIGURE 11.2.   The Power I (left),
Asterisk Man (middle), and the
Advertising Option Icon (right).

Participating advertisers would put a small Advertising
Option Icon in their ad, and clicking it took consumers
to the AdChoices page. This assumed that consumers would notice it *and* know to click it
(Figure 11.3). By 2011, the industry claimed that already more than one thousand companies
were participating, but by 2013 a survey found 73 percent of consumers did not recall the
icon and only 1 percent could correctly identify it (Richards & Fernandez 2014).

Data collection wasn't confined to consumers' interactions with ads. The Internet of
Things meant data soon was coming from every direction.

Consumer targeting now was based
on data derived from actual consumer
behavior. The industry, starting in 2007,
called this "Online Behavioral Advertising" (OBA). It seemed SUN Microsystems'

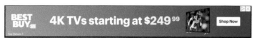

FIGURE 11.3.   A 2018 banner ad with the
Advertising Option Icon in the upper-right corner,
next to the [x] closure box.

chairman, Scott McNealy, was correct when in 1999 he declared, "You have zero privacy
anyway. Get over it!"

OBA was used when Target, running a sophisticated computer model of customer tracking, went a bit wrong. This model identified twenty-five products that, when purchased in a
given time period, suggested a woman was pregnant. Parents of newborns buy a lot, so this
held the potential for Target to sell many products. A man came into Target demanding to
see a manager. He was incensed his teenage daughter was getting Target coupons for baby-
related merchandise. "Are you trying to encourage her to get pregnant?" he demanded. The
man later apologized after discovering his daughter was in fact pregnant (Duhigg 2012).

Aside from losing privacy to advertisers, telling them things you don't want them to know,
there are major data breaches that open data caches to criminals. Yahoo had 3 billion accounts hacked in 2013, and 500 million the next year. Equifax, the consumer credit reporting
agency, in 2017 had a hacker tap into 146 million accounts. Those are just examples. That
data might include passwords, and most certainly included personal information that could
lead to identity theft. This information has great value to advertisers—and thieves.

By the twenty-first century's second decade, advertisers had immense volumes of data,
facilitating targeting that approached a waste-free advertising ideal. Advertising now was
more scientific than anyone a century earlier likely could have envisioned.

CONCLUSION

In 1919, a celebration recognizing the fiftieth anniversary of N.W. Ayer and honoring F. Wayland Ayer, its founder, was held. Former US president William Howard Taft spoke, saying:

We are honoring a man who has made advertising a science, who has made it useful, and who has robbed it of many of its evil tendencies, and who has a right to be proud of the record he has made . . . we owe a debt of gratitude to Mr. Ayer, for having rendered a form of publicity so useful and elevating, which might have been vicious and deplorable.

Contrary to Taft's words, the science of advertising was still in its infancy, though the twentieth century made great strides toward that goal. But science is not an endpoint, it is a continuing process. The science of advertising doubtless will continue to advance. Of course, the same can be said of the laws applied to it.

12

Criticism, Law, and Policy

It is a notorious fact that there has been so much trickery and dishonesty in the advertising business that a man engaged in it sometimes feels embarrassed when he is asked what business he is in.

—*Charles Austin Bates*

Advertising has a long history of criticism, leading to laws aimed at limiting where, when, or what advertisements can do. It is easy to imagine advertising restrictions so onerous that an ad industry would never survive. But there are limits to how far laws can go, quite evident in the US legal system. The laws of two hundred countries can't be described here, and the United States produces the largest percentage of advertising, so my focus will be confined to the United States.

CONSTITUTIONAL LIMITS
The US Constitution serves as the governor on advertising laws. That document defines the rights of citizens against excessive interference. The US Supreme Court interprets the Constitution, and it is the First Amendment of the Constitution that has the greatest impact on advertising, since it protects free speech.

The First Amendment was adopted in 1791, but the first Supreme Court case to involve advertising wasn't until 1942. Until then, it was assumed that advertising wasn't protected speech. In that case, *Valentine v. Chrestensen* (1942), Chrestensen had passed out handbills in New York City promoting submarine tours. The court declared "purely commercial advertising" wasn't protected by the First Amendment. For many years afterward the assumption continued that advertising was not free speech.

The first case to slightly change that assumption was *New York Times v. Sullivan* (1964), involving a political protest published as an ad (Figure 12.1). There the court decided that advertising resembling an editorial, like promoting a cause, is protected. An editorial would be protected, so that same content in paid advertising space should not undermine

97
APPENDIX B

> *"The growing movement of peaceful mass demonstrations by Negroes is something new in the South, something understandable.... Let Congress heed their rising voices, for they will be heard."*
>
> —*New York Times editorial*
> *Saturday, March 19, 1960*

Heed Their Rising Voices

As the whole world knows by now, thousands of Southern Negro students are engaged in widespread non-violent demonstrations in positive affirmation of the right to live in human dignity as guaranteed by the U. S. Constitution and the Bill of Rights. In their efforts to uphold these guarantees, they are being met by an unprecedented wave of terror by those who would deny and negate that document which the whole world looks upon as setting the pattern for modern freedom....

In Orangeburg, South Carolina, when 400 students peacefully sought to buy doughnuts and coffee at lunch counters in the business district, they were forcibly ejected, tear-gassed, soaked to the skin in freezing weather with fire hoses, arrested en masse and herded into an open barbed-wire stockade to stand for hours in the bitter cold.

In Montgomery, Alabama, after students sang "My Country, 'Tis of Thee" on the State Capitol steps, their leaders were expelled from school, and truckloads of police armed with shotguns and tear-gas ringed the Alabama State College Campus. When the entire student body protested to state authorities by refusing to re-register, their dining hall was padlocked in an attempt to starve them into submission.

In Tallahassee, Atlanta, Nashville, Savannah, Greensboro, Memphis, Richmond, Charlotte, and a host of other cities in the South, young American teenagers, in face of the entire weight of official state apparatus and police power, have boldly stepped forth as protagonists of democracy. Their courage and amazing restraint have inspired millions and given a new dignity to the cause of freedom.

Small wonder that the Southern violators of the Constitution fear this new, non-violent brand of freedom fighter ... even as they fear the upswelling right-to-vote movement. Small wonder that they are determined to destroy the one man who, more than any other, symbolizes the new spirit now sweeping the South—the Rev. Dr. Martin Luther King, Jr., world-famous leader of the Montgomery Bus Protest. For it is his doctrine of non-violence which has inspired and guided the students in their widening wave of sit-ins; and it this same Dr. King who founded and is president of the Southern Christian Leadership Conference—the organization which is spearheading the surging right-to-vote movement. Under Dr. King's direction the Leadership Conference conducts Student Workshops and Seminars in the philosophy and technique of non-violent resistance.

Again and again the Southern violators have answered Dr. King's peaceful protests with intimidation and violence. They have bombed his home almost killing his wife and child. They have assaulted his person. They have arrested him seven times—for "speeding." "loitering" and similar "offenses." And now they have charged him with "perjury"—a *felony* under which they could imprison him for *ten years.* Obviously, their real purpose is to remove him physically as the leader to whom the students and millions of others—look for guidance and support, and thereby to intimidate *all* leaders who may rise in the South. Their strategy is to behead this affirmative movement, and thus to demoralize Negro Americans and weaken their will to struggle. The defense of Martin Luther King, spiritual leader of the student sit-in movement, clearly, therefore, is an integral part of the total struggle for freedom in the South.

Decent-minded Americans cannot help but applaud the creative daring of the students and the quiet heroism of Dr. King. But this is one of those moments in the stormy history of Freedom when men and women of good will must do more than applaud the rising-to-glory of others. The America whose good name hangs in the balance before a watchful world, the America whose heritage of Liberty these Southern Upholders of the Constitution are defending, is *our* America as well as theirs ...

We must heed their rising voices—yes—but we must add our own.

We must extend ourselves above and beyond moral support and render the material help so urgently needed by those who are taking the risks, facing jail, and even death in a glorious re-affirmation of our Constitution and its Bill of Rights.

We urge you to join hands with our fellow Americans in the South by supporting, with your dollars, this Combined Appeal for all three needs—the defense of Martin Luther King—the support of the embattled students—and the struggle for the right-to-vote.

Your Help Is Urgently Needed . . . NOW !!

Stella Adler
Raymond Pace Alexander
Harry Van Andale
Harry Belafonte
Julie Belafonte
Dr. Algernon Black
Marc Blitzstein
William Branch
Marlon Brando
Mrs. Ralph Bunche
Diahann Carroll

Dr. Alan Knight Chalmers
Richard Coe
Nat King Cole
Cheryl Crawford
Dorothy Dandridge
Ossie Davis
Sammy Davis, Jr.
Ruby Dee
Dr. Philip Elliott
Dr. Harry Emerson Fosdick

Anthony Franciosa
Lorraine Hansbury
Rev. Donald Harrington
Nat Hentoff
James Hicks
Mary Hinkson
Van Heflin
Langston Hughes
Morris Iushevitz
Mahalia Jackson
Mordecai Johnson

John Killens
Eartha Kitt
Rabbi Edward Klein
Hope Lange
John Lewis
Viveca Lindfors
Carl Murphy
Don Murray
John Murray
A. J. Muste
Frederick O'Neal

L. Joseph Overton
Clarence Pickett
Shad Polier
Sidney Poitier
A. Philip Randolph
John Raitt
Elmer Rice
Jackie Robinson
Mrs. Eleanor Roosevelt
Bayard Rustin
Robert Ryan

Maureen Stapleton
Frank Silvera
Hope Stevens
George Tabori
Rev. Gardner C. Taylor
Norman Thomas
Kenneth Tynan
Charles White
Shelley Winters
Max Youngstein

We in the south who are struggling daily for dignity and freedom warmly endorse this appeal

Rev. Ralph D. Abernathy
(Montgomery, Ala.)
Rev. Fred L. Shuttlesworth
(Birmingham, Ala.)
Rev. Kelley Miller Smith
(Nashville, Tenn.)
Rev. W. A. Dennis
(Chattanooga, Tenn.)
Rev. C. K. Steele
(Tallahassee, Fla.)

Rev. Matthew D. McCollom
(Orangeburg, S. C.)
Rev. William Holmes Borders
(Atlanta, Ga.)
Rev. Douglas Moore
(Durham, N. C.)
Rev. Wyatt Tee Walker
(Petersburg, Va.)

Rev. Walter L. Hamilton
(Norfolk, Va.)
I. S. Levy
(Columbia, S. C.)
Rev. Martin Luther King, Sr.
(Atlanta, Ga.)
Rev. Henry C. Bunton
(Memphis, Tenn.)
Rev. S. S. Seay, Sr.
(Montgomery, Ala.)
Rev. Samuel W. Williams
(Atlanta, Ga.)

Rev. A. L. Davis
(New Orleans, La.)
Mrs. Katie E. Whickham
(New Orleans, La.)
Rev. W. H. Hall
(Hattiesburg, Miss.)
Rev. J. E. Lowery
(Mobile, Ala.)
Rev. T. J. Jemison
(Baton Rouge, La.)

Please mail this coupon TODAY!

Committee To Defend Martin Luther King
and
The Struggle For Freedom In The South
312 West 125th Street, New York 27, N. Y.
UNiversity 6-1700

I am enclosing my contribution of $_____ for the work of the Committee.

Name _____ (PLEASE PRINT)

Address _____

City _____ Zone ____ State ____

☐ I want to help   ☐ Please send further information

Please make checks payable to:
Committee To Defend Martin Luther King

COMMITTEE TO DEFEND MARTIN LUTHER KING AND THE STRUGGLE FOR FREEDOM IN THE SOUTH

312 West 125th Street, New York 27, N. Y. UNiversity 6-1700

Chairmen: A. Philip Randolph, Dr. Gardner C. Taylor; *Chairmen of Cultural Division:* Harry Belafonte, Sidney Poitier; *Treasurer:* Nat King Cole; *Executive Director:* Bayard Rustin; *Chairmen of Church Division:* Father George B. Ford, Rev. Harry Emerson Fosdick, Rev. Thomas Kilgore, Jr., Rabbi Edward E. Klein; *Chairman of Labor Division:* Morris Iushewitz

FIGURE 12.1. From *New York Times v. Sullivan,* the "Heed Their Rising Voices" editorial ad, published March 29, 1960.

that protection. This protected "editorial advertising," while leaving "commercial" advertising unprotected.

Several years later, *Pittsburgh Press v. Pittsburgh Commission on Human Relations* (1973) addressed gender bias of headings in a newspaper's classified advertising section, declaring "Jobs—Male Interest" and "Jobs—Female Interest." The court used the *Valentine* rule, finding this was unprotected commercial advertising, but leaving the door open a crack. It implied there *might* be protection where the ad's commercial interest outweighs the government's interest in regulating it.

Bigelow v. Virginia (1975) found that crack. A "commercial" ad for an abortion clinic ran in the *Virginia Weekly* newspaper. The newspaper's managing editor was charged with violating a law prohibiting "encouraging" abortion. The court recognized that abortion was a hot topic, declaring this ad *did more* than merely propose a commercial transaction—it contained material of a clear "public interest." Besides, abortion was legal in New York, the clinic's location, and Virginia couldn't regulate businesses in New York. The justices didn't approve of Virginia trying to keep its citizens ignorant of abortions in New York and decided the ad was constitutionally protected.

The next year, *Virginia Board of Pharmacy v. Virginia Citizens Consumer Council* (1976) was about pharmacies advertising drug prices, violating state law. Consumers sued, wanting prices in the ads. That consumers were pushing this showed the court there was a clear "public interest" in this information, just like in the *Bigelow* case. And like *Bigelow*, Virginia wanted to keep its citizens in the dark. The decision, a landmark, announced that even commercial advertising is protected "speech" under the First Amendment.

That didn't mean no advertising restrictions were permissible, but the bar was raised. In *Linmark Associates, Inc. v. Township of Willingboro* (1977), to stop public perception of "white flight" from Willingboro Township, New Jersey, an ordinance barred use of "For Sale" signs everywhere except for model homes. The court declared this limited homeowners' free speech, suggesting the township encourage using "Not For Sale" signs instead.

Ohralik v. Ohio State Bar Association (1978) then opened the door to more regulation of advertising than was allowed on other forms of speech, noting a "common-sense" difference between commercial and non-commercial speech. It suggested commercial speech deserves more "limited measure of protection." What regulations were permissible wasn't clear.

Drawing that line was the subject of *Central Hudson Gas and Electric v. Public Service Commission of New York* (1980). Public electric utilities were prohibited from using "promotional" advertising during the 1973 fuel shortage. Even after the shortage ended, that ban was maintained. Central Hudson was subject to the ban, but some of its competitors weren't public utilities and therefore not restricted, so it sued.

The justices noted that advertising is protected, but less protected than other speech types, so the government can prohibit speech that is more likely to deceive than inform. They provided a "test" to help determine when a restriction on *commercial speech* (i.e., "advertising") would be allowed:

Is the speech lawful and not misleading?

Does the government have a substantial interest in regulating it?

Does the regulation directly advance that substantial interest?

Is the restriction not more extensive than necessary?

These were four hurdles legal authorities must leap before imposing ad restrictions. The court determined the prohibition on promotional advertising was unconstitutional. The *Central Hudson* test became the border between allowable and illegal ad regulations.

An attorney in 1985 ran a newspaper ad offering to represent women harmed by an intrauterine device, which included a drawing of the device. He was found guilty of violating attorney advertising standards by including that illustration, deemed undignified and inappropriate for lawyer ads, even when entirely truthful. There was no clear "substantial interest," required by the *Central Hudson* test, so the ad was constitutionally protected.

In 1986, Chief Justice Warren Burger retired, and William Rehnquist went from associate to chief justice. One of Burger's final decisions was *Posadas de Puerto Rico v. Tourism Company* (1986). Rehnquist, already announced as the new chief, ended up authoring the court's decision. It is worth noting that he previously disagreed with every prior court decision that protected commercial speech.

The US commonwealth of Puerto Rico had legal casino gambling, but prohibited casinos from targeting ads at the Puerto Rican people while allowing them to target tourists. Posadas de Puerto Rico was a casino using minimal advertising, but those ads were not clearly limited to tourists. Justice Rehnquist's decision seemed to apply the *Central Hudson* test, even though he disagreed with that decision, but he gave great deference to the Puerto Rican legislature, concluding the legislature's approach was reasonable. The casino lost. This raised the question of whether the *Central Hudson* test would continue to protect advertising (Richards 1997).

Subsequent cases, including *S.U.N.Y. v. Fox* (1989) and *U.S. v. Edge Broadcasting* (1993), increased concerns about the Supreme Court undermining the *Virginia Pharmacy* decision. Then came *44 Liquormart v. Rhode Island* (1996). Rhode Island prohibited advertising alcoholic beverage prices. When a liquor store ran an ad with pictures of bottles and the word "WOW" beside some, the Liquormart was charged with violating that law by implying low prices. The court's decision here changed the game.

This decision said the only reason commercial speech is subject to more regulation is to ensure a "fair bargaining process." If not about fair bargaining, a regulation must be carefully scrutinized:

Precisely because bans against truthful, nonmisleading commercial speech rarely seek to protect consumers from either deception or overreaching, they usually rest solely on the offensive assumption that the public will respond "irrationally" to the truth. . . . The First Amendment directs us to be especially skeptical of regulations that seek to keep people in the dark for what the government perceives to be their own good. That teaching applies equally to state attempts to deprive consumers of accurate information about their chosen products.

The store won. This was a strong declaration protecting advertising from spurious regulatory attacks.

There are many decisions not mentioned here, but they tend to be less significant. The *Central Hudson* test is still the litmus for regulations, but *44 Liquormart* stands as a bulwark against diluting that test, contrary to *Posadas* (Richards 1997). Regardless, claims violating the fair bargaining process, including misleading claims, continue to be regulable.

DECEPTION AND UNFAIRNESS

Preston (1975) traced laws regulating deceptive advertising back to the law of misrepresentation in England, circa 1367 CE. A man stole some cows and sold them as if he owned them. He was found guilty because he *knew* he didn't own the cows. "Knowledge" of the falsity became a basic principle of misrepresentation.

In 1843, a court decided that making a claim *without knowing it was true* also should be a misrepresentation. And in 1867 another English court decided making a claim *without a reasonable ground to believe it*—even if the seller does believe it—likewise is misrepresentation. Other courts wouldn't go that far, until US courts adopted it in 1898. English courts resisted that principle until 1963.

The law of misrepresentation is common law—that is, court-made law. Under this law the truth/falsity of a seller's claim is important only if a consumer "reasonably relied on the misrepresentation to his or her detriment." This is an important, but not perfect, law. It required each victim to sue. An ad misleading thousands would never be sued by every victim.

This laid the foundation for the FTC Act, enacted in 1914. It allowed the FTC to sue on behalf of all victims. Section 5 of the Act is most important for advertising, declaring, "Unfair methods of competition in commerce are hereby declared unlawful." Advertising isn't mentioned, but the first FTC decisions, in 1916, included advertising. FTC commissioners found that deceiving consumers is an unfair method of competition (Richards 1990).

This was during the Truth-in-Advertising movement, and at the start of the consumer movements, so there was public pressure nudging the FTC toward advertising regulation. In 1915, the Associated Advertising Clubs of the World's president appeared before the commission discussing deceptive advertising as an unfair method of competition (Kenner 1936).

An appeals court in 1919 affirmed FTC authority to interpret "unfair methods of competition" broadly, stating the commission's mission included stopping practices "that have a capacity or tendency to injure competitors directly or through deception of purchasers." But the Supreme Court in *FTC v. Gratz* (1920) and *FTC v. Raladam* (1931) reminded the FTC it was a competition protection agency, not a consumer protection agency.

In 1938, Congress fixed it, giving the FTC authority over both competitor and consumer protection by passing the Wheeler-Lea Amendment to the FTC Act. It altered wording of Section 5 to, "Unfair methods of competition in commerce, and unfair or deceptive acts or practices in commerce, are hereby declared unlawful." That gave the agency permission to regulate advertising, even with no clear impact on competition. It was slightly re-worded again in 1975, changing "in commerce" to "in or affecting commerce" (Richards 1990).

The FTC now could regulate (1) unfair advertising and/or (2) deceptive advertising. The deceptiveness standard asked whether claims had a "capacity or tendency" to mislead consumers. Also, that deception must not be trivial; it must be "material." That meant "the natural and probable result of the challenged practices is to cause one to do that which he would not otherwise do."

In 1969, both the American Bar Association and consumer activist Ralph Nader published reports harshly criticizing the FTC for doing little to protect consumers, kicking off a decade of more aggressive agency action. The FTC encouraged states to enact "Little FTC Acts" so states could do some of that regulation, as the agency couldn't do it alone. By the decade's end there were complaints that the FTC was too aggressive (Pertschuk 1982).

An idea was presented in the early 1970s by a group of law students: "corrective advertising." Previously, an advertisement found deceptive normally resulted in an order that the advertiser stop ("cease and desist") running the ad. The commission had no power to fine or punish advertisers. Around 1950 the FTC began sometimes ordering that more information be provided in the ad, rather than stopping the ad. This was known as "affirmative disclosure." Corrective advertising was similar but went further, requiring that information be disclosed to repair a misimpression, becoming the third remedy available to the FTC.

In 1975, the FTC Improvements Act gave the commission authority to approach courts for help. The FTC could request a temporary injunction, stopping an ad pending a final decision regarding whether it broke the law. This had other important consequences, because it gave the case to a court, allowing it to order remedies beyond the FTC's powers. So courts began ordering "consumer redress," meaning advertisers were forced to repay consumers for losses. This was revolutionary for the FTC.

Ronald Reagan, running for president in 1980, promised to reduce federal regulation. Immediately after taking office, he appointed James Miller, an economist, as chairman of the FTC. Miller believed too much regulation is counterproductive and tried to curb FTC activities.

He pushed Congress to define "deception" in the FTC Act, with no success, so in 1983 he pushed the commissioners to craft a Policy Statement on Deception, reframing its meaning. The statement claimed the previous standard was a "capacity and tendency" to mislead, the same as a "likelihood" to mislead. The new definition was:

1. There is a representation, omission or practice that,
2. Is likely to mislead consumers acting reasonably under the circumstances, and
3. The representation, omission, act or practice is material.

The commission explained that "a material misrepresentation, omission, act or practice involves information that is important to consumers, and, hence, likely to affect their choice of, or conduct regarding, a product." This, too, was a re-definition. This new standard seemed more restrictive (i.e., less protective) than the old approach, consistent with Reagan's promises.

The FTC power over "unfairness" also encountered a realignment. Unfair acts or practices were defined as "immoral, unethical, oppressive or unscrupulous," such as practices taking advantage of children or the elderly. Some advertisers felt this broad definition gave the FTC too much power. So in 1980 some US senators pressed the FTC for its unfairness definition, resulting in a Policy Statement on Unfairness. This new statement, too, seemed to diminish FTC power.

That still was unsatisfactory to some, setting off years of debate. In 1994, Congress wrote an unfairness definition into the FTC Act, declaring an act or practice unfair if it:

1. Causes or is likely to cause . . . substantial injury to consumers, which is
2. Not reasonably avoidable by consumers themselves and
3. Not outweighed by countervailing benefits to consumers or to competition.

This clearly shows a cost/benefit analysis typical of economists' thinking, likely from James Miller's 1981 appointment.

The FTC decision in *Pfizer, Inc.* (1972) announced an advertiser should have sufficient reason to believe a claim is true *before* making it. It must be "substantiated." Advertisers always were responsible for deceptiveness, but previously advertisers could make claims without proof. If the FTC challenged it, they could seek proof. *Pfizer* meant any advertiser making a claim must have proof of that claim in their possession when the claim is made. *Without proof in hand* when the claim is made, the advertiser would be guilty of deceptiveness, even if the claim is true. The FTC issued a Policy Statement Regarding Advertising Substantiation in 1984, further clarifying it.

By the mid-1980s, as Reagan's push for FTC deregulation took hold, many deceptive advertising complaints were ignored, so states began filling the void. Since each state had different ideas about regulation, laws had the potential to conflict. So in 1987 states' attorneys general began working together through the National Association of Attorneys General (NAAG), creating guidelines for advertisers. The FTC wasn't thrilled, since it was intent on deregulating and states were obstructing that. By 1989, it was clear states would continue augmenting FTC regulation (Richards 1991).

The commission continued being the primary US advertising regulator but, besides states, there were other authorities with authority over advertising. One of those agencies was the Food and Drug Administration (FDA).

FOOD AND DRUGS

Historically, so-called "patent" medicines rarely broke laws, because no law barred sale of quack remedies. Some were as much as 30 percent alcohol. Some included cocaine, heroin, opium, or other toxic materials, but no law was broken. The first US law to deal with this was the Pure Food and Drug Act of 1906 (PFDA). Before that, the patent medicine industry, via lobbying, had blocked every regulatory attempt (Sobel 2002). By then, exposés in *Ladies' Home Journal* and *Collier's* created a groundswell of support for such regulations. Upton Sinclair's *The Jungle*, a powerful exposé on meat packing, helped make food and drug restrictions inevitable.

Drugs roughly fell into two categories: (1) "ethical" drugs, and (2) patent medicines. Drugs in the first group were listed in the United States Pharmacopoeia (USP). The second group included questionable ingredients. The American Medical Association (AMA) in 1905 created a Council on Pharmacy and Chemistry, to set standards for drugs and to steer patients toward effective (not bogus) drugs (Donohue 2006). The council was a foundation for the Food and Drug Administration.

Patent medicines were advertised to consumers, but "ethical" drugs were not. The AMA discouraged doctors from prescribing patent drugs, and medical journals were discouraged from running such ads. Self-medication was considered bad, so pharmaceutical companies were encouraged to target ethical drugs at physicians, not patients. But the PFDA focused on creating more informed consumers, not reducing self-medication. It prohibited false or misleading labeling ("misbranding") and required that the presence and amount of certain dangerous ingredients be clearly identified (Donohue 2006). The Supreme Court in *U.S. v. Johnson* (1911) decided the restriction on false labeling didn't mean you couldn't lie about a drug's effects. It meant you weren't permitted to lie about drug ingredients or identity.

This was a serious limitation of the PFDA, so Congress passed the Sherley Amendment in 1912. It was designed to prohibit fraudulent therapeutic claims, though it was flawed, prohibiting "intent" to defraud. Proving advertiser intent was nearly impossible, so the amendment had little effect (Donohue 2006).

One case pursued under the PFDA was Clark Stanley's Snake Oil Liniment, a patent medicine. Stanley claimed he learned the miracle of rattlesnake oil from Hopi Indians. At the 1893 Chicago World Colombian Exposition, with a crowd watching, he pulled a snake out of a bag, cut it open, and threw it into boiling water. He skimmed the fat off the water, suggesting that was how he made Snake Oil Liniment. A shipment of it was seized and tested in 1916, finding this product—claimed as a cure for nearly everything—was a mix of mineral oil, another fatty oil, capsicum, and a tiny bit of camphor and turpentine. It had no snake oil in it and so was declared misbranded. Stanley pleaded "no contest" and paid a $20 fine (Gandhi 2013).

The PFDA was inadequate, though, in dealing with Eben M. Byers. In 1927, Mr. Byers had an elbow injury, and his doctor recommended Radithor, a patent medicine (Figure 12.2). It was a mix of radium and distilled water, a genuine "energy" drink. Radium wasn't a PFDA-controlled substance. It was labeled "radioactive water," making it true, not misbranded, and therefore legal. It was advertised as "A Cure for the Living Dead," which likewise was sadly truthful.

Byers claimed it made him feel more energetic, recommending it to friends. He consumed something like 1,400 bottles, losing his jaw from radiation and dying in 1932 from radiation poisoning. He was buried in a lead-lined coffin (Brumfield 2019). Dangerous patent medicines continued posing public health risks.

In fall 1937, thirty-four children and seventy-one adults died from Elixir Sulfanilamide, which promised to cure ills from sore throat to gonorrhea (Akst 2013). The drug's maker, S. E. Massengill Company, did nothing illegal except calling it an "elixir." That term was reserved for ethanol products. The FDA, back then, had no authority over drug safety.

Public outrage over the "Elixir" deaths also helped nudge Congress toward passing the Food, Drug, and Cosmetics Act of 1938 (FDCA).[1] This Act gave the FDA responsibility for drug safety. While the agency began safety oversight, it didn't create a distinction between over-the-counter (OTC) and prescription drugs. Few drugs were prescription-only, with most being left to the manufacturers' discretion (Donohue 2006).

FIGURE 12.2.   Radithor, a patent medicine from the 1920s.

Recall that 1938 was the year Congress passed the Wheeler-Lea Amendment to the FTC Act. Besides blessing FTC authority over consumer protection, the amendment likewise gave the FTC authority over food, drugs, diagnostic and therapeutic devices, and cosmetics advertising. This put labels under FDA control but ads under the FTC, though the FDA did try to regulate ads. In 1954, the two agencies struck cooperative working agreements.

The principal focus here is law in the United States, but quack medicines were extant in Britain, too. Many ad claims promised cures for cancer, so Parliament passed the Cancer Act in 1939, banning such claims. And the Pharmacy and Medicines Act of 1941 banned false treatments for a range of illnesses, from cataracts to diabetes to tuberculosis.

The US Congress in 1951 passed the Durham Humphrey Amendments to the FDCA, including a definition of "prescription drug." Finally, significant control over medication was wrestled from patients and put into physicians' hands. This also facilitated banning dangerous substances.

Pharmaceutical advertising did arise in congressional hearings in 1959 and 1960, even with those ads targeted at physicians. Some ads downplayed drug side effects, boasting unproven efficacy. There also were concerns advertisers would influence medical journals that ran their ads, since physicians might rely on biased information (H. M. 1961).

More tweaks to the FDCA occurred in 1962: the Kefauver-Harris Amendments. Now, drugs must be proved not only safe but also effective! The FDA was the final arbiter. Responsibility for *prescription* drug advertising moved from the FTC to the FDA, leaving OTC drug ads oversight to the FTC. In 1969, the FDA adopted regulations on prescription drug ads, requiring a "true statement of information in brief summary relating to side effects, contraindications, and effectiveness" and a "fair balance" of information about drug side effects versus effectiveness (Donohue 2006).

The Drug Research Corporation was producer of Regimen Tablets, supposed weight loss pills sold from the mid-1950s until 1962, when the FDA ordered them off the market. They were advertised as a "wonder drug for fat people," promising weight loss without dieting. The firm's ad agency, Kastor, Hilton, Chesley, Clifford & Atherton, moved the ads from direct mail to newspaper and television, adding endorsers showing off their weight loss and claiming they "never felt better." The claims were false. The Drug Research Corporation was found guilty of fraudulent claims (*U.S. v. Andreadis* 1966). But, most important for us, this was the first time an advertising agency was held guilty for advertising fraud on a client's behalf. The fine was $50,000. Until then, only clients were held guilty. Renowned adman Emerson Foote tried saving the agency, but in 1967 it closed. The conviction killed its reputation.

Until the 1980s, direct-to-consumer advertising (DTCA) for prescription drugs was nonexistent. Ads for prescription drugs previously went only to physicians. But in 1981 Merck, Sharp & Dohme broke the unwritten rule by running a print ad for a pneumonia vaccine called Pneumovax in *Reader's Digest* magazine (Figure 12.3). This was the first prescription drug ad aimed at consumers. And in 1983 Boots pharmaceuticals introduced the first TV ad for a prescription drug, a pain reliever called Rufen (Scott 2015).

In 1982, the Eli Lilly pharmaceutical company took an aggressive PR approach, issuing press kits with video to TV and radio stations for Oraflex, an anti-arthritic prescription. The press reported it might prevent arthritis progression, going beyond FDA-approved label claims (Donohue 2006). FDA regulations didn't address DTCA then, but in 1985 it began requiring the same disclosures in DTCA that it did in ads directed at physicians.

This decision effectively stopped broadcast ads, because of the disclosures. Even in print, disclosures often required more space than the actual advertising claims. Physicians in the 1980s were overwhelmingly opposed to DTCA, as were some consumers (Donohue 2006). But as "managed health care" sought cheaper treatments, the pharmaceutical industry found benefits in directly lobbying consumers.

The Nutrition Labeling and Education Act of 1990 created a new format for food labels, dictating specific label details. Noncompliance made the food "misbranded." While the FDA permitted some visual variation, the Act's goal was standardization, so consumers could instantly scan labels for specifics, like calories.

The industry found work-arounds to FDA disclosure requirements for television, using techniques like "help wanted" commercials that just happened to mention their drug's name. Under pressure, the FDA in 1997 published draft guidelines for broadcast DTCA, offering alternatives to extensive labeling requirements by allowing manufacturers to refer consumers to websites or toll-free telephone numbers for more information.

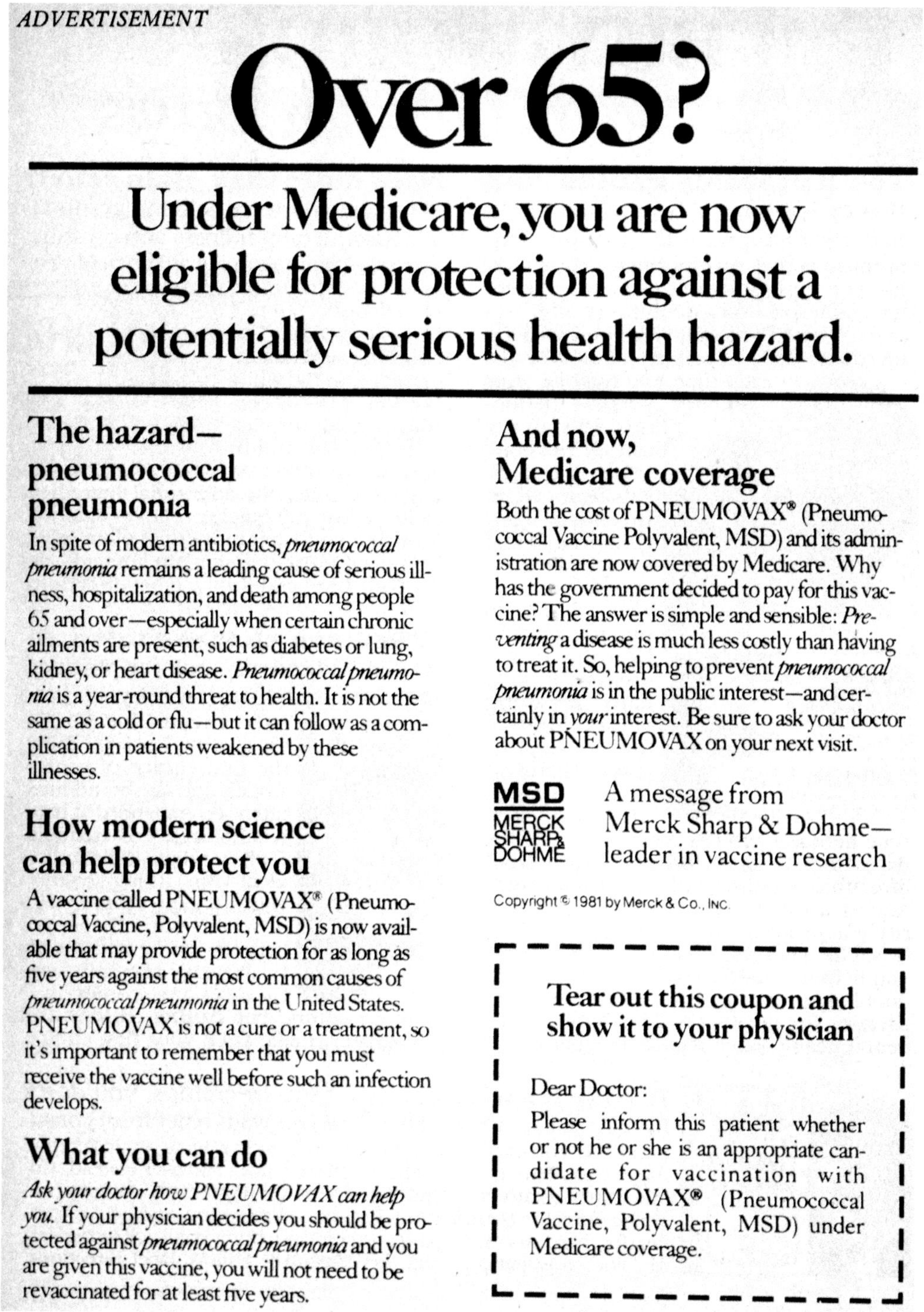

Over 65?

Under Medicare, you are now eligible for protection against a potentially serious health hazard.

The hazard—pneumococcal pneumonia

In spite of modern antibiotics, *pneumococcal pneumonia* remains a leading cause of serious illness, hospitalization, and death among people 65 and over—especially when certain chronic ailments are present, such as diabetes or lung, kidney, or heart disease. *Pneumococcal pneumonia* is a year-round threat to health. It is not the same as a cold or flu—but it can follow as a complication in patients weakened by these illnesses.

How modern science can help protect you

A vaccine called PNEUMOVAX® (Pneumococcal Vaccine, Polyvalent, MSD) is now available that may provide protection for as long as five years against the most common causes of *pneumococcal pneumonia* in the United States. PNEUMOVAX is not a cure or a treatment, so it's important to remember that you must receive the vaccine well before such an infection develops.

What you can do

Ask your doctor how PNEUMOVAX can help you. If your physician decides you should be protected against *pneumococcal pneumonia* and you are given this vaccine, you will not need to be revaccinated for at least five years.

And now, Medicare coverage

Both the cost of PNEUMOVAX® (Pneumococcal Vaccine Polyvalent, MSD) and its administration are now covered by Medicare. Why has the government decided to pay for this vaccine? The answer is simple and sensible: *Preventing* a disease is much less costly than having to treat it. So, helping to prevent *pneumococcal pneumonia* is in the public interest—and certainly in *your* interest. Be sure to ask your doctor about PNEUMOVAX on your next visit.

 A message from Merck Sharp & Dohme— leader in vaccine research

Copyright © 1981 by Merck & Co., INC.

Tear out this coupon and show it to your physician

Dear Doctor:

Please inform this patient whether or not he or she is an appropriate candidate for vaccination with PNEUMOVAX® (Pneumococcal Vaccine, Polyvalent, MSD) under Medicare coverage.

FIGURE 12.3. This Pneumovax ad, from the October 1981 *Reader's Digest* magazine, was the first DTC prescription drug ad.

US DTCA accounted for $363 million by 1995, nearly seven times that of 1991, and by 2005 it reached $4.2 billion (Donohue 2006). By 2016, it was roughly $10 billion (Dunn 2019). All that from one small print ad in 1981. Aside from the United States, as of 2020, only New Zealand allowed DTCA.

I ADVERTISED, BUT I DIDN'T INHALE

Tobacco always seemed to be the front line of advertising criticism. Many people lost loved ones to cancer and emphysema from tobacco use. The products were hated, and tobacco advertising was the public face of those prod-

FIGURE 12.4. The 1926 Chesterfield cigarette ad believed to be the first to clearly target women.

ucts. The general public believed tobacco companies advertised to encourage smoking. Not surprisingly, tobacco advertising experienced more than a few legal attacks.

Tobacco was targeted as early as the 1500s (Richards 1987). But its advertising wasn't a big issue until the twentieth century. By 1919, *Printers' Ink* magazine was warning of "an insidious campaign to create women smokers" (Norris 1990), though Chesterfield is credited with the first cigarette ad targeted at women, in 1926 (Figure 12.4).

FIGURE 12.5. In 1937, Philip Morris began making claims that medical studies found its cigarettes could help cure throat irritations.

Between 1914 and 1928, the number of smokers increased by a factor of seven (Printers' Ink 1938). That increase was partly caused by changed tobacco blends, but advertising also was a factor. Both pipe tobacco and cigar use dropped, but cigarette use soared (Fox 1984).

In 1927, an English physician noted that nearly all of his lung cancer cases were smokers, and in 1936 the *Journal of the American Medical Association* found that of 135 men with lung cancer, 90 percent were chronic smokers (Richards 1987). Evidence was mounting against tobacco.

In 1937, Philip Morris was claiming that its cigarettes would help clear up cases of throat irritation (Figure 12.5). And by 1946 R. J. Reynolds was implying medical superiority by claiming more doctors smoked its Camel brand. So in 1955 the FTC published industry guides indicating cigarette sellers should not state in ads, explicitly or implicitly, that smoking had any medical approval. And in 1953 the American Medical Association banned tobacco ads from its publications (Richards 1987).

By then, cigarette makers were some of the biggest advertisers of all time. Some magazines found much of their revenue originated from them. Many famous people were models for those ads. Ronald Reagan, a B-movie star in 1951, was the first advertising model to later become US president (Figure 12.6).

But in 1962 the British Royal College of Physicians declared smoking caused lung cancer, and the US Surgeon General created an Advisory Committee on Smoking and Health. That committee's report, in 1964, agreed with the British. Some magazines, including the *New Yorker* and *Saturday Review*, immediately banned tobacco

I'M SENDING CHESTERFIELDS to all my friends. That's the merriest Christmas any smoker can have — Chesterfield mildness plus no unpleasant after-taste

Ronald Reagan

CHESTERFIELD *Buy the beautiful Christmas-card carton*

FIGURE 12.6.   Ronald Reagan as a cigarette model in 1951, three decades before becoming US president.

advertising within their pages. Bill Bernbach and David Ogilvy both announced their agencies were out of the tobacco ad business, while the chairman of McCann Erickson, Emerson Foote, quit the agency because it wouldn't reject tobacco accounts.

The FTC adopted a regulation mandating all cigarette ads and packages contain a warning that smoking is dangerous to health, effective 1965. The commission was accused of abusing its authority. It suspended that regulation, but Congress passed its own cigarette advertising and labeling law in 1965, requiring packages (not ads) include "Caution: Cigarette Smoking May Be Hazardous to Your Health" (Richards 1987). In 1970, the wording changed to "Warning: The Surgeon General Has Determined That Cigarette Smoking Is Dangerous to Your Health." An agreement between the FTC and the six major US cigarette makers extended warnings to ads, beginning in 1972 (Richards 1987).

Tobacco advertising was banned from UK television in 1965 and from Canadian television and radio in 1969. A US broadcast ban of tobacco advertising began in 1971. More than $200 million a year could now be diverted to other media, mostly at television's expense.

Once off broadcast, public attention and criticism of tobacco died for several years, reigniting in 1984. A new law required that health warnings on packages and ads be replaced with four rotating warnings. And in late 1985 the US Surgeon General proclaimed cigarette smoking was the leading cause of death and disability, suggesting cigarette advertising be banned altogether. Proposed legislation followed, but failed, and was reintroduced in some form repeatedly for about ten years.

FIGURE 12.7. Joe Camel, from 1990. Joe represented the brand from 1987 to 1997.

Tobacco advertising continued under attack, but Camel cigarettes' "Joe Camel" became the poster boy for tobacco's hazards. Joe was a cartoon character, so critics believed his purpose was to seduce children to smoke (Figure 12.7). A 1991 study found Joe was as familiar to six-year-olds as Mickey Mouse, fueling the fire. The FTC was pushed to ban Joe, but it declined. The FDA then tried to regulate Joe (Richards 1996). That, too, failed, and those repeated federal failures eventually led to state government involvement.

The federal government kept running into the First Amendment. Tobacco advertising (including Joe) was protected speech. The states found a work-around by threatening to sue tobacco companies for the health cost borne by them. Instead, they settled. In 1998, the four largest US cigarette manufacturers signed a Master Settlement Agreement (MSA) with forty-six states, five US territories, and the District of Columbia. The companies agreed to pay states $206 billion total.

Importantly, the MSA forbade those companies from targeting kids, banned a variety of advertising techniques, and prohibited major sponsorships. Because it was done by contractual agreement, it avoided First Amendment obstacles. Beginning in 1999, tobacco stopped appearing on billboards, sampling disappeared, and tobacco-branded merchandise ended. States proved successful where the federal government was impotent.

SPIRITED ADVERTISING

Like tobacco, some people are averse to alcoholic spirits. Organizations like Mothers Against Drunk Driving (MADD) have dedicated great energy to fighting alcohol abuse. No surprise, then, alcohol ads are treated like tobacco ads.

The US Constitution's 18th Amendment, ratified in 1919, prohibited producing, selling, and transporting intoxicating liquors. The Volstead Act then triggered years of Prohibition, along with bootlegging and other lawlessness. It ended with the 21st Amendment's ratification in late 1933, repealing the 18th Amendment. Alcoholic beverages were again legal, but some people were uncomfortable with this legalization. Wine and beer, with lower alcohol content, caused less concern. "Hard" liquors had to be extra cautious not to trigger political blowback.

With radio's rise, in 1936 liquor producers adopted a voluntary ethical "Code" to not advertise on radio. As television took off after World War II, in 1948 the liquor industry extended that ban to TV. They stuck to print advertising. The wine industry was smaller and did far less advertising. The beer industry, however, adopted broadcasting for its ads, much of which was sporting event sponsorship. In 1953, the Anheuser-Busch brewery bought the St. Louis Cardinals baseball franchise. Fear of returning to Prohibition faded, and beer owned the airwaves for decades.

Government began closer scrutiny of alcohol advertising in the 1970s, when Congress investigated its role in alcohol abuse. Because the 21st Amendment gave states power over alcohol sales within their borders, some states adopted restrictions on alcohol advertising. Those restrictions were legally challenged (Sterchi 1985).

Most notable of those was an Oklahoma statute in 1981, banning alcoholic beverage ads within the state, except a single sign at liquor stores stating "Retail Alcoholic Liquor Store." A lawsuit ensued, and the state won. This coincided with Supreme Court decisions bolstering constitutional protection of advertising.

The state then amended its constitution in 1984 to include that same ban. But another lawsuit led a district court to declare this amendment unconstitutional under the US Constitution, because there was no evidence alcohol advertising caused alcohol abuse (*Oklahoma Broadcasters Association v. Crisp* 1985). State regulatory initiatives died down after that.

The sixty-year voluntary broadcast liquor advertising ban changed over the years, including a 1988 modification allowing "spirits coolers" advertising on TV. But the ban really ended in March 1996, when Crown Royal ran a thirty-second commercial on the Prime Sports Network, a small cable channel, becoming the first broadcast commercial for liquor (Figure 12.8). The voluntary Code prohibited commercials but allowed event sponsorships, and Seagram argued this was a sponsorship "message," not a commercial (Gellene 1996).

Both President Clinton and the Center for Science in the Public Interest expressed concerns, resulting in extra publicity for Crown Royal. A few months later, the Dis-

Obedience School Graduate.   Valedictorian.

Those who appreciate quality enjoy it responsibly.

FIGURE 12.8.   The first broadcast commercial for liquor was a video version of this print ad.

tilled Spirits Council of the United States (DISCUS) officially changed the Code, allowing broadcast commercials. The major television networks all promised to continue their own ban (Elliott 1996).

NBC was first to change that policy, in 2001, but in 2002 went back to forbidding liquor ads. This presented opportunities for local, independent, and cable channels. After Crown Royal, a range of whiskey, vodka, gin, and tequila brands pursued advertising on radio and TV. Finally, in 2011, CBS allowed liquor ads late at night. Soon after that, ABC and NBC followed, but cable stations continued getting most of those advertising dollars (Schultz 2012).

The DISCUS Code continues to restrict liquor advertising, such as prohibiting use of cartoon figures or portraying sexual prowess as derived from these drinks (Elliott 1996). States continue their authority over alcohol, so different states have different restrictions, like limiting appeals to children or billboard placement near playgrounds or schools, and more.

LITTER ON A STICK

Tobacco and alcohol have been front-line content for regulatory attacks, but the front line for advertising media often includes billboards. The story of billboard regulation really begins in the 1900s. The first laws aimed at controlling outdoor ads along public highways were in Great Britain.

An American, Henry Crowell, in 1900 put an enormous Quaker Oats sign atop the white cliffs of Dover, visible from France! A storm of letters to the newspaper followed, and the National Society for Checking the Abuses of Public Advertising argued England's landscape was being disfigured.

Several laws were passed, including the Advertisements Regulation Acts in 1907 and 1925, and the Town and Country Planning Act of 1947. The latter law dictated that outdoor ads couldn't be erected without local planning commission approval, with limited exceptions. This put substantial authority in localities, while creating a nationwide push toward regulation. Under this law, advertising can be restricted for purposes of public safety "and amenity" (i.e., aesthetics) and allowed total signage bans in "areas of special control."

With motor vehicles came billboards along highways. Long after Henry Crowell, boards were still denounced as "visual pollution." Some critics dubbed them "litter on a stick" (Taylor 1997). And concerns were not limited to Britain.

The Missouri Supreme Court heard a case in 1911 about billboards (Taylor 1997). The argument: Robbers could hide behind them! Later they were criticized as traffic hazards. Vespe (1997) says:

> It is also likely that America's rush to "uglify" the landscape has serious safety and health consequences. Most studies have found—and most traffic engineers will concur—that roadside "distractors," such as billboards, make it more difficult for drivers to find traffic signs and pay attention to the road.

Research has disproved it, but the "road hazard" myth persisted (Taylor 1997). "Uglification," frankly, had some merit.

Municipalities like New York began issuing their own rules, but their authority ended at the city limits. Congress first addressed outdoor advertising with the Bonus Act, part of the Federal-Aid Highway Act of 1958. It offered monetary rewards to states for restricting billboards to 660 feet from primary highways. States could remove non-complying signs, but must pay sign owners fair compensation, most of which was covered by the federal government. Twenty-five states participated.

With nudging from Lady Bird Johnson, in 1965 the Highway Beautification Act (HBA) replaced that law, while continuing bribes to states. It included removal of certain sign types, strictly controlled signs within 660 feet of primary highways, and limited sign size, lighting, and spacing. There were exceptions, like on-premises business signs and signs in industrial areas. Subsequently, several amendments adjusted those requirements.

One issue that arose involved "changeable" signs. Technologies developed for changing signs without manually stripping the old, and pasting new, ones. In the 1920s, a method using fourteen moving louvers was created, and another louver-type came in the 1950s, but both had problems (Laible 1997). By the 1990s, billboards with three-sided slats were popular. They could rotate three different ads.

HBA Amendments in 1978 permitted these changeable techniques for a business's on-premises signs but not for others, creating a two-tiered system. The Federal Highway Administration (FHWA) in 1990 declared that "signs . . . irrespective of the method used to display the changing message are prohibited," responding to a question about using lights, rotating slats, glow cubes, and so forth (Laible 1997). Again, evidence suggested these methods weren't traffic hazards, contrary to assumptions.

In 1996, the FHWA began allowing changeable billboards in commercial/industrial areas, with state approval. But even then, digital billboards weren't anticipated by lawmakers. They arrived in 2005, and municipalities started making up rules. Indianapolis banned digital billboards (aka changeable electronic variable message signs, or CEVMS) in 2003, *before they arrived*, declaring them visual clutter and road hazards. The FHWA studied the situation. Digital boards promised to display five to seven different ads in rotation on a single structure, increasing revenue (Schoettle 2007).

The FHWA published a policy clarification regarding electronic signs in 2007, stating they didn't violate the law. In 2016, a federal appeals court concluded that clarification was in accordance with the HBA. State and local authorities could ban or restrict signs, but the federal position was that digital billboards are permissible.

Those laws concerned advertising along national highways, but signs are everywhere. San Diego prohibited putting outdoor advertising signs within the city "to eliminate hazards to pedestrians and motorists brought about by distracting sign displays" and "to preserve and improve the appearance of the City" (*Metromedia, Inc. v. City of San Diego* 1981). There were two exceptions: (1) a business's on-premises signs, and (2) twelve categories of signs, like bus stop signs, government signs, and so on.

The US Supreme Court agreed billboards present problems and are regulable but said, "The occupant of property may advertise his own goods or services; he may not advertise the goods or services of others, nor may he display most noncommercial messages." It also agreed billboards can be ugly and might be traffic hazards. This law's problem was that, while allowing on-premises commercial signs, it didn't allow noncommercial signs. It protected commercial speech more than noncommercial, which was unconstitutional.

In *City of Ladue v. Gilleo* (1994), Margaret Gilleo put a sign on her lawn protesting the Persian Gulf War, but it was stolen. A second was knocked down. She called the police. They told her she was violating city sign laws. She sued and put a sign in her second-story window. The city rewrote its law to include ten exceptions, but it prohibited window signs.

The court said city sign regulations must be reasonable and not designed to censor content. Ladue's wasn't a blanket ban; it provides exceptions, protecting some speech over others. And it bans important speech at an important location: the home. Yard and window signs convey a message, but also (1) say something about the speaker, and (2) each has a particular audience: neighbors. It's also cheap. This law, therefore, unconstitutionally treads on residents' liberties.

A later case helped clarify the thinking and legal status of outdoor signs. In *Reed v. Town of Gilbert* (2015) the town only prohibited signs *without a permit*, providing twenty-three exceptions, including "ideological signs," "political signs," and "temporary directional signs relating to a qualifying event." Each had different requirements; for example, directional signs could be six square feet, while political signs could be thirty-two.

A church moved locations week to week, using temporary signs to direct its congregation to the week's location. The city cited the church for ordinance violation. The third time, the city confiscated the sign. The Supreme Court stated government cannot restrict expression based on its subject matter or content, and those exceptions varied by content. More important, the court said, "A regulation that targets a sign because it conveys an idea about a specific event is no less content based than a regulation that targets a sign because it conveys some other idea." This law also wasn't narrowly tailored, so it failed the fourth step of the *Central Hudson* test. Again, a city's laws violated the First Amendment. In this case, laws favoring one type of content over another aren't allowed.

Outdoor signs of all types will continue as targets of legal attack. But laws aren't the only form of control.

SELF-CONTROL WITH ADVERTISING

Where law leaves off, self-regulation starts. On the heels of the (mostly) American Truth-in-Advertising movement and the consumer movements, a pro-regulatory climate continued. In 1969, *The Nader Report* and the *Report of the ABA Commission to Study the Federal Trade Commission* both lambasted the FTC as too passive. The stage was set for more aggressive regulation, and the ad industry read that writing on the wall.

In 1971, the three leading ad industry organizations—the American Advertising Federation (AAF), the Association of National Advertisers (ANA), and the American Association of Advertising Agencies (AAAA)—joined with the Council of Better Business Bureaus (CBBB) to create a mechanism for self-regulation called the National Advertising Review Board (NARB). Zanot (1979) credits this mechanism as the brainchild of Howard Bell, former AAF president. The idea was a system to act as the industry's self-regulatory governor, applying certain standards uniformly to all national advertising.

The NARB would be composed of seven to fifteen people, with most representing the public's interest. Existing codes, including the Creative Code of the AAAA, and the Advertising Code of American Business, were to serve as the system's standards (Zanot 1979).

It was inspired by the Advertising Standards Authority (ASA) in Britain. That organization, established in 1962, had a head start. By 1971, the ASA handled about three hundred cases per year, apparently successfully. If the ASA found an advertiser violating standards, the advertiser could be added to a blacklist and media would refuse its ads. The American system, legally, couldn't exactly duplicate the ASA (Zanot 1979).

The NARB created a National Advertising Division (NAD) of the CBBB to receive advertising complaints. It would assess the complaints and decide whether action was necessary. If so, it would approach the advertiser for changes. If advertisers disagreed, they could appeal to the NARB, which now had fifty members: thirty advertisers, ten agency executives, and ten "public" members. A panel of five, drawn from that pool in those proportions, would hear the appeal. If it determined the ad needed changes but the advertiser refused, the decision could be announced to media and the case sent to the FTC. In addition, a National Advertising Review Council (NARC) was created to oversee the whole program, made up of leaders of the four founding organizations (Zanot 1979).

Soon, a parallel system was created for *local* advertising. Local Advertising Review Boards (LARBs) were established in several cities, with the first being in Phoenix, Arizona (Zanot 1979). In 1974, the NARB also created a Children's Advertising Review Unit (CARU) as a part of the NAD.

The NARB was mostly focused on deceptive advertising, but it also issued a report on advertising and women, and a statement on advertising to the elderly. In just five years, it handled one-thousand-plus complaints (Zanot 1979).

It was successful, and in 2004, adapting to the internet, another initiative started: the Electronic Retailing Self-Regulation Program (ERSP). This was a self-regulatory program for direct response advertising, to instill greater consumer confidence in electronic advertising. In 2011, the Online Interest Based Advertising Accountability Program was established, to enhance consumer trust in "online behavioral advertising" by making it more accountable.

Over time the system became known as NARC, even though "narc" was popular shorthand for narcotics agent, meaning to act like a police informant. But in 2012, the system's name became the Advertising Self-Regulatory Council (ASRC).

An unrelated Network Advertising Initiative (NAI) was founded in 2000. Its focus was online data gathering for use in digital advertising, policing data collection and use. The NAI added a Mobile Application Code in 2013, to encompass data collection via mobile devices.

Other countries self-regulated advertising over the years. In 1974, the Japan Advertising Review Organization (JARO) and the Advertising Board of the Philippines (Adboard) both began. The Advertising Council of Nigeria followed in 1977, the Brazilian National Council for Self-Regulation (Conselho Nacional de Autorregulamentação Publicitária, CONAR) in 1980, and the European Advertising Standards Alliance in 1991.

Self-regulation's advantage is it can reach where the law can't. The US Constitution, for example, prevents laws from dealing with certain issues because of free speech protections. Some issues, like offensive or tasteless topics, can be reached only through self-policing.

EVOLVING TASTE AND ETHICS

Just because something is unethical doesn't mean it's illegal, and vice versa. One reason is that ethics vary from person to person, leading to disagreement when crafting legal or self-regulatory policies regarding some subjects. So a bit should be said about advertising ethics.

Breadth

A subject evoking varied opinion is sex. Some feel that no sexuality, overt or covert, should appear in ads, while others accept it. One sex-related topic of hot debate has been contraception. Advertisers want to make friends, so most will choose the path of least objection. Consequently, the first condom commercial wasn't until 1975. It ran, briefly, on the NBC station in San José, California, KNTV, and encountered criticism. Earlier in the century, contraceptives and contraceptive advertising had a complicated legal relationship (Treichler 2014), but the topic remained socially taboo. That wasn't limited to the United States. The first condom commercial in the UK was for Durex brand in 1986.

Then there's underwear. Until 1982 the National Association of Broadcasters prohibited portraying live models on TV wearing underwear. Underwear manufacturers made commercials using mannequins (Rotfeld 2001). On May 4, 1987, also on NBC, the first commercial with a live model wearing a bra ran. Public acceptance had evolved, and condom commercials helped develop acceptance (Horovitz 1987).

Sexual content, though, isn't the only advertising controversy. I already mentioned Benetton's "shockvertising." By 1988, Benneton was pushing boundaries of advertising ethics by intentionally creating controversy, some including sex. The first real "shock" was a picture of an exposed breast, but in 1989 an ad was run of a Black woman breastfeeding a White baby. It, too, included an exposed breast, but it also crossed a racial barrier (Hubbard 1993). Another ad showed the hands of two men handcuffed together. One was White and one Black, leaving it to viewers to decide which was a prisoner.

Yet another ad depicted a family with their son dying of AIDS. Then there was an albino Zulu woman being stared at by her village, who were all Black. Every ad plucked at tender spots in society. Sex continued as a go-to topic. One Benetton ad showed two horses copulating. But perhaps the ad that crossed furthest over a boundary of taste was in 2011, depicting world leaders kissing (e.g., Barack Obama kissing China's Hu Jintao). It was the image of Pope Benedict XVI kissing an Egyptian imam that caught hell. The Vatican condemned it (Figure 12.9).

Benetton deserves credit as the originator of this form of advertising, but a UK "master of shockvertising," Trevor Beattie, also contributed. In 1991, Beattie did a campaign for French Connection UK, with "FCUK Fashion!" as a headline. Beattie's response to criticism was "These ads aren't shocking; what is shocking is the rank mediocrity of 90 per cent of British

advertising, which means that anything remotely different stands out" (Tungate 2007). The rise of shock advertising illustrates the evolving nature of taste and ethics.

Church

The Catholic Church weighed in regarding ad ethics in
1997. The Pontifical Council for Social Communications
studied advertising's effects on society, resulting in *The
Catholic Church's Handbook on Ethics in Advertising.* It
identified supposed cultural, moral, and religious harms
from advertising, followed by some ethical principles.
Surprisingly, it concludes:

> Many women and men professionally engaged in ad-
> vertising do have sensitive consciences, high ethical
> standards and a strong sense of responsibility. But even
> for them external pressures—from the clients who com-
> mission their work as well as from the competitive inter-
> nal dynamics of their profession—can create powerful
> inducements to unethical behavior. That underlines the
> need for external structures and systems to support and
> encourage responsible practice in advertising and to
> discourage the irresponsible. . . . We do not wish, and

FIGURE 12.9. Another ad from
the 2011 Benetton "*UNHATE*"
campaign included a doctored
image of Israeli Prime Minister
Benjamin Netanyahu kissing
Palestinian Authority President
Mahmoud Abbas. It was displayed
on an enormous billboard in Tel
Aviv, to the displeasure of many.

certainly we do not expect, to see advertising eliminated from the contemporary world. Advertising is an important element in today's society, especially in the functioning of a market
economy, which is becoming more and more widespread. (Foley et al. 1997)

Seifert Does Ethics

In spite of ad professionals who adhere to high ethical standards, there are exceptions. A
notable example was Shona Seifert, 2004–2005 president of TBWA/Chiat/Day and former
senior partner and executive group director at Ogilvy & Mather New York. At Ogilvy she
ordered employees to falsify time sheets, and more, for the Office of National Drug Control
Policy, 1999–2000. She and a colleague were guilty of overbilling, and she received eighteen
months in prison and a fine of $125,000, and she was ordered to write a code of advertising
ethics (Warner 2005). She submitted an eighteen-page document to the judge, but the Seifert
Code was never embraced by the industry.

Institute for Advertising Ethics

In 2010, the AAF created an Institute for Advertising Ethics (IAE), with Wally Snyder,
former president and CEO of the AAF, as its executive director. The next year, it published
its *Principles and Practices for Advertising Ethics,* with eight principles:

1. Advertising, public relations, marketing communications, news, and editorial all share a common objective of truth and high ethical standards in serving the public.
2. Advertising, public relations, and all marketing communications professionals have an obligation to exercise the highest personal ethics in the creation and dissemination of commercial information to consumers.
3. Advertisers should clearly distinguish advertising, public relations, and corporate communications from news and editorial content and entertainment, both online and offline.
4. Advertisers should clearly disclose all material conditions, such as payment or receipt of a free product, affecting endorsements in social and traditional channels, as well as the identity of endorsers, all in the interest of full disclosure and transparency.
5. Advertisers should treat consumers fairly based on the nature of the audience to whom the ads are directed and the nature of the product or service advertised.
6. Advertisers should never compromise consumers' personal privacy in marketing communications, and their choices as to whether to participate in providing their information should be transparent and easily made.
7. Advertisers should follow federal, state, and local advertising laws, and cooperate with industry self-regulatory programs for the resolution of advertising practices.
8. Advertisers and their agencies, and online and offline media, should discuss privately potential ethical concerns, and members of the team creating ads should be given permission to express internally their ethical concerns.

Note that it took a full century from the Truth-in-Advertising movement's start for a *general* set of ethical principles to emerge for the US advertising industry.

Codes

Don't misunderstand—a long list of ethical codes had developed in specific contexts, including the AAAA creative code in 1924. That was limited to AAAA member agencies. Britain's Association of Publicity Clubs did the same in 1925. The International Chamber of Commerce developed an International Code of Standards in 1937, later called the ICC Marketing Code. Again, it applied only to ICC members. The American Marketing Association created a Statement of Ethics, which originally was rather abstract (O'Boyle & Dawson 1992), and the Word-of-Mouth Advertising Association (WOMMA) has its own code of ethics.

Some industries even have their own codes. The tobacco industry has a Cigarette Advertising Code, the distilled spirits industry has its Code of Responsible Practices for Beverage Alcohol Advertising and Marketing, and the Beer Institute has an Advertising & Marketing Code. Even the American Association of Endodontists and the American Association for Respiratory Care have advertising codes. Facebook and Amazon.com also have codes. Of course, other countries have sets of standards. The matrix of ethical codes on just one continent is daunting.

Recall it was the *American Agriculturist* magazine in 1860 that took the first ethical stand against deceptive ads. And in 1880 the *Farm Journal of Philadelphia* published a "Fair Play Notice," guaranteeing the advertisers in its pages. So magazines published the first ethical codes of any sort.

But the Curtis Advertising Code in 1910, by the *Ladies' Home Journal* publisher, was the first fully articulated set of standards, covering more than deceptive ad claims. After that, many publications adopted similar codes.[2]

In 1935, the Columbia Broadcasting System (CBS) published a self-regulatory Radio Code that included advertising, followed by the National Broadcasting Company (NBC) in 1934 (Spring 1992). Those codes eventually included television, and networks later established advertising acceptability departments.[3]

Other Notable Cases

A few industry missteps deserve mention. One, in 1974, was more of a marketing than advertising error, but ads played a tragic role. A report, "The Baby Killer," was published that year by a UK organization called War on Want, accusing Nestlé Infant Formula of causing illness and death of babies in third world countries. It blamed Nestlé's advertising and marketing. Basically, many women in those countries were poor, even undernourished. This product promised to help give their babies needed nourishment. Women fed their babies formula *in lieu* of breast milk. The ads promised healthy and happy babies.

But underprivileged families had unique problems, like unsanitary water. The powdered formula was mixed with that water, effectively poisoning babies. Also, poor families would dilute the formula to save money, thereby starving their babies (Solomon 1981). Written instructions told parents not to do those things, but literacy in these areas was very low. Babies died. Dr. Derrick Jelliffe called this "commerciogenic malnutrition," pointing his finger at marketing and advertising entities pushing this product into a market unprepared to properly use it.

Another lapse happened in 1989, which got the Young & Rubicam (Y&R) agency into trouble. Pursuing the Jamaica Tourist Board account, Y&R did what most agencies had done forever: hire a local "consultant" to grease the skids. That consultant forwarded money to Jamaica's minister of tourism. Winning tourism accounts often required "helping" local officials. Such bribery was illegal under US law—the Foreign Corrupt Practices Act—but government always turned a blind eye. The first Bush administration apparently decided to tighten the rules, holding Y&R up as the poster child (Rothenberg 1990). Y&R was fined $500,000 and was the first agency ever indicted under the Racketeer Influenced and Corrupt Organizations Act.

By the 1980s, the Scali, McCabe, Sloves agency was a major mover. But developing a campaign for its oldest client in 1990 overstepped law and ethics. Volvos were promoted for years as strong and safe cars. The agency heard about a "monster truck" rally in Vermont, where trucks had rolled over and crushed car after car, but not a Volvo. They decided to re-create it.

Shooting both film and still photos in an arena in Austin, Texas, a monster truck rolled over—and crushed—the Volvo and other cars. So they built a heavy wooden cage, inserted it in another Volvo, and filmed again. That Volvo collapsed too. Next, they welded a steel cage into a Volvo, cutting the roof supports on all the other cars to guarantee their collapse, and shot it. It worked (Figure 12.10). But an "extra" actor, in the rally crowd, walked around taking

FIGURE 12.10.   A print ad from the Volvo shoot appeared in *Car & Driver* magazine, among others.

pictures between the filming. His dozens of photos documented everything, serving as evidence when the State of Texas sued Volvo. The ads didn't disclose that this was a re-creation, implying this was an actual rally. Volvo pulled the ads, but not before they'd run at least once, and ended up paying Texas $316,250. The agency resigned Volvo's account (Foltz 1990).

The next example might be blamed on the magazine, but it involved the publication's advertising department. *Soldier of Fortune* ran this classified ad in June 1985:

> GUN FOR HIRE: 37-year-old professional mercenary desires jobs. Vietnam veteran. Discrete and very private. Body guard, courier, and other special skills. All jobs considered.

Two men hired him to kill a business associate, which he did. All were convicted of murder, but the deceased man's family sued the magazine. The magazine lost $4.37 million in 1992 because it was clear the advertiser was willing to commit crimes (Smothers 1992).

Approaches to Ethics Have Changed

Throughout the twentieth century, media, not the advertising industry, probably had the greatest impact on limiting unethical advertising practices. The IAE created a set of principles, but this organization aims at guiding the field's dedication and adherence to greater ethicality. In 2014, it created an Advertising Ethics Certification program, encouraging practitioners to participate in an ethics training program. But this is only a start.

PLEASE DON'T CALL OR WRITE

People often find advertising annoying, especially when it's unsolicited. Options to address this problem have arisen.

The Direct Mail Association (DMA) created a Mail Preference Service (MPS) in 1971, making it possible for people to remove their names from American mailing lists by "opting out." They receive direct mail unless they take action to register with the MPS. An approach not adopted would let people "opt in" to mailing lists, meaning they would *not* receive the mail unless they took action. Direct mail companies didn't like that approach. It would provide far fewer names for their lists. Some people have suggested the industry actively seeks to discourage MPS use. This was before email, so it applied only to the US Postal Service.

Other countries followed suit. The UK's MPS began in 1983, along with one in France called "Stop Publicité." Soon all of Europe jumped aboard. They were called "Robinson Lists," named after Daniel Defoe's Robinson Crusoe, because when Crusoe shipwrecked on an island with cannibals, he intentionally distanced himself from his neighbors.

Those lists were "junk" mail, but unsolicited ads also came via telephone. Like direct mail, telemarketing firms met their equivalent of MPS when the US Congress passed the Do-Not-Call Implementation Act of 2003. The FTC implemented it by forming a National Do Not Call Registry. Consumers could register to prohibit telemarketers from calling their number for five years. In 2007, that duration was extended indefinitely.

In 2003, Congress also passed the Controlling the Assault of Non-Solicited Pornography and Marketing (CAN-SPAM) Act, to cover electronic mail. This wasn't the first time advertising and pornography were lumped together. There was a push to create a national do-not-email list, which consumers wanted, but industry pushed back hard. CAN-SPAM didn't go that far, though it did set standards for email, but barred states from passing laws prohibiting email. CAN-SPAM, enforced by the FTC, requires accurate headers and subject lines identifying the email as an ad; a mailing address must be included, and it must give recipients a way to opt out of future emails.

Again, the industry forced consumers to opt out rather than opt in. Also, some argued CAN-SPAM was weakly enforced and thus not a particularly effective solution to all the unsolicited email. The FTC was against a do-not-email registry, arguing it would be ineffective because most unsolicited email originated from unscrupulous advertisers who would ignore the law and use the list for their own mailings.

Finally, websites also were a concern, not because of intrusiveness, like email, but because they collected personal data of visitors. As of 2020, there still was no option for consumers to opt out of having their data collected. Private industry offered some solutions; for example, the StopDataMining.me website provided consumers information about how to opt out, but this still required the consumer to visit site after site to exercise their right to opt out.

MORE DIGITAL SOLUTIONS

Advertising, particularly media buying, has encountered fraud. Digital media have led to controversies about numbers of impressions, with calculation methods that vary significantly. Data breaches are another problem. And programmatic buying has multiple weaknesses, including the risk of putting a brand's ad next to brand-inconsistent (even offensive) content. All are legal or ethical dangers.

The bitcoin, a form of cryptocurrency, changed everything. To work, it had to be secure. This led to development of "blockchain" technology, which holds great promise for the ad industry. Blockchain enables dealing with someone while removing risk. The "secured chain of blocks" concept appeared in 1991, but the first practical application was bitcoin in 2009.

Then came the "smart contract," a part of something called "Ethereum," basically blockchain 2.0, in 2014. It expanded blockchain to handle more financial instruments than just bitcoin.

More developments continue, but, most important, these technologies provide a new level of clear, fixed, transparent, and secure transactions. In simple terms (i.e., terms even I understand), blockchain creates a transactions ledger that everyone involved in the transaction can access. When anything is entered in the ledger, it is permanent, can't be altered, and is visible to everyone. If a mistake occurs, another entry must be created to fix it, so everyone can see the correction was made. Finally, the smart contract can contain rules, computer programs that specify actions in response to meeting certain conditions.

Relevance? Advertisers or agents, by connecting with all of their publishers (e.g., websites) in blockchain, can reduce the number of intermediaries and prevent publishers from scam-ming them since all the data are visible by everyone (Dedovic 2019). Even audience impressions and their specific sources can be included in the ledger. The smart contract feature also can guarantee near instantaneous payment. Theoretically, fraud becomes impossible, and it could cut down on spam (Dedovic 2019).

By 2017, the ad industry already was being transformed by blockchain, in unimaginable ways. One company, Cryptibles, launched a cryptocurrencies app that year for advertisers to provide consumers with digital collectibles or tokens (promotional products). The collectibles were tied to the blockchain, so they couldn't be stolen or copied. Security is the key promise of blockchain. Bigger players like IBM and Toyota quickly jumped onto this bandwagon, and the Havas Group of agencies established its own Havas Blockchain company in 2018.

Blockchain (and probably technologies still undiscovered) is an automated set of digital solutions to some legal and ethical problems. It is a form of self-regulation. It won't solve sexism and racism in advertising, but holds great promise for reducing some current and future problems.

CONCLUSION

As the Victorian era closed, advertising law was simplistic, and ad ethics were the cause *du jour* of magazines. Advertising's changes since 1900 are both massive and complex. The legal and social consequences follow that same pattern. And both laws and ethical standards have evolved to meet these shifting sands. Advertising professionals today must be constantly on guard for new liabilities and public relations nightmares.

13

Improving on the Old

I think that I shall never see
A billboard lovely as a tree.
Indeed, unless the billboards fall
I'll never see a tree at all.

—Ogden Nash, "Song of the Open Road," 1933

The majority of media and methods from previous centuries continued in the twentieth century, but advances in technologies enhanced them. Echoes of the Industrial Revolution continued to evolve the industry, as found in signage of this period.

ADVER-LOGICAL SIGNS

Signage is all about finding ways to draw more attention, and billboards proved especially effective. However, sizes varied all over the place, so ads had to be tailored to each board used. In 1900, standardized structures were agreed upon in the United States, opening doors to regional (or even national) mass-produced signs, allowing assurance that the signs would fit boards everywhere. The timing was fortuitous, since eight years later Henry Ford created his Model T automobile, mobilizing the middle class.

Soon, electric lighting pushed the sign industry forward. In 1910, neon lights first appeared, at a Paris Auto Show, thanks to Georges Claude. This development drastically altered the playing field for lighted displays, as more and more lighting was used on signs. That year a "great chariot race" electric sign promoting Washburn-Crosby's Gold Medal Flour appeared on a seven-story building in Herald Square, New York City (Figure 13.1). It combined size, complexity, and motion, using 20,000 bulbs and 2,750 switches to shine on Manhattan. A movement of horses, drivers, and whips was created by lights. It was one of the world's most famous electrical signs (Anonymous 2016).

FIGURE 13.1. The "great chariot race" electric sign at Herald Square in New York City, circa 1910.

A sign the Guinness Book of Records declared the world's biggest advertisement was erected in 1925. The Citroen automobile company rented the Eiffel Tower as a billboard, with "Citroen" on the tower's side, facing the Seine waterway (Figure 13.2). It used 250,000 bulbs and 600 kilometers of cabling, and was there until 1934. It was so bright that on his history-making trans-Atlantic flight of 1927, *Charles Lindbergh used this ad for navigation into Paris.* Advertising was his guide!

Innovations in billboards and large signs are many. The first photograph appearing on a billboard was in 1919, for Yucatan Gum. Many believe a 1931 billboard changed Christmas forever. Coca-Cola hired Haddon Sundblom to create a holiday billboard with an image of Santa Claus. That image didn't resemble a thinner Father Christmas used previously. The jolly old elf was never the same.

Then there is the "smoking" billboard that appeared in Times Square, New York City, in 1943. Camel cigarettes erected it, with an enormous face of a man actually blowing five-foot-wide smoke rings every four seconds (Figure 13.3). In reality steam rings, they continued to puff from the billboard until 1966.

Billboards aside, most signs prior to the 1930s were wood, metal, or baked porcelain. When lighted, most used incandescent bulbs, but after that neon spread in more detailed and colorful ways (Taylor, Claus, & Claus 2005). And Daniel McFarlan Moore had developed the "Moore Light" in 1896, setting the stage for General Electric's "flourescent" lighting in the 1930s, providing advertisers another option. In the 1940s, neon signage added flashing, animation, larger sizes, and more (Anonymous 2016).

There was no "circulation" of signs, so the outdoor industry began searching for ways to estimate viewership (Turner 1953). The Traffic Audit Bureau, founded in 1933 to audit circulation claims, joined that search (Taylor, Claus, & Claus 2005).

FIGURE 13.2. Citroen rented out the Eiffel Tower from 1925 to 1934 as an advertising medium.

The 1940s and 1950s brought plastics to signs. This reduced sign production costs, and plastic signs required less attention (e.g., re-painting). In addition, it was easy to adapt various lighting methods to plastic signs. In time, several different plastic varieties developed.

The field matured, so more coordination and structure became attractive. This started when the International Bill Posters' Association of North America was estab-lished in 1872, and in 1891 the Associated

FIGURE 13.3. The famous Camel "smoking" billboard in Times Square, in 1943.

Bill Posters' Association of the United States and Canada followed. In 1916, a new association formed: the National Outdoor Advertising Bureau. In 1925, the Poster Advertising Association and the Painted Outdoor Advertising Association merged, creating the Outdoor Advertising Association of America. By then the term "outdoor advertising" became trade terminology.

Digital technologies took over advertising of all sorts by the twenty-first century, including outdoor forms. For billboards, changing the image or the advertiser was instantaneous, replacing sending a crew out to paste a new image over an old one. And the advertiser now shared the board with other advertisers.

As of 2005, billboards began converting to digital when Clear Channel Communications erected seven LED (light-emitting diode) boards around Cleveland, Ohio. By 2007, there were about 700 in the United States. By 2019, that number was 8,800. Also in 2007, the US Federal Highway Administration approved use of digital billboards.

The quality, resolution, and brightness of the boards advanced greatly. Perhaps the most important advance was using real-time data to deliver the right billboard image at the right time. If highway traffic is moving slowly, the board can deliver different ad messages than if traffic is moving quickly (Marshall 2016). As data improves, so will abilities to target audiences with the optimum messages.

In 2007, signs on buses started being GPS-enabled. This allowed automatic changes in the ads displayed, depending on the neighborhood, to serve ads better meeting the needs of different audiences.

In 2017, another innovation came thanks to Maltesers chocolates. A London bus shelter included a "Braille billboard" promoting diversity. Its message, "Caught a really fast bus once, turns out it was a fire engine," emphasized the brand's "light side" (Figure 13.4). An audio message directed people to the brand's Facebook page. It was introduced on World Braille Day (Handley 2017).

FIGURE 13.4. A Braille billboard that appeared in London in 2017.

By then the term "outdoor advertising" was replaced by "out-of-home advertising." Many ads in this category, like kiosks and posters, aren't always outdoors, so the former term seemed limiting. In 2019, the Outdoor Advertising Association of America replaced "Outdoor" in its name with the new term.

THE LEGEND OF A SERIAL SELLER

One chapter in sign history deserves special attention, because the signs were a notable part of culture. They were entertainment and a way to shorten a trip, and fostered fond memories.

Burma-Shave shaving cream emerged from the Burma-Vita company in 1925. And soon its signs appeared along two roads out of Minneapolis: Route 65 and the road to Red Wing. Popular cars at the time included Model T Fords, Lincolns, Packards, Auburns, the Pierce-Arrow Model 80, and the Stutz Bearcat. Highways were two lanes, but quality was improving. A normal cruising speed was often thirty-five miles per hour, though speedsters went up to fifty miles per hour. And families now were taking road trips for vacations.

Burma-Shave was the company's 143rd shaving cream formula. Its owners tried selling it by giving out samples, where a customer paid only if they liked it. It didn't work so well. Allan Odell, a company executive, came up with a better approach after seeing serial signs promoting a gas station. One sign said "gas," another said "oil," then "restrooms," and so forth (Rowsome 1965). He said, "Every time I see one of these setups, I read every one of the signs. So why can't you sell a product that way?" Advertising people said it would never work, but Allan was determined.

FIGURE 13.5. One serial series of ads that appeared in 1938.

The first Burma-Shave signs were on secondhand boards, with no rhymes. Four small consecutive signs might say, SHAVE THE MODERN WAY / FINE FOR THE SKIN / DRUGGISTS HAVE IT / BURMA-SHAVE. It was year-end 1925 and getting cold. But the signs worked, so they created a sign shop in early 1926. Allan and his father became copywriters (Rowsome 1965).

Most ads of the time were serious, long copy, and hard sell. The Odells went the other way, injecting humor and irreverence, such as DOES YOUR HUSBAND / MISBEHAVE / GRUNT AND GRUMBLE / RANT AND RAVE / SHOOT THE BROOT SOME / BURMA-SHAVE. A six-sign series became the default. The signs carried a jingle cadence while controlling the reading speed and pauses (Rowsome 1965). Families would drive down the road reading the signs aloud, in unison, usually laughing (Figure 13.5).

The Odells soon ran low on creative spark, so Allan had another idea. By 1932, they sponsored annual verse contests, paying $100 for every jingle used. They advertised the contests on radio and in print. For some contests entries exceeded fifty thousand. They hired copywriters to sort through the entries.

Allan authored a public service jingle in 1935: KEEP WELL / TO THE RIGHT / OF THE ONCOMING CAR / GET YOUR CLOSE SHAVES / FROM THE HALF-POUND JAR. The signs became iconic of Burma-Shave, allowing it to use jingles having nothing to do with shaving. It followed with many signs promoting highway safety—for example, REMEMBER THIS / IF YOU'D / BE SPARED / TRAINS DON'T WHISTLE / BECAUSE THEY'RE SCARED.

The signs were so integral to travel that cartoons and radio comedians poked fun at them. This was a uniquely American advertising form. In time, Burma-Shave had about seven thousand sets of signs in forty-five states.

Soon television was the newest and brightest advertising bauble, and the Odells reduced use of the signs. Also, the Federal-Aid Highway Act of 1956 led to a US Interstate Highway System, quickly changing travel speeds and proximity of private land to travelers, making small signs less readable. When Philip Morris bought the company in 1963, Burma-Shave serials ended. But they left their mark on advertising history.

MORE SKY-HIGH ADVERTISING

While nineteenth-century advertising reached high, the twentieth century took it to new heights. The Wright Brothers, who flew an airplane at Kitty Hawk in 1903, usually get credit for inventing powered flight. It appears credit really belongs to Gustave Whitehead, in 1901. The first newspaper advertisement to sell an airplane wasn't until June 1909, for the Herring-Curtiss Aeroplane.

The first aerial advertising by an airplane may have been in 1908. Several sources indicate it promoted a Broadway play, though detail is sparse (e.g., Cox 2008). While not mentioning that, an article published March 17, 1909, in the *Boot and Shoe Recorder*, mentions the benefits of airplane advertising. By 1919, airplanes were regularly used for advertising, including dropping handbills or tokens on audiences and otherwise attracting publicity for businesses (Frank 1919).

A rigid balloon airship came first (see Chapter 7), but the non-rigid "blimp" airship was conceived in 1902. The first non-rigid airship used for advertising was the "Suchard" airship, with that name across its side. It was financed by the Suchard Swiss chocolatiers. In 1913, it was scheduled to fly from the Canary Islands to the United States, crossing the Atlantic, but that never happened.

The first Goodyear blimp used for advertising was called *Pilgrim*, in 1925, the first to use helium rather than the flammable hydrogen of the *Hindenburg*. The *Pilgrim* and its sister ship, *Puritan*, carried displays on both sides while ferrying hundreds of passengers around the 1933–1934 Chicago World's Fair. The Goodyear blimp elevated the company's brand (Figure 13.6).

FIGURE 13.6. The Goodyear blimp as seen in 2008.

Airplane skywriting for advertising began in May 1922, over the Derby at UK's Epsom Downs Racecourse. Royal Air Force Captain Cyril Turner wrote "Daily Mail" above the track, promoting the newspaper of that name. The newspaper, the next day, devoted much of its space to that event. The invention was created by Major J. C. Savage of the Royal Fly-

ing Corps, after nine years working on it (Turner 1953). In November, another demonstration occurred over New York City. By the Chicago World's Fair of 1933–1934, it was popular (Russell 1937).

FIGURE 13.7. Aerial banners have been used for nearly a century.

When thinking of airplane advertising today, we might envision planes pulling banners across the sky (Figure 13.7). That didn't begin until about July 1930, when a banner flew over Hanworth Air Park as a demonstration (Turner 1953). This continues to be a top contender for the "most dangerous" advertising delivery method (Schroeder 2015).

SPACE NEEDED!

How can a man in a $27,000 suit settle for a $235 watch?

The Apollo-Soyuz spacesuits, like those for every preceding space mission, were designed especially for the job. Not surprising either. You'd hardly expect to find the equipment for the flight through space to this historic America-Russia meeting ready-invented in the shops.

Yet that's how the astronauts found the Omega Speedmaster, their watch.

In 1965 NASA picked up a Speedmaster, as simply as you do in your local jewellery shop. And they made it standard flight equipment for every astronaut because, unlike any other chronograph tested, whatever NASA did to the Speedmaster, it stood up.

If you're wearing an Omega Speedmaster you can be proud of it – numerous space missions, six moon landings, and now, almost unbelievably, America and Russia together. For any other watch, the shock would be too much.

1. Omega Speedmaster Professional Chronograph. Standard issue to the American astronauts.
2. Omega Speedmaster 125. Officially certified automatic chronograph chronometer.
3. Omega Speedsonic (300). Officially certified electronic chronograph chronometer.

Ω OMEGA

FIGURE 13.8. Many products were linked to space in ads, but the Omega Speedmaster actually was the first wristwatch worn on the moon, on the outside of a space suit.

Those aerial advertising approaches continued throughout the century, but in 1961 Yuri Gagarin of the Soviet Union became the first human in space, soon followed by Alan Shepard of the United States, starting the "space race." On July 20, 1969, Neil Armstrong and Buzz Aldrin were first to set foot on the moon. Various products and services used space imagery, some with legitimate ties to space travel, for decades space-related advertising remained earthbound (Figure 13.8).

In 1990, advertising went through the stratosphere, literally. Tokyo Broadcasting System bought a seat on Soyuz TM-11 for Toyohiro Akiyama, a reporter, for $10 million. As part of the deal the company's logo was prominently displayed on the launch vehicle. Logos for Sony, Otsuka Pharmaceutical, and Unicharm also appeared. This marked the beginning of advertising beyond this planet. These ads had astronomical reach!

The space billboard project, in 1993, was conceived to establish a kilometer-long illuminated billboard in Earth's low orbit. From Earth it would appear about the size and brightness of the moon. Outrage followed. People didn't want a permanent lighted obstruction in the sky. So a bill was introduced in Congress to ban US advertising in space. The law was passed, but only after an amendment to restrict only "obtrusive" advertising, meaning ads on rockets and astronaut clothing would still be permitted.

Pepsi Cola in 1996 paid the Russian space program about $5 million to have a cosmonaut float a four-foot Pepsi can replica outside the Mir space station. Pepsi had a long-standing interest in aerial advertising (Figure 13.9). In 1940 alone, it used skywriting 2,225 times over the Americas (Koren 2019).

FIGURE 13.9.   Suzanne Asbury-Oliver was a Pepsi skywriter beginning in 1980.

In 1997, the Israeli company Tnuva made a milk commercial. It was the first advertising commercial filmed in space, shot aboard the Mir station.

Pizza Hut made news in 2000 by paying about $1 million to put its logo on a Proton rocket launched from Russia. The launch was viewed by five hundred million people, making the cost per viewer pretty cheap. The very next year it became the first company to deliver a pizza to people living in outer space (cosmonauts) when it sent a six-inch salami pizza to the International Space Station. The small size was necessary to fit the station's oven. Pizza Hut claimed it checked and rechecked the address before attempting the delivery.

In February 2018, private space company SpaceX delivered perhaps the greatest publicity stunt ever. SpaceX's CEO, Elon Musk, also was CEO of Tesla Motors, the electric automobile company. As SpaceX conducted its first launch test of a Falcon Heavy rocket, Musk boosted his personal Tesla Roadster into space with a dummy driver. As the car was released into space, it was photographed, and the photos were used in ads (Figure 13.10). Criticized as a stunt car commercial by some, others dubbed it the "world's best car ad."

FIGURE 13.10.   An actual photo of Elon Musk's car once it arrived in space.

Other products have reached space, but not all managed to capitalize on the publicity potential. Astronauts seem to like chocolate, so lots of candies have reached orbit: M&M, Toblerone, Ghirardelli, Kit Kat, Reese's Cups, and, of course, Milky Way, are some.

In 2013, NASA rocketed three HTC Nexus One smartphones into orbit as satellites to photograph Earth. Also, a Kentucky Fried Chicken (KFC) sandwich reached space, propelled not by a rocket but by a balloon, in 2017. That one *was* used in an advertising campaign.

COMICS AND CARTOONS

Comic books in America have been traced to a hardcover book in 1842. But comic *strips* are older. As "sequential art," they started as cave drawings and then Egyptian hieroglyphs. Some devices that we attribute to comics, like word balloons, came in the late eighteenth and early nineteenth centuries. Comic strips in newspapers arose in the late 1800s.

Use of cartoonish styles in advertising probably began with 1800s trade cards. They really pushed the boundaries of color and art styles in advertising, and cartoons were perfect for both. The first advertising comic book probably was Kellogg's *Funny Jungleland Moving-Pictures* in 1909, given away with cereal.

The first comic *strip* advertisement, for Colgate Ribbon Dental Cream, was on the back cover of *The Youth's Companion* on November 5, 1914 (Figure 13.11). Colgate, also in

FIGURE 13.11. The first known comic strip ad.

1914, published a comic book, *The Jungle School*, pretty clearly drawn (read: ripped off) from the very successful Kellogg comic book (Figure 13.12). Colgate clearly believed in comics.

Comic strip and comic book approaches allowed advertisers to tell stories beyond the confines of a static ad. Stories progressed through multiple frames, instead of squeezing one into a single frame. In essence, comics offered a unique and enhanced messaging style, a unique aesthetic approach, and, as in comic books, a unique medium. They frequently included humor! Any of these factors could explain their popularity for advertising.

The "golden age" of comic books began in 1938 and 1939 when superheroes emerged. Even before Superman (1938), Batman (1939), Flash (1940), and Green Lantern (1940), and long before Spider-Man (1962), the comic book industry was getting traction. With some success

FIGURE 13.12.   Colgate's *The Jungle School* comic book from 1914.

printing comics for Sunday newspapers in 1932, in 1933 the Eastern Color Printing company began publishing *Gulf Comic Weekly* (renamed *Gulf Funny Weekly*), a four-page tabloid with full-color comic strips, used as a giveaway promotional product at Gulf Oil gasoline stations (Figure 13.13). This was an advertising comic booklet.

In addition, Eastern Color Printing published a booklet for Standard Oil gasoline stations, *Standard Oil Comics*, in 1933, when it also began printing the eight-page *Funnies on Parade*. It really was four pages, like the others, but folded to create eight smaller pages, the format of modern comics, and many consider it the first modern comic. Like the other two, it was a promotional product, but for Procter & Gamble. Eastern created comic books for other advertisers, too.

Advertising comic books and strips continued, and several companies have used comic books as advertising, including B.F. Goodrich, Big Boy Restaurants, Servicemaster, Baskin & Robbins, Carvel, Schwinn,

FIGURE 13.13.   The *Gulf Funny Weekly* from July 1934.

FIGURE 13.15.   A portion of a Hostess Fruit Pies ad featuring the Incredible Hulk in 1980.

FIGURE 13.14.   *Adventures of the Big Boy* comic for Big Boy Restaurants, from 1959.

Poll-Parrot, Buster Brown, Osterizer, and more (Figure 13.14). Even heroes and superheroes have become cartoon product spokes characters (Figure 13.15). The Incredible Hulk and others used their star power endorsing products, but real people also sometimes did the endorsing.

ENDORSEMENTS/TESTIMONIALS

Probably even in ancient times there were product or merchant endorsements. In a 1752 ad, a girl's boarding school headmistress, Elizabeth Gardiner, recommended bodices sold by a Mr. Parson (Robertson 2011).

Even royal endorsements reach back to the 1760s. Josiah Wedgwood and Sons in 1765 made a cream-colored tea set for Queen Charlotte, wife of King George III. Wedgwood thereby became "Potter to Her Majesty."

The era of celebrity endorsements started in 1882. Thomas J. Barrett, of A&F Pears, convinced a famous actress (and mistress of the Prince of Wales, later known as King Edward VII), Lillie Langtry, to endorse Pears' Soap. She is quoted, "I prefer PEARS' SOAP to any other." She became the first actor to endorse a product in an ad (Figure 13.16).

I'm drawing a fine line between endorsements and testimonials. The former tend to be paid, while the latter are not. Endorsements connote using an established brand to enhance another brand. So endorsements are from the famous, while testimonials are from the less-than-famous.

FIGURE 13.16.   Lillie Langtry's endorsement of Pears' Soap, from 1882.

Patent medicines used testimonials of common users; for example, Dr. Kingsley's Cancer Cure used supposed testimonials in 1881, if not earlier.

People endorsing or testifying regarding a brand were known as "spokes characters," or "trade characters," though this might imply characters *created* for trade purposes. Having characters speak for the brand soon caught on, but characters certainly varied.

ADVERTISING HAS CHARACTER(S)

Trade characters (or "icons") gained popularity in the late 1800s. These include any sort of "character"—human, cartoon, animal, or even inanimate object—used to represent a brand. Some are "spokes" characters, if they speak, but some are silent. Some move while others are stationary. All lend a personality to a brand, distinguishing it from competitors (Figure 13.17).

The wooden cigar store "Indian" was a trade character, but represented a product *category* rather than a brand. Early signs for pubs and inns featuring a dog or duck or king or grasshopper image were using it to distinguish that business. The rabbit of Jinan Liu around 1200 CE advertising his needle shop was a trade character. So trade characters have existed for at least eight centuries.

What changed in the late nineteenth century was the advertising through which those characters were conveyed. They now live longer and reach farther. Technological developments made reproduction of character images easier and more consistent, and twentieth-century technologies enabled character speech and movement. Characters now could be legally protected as trademarks or parts of trademarks. All of these developments made characters more attractive as advertising devices.

FIGURE 13.17. An iconic cartoon-type character, Reddy Kilowatt was created in 1926 for Alabama Power Company, was later used by Duke Energy, and more recently has been owned by Xcel Energy.

Society had changed. While a sports figure or actor might previously have had fame within a relatively confined area, now magazines reached across entire nations, so fame became bigger for those people. This made them even more attractive as spokes characters. In 1910, Gillette, a safety razor company, began using professional athletes in its ads, giving testimonials (Figure 13.18). Use of both real people and fictional characters was spreading.

Today, trade characters are found everywhere. The list in Table 13.1 includes most well-known ones, as well as ones that once were well known.

Human characters have struck gold for advertisers. In 1984, a character even stepped onto the US presidential campaign stage. Clara Peller, an eighty-year-old manicurist, acted in a series of commercials. She was hard of hearing with a gruff voice, but that was perfect for a Wendy's restaurants commercial portraying three elderly ladies visiting a competing restaurant (Figure 13.19). Two of them are busy commenting on a competitor's enormous bun, when Peller yells, "Where's the beef?!"

DONOVAN of Detroit   CHANCE of Chicago   KLING of Chicago   WAGNER of Pittsburg   JENNINGS of Detroit

The men who uphold the standards of American sport today are clean men—clean of action and clean of face. Your baseball star takes thought of his personal appearance—it's a part of his team ethics. He starts the day with a clean shave—and, like all self-reliant men, he shaves himself.

Wagner, Jennings, Kling, Donovan, Chance—each of the headliners owns a Gillette Safety Razor *and uses it.* The Gillette is typical of the American spirit. It is used by capitalists, professional men, business men—by men of action all over this country—*three million of them.*

Its use starts habits of energy—of initiative. And men who *do* for themselves are men who *think* for themselves.

Be master of your own time. Buy a Gillette and use it.

You can shave with it the first time you try. The one perfectly *safe* razor and the only safety razor that shaves on the correct hollow ground shaving principle.

No stropping, no honing.

Send your name on a post card for our new Baseball book. Schedule of all League games—batting records—24 pages of interesting facts and figures. Every fan should have it. It is free.

King C Gillette

GILLETTE SALES COMPANY, 22 W. Second Street, Boston
New York, Times Building Chicago, Stock Exchange Building Gillette Safety Razor, Ltd., London
Eastern Office, Shanghai, China   Canadian Office, 63 St. Alexander Street, Montreal

GILLETTE SALES COMPANY, 22 W. Second Street, Boston
Factories : Boston, Montreal, Leicester, Berlin, Paris

FIGURE 13.18. The first use of sports figures to endorse a product in an ad, in 1910.

Table 13.1. **Trade Characters of Some Note**

Character	Product	Year
Johnny Walker	Johnny Walker whiskey	1820
Quaker Oats Man	Quaker Oats	1877
Gold Dust Twins (Goldie & Dustie)	Gold Dust scouring powder	1892
Aunt Jemima	Aunt Jemima pancake mixes and syrup	1893
Rastus (chef)	Cream of Wheat	1893
Psyche	White Soda Rock	1894
Nipper	Radio Corporation of America (RCA)	1895
Michelin Man (aka "Bibendum")	Michelin tires	1898
Buster Brown & Tige	Buster Brown shoes and hosiery	1904
Campbell Kids	Campbell's Soups	1904
Sweetheart of the Corn	Kellogg Company	1907
Old Joe	Camel cigarettes	1913
Dutch Boy	Dutch Boy paints	1914
Morton Salt Girl	Morton Salt	1914
Cracker Jack & Bingo	Cracker Jack caramel popcorn	1916
M-G-M Lion	Metro Goldwyn Mayer	1916
Mr. Peanut	Planter's Peanuts	1916

Character	Product	Year
Uncle Sam	US Army	1917
Johnny the Bellhop	Philip Morris cigarettes	1919
Buddy Lee	Lee Jeans	1920
Betty Crocker	Betty Crocker food products	1921
Messenger Boy	Whitman's chocolates	1921
Reddy Kilowatt	Alabama Power Company	1926
Jolly Green Giant	Green Giant vegetables	1928
Dino the Dinosaur	Sinclair oil and gasoline	1930
Snap! (of Snap! Crackle! & Pop!)	Rice Krispies cereal	1933
Aristocrat Tomato Man	Heinz Ketchup	1934
Willie and Millie Penguins	Kool cigarettes	1934
Pep Boys—Manny, Moe, & Jack	Pep Boys auto parts stores	1935
Big Boy	Bob's Pantry restaurant	1936
Elsie the Cow	Borden dairy products	1939
Chesty Boy	Chesty Potato Chips	1940s
Crackle! (of Snap! Crackle! & Pop!)	Rice Krispies cereal	1941
Lil' Squirt	Squirt soft drink	1941
Pop! (of Snap! Crackle! & Pop!)	Rice Krispies cereal	1941
Chiquita Banana	Chiquita bananas	1944
Smokey the Bear	US Dept. of Forestry	1944
Uncle Ben	Uncle Ben's Rice	1944
Chef Boy-Ar-Dee	Chef Boy-Ar-Dee canned spaghetti	1945
Speedee	McDonald's restaurants	1950
Piggly Wiggly	Piggly Wiggly grocery stores	1951
Speedy Alka-Seltzer	Alka-Seltzer	1951
Tony the Tiger	Kellogg's Sugar Frosted Flakes	1951
Tropic-Ana	Tropicana Orange Juice	1951
Bazooka Joe	Bazooka bubblegum	1953
Exxon Tiger	Exxon gasoline	1953
Farfel (dog puppet)	Nestle's Quik	1953
Playboy Bunny	Playboy magazine and clubs	1953
Willie Wiredhand	National Rural Electric Cooperative	1953
Burger King	Burger King restaurants	1954
Hamm's Bear	Hamm's beer	1955
Marlboro Man	Marlboro cigarettes	1955
Kool-Aid Pitcher	Kool-Aid powdered soft drink	1956
Marky Maypo	Maypo cereal	1956
Buffalo Bee	Nabisco Rice Honeys	1957
Cornelius (the rooster)	Kellogg's Corn Flakes	1957
Mr. Clean	Mr. Clean all-purpose cleanser	1957
Juan Valdez	Nat'l Fed'n of Coffee Growers of Colombia	1958
Little Oil Drop	Humble Oil	1958
Little Miss Coppertone	Coppertone suntan lotion	1959
Sugar Pops Pete	Kellogg's Sugar Pops cereal	1959
Trix Rabbit	Trix cereal	1959
Mr. Magoo*	General Electric bulbs	1959
Choo-Choo Charlie	Good & Plenty	1960
Charlie the Tuna	Star-Kist Tuna	1961
Mr. Bubble	Mr. Bubble bubble bath	1961
Punchy (and Oaf)	Hawaiian Punch soft drink	1962
Raid Bug	Raid insecticide	1962
Cap'n Crunch	Cap'n Crunch cereal	1963
Ronald McDonald	McDonald's restaurants	1963

(continued)

Table 13.1. *Continued*

Character	Product	Year
Funny Face	Funny Face Pillsbury powdered drink mix	1964
L. C. "Lucky" Leprechaun	General Mills' Lucky Charms cereal	1964
Mr. Salty	Nabisco pretzels	1964
Sugar Bear	Post Sugar Crisp cereal	1964
Toucan Sam	Kellogg's Froot Loops cereal	1964
Pillsbury Doughboy (Poppin' Fresh)	Pillsbury foods	1965
Quake	Quake cereal	1965
Quisp	Quisp cereal	1965
Mr. Wiggle	General Foods' Jell-o Gelatin	1966
Maytag (Repair) Man	Maytag appliances	1967
Frito Bandito	Frito-Lay Corporation	1967
Keebler Elf	Keebler cookies and crackers	1968
Little Green Sprout	Green Giant vegetables	1968
Bud Man	Budweiser beer	1969
Count Chocula	General Mills' Count Chocula cereal	1971
Frankenberry	General Mills' Frankenberry cereal	1971
Twinkie the Kid	Hostess Twinkies	1971
Dig'Em (the frog)	Kellogg's Sugar Smacks cereal	1972
Scrubbing Bubbles (Scrubby, Mindy, Poppy, and Sudsy)	Dow Brands	1972
Boo Berry	General Mills' Boo Berry cereal	1973
Nesquik Bunny (Quicki)	Nestle's Nesquik powdered drink mix	1973
A&W Bear	A&W Rootbeer	1974
Joe Camel	Camel cigarettes	1974
Chuck E. Cheese	Chuck E. Cheese Pizza	1977
McGruff the Crime Dog	Ad Council	1978
Spuds MacKenzie	Bud Light beer	1983
Crash Test Dummies (Vince & Larry)	Ad Council	1985
Max Headroom	New Coke	1985
California Raisins	California Raisin Advisory Board	1986
Mac Tonight	McDonald's	1986
Noid	Domino's Pizza	1986
7-Up Spot	Seven-Up soft drink	1987
Energizer Bunny	Eveready Energizer batteries	1989
Chipper (friend of Nipper)	RCA	1991
Coca-Cola Bears	Coca-Cola	1993
Jack Box	Jack-in-the-Box restaurants	1993
Budweiser Frogs	Budweiser beer	1995
General	General Auto Insurance	1997
Budweiser Lizards	Budweiser beer	1998
Taco Bell Chihuahuas	Taco Bell restaurants	1998
Geico Gecko	Geico Insurance	1999
Pets.com Sock Puppet	Pets.com	1999
AFLAC Duck	Aflac Insurance	2000
Geico Caveman	Geico Insurance	2004
Mr. Mucus	Mucinex	2004
Flo	Progressive Insurance	2008
Geico Stack of Money	Geico Insurance	2008
Allstate Mayhem	Allstate Insurance	2010
Geico Pig (Maxwell)	Geico Insurance	2010
Geico Camel	Geico Insurance	2013

*Created prior to this date, but adopted for advertising purposes at this time.

That line, and Peller, gained celebrity status. Wendy's profits jumped 31 percent. Because it was a presidential election year, one candidate, former vice president Walter Mondale, used Peller's line against Senator Gary Hart when vying for the Democratic nomination. It was replayed again and again throughout the campaign, reminding audiences of Wendy's.

But live characters—people—aren't perfect. Around 1971, Procter & Gamble had an attractive young woman pose holding a baby, as a "mother and child" image for Ivory Snow laundry detergent (Figure 13.20). That woman, Marilyn Ann Briggs, became renowned in 1972

FIGURE 13.19. Wendy's classic commercial with actress Clara Peller on the right.

for "acting" in *Behind the Green Door*, a pornographic film. She became known as Marilyn Chambers (McLellan 2009).

In 1975, football star O. J. Simpson began making ads for Hertz Rent-A-Car. He later was in ads for several brands (Figure 13.21). One survey found Simpson to be the most popular athlete spokesman of any brand (Schwab 2016). As a trade character, he seemed ideal. He was African American, and yet White Americans liked the commercials!

Although Simpson hadn't appeared in Hertz ads for years, the ads were recalled by the press when Simpson was charged with killing his ex-wife and her friend in 1994, especially since he still was under contract to Hertz (Murray 1994). Hertz distanced itself from Simpson, but

FIGURE 13.20. Marilyn Chambers, on the Ivory Snow box circa 1970, became a star in pornographic films.

the damage already was done, since he was so indelibly linked to the brand. That incredible earlier success was now a brand image crisis. Simpson was acquitted, but the damage remained. In 2008, Simpson was convicted of armed robbery, and the damage continued (e.g., Bekiempis 2019).

The list of live trade character failures is long. Jared Fogle was an enormous success for Subway restaurants, until he was convicted of child porn and soliciting minors for sex (Chappell 2015). Actor Charlie Sheen was dropped as spokes character for Hanes underwear upon being arrested for domestic violence (Wang 2010).

Not all failures were legal convictions. Golf pro Tiger Woods had an automobile accident, exposing him for marital infidelity, paying prostitutes, and more. Numerous advertisers pulled ads with Woods in them, and some permanently jumped ship (Edwards 2009). Van-Hooker (2015) lists several other spokespeople who screwed up, while Stampler (2012) offers a different list, and together they compile far from an exhaustive record.

FIGURE 13.21. O. J. Simpson became so popular as a spokes character that he even bridged the gap between live and comic character. This ad appeared on the back cover of a comic book in 1980.

It's a wonder there isn't greater reliance on cartoon characters, since they can't easily go rogue. And they have added benefits like never aging, and never dying. Potentially, they can last centuries.

Many ad agencies, and advertisers, have created memorable characters. Leo Burnett, in particular, built a reputation around this. It invented the Marlboro Man, the Jolly Green Giant, Tony the Tiger, the Keebler Elves, and many more.

Some non-human characters, like the California Raisins, reached "star" status for a time. The Raisins were created using a new animation technique called "claymation." Foote, Cone & Belding in San Francisco introduced them in 1986 to represent the California Raisin Advisory Board. They sang and danced, becoming pop culture phenomena for a previously unexciting brand.

And then came a sock puppet. In 1999, Pets.com, an online pet supply store, used the puppet as a spokes character—microphone and all—reaching near cult status. It

FIGURE 13.22. The Pets.com sock puppet became such an icon it even appeared on the cover of *Mad Magazine.*

was in the Macy's Thanksgiving Day Parade that year and in a Super Bowl ad in 2000 (Figure 13.22). But even a popular character won't save a flawed brand. Pets.com's stock dropped from $14 per share to 22¢ per share in less than a year.

In 2017, State Street Global Advisors (SSGA), a financial firm representing gender-diverse companies with strong female leadership, made a statement for International Women's Day. A bronze statue was installed in New York City the day before: a girl standing fearlessly in front of the financial district's famous *Charging Bull* statue (Figure 13.23). *Fearless Girl* became a symbol for girls and women, far beyond representing the SSGA brand. It represented empowered women, and as an ad it won eighteen Cannes Lions awards at the 2017 Cannes Lions International Festival of Creativity (and several other awards). Originally it had a one-week permit, but it stood on that spot for more

FIGURE 13.23. *Fearless Girl*, while still facing the bull, in 2018.

than a year and a half. The bull's sculptor was unhappy about it, so *Fearless Girl* was moved permanently to the New York Stock Exchange.

PRODUCTS AS ADS

The idea of using small, cheap, or free items to promote brands has had multiple names. "Novelty advertising" was an early name, though some criticized this as a misnomer. "Tangible advertising," "connective advertising," "supplemental advertising," or "personal advertising" also were used in the early 1900s (Bunting 1925). Less formal terms include "giveaways" (for the free ones) or "tchotchkes." The most pejorative term, used by ad practitioners with limited respect for them, probably is "trinkets and trash."

For several decades the preferred term was "advertising specialties." Much later the industry adopted "promotional products" (PP). Whatever it's called, there are few people alive who don't possess a pen, key fob, T-shirt, or other item with a brand name printed on it representing some *other* product or service.

Booklets, playing cards, and folding fans from the late 1600s and early 1700s already were mentioned as PP. Calendars, bags, matchbooks, and so forth followed in the late 1800s. But the 1900s is when this really became a full-blown industry.

There was traction for this method of advertising when that century began, as noted in *Fowler's Publicity*:

> Advertising clocks and thermometers are expensive, but their advertising value is permanent. The fact that many of the most conservative of progressive advertisers distribute large quantities of thermometers seems to indicate that this method of advertising has a definite, intrinsic value of the most permanent character. (p. 1904)

A device to imprint text on wooden pencils, developed in 1908, made one of the world's most frequently used and cheapest products into a PP. Writing instruments became mainstays of the PP industry.

Radio helped promote the PP business. In the 1920s, when commercial radio was an infant, program sponsors would give souvenir products to listeners who wrote them (Hettinger 1933).

Recall that Kellogg used a children's book as a giveaway in breakfast cereal beginning in 1909, and comic books as ads in 1933. From the start advertisers employed products that could promote all manner of business.

By the late 1930s, Wheaties invited customers to collect cereal box tops to mail in for a "Jack Armstrong Egyptian Whistle Ring." PP in exchange for proofs of purchase, or toys hidden in cereal boxes, became common. This approach has gone through popularity cycles but continued into the twenty-first century (Figure 13.24).

The development of polyurethane and hard plastics made production of cheap products, like stress relievers and children's toys, feasible. As more advertisers sought products not already owned by prospective customers, PP vendors were forced to become creative, offering new options every year. Soon catalogs of products gave merchants hundreds of choices.

A few products deserve special mention, including the Mickey Mouse Watch. The Walt Disney company created it in 1933, for sale at the Chicago World's Fair for $3.25. Mr. Disney originally argued that it would never sell. He was wrong. In 1957, he was presented with the twenty-five-millionth Mickey watch. It became iconic of Disney's company.

FIGURE 13.24. A promotional product used as a breakfast cereal premium is depicted on this 1990 box.

Another notable PP came in 2004. Lance Armstrong, reigning champion of the Tour de France bicycle race, created the Lance Armstrong Foundation charity in 1997. In 2003, it be-

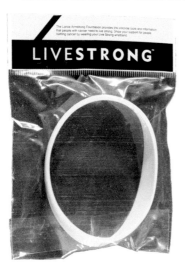

FIGURE 13.25. The Livestrong bracelet.

came the Livestrong Foundation, and in 2004 it introduced a yellow silicone-gel wristband, emblazoned with "Livestrong," as a fund-raiser (Figure 13.25). They sold for $1 apiece, costing just cents each to produce. Within ten years eighty million bracelets were sold. Hundreds, maybe thousands, of other organizations copied the idea.

In 2016, US presidential candidate Donald Trump put his campaign slogan, "Make America Great Again," on red baseball-style caps (Figure 13.26). Those caps were iconic of his campaign and became perhaps the most memorable presidential campaign device ever used.

The first organization to represent the PP industry was the Advertising Novelty Manufacturers Association (ANMA), formed by a dozen PP manufacturers in 1904. The Advertising Federation of America didn't recognize it as a legitimate advertising approach until 1912. The ANMA merged with the Advertising Specialty Guild in 1964. By blending with the guild, formed in 1953, the association was renamed the Specialty Advertising Association. In 1970, it became the Specialty Advertising

FIGURE 13.26. Donald Trump's 2016 campaign hat.

Association International, and in 1992 it evolved into the Promotional Products Association International (PPAI).

The association had 12 members initially, but it grew to 56 by 1906. In 1928, it had 132 members, by 1966 it was 1,211, and in 2020 it exceeded 15,000.

The Advertising Specialty Institute (ASI) began in 1950. It originally was conceived as a mechanism to find specific products, publishing a directory called the "Advertising Specialty Register." Over time its mission overlapped with the PPAI. ASI was a member of PPAI until 2005, when it was pushed out.

DISCOUNTS AND LOYALTY

Products and services often are promoted with discount programs designed to encourage customer loyalty. The most common is couponing.

Coupons

Coupons come in different forms, though we usually think of some certificate offering a discount. Some coupons, though, offer a PP as a "premium," and others offer access to more information. No matter their promise, coupons almost always are a form of brand promotion that may or may not carry other attributes (e.g., brand logo) as advertising.

The birth of coupons is hard to determine. The "Lipton Pounds" of 1877, by Thomas Lipton (Chapter 7), promised goods worth one pound for fifteen shillings. That constituted a form of coupon. When B. T. Babbitt sold packaged soap in 1851, he included certificates in the wrapper allowing consumers to redeem a certain number of them for art. The Grand Union Tea Company in 1872 issued tickets (coupons) for its products.

Recall that the trade tokens of the seventeenth or eighteenth centuries acted as money, dedicated to specific stores, though we don't know whether they ever were given away as discounts. Figure 13.27 depicts a one-cent token of 1874 from the FREMAD Association, a coopera-

FIGURE 13.27. A one-cent token from the FREMAD Association, 1874.

tive store in Minnesota, which seems a *de facto* metal coupon.

Murchison (1919) claims:

About 1885 the coupon system began to assume proportions which made it an imposing factor in merchandising. So rapid has been its growth that, according to recent estimates, merchandise premiums to the value of $125,000,000 annually are distributed in redemption of trading stamps and coupons, exclusive of the slips which are redeemed in cash or other methods. On this basis it is calculated that premiums figure in the selling of five billion dollars' worth of merchandise annually. It is also calculated that of the 20,000,000 families in the United States, 10,000,000 are redeeming coupons, through some member of the families or through the servants who handle the family groceries.

Many authors (e.g., FitzPatrick 2008; Tuttle 2010) suggest Asa Candler, who bought the Coca-Cola formula from its inventor, John Stith Pemberton, first developed coupons. The Coca-Cola Company confirms that first coupon was in 1888. Candler gave out "tickets" for one free glass of Coke. By 1913, consumers had redeemed 8.5 million.

C. W. Post is credited with being the next adopter of this tool. He invented a "healthy" breakfast cereal, Grape-Nuts, in 1897. He took Candler's coupon idea and created a grocery discount coupon, with a penny off the going price (Klaffke 2003; Glanton 2005).

It's clear one variety of coupon was common by 1902, the "return coupon," a mail-order device. Scott (1902) notes advertisers developed this to track the multiple periodicals in which they published ads. Starch (1926) reflects, "The return coupon came into more common use about 1900 and since then has been used with increasing frequency until today it is used very generally." This wasn't originally a discount coupon, but a mechanism for ordering a product or requesting additional information. But it laid the foundation for other coupon types.

The original "corner coupon" was developed by Ralph Tilton (Dyer 1905), first published in the *New York Herald* in 1899. It commanded readers to "Cut This Corner" (clip the coupon), encouraging them to send it to John Wanamaker's store for a sales brochure about joining a half-price club. It also served as a discount offer (Scott 1902). This made coupon clipping a habit, while establishing conventions like dotted lines as a clipping guide.

A factor that led to coupons being clipped, not torn, from ads was postal regulations. A US regulation of 1908 required that coupons in advertising material, to qualify as second-class mail, must not be perforated for easy detachment. Otherwise, they'd require the higher third-class postage rate. Clippable coupons qualified for second-class postage so long as they didn't occupy more than 25 percent of the ad, making them a mere "incidental feature" of the ad (Post Office Department 1912).

Coupon books began arriving at least by 1890 (Figure 13.28). Early coupon books frequently were a collection of multiple coupons for one merchant, though some covered multiple sellers. Some had sufficient perceived value that they were sold to consumers, and some involved schemes that asked consumers to sell the books in exchange for a prize.

Coupon use grew, really taking off in the 1930s Depression. During World War II, the government issued vouchers labeled "ration coupons," to control consumption of goods. But true commercial couponing continued, and in 1957 the Nielsen Coupon Clearing House began as a universal redemption center.

"Shared mail" coupons arrived in 1968, when Terry Loebel created Valpak, a packet

FIGURE 13.28. A coupon book dated 1890 offers five-cent coupons from various merchants, from the Novelty Advertising Company.

of coupons mailed directly to consumers. Another version, the free-standing insert (FSI), later known as preprint advertising, arrived in 1972, thanks to George F. Valassis. Discount coupons were collected by Valassis and a deal struck with several newspapers to insert coupons in the papers for easy distribution. This not only became a coupon delivery system but also made newspapers with the preprint material more popular among readers who used those coupons.

Then 1974 brought "blow-in cards." These cards were machine-inserted into magazines, so they would fall out when the magazine was opened.

It is estimated that in 1980 more than eighty billion coupons were printed, expecting about 20 percent to be redeemed (McChesney 1982). By that time many consumers were true coupon collectors, organizing their shopping around coupons.

Introduction of the Universal Product Code (UPC) in 1974 brought change. This scannable bar code carried product information that machines could read. Initially that information was used for inventory control, scanning to record how many units were in stock. But the 1980s saw computers and software become accessible and affordable, and computer-generated coupons arrived around 1990.

Computer Age Coupons

Initially these were coupons printed at a store checkout, or from machines attached to store shelves, using the UPC. That year the Winn Dixie grocery chain participated in a trial of electronic couponing (Sloane 1990). Consumers received coupons at the register, for a brand competing with the brand they purchased, or a coupon for re-purchase of their chosen brand. Some stores had machines in shopping aisles where consumers could push a button to print a coupon.

Next came emailed coupons. Email, for most people, began in the early 1990s, and by the late 1990s email was a common means of reaching customers. That is when printable coupons began appearing on websites. Some merchants posted them on their own sites, but specialty coupon websites like ValuPage.com arrived by 1997. These were aggregation sites, where multiple advertisers posted coupons, catering to heavy coupon users. Coupon codes' (aka promotional codes, key codes, reward codes, etc.) popularity exploded, making it even easier to apply discounts to online purchases.

The Quick Response (QR) Code emerged in 1994, a step toward easy scanning by consumers. Once the iPhone was introduced in 2007, mobile coupons soon became reality. Consumers could access discount coupons even while waiting in the checkout line.

Coupons have monetary value, so a real problem is coupon fraud and theft. In 1980–1981, nineteen people were convicted of coupon fraud in the San Diego–San Francisco area alone. Common methods of fraud include submitting expired coupons or redeeming coupons for products not purchased (McChesney 1982). But this crime goes beyond store customers.

In 2019, the owner of a Shop 'n Save supermarket was charged with stealing more than $300,000 through coupons. He had employees cut coupons from unsold newspapers, and then he would send them for redemption as if customers had submitted them toward product purchases (Braine 2019). The preprint coupons inserted in high-circulation weekend newspapers can represent millions of dollars in piles awaiting insertion in those papers. Believe it or not, people have jobs guarding advertising.

Trading Stamps

I must mention trading stamps, as these were *de facto* coupons. Such stamps were given away with purchases from participating merchants. The more you bought, the more stamps you received. Schuster's Department Store, in Milwaukee, Wisconsin, was likely the birthplace of trading stamps, issuing its first stamps in 1890.

In 1896, Sperry & Hutchinson got into this business, serving multiple stores with its S&H Green Stamps (Figure 13.29). Top Value stamps, Gold Bond stamps, and many more developed over the years. By 1919, there were thirty-five to forty US trading stamp companies, with more than sixty-five thousand participating retailers (Murchison 1919).

Consumers were encouraged to collect stamps and, upon reaching a certain number, pasted into a booklet, exchange the booklet for merchandise selected from a catalog. This was an early frequent-shopper program, lur-

FIGURE 13.29. An S&H Green Stamp from 1897, the second year they were available.

ing a consumer to a retailer again and again. The trading stamp craze lasted until the 1970s, when retailers began competing on price instead of premiums. Discount coupons were a better fit for this new climate.

Trading stamps continued to exist, but were far less common. As with everything else, they went digital. Around the year 2000, the leading brand, S&H Green Stamps, became S&H Greenpoints.

Box Tops, Soup Labels, and Receipts

The Betty Crocker brand is credited as the initiator of box top collecting. In 1929, it put coupons in its product boxes, to be collected and redeemed for spoons to eat the product. The offerings expanded, and in 1937 the company began printing coupons on box tops. Like the stamps, a reward catalog developed to encourage people to collect box tops. Betty Crocker's program continued until 2006.

Other companies followed with box top programs, which were popular for decades. They gained new life in 1996, when General Mills (owner of Betty Crocker) started "Box Tops for Education," encouraging schoolchildren and their families to collect box tops, turning them into their school. Schools redeemed them for cash. Campbell Soup Company had a similar program with soup labels back in 1973, allowing schools to redeem labels for athletic equipment and other needed school supplies. In 1998, Hy-Vee stores created a similar "Cash 4 Students" program, based on collecting store receipts.

Loyalty Programs

Computer-generated coupons brought computers into the mix, which also led to frequent-shopper cards. The Wegman's supermarket chain was an early adopter of "loyalty cards" in 1991 (Kleinfield 1991). These cards could electronically track a consumer's purchases and provide instant coupon-like discounts when certain thresholds (e.g., one free for every ten purchased) were met.

In 1998, eBates.com, among the first wholly digital coupon and "promo code" platforms for online shopping, offered cash-back opportunities as well. By purchasing from one of its affiliated merchants through an eBates link, a commission is paid to eBates, and it splits that commission with the consumer. This creates a guaranteed discount simply by using eBates as a portal. Being listed on the eBates site also promotes advertisers. The company was acquired by Rakuten in 2014. Several competitors quickly arose.

Coupon and stamp programs served consumers' interests with a discount, and sellers' interests by promoting products and building consumer brand loyalty. Many also benefited sellers by collecting data, such as the consumer's name and contact information. By contrast, loyalty cards made data gathering the primary objective, and the amount of data was mountainous, compared to prior approaches. Merchants now could track individual shoppers' spending in the store—what they bought and when—the way online purchases could be tracked.

CONCLUSION

Methods that appeared in earlier times, almost without exception, both expanded and evolved in the twentieth century. These methods—print, personalities, and products—continue to be powerful techniques, even amid the newest and shiniest approaches.

Newest Media and Methods

Television won't be able to hold on to any market it captures after the first six months. People will soon get tired of staring at a plywood box every night.

—*Darryl F. Zanuck, president of 20th Century Fox, 1946*

The old methods of reaching consumers completely changed in the twentieth century, but it is the new media that are the real story. They even changed the ways people talked about advertising.

THE LANGUAGE OF MODERN ADVERTISING

Recall that the word "advertise" emerged in the fourteenth century and "marketing" in the sixteenth century. Most terms mentioned earlier are still in use today, with a few exceptions. Today's lexicon is much bigger, and new terms sprout almost every day.

The term "public relations" was a more recent creation. Its first use had a slightly different meaning, referring to public welfare. Attorney Dorman Eaton is credited with using it in his 1882 speech at Yale Law School titled "The Public Relations and Duties of the Legal Profession." But Guth & Marsh (2003) claim Thomas Jefferson used it in an 1807 address to Congress, talking about Congress's obligations to citizens. Use within the PR profession, though, was not the norm until around 1913. Even then, "propaganda" was still common.

The earliest documented use of "direct mail" was in 1893. T. B. Russell's article, "With English Advertisers," used it in *Printers' Ink*. The term "direct marketing," came later, in 1958, by Lester Wunderman. His agency, Wunderman, Ricotta & Kline, was founded that year to more directly tie advertising to results.

First use of "consumerism" was in 1915, just before the consumer movement began. Marchand (1985) says "Madison Avenue" was first used, meaning the ad industry, in 1923. The word "commercial," meaning a broadcast ad, began in 1935. "Creative," as a noun referring to a creative person, started in 1938. And "commercial speech," a legal term referring to advertising and related expressions, was coined by Judge J. Skelly Wright in 1971.

Other additions to our vocabulary are[1] television (1900), radio (1903), advertorial (1917), junk mail (1921), narrowcasting (1932), video (1934), telemarketing (1963), psychographics (1968), infomercial (1981), guerrilla marketing (1984), integrated marketing communication (1989), e-commerce (1993), m-commerce (1997), clickbait (1999), and native advertising (2011).

Terms relevant, but not confined, to advertising include "artificial intelligence," beginning in 1955, and "artificial reality," coined by Myron Kruegere in 1969. "Virtual reality" came later, in 1987; "World Wide Web" and "augmented reality" both arrived in 1990. The "information superhighway" is harder to trace. Nam June Paik claims to have invented it in 1974, but *Merriam-Webster* claims it was coined in 1983. Former vice president Al Gore also is credited with inventing it in 1978, or 1985, or 1994. The most solid source appears to be *Merriam-Webster*, based on an article in the January 3, 1983, *Newsweek* magazine, which is easily traceable. The "Internet of Things" was first mentioned in 1999 by Kevin Ashton.

Advertising jargon has increased exponentially, making it impossible to cover all of it. The bucket of terms is now an ocean.

WHEN RADIO WAS "NEW MEDIA"

Never before the advent of radio did advertising have such a golden opportunity to make an ass out of itself. Never before could advertising be so insistent and so unmannerly and so affront its audience.

—*William J. Cameron (1938), director of public relations for Ford Motor Company*

A Sound Approach

The seeds of audio recording and broadcasting arrived in the late 1800s. The first audio recording, of someone singing, was in 1860, by inventor Edouard-Leon Scott de Martinville. It used paper as the recording medium. Sound was recorded on magnetic media in 1899. And in 1891 Thomas Edison received a patent to transmit electric signals (radio). These set the stage for the next big thing in advertising.

The earliest advertising medium approximating radio was the telephone. Alexander Graham Bell created his phone around 1876. By 1899, Budapest had 6,200 telephones routed through a central switchboard. From 10:30 a.m. to 10:30 p.m., it was treated much like our radio, with news broadcast over the wires (Printers' Ink 1938). Merchants bought commercial time, making it the earliest form of telemarketing! Marconi invented radio in 1894, but it took decades to become a viable ad medium.

The first radio available for purchase by the public was advertised in *Scientific American's* January 13, 1906, issue (Figure 14.1). The brand, Telimco, cost $8.50 and was promoted as a "wireless telegraph." It mostly was for hobbyists, but government already was involved.

Proof of the medium's value came when New York City department store owner John Wanamaker set up a radio on his store's roof. David Sarnoff operated it, receiving messages on April 1912 from ships rescuing people as the *Titanic* sank. He contacted the press with that breaking news.

President Theodore Roosevelt created the Interdepartmental Board of Wireless

FIGURE 14.1. The first ad selling a radio, from *Scientific American*, January 13, 1906.

Telegraphy in 1904, taking the first step toward regulating radio. Then came the Wireless Ship Act (1910), the Radio Act (1912), the Radio Act (1927), and the Communications Act (1934). So radio as a commercial medium was built around a regulatory system that was forming alongside the medium itself. That might be the last time government acted so quickly.

A couple of things worthy of note came out of the 1927 law. It created the Federal Radio Commission (FRC), and it established that radio waves, over which sound is carried, are publicly owned. It wouldn't prevent radio stations from using those waves, and stations weren't required to pay rent for their use (Scott 2000). But it led to licensing stations, and implied responsibility to citizens-as-owners. The 1934 act replaced the Federal Radio Commission with a Federal Communications Commission (FCC).

The first real move toward commercial radio might be 1907, when the first broadcast of music occurred. Two years later, Dr. Charles David Herrold created the oldest radio station still existing in the United States (San Jose, California), now called KCBS. It started as an experimental station, with just fifteen watts of power, receiving its first license in 1915, with call letters 6XF, and in 1921 became KQW with a commercial license. CBS bought it in 1949, changing it to KCBS effective 1951.

In 1919, a Westinghouse engineer, Frank Conrad, broadcast music from his garage in Pittsburgh, Pennsylvania, which piqued interest in kits to build radios at home. David Sarnoff then was seeking support to develop radio, but one response was "The wireless music box has no imaginable value. Who would pay for a message sent to nobody in particular?"

Enter: Advertising

In 1920, Westinghouse executive H. P. Davis saw a department store ad selling radio receivers for listening to Frank Conrad's music. He realized Westinghouse could create a market for receiving sets by broadcasting (Hettinger 1933). Westinghouse invested in Conrad's transmitter, establishing a broadcast station, KDKA, on November 2, 1920. By 1921, the station already was broadcasting baseball games and prizefights. Almost simultaneously, the Detroit News set up a station (Scott 2000). Conrad's station, however, was the first station to receive a federal commercial license, on October 27, 1920. The Detroit station, initially WBL but almost immediately changed to WWJ, received its license in October 1921.

While radio found its foothold in the United States, Radio Moscow began broadcasting in 1922. At twelve kilowatts, it easily was the world's most powerful station. BBC Radio also began daily newscasts that year in Britain. Thailand's radio started in 1930 (Pongsapitaksanti 2010). But it wasn't until 1959 that commercial radio finally reached Korea.

Initially, the idea of radio becoming an advertising medium was not popular. Even Herbert Hoover, then secretary of commerce, felt it inappropriate (Gale Group 2000). He once said it was "inconceivable that we should allow so great a . . . service to be drowned in advertising clatter" (Mierau 2000). Yet there was much talk about monetizing this technology, and many new stations failed for lack of funding. *Printers' Ink* magazine even lambasted advertising on radio (McLaren & Prelinger 1998). The British considered radio commercials offensive (Turner 1953).

J. C. McQuiston, head of publicity for Westinghouse, in August 1922 said:

The broadcasting to thousands of homes of advertising information concerning, say: "Things for women and things for men," probably the butcher with his meats; the baker with his bread; the tailor with his clothes; and the grocer with his crackers and cheese—what kind of a home will it be anyhow? You may say you can turn it on at will and turn it off when you want to, but even so, who will want it? How valuable will be the media if the public will not support it? Personally, I don't think they will support it. (Fredericks 2007)

The American Newspaper Publishers Association joined this chorus (Wood 1958). But there was no existing model for electronic broadcasting. Nonetheless, it took little time for advertising to find a home in radio.

The first radio commercial was unpaid. Vincent Lopez and his orchestra broadcast live from the Pennsylvania Grill, New York City, in 1921. In an early broadcast Lopez invited people to call the Grill for reservations to see his orchestra live.

One could argue the first print ad transmitted by radio was more than a year earlier, as reported in the *Detroit News* on September 4, 1920. Albert Allen's station, 8WA, transmitted an ad, but this is what was broadcast: "Detroit News—Please insert the following want ad and send the bill by mail: 'For sale—One pair of prism binoculars, 12 power. James P. Allen, 435 Bragg street.'"

In late 1922 or early 1923, WEAF, owned by American Telephone and Telegraph (New York City), began offering advertisers opportunities to broadcast sales messages for $100 per ten minutes. This is how paid radio advertising began (Hettinger 1933). Known as "toll broadcasting," anyone could pay the toll and be transmitted, not just advertisers. At first the sales pitches were required to be oblique, mentioning the advertiser's name but not a specific product or price. Gillette provided a talk on beards, rather than talking about shaving products (Clark 1988).

Finally, It's Legal!

The first *paid* radio commercial was one of those WEAF slots, a commercial for a Long Island real estate company, the Queensboro Corporation. Recall that one of the first newspaper ads in America, in 1704, was for real estate on Long Island. And the first electric spectacular, in 1891, also was about Long Island real estate. Rather than Madison Avenue, it seems Long Island real estate is the center of the advertising universe!

In 1923, WEAF New York connected with WNAC Boston to create the first radio network: Red Network. Networks aided in attracting advertisers, because they had more resources for developing attractive programming. The National Broadcasting Company (NBC) was founded in 1926, and the United Independent Broadcasters (later called Columbia Broadcasting System) in 1927.

A clothing store, Browning, King and Company, in 1923 became the first advertiser to sponsor an entertainment show, an hour of dance music (Hettinger 1933). Music was central to radio's success, but it wasn't alone. That same year *The Eveready Hour*, often credited as first, became a sponsored radio program. Eveready Batteries was the sponsor (Figure 14.2). This show involved more entertainment content than just music. Other sponsors began naming shows reflecting their brand—for example, the *Palmolive Hour* in 1927. The Lucky Strike Dance Orchestra, sponsored by Lucky Strike cigarettes, debuted on thirty-nine NBC radio stations in 1928. The *Amos 'n' Andy Show* arrived in 1929, sponsored by Pepsodent toothpaste. It was the first radio situation comedy, and it was a hit. The first radio soap opera, *Painted Dreams*, also in 1929, ran for nearly a year before landing a sponsor. Ironically, its sponsor was a meat packer, not a soap.

Procter & Gamble sponsored a soap opera, *Ma Perkins*, in 1933. P&G also produced the program. P&G's Oxydol soap was the sponsor, making this a genuine *soap* opera. By producing it, the advertiser had complete content control, in ways no other previous program permitted. This idea quickly caught on. Meyers (2011) states, "During the 1930s and 1940s, a majority of national broadcast sponsored radio programs were produced by top advertising agencies." The downside was that it gave *too* much control to advertisers, pulling things like quality control away from broadcasters.

Radio advertising revenue reached about $14 million in 1929 (Printers' Ink 1938). By then, 90 percent of commercial stations were selling ad time (Scott 2000). Radio delivered audiences for advertisers. It seemed to transcend the economic tragedy of that period, the Great Depression, in part because radio offered escape from hard times (Fox 1984). Never before was there such a cheap source of entertainment, aside from reading. By 1938, its ad revenues surpassed magazines.

There remained resistance. The National Association of Radio Broadcasters (NARB, which would mean something different later) began in 1923. In 1928, it dictated that commercials were not to be broadcast during the "family hour," 7 p.m. to 11 p.m. For years even mentioning certain products (laxatives, depilatories, etc.) was prohibited. Networks forbade mentioning prices. But NBC, then CBS, in 1932 got rid of the price ban (Hettinger 1933).

Eveready Hour—Every Tuesday at Nine P. M.

[*Eastern Standard Time*]

"EVEREADY HOUR." Nine o'clock (Eastern Standard Time) every Tuesday evening is the hour set apart for the simultaneous broadcasting of Eveready programs through a chain of prominent interconnected radio stations. You can easily tune in one of these stations and listen to the delightful programs of the "Eveready Group." You will laugh at the light comedy. You will be thrilled with the harmonies of the vocal and instrumental programs. Dance music will set your toes a-tingling.

Be sure that the batteries for your radio receiver are full of power and pep, so that your enjoyment may be complete. Use Eveready "A" Batteries for lighting the vacuum tubes.

Eveready "B" Batteries for detector and amplifying tubes. Eveready "C" Batteries to clarify tone and prolong "B" Battery life.

Try the new 45-volt Heavy Duty Eveready "B" Battery (No. 770) for receivers with four or more tubes. Because of their longer life they cut "B" Battery costs in half and even more. Dry "B" Batteries are an economical, dependable and convenient source of plate current.

Use Eveready Radio Batteries for all radio purposes—they last longer.

Manufactured and guaranteed by

NATIONAL CARBON CO., INC.

Headquarters for Radio Battery Information

New York   San Francisco

Canadian National Carbon Co. Limited, Toronto, Ontario

FIGURE 14.2.   January 1925 advertisement for *The Eveready Hour*.

Putting Them on the Spot, and on the Move

Small advertisers often couldn't afford to run commercials on networks, so they began "spotting" time in limited areas, buying locally instead of network-wide. A network might cover multiple states, while the advertiser need reach only a few spots within that area. Thus began "spot broadcasting," a more affordable approach that avoided waste when networks reached markets where the advertiser had no stores.

Most stations had no sales representatives, but "radio brokers" helped merchants find their spot options. Over time, many stations contracted with exclusive representatives (Printers' Ink 1938).

Automotive dashboard radios appeared in 1930, allowing advertisers to reach audiences in transit. Named the "Motorola" (from "motorcar Victrola"), it was first demonstrated in a Studebaker. FM radio was invented in 1933, though the first commercial FM radio license wasn't until 1941, providing higher fidelity sound than previous (AM) radio.

By 1951, television pulled audiences away, so the Broadcast Advertisers Bureau (later called the Radio Advertising Bureau) was formed to promote radio. The first mass-produced pocket radio, the Regency TR-1 transistor radio, came in 1954 (Figure 14.3). Again reaching a new audience, listeners now were found on beaches, in backyards, and in places where bulky plug-in radios were

FIGURE 14.3. The TR-1 transistor radio, introduced in 1954.

impractical, and television couldn't reach. This took off when Sony introduced its TR-63 radio in 1957, and advertisers could reach almost anywhere.

Internet, Satellite, and Digital

Radio changed little until the 1990s, when other portable electronics presented new competition. In 1992, the radio industry moved toward a Digital Audio Radio Service (DARS), setting aside part of the broadcast spectrum for satellites. Finally, in 2001, the first radio satellites reached orbit for XM Satellite Radio, followed by Sirius Satellite Radio. The two companies merged in 2007, forming Sirius XM Satellite Radio.

The principal benefit of satellite radio is the enormous number of stations, rather than a few stations in any geographic area. And much of it is commercial-free, because it is subscription-fee supported. Originally designed for automotive use, it expanded to hotels and other businesses. In 2016, it boasted thirty-one million subscribers.

In 1993, the first internet radio service began, allowing users to listen to broadcasts via computers and, later, mobile devices. In 1994, WXYC-FM in North Carolina was the first regular radio station to send its signal via the internet. The first internet-only radio network, NetRadio.com, began in 1995.

Internet radio quickly outstripped satellite radio, even before the rise of mobile devices. It no longer was necessary to carry radios, since so many other devices received those stations. For broadcasters, this helped circumvent regulatory authorities, since it doesn't use the broadcast spectrum. For advertisers, it meant access to more audience data, making personalized advertising possible in ways not possible on broadcast.

In 2002, the Federal Communications Commission approved use of HD Radio (HDR) in the United States. "HD" was adopted because television used that to mean "high definition," a much higher quality than traditional television. For radio, HDR offered higher-quality sound, with less noise, while enabling broadcasters to transmit digital information alongside the regular (analog) radio signal. But HDR uses more bandwidth, meaning fewer radio stations can operate in a market. It wasn't widely adopted by consumers. Some other countries adopted different formats: Digital Audio Broadcasting (DAB) and Digital Radio Mondiale (DRM).

For advertisers, a single HDR station can carry "side channels," meaning advertisers can negotiate for exposure on multiple channels while dealing with one station. HDR also offers the "Artist Experience." HD Radios with a screen—common in automobiles by 2018—could display static images on those screens, like mini electronic billboards transmitted with the audio content.

Over a century, radio went from being media king to struggling for survival. The internet and satellite have helped it avoid demise. But technologies like smartphones, allowing listeners to carry thousands of songs in their pocket while getting both written and video news reports, mean radio no longer dominates mobile news and music options.

THE PROMOTING OF FREDERICK R. EWING

This is a story about the amazing power of false advertising well told. Some called it the hoax of the century.

Shep (Jean Shepherd) was a New York radio personality on WOR in 1956. Radio was struggling to compete with television. Shep invited listeners to call and chat on air, and one night the *New York Times* bestseller book list was discussed. Shep argued such lists held powerful sway over people and proposed his listeners play a game in which they asked for a book, to see whether they could get that book on the list. And the book wouldn't even exist.

Shep invented the title (*I, Libertine*), the author (Frederick R. Ewing), and the author's backstory. None was real! Then he turned his listeners loose. They requested the book at bookstores and brought back hilarious stories. One bookstore clerk supposedly said, "Frederick R. Ewing? It's about time people began noticing his work." A listener also brought it up in a bridge club meeting. Some members claimed they read it and argued over which chapters they preferred. That summer the book appeared on the *Times* bestseller list.

So Shep and a friend wrote the book, under the Ewing name (Figure 14.4). That *real* book also appeared on the bestseller list! It was a romance novel, of sorts. Like the Lord of Montegu in 1749, Shep conducted a wager—an experiment—regarding advertising's power, with the same results.

RADIO WITH PICTURES (AKA TELEVISION)

Television is the first truly democratic culture—the first culture available to everyone and entirely governed by what the people want. The most terrifying thing is what people do want.

—*Clive Barnes,* New York Times, *December 30, 1969*

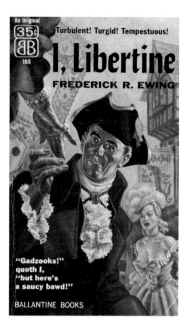

FIGURE 14.4. The book that eventually did get written by Jean Shepherd and his friend Ted Sturgeon.

Mechanical versus Digital

John Logie Baird publicly demonstrated television in January 1926 in London, but he called it the "televisor." Two years later, he repeated it, but in color! Between those years, he transmitted a signal over 438 miles, from London to Glasgow, but Bell Laboratories already had transmitted 225 miles, from New York to Washington, DC, a month earlier. Baird's approach was a "mechanical" television. Philo Taylor Farnsworth invented an "electronic" television in 1927.

Radio Corporation of America (RCA), founded in 1919, was a radio equipment leader by the 1930s. It invested in developing Farnsworth's television. In 1939, a speech by President Franklin D. Roosevelt was televised, making him the first president on TV. RCA began selling televisions later that year. The screens, black and white, were five by twelve inches. In May of that year, RCA began regular broadcasts. The first was a baseball game.

Two years later, CBS joined, telecasting news. With the advent of World War II, television's growth slowed, but from 1947 to 1950 many television programs began, including the children's program *Howdy Doody*. Children were key to selling televisions. Many of those early programs were advertiser sponsored, as reflected in their titles, such as *Gillette Cavalcade of Sports, Kraft Television Theatre, Texaco Star Theater, Camel News Caravan,* and *Philip Morris Playhouse*.

The British launched the BBC Television Service in 1936. Other countries were slower to follow. Japan began in 1951, Spain in 1956, Beijing and Shanghai in 1958, and India and the Netherlands in 1959.

Commercials Before TV Was Commercial

The first television commercial actually preceded true commercial broadcasting, when TV still was experimental. Charles Francis Jenkins, who contributed to television's development, created the first TV station, W3XK, in 1928, using Baird's mechanical process. Jenkins began broadcasting radiomovie picture stories, told with simple silhouettes of people. His

FIGURE 14.5.   A silhouette of the Old Dutch Cleanser girl was telecast by Charles Jenkins in 1930.

lab workers acted in them. One, in 1930, depicted the "Old Dutch Girl" image from Old Dutch Cleanser, effectively creating a commercial (Figure 14.5). Jenkins was fined by the FRC for violating the station's license.

The date of Jenkins' broadcast is unknown, so it's possible the first commercial was November 5 of that year, by Baird's company. It transmitted from the Hairdressing Fair of Fashion in London, and included a promotion of the "Eugene Method of Permanent Hair Waving."

On December 7, the W1XAV station in Boston televised the CBS Radio orchestra, in which it ran a commercial for I. J. Fox Furriers. W1XAV, too, was fined for violating its license. No matter which commercial actually was first, undoubtedly the first TV commercial was in 1930.

In 1939, a big network experimented with commercials. NBC's W2XBC station, New York, did it before a Cincinnati Reds and Brooklyn Dodgers baseball game. Commentator Walter J. "Red" Barber did unscripted promotions for Socony Vacuum Oil (Mobil), General Mills, and Ivory Soap. Barber recalled, "For the gasoline sponsor, I put on a filling station man's hat and spieled about gas. For the breakfast cereal spot, I poured some of the stuff into a bowl. There wasn't much I could do for the soap sponsor. I just held up a soap bar and extolled its virtues" (Robertson 2011).

FIGURE 14.6.   For ten seconds, this image appeared on television before a baseball game in 1941.

The first *legal* television commercial (after the experimental TV phase) was on July 1, 1941, just two months after the FCC first issued commercial licenses. The commercial was ten seconds, for Bulova watches, on NBC's WNBT station (Figure 14.6). It was a static image that Bulova paid a whopping $9 to run before the Brooklyn Dodgers–Philadelphia Phillies baseball game at Ebbets Field, New York (Newman 2016).

In September 1941, the first animated television commercial ran. Botany Mills ties created it, with its Botany Lamb prancing around the screen. Seven ads were created and run through the next six years. Each ended with the Lamb predicting the weather, looking through a telescope (McDonough & Egolf 2002). The animation was by Otto Messmer, who created the Felix the Cat cartoon character. In 1947, "Reddy Kilowatt" was animated for commercials by Walter Lantz, using a "cel animation" technique. Lantz was also a famous cartoonist, creating Woody Woodpecker years earlier. Animated commercials became commonplace.

Television advertising didn't catch on immediately. Neither advertisers nor agencies really knew how to capitalize on this medium—obvious from that static Bulova commercial. Ad professionals tried moving print or radio ads into television form, not knowing how to use video. But by the 1950s TV advertising really took off.

Sponsored programming dominated early radio and became TV's revenue model. But as of the late 1950s, few still used the sponsorship model (Meyers 2011). Broadcasters and producers wrestled programming control back from advertisers, and the "commercial break" now included multiple ads for multiple advertisers, diffusing the power of one advertiser.

Some Notable Firsts

Many "firsts" could be listed here (e.g., first car commercial, first bicycle commercial), given unlimited pages, but I'll mention a couple. The first African American television commercial was in 1948, for Jax Beer, titled "Whistle up a Party." Yes, there were titles back then (Figure 14.7). And the first computer commercial, in 1954, was for the UNIVAC computer, a "giant brain" that "cannot make a mistake," the "world's first electronic computer practical for commercial use."

FIGURE 14.7. A 1948 Jax Beer commercial is the first TV commercial using an all African American cast.

Television advertising had obstacles. When Communists conquered China in 1949, they began removing advertising. During China's Cultural Revolution, beginning in 1966, the remaining advertising virtually disappeared (Li 2017). This wasn't confined to television, since TV wasn't a factor there until 1959. Billboards were repurposed for government messaging. So TV commercials didn't get traction in China until much later.

Technological developments mustn't be ignored. In 1938, Philco Radio & Television Corporation announced the remote control: the Philco Mystery Control! It was for radio at that time. There were other remote radio controls, but they were all wired, while Philco's was wireless. The first wireless control designed for television was in 1955 by Zenith, called the "Flash-matic" (Figure 14.8).

FIGURE 14.8. An advertisement for the Zenith Flash-matic, the first real remote control for television.

Cable and Color

In 1947, John Watson owned an appliance store in Mahanoy City, Pennsylvania. Televisions weren't selling well, as home antennas couldn't pick up broadcast signals well in that location with the surrounding mountains. Watson erected an antenna on a mountaintop, running a wire from there to his store. TV reception in his store improved greatly. He subsequently allowed others to hook into his setup for $100, plus $2 per month. He'd invented cable television (Parsons 1996).

Cable expanded in the United States, but didn't reach Britain until 1972. By 1987, half of US homes with TVs were on cable, while in Belgium penetration was 80 percent. By 2000, more US advertisers were buying time on cable stations than on broadcast stations.

Color was important, too. Although Baird had demonstrated color back in 1928, further development was slow. Even in 1945, the FCC prohibited selling color televisions. But on June 21, 1951, CBS broadcast a TV program in color. There were just twenty-five color TVs in use then, and the twelve million black-and-white TV owners saw only blank screens during that broadcast.

FIGURE 14.9.   The first TV commercial to run in the United Kingdom, in 1955.

Also in 1951, the first color TV commercial ran, for Jell-O Pudding & Pie Filling. Pabst Blue Ribbon ran the first color beer commercial that year.

British broadcast regulators still resisted allowing television advertising. The first TV commercial (black and white) in the UK wasn't until 1955. A sixty-eight-second commercial for Gibbs SR Toothpaste ran at 8:12 p.m. on September 22 (Figure 14.9). The first Australian TV commercial was in 1956 (Crawford 2008), and the first Russian TV commercial—promoting corn consumption—was in 1964, in color (Barsanti 2016). India's first commercial was in 1978.

But 1951 also marked the first live transcontinental TV broadcast, at the Japanese Peace Treaty Conference in San Francisco. The Treaty of San Francisco was signed then, as a follow-up to World War II.

The number of US households with television in 1952 reached twenty million, which grabbed attention on Madison Avenue. Some agencies were more adept at this new medium than others, which led some big clients to change agencies. Audience attention was assumed, so ads often went directly to the sales pitch (Fox 1984).

And 1952 is when the National Association of Radio & Television Broadcasters adopted a regulatory television code, nearly half of which was directed at commercials. By 1953, there were about four hundred American television stations (Turner 1953).

During this time, RCA sued CBS to stop its color broadcasts, and the CBS approach to color failed. The RCA approach received FCC approval, so in 1954 it began selling color TV sets with a twelve-and-a-half-inch screen. Regular US color broadcasts began that year.

NBC broadcast the Tournament of Roses Parade in the first coast-to-coast telecast. The first Dutch color television programs began in 1956.

The first local color TV commercial was telecast, also in 1954, on WNBT-TV New York, for Castro Decorators. It began a trend of outlandish spokespeople, claiming "Mad Max Castro" was insane for selling at such low prices.

Culture and Sound

Important to TV culture, in 1954 C.A. Swanson & Sons introduced TV Brand Frozen Dinners, in aluminum trays. A full meal could be heated in the oven and eaten while watching television, with only silverware to wash. This gave people permission to eat in front of the TV.

Throughout the 1950s experiments were conducted for stereo TV sound. Televisions supported just one sound channel, so techniques like using the TV for one channel and a radio station for another were tried. In 1959, ABC ran "The Peter Tchaikovsky Story" on *Walt Disney Presents*, using ABC-affiliated FM radio stations for the right channel and AM for the left. True "simulcasting" of left and right for FM stereo was introduced in 1961.

In 1955, American television became more multicultural. Raoul A. Cortez had pioneered Spanish language radio nine years earlier, and after years of trying he received a TV broadcast license for KCOR-TV (changed to KWEX-TV in 1961). Although a few Spanish programs had run on US stations in 1951, this was the first all-Spanish station (Albarran 2009). It was an ultra-high-frequency (UHF) station, rather than the very high frequency (VHF) used by major networks, meaning viewers needed a special converter to watch it (Figure 14.10). Slowly, Cortez found advertisers willing to spend money reaching the Latino market.

FIGURE 14.10. KCOR-TV advertised to encourage people to get their TVs converted so that they could receive this UHF station.

It's likely the first Spanish TV commercial in America was in 1955 on KCOR-TV; the first Spanish commercial on English-language US stations was in 1989. Pepsi created it to run during the Grammy Awards on CBS. This was a year after the first English commercial in the Soviet Union (Mull 1988). To date, no Russian commercial has run on American stations.

Language issues aside, US television made a step toward internationalization in 1962, when the Telestar 1 satellite launched, enabling long reach by broadcast stations. The first live television program was sent from the United States to Europe.

In 1964, WOR-TV New York ran a program entirely composed of commercials, uninterrupted, about Clio award winners. Subsequently, programs dedicated to advertising became relatively common.

Networks had telecast some shows in color for about a decade, but in 1965 NBC became "The Full Color Network." This nudged ABC and CBS to up their use of color. By fall 1966, all three networks were full color for "prime time" (evening) programming.

Most television commercials were sixty seconds long. But in the 1960s some adopted a shorter format. By 1971, the thirty-second commercial was considered the norm. The fifteen-second commercial began in 1985.

The longest commercial in history, to date, was fourteen hours. On December 8, 2018, Procter & Gamble's Old Spice brand antiperspirant ran it to promote a new Durascent technology. It was a composite of around 1,600 shorter commercials spliced together with a recurring, "Smell Amazing Forever with the New Old Spice." The unstated message was that the commercial might last as long as this antiperspirant protection. It ran from 6 a.m. to 8 p.m. in São Paulo, Brazil. Before that, the longest commercial was thirteen hours, five minutes, and eleven seconds, for Arby's Smokehouse Brisket sandwich, run on KBJR-TV Duluth, Minnesota, in 2014.

A new product in 1982 represented another move toward mobility: the pocket television. Sony was first to mass-produce one, the Sony Watchman FD-210. It was black and white with a 2-inch screen, battery operated, and fit in a pocket (albeit an enormous one, at nearly 8 inches tall). Other manufacturers followed, then color, and then larger screens. In 1983, Seiko introduced a television wristwatch with a 1.2-inch screen. Within a couple of years, a portable TV to install in cars also was available.

In 1996, broadcasters and manufacturers, pushing resolution limits, ran the first public high-definition television (HDTV) broadcast. TV signal resolutions had changed over the decades, and varied by country, but the standard US broadcast in 1990 was about 640×480 pixels, while HD ranged from 1280×720 to 1920×1080. This was a big jump. Then came 4K *ultra* high definition, or UHDTV, at 3840×2160 pixels, with the LG model 84EM9600 being first, in 2012. Sharp demonstrated an 8K television, at 7680×4320 pixels, in 2012. As resolution improves, both programs and ads become more impressive. European HDTV broadcasts began in 2004.

And the Price Goes Up

From a 1941 $9 Bulova commercial, probably considered a risky investment, in 2004 Chanel No. 5 perfume created the most expensive TV commercial: $33 million. It was a four-minute film by Baz Lurhmann, starring Nicole Kidman. She played an actress chased by paparazzi. It debuted in movie theaters on November 1, and on US television in mid-November.

Advertisers embraced TV as a medium, and yet there remained one ad-free zone: public service broadcasting. In 2011, the British Broadcasting Corporation publicly apologized for accidentally airing its first ever thirty-second commercial. Televising the Wimbledon tennis tournament, an ad appeared encouraging viewers to "log on now and get your tickets today" to an upcoming tournament. The ad mentioned Barclays, the financial services company. A complaint spurred this apology, not from general viewers but from ITV, a British commercial TV network (Foster 2011).

Over the late twentieth century, and into the early twenty-first, the number of commercials also increased. A typical 1960 US "one-hour" program was fifty-one minutes, with nine minutes for commercials. By the century's end, commercials averaged about sixteen minutes and could reach twenty-two minutes at times. Commercials approached one-third of televised content. Obviously, financial realities had changed markedly since that original Bulova commercial.

Television, whether wireless, cable, or via internet, became the twentieth century's defining medium. The Vietnam War has been labeled the first televised war. In July 1969 the world watched as man first leaped onto lunar soil. And August 1974 had audiences watch in disbelief as Richard Nixon resigned the US presidency on television. On June 5, 1989, audiences watched live protests in Tiananmen Square, Beijing, as one man stood bravely before a tank. A few months later, on November 9, 1989, *NBC News* televised from East Berlin as crowds tore down part of the Berlin Wall. TV became a culture in itself.

TV reached more people than previous media. The largest audience of any television program was Super Bowl XLIX, reaching 114.4 million viewers. Radio's largest was a fraction of that. The largest circulation newspaper was the *New York Times*, at 7.5 million, in 2020. No medium comes close to TV, and no medium delivers as many eyes or ears to advertisers.

IS IT LIVE OR IS IT MEMOREX?

With older media such as newspapers, the information transmission mechanism is a storable record. Radio and TV initially had no storage method, other than writing about it.

Music used written musical notes. Music boxes brought those notes to life, emulating the way in which it had been played. The early 1800s invention of photography added a new method of visual recording. These weren't perfect recordings, but over time we came closer.

Audio recording began in 1857 on a phonautogram, a soot-on-paper recording, but there was no way to play it back. The phonograph cylinder came in 1877, allowing both recording *and* playback, thanks to Thomas Edison.

The disc record, and gramophone to play it, came in 1887. This became the standard, and "records" dominated home music playback through the twentieth century. Soon, in 1892, Edison recorded moving pictures.

Electrical transcription was a disc variation used mostly for commercial radio broadcasting, starting in 1924, through an electrical, not mechanical, method and with higher audio quality than consumer records. For advertisers, it was transformative. Instead of performing live commercials on each station, discs could be sent to several stations. The commercial would be identical on each, and could be played any time of day or night.

Next came phonofilm, in the 1920s, optically putting sound on photographic film. This was adopted by the motion picture industry.

Magnetic wire recordings became popular in the 1920s, though invented in 1898. Steel tape then replaced wire, but turned out to be rather dangerous.

Next was magnetic tape, by BASF in 1934. The first commercial recorder was the 1938 Magnetophon K4, by AEF in Berlin. The first in the United States was the 1948 Ampex 200A. Ampex produced a *video*tape recorder in 1951, enabling advertisers to distribute recorded TV commercials in place of live or filmed performances.

In 1935, Eastman Kodak announced its Kodachrome photographic film, the first commercially available color film, allowing still and motion pictures in color. But the earliest color motion picture (only a test) was in 1902 by Edward Raymond Turner, who had patented his process in 1899. The first color film shown to audiences was *The World, the Flesh and the Devil*, a British Kinemacolor film, in 1914. Kinemacolor used black-and-white film projected through quickly alternating color filters.

Compact cassette tape appeared in 1962 (Figure 14.11), and 8-track tape in 1964. These were more practical for consumers. Automotive players were developed for both, so listeners could carry their preferred music with them.

The music compact disc (CD) arrived in 1982, using lasers to read digital (not analog) recordings, but they weren't consumer recordable. The major advantage was purity of sound, without the noise heard on previous records.

Consumer videotape cassettes were introduced in two forms: VHS (1971) and Betamax (1975). A format war ensued. By 1985, one-third of American homes had a video cassette recorder (VCR), as did 45 percent of British homes, 60 percent of

FIGURE 14.11.   Part of a famous Memorex campaign for its cassette tapes, circa 1974.

Japanese, and 83 percent of United Arab Emirates homes (Clark 1988). VHS was cheaper, so Betamax lost the war, ceasing production in 2002. Digital video recorders (DVRs)—solid-state VCR alternatives—arrived in 1999, with TiVo as leader.

The optical laserdisc, conceived in 1958, wasn't available until 1978. It was a playback-only video disc. Phased out in 2001, the smaller digital video disc (DVD) effectively replaced it in 1996.

The computer industry added recording media, like IBM's hard drive, with the RAMAC 305 computer system, in 1956. It was huge. A smaller version, the IBM 2311, appeared in 1964. IBM created the 8-inch floppy disk drive in 1967, reduced to 5.25 inches in 1976 and 3.5 inches in 1982.

The CD-ROM, in 1985, like the music CD, offered "read-only memory" (ROM), so users couldn't write to it. Later versions (CD-R and CD-RW) allowed users to record data.

Digital recordings soon were written to memory chips, aided by an algorithm, MP3, which compressed the data. Consumer MP3 players appeared in 1997, followed by Apple's iPod in 2001. USB "flash drives," in 2000, soon became the medium of choice for digital data recording (Figure 14.12). Compact Flash (1994), Secure Digital (1999), and other memory cards also became common.

FIGURE 14.12. Flash drives sometimes include promotional content, but this one, like most, is simply branded using the exterior. In this case even the shape is suggestive of the advertised product, a key for a car.

Digital cameras had a crude start in 1975 at Eastman Kodak. The Dycam Model 1 came to market in 1990, with less than one megapixel resolution. Image quality and price made for slow adoption.

Each recording medium was an opportunity to save and/or deliver advertising. Film, after print, was among the earliest means of recorded advertisements. The first movie trailer, an advertising movie about a movie (actually a play, in this case), appeared in theaters on November 1913. Marcus Loew theaters' publicist created the film about the Broadway musical *The Pleasure Seekers*, from film shot during rehearsals. Running advertisements between films became popular with theater owners.

The first advertising "talkie" (recorded motion and sound) was *Meet Mr. York* in 1929. Over six minutes long, it promoted the York Milk Bar, chocolate by Rowntree's of York, England (Figure 14.13), just two years after the first talking motion picture, *The Jazz Singer*.

FIGURE 14.13. The very first advertising "talkie" film, promoting a candy bar.

Renowned singer/actor Bing Crosby funded some development of videotape. Its first use was for a time-shifted "live" broadcast of the Bing Crosby Pebble Beach Golf Tournament of 1956, so all time zones saw it at 2 p.m. Easy Washing Machine Company wanted to use videotape for a commercial during the tournament and inquired about Crosby doing "welcome to my tournament" as part of it. Crosby agreed, at no cost, since it was his tournament. The only cost was $500 for equipment rental, making the first tape-recorded TV commercial incredibly inexpensive (White 1995).

FIGURE 14.14. Buick's "road test" of the new Reatta in 1988.

Upon their arrival, floppy disks became advertising media. Automotive manufacturer Buick, for example, distributed virtual "road test" disks for the 1988 Buick Reatta (Figure 14.14). USB flash drives (2000) soon became devices to distribute advertising and PR materials.

Broadcast no longer was the sole option. Advertisers had new choices for reaching consumers with commercials.

IS IT ADVERTISING . . . OR BRIBERY?

Around 1900, payola became a problem. If you visited a music store, you might find someone playing piano, demonstrating sheet music. Songs chosen influenced what music sold. In 1916, *Variety* magazine began fighting sheet music companies that paid musicians to play their music, not someone else's music (McLaren & Prelinger 1998).

"Payola" combined "pay" and "ola," with the latter taken from Victrola, Pianola, Motorola, and other music equipment. It was paid advertising but became an illegal form of bribery.

Once radio took off, payola found a new home. Stations could select songs to play without restrictions, so music companies could pay to get theirs played. Services publishing weekly "Top 40" song lists might also accept "valuable" input from music publishers.

The most famous payola scandal in radio involved disk jockey (DJ) Alan Freed. Other DJs were involved, but Freed became radio's payola poster boy because he was disliked by some. Congressional hearings in 1959 revealed that 335 DJs across the United States had accepted more than $263,000 in advertisers' "consulting fees." Wesley Hopkins of KYW Cleveland received $12,000 in "listening fees" over two years for "evaluating the commercial possibilities" of records. The US annual household income at the time averaged $5,100. A Chicago DJ accepted $22,000 to play one record.

Freed ended up paying fines and getting a jail sentence (suspended). The famous Dick Clark was implicated, but, well liked, he got a "slap on the wrist" (Hutchinson 2015). Freed was forced out of radio.

But what drew attention to payola was television. In 1955, CBS introduced a Revlon-sponsored and immensely popular game show, *The $64,000 Question*. Others followed. NBC's *Twenty-One* had a contestant, Charles Van Doren, with a $3,600 annual salary. He won $129,000. Some later contestants won even more.

In 1958, another show's guest found a piece of paper listing answers to that day's twenty-one questions. An investigation and trial followed. A show producer had given Van Doren advance answers and was indicted for perjury.

Congress then held hearings on game show legitimacy. Van Doren admitted he cheated, and a law followed to make this illegal. All three TV networks canceled game shows en masse (Hinckley 2017). Hearings also followed for radio payola.

The payola story doesn't end there. In 2002, radio stations owned by Infinity Broadcasting offered listeners chances to meet singer Celine Dion, for an Epic Records promotion promising winners would be flown to Las Vegas for a Dion performance. To participate, stations promised to play Dion's latest single (Lewis 2016). It was the same payola scheme. But now payola was clearly illegal.

Another case three years later also involved Epic Records, a division of Sony, paying bribes to radio stations and their employees for favorable play of Sony music (Leeds & Story 2005). Instead of "payola," it now was called "pay-for-play."

The draw of paying for better exposure continues to seduce the music industry and others. It exists in forms that are not illegal. Food producers, for example, are charged "slotting allowances" to obtain better store shelf space, so their brand will be at eye level while others are pushed to a high or low shelf, or pushed out entirely. This is "pay-to-stay" (Edwards 2016).

IT'S A GAME . . . IT'S A BIG GAME . . . IT'S SUPER COMMERCIALS!

The biggest audience ever to watch a television broadcast was a Super Bowl game drawing 114.4 million viewers. That's an advertiser's dream.

The Super Bowl was first played in 1967 and appeared on two TV networks: NBC and CBS. Since then, its popularity has exploded. In 1967, the price for an advertising slot was $75,000 (NBC) or $85,000 (CBS) for sixty seconds. A thirty-second slot was $42,000. By 2020, a thirty-second slot (not including production) cost $5.6 million! The Super Bowl became the "Super Bowl of Advertising." It's said that people watch the Super Bowl as much for the commercials as for the game. Some of history's most memorable TV commercials appeared there.

Coca-Cola ran a commercial on Super Bowl XIV that became a slice of popular culture. In it, football player Mean Joe Greene is handed a Coke by a young boy as Greene limps off the field. In response, Greene (not so Mean) tosses the boy a team jersey.

Super Bowl XVIII is remembered as the Apple Macintosh "1984" game. It reimagined George Orwell's book, *1984*, in sixty seconds. After striking imagery, it ended with "On January 24th, Apple Computer will introduce Macintosh. And you'll see why 1984 won't be like '1984.'" Instantly, it was one of the most famous commercials of all time.

Budweiser beer ran commercials regularly for years, some becoming classics, but one during Super Bowl XXXVI was months after New York's World Trade Center's destruction on 9/11. The commercial appeared just once, depicting the Budweiser Clydesdales approaching New York City. It ends with the horses facing where the Trade Center is missing, bowing in respect. It was memorable.

FIGURE 14.15.   Volkswagen Passat commercial from the 2011 Super Bowl, with little Darth Vader.

Super Bowl XLV had Volkswagen make a splash with a little boy wearing a "Darth Vader" (*Star Wars* character) costume, pretending to have "the force" and trying to use that force on an exercise bicycle, the family dog, his sister's doll, and so forth. When he tries it on the Volkswagen Passat in the driveway, the car starts . . . with a little help from dad's remote starter (Figure 14.15).

This discussion omits numerous deserving mentions, but illustrates the Super Bowl's importance to advertising. Television specials and news reports before the game focus on the ads, and many organizations conduct Super Bowl ad rankings.

ADS MAKE SENSE . . . AND SCENTS

Radio tapped hearing, and television offered vision. But merchants know smell also can sell. A grilling steak or fresh yeast donuts have valuable odors. The challenge: finding an olfactory delivery system. Some restaurants use fans to broadcast smells through the neighborhood. Reaching other neighborhoods, or towns, remains elusive.

The motion picture industry tried bringing smells to viewers in 1916, when a Pennsylvania theater used odor-infused cotton balls during movies (Brownlee 2006). The lingering smell required heavy ventilation between film showings, making it impractical.

Later technologies made movies stink (beyond bad writing and acting): Odorvision, Smell-O-Vision, AromaRama, Odorama, Sensorama, SpotScents, and, later, iSmell and SmellIt. The first, Smell-O-Vision (1939), emitted up to thirty different odors. It was used once, in 1960. AromaRama, with thirty-one odors, was used with a 1959 film.

One system pumped odors through air conditioning, another pumped them to individual seats, while another dispensed smells from hanging canisters (Schmeisser et al. 2013). None was especially successful for movies, but some found success in other venues.

The film industry saw potential in an immersive audience experience, as did the advertising industry. It had a bit more success.

For centuries newspapers were entirely visual. The *Washington Daily News* in 1937 was the first newspaper to publish a perfumed advertising page. It didn't work well, as the perfume smell at breakfast led to accusations of extramarital affairs.

Scratch 'n' Sniff, invented in 1965, was the first practical method of making ads stink. Strips were attached to print ads and readers could scratch them to release odors (Figure 14.16). By the early 1970s, the ad industry enthusiastically adopted this technique. In 1979, "peel-apart strips" added another method, and 1990 brought "fragrant ink" or "fragrant varnish" technology (Figure 14.17).

The sniff that launched a million sips.

Scratch the tape then sniff the tape for the world's driest martini.

Back in 1870, Fleischmann developed the world's first dry gin. And today we still make the driest.

To tempt you to try it, we've even taped the scent of a Fleischmann's martini right on this page. Merely scratch the piece of tape below and then sniff it.

We hope that once you have taken a whiff of our martini, you won't be satisfied until you have a taste.

Then you'll be extremely satisfied.

scratch n' sniff

Fleischmann's. World's driest gin.

DISTILLED FROM AMERICAN GRAIN · 90 PROOF · THE FLEISCHMANN DISTILLING CORP., N.Y.C.

FIGURE 14.16. Fleischmann Gin offered readers a chance to sniff the aroma in 1972, using the original Scratch 'n' Sniff technology.

NORDSTROM

"Subtle and sensual, a frag... ...ould be an aura that surrounds...
Giorgio Armani

black code

Open here ▶
to discover
armani black code

FIGURE 14.17. The left side of this fragrance ad peels open to release the scent using a newer technology.

Still used today, scent strips are "passive," using microencapsulation to hold smells until customers release them. The theater approach is "active," stinking without audience action.

Noseworthy advertising led to "olfactive branding" or "scent marketing." Marlins Park stadium in Miami uses caramel popcorn smell for a "whimsical, family atmosphere" throughout the park, but it uses black orchid aroma in its Diamond Club, for a sophisticated atmosphere, and orange smell in its team store to evoke Orange Bowl memories (Elejalde-Ruiz 2014).

A sense beyond smell is now reached by magazines: sound. When readers opened a *People* magazine in 2008, they heard Natasha Bedingfield sing in an ad for a Verizon Wireless music download service. Electronics were embedded in the page.

But the first sound in magazine advertising was in a Texas Instruments (TI) ad in *Business Week* in October 1989. It talked (Figure 14.18), saying, "I am the talking chip, one of many Texas Instruments MegaChip Technologies that are changing the way the world lives, works and plays." This was the first talking magazine ad.

The first newspaper talking ad was in the *Times of India* and *The Hindu* (2010) for Volkswagen's Vento model. Opening the newspaper's last page activated a light sensor, triggering a voice chip. Delhi police received calls from panicked readers, and in Mumbai a bomb squad responded. Printed on the ad was "Feel the shiver of excitement?" Apparently many did.

Toyota came to its senses in 2018. In *InStyle* magazine was a "pop-up" 3D ad resembling Toyota's new Camry's dashboard. Readers put their thumbs on a door handle to open the ad, activating a new car smell (Figure 14.19). Sensors in the handle registered readers' pulses and lit an LCD monitor, so readers could *see* and *hear* their heartbeat, reaching three senses!

Here's what makes this ad talk.

This device complies with Part 15 of the FCC Rules. Operation is subject to the following two conditions: (1) this device may not cause harmful interference and (2) this device must accept any interference received, including interference that may cause undesired operation. The electronics in this ad radiate small amounts of radio signals until the batteries run down. These digital circuits comply with the Class B limits of the FCC Rules designed to provide reasonable protection against harmful interference to radio and television in a residence, although there is no guarantee that interference will not occur. If interference is suspected, reorient the receiving antenna and increase the distance between the ad and the receiver. Modification of the circuitry in this ad will void the user's FCC authority to operate this device.

FIGURE 14.18. The Texas Instrument ad that talked also provided an explanation on the back of the ad.

FIGURE 14.19.   This Toyota Camry insert has sensors on the door handles that activate a heart monitor.

Gains in *active* delivery methods also developed. In 2010, a billboard on River Highway, North Carolina, displayed a huge piece of steak on a fork while cooking steak fragrance pumped out for passing motorists (Frucci 2010), becoming the first scented billboard! Two years later, Dunkin' Donuts, in Korea, used something like an air freshener, releasing coffee aroma in city buses whenever the bus radio played a Dunkin' Donuts advertisement (Garber 2012).

And in 2007 a company called First Flavor introduced something like Scratch 'n' Sniff for taste (Figure 14.20). Peel 'n' Taste strips were first put into use by Welch's Grape Juice in February 2008, attaching them to an ad in *People* magazine (Zmuda 2008). Some advertisers had a taste for it. Sunny Delight in 2009 used it to promote SunnyD Orange Whirl and Strawberry Swirl smoothies (Bruce 2009). Not too many ads, though, ask you to lick them.

FIGURE 14.20.   Welch's Peel 'n Taste Grape Juice ad from 2008.

In 2013, Coca-Cola introduced another variation in the Middle East: the first fully edible magazine ad (Figure 14.21). For Fanta brand drinks, Coke wanted to encourage trial of its improved flavor. The solution: an edible advertisement printed on rice paper infused with the new flavor (Gianatasio 2013).

Using "touch," as "tactile marketing" or "haptic advertising," usually is subtle, like printing an ad on different paper so it *feels* special. Or it uses ink with a distinct feel. Probably the oldest tactile ad method embossed the ad's paper. Promotional products, too, can be slick or rough or squishy experiences for the right product. A slogan like "Ford Tough" might use a hard, heavy, promotional toy to reinforce that message.

A broader term describing tapping all senses is "sensory marketing." Advertising as a complete sensory experience is an ideal. Today we can create a 360-degree sensory brand experience.

The internet turned consumers' attention away from traditional media in part because of this, conveying text, sound, and video. So there was talk of media "convergence." But old media didn't disappear; the internet expanded them. Literally millions of new media experiences were possible on the internet alone. In a way, it was really media "divergence."

These smellable, lickable, loud, haptic ads enabled "multi-sensory advertising." The internet was limited to sight and sound, but electronically conveyed smell, taste, or touch is not impossible. But even print is more innovative than previously.

Schwartz Spices introduced a poster in 2014 for its "The Sound of Taste" campaign. It applied synaesthesia, blending sight, sound, and taste into a "sonic poster" called Feel Flavour. The poster used touch-sensitive inks, making an interactive "app out of the paper," connecting to viewers' phones and playing musical chords as it is touched. Different herbs and spices were assigned chords, giving each taste a unique sound and multi-sensory advertising experience: touch, taste, sound, and vision.

FIGURE 14.21. Fanta's 2013 edible advertisement.

Around 2000, more means of engaging consumers were occurring, using methods that didn't exist a few years earlier, thanks to multi-sensory advertising. But it also resulted from a move toward "brand activations."

INNOVATIONS AND ACTIVATIONS

Brand activations, basically, are ads or promotions driving consumer interaction with brands. Getting consumers to do more than passively watch or listen to an ad is the goal, so consumers "actively" engage with the product. Product sampling and promotional products are common forms of activation, but any brand-related action potentially constitutes activation, even pushing a button. But not all innovations entail activation.

In 2008, *Esquire* magazine celebrated its seventy-fifth year with a cover using new(ish) E-Ink technology. In it, an ad for Ford Flex also applied E-Ink, with three areas flashing in rotation. That magazine's one hundred thousand copies sold at 150 percent of the normal price. Motion was added to print: an innovation, not an activation.

Peugeot created an ad promoting an automobile's safety, running it in *Exame*, a Brazilian business magazine, in 2011. It invited viewers to "Hit this spot hard and find out why the new Peugeot 408 provides a lot more safety." On the car's image a spot, when hit with a fist, caused a mini airbag to inflate, opening a two-page ad. Hitting the ad is a clear activation, causing consumer interaction with both ad and brand.

Nivea sunscreen in 2013 ran an ad in Brazil's *Veja Rio* magazine that included an operational solar panel with a phone plug, inviting readers to charge their phones. This likewise is an activation.

In 2014, Nivea, again in *Veja Rio*, had an ad to help parents with small children. A humidity-resistant paper wristband with electronics, on the ad, could be put on a child's wrist with a Velcro fastener. Downloading an app to parents' mobile phone let them track their child, another activation.

Wired magazine's readers in New York or Chicago, in January 2014, found an ad for Motorola's Moto X mobile phone. The ad used LED lights and plexiglas, allowing viewers to "customize" the pictured smartphone's color by pressing buttons on the ad. Motorola inserted ads in 150,000 magazines.

Brazil's *Contigo!* magazine in 2014 published an ad for the C&A fashion store with "like" buttons under pictures of different outfits. The buttons lighted when pushed, while posting an image of the liked outfit to the reader's personal Facebook timeline, bridging the gap between a print magazine and internet social media.

Glacial, a Kirin Brazil beer, in 2015 ran ads printed on paper embedded with salt particles. Instructions told users to soak the ad in water, wrap it around their beer, and then stick it in the freezer to chill the beer in half the normal time (Figure 14.22).

In 2015, Chevy promoted its Colorado truck with an interactive digital video ad in *Esquire* and *Popular Mechanics* magazines (Figure 14.23). Viewers could watch three short videos on the magazine page. Again, this is an activation. But Chevy wasn't first to put video in a magazine ad. Dolce & Gabbana did it in October 2012 in some UK issues of *Marie Claire* magazine.

Beyond magazines, an activation tapping one sense mentioned earlier illustrates the creativity applied to find new touch points with consumers. In 2010, the White Castle ham-

FIGURE 14.22.   Glacial Beer used its ad as a mechanism to ensure the beer is cold.

FIGURE 14.23.   A 2015 Chevy Colorado digital video ad. The video screen can be seen, running, in the upper right corner.

burger chain sold hamburger-scented candles. They were in ceramic replicas of the boxes in which the brand's hamburgers were served (Figure 14.24).

In 2018, Oreo cookies sold a music box that "played" Oreos as if they were vinyl music records spinning on a turntable (Figure 14.25). The song isn't really encoded onto the cookie, but it gives that impression by sensing whether a cookie is present before emitting sound (Pomranz 2018).

Television, too, has experienced some experimentation. In 2007, KFC ran a commercial that included a very high-frequency "Mosquito Tone." Only children and adolescents

FIGURE 14.24. A candle scented with hamburgers and onions.

could hear those tones, so KFC offered gift certificates to the first one thousand people to identify where in the commercial the tone was used. The activation involved everyone who tried to be among those one thousand.

FIGURE 14.25. The Oreo Music Box seems to play music from cookies.

The years 1980 to 2020 were a watershed period. This list is but a sample of the innovative advertising methods during that time, but it shows how times had changed.

POINT-OF-PURCHASE AND POINT-OF-DECISION

"Point-of-purchase" (POP), aka "point-of-sale" (POS), is advertising at the point where shoppers choose between products or brands. This frequently is in-store advertising, as competing brands sit on shelves side by side. Packaging is POP advertising that can influence a shopper's selection. In social media and text messaging, POS has a different—and less positive—meaning, so I will adopt the POP acronym.

As packaging developed in the late 1800s, it awakened merchants to the potential of POP advertising. Customers sometimes came shopping with a specific brand in mind, but made decisions when looking at the merchant's offerings. This is, effectively, the last chance to make a sales pitch. In time other POP techniques were added. But one form of POP already well developed was the window display.

By the late 1700s, in big cities like London, there were stores with large windows. Products would be hung for display to passersby. Shoppers learned about products "through trade cards, the shop window, and the display of goods inside shops" (Walsh 1995).

Window displays probably were entirely retailer-driven, since product branding hadn't yet taken root. Most merchants knew a lot about salesmanship but had no incentive to push one supplier's product over another's. But street lighting made street-facing space important, since consumers could "window shop" after stores closed. The ascent of department stores brought both larger windows and more goods to showcase.

By the late 1800s, manufacturer-driven displays were gaining traction, including both meticulous product arrangements and window signs (Figure 14.26). A window decorator's profession now existed. In fact, L. Frank Baum, author of *The Wizard of Oz*, started the first

Meyercord Decalcomania Window Signs

Goods sold to the dealer are only half sold. There is still a certain important something needed to insure maximum success for every sales campaign. Competition and the complexities of modern distribution are responsible. It is now necessary to guarantee the *salability* of your goods—*to the dealer*—as well as their quality. **Meyercord Signs** supply this needed force. They move your goods from his shelves.

National advertising without a cent for space

MEYERCORD SIGNS enable you to utilize the valuable advertising space offered by the dealer's windows—*free*. You can take advantage of this wonderful medium of publicity at a trifling cost.

Like hand-painted signs

Meyercord Window Signs are finished in open-lettered sign writers effect—*in pure oil colors and gold*. Look as handsome and expensive as real hand-painted, oil color signs. They are easily applied and won't rub off; Washing brightens them up. Can be read from within or without—by day or night. The dealer gives you the space; keeps the sign clean; pays for their illumination. Can you get the same utility of service from any other medium of publicity—can you say as much for any other sign?

Send us a sample of your trade-mark or trade-slogan and learn how Meyercord Sign advertising will benefit you.

THE MEYERCORD COMPANY, Inc.
Main Office, 1107-1112 Chamber of Commerce Bldg., CHICAGO, Ill.
Branches in all large cities.

Actual Size 11 x 19 in.
Eight Colors and Gold.

When writing to Advertisers, please mention THE SPICE MILL.

FIGURE 14.26. A 1915 advertisement promoting signage for a window display, depicting a coffee sign.

window trimmers' trade journal, *The Show Window*, in 1897. The National Association of Window Trimmers first met in August 1898 (Norris 1990).[2] By around 1911, some were using fancy "motion displays" using clockworks to move parts around, or even setups so expensive they were only loaned to store owners as "itinerant" displays (Printers' Ink 1938). By 1943, the US War Department claimed, "There is no surer or less expensive way to stimulate business than by improving the technique of window display" (Rowse & Fish 1943).

Displays spread from windows to counters. This trend took off in 1914 (Printers' Ink 1938). But merchants often were perceived by manufacturers as putting little effort into selling their products, so "dealers' aids" such as demonstrations and store cards were invented (Tipper & Hotchkiss 1914). These dealers' aids were mostly what later became known as POP displays, intended to nudge retailers into promoting one brand over others. "Store cards" were the simplest early counter displays, basically a small cardboard sign promoting a brand.

A 1915 "Sales Helps for Grocers" details dealers' aids available from producers of groceries and related goods; for example:

> The A.I. Root Co., Media, O., makers of "Airline" honey. Furnish two-color store cards, series of 10; cloth signs 18x48; window display set with live bees in observation hives; 64-page Airline Honey Cook Books; newspaper cuts; lantern slides; display fixtures; letters and samples of honey to dealer's customers.

Live bees? Bees as advertising. Sweet! That broad set of options represented just one producer from a list of ten published in the July issue of *Simmons' Spice Mill* newsletter.

Some window displays, even before 1900, could be novel. Merchants didn't always grasp the optimal uses of space, though. One store displayed a mummified cat with a rat in its mouth. A picture dealer had a donkey, its body hidden behind curtains, sticking its head out of a framed canvas (Scott 1895).

Hall (1926) describes dealers' aids that included moving pictures, merchandise holders, blotters, books, all manner of signs, and giveaways ("specialty advertising"). POP was fully engaged by then.

Manufacturers liked this advertising method and quickly buried shopkeepers in them, and a lot was wasted (Tipper & Hotchkiss 1914). But some manufacturers began asking retailers to pay for particular items, such as display cases. Some paid retailers for space, like in the window display (Hall 1926).

The "shelf talker" or "shelf screamer," a sign generally hanging or projecting from the shelf's front edge, is one form of POP. It allowed a brand, displayed among other brands, to stand out from the competition. By 2014, electronic versions—even "*video* shelf talkers" (VST)—arrived. Now they really could scream, if the advertiser desired.

The endcap display, where merchandise and signage for a single brand sits on the end of a store aisle, became prime real estate for display. The free-standing display unit (FSDU), usually a brand-dedicated display that brings its own shelf space, and "dump bins," where products can be grabbed out of a large box or barrel, were other forms. These are a few POP types, but each spawned even more creative variations. By 2000, a list of unique POP displays could fill a library. Advertisers proved to be a creative lot.

By the 1990s, advertising professionals recognized that purchase decisions aren't just made either (1) far in advance of purchase or (2) at the point of purchase. There is a continuum of decision points between those extremes. Some purchase decisions are made early, and some later. Even in-store decisions may vary from one part of the store to another. The "point-of-decision" (POD) was more important than the POP.

In the 1990s, this specialty became known as "shopper marketing," with an objective of better understanding a shopper's decision points. Shopper marketing came to rely heavily on research and data analysis, so even POP advertising had become more of a science.

One form of POP/POD needs more space here. It began, really, in the mid-1800s: product packaging.

SOMETIMES A BOX IS NOT JUST A BOX

The earliest packaging with advertising on it was for paint in China, around 1300 CE (see Chapter 3). A package design, beyond the functional, wasn't a big concern before branding's rise in the 1800s. Recall that Babbitt's Soap was the first soap sold in a wrapper, in 1851 (see Chapter 6). That was a watershed for the future packaging industry.

The first real packaging innovation came in 1805, during the Industrial Revolution. Napoleon Bonaparte offered a reward for improving food preservation, to keep his armies fed. Nicholas Appert did that by "canning" food—boiling it and sealing it in jars—making him the "father of canning." Peter Durand extended the idea to tin cans in 1810. The first cardboard box came in 1817. These inventions led to previously unimaginable food sales.

Soon, products were packaged in paper, cardboard, glass, and metal containers. But options for product protection and preservation continued to expand. Some developments were more relevant to advertising than others. Beverages were packaged in bottles until 1935, when it became possible to put soda, beer, and so on in steel cans. Then, in 1959, aluminum cans entered the picture. In the 1960s, clear cellophane made virtually invisible and windowed packages possible, so the product itself became a part of the advertising.

Next was the "dual use" package. Originally, packages were functional and disposable. But some producers began considering packaging with an afterlife. One was the Dixie Queen company, which sold tobacco. In the 1860s, it created metal tins that resembled picnic baskets, for use storing tobacco but *also* for storing other items. This packaging had life beyond delivery of fresh tobacco, a "dual use." Other companies adopted this approach, so the package's advertising value continued beyond product delivery.

Flexographic printing arrived in the 1930s. Until then, printers could only print on limited items. Flexography, though, vastly increased the shapes and types of materials, including packaging, on which they could print. Now milk cartons, metallic films, and more could receive printing inks.

But the designs on the packaging are most important to us. With branding came competition. Brands with near monopolies now found themselves under increasing competitive pressure. Packaging offered ways to distinguish brands from one another (Norris 1990).

One early manufacturer to recognize package design as an advertising tool was the Campbell Soup Company, using labels on its cans. Uneeda biscuits, for its boxes, was another. But few companies adopted this method of advertising until after 1900 (Printers' Ink 1938).

Smith Brothers Cough Drops were advertised with the brothers' images in 1866, but package design was not a concern then. Success of their product, though, led to knockoffs. Others began selling cough drops, even under similar names, so the brothers started putting their images on the package, where consumers could connect the ads to the packages. This helped brand advertising on packages take off.

The UPC barcode appeared on packaging in 1974. The first product barcode scanned was a Wrigley's gum in Troy, Ohio. Hence, packages became a vital feature in advertisers' consumer data collection. A more advanced barcode version emerged in 2010.

Another scan code was announced in 1994 by the Toyota automotive company: the Quick Response Code (QR Code). It didn't become important until about 2005, when its adoption really began. This code facilitated rapid consumer access to product information via the internet. Later it was printed on print advertisements, packages, and package inserts. Codes allowed two-way information flow, benefiting both advertisers and consumers.

In the 1970s, an anti-branding fad developed with the "generic" brand. In the 1980s, this trend caught a tail wind, as advertisers competed more and more on price. The generic brand concept was to invest little in advertising, reflected by very plain packaging, usually a white package with simple black text and no color or imagery. Product prices were much lower than branded alternatives. By the 1990s, generic brands evolved into store brands, even premium store brands. Costco's Kirkland Signature brand was born in 1995.

A trend in the twenty-first century was "green packaging"—that is, environmentally friendly packages. Concern over the polluting influence of packaging materials became a wide concern. Biodegradable packaging, recycling programs, and reusable containers all enjoyed new popularity.

Packaging technologies continue to evolve, as does the advertising on and in packages. Options like augmented reality were implemented on packages, as in other ad forms. And as the "Internet of Things" (IOT) expanded, with cars, doorbells, refrigerators, and more becoming part of our electronic monitoring, it likewise appeared in some packaging approaches.

One clever application (and "activation") of IOT was by Frito-Lay's Tostitos, just before the 2017 Super Bowl, with a limited-edition "Party Safe" product package that had a sensor to detect alcohol on anyone's breath by blowing on the bag. A green circle on the bag turned red and a "Don't Drink and Drive" warning appeared if alcohol was detected (Figure 14.27). By tapping the bag against a phone (using Near-Field Communication technology), it called the Uber ride-hailing company, with a $10 discount, for a safe ride home.

FIGURE 14.27. The "Party Safe Bag" for Tostitos, before and after exposure to alcohol breath.

Each new package technology opens up possibilities for creative advertising approaches. Packages have moved from playing passive advertising roles to more actively engaging consumers.

BEING DIRECT ABOUT GOING POSTAL

Recall Ben Franklin started the first real mail-order business in 1744, though brides apparently were "ordered" by mail as far back as 1607. The New York Life Insurance Company used direct mail promotions in 1872. But mail-order sales and mailed catalogs, combined with Rural Free Delivery, made direct mail (DM) advertising—often including mail-order sales—take off in the late nineteenth century (Calkins & Holden 1912).

By 1900, DM was common. A book called *Secrets of the Mail-Order Trade*, by Samuel Sawyer, declared:

> Back forty years ago, a farmer would never have thought of writing from his home in St. Lawrence County, New York, to a concern in Chicago, sending two dollars by registered letter for a patented alarm clock. Now, such procedure is almost as likely as it is that the granger will wait until he goes down to Ogdensburg, Malone or some other trading center. People living in the South, send money to the North for shoes, now, to a considerable extent, making their selection from the extensively varied stocks of dealers who cater for mail orders. (Sawyer 1900)

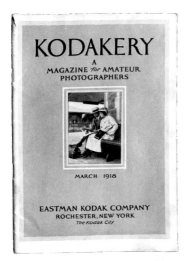

FIGURE 14.28. A "Photographic Magazine" dedicated to Kodak products, from 1918, was a house magazine probably used to secure the second-class postage rate.

In 1863, Congress created a new class of mail for printed matter, lowering DM costs. The 1879 US Mail Classification Act went further, dividing printed matter into second- and third-class mail. While "legitimate" publications like newspapers and magazines were second class, "publications designed primarily for advertising purposes, or for free circulation, or for circulation at nominal rates" were third class (Kielbowicz 1993).

Third-class rate was eight times higher than second. Discriminating against advertising, it was like the old British stamp duty. But advertisers proved willing to bear the costs. This proved an incentive for disguising some DM pieces for the cheaper second-class rate. So by sending ads in the form of corporate house magazines or newspapers—known as "technical and trade-paper advertising"—advertisers could save substantial costs (Figure 14.28). An assistant postmaster general in 1906 observed that "more than 60 per cent of the newspapers and up to 80 per cent of the magazines receiving the subsidy were not entitled to it" (Petty 2013).

DM was controversial almost from the start. The third-class mail status, in spite of higher cost, became part of the controversy. A 1917 magazine editorial remarked:

[A] pestiferous circular, weighing quite as much [as a letter], is carried through the mails for a cent . . .

More than ninety per cent of the mail matter passed as third class is sheer waste and promptly goes, unopened, unread and unconsidered, into the wastebasket . . .

To contend that the printed circular is a necessary or even valuable adjunct to the business of the country is absurd . . .

Mail solicitation of business by printed circular has become an intolerable annoyance, to which all are subjected whose addresses appear in the directory or the telephone books. (Kielbowicz 1993)

DM prepared consumers for door-to-door salesman visits, drawing consumers to retailers, bypassing retailers, bypassing newspaper publishers, or simply supplementing other advertising. Even at the start of the twentieth century, DM ranged from catalogs to advertising flyers, to company magazines, to postcards or letters, to free samples (Hall 1926).

Back then, DM was considered the most effective advertising method to reach people in rural areas, and it was used principally by mail-order houses. This preceded radio and television, so there were limited ways to reach those living outside cities, and mail order was the way rural families bought products unavailable in small-town stores (Calkins & Holden 1912).

DM helped initiate mailing list development, or, put another way, it created some of the earliest forms of consumer database. Sawyer (1900) described the need to develop mailing lists when The Multi-Mailing Company of New York in 1903 became one of the first companies to specialize in creating and supplying such lists, starting with "lead lists" of potential customers it compiled by pulling names and addresses from telephone directories.

Some agencies had begun incorporating DM into their work when the "father of direct mail," Homer J. Buckley, in 1905 created the first real direct mail advertising agency (Figure 14.29). Founder of Buckley, Dement & Co., he established the Direct Mail Advertising Association in 1917, and four years later the National Council of Business Mail Users. DM became a distinct specialty within advertising.

Buckley, like George Rowell decades earlier, pushed this discipline forward by publishing the *Direct Mail Data Book and Mailing List Catalog*. This sorted prospective buyers by profession. Its 1924 catalog helped advertisers reach 46,000 insurance agents, 140 manufacturers of axe handles, 1,200 bedding and mattress makers, and so on (Case 2015). Data lists were now a central element of the profession, and list brokers became an industry on their own.

A factor in the spread of mail order, which affected DM advertising, was credit. Sears, Roebuck & Company first offered charge accounts in 1911. With credit, consumers could buy more, meaning merchants had incentives to send promotional flyers and catalogs. The

Homer J. Buckley

Secretary-Treasurer Buckley, Dement & Co.
Direct Mail Advertising Specialists

Oh, here is the man who invented
The one-cented drive and two-cented,
And clutters the mails
With bushels and bales,
Till the mailmen are Buckley-demented.

FIGURE 14.29. A promotional piece for and by Homer J. Buckley.

credit card was born in 1958, with Bank of America creating "Bank Americard," the precursor to the Visa card. Master Charge (later MasterCard) followed in 1966. These made payment by mail easier, helping direct sales grow.

The US Congress in 1912 passed a law creating the parcel post service. Previously, packages were delivered by private companies, now the US Postal Service could handle packages, making it easier to send larger items to consumers. The mail system became a significant advertising medium.

"Bulk rate" third class, introduced in 1928, gave advertisers another low-cost ad mail tool. Today, if you look up "bulk mail" on Wikipedia, it says, "Bulk mail broadly refers to mail that is mailed and processed in bulk at reduced rates." The term is sometimes used as a synonym for advertising mail. "Junk mail" was a term first used in 1921.

DM was popular with advertisers, since it could reach consumers too dispersed to reach via other media. It allowed delivery of more information, personally tailored material, or memorable items than possible otherwise. It could be used by a wide range of advertisers.

Maxwell Sackheim worked in traditional advertising for years, but found his passion in DM. He initiated the "Book-of-the-Month Club" in 1926, inventing the "negative option plan," likely the first opt-out plan. A club member would receive advance notice about a book and, unless they sent a "no," they automatically received the book. Both club and plan went on to be platforms from which many other companies launched programs in later years.

Dwight Eisenhower conducted the first national direct mail political campaign for his election in 1952 (Godwin 1988). And DM has been used continuously for politics since.

A DM controversy occurred in the 1950s. The US Postal Service conducted an experiment in 1952. Instead of addressing every piece of mail, advertisers could simply send enough pieces for every address in a market, so the carrier made sure everyone received a copy. This was called "patron mail." Mailing lists were no longer needed, since no specific group was targeted (Kielbowicz 1993).

Newspapers and magazines felt threatened, since this helped advertisers bypass them to reach a broad audience. Publications began describing it as "junk mail" to their readers. Some made misleading remarks about such advertising, disparaging the fact that third-class postage was cheaper than first class, even though newspapers and magazines received an even more preferential postage pricing (Kielbowicz 1993).

Other techniques evolved. Over the years marketers included free items in their mailings, even things like free postal stamps, to encourage response by recipients. In 1955, *Reader's Digest* magazine went further by including two copper pennies that could be seen from outside the envelope, for a total of forty million pennies. Finding that many did not prove easy. This was the first instance of sending legal currency as a direct mail attention grabber. This promotion brought a million new magazine subscribers, along with another million members added to its book club (Case 2015).

Direct mail letters' importance as an ad method never changed. A letter offering a special opportunity to recipients continued as an incredibly effective tool (Case 2015).

Lester Wunderman, another DM leader, rose to prominence in the 1950s and 1960s. Wunderman found wonder in DM, when others in advertising avoided it. One of his innovations was mail-in subscription cards in magazines. And if anyone moved the industry terminology from "mail order" to "direct marketing" (DMktg), it was Wunderman, coining this term in 1967.

This new term made more sense, because the industry already was using more than just traditional mail. "Direct response," including mail-in cards blown or stitched into magazines, for example, was part of the field. By the 1990s, the industry staked out internet-based banner ads, electronic mail, and text messaging as the province of DMktg.

Unsolicited mail had a poor reputation, and the name "junk mail" (later, "spam"), so most ad practitioners thought it a less legitimate promotional method. But they tended to underestimate its influence. About 41 percent of the world's mail is US-based. Nearly half of that is advertising. By 2015, advertising mail brought $19 billion in revenue to the US Postal Service, on eighty billion pieces delivered.

The industry organized under the Direct Mail Advertising Association in 1917. In 1973, its name changed to the Direct Mail Marketing Association, and in 1983 it became the Direct Marketing Association. But the world changed, so it again found need to change its name in 2016, to the Data & Marketing Association. In 2018, it became a division of the Association of National Advertisers.

BRANDS BECOME MOVIE STARS

"Product placement" (PP) is advertising a product by placing it into entertainment productions, such as film or television. The earliest product placement was in 1896, when the Lumière brothers and Francois-Henri Lavanchy-Clarke produced and distributed motion pictures filmed in Switzerland. Lavanchy-Clarke represented Lever Brothers, makers of Sunlight Soap, resulting in a Lumiére film titled *Washing Day*, featuring women washing laundry in tubs with soap boxes sitting in front, labeled "Sunlight Savon" (the soap's French brand) and "Sunlight Seife" (the German brand). Later that year Sunlight Soap appeared in another film, *Défilé du 8e Battalion* (Newell et al. 2006).

There is disagreement regarding when "organized" PP began, but movies in the 1930s and 1940s were doing placements. PP's birth often is attributed to the insertion of Reese's Pieces candy in the 1982 movie *E.T., the Extra-Terrestrial*. But there were many film placements before then. In 1977, the Pontiac Trans Am automobile had a starring role in *Smokey and the Bandit*, and the 1964 James Bond film, *Goldfinger*, made a star of an Aston Martin. Another Bond movie, *Live and Let Die*, in 1973, promoted the new Pulsar P2 digital wristwatch when Bond wore it in a close-up (Figure 14.30). In 1968, Disney's *The Love Bug* starred the Volkswagen Beetle (Figure 14.31).

Many films had more "cameo"-type roles for brands. In 1970, *A Clockwork Orange* had scenes displaying the *Daily Telegraph*, *Daily Mirror*, and *Daily Mail* newspapers. The classic 1946 Christmas movie, *It's a Wonderful Life*, had a Coca-Cola sign behind a young George Bailey while working at a soda fountain. In fact, Coke signs appear in many films. Opening credits of *Grease* in 1976 depict several commercial brands: *Mad Magazine*, Reese's candy, Firestone tires, and Pepsi-Cola are easily seen.

FIGURE 14.30. Pulsar P2, the first mass-produced digital wristwatch, was part of a 1973 James Bond movie, and this ad followed in print.

But in the 1980s this industry did become more organized and visible. Many earlier placements were barter arrangements; for example, a soft drink company provided drinks for cast and crew during filming in exchange for catching the drink on camera when filming. Now producers realized they could put a price on inclusion. The term "product placement" was coined in 1982, with terms like "tie-ups" or "tie-in advertising" used earlier (Newell et al. 2006).

Brands other than cars began taking on larger roles in films. In 2004, *Harold & Kumar Go to White Castle* featured the White Castle restaurant chain, and *Demolition Man* in 1993 had Taco Bell restaurants play a starring role.

Much discussion of PP entails feature films, but the principle also applies to television and radio. The sponsored programs in the twentieth century's first half didn't always confine the brand mentions/depictions to commercial breaks; there also were skits involving brands. Throughout the 1950s there were arguments over PP between networks and advertisers when pushing for placements. One source from 1951 said:

FIGURE 14.31. Promotion for 1968's *The Love Bug* shows the product (VW Beetle) that was the star of the film.

Radio and TV gagwriters have found a new way to make a buck if they can get away with it. The gimmick is to mention a commercial product in a gig. Standard price is $250 a mention. On Berle's show the other night, Joey Fay had a five-minute bit in which he mentioned five products. That was a quick $1,250 some writer made on the deal. (Newell et al. 2006)

PP benefits are numerous, to both the advertiser and the film/show producer. It is a revenue source for producers and can be low-cost advertising for brands. It can imply endorsement by characters using it on film. It can be shown where there are no other advertisements.

It is blended into the story line, so viewers are less likely to leave the room when the product is on screen, and more (Turcotte 1995).

PP isn't without criticism. Not all brand portrayals reflect positively on those brands. In 1994's *Clear and Present Danger*, the drug lord's security chief drives an Infinity automobile, which could bring negative connotations. Some social critics believe placements are a covert, potentially unethical advertising form. Some producers dislike placement, feeling it over-commercializes films or weakens the film's integrity by injecting a special scene to show a product (Turcotte 1995).

This advertising technique is unlikely to diminish. As advertisers face an increasingly cluttered promotional landscape and technologies that facilitate options for audiences to avoid advertisements, integrating products into storylines becomes more and more attractive.

ADVERTISING GOES NATIVE

Product placement really is a form of "native advertising." This term was introduced in 2011 by Fred Wilson at a conference, but the concept is older. Initially it described online media, but the phenomenon had been occurring in other media for more than a century.

Creating ads that resemble magazine or newspaper articles is nothing new. In 1946, it acquired the name "advertorial"—advertising looking like editorial content. But Esner (2019) found an advertorial dating from 1898. The "article" was about a series of visits to art studios. It was an advertorial because it was designed to sell artworks from those studios. And this probably wasn't the first advertorial.

A magazine advertorial targeted at women might look like an article about beauty regimens, while promoting a makeup brand. In *Popular Mechanics* it might be an "article" about woodworking, promoting a tool brand. Newspapers do the same, but they also have "special sections." So a "Home" section that runs weekly might be written entirely by a real estate agent, rather than by journalists.

One argument for using advertorials is that readers' minds process editorial information a certain way, and advertising disrupts that processing, forcing their minds to reorient. So, making an ad more like the surrounding material makes it easier to process the information.

The counter-perspective is that advertorials are covert advertising, intended to fool readers into thinking they're getting unbiased editorial or entertainment material. Some call advertorials "information pollution" (e.g., Ellerbach 2004; Cameron et al. 1996) since it borrows credibility from surrounding journalistic content. The concern is readers being deceived, at least where advertorials aren't labeled as advertising (see Hausknecht, Wilkinson, & Prough 1991; Kim, Pasadeos, & Barban 2001).

In 1982, the American Society of Magazine Editors (ASME) adopted guidelines designed to ensure advertorials are "clearly and conspicuously" labeled as ads. In 1997, ASME added electronic editorial materials to the guidelines. In 2014, the guidelines were further updated to include the term "native advertising." By then, most magazines were putting some or all content online, so drawing a line between advertorials and native ads was impossible.

The trouble with self-regulatory guidelines is enforcement. The primary pressure exerted by ASME was that any magazine violating the guidelines could be disqualified from its national awards. But magazines with no aspiration for such awards could ignore the guidelines, and they apply only to magazines.

Native ads, now including advertorials, continued breaking new ground beyond 2000. *Forbes* magazine got noticed when an advertorial for Fidelity financial services got space both on the cover and inside (Figure 14.32). It was perceived by some as crossing the line that divides magazines' business and editorial sides (Dvorkin 2015).

Sometimes the term "advertorials" has been used for broadcast (e.g., Perelló-Oliver & Muela-Molina 2019), but the common term is "infomercial." That was coined in 1950, not long after the first television infomercial, demonstrating the Vitamix kitchen blender, in 1949 (Figure

FIGURE 14.32. A native advertisement appeared on the cover of *Forbes* on its March 2, 2015, edition. The "ad," for Fidelity, is shown enlarged to the right.

14.33). Some are short, but many infomercials are thirty minutes, or longer. The Vitamix example was a product demonstration that probably wouldn't have been mistaken for regular programming. But many infomercials emulate talk shows or news broadcasts, so, like advertorials, they have a covert nature.

Some famous infomercials broadcast in the 1970s and 1980s included the Popeil Pocket Fisherman, a small fishing pole about nine and one-quarter inches long when folded. Ron Popeil, who also promoted products under the brand Ronco, actually had numerous infomercials of some fame, including the Veg-o-Matic, Mr. Microphone, Hair-in-a-Can Spray, the Buttoneer, and more. Some became fodder for TV comedy skits.

Another infomercial, around 1978, promoted the Ginsu Knife, a serrated blade knife claimed to cut most anything.

FIGURE 14.33. The very first infomercial, for the Vitamix blender, is not that different from many infomercials seventy years later, though in black and white with lower resolution.

Most infomercials were shown late at night. The Chia Pet, a terra cotta figurine on which chia seeds were planted, appeared on another infomercial. Then came the LifeCall medical alert system, where an elderly woman falls on the ground and pushes a LifeCall button on a necklace, crying, "I've fallen and I can't get up!" These ads were notable in the buzz created for each advertiser.

FIGURE 14.34.   The Yahoo! website lists links to news and entertainment articles, but among them are native ads. In this listing from January 3, 2020, the center of the three listings is an ad. Above the headline, in gray type, it says, "Ad CompareCards.com."

The "native advertising" label was developed because online media quickly started making advertising resemble editorial content, raising the need for guidance as to what was appropriate and what wasn't. The Interactive Advertising Bureau (IAB), the US Federal Trade Commission (FTC), and the Institute for Advertising Ethics, among others, all studied this evolving situation. A primary concern was how to accomplish business goals without misleading consumers. So far, no single set of guidelines has emerged.

By 2020, most online media were labeling native advertisements in some way, but labels varied greatly. Some put colored backgrounds behind, or borders around, ads to separate them from editorial content. We don't know whether consumers notice these characteristics (Figure 14.34).

Whether called product placement, advertorials, infomercials, or native advertising, every attempt to blend advertising into other media content has encountered criticism. Nonetheless, there is no end to it in sight.

JINGLE SELLS

Recall that there were jingles well before the twentieth century. But they only had music if consumers added it, or if sung by town criers, since they couldn't be recorded or transmitted until the late 1800s. Those songs of criers centuries earlier make clear the value of catchy songs and jingles.

Most credit the "first jingle," erroneously, to Oldsmobile. The song was "In My Merry Oldsmobile," dating to 1905, though it might be the first *modern* jingle. Its music was a hit song (McLaren & Prelinger 1998), but the car's maker couldn't broadcast it over radio for more than two decades. It appears General Mills actually created the first broadcast commercial jingle in 1926, which initially aired Christmas Eve in Minneapolis. Four men, "The Wheaties Quartet," sang:

> Have you tried Wheaties?
> They're whole wheat with all of the bran.
> Won't you try Wheaties?
> For wheat is the best food of man.

Have you tried Wheaties?
They're whole wheat with all of the bran.
Won't you try Wheaties?
For wheat is the best food of man.

They're crispy and crunchy
The whole year through,
The kiddies never tire of them
and neither will you.

So just try Wheaties,
The best breakfast food in the land.

Some claim this jingle actually saved the brand from extinction, with General Mills having planned to end the brand in 1929.

The first "singing commercial" to start the musical jingle craze, and the first *nationally* broadcast commercial jingle, likely was for Pepsi-Cola in 1939. Set to a nineteenth-century tune, "D'ye ken John Peel," was this verse:

Pepsi-Cola hits the spot,
Twelve full ounces, that's a lot.
Twice as much for a nickel, too
Pepsi-Cola is the drink for you!
Nickel, nickel, nickel, nickel,
Trickle, trickle, trickle, trickle.

It became annoyingly popular, broadcast over 469 radio stations 296,426 times and in jukeboxes (Turner 1953). It also became the soundtrack of an animated short film called *Pepsi and Pete's Snowman*, shown in theaters. The Chiquita Banana jingle followed in 1944, also becoming a jukebox hit (McLaren & Prelinger 1998).

Table 14.1 lists some of the most well-known jingles of (mostly) the twentieth century.

Development of popular jingles sometimes comes with a backstory. One popular novelist of the late twentieth and early twenty-first centuries is James Patterson. Numerous popular book series and television programs sprang from him. It turns out he also authored one of those well-known jingles. Having gotten his college degree in English literature in 1971, he went to work at the J. Walter Thompson ad agency as a copywriter. His novel career began there, and that is where, at age thirty-four, he wrote the jingle "I'm a Toys R Us kid!" He worked with Linda Kaplan Thaler, who went on to develop jingles for several other brands.

A popular singer of the 1970s and 1980s was Barry Manilow. Before becoming a pop icon, he wrote and sang jingles. From the list above alone, he wrote "I'm stuck on Band-Aid" and State Farm's "Like a good neighbor," as well as McDonald's "You deserve a break today." That's three from a short list.

Table 14.1. Popular Advertising Jingles

Brand	Song/Jingle	Year
Olds Motor Vehicle Co.	In My Merry Oldsmobile	1905
Wheaties cereal	Try Wheaties	1926
Pepsi-Cola	Nickel, Nickel	1939
Chiquita Banana	I'm a Chiquita Banana	1944
Brylcreem	A little dab'll do ya'	1949
Chevrolet	See the USA in your Chevrolet	1950
Peter Paul Mounds/Almond Joy	Sometimes you feel like a nut, sometimes you don't	1953
Pepsodent toothpaste	You'll wonder where the yellow went when you brush your teeth with Pepsodent	1953
Winston cigarettes	Winston tastes good like a cigarette should	1954
Nestle's chocolate	N-E-S-T-L-E-S, Nestlé's makes the very best . . . chocolate	1955
Roto-Rooter	Away go troubles down the drain	1956
Pillsbury	Nothing says lovin' like somethin' from the oven	1957
Wrigley's Doublemint Gum	Double your pleasure, double your fun	1959
Green Giant	In the valley of the jolly—ho-ho-ho!—Green Giant	1959
Rice Krispies cereal	Snap, Crackle & Pop	1961
Rice-a-Roni	Rice-a-Roni, the San Francisco treat	1961
Coca-Cola	Things Go Better With Coke	1963
Oscar Meyer	I wish I were an Oscar Mayer Wiener	1965
Armour Hot Dogs	Hot dogs, Armour hot dogs	1967
Coca-Cola	It's the Real Thing	1970
Budweiser beer	When You Say Budweiser, You've Said It All	1970
Coca-Cola	I'd Like to Teach the World to Sing	1971
Miller High Life beer	If You've Got the Time, We've Got the Beer	1971
State Farm	Like a good neighbor, State Farm is there	1971
McDonald's	You Deserve a Break Today	1971
Budweiser	Here Comes the King	1971
Sara Lee	Nobody doesn't like Sara Lee	1972
Ace Hardware	Ace is the place with the helpful hardware man	1974
Burger King	Have it your way	1974
Oscar Mayer Bologna	My bologna has a first name, it's O-S-C-A-R	1974
Libby's food	When it says Libby's, Libby's, Libby's on the label, label, label you will like it, like it, like it on your table, table, table	1974
McDonald's	Two all-beef patties, special sauce, lettuce, cheese, pickles, onions, on a sesame seed bun	1975
Ralston Meow Mix	Meow, meow, meow, meow	1976
Band-Aid	I'm stuck on Band-Aid, 'cause Band-Aid's stuck on me	1976
Dr. Pepper	I'm a Pepper	1977
Empire Carpets	800, 5-8-8-2-300, Empire	1977
Lowenbrau	Here's to good friends	1978
Alka-Seltzer	Plop plop, fizz fizz, oh what a relief it is	1978
Toys R Us	I'm a Toys R Us kid	1982
Klondike ice cream bar	What would you do for a Klondike bar?	1983
Folgers Coffee	The Best Part of Waking Up is Folgers in Your Cup	1984
Kit Kat candy bar	Give me a break	1986
Chili's restaurant	I want my baby back, baby back, baby back ribs!	1986
Huggies Pull-Ups	I'm a Big Kid Now	1994
Subway	Five. Five dollar. Five dollar foot-long	2008

Finally, there's Keith Reinhard, who later was chairman of the DDB Worldwide ad agency and creator of the Omnicom super-agency. Reinhard actually worked with Manilow on two of those three songs. He also wrote the McDonald's "Two all-beef patties" jingle in 1975, mentioned earlier. Reinhard claims that one was a virtual accident. He'd written something the client didn't like, saying, "But it doesn't tell people what's in it!" So Reinhard, to show the client how silly a listing of contents would be, wrote this jingle. The client loved it, and it became a jingle consumers memorized!

Indeed, sometimes jingles become part of popular culture. The Chili's "Baby Back Ribs" jingle was later used as a comedic bit in the motion picture *Austin Powers*, by a character named Fat Bastard. Among teens, this resonated to the point they were repeating it for weeks after seeing the movie.

In the minds of many, the top commercial jingle/song of the twentieth century would be Coke's "I'd Like to Teach the World to Sing," in 1971. The Vietnam War was in full swing, and it came on the heels of the 1960s peace and love movement. It was one of the most expensive commercials ever produced, bringing together a large, diverse group of singers on a hilltop in Manziana, Italy. The television commercial (also a radio version) had the camera focus on one singer, then as others joined in harmony the camera panned across the large crowd, then back to show them on the hillside. People thirsted for world harmony then, and Coke was presented as a bridge to peace, unity, and . . . of course . . . harmony. It was the brainchild of creative director Bill Backer. Coca-Cola bottlers received one hundred thousand letters about this commercial. The song later was revised to delete brand references, and it became a hit single. Bill Backer also wrote "It's the Real Thing" and the Miller High Life jingle.

Jingles, and even music without words, proved so evocative of memories that many brand identities became locked into sounds. In 1961, a copywriter named Richard Blake worked with Epic Records and the Lester Lanin Orchestra to produce a music album, "Lester Lanin and His Orchestra Play the Madison Avenue Beat" (Figure 14.35). The album played the sounds of fifty-eight radio and television commercials (McLaren & Prelinger 1998).

FIGURE 14.35. You know commercial songs and jingles have reached the level of popular culture when a record album of them can be purchased. This one was in 1961.

Jingles didn't disappear in the twenty-first century, although their popularity sagged. But people recall a good jingle for years after it ends, guaranteeing their return.

WHERE THERE ARE EYES . . .

Advertising options continued to expand unimaginably. Dr. John Leckenby, at the University of Texas, espoused his "blob theory" of advertising, based on the 1958 Steve McQueen movie, where an alien monster of gelatinous goo was impossible to avoid. It could seep into every crevasse and under every door. Leckenby's theory was that advertising likewise seeps into any gap and is inescapable.

The advertising blob has oozed onto vehicles. From 1829, London omnibuses carried signs, and soon brand names and logos were on them. Wagons and other vehicles also added them as the century progressed. When automobiles and motor buses arrived, it carried over to them.

When vinyl was invented, in 1926, die-cut vinyl letters and paint-on vinyl were possible for applying ads to vehicles. That was a more expensive process, so paint continued as the norm.

Signs on vehicle bumpers started in 1946. Screen printer Forest P. Gill is credited with creating the first bumper sticker. He had the idea of using adhesive, and used it to promote tourist attractions like Missouri's Meramec Caverns and Florida's Marine Gardens (Gupta 2009).

Development of computers and inkjet printers was a big moment for vehicles-as-signs. Now consistent and repeatable imagery was possible, and computers could model surfaces, allowing printing on curved surfaces. So the vehicle "wrap" was invented. Printing was on enormous vinyl sheets that were then glued onto vehicles, covering them entirely, with see-through options for windows. These were great for buses that constantly move through neighborhoods, being viewed by thousands each day. The first true bus wrap ad was in 1991, in New Zealand, promoting the Pan Pacific Hotel (Eff 2013). And Pepsi sponsored the first fully digital printed bus wrap to promote its Crystal Pepsi product in 1993.

But buses weren't the only application. Taxis were used, and even consumers could rent out their own cars as moving billboards, with advertisers paying them (Atkinson 2016). Wraps might even be applied to more than just vehicles.

Advertising also oozed into bathrooms: onto the walls of stalls, on paper dispensers and mirrors, and even in urinals of commercial businesses. This started in 1970s Europe, reaching America around 1981. These ads have captive audiences. Although some consumers dislike it, a 1995 survey found that 77 percent of people approved.

Advertising now is found even in the holes on golf courses. In 1992, Gerard M. Hannon created a way to put removable signs in the cups. It seems wherever eyes can be found, an ad will fit there.

Perhaps the most intriguing example of ad creep is "skinvertising." In the 1990s, a few companies gave away free temporary tattoos that included their logo. Calvin Klein in 1996 put free CK tattoos in back-to-school materials for children (Stead 1997). But actually paying someone to wear branded tattoos was the idea of adman John Carver in 2003, calling it ForeheADS (forehead advertising). His first clients were *FHM* magazine and CNX cable TV. People were paid to wear temporary tattoos on their heads, where others couldn't avoid seeing them. A company that copied the idea paid $150 per week per forehead. In 2004, Toyota used this method to promote its new Scion tC.

Around 2005, skinvertising went to the next level: *permanent* tats. One man supposedly earned $200,000 selling his skin. A woman, Kari Smith, auctioned her forehead on eBay.com. A gambling casino paid her $10,000 to permanently ink "GoldenPalace.com" on her forehead (Figure 14.36). Ironically, many advertisers paying for permanence went out of business. A lot of the early advertisers adopting this trend were dot-com businesses, flush with cash at that moment. They didn't last as long as the tattoos.

FIGURE 14.36.   A permanent "skinvertisement," from an eBay auction.

The advertising monster creeps everywhere. Clearly, where there are eyes, there are—or soon will be—ads.

CONCLUSION

Sound recording and motion picture technologies swept the advertising world in the first half of the twentieth century. Radio was the big dog for a quarter century, followed by television for the next half century. Both continued to be important, but electronics led to computers, setting the course for events in the next chapter.

15

Living in a Virtual World

The internet is a solution looking for a problem.

—*Bill Towler, of Towler Data Services, 1995*

TV will forever outreach interactive media, and individual television programs will forever outreach any individual Web site or Web program.

—*Jonathan Bond and Richard Kirshenbaum, 1998*

Pop-up ads are a great idea! It reminds me of the little boy who liked a girl so he dipped her pigtails in an inkwell. It's always a good start on a relationship to piss off the person you want to seduce.

—*Jef I. Richards, 2002*

I'm about to discuss what commonly is called "new media," but I used that descriptor for other media that were new in the twentieth century. The material here is even a more profound leap forward from the nineteenth century, with so many moving parts, that I feel it *virtually* begs for its own chapter.

WEAVING A WEB

Math professor Charles Babbage is credited with the earliest concept of computers, known as the Analytical Engine, in 1837. The Turing Machine, created by Alan Turing in 1936, was a mathematical model that theoretically could compute anything presented to it. It was the inspiration behind today's computers.

But the first electronic digital computer was in 1937, by John V. Atanasoff and Clifford Berry, the Atanasoff-Berry Computer (ABC). A computer named Colossus followed in 1943 for the US military, replaced in 1946 by the general-purpose Electronic Numerical Integrator and Computer (ENIAC), which had 17,500 vacuum tubes, filled a fifty-foot room, and weighed thirty tons. The Computer Age had begun.

Computers increased in speed and abilities, while decreasing in size, but still they were large and expensive. The earliest personal computers were kits for hobbyists, beginning with the MITS Altair 8800 in 1975. Others followed, notably the 1976 Apple I, and in 1977 the Apple II. Apple went on to introduce the Macintosh in 1984. Several companies introduced computers in the interim, most important being the IBM PC in 1981, with 16 KB of memory and two 5.25-inch disk drive bays.

Related was introduction of the handheld four-function electronic calculator in 1970, which led to a more advanced handheld calculator, the HP-35, in 1972. The HP became the tool of choice for many engineers, being a computer they could hang from their belt. Also, the Pulsar P2 wristwatch appeared in 1973. It was the first mass-distributed electronic digital wristwatch, promoted as a "time computer." These were the first computer-type devices in reach of normal people.

Even before personal computers, computers affected ads. One devised for 7-Up soft drink, in 1974, is generally accepted as the first computer-assisted design of a commercial. Called "Bubbles," the same name as that Pears' Soap ad a century earlier, it was a fantasy where winged women were shown swimming in 7-Up. Three years later, a commercial for Kawasaki motorcycles, called "The Ultimate Trip," had a bike drive through computer-generated scenery (Sivulka 1998). All of this preceded the internet.

In 1945, in the October issue of *Wireless World*, novelist Arthur C. Clarke described a worldwide communication network using satellites spaced around the planet in geosynchronous orbit. This was the first conception of the internet. In October 29, 1969, with introduction of the Advanced Research Projects Agency Network (ARPANET), it began taking shape. ARPANET connected a computer at the University of California–Los Angeles to one at Stanford University, about 350 miles away, using a satellite, as Clarke proposed. Its purpose was military.

Thanks to a 1978 blizzard, Ward Christensen and Randy Suess created the first computer bulletin board system (BBS), using a corkboard, where notices were posted, as their model. The new personal computers made it accessible using telephones and signal-to-sound converters called dial-up modems. They were slow, but they worked. This led to a community of non-military internet users.

The next year, 1979, ushered in an internet service for non-military, non-expert users: Compu-Serve. It had existed since 1969 but only served businesses. Now it targeted personal computer users with a sort of time-sharing, putting Golden United Life Insurance's computers to work for profit when that company wasn't using them. It provided something new: an electronic mail (email) system for consumers.

The military continued controlling ARPANET, but in 1984 a separate military network, MILNET, was born. ARPANET ended in 1990, but the internet was built on ARPANET's bones. In 1990, Tim Berners-Lee invented the World Wide Web (WWW), enabling creation of websites and hyperlinks between sites.

Also in 1984 came Prodigy, a more user-friendly collection of news, email, bulletin boards, and so forth. Prodigy used a graphic user interface before Compu-Serve, attracting computer users intimidated by command-line (text only) interfaces. Prodigy's service *included advertising*. Its original business model depended on advertising and online shopping for revenue, more than its user subscription fees. It was the first online service that depended on advertising for funding.

Sears and IBM invested in Prodigy, which ensured them ad space. Initially those ads weren't clickable. This was before the internet opened to commercial use, but Prodigy was an internet "doorway," so ads were on this metaphorical door rather than on the internet. Subscribers would connect their computer to their telephone to call Prodigy, which then opened that door.

When ARPANET was decommissioned in 1990, it became possible for the "Net" to become commercially supported. In 1991, the US National Science Foundation established a framework for that, ensuring the costs of the internet "backbone" were covered. Businesses slowly dipped their toes in this digital tidepool.

While Prodigy had served up ads for years, the first clickable web ad was in 1993. The Global Network Navigator (GNN) sold the ad to a Silicon Valley law office, Heller Ehrman LLP. The first commercial website was GNN's own site that same year. And in 1994 Heller Ehrman LLP created the first law office website.

The world's first banner advertisement went live on October 27, 1994. A mere 468×60 pixel graphic, it was an ad for AT&T, as part of its "You will" campaign (Figure 15.1). For two years, AT&T ran a campaign asking provocative questions like "Have you ever tucked your baby in? From a phone booth?" The ads ended with "You will." This banner appeared on *Wired* magazine's website, Hotwired.com. An amazing 44 percent of visitors clicked the banner. Hotwired was paid $30,000 to display it for three months (Cook 2016).

FIGURE 15.1. The first ever banner ad, for AT&T, appeared on October 27, 1994.

In 1994, the first person-to-person text message was sent, and the Netscape Navigator web browser was launched. Both encouraged consumer internet use. And the computer "cookie" also was invented, helping advertisers by leaving crumbs of information on the computer that advertisers later could access, identifying how many times (and when) a visitor came to a website.

Much happened in 1995. Ragu pasta sauce became the first packaged goods brand to open a website. Brand websites quickly became electronic brochures, catalogs, and even virtual stores and marketplaces. The first US online purchase was in 1994, even before Ragu's website. It was a music CD purchased through an electronic commerce (e-commerce) portal, NetMarket. The first online purchase in China was in 1998, not far behind the United States. Amazon.com also opened in 1995, to become the leader in online commerce. It also led the creation of online-only stores, like the Zappos shoe store in 1999.

Also in 1995 was the birth of the Internet Advertising Council, created to promote the internet as an advertising vehicle and create guidelines for its use. Meanwhile, Jeffrey Zeldman started the first advertising blog, *The Ad Graveyard*. The University of Texas was the first university to offer an internet advertising class. And Craigslist began, which led to the rapid decline of classified newspaper advertising, although it wasn't a national factor until early the next decade.

FIGURE 15.2.   The first animated banner was based on the arcade game "Pong," which simulated table tennis (aka Ping-Pong). The white vertical rectangle on each end is a paddle, and the white square on the left side is the ball. The paddles move up and down via keystrokes.

A very early arcade video game was "Pong" in 1972. Unlike others, this game became wildly successful. In 1996, the Hewlett-Packard company created the first animated banner advertisement, for one of its printers, based on Pong. The ad was an actual game (though simple) the viewer could play (Figure 15.2).

Over succeeding years banners became aesthetically more refined, even with what appeared to be video (Figure 15.3). Some even had sound! The first banners including audio probably were thanks to the radio website Spinner.com. No method for incorporating sound in banners existed in 2002, so Spinner.com synchronized an audio file with displaying a banner between songs on its website. It called this "ActiveAudio."

Ethan Zuckerman takes credit for designing "one of the most hated tools in the advertiser's toolkit," the first pop-up advertisement, in 1997. These ads suddenly appear on top of material you're trying to see, obstructing your view (Figure 15.4). He explains:

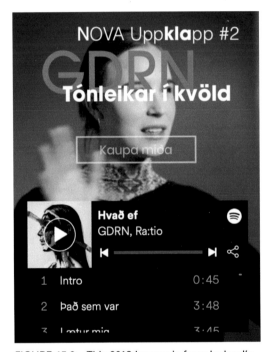

FIGURE 15.3.   This 2018 banner is from Iceland's Nova telecom company, and it includes video as well as moving text.

> It was a way to associate an ad with a user's page without putting it directly on the page, which advertisers worried would imply an association between their brand and the page's content. Specifically, we came up with it when a major car company freaked out that they'd bought a banner ad on a page that celebrated anal sex. I wrote the code to launch the window and run an ad in it. I'm sorry. Our intentions were good. (Zuckerman 2014)

Admittedly, there is dispute as to whether Zuckerman was first. John Shiple, project manager at GeoCities, is credited by some as inventor that same year, having developed a pop-up as a mechanism for GeoCities to make money. Other variations—for example, the "pop-under"—followed.

By the waning months of the 1990s, advertisers everywhere sought an on-line presence, creating a "dotcom frenzy" (Tungate 2007). Internet investments were at an all-time high, though some was non-strategic (read: foolish). Thus came the dot-com crash in 2000.

For advertisers, 2002 was a dark time because AdBlock, the first broadly adopted internet ad blocking software, was intro-

FIGURE 15.4.   A modern example of a pop-up ad.

duced. The internet equivalent of a remote control, it let viewers avoid ads. Its author claims to have made no profit from it, but it was popular (O'Reilly 2015). It effectively stifled the sources of revenue for many websites.

The internet became a blend of newspaper, radio, television, and other media accessible through a single digital device. As transformative as radio and then television were in the twentieth century, the internet represented a previously unimaginable change for advertising. This wasn't just a new medium; it was a whole new way of thinking about media options.

The internet was considered "the new medium" of the 1990s, but really it was a *collection* of new media, just as Gutenberg's press turned "print" into newspapers, magazines, handbills, and more. We likely don't even know all the media that will be internet spawn, but I need to address some that have affected the advertising business.

COMING TO LOGGER ADS

One internet-based medium was the blog, which generally refers to a public diary, thought journal, or rant site. The Lexico dictionary defines it as "a regularly updated website or web page, typically one run by an individual or small group, that is written in an informal or conversational style." Many believe blogs began with the Links.net site started by Justin Hall in 1994. It was a paradigm shift, giving a formerly unknown individual like Hall the power of creating an advertising vehicle.

The term began in 1997 as "weblog," coined by Jorn Barger, abbreviated as blog in 1999 by Peter Morholz. It was Barger's online "log" of his thoughts, making him the first web logger.

Commercial use followed, with the *Charlotte Observer* newspaper's blog in 1998. But blogs spread slowly. In 1999, five years after Hall's, a directory of blogs listed only twenty-three. But that year Blogger and LiveJournal both launched, offering places to post blogs. By 2001, blogs seemed to be everywhere. Platforms to help create blogs were popping up:

Movable Type (2001), WordPress (2003), TypePad (2003). Now any individual, or business, could easily create a blog.

In 2002 came Audioblogger, an audio-based blog site, inventing podcasting. Ben Hammersley coined that term in 2004. PodTrac was founded in 2005 to facilitate ad sales on podcasts, as well as providing audience tracking data (McGowan 2010). Podcasts, unlike radio, could be heard on demand, in locations where radio signals were limited, and on topics too specialized to get radio play.

A video version came in 2004, the "vlog." It took off once YouTube formed in 2005, becoming the *de facto* means of posting "how-to" and product review videos. YouTube became the world's largest video ad vehicle, and was bought by Google in 2006 for $1.65 billion. That year YouTube created "brand channels" for commercial users. It entered an advertising partnership with NBC, too. By 2009, YouTube allowed ads in seven formats (Jackson 2011).

In China, at the end of 2006, a YouTube knock-off, Youku, was announced. But Youku didn't remain China's top vlog site. By 2020, iQiyi, launched in 2010, was leading in China, and it was one of the world's largest video sites.

BlogAds, in 2002, offered to help advertisers reach specialty audiences carved out by some blogs, becoming the first blog advertising broker. In 2003, Google introduced AdSense, designed to be an advertising server that sends ads to websites in Google's network, including some blogs. Blogs were now an advertising medium. That same year political advertising jumped into blogs in a big way. Suddenly bloggers were making real money.

In 2004, "blog" became *Merriam-Webster* dictionary's "Word of the Year." By 2005, about $100 million of ads appeared on blogs, and 32 million Americans were reading blogs. It also was 2005 when the first blogger obtained White House press credentials. By 2010, around 152 million blogs existed. Audiences, often skeptical of advertising, found many blogs to have authenticity not found in most ads (Newman 2015). Blogs went from a viable medium to an important one, as did vlogs and podcasts. By 2019, 144 million people were podcast listeners.

Blog advertising became a global phenomenon. In China, famous bloggers known as Wang Hong ("internet celebrity"), like their American counterparts, found lucrative careers online, earning even more than the country's highest paid actors (Tsoi 2016). Many US blogging services were blocked in China, so Weibo, a blogging ("microblogging") website, started in 2009. It was valued in 2018 at $30 billion.

But blogs were not alone as new media. A related medium was growing alongside them: social media.

BECOMING SOCIAL

"Social media" turned up the fire under online advertising.[1] This medium arrived in 1997, with SixDegrees.com, which allowed users to add friends and build a network. It wasn't an enormous success but laid the foundation for others, like Friendster.com in 2002. This site, too, helped users build networks of friends while sharing pictures, videos, and more. This effort was more successful, but neither site welcomed advertising.

A Swedish social media site began in 2000: LunarStorm. It was advertising supported from its very start (Edosomwan et al. 2011), making it the first social media site to accept advertising.

Then came LinkedIn, at the end of 2002. MySpace arrived in 2003, becoming the biggest social media platform for a brief time, 2005–2008, supposedly worth $12 billion in 2007, due to tremendous advertising potential. But Facebook, in 2004, achieved a million users in its first year. Facebook was primarily aimed at college students, the market initially pushed to advertisers, so its first ads were campus flyers. Two years later, welcoming a broader market, Facebook started actively seeking advertising, with J.P. Morgan Chase as its first major advertiser. Its first ads were the small display type, along with sponsored text links (Cook 2016).

Microsoft bought a 1.6 percent interest in Facebook in 2007 for $240 million. By 2008, it was the top online social network. And by 2009 it offered advertisers advanced consumer-targeting opportunities. In 2011, MySpace sold for only $35 million, a drop from 2007's value.

Part of Facebook's 2007 deal with Microsoft (MS) gave MS the right to place international ads on the site. Also, Facebook offered "Sponsored Stories" in 2011, and its "Social Graph" gave advertisers new data access in 2012. "Video Ads" followed in 2013, as well as "Lookalike Audiences," helping advertisers find prospects similar to current customers. "Carousel Ads" came in 2014, along with "Dynamic Product Ads," "Lead Ads," and "Canvas Ads" in 2015. New possibilities continued to emerge, with Facebook finding new carrots to dangle in front of advertisers.

Twitter happened in 2006 as the first major "microblog," more closely resembling social media than most blogs. Blogs allow authors to write endlessly, whereas microblogs limit the number of characters. Twitter confined posts ("tweets") to 140 characters, allowing quick social connections. At first it shunned ads, but in 2010 it allowed "Promoted Tweets," ads that looked like tweets (native advertising), followed by "Promoted Trends," which permitted including brand

"To infinity and beyond"! Toy Story 3 hits theaters Friday, June 18. Did you get your tickets yet? www.disneyticketstogether.com #toystory3

FIGURE 15.5. The first Twitter "Promoted Trend" ad, from Disney-Pixar, promoted the motion picture *Toy Story 3*. The brand hashtag: #toystory3.

hashtags (Figure 15.5). New options continued, like "Promoted Accounts" (2010), "Conversion Tracking" (2013), and "Twitter Analytics" and "Tailored Audiences" (2014).

Instagram, social media with photo and video sharing, launched in 2010. Pinterest, for posting and sharing images in topical collections, arrived in 2011. Snapchat, another photo-sharing site, began in 2012. Instagram and Pinterest first offered advertising placement in 2013, while Snapchat followed in 2014.

By 2018, US social media ad spending reached $27 billion per annum. Globally it was $58 billion. By contrast, global television ad spending was $140 billion, so social media was approaching TV's halfway mark. But total global internet ad spending was an impressive $404 billion. Traditional media like television were still important, but had become a smaller piece of the story than previously.

SAMPLE THIS!

Almost anything can be ad media. Giving away samples is especially effective advertising for good products (though not for bad ones). In Chapter 3, I mentioned that town criers in France provided free wine samples in the twelfth century CE. The poem "Piers Plowman" talked of innkeepers giving away food samples in the fourteenth century. B. T. Babbitt apparently gave out soap samples in the mid-nineteenth century, too. Product sampling isn't new, and by the twentieth century it was a well-worn technique. And it fit later ideas regarding "activation"—getting consumers actively involved with products.

In the twenty-first century anyone who buys groceries has encountered free food samples for promoting packaged goods. "Trial size" samples of shampoo, toothpaste, and so on also are frequently distributed. Before public and legal pressures to abandon it, this approach was common for cigarettes.[2] Some of the world's strongest brands have been built with sampling.

Coca-Cola claims its earliest promotional effort involved sampling, in 1888. That sampling entailed distributing coupons for free samples. And 130-plus years later, sampling is still used. Visiting Coca-Cola headquarters leads to a room full of machines letting visitors sample more than one hundred of the company's beverages.

Clorox bleach started in 1914, but the product wasn't for home users. Annie Murray had the idea of a less concentrated bleach for homes, and she used sampling, giving away fifteen-ounce bottles of bleach at a grocery store. That brand survives today.

A purchaser of Johnson & Johnson's shaving stick, circa 1907, would find a postcard inside its wrapper, suggesting the buyer submit a friend's name, who would receive a free sample stick. This was direct mail aimed at building a prospect list. It was about data collection, with the sample as payment for that data. By using the referral, the original purchaser offered the friend a testimonial regarding the product.

In the 1990s, with the rise of the internet, sampling jumped aboard this train. Many products were now digital—software, electronic books and music, newspapers, and more—all of which were deliverable by the internet. This quickly became the norm, and most digital products were subsequently promoted via sampling. Many non-digital products, in a spin on Johnson & Johnson's approach, offered to mail samples to those providing their name and address on a website or social medium.

There also is virtual sampling. Virtual and augmented reality really began at the start of the twenty-first century, though its merits were recognized much earlier. Even around World

War I, advertisers were beginning to appreciate the use of color, beyond just attention grabbing, because color made product images more realistic. For some products, color photos were the closest thing to a product sample (Printers' Ink 1938). Higher-resolution photography, the advent of motion pictures, and, later, higher-definition television all did the same, moving consumers closer to realistic viewing, and almost touching, products.

Virtual sampling, though, came closest to reality as it moved from two-dimensional to three-dimensional product representations. Several technologies took us in that direction.

WHERE REALITY ENDS

In Chapter 7, the genesis of three-dimensional (3D) photography was covered, with introduction of the stereoscope in 1838, anaglyph 3D in 1853, and the first anaglyphic motion pictures in 1889. Both stereoscopic and anaglyphic techniques continued in use, laying the foundation for today's virtual reality (VR).

Because anaglyphic 3D used eyeglasses for the depth effect, a 1935 novel by Stanley G. Weinbaum, *Pygmalion's Spectacles*, described a world where goggles allowed wearers to enter a virtual world. The eyewear allowed users to experience both 3D and virtual smells, taste, and touch. This is the earliest imagining of VR ever publicly described.

Three years later, Antonin Artaud published *Le théâtre et son double*, a compilation of essays in which theater was described as "*la réalité virtuelle*," creating the term "virtual reality." "Artificial reality" (AR) was coined by Myron W. Krueger circa 1969, followed in 1990 with Tom Caudell coining "augmented reality."

Technology of the time confined virtual reality to 3D images, but developments continued. Late 1952 brought color to 3D movies. The first stereoscopic color feature film was *Bwana Devil*. The 1950s became the heyday of 3D movies.

Morton Heilig in 1957 invented the "Sensorama Simulator," a multi-sensory virtual experience. It was large, but someone could sit with their head surrounded, experiencing 3D *plus* "sounds, breezes, odor and tactile sensations." It was the most immersive VR experience ever. Only one was ever built, because of finances.

Heilig went on to create the "Telesphere Mask" in 1960, the earliest form of VR head-mounted display (HMD), displaying a 3D image with stereo sound. Long before computers were used for complex images, this relied on film. A computerized HMD came in 1968. Ivan Sutherland introduced the "Sword of Damocles," a head-mounted computer display, though still crude in its graphic capabilities.

In 1947, another visual technology was invented when Dennis Gabor developed "wavefront reconstruction," aka holography. He created the world's first hologram in 1948. Previous 3D imagery methods were effectively simulated; holography was real 3D photography. Special glasses weren't needed, nor did it require two separate cameras to simulate viewers' two eyes. But it required "coherent" light, so it wasn't until lasers were invented in 1960 that it became practical. It actually happened in 1962, but one almost needed to be a physicist to practice holography.

Gabor's was a "transmission" hologram, requiring observers to view the image by looking *through* the photographic film on which it was recorded. A laser was needed both to record and to transmit the image, which limited adoption of holography. But in 1958 Yuri Denisyuk invented "volume holography," which used white light for viewing. The light reflected off the image, so it was a "reflection" hologram, the form of hologram later used on credit cards. In 1979, a technique to produce reflection holograms by embossing was found, increasing potential for advertising uses.

With exception of the stereoview cards of the 1800s, advertising didn't jump on 3D methods. But in 1964 Eastman Kodak, the leading photographic and chemical supply company, ran an ad in *Look* magazine that included an attached card with a 3D image on it. It was the "first ink-printed postcard sized parallax panoramagram" (Figure 15.6), using Kodak's "Xograph" process. It used a lenticular plastic screen laid over the image, so a viewer's left eye saw a different image than their right eye. The ad called it "the first full color picture made in a new dimensional process." It certainly was the first lenticular 3D magazine advertisement, promoting both Kodak's Xograph process and the new Kodel fiber product.

By the 1970s, advertisers were using the anaglyphic process (Figure 15.7), which required viewers wear glasses with one blue and one red lens to see the 3D effect. Also in the 1970s General Motors had (probably) the first transmission holographic advertisement. In its building lobby in Manhattan, visitors would walk around a plexiglas box with a car inside. The car was transparent, but walking around the box you could see every side of the car as if it were really there. It was like a *partially* invisible toy car was there, but it was a hologram.

In 1987, Toyota applied the original stereoscope approach, distributing a 3D viewer with a film image inserted, depicting its Corolla automobile. Then, in 1988, the cover of *National Geographic* was a reflection hologram. The first reflection holographic magazine advertisement,

FIGURE 15.6.   The Kodak Parallax Panoramagram, front and back, as it appeared in the ad.

The Non-Giant Economy Size.

Unlike so many of our giant competition, Sherwood doesn't make a full line of audio equipment. No radios. No tape decks. No headphones. No turntables. Versatility may never be our claim to fame.

But the limited scope of our output does have benefits. We can concentrate on refining each of our products, engineering them for maximum performance.

A case in point is the S7310. It has minimum RMS power output @ 0.5% total harmonic distortion, both channels driven, of 38 watts per channel @ 8 ohms, 20-20,000 Hz. Which means that this receiver outpowers all other units in its price range. With exceptional selectivity and sensitivity ratings.

We also utilize only the finest and most advanced of proved componentry: Dual gate MOS FET's and phase lock loop circuitry, the latest integrated circuitry and Solid-State FM IF Ceramic Filtering devices. Equally important, we've eliminated the gimmickry and gadgets that add nothing to the equipment except a potential for malfunction.

In short, if you look at receivers that do as much as Sherwood's S7310, they probably cost more than $369.95. Or, if they cost the same, do less.

Which only proves that, in hi-fidelity manufacturing, good things come from small packagers.

Sherwood Electronic Laboratories
4300 N. California
Chicago, Illinois 60618

Sherwood.

The word is getting around.

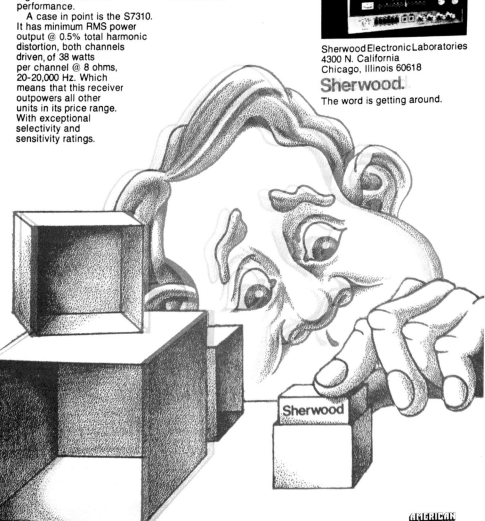

FIGURE 15.7.   A 1975 anaglyphic 3D advertisement for Sherwood audio equipment.

FIGURE 15.8. The back cover of the December 1988 *National Geographic* magazine.

and first holographic ad on a magazine cover, was on the back cover, promoting McDonald's restaurants (Figure 15.8).

Omni magazine in 1990 created a scandal over a 3D ad by publishing a reflection hologram ad for Motorola cellular telephones. The ad was just inside the cover, with a hole cut in the cover allowing the 3D image of Motorola's phone to be seen. Two of the magazine's editors quit, arguing this blurred the traditional line between editorial and advertising content (Figure 15.9).

While AR began with the Sword of Damocles in 1968, it gained momentum in 1992. Louis Rosenberg created a fully immersive AR system, but advertising use didn't happen until 2008 when the Mini automobile company issued a magazine ad for the Mini Cabrio. Holding that ad up to a computer camera, a virtual model appeared on the computer's screen and could be viewed at various angles by moving the ad.

In 2009, New York Fries created the first AR advertising application on Facebook. By printing a graphic from the Facebook ad and pointing a computer camera at it, a bobblehead of actor Gary Coleman would predict the next twenty-five years of the user's future. Over the succeeding decade, advertisers jumped on the AR approach in droves.

In one clever twist in 2013, Kontor Records in Germany applied AR to advertise its music to ad agencies. Instead of sending promotional CDs to agencies, to be ignored, Kontor sent full-size vinyl LP records in envelopes that unfolded to create paper "office turntables." Putting the disk on the turntable and then scanning a QR code with their phone caused the record to play while showing the disk revolving on the turntable (Martins 2013).

In 2015, the leading VR viewer, Oculus Rift, cost about $1,500. The *New York Times* newspaper distributed to its print subscribers a cardboard virtual reality viewer, created by Google (Figure 15.10). Some people initially thought it was a joke, but the device worked. By inserting their mobile telephone into the viewer, users could view

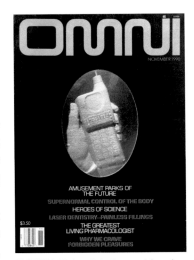

FIGURE 15.9. A holographic ad can be seen peeking through the cover of the November 1990 *Omni* magazine.

VR material from the newspaper's app (Somaiya 2015). A million viewers were given
away, almost singlehandedly popularizing
VR throughout the United States. So General Electric posted a VR animated video
advertisement on that app.

The IKEA furniture company had distributed a smartphone app since 2011 that
worked with its print catalog. Then, in
2014, it added AR to the app. Find a piece
of furniture you like in the catalog, place

FIGURE 15.10. The Google virtual reality viewer
distributed by the *New York Times* newspaper.

that page on the floor where you'd like that furniture, and the app displays your room with
the furniture in it. This laid track for many other companies in the future.

In 2015, Facebook enabled 360-degree videos. While different from these other technologies, it allowed viewers to scroll side to side, seeing photographs as if they were standing in
the photo and turning on the spot to look around. This is another dimension of VR that presented great opportunity, which Nickelodeon, ABC News, Buzzfeed, and others immediately
used for advertising (Peterson 2015).

As both VR and AR became the present and future of advertising, reality would never be
the same again.

MEDIA PLANNING AND BUYING IN THE TWENTY-FIRST CENTURY

Until the twentieth century's end, planning and buying media for advertising was pretty
straightforward. The first major change was cable television, which multiplied the number
of broadcast channels and allowed advertisers to reach more specific consumer targets. But
the internet (and other digital media) both improved and complicated things. Banners, pop-
ups, ad blockers, and more affected how consumers could be reached electronically. It was
nothing like the 1960s when media planners had far more limited options.

Basic media planning and buying isn't brain surgery. You figure out who should see or hear
your ad (the "target"), then you determine what media that target uses (newspapers, television, etc.). Finally, you find the price that gets the most bang for your buck to reach that group.

The earliest attempts at targeting specific groups—"segmenting" people—divided
groups into "demographic" categories: age, gender, race, education level, marital status,
and so on. This was fairly common by the 1920s (Tedlow & Jones 1993). A couple of decades earlier, advertising generally was published without a plan. Demographic segmentation was about reducing waste, putting ads where those likely interested would see them.
As industry invested more in consumer research, which took off in the 1920s, this became
more accurate and useful.

Segmentation took a turn in the mid-1960s. Researcher Daniel Yankelovich in 1964
pushed to describe consumers beyond demographics, and in 1965 Emanuel H. Demby
coined the term "psychographics" to describe things like feelings, beliefs, and attitudes for
use in segmentation. The Values Attitudes and Lifestyles (VALS) model created by SRI International in 1978 offered a systematized approach to psychographic segmentation.

Tools for determining who uses what media vehicles would fill catalogs. But again, the concept is not difficult. We simply need to know who uses what medium (e.g., newspaper) and, within each, what specific "vehicle" (e.g., the *Chicago Tribune*). The first step was circulation of print media, which you'll recall was a struggle until the Audit Bureau of Circulation (ABC) filled that niche. Then, for radio and TV, came ratings. A. C. Nielsen was a leader in this, beginning with its Radio Index in 1936, first used in the United States in 1942. Its Television Index followed in 1950.

Techniques improved, and the richness of the data increased. This led to concepts like "households using television" (HUT), "share of audience," "gross rating points," and "gross impressions." And media cost data led to "cost per thousand" (CPM), "cost per rating point," and so on. Companies like Standard Rate and Data Service (SRDS), formed in 1919, compiled this cost data.

Understanding consumers was important, so surveys, census data, and research companies like Mediamark Research, Inc. (MRI), W. R. Simmons, Yankelovich, and others offered consumer insights, for matching to that media data. It also provided psychographic insights into issues like how each medium was used. For specific media plans, different variables would apply. Really, media planning was the first advertising discipline relying almost entirely on data collection. But data availability hasn't been uniform, being more accessible in the United States and United Kingdom than in most countries.

The internet introduced new data collection methods and new ways to deliver ads. The media world entered a wholly new dimension in the 1990s.

WebConnect was the earliest entry into online ad placement in 1995, offering a Site Price Index allowing advertisers to compare costs for placing ads on various websites. WebConnect was the first "ad network," where a company acted as broker for multiple websites (aka "publishers").

Introduction of Doubleclick in 1996 helped systematize internet ad space purchasing. Businesses were just beginning to advertise on the internet, but how to find the best websites and negotiate advertising on each site, how to track who is viewing the ad, and more, were unknowns. It also was hard for websites to know how to attract advertisers. There was no Audit Bureau or Nielsen for websites, and the number of websites was reaching toward infinity, so it was complicated.

DoubleClick was the first online ad server, developing a website network from which it would serve banner ads in real time. An advertiser need only deal with DoubleClick to reach many appropriate websites. And in 1996 it introduced the Dynamic Advertising Reporting and Targeting (DART) system for tracking when ads were clicked. It also started building its own consumer activity database, then buying other databases to blend with it (Oberoi 2013). Pricing, like print ads, was based on CPM impressions. DoubleClick quickly built an enormous network, giving it substantial sway over the online ad market. By 1999, it served billions of ads.

The GoTo.com search engine, in 1997, came from a startup incubator called Idealabs, run by Bill Gross. Gross had bought a defunct search engine to resurrect. He wanted to let advertisers sponsor searches by purchasing keywords. This was the "paid placement model"

(PPM). Gross also instituted an automated auction where advertisers could bid on keywords. Word buyers would pay GoTo only when someone clicked on a link resulting from that keyword search. This became the start of something called "pay per click" (PPC). And GoTo made a lot of money!

The paid-search approach was partly designed to address a problem with "spam results." By repeating a word on a webpage enough times, searches for that word would bring that page to the top of search results. So a porn website could bury the word "children" over and over on pages, and a search for something like children's clothes would find that porn site. By allowing keywords to be purchased, the purchasers' sites would populate the results instead (Oremus 2013). Advertising helped push out the spammers.

PPC became a revenue source for search engines. Google, a brand-new search engine launched in 1998, sought a financial support model. By 1999, the company bled money, and revenue still was elusive. It introduced AdWords in 2000, where advertisers paid for text ads to pop up with search results. In 2002, AdWords was replaced with PPC called AdWords Select. When it went public two years later, Google was valued at $27 billion. In 2007, Google bought DoubleClick for $3.1 billion.

Consequently, PPC became an alternative to CPM pricing. CPM measured how many people saw an ad, while PPC measured how many acted on that ad, clicking it. Like targeting, this was about eliminating waste, by avoiding people who had no real interest in the advertised material. And the number of clicks (click-through rate) is an indicator of the ad or placement quality.

Both PPC and CPM options continued. But media buying became more automated.

ENTER PROGRAMMATIC ADVERTISING

Right Media arrived in 2003 as a media buying agency, but it became the first advertising exchange. This was a marketplace where media buyers and sellers could do business, reaching many sellers/buyers quickly. The focus is principally on the supply side, and how many ad spaces or "impressions" are available to buy. Right Media quickly added a "yield manager" to predict the probability of a click, given buyer specifications. Buying and selling were both getting smarter. Yahoo bought what was now called the RightMedia Exchange (RMX) in 2007. Other ad exchanges followed.

MediaMath was born in 2007, representing another sea change. It was the first "demand-side platform" (DSP), a software approach to buying online media. Before MediaMath, ads were bought and sold by real humans. This helped automate media buying and selling, letting computers deal with ad exchanges like RMX to get the desired ad impressions at the lowest price.

Once DSPs worked for advertisers, publishers needed similar automation to maximize their revenues. They automated ad placement (impressions) inventories for sale using "supply-side platforms" (SSPs).

This is where the process went into overdrive, with the introduction of "real-time bidding" (RTB) for impressions in 2009. The moment impressions became available for purchase, bidding happened in "real time." When a user clicked a link to load a page on a browser, the website publisher sent a call for bids, engaging some combination of DSPs, exchanges, and SSPs—including some user information. Calculations were made and bids were placed. The winner's ad was then loaded on the page.

This whole process is called "programmatic buying." Because both buyer and seller are represented, it is viewed as an ROI (return on investment) optimization mechanism. However, it's still evolving. The first software was for desktop computers, but mobile computing presented another factor, since screen real estate on a seventeen-inch computer monitor was quite different from a mobile telephone's. And mobile phones didn't use "cookies" like desktop computers.

Mobile platforms arrived in 2007 with Apple's iPhone, the first modern smartphone. Advertisers soon sought to optimize ad exposure on phones. By 2014, mobile web browsing passed desktop browsing, making it a vital ad delivery system.

Simultaneously came automations for matching ads to users. Google's AdSense was the leader. In 2010, it began mining user search history data, through computer cookies, to perform "contextual matching" fitting consumers to more relevant advertisements (Schwartz 2010).

All this automation in internet media buying was timely. In 2009, internet advertising first surpassed television ad spending.

Some history of audience targeting was mentioned above, but there is more to that story. New technologies brought new means to both create and apply targeting.

GOOD COOKIES MAKE GREAT FENCES

Prior to the internet's commercialization, collecting consumer data almost entirely required manual collection techniques like surveys, focus groups, diaries, and so on. The information was an essential part of media planners' toolboxes for ad targeting. A few automated methods were developed by companies like Nielsen, for TV/radio ratings, but most data gathering was by hand.

A significant data collection method change came in 1994 when Lou Montulli invented computer "cookies." A cookie was a bit of data saved to users' computers at the request of a website. When visiting a website, you might give your name and more. That information is written into a "cookie" file on your computer so next time you visit that website it doesn't ask the same questions again. Advertisers found more uses for this cookie-writing ability, including storing your interests, preferences, browser search terms, the type of computer you were using, even your spending habits. It was an intelligence file on the user. The data was stored there and later used for targeting (among other things), all through automation.

Cookie data enabled something called "behavioral targeting." Like using psychographic and demographic data for targeting, it uses data on consumers' actual behavior. So, for example, a user searching for high-end hunting equipment, and buying certain types, leaves digital footprints that are then used to send specific product ads to that user and help tailor the ad content.

Never before had a consumer's behavior been so accessible to advertisers, so this allowed new levels of precision in eliminating waste by precise targeting. This led to the concept of "micro-targeting," aiming at smaller and nearly waste-free target audiences. Cookies put this within reach. But there was more to come.

Built on technologies dating to at least 1989, another development occurred in 1999. The Palm VII personal digital assistant (PDA) gave consumers their first taste of location-based services (LBS). This is a set of policies that enable various technologies, including Global Positioning Systems (GPS), to identify a device's physical geographic location. This became invaluable with introduction of the iPhone in 2007. Not only could a certain type of person be targeted, but it could also be confined to a specific geographic area: "geo-targeting." Geo-targeting did exist before that time, since most ads were published in specific geographic areas, like specific cities, but this was more precise, immediate, and dynamic targeting than previously possible.

That led to "geo-fencing," putting boundaries around a geographic area. So a baseball field could be geo-fenced, targeting only people at today's baseball game. By 2010, this was part of the advertising repertoire. That year Where Inc. received a US patent for location-based services,[3] which mentioned one use was offering coupons to people entering geo-fenced areas (Schonfeld 2010). However, location services constant use was taxing on mobile devices' batteries in 2010, so it took a couple of years before it caught on.

As better technologies enter the market, even greater targeting precision is likely. But more questionable targeting techniques also may follow.

FISHING FOR RESULTS

Online advertising has had some controversies. Both "clickbait" and "chumbox" are terms for methods websites use to fish for viewers. Headlines are the bait.

Clickbait has a long history in journalism, with newspapers upping circulation numbers via sensational headlines, even deceptions, to grab readers who otherwise wouldn't touch the newspaper. Newitz (2014) argues this reaches at least to 1888, and has been called "yellow journalism." Wikipedia defines today's version:

> Clickbait is a form of false advertisement which uses hyperlink text or a thumbnail link that is designed to attract attention and entice users to follow that link and read, view, or listen to the linked piece of online content, with a defining characteristic of being deceptive, typically sensationalized or misleading.

While that confusingly commingles "deceptive" and "sensationalized," the essence is exaggeration or hyperbole.

A typical clickbait heading might be "You won't believe what these 1980s child stars look like today!" This has been used online since CPM impressions were adopted for ad sales in the mid-1990s.

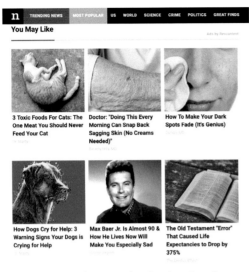

FIGURE 15.11.   An example of a chumbox from the Newser.com website. In light gray text, in the upper right corner, it says "Ads by Revcontent."

Chumbox is newer, but with a similar twist. It was first used for online advertising around 2014–2015 (e.g., Mahoney 2015). In fishing, "chum" is bits of fish thrown into the water to attract larger prey, like sharks. A chumbox is a box of rotting fish. In internet parlance it is a grid of "ads"—thumbnail image links to stories—with provocative headings (Figure 15.11). Like the fishing metaphor, this is a box (albeit 2D) of clickbait, to attract info-hungry passersby. The chumbox industry doesn't like that name, preferring something like "content recommendation platforms."

So now we have "chumvendors." As DoubleClick served ads to various websites, rotating them with other ads, chum-vending did the same with clickbait ads. Chumboxes could be different each time you turn to that website, and those same boxes might appear on other sites.

WHERE YOU GO, THEY WILL FOLLOW

Mobile computing started in the form of "personal information managers" (PIMs). These devices, designed to hold, for example, appointments and telephone numbers, really began in the early 1990s. The first prototype PIM in the 1970s, the Dynabook, never made it to market. The first functional PIM was the Psion Organiser in 1984, resembling a large handheld calculator, using removable "datapaks" for simple data storage. More functionality came later.

As the 1990s began, companies like Casio began offering basic PIMs. The first to be called a "personal digital assistant" (PDA) was the Apple Newton in 1993. It was groundbreaking but, thanks to its high price, a failure that ended in 1998. Still, it influenced the direction of pocket computers.

The Palm Pilot appeared in 1996, adopting some ideas from the Newton, but it was cheaper and an open platform permitting programmers to write their own programs. It succeeded, but also showed others what would sell, so PDA competition exploded. The mobile computer, in its simplest form, was now reality. Wireless connections with the outside world came in 1999 with the Palm VII. And that capability almost instantly became standard on PDAs.

Next came the tablet computer. Laptop computers had existed since the 1980s, but the tablet initially was more like a PDA than a computer. It was far more mobile, but with limited functions. It had a larger screen than PDAs, with a variety of small programs. The Microsoft Tablet PC was first sold in 2000. But Apple introduced the iPad in 2010, and tablets became popular.

Mobile telephones go back farther. Wireless radios initially were used for person-to-person communication, and sometimes called "wireless telephones." The first patent using that term was in 1908. And in 1910 the "mobile telephone" was created by a Swedish engineer named Ericsson. He installed it in his car, but he had to stop along the road and connect wires to telephone poles for it to work. It didn't catch on.

The first "mobile wireless telephone" was from Western Electric Corporation in 1946. It was more wireless radio than telephone but linked into the telephone system so users could call, or be called by, people with normal telephones. The rich and powerful adopted it, generally as a car telephone.

Finally, in 1973, Motorola developed the first *handheld* mobile telephone. But mobile phones were rare until the "cellular" phone in 1983: the Motorola DynaTAC 8000x. It was both large and expensive, but smaller and cheaper mobile phones followed year after year. Those worked on an analog (first-generation) cellular network, but digital (second-generation) cellular systems began in 1991.

The PDA and mobile phone merged into the smartphone, really starting with IBM. It developed one in 1992, available for purchase in 1994: the Simon Personal Communicator. It could send email, and had an address book and a scheduler, but it was large. More smartphones followed, but the watershed was in 2007 with Apple's iPhone. It could browse the internet on the go and run a large number of software applications ("apps"). It was pocket sized, had a virtual keyboard, and allowed up to eight hours of talk time. This phone became the standard bearer against which others competed.

Smartphone features made mobile advertising feasible. The first mobile ad used one such feature: text messaging.[4] In 2000, a Finnish news provider sent news headlines by text, sponsored by an advertiser. Texting became a well-worn method for advertisers to communicate with consumers. The first mobile advertising conference also was that year, hosted by the Wireless Marketing Association.

The iPhone made wider varieties of mobile ads possible, even delivering ads aimed at desktop computers. Full display and banner ads with color images, and television-type commercials, became the norm. Tablets like the iPad made them bigger. Mobile advertising was soon limited only by advertisers' imaginations.

Above I mentioned how online advertising came to rely on supply-side and demand-side networks. In 2006, the first *mobile* ad network, as a marketplace between supply and demand sides, was called AdMob. In 2009, it was purchased by Google. Over time many mobile ad networks appeared, such as Applovin, ironSource, UnityAds, ConsoliAds, and Adsperfection. Mobile advertising had gone beyond a mere game.

GAMIFICATION OF ADVERTISING

Beyond all these varieties of computer, dedicated electronic gaming systems—both console and portable—were created. The first home video game system was the Odyssey by Magnavox in 1972. Atari followed in 1977, and Nintendo in 1985. Games also were being developed for computers. Still more dedicated game systems kept arriving. Over time, games actually appeared on all of these platforms.

Both children and adults always have loved games. Games were some of the first programs developed for personal computers. Not surprisingly, eventually games came to incorporate advertisements. A game designed to promote a brand, where the game is itself an ad, is an "advergame." But allowing brands to advertise within a game is called "in-game advertising" (Gross 2010). That distinction is not always recognized, but both gamify advertising.

The very first in-game advertising was likely a joke, and it wasn't developed for kids. It came before personal computers. Digital Equipment Corporation in 1973 had the game "Moonlander" (later released as "Lunar Lander" by Atari) developed for its GT40 Graphics Display Terminal. It showcased this "intelligent terminal's" abilities. A version of the game had a hidden "easter egg" (surprise). The game's objectives included landing a lunar module on the moon. If you landed in one particular spot a McDonald's restaurant appeared, the astronaut emerged and walked to McDonald's for a Big Mac (to go) and then walked back, and the module would lift off. It's not clear whether McDonald's was involved in its creation.

FIGURE 15.12. The first real advergame, from 1983.

"Polo" nearly became the first advergame. It was being developed in 1978 for the Polo brand. But it never was finished.

By 1983, personal computers and dedicated gaming machines were both gaining popularity. Nintendo released its Family Computer (Famicom) gaming system in Japan, but it took a couple of years to reach the United States. Atari had a gaming system already in the United States. That year M Network released a game for Atari's 2600 machine, believed to be the first true advergame: "Kool-Aid Man" (Figure 15.12). The title character was the "mascot" of Kool-Aid beverages, and the game promoted that brand, with success.

Parker Brothers also developed an advergame that year, and it again involved McDonald's. In it, Ronald McDonald would feed hungry aliens. The aliens would chew on the Golden Arches if not fed fast enough. This game was tested, but a narrow age group liked it, so it was cancelled.

Simultaneously, Coca-Cola worked with Atari on a version of "Space Invaders," where players shot at the enemy: Pepsi. The game "Tapper" was an arcade game developed for Budweiser, in which the player serves beer and collects empty glasses before they fall to the floor.

Johnson & Johnson created a "Tooth Protectors" game where the Protector used a toothbrush, floss, and dental rinse to fight Snack Attackers. Ralston Purina turned its Chuck Wagon dog food commercials into a "Chase the Chuck Wagon" game. All occurred about the same time as "Kool-Aid Man," so validity of its "first" title is subject to debate.

Since then, many games promoting brands have been crafted (Figure 15.13). Regarding smartphones, Wong (2018) reported that "mobile games monetize in-app ads four times more often than non-gaming apps." Games make more money from ads than non-games! An entire industry developed around placing advertisements in games.

SPAM, A LOT

A pejorative term describing some advertising is "spam," referring to unsolicited, unwelcomed advertising. The word comes from a television comedy skit: *Monty Python's Flying Circus*. First used in 1990, referring to unsolicited electronic mail, the first unsolicited ads were sent long before that.

FIGURE 15.13. A 2006 advergame for the XBox gaming system, promoting Burger King restaurants.

The first unsolicited commercial appeal goes back to the telegraph. One evening in May 1864, a telegram was delivered to several British politicians. At such an hour they might assume it something quite serious! But this message was something else: an ad for the dental practice of Messrs Gabriel, at 27 Harley Street, open "10 till 5."

Some recipients didn't take it so well, writing scathing letters to the *Times* newspaper (Anonymous 2007). One recipient, in his letter, said, "I have never had any dealings with Messrs. Gabriel, and beg to ask by what right do they disturb me by a telegram which is evidently simply the medium of advertisement?"

A later form of spam came from the first telemarketing company, DialAmerica, in 1957. But even before that, the telephone likely was used for unsolicited promotions. One story has it this began with housewives trying to sell cookies.

Records are sparse, but it is likely the first telephone spam was not long after the telephone was invented. In 2020, several years after the US Federal Trade Commission established its "Do Not Call" registry prohibiting unsolicited calls to anyone on that list, there still were billions of illegal spam calls every month. Many, or most, of these weren't legitimate advertisers, but those engaged in telemarketing fraud—that is, scam artists.

In May 1978, before the internet, the ARPANET became a medium for spam. A marketing manager for Digital Equipment Corporation, Gary Thuerk, sent email to four hundred ARPANET users promoting a new product. It was the first email spam (Figure 15.14). Complaints came almost immediately, and Thuerk was chewed out by someone representing ARPANET. People still think of him as the "father of spam."

Another notable case of internet spam was in April 1994. Laurence Canter and Martha Siegel Legal Services sent out mass advertising about the "green card lottery," for immigrants seeking a "green card" for residence in the United States, to more than five thousand

DIGITAL WILL BE GIVING A PRODUCT PRESENTATION OF THE NEWEST MEMBERS OF THE DECSYSTEM-20 FAMILY; THE DECSYSTEM-2020, 2020T, 2060, AND 2060T. THE DECSYSTEM-20 FAMILY OF COMPUTERS HAS EVOLVED FROM THE TENEX OPERATING SYSTEM AND THE DECSYSTEM-10 <PDP-10> COMPUTER ARCHITECTURE. BOTH THE DECSYSTEM-2060T AND 2020T OFFER FULL ARPANET SUPPORT UNDER THE TOPS-20 OPERATING SYSTEM.

THE DECSYSTEM-2060 IS AN UPWARD EXTENSION OF THE CURRENT DECSYSTEM 2040 AND 2050 FAMILY. THE DECSYSTEM-2020 IS A NEW LOW END MEMBER OF THE DECSYSTEM-20 FAMILY AND FULLY SOFTWARE COMPATIBLE WITH ALL OF THE OTHER DECSYSTEM-20 MODELS.

WE INVITE YOU TO COME SEE THE 2020 AND HEAR ABOUT THE DECSYSTEM-20 FAMILY AT THE TWO PRODUCT PRESENTATIONS WE WILL BE GIVING IN CALIFORNIA THIS MONTH. THE LOCATIONS WILL BE:

TUESDAY, MAY 9, 1978 - 2 PM
HYATT HOUSE (NEAR THE L.A. AIRPORT)
LOS ANGELES, CA

THURSDAY, MAY 11, 1978 - 2 PM
DUNFEY' S ROYAL COACH
SAN MATEO, CA
(4 MILES SOUTH OF S.F. AIRPORT AT BAYSHORE, RT 101 AND RT 92)

A 2020 WILL BE THERE FOR YOU TO VIEW. ALSO TERMINALS ON-LINE TO OTHER DECSYSTEM-20 SYSTEMS THROUGH THE ARPANET. IF YOU ARE UNABLE TO ATTEND, PLEASE FEEL FREE TO CONTACT THE NEAREST DEC OFFICE FOR MORE INFORMATION ABOUT THE EXCITING DECSYSTEM-20 FAMILY.

FIGURE 15.14.   Computer spam began in 1978, with this email message.

USENET discussion groups. The response wasn't entirely positive. Canter and Siegel later claimed they gained one thousand new clients.

Canter was later disbarred, partly because of his advertising violating laws governing attorney advertising. It is believed he was the first lawyer ever disciplined for illegal internet advertising (Craddock 1997).

Like telemarketing, email spam grew until becoming an overwhelming problem. In 2018, 14 billion spam emails were sent on a daily basis, with only one response out of every 12.5 million emails sent. While not very efficient or effective advertising, the sheer volume made it worthwhile for many.

CONCLUSION

Commerce now exists largely in a world transcending brick and mortar, and advertising was the sail that pushed it into these new waters. This is a brave new, virtual, world for the ad industry, unlike any challenge—or *set* of challenges—faced in the past. It is a new paradigm, changing every aspect of advertising.

16

Ads and Culture

The destiny of our Western civilization turns on the issue of our struggle with all that Madison Avenue stands for more than it turns on the issue of our struggle with Communism.

—*Arnold Toynbee, British historian, 1963*

Whether you like or dislike advertising, there is no denying it has profound effects on society. Its pervasiveness ensures its impact. Those effects deserve serious attention here. Let's begin by looking at one thing making ads so memorable and influential: slogans.

SLOGANS THAT JUST DO IT!

Slogans (or "taglines" or "straplines")[1] really came into vogue in the late 1800s. The way was led by quacks selling junk cures (Elliott 1962). But politicians helped, too. Or perhaps that's redundant.

The 1890s saw the rise of slogans. G. Herb Palin, for example, would write ten slogans for $100 (Presbrey 1929). It makes sense the slogan's rise would track the rise of trademarks. Recall that trademark laws were a product of the late nineteenth century.

A well-known US presidential slogan dates to 1840, when William Henry Harrison used "Tippecanoe and Tyler, too" to beat Martin Van Buren. Tippecanoe reminded voters that Harrison defeated a Shawnee tribe at the Tippecanoe River in 1811. Tyler was John Tyler, his running mate. Memorability is essential for a good slogan (Ries 2015), and that was memorable. It's still recalled today!

In the twentieth century, slogans became key advertising tools. They could convey a brand's essence, or differentiate it, or just make the brand memorable. Some slogans come with stories.

The Maxwell House coffee slogan that started in 1915, "Good to the last drop," supposedly was taken from a comment by President Teddy Roosevelt in 1907. The 1933 "Breakfast of Champions" Wheaties cereal slogan was hastily written by ad exec Knox Reeves when

369

asked what to put on a sponsor board at a Minneapolis Millers baseball game. And the 1962 Avis rental car slogan "We try harder" originated when ad legend Bill Bernbach asked Avis president Robert Townsend how his company—#2 in the market—differed from #1, Hertz. That was his response. Apparently not all slogans take months of deliberation and research.

In 1997, Apple Computer's "Think Different" slogan was first used in its "Here's to the Crazy Ones" commercial. Apple president Steve Jobs called that commercial's script "shit," but the commercial was made. It and the "Think Different" slogan led to the company's turnaround. The client isn't always right.

An exhaustive collection of product slogans would take volumes. Some notable ones, though, are in Table 16.1, with political slogans in Table 16.2.

Table 16.1. Slogans Over the Years

Advertiser	Slogan	Year
Beecham's Pills	Worth a Guinea a Box	1859
Dr. C.M. Townsend	Why let pain your pleasures spoil, for want of Townsend's Magic Oil?	1875
Dr. Williams	Dr. Williams' Pink Pills for Pale People	1890
Hires Root Beer	Delicious Temperance, Thirst-quenching, Health-Giving Drink.	1890
Hires Root Beer	The Great Health Drink.	1892
Coca-Cola	1. The Ideal Brain Tonic. 2. A Delightful Summer and Winter Beverage. 3. For Headache & Exhaustion.	1892
Heinz	57 Varieties	1892
New York Times	All the news that's fit to print.	1896
Oldsmobile automobiles	Practically noiseless and impossible to explode.	1897
National Biscuit Co.	Lest you forget, we say it yet, Uneeda Biscuit.	1898
Coca-Cola	For headache and exhaustion, drink Coca-Cola.	1900
Victor Talking Machine	His Master's Voice	1901
Quaker Oats	It Puts Off Old Age.	1902
Packard automobiles	Ask the man who owns one.	1902
Pepsi-Cola	Exhilarating, Invigorating, Aids Digestion.	1903
Coca-Cola	Delicious and refreshing.	1904
Cadillac automobiles	You Can Kill a Horse but Not a Cadillac.	1905
Coca-Cola	The favorite drink for ladies when thirsty, weary, and despondent.	1905
Coca-Cola	The Great National Temperance Drink.	1906
Coca-Cola	Good to the last drop.	1908
Pepsi-Cola	Delicious and Healthful.	1908
Oldsmobile	The logical car at the logical price.	1909
Morton Salt	When it rains, it pours.	1911
Woodbury Soap	A skin you love to touch.	1911
Cadillac	The Penalty of Leadership.	1915
Maxwell House Coffee	Good to the last drop.	1915
Sunkist Orange Drink	Drink an Orange.	1916
Florist's Transworld Delivery (FTD)	Say it with flowers.	1917
Lucky Strike cigarettes	It's Toasted.	1917
Pepsi-Cola	Pepsi-Cola—It Makes You Scintillate.	1919
Smith Brothers Cough Drops	A Cough is a Social Blunder.	1919
Steinway Pianos	The instrument of the immortals.	1919
Camel cigarettes	I'd walk a mile for a Camel.	1921

Advertiser	Slogan	Year
Listerine mouthwash	1. Often a bridesmaid—but never a bride.	1923
	2. For Halitosis, Use Listerine.	
Outdoor Advertising Agency of America	The highway has become the buyway.	1923
US School of Music	They all laughed when I sat down at the piano, but oh!, when I began to play . . .	1925
Listerine mouthwash	Often a Bridesmaid, Never a Bride.	1925
Coca-Cola	Stop at the red sign.	1926
Pepsi-Cola	Peps You Up!	1928
Guinness Beer	Guinness is Good for You!	1928
Beech-Nut Peanut Butter	Give me a big one every time.	1929
Coca-Cola	The pause that refreshes.	1929
Kellogg Rice Krispies	Snap, Crackle, Pop!	1932
Oldsmobile	Outstanding General Motors values in the medium price field.	1932
Wheaties cereal	Breakfast of Champions.	1933
Haig Scotch Whisky	Don't be vague. Ask for Haig.	1934
Hallmark Cards	When you care enough to send the very best.	1934
Campbell's Condensed Soups	M'm M'm Good.	1935
Guinness Beer	My Goodness. My Guinness.	1935
Coca-Cola	Cold Refreshment.	1937
Heinz Fresh Cucumbers & Pickles	What food these morsels be!	1938
Pepsi-Cola	Twice as Much for a Nickel.	1939
Coca-Cola	Thirst Asks Nothing More.	1939
Pepsi-Cola	Bigger Drink, Better Taste.	1943
Arpege Cologne	Promise her anything, but give her Arpege.	1945
Colgate Toothpaste	It cleans your breath while it cleans your teeth.	1945
Madman Muntz, used car dealer	I wanna give 'em away but Mrs. Muntz won't let me. She's crazy.	1946
De Beer Consolidated Mines	Diamonds are forever.	1947
US Forest Service	Only YOU can prevent forest fires.	1947
Brylcreem hair dressing	A little dab'll do ya.	1949
Maidenform bras	I dreamed I went shopping in my Maidenform bra.	1949
Pepsi-Cola	Why Take Less When Pepsi's Best.	1949
Pepsi-Cola	More Bounce to the Ounce.	1950
Kellogg Frosted Flakes	They're GR-R-REAT!	1951
Cadillac	It's a Who's Who of the Highway!	1952
Coca-Cola	The gift of thirst.	1952
Pepsi-Cola	Any Weather is Pepsi Weather.	1952
Gimbel's Department Store	Riddle: What's college? That's where girls who are above cooking and sewing go to meet a man they can spend their lives cooking and sewing for.	1952
Kentucky Fried Chicken (KFC)	It's finger-lickin' good.	1952
Cadillac	Standard of the world.	1953
Peter Paul Candies	Sometimes I feel like a nut. Sometimes I don't.	1953
Pepsodent Toothpaste	You'll wonder where the yellow went, when you brush your teeth with Pepsodent.	1953
Coca-Cola	Dependable as sunrise.	1954
M&M Candies	The milk chocolate melts in your mouth—not in your hand.	1954
Alka-Seltzer	Speedy is its middle name.	1954
Winston cigarettes	Winston tastes good like a cigarette should.	1954
Indianapolis 500 Mile Race	The Greatest Spectacle in Racing.	1955
Birdseye Peas	Sweet as the moment when the pod went "pop."	1956
Kentucky Fried Chicken	We fix Sunday dinner seven nights a week.	1956

(continued)

Table 16.1. *Continued*

Advertiser	Slogan	Year
Timex Watches	It takes a licking and keeps on ticking.	1956
Roto-Rooter	Away go troubles down the drain.	1956
Coca-Cola	Sign of good taste.	1957
De Soto automobiles	This baby can flick its tail at anything on the road!	1957
Crest Toothpaste	Look, Ma! No cavities!	1957
Greyhound Bus Lines	Leave the driving to us.	1957
Kit Kat candy	Have a break . . . Have a Kit Kat.	1957
Pillsbury	Nothing says lovin' like somethin' from the oven.	1957
Cadillac	Finest Expression of Motordom's Highest Ideal!	1957
Rice-A-Roni	Rice-A-Roni, the San Francisco Treat.	1958
Cadillac	World's Best Synonym for Quality!	1959
Volkswagen	Think small.	1959
Trix cereal	Silly rabbit! Trix are for kids.	1959
Kellogg	The best to you each morning.	1959
Wrigley's Doublemint Gum	Double your pleasure, double your fun.	1959
Bounty Paper Towels	The Quicker Picker Upper.	1960
Coca-Cola	1. Relax with Coke.	1960
	2. Revive with Coke.	
McDonald's restaurants	Look for the Golden Arches.	1960
Milky Way candy	The sweet you can eat between meals without ruining your appetite.	1960
IBM Tabulating Cards	IBM cards: working paper . . . not paper work.	1960
Plaza Hotel	The Rendez-vous is so romantic . . . it's downright dangerous.	1960
Avis Rental Cars	We Try Harder	1962
Clairol Hair Coloring	Is it true blonds have more fun?	1965
Foster Grant Sunglasses	Isn't that you behind those Foster Grants?	1965
Mars candy bars	A Mars a day helps you work, rest and play.	1965
Raid insecticide	Kill bugs dead.	1966
United Air Lines	Fly the friendly skies of United.	1966
Heinz Baked Beans	Beanz Meanz Heinz.	1967
One-A-Day Multiple Vitamins plus Iron	The Other Pill.	1967
Pepsi-Cola	Taste that beats the others cold.	1967
M&M candies	Melts in your mouth, not in your hands.	1967
McDonald's restaurants	The closest thing to home.	1967
Public Service Announcement	Do you know where your children are?	1967
Listerine mouthwash	You want to knock 'em dead, but not with your breath.	1968
Wisk Laundry Detergent	Ring around the collar.	1968
Coca-Cola	It's the real thing.	1969
Pepsi-Cola	You've Got a Lot to Live, and Pepsi's Got a Lot to Give.	1969
Nationwide Insurance	Nationwide is on your side.	1969
Encyclopedia Britannica	Dick and Jane is dead.	1970
Wendy's restaurants	Quality is Our Recipe.	1970
Oldsmobile	The Escape Machines. Escape from the Ordinary.	1970
Budweiser beer	When You Say Bud You've Said It All.	1970
Frank Perdue Poultry	It takes a tough man to make a tender chicken.	1971
Chiffon Margarine	It's not nice to fool Mother Nature!	1971
Heinz Ketchup	Slowest Ketchup in the West.	1971
Alka-Seltzer	I can't believe I ate the whole thing!	1972
John Deere	Nothing runs like a Deere.	1972
Memorex Recording Tape	Is it live, or is it Memorex?	1972
Sara Lee Food Products	Nobody doesn't like Sara Lee.	1972
Burger King restaurants	Have it your way.	1973

Advertiser	Slogan	Year
Carlsberg Beer	Probably the best lager in the world.	1973
Cutty Sark Whisky	Don't give up the ship.	1973
American Broadcasting Co.	Wide World of Entertainment.	1973
L'Oreal	Because I'm worth it.	1973
Merrill Lynch	Merrill Lynch is bullish on America.	1973
Pepsi-Cola	Lipsmackin' thirstquenchin' acetastin' motivatin' goodbuzzin' cooltalkin' highwalkin' fastlivin' evergivin' coolfizzin' Pepsi.	1973
Seven-Up soft drink	The Uncola.	1973
Miller Light Beer	Tastes great, less filling.	1974
Heineken Brewery	Heineken. Refreshes the parts other beers cannot reach.	1974
American Express Card	Don't leave home without it.	1975
BMW automobiles	The ultimate driving machine.	1975
Hebrew National meat	We answer to a higher authority.	1975
Meow Mix cat food	Tastes so good cats ask for it by name.	1976
Alka-Seltzer	Plop, plop, fizz, fizz, oh what a relief it is!	1976
Rolaids antacid	How do you spell relief?	1976
New York Dept. of Economic Development	I love NY.	1977
Cadbury Fruit & Nut candy	Are you a Cadbury's Fruit & Nut Case?	1978
E.F. Hutton Financial Services	When E.F. Hutton talks, people listen.	1978
AT&T	Reach out and touch someone.	1979
Coca-Cola	Have a Coke and a smile.	1979
NyQuil Cold Medicine	Nighttime sniffling, sneezing, coughing, aching, stuffy head, fever, so you can rest medicine.	1979
Fiat Strada	Hand-built by robots.	1979
Van Camp Pork & Beans	If you think asparagus has a lot of iron, you don't know beans.	1979
General Electric	We bring good things to life.	1979
McDonald's	You deserve a break today.	1980
Lay's Potato Chips	Betcha can't eat just one.	1981
United States Army	Be all that you can be.	1981
Grey Poupon	Pardon me, do you have any Grey Poupon?	1981
A&W Root Beer	That frosty mug sensation.	1982
Coca-Cola	Coke is it!	1982
Federal Express	When it absolutely, positively has to be there overnight.	1982
Skittles candy	Taste the Rainbow.	1982
Dunkin' Donuts	Time to make the donuts.	1982
Pepsi-Cola	The choice of a new generation.	1984
Wendy's	Where's the beef?	1984
Folgers Coffee	The best part of waking up is Folgers in your cup.	1984
McDonald's	It's Mac Tonight.	1985
Texas Dept. of Transportation	Don't mess with Texas.	1985
Castlemaine XXX Lager	Australians wouldn't give a XXXX for anything else.	1986
Chevrolet	The Heartbeat of America.	1986
Kit Kat candy	Gimme a break.	1986
Sure antiperspirant	Raise your hand if you're Sure.	1986
Nike	Just Do It.	1987
Partnership for a Drug-Free America	This is your brain. This is your brain on drugs. Any questions?	1987
National Pork Board	Pork. The Other White Meat.	1987
Adelma Mineral Waters	Fresh Squeezed Glaciers.	1988
Visa credit card	Visa—It's everywhere you want to be.	1988

(continued)

Table 16.1. *Continued*

Advertiser	Slogan	Year
Ace Hardware	Ace is the place with the helpful hardware man.	1989
Gillette	The best a man can get.	1989
Saturn automobiles	A Different Kind of Company. A Different Kind of Car.	1989
Energizer Batteries	It keeps going . . . and going . . . and going.	1989
Chevrolet Trucks	Like a Rock.	1991
Maybelline Cosmetics	Maybe she's born with it. Maybe it's Maybelline.	1991
Beef Industry Council	Beef. It's what's for dinner.	1992
Coca-Cola	Always Coca-Cola.	1993
California Milk Processor Board	Got Milk?	1993
McDonald's	Do You Believe in Magic?	1993
Miller Beer Racing Teams	We race for beer.	1996
Apple Computer	Think Different.	1997
Mastercard credit card	There are some things money can't buy. For everything else, there's Mastercard.	1997
Taco Bell restaurants	¡Yo Quiero Taco Bell!	1997
Kay Jewelers	Every kiss begins with Kay.	1997
Ant-Stop Orthene Fire Ant Killer	1. And here's the really good part: everybody dies, even the queen! 2. Kick Fire Ant Butt!	1999
McDonald's	We love to see you smile.	2000
United Parcel Service	What Can Brown Do For You?	2002
Wendy's	It's Good to Be Square.	2005
Simply Orange juice	Simply unfooled around with.	2006
Old Spice fragrance	Smell Like a Man.	2008
Procter & Gamble	Proud Sponsor of Moms.	2010

Table 16.2. Presidential Political Slogans

Advertiser	Slogan	Year
William Henry Harrison	Tippecanoe and Tyler, too.	1840
Franklin Pierce	We Polked You in '44, We Shall Pierce You in '52.	1852
Abraham Lincoln	1. Free land, free speech and free men. 2. Vote Yourself a Farm.	1860
Abraham Lincoln	Don't change horses in midstream.	1864
Ulysses S. Grant	Vote as you shot.	1868
Franklin D. Roosevelt	In Hoover we trusted, now we are busted.	1932
Franklin D. Roosevelt	1. We millionaires want Willkie. 2. Better a Third Termer than a Third Rater.	1940
Wendell L. Willkie	1. No Third Term. 2. Roosevelt for Ex-President.	1940
Thomas E. Dewey	Dewey or don't we.	1944
Franklin D. Roosevelt	Don't swap horses midstream.	1944
Harry S. Truman	I'm just wild about Harry.	1948
Thomas E. Dewey	Dew it with Dewey.	1948
Dwight D. Eisenhower	I like Ike.	1952
John F. Kennedy	A time for greatness 1960.	1960
Richard M. Nixon	For the future.	1960
Richard M. Nixon	This time, vote like your whole world depended on it.	1968
Hubert Humphrey	Some People Talk Change, Others Cause It.	1968
Richard M. Nixon	Nixon Now.	1972
Jimmie Carter	Not just peanuts.	1976
Ronald Reagan	It's morning again in America.	1984

Advertiser	Slogan	Year
Bill Clinton	1. For People, for a Change. 2. It's the economy, stupid.	1992
George H. W. Bush	Don't Change the Team in the Middle of the Stream.	1992
Bill Clinton	Building a bridge to the twenty-first century.	1996
Bob Dole	Bob Dole. A Better Man. For a Better America.	1996
George W. Bush	Compassionate Conservatism.	2000
Al Gore	Leadership for the New Millennium.	2000
George W. Bush	A Safer World and a More Hopeful America.	2004
Barack Obama	Change we can believe in.	2008
Mitt Romney	Believe in America.	2012
Barack Obama	Forward.	2012
Donald J. Trump	Make America Great Again.	2016
Hillary Clinton	Forward Together.	2016

Once advertisers began using slogans, they were here to stay. After transportation moved off horseback, products formerly sold only in confined areas began competing with similar products in other geographic areas. Slogans helped differentiate one brand from another, making a brand more memorable, often highlighting a major selling point, or even touching consumers' hearts. Today, most wise advertisers use slogans. In the words of brand Nike, "Just Do It."

POLITICS OF PRESIDENTS

Aside from the slogans above and buttons (Chapters 4 and 7), and direct mail (Chapter 14), political advertising has a notable presence in advertising history. And the twentieth century brought new opportunities to politicians.

Radio brought presidents closer to voters. When Herbert Hoover gave his presidential nomination acceptance on radio in August 1928, it was probably the first time such large numbers of people heard a president-to-be speak, though not the first time a presidential candidate's message was broadcast over radio. The 1924 campaigns used radio to promote candidates. Republicans especially used the new technology to reach voters, even sponsoring a program: "Midnight Theatrical Revue." By the 1928 election, the parties could reach up to forty million people on election eve alone (Nicolaides 2006). By 1932, radio advertising was a fixture in American presidential campaigning.

When television was added, politics was forever changed. In 1952, Rosser Reeves produced the "Eisenhower Answers America" campaign for presidential candidate Dwight Eisenhower. This was the start. Politicians had made speeches on TV before that, but they never bought space for commercials. These were thirty-second spots, when sixty-second spots were common. Reeves' research indicated that repeated short messages were more effective than a single long message. And, in retrospect, they seemed quite effective. Eisenhower's opponent, Adlai Stevenson, did little with short TV commercials and lost in a landslide. After that, presidential candidates couldn't avoid this approach.

FIGURE 16.1. The "Daisy" commercial for LBJ ran on September 7, 1964.

The most famous political commercial in history was in 1964, though it ran only once then, September 7, on NBC. Run by Lyndon B. Johnson, it was titled "Daisy" (Figure 16.1), depicting a little girl pulling petals off a flower and counting. Her count becomes a man's voice in a countdown. The camera zooms in on her eye, and we see a nuclear explosion. We hear LBJ say, "These are the stakes . . . ," implying a vote for Barry Goldwater, his opponent, could mean nuclear holocaust. This commercial still is held up as the quintessence of negative political advertising.

In 1984, Ronald Reagan ran a reelection commercial titled "Prouder, Stronger, Better," better known as "Morning in America." The ad, by Hal Riney, was entirely positive, portraying Americans going to work and suggestive of the strong US economy, while questioning reasons to change direction. It was the economic equivalent of "Daisy."

Advertising also played an important role in the George H. W. Bush campaign of 1988. Often called the "Willie Horton ad," really two different but related ads run by Bush—"Weekend Passes" and "Revolving Door"—warned that Michael Dukakis' policies as governor showed he released criminals to commit more crimes. This message, too, implied disaster for the country if his opponent was elected. Johnson, Reagan, and Bush all won.

FIGURE 16.2. Barack Obama's 2008 poster by Shepard Fairey.

Television commercials aren't the only influential political promotions. In 2008, street artist Shepard Fairey created a poster of Barack Obama (Figure 16.2). He did it in one day, and it was so popular that many derivative copies were created. It was so iconic of that campaign the Smithsonian Institution placed the original in its National Portrait Gallery. Unfortunately, Fairey drew the poster from an Associated Press photo and was sued. In 2012, he was found guilty of destroying evidence.

Another presidential campaign's advertising practices got notice, but not because of a particular ad. In 2016, presidential candidate Donald Trump hired political data firm Cambridge Analytica (CA) to help guide his advertising. CA tapped Facebook to pull data on fifty million people. Facebook allowed use of its data for academic research but barred use for advertising purposes. CA crossed that line in service of Trump's campaign, resulting in serious privacy concerns (Granville 2018). This issue elevated public concerns over data access by advertisers, raising questions about Facebook and other companies with major consumer data access.

In 2016, about $6.3 billion was spent on US political campaigns, and closer to $10 billion in 2020. With such investment in political ads, politics will continue having major influences on this profession.

LAWYERS CAN SPEAK

In the past, some professions prohibited advertising. For some it was more peer pressure suggesting advertising was undignified. Some professions, though, used laws to enforce this ban.

Lawyers advertised before 1908. Trade tokens from 1794 prove lawyers advertised then (Figure 16.3). Abraham Lincoln and partner William Herndon ran newspaper advertisements (Figure 16.4).

In 1908, the American Bar Association enacted ethical canons declaring lawyer advertising unethical. Canon 27 stated:

FIGURE 16.3. A trade token promoting Thomas Erskine and Vicary Gibbs, lawyers, from 1794, hailing their win of a famous treason trial. This is one of the earliest lawyer ads still in existence.

FIGURE 16.4. An advertisement for Abe Lincoln and William Herndon from 1859.

The most worthy and effective advertisement possible, even for a young lawyer, and especially with his brother lawyers, is the establishment of a well-merited reputation for professional capacity and fidelity to trust. This cannot be forced. . . . [S]olicitation of business by circulars or advertisements . . . is unprofessional. . . . Indirect advertisement . . . and all other like self-laudation, defy the traditions and lower the tone of our high calling, and are intolerable. (Taggart 1977)

Failure to comply could result in censure, or disbarment, since state courts enforced this.

For nearly seven decades lawyer advertising was confined to business cards, signs labeling law offices, and listing numbers in telephone directories. This ended in 1977 when the US Supreme Court declared attorney advertising protected under the First Amendment, the year after deciding pharmacist advertising was protected.

CONSUMERS IN TRAINING

Magazines

Children have long been viewed as consumers, principally for toys. The history of toys goes back thousands of years. In the 1700s, as more specialty stores appeared in cities, toyshops were among them. One historian said, "By 1780 toyshops abounded everywhere." As greater attention was given to pre-adults, the publishing industry noticed. In 1789, *The Children's Magazine: Calculated for the Use of Families and Schools* was the first periodical specifically for children, but it lasted only four issues. More kids' magazines appeared soon, but they also experienced sudden death almost immediately.

In the late nineteenth century the children's market took off, in the wake of the Industrial Revolution and the new ideas it brought, along with the national and international sales reach it introduced. By then the children's market went beyond toys, now including bicycles, clothes, and foods preferred by kids. Recognizing this, the British Parliament passed a law in 1874 protecting children from merchants trying to seduce them into buying products and building debt.

One of the earliest *successful* kids' magazines, *The Youth's Companion*, began in 1827. By 1885, its circulation reached 385,000, and it included advertising.

Another successful children's publication, *St. Nicholas*, started in 1873. It's interesting to note that the magazine was directed at kids but the advertisements generally weren't. The January 1877 issue, for example, contains a page with four ads that clearly are for adults: Royal Baking Powder, Violet Toilet Water, Rogers' Statuary, and Brook's Spool Cotton, with just one ad for children: Eagle Soap Bubble Toy. That ad says, "Look here, Children! If you want lots of fun, get one of the new Eagle Soap Bubble Toy" (Figure 16.5).

Over time the magazine became more savvy at reaching children. In October 1900 *St. Nicholas* offered advertising competitions for children, to encourage them to study the ads in each issue. By then more than 236 US children's magazines had been published, so there was competition. In the March 1905 issue of *Profitable Advertising*, an advertising trade

FIGURE 16.5. A page from *St. Nicholas* magazine of Jaunary 1877, a children's magazine, with most ads aimed at adults.

magazine, *St. Nicholas* ran an ad offering, "Here is a fine school of young fish! Aren't they worth a little bait?" The children's market potential was fully realized.

Parents weren't entirely on board with children's ads, and ads in children's magazines seemed especially offensive. But advertisers had children in their crosshairs. One children's magazine, *Jack and Jill*, catered to parental concerns by announcing in 1938 that it would not publish ads. It avoided advertising until 1963. Some covert forms of advertising did, however, seep into the magazine, regardless of that promise (Holiday 2019).

FIGURE 16.6. The first cereal premium, from Kellogg in 1909.

Promotional Products

Children read books—or parents read to them—so the first free premium with breakfast cereal was a booklet. In 1909, Kellogg gave away *Funny Jungleland Moving-Pictures* with Toasted Corn Flakes (Figure 16.6). It was so sought after that it later was sold by mail order for ten cents. By early 1912, Kellogg had distributed 2.5 million of these, and this continued until 1932. Magazines were no longer the sole method of advertising to kids.

Schools

By the 1930s, advertisers were finding more ways to reach children. And the place they could be reached in large numbers was schools. General Motors published four books for use in science classrooms. Heinz, General Foods, American Can, and others also found their way into schools. Some sold teaching aids, but others gave materials at no cost. The 1934 Lifebuoy Wash-Up Chart, featuring Lifebuoy soap, was requested by two hundred thousand adults and nine million children (Stole 2006). Home Makers' Educational Service was a company whose sole purpose was funneling advertisers' materials to students.

Advertising through schools continued, but on a limited scale. But in 1988–1989, when US schools suffered a funding crisis, corners were cut in purchasing the latest audio-visual (A/V) equipment, like video recorders and TVs. Chris Whittle, of Whittle Communications, came to schools as a savior, introducing Channel One.

Whittle offered schools new, free A/V equipment if they'd show students a twelve-minute news show daily. His company produced the show with kid reporters and news that kids could understand. Schools would make students aware of current events while getting free equipment. The show had commercials, so schools were effectively forcing students to watch commercials (Richards, Wartella, Morton, & Thompson 1998). Some parents hated this arrangement, but without higher taxes, this was the best option for schools.

Other companies followed Whittle's lead. Star Broadcasting offered public address equipment in exchange for allowing the company to program music, news, and other content to play at lunch and between classes. Other companies offered videos, lesson plans, and handouts to teachers, showcasing their brands. Sponsorship on athletic uniforms, in gymnasiums, and more increased. Advertising began appearing on school buses. Some schools printed advertisements on students' report cards and lunch menus. These ideas weren't entirely new, since ads had appeared on some report cards and covers as early as the 1920s (Figure 16.7). Companies offered teachers and schools something they needed in exchange, from cash to volleyballs.

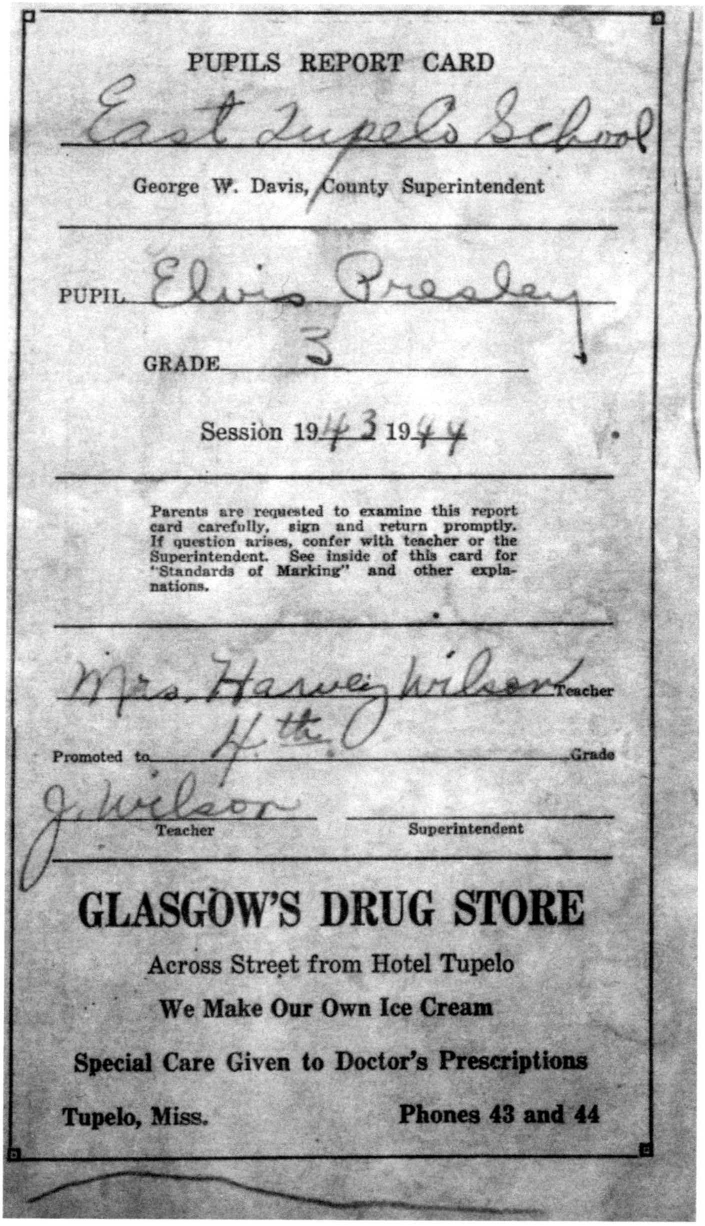

PUPILS REPORT CARD

East Tupelo School

George W. Davis, County Superintendent

PUPIL Elvis Presley

GRADE 3

Session 1943 1944

Parents are requested to examine this report card carefully, sign and return promptly. If question arises, confer with teacher or the Superintendent. See inside of this card for "Standards of Marking" and other explanations.

Mrs. Harvey Wilson Teacher

Promoted to 4th Grade

J. Wilson
Teacher Superintendent

GLASGOW'S DRUG STORE

Across Street from Hotel Tupelo

We Make Our Own Ice Cream

Special Care Given to Doctor's Prescriptions

Tupelo, Miss. Phones 43 and 44

FIGURE 16.7. Singer/actor Elvis Presley's third grade report card from 1943–1944 had advertisements on front and back.

Television and Kid-Vid

Although television began in the 1920s, commercial television wasn't until 1941, and it didn't gain traction until after the war, when television sets started selling, growing from about six thousand in existence in 1946 to twelve million five years later. One early tactic for selling televisions was broadcasting children's shows, like *Howdy Doody*, to draw kids' attention. That drew family attention. By the 1960s, there were scores of children's programs being produced, and advertisers followed.

One of the earlier shows was *Miss Frances' Ding Dong School* in 1952, for preschool children. At the program's end Miss Frances would ask children to get their parents, dismissing the kids. She'd pitch the parents for her sponsor—for example, Kix cereal (O'Barr 2008).

Another show, *Rootie Kazootie*, directly pitched products, such as a candy bar, to kids. The show's main characters did the selling. They generally had a single sponsor, limiting competition for kids' eyes and ears. But by the 1960s the sole-sponsor approach was gone, and "pods" of multiple commercials ran during scheduled program breaks.

Concerns about television's impact on children, and advertising's effects, took root quickly. In 1968, a small group of Massachusetts housewives took action to limit children's advertising. The group, led by Peggy Charren, called itself Action for Children's Television (ACT). It petitioned a local television station about a children's program, and soon was aggressively fighting to protect children. By 1970, ACT proposed guidelines to the FCC seeking to ban advertising on children's TV shows, which would cost networks at least $83.5 million (Ranly 1976). ACT kept pushing for limits, and children's television gained the nickname "kid-vid."

In 1972, the National Association of Broadcasters (NAB) agreed to reduce advertising time on children's programs from sixteen to twelve minutes. This was a modest, but important, win for ACT. The FCC adopted the NAB guidelines as a legal requirement for broadcasters in 1974, which now further limited ads on weekends to ten minutes per hour.

Simultaneously, the Council of Better Business Bureaus' National Advertising Review Council (NARC)—the principal US self-regulatory advertising mechanism—created the Children's Advertising Review Unit (CARU) to oversee ads aimed at children, funded by major children's advertisers. Also, the FTC formed the Children's Television Advertising Project (CTAP) to develop policies regarding children's advertising.

An *FTC Staff Report on Television Advertising to Children* was published in 1978, concluding "that television exerts a uniquely powerful influence over children" and recommending a ban of children's television ads. The National Science Foundation also conducted a kids' television advertising study, concluding that before enacting an advertising ban, more understanding of television's effects on kids was needed. In the end, no ban was enacted (Curran & Richards 2000).

One phenomenon that developed from radio programming, circa 1932, was that marketers recognized that programs popular with children could lead to selling program-related products. A children's radio program, *The H-Bar-O Rangers*, generated books, comics, cereal bowls, and more for Hecker H-O Cereal Company. These products advertised the show, sometimes creating extra revenue streams.

For television, the *Howdy Doody* show was first, in 1948, issuing "I'm for Howdy Doody" buttons for children who wrote letters supporting the show (Figure 16.8).[2] It was used to measure audience size. The producer ordered 10,000 buttons but eventually gave away 250,000, proving products tied in to popular TV programs had value. *Howdy Doody* then produced and sold many products, and many other programs produced tie-in products.

FIGURE 16.8. The original *Howdy Doody* television program tie-in button from 1948.

In 1983, "tie-ins" were taken to another level when the *He-Man* television show aired. *He-Man* was unique because it was developed *after* the He-Man figurine was on store shelves (Figure 16.9), the opposite of normal tie-in products (Clark 1988). In effect, the show was a thirty-minute commercial for the figurine. As new characters appeared on the show, new action figures were available for purchase in stores. It was successful. Between 1982 and 1987, seventy-three new tie-in programs were created.

This wasn't new. A *Hot Wheels* cartoon aired from 1969 to 1971, promoting Mattel's toy cars. Other toy makers complained to the FCC, which responded by requiring stations to log part of the show as advertising time (Clark 1988). But tie-ins during the 1980s were enabled by the FCC loosening broadcaster rules in an era of deregulation. The number of commercials per hour of children's programming also doubled.

By 1987, many parents, angry with the overt connection of programming and product sales, called for congressional action. When Mattel sponsored the *Captain Power and the Soldiers of the Future* (Figure 16.10), it sold a $40 plastic gun for viewers to shoot Captain Power's enemies. The gun registered a "hit" when they succeeded but was fairly worthless without the TV show, and the show wasn't as much fun without the gun. Children begged parents for the gun. Like *He-Man*, new products were introduced within the show. Both Congress and CARU got involved, and the program was pulled from broadcast with rebates offered for the gun.

FIGURE 16.9. *He-Man* toy from the mid-1980s.

A bill was submitted in Congress in 1988 to force the FCC to reinstate restrictions on children's advertising. It failed, so another was offered in 1989. Finally, in 1990, the Children's

DON'T JUST STAND THERE. FIRE BACK!

Lord Dread™ is threatening the future of the human race! Captain Power™ battles him every week on TV and he needs your help.

Grab your PowerJet XT-7™... fire invisible beams at enemy targets on his TV show... and SCORE! Or be hit! This is not a test. The TV show WILL FIRE BACK! Sure, you're good... but are you great? Get Captain Power interactive video-

tapes with three different skill levels. Practice with the PowerJet XT-7. And practice some more.

Are you going to help Captain Power and the Soldiers of the Future™? Or are you just going to stand there?

The power of the future is in your hands!

CAPTAIN POWER and associated trademarks are owned by Landmark Entertainment Group, used under license by Mattel.

Figure, jet and videotapes each sold separately. Batteries not included. ©Landmark Entertainment Group 1987. All Rights Reserved.

Watch for the futuristic military adventures of Captain Power and the Soldiers of the Future on TV this fall.

FIGURE 16.10.   An ad for *Captain Power and the Soldiers of the Future*, from 1987.

Television Act passed, giving the FCC a year to enact restrictions. In fall 1991 new limits restricted TV broadcasters to ten and a half minutes of advertising per hour during weekends and twelve minutes during weekdays. The FCC didn't put restrictions on tie-ins.

Criticisms about children's television advertising span many topics. Commercials for sweetened food products (cereal, soft drinks, candy) is one. Blurring lines between programming and advertising, especially using program characters, is another, as is use of cartoon characters to sell products. It's a long list.

Internet

The World Wide Web was invented by Tim Berners-Lee in 1989, which effectively opened the internet to commercial traffic and advertising. Almost immediately it attracted children. Dangers to innocent children were apparent. Of particular concern was that the internet was almost entirely a lone activity. No one was watching what the child faced.

The industry wanted self-regulation, and the CARU and Direct Marketing Association published guidelines for businesses, to protect kids. The FTC subsequently reviewed children's websites and found they weren't following either set of guidelines. Websites could collect private information from children, with no parental controls (Curran & Richards 2000). So in 1998 Congress passed the Children's Online Privacy Protection Act (COPPA), effective April 2000, requiring website operators to publish a privacy policy and obtain verifiable consent from parents/guardians before collecting private information. The FTC issued more specific requirements for complying with COPPA.

Other

In the late twentieth century and early twenty-first, advertisers found new ways to reach children. Some manufacturers offered collaboration with other advertisers. Barbie dolls offered Coca-Cola Barbies and NASCAR Barbies, and even Barbie holding a MasterCard credit card (Figure 16.11). Some adult magazines created kids magazines—for example, *Time for Kids*. Children were targeted with nearly the same vigor as adults.

AFRICAN AMERICANS IN MODERN ADVERTISING

In early twentieth-century America, dark-skinned people of African descent were free but overwhelmingly poor. They were not yet a major consumer force, but they did affect the marketplace. Until the 1930s, Black children were

FIGURE 16.11.   Cool Shoppin' Barbie, from 1997, makes Barbie a sales clerk behind a cash register while holding a MasterCard.

commonly labeled "pickaninnies," and a Pickaninny brand peanut butter was sold (Kern-Foxworth 1994). Blacks were depicted in ads in cleaning, cooking, train porter, or other serving roles, echoing earlier subservient stereotypes.

Publications targeting African Americans were growing, many in technical or business fields where these people were portrayed in professional roles. Black-owned companies also were appearing, including Black-owned newspapers like *Negro World*, also portraying them in positive and professional roles (Moss 2003). Recall that Jax Beer created the first African American television commercial, in 1948, with an all-Black cast having a party. It was positive imagery, clearly aimed at Black audiences. So the portrayals differed with the intended audiences.

Black-owned businesses and publications needed agencies for their distinct market. Supposedly, the first Black-owned ad agency, the Vomack Agency, began in 1940s Inwood, New York. But Alton Davis, Consuelo Young, and James D. Powell are claimed to have formed Davis, Young and Powell in 1930s Chicago (Groark 2000), and in 1943 David J. Sullivan opened the Negro Market Organization in New York City. Who was first remains subject to debate.

Opportunities for African Americans in major ad agencies were nonexistent. One executive explained, "Agencies shy away from hiring Negroes because they're afraid an account in the South might object" (Fox 1984).

But in 1952 BBDO hired Clarence Holte to oversee "Negro Markets," as the Black executive at a major ad agency. Young & Rubicam in 1955 hired Roy Eaton as the first Black "creative" at a major ad agency. And Ted Bates in 1963 hired its first full-time Black copywriter, Thomas Richardson.

Vince T. Cullers opened Vince Cullers Advertising in 1956. Some believe it was the first *full-service* Black-owned agency. He specialized in the African American market but is remembered for his agency's outstanding work. Cullers fought in World War II, becoming a combat artist. He later sought work as an advertising art director. He was offered a job based on his portfolio, but when he showed up for work and they saw he was Black, the job evaporated. He tried other Chicago agencies with no luck but freelanced and saved money to start his own agency.

The 1960s American Civil Rights Movement opened some doors for African Americans. BBDO in 1963 created the first daytime general audience television commercial with Black actors, for Wisk Laundry Detergent. In it, White and Black boys played ball together, though the White boy was the main character and the Black boy appeared briefly. It aired during the CBS show *Password*, thanks to urging by New York's Congress of Racial Equality (Samuel 2001).

After 1965 Black characters appeared on more television shows, even as stars (Moss 2003). This helped normalize use of non-White characters for advertising as well.

In 1966–1967, the New York City Commission on Human Rights examined a year of commercials from forty agencies. It found that Foote, Cone & Belding used a Black actor in 1 of 177 commercials. Six months later, the numbers jumped to 11 in 73. The commission also found, in August 1967, that only 3.5 percent of employees in those forty agencies were Black, and most were low-level employees (Fox 1984).

Jock Elliott, chair of Ogilvy & Mather US, called for New York agencies by close of 1972 to have at least 13 percent minority professional employment. *Advertising Age* magazine in 1992 published "The Ad Industry's 'Dirty Little Secret,'" declaring that only 5.2 percent of US ad agency employees were African American, and just 3 percent of managers in advertising, marketing, and public relations were Black. Fewer than 1 percent of creative staff in the top twenty-five agencies were Black. The US Census in 2000 found five hundred thousand people working in advertising and related fields. About 6 percent were African American. The 2010 Census found that of all *managerial* positions in advertising and promotions, Blacks filled only 0.8 percent. Public relations was better, at a whopping 4.4 percent. It seems the industry still had a dirty little secret.

Another contributor to African Americans in advertising, Barbara Juanita Gardner Proctor created the Proctor and Gardner Advertising agency in 1970, becoming the first Black woman to own an ad agency. She had been in the ad business only six years before that but won twenty-one awards in three of those years. She was named "Chicago Advertising Woman of the Year" for 1974. Before that she worked for VeeJay Records and wrote freelance articles for *Downbeat* magazine. She's credited with bringing the Beatles to the United States in 1962. Ronald Reagan mentioned her in his 1984 State of the Union address.

In 1971, Thomas J. Burrell formed Burrell McBain with partner Emmett McBain. McBain left just three years later. Burrell won major accounts like Philip Morris, Coca-Cola, McDonald's, and Crest Toothpaste. His agency became a leader for African American–targeted ads. He famously declared, "Black people are not dark skinned white people."

By the 1980s, Black celebrities were a major presence. Michael Jackson was a top music performer, and his *Thriller* album became a major cultural force. Actor Bill Cosby had the top-rated situation comedy on television, *The Cosby Show*. And Michael Jordan was the biggest name in basketball. This wedged the door open further for Black actors in advertising (Kern-Foxworth 1994).

Public relations, though as a profession started later than advertising, was ahead in terms of racial integration. Joseph Varney Baker founded the first Black-owned US PR firm in 1934, nearly a decade before advertising. He was the first African American accredited by the Public Relations Society of America (PRSA). In 1958, he became the first Black president of the PRSA Philadelphia Chapter, being elected by a unanimous vote.

Barbara C. Harris worked for Baker. She was the first Black woman to manage PR for major corporate accounts, and in 1958 she took over as agency president. Like Baker, she became president of the PRSA Philadelphia Chapter in 1973. She also made another mark on history in 1988, becoming the first woman Anglican bishop.

African Americans' progress was in some ways staggering, but in other ways minimal. By the 1960s, they were appearing in advertising, but negative depictions simply became more subtle. For example, some products targeted at them promised to whiten their complexion, as if whiteness should be an aspirational goal (Figure 16.12). Others offered to straighten their hair (Figure 16.13).

Lever Brothers made a splash in 1963. At a time of social unrest, the company concluded it had done a poor job of representing minorities. A cover story in *Advertising Age*

FIGURE 16.12.   This 1963 ad offers a "skin tone cream" that promises "lighter, lovelier skin beauty."

FIGURE 16.13.   Also from 1963 is this hair straightener advertisement.

reported, "Lever Bros., one of the country's biggest advertisers, has asked all its agencies to come up with suggestions for more effective use of Negroes and members of other minority groups in the company's advertising" (Christopher 1963). This could not be ignored, since the previous year the company had spent $42 million on TV time alone. This was a turning point for advertising.

Even in the twenty-first century, depictions of African Americans attracted controversy. In 2013, Cheerios breakfast cereal ran a television commercial about a little girl with a White mother and a Black father. Comments on the commercial's YouTube debut had to be disabled because so many racist remarks were posted (Stump 2013). In 2017, Kellogg's Corn Pops cereal's box was condemned as racist. It depicted many corn pop characters playing and having fun, with a single character, appearing to be a janitor, cleaning up after the others. Every figure was light in color, except the janitor (Figure 16.14). Kellogg immediately went into redesign mode.

hey @KelloggsUS why is literally the only brown corn pop on the whole cereal box the janitor? this is teaching kids racism.

11:02 AM · Oct 24, 2017 · Twitter for iPhone

FIGURE 16.14.   This tweet is typical of the criticisms received by Kellogg's Corn Pops and shows a portion of the cereal box that created the controversy.

Also in 2017, Nivea skincare products, promoting deodorant, created a campaign called "White Is Purity." One ad showed a woman in a white outfit, suggesting this deodorant wouldn't stain her clothes. It didn't go over well (Wang 2017), becoming the official deodorant of White supremacists. The same year Dove, another skincare company, placed an ad on Facebook depicting a Black woman removing her T-shirt to reveal a White woman beneath it, implying Dove's product caused the change. This ad, too, was a fail (Astor 2017). In both cases, the problem should've been caught before publication, since it was as clear as black and white.

An immense gulf continued to exist between White and Black Americans. This is true whether talking about their portrayals in ads, or their ad industry jobs. As of 2019, African Americans comprised 13.4 percent of the US population but still were underrepresented.

In 2020, after multiple incidents of Black citizens killed by police, a "Black Lives Matter" (BLM) movement gained momentum. It unearthed latent racism in advertising and other business practices.

One consequence of BLM was a "15 Percent Pledge," where merchants committed 15 percent of shelf space to products from Black-owned businesses. Sephora was one of the first store chains taking the pledge (Marheshwari 2020). And the Aunt Jemima brand, after 131 years, announced it would change its name because of racial stereotyping on which it was based (Kesslen 2020). Other brands with similar backstories, including Uncle Ben's rice and Cream of Wheat breakfast porridge, announced they, too, would review their brand's image. But not everyone, including descendants of the original Aunt Jemima model, supported the move to cancel the brand's history.

Johnson & Johnson announced it would stop sales of skin-whitening products (Cramer 2020). Other companies announced they were pulling ads off social media websites like Facebook, because the sites didn't prohibit "hate speech" aimed at African Americans and others (Mansoor 2020). The BLM movement was being aided by advertising, while having clear effects on advertising. But this population has not been alone in its relationship with advertising.

YO QUIERO ADVERTISING

Like Blacks, Latinos have a history of mistreatment in America. This probably began when Spain discovered the Americas, since much of America first became part of the Spanish Empire. Multiple wars were fought over Spanish rule between 1808 and 1833. And the Mexican-American War came in 1846, followed by the Spanish-American War of 1898. Some of those hostilities, and a sense of US superiority over Latin America, continued to simmer.

A 1910 movie called *The Thread of Destiny* portrayed Mexicans as "banditos," even using the term "greaser." Stereotypes had left the starting gate. Male Hispanics were often depicted as untrustworthy, lazy, or stupid, and the women as hyper-sexualized *senioritas*. More positive depictions usually dealt with music and dancing.

In advertising, Latinos were notable for their near absence until the mid-twentieth century. One of the earliest Latino advertising spokes characters was the Chiquita Banana in 1944. She was half-woman, half-banana, and danced and sang the "Chiquita Banana" jingle with a Spanish accent. She became fully human in 1987.

The National Federation of Coffee Growers of Columbia in 1958 introduced Juan Valdez, created by Bill Bernbach. Valdez appeared as a humble coffee grower, usually with his mule. This was a relatively positive image. But in 2009 a cartoonist offended the Federation when a cartoon said, "Y'know, there's a big crime syndicate in Colombia. So when they say there's a little bit of Juan Valdez in every can, maybe they're not kidding." The stereotype here wasn't created by the advertiser.

In 1967, a TV commercial was created for Frito-Lay Corporation, starring a cartoon character called the "Frito Bandito." He was short and chubby; wore a handlebar-type mustache, a huge sombrero, and pistols; and spoke with a Spanish accent.

A simultaneous magazine campaign featured a "Wanted" poster of the Frito Bandito (Figure 16.15). It declared, "He loves cronchy Fritos corn chips so much he'll stop at nothing to get yours. What's more, he's cunning, clever—and sneaky!" Mexican Americans weren't thrilled, calling for a ban, arguing the ads were racist. They felt Mexicans were being pictured as sneaky thieves.

William Raspberry, in the *Washington Post*, stated, "The point is that the ethnic stereotypes, bad enough no matter who they depict, are intolerable when they pick on people who are daily victims of American racism. And if the point had escaped those who created the Frito Bandito ads, the complaints from Mexican Americans have removed whatever innocence there may have been." The campaign lasted until 1970.

FIGURE 16.15.   A Latino
advertising character, the "Frito
Bandito," circa 1967.

In 1988, the Taco Bell restaurant chain introduced its "Run for the Border" campaign. Implying that going to Taco Bell was a metaphorical trip to Mexico, the Latino community disliked this allusion. The theme, some felt, conjured images of drug running, or escaping the law, thereby suggesting Mexico was full of illegals.

And in 1997 Taco Bell went to the dogs. A chihuahua named Dinky was tapped as the brand's spokes-character. All it said was "¡Yo Quiero Taco Bell!" (translated: "I want Taco Bell!"). Again, Mexican Americans called for a ban (Reyes 1998). But the dog's refrain became part of popular culture, used by seemingly everyone. It ended in 2000.

The Mac Haik Ford Lincoln Mercury dealership outside Austin, Texas, sent an email ad in 2007 that wasn't well received. On the ad's top was "Tired of Wet Backs????" Although air-conditioned seats were mentioned in the ad, the term "wetbacks" had been an ethnic slur aimed at Latinos for decades.

And in Holt, Michigan, in 1994, the WJXQ-FM radio station ran a Cinco de Mayo tongue-in-cheek contest promising listeners their "own personal Mexican." Here's the script:

Some are giving trips to Mexico City but, we are bringing Mexico to you, that's right, we're giving away Mexicans, real live Mexicans. Ay Carramba. We'll be smuggling illegal aliens across the border in the wheel-well of a station van then we'll give one to you. Imagine, your own personal Mexican, they'll wash your car, clean your house, pick your crops, anything you want because if they don't, you'll have them deported. Adios Amigos. Be the fifth caller when you hear this sound (mooing cow, sound effect), and win a Mexican. Members of this station and their families are not eligible to own Mexicans—bathing and delousing of Mexicans is winners responsibility. Station assumes no liability for infectious diseases carried by Mexicans. Celebrate Cinco de Mayo in your own home everyday, with your very own Mexican. Keep listening to win. The breakfast club.

Apparently it was an ad for *The Breakfast Club* radio show. But it reveals the bias and stereotypes the Latino community faced.

It's not surprising Hispanics encountered barriers to creating a presence in advertising. The first US radio station licensed to a Latino was in 1946, and the first Hispanic television station was in 1954 in San Juan, Puerto Rico (WKAQ-TV). A second opened in 1955, in Los Angeles (KCOR-TV), though it was of the weaker UHF variety. These stations catered to a Latino audience, with ads using Latino actors. This created a demand for advertisers and agencies covering that market.

The first US Latino agency wasn't until 1962. Called Spanish Advertising and Marketing Services (SAMS), Luis Diaz-Albertini founded it. He started his career at McCann Erickson, Havana, in 1948. After his years at SAMS, he went on to head Uniworld Hispanic in 1982.

Coincidentally, the first person to win a Clio award for a Hispanic-owned agency, in 1987, was Sara Sunshine, a Cuban immigrant who had been head copywriter and art director of SAMS since its start. DeGarmo Advertising took over SAMS around 1976, acquired by D'Arcy-MacManus & Masius in 1980.

The Conill agency was founded by Alicia and Rafael Conill in 1968 to serve the large Puerto Rican population in Miami. Both had worked at Mestre Conill Publicidad in Cuba before moving to the United States. In 1987, their agency was bought by Saatchi & Saatchi.

Leaving Cuba during the Castro revolution, Tere A. Zubizarreta entered advertising as a secretary at McCann/Marshalk Advertising. But in 1976 she formed a Miami agency: Zubi Advertising Services. Her agency had hundreds of millions of dollars in billings, with over one hundred employees. Zubizarreta was inducted into the Advertising Hall of Fame in 2012.

Other agencies formed after that, but one especially worth mentioning was formed by Lionel Sosa, Ernest Bromley, and Al Aguilar, in 1981: Sosa, Bromley, Aguilar & Associates. Located in San Antonio, Texas, this agency became a major player in Latino markets nationwide, eventually becoming America's largest Hispanic agency. In 2005, Sosa was named "one of the 25 most influential Hispanics in America."

Alex Lopez Negrete and his wife, Cathy, in 1985 formed Lopez Negrete Communications in Houston. It became the largest Hispanic-owned full-service advertising agency, with 250-plus employees.

In 1996, a number of Hispanic agencies established an Association of Hispanic Advertising Agencies (AHAA). Forty-one agencies were represented at its first meeting, with Hector Orci, head of La Agencia de Orci & Asociados (Los Angeles), serving as AHAA's founding president. Orci also was inducted into the Se Habla Español Hall of Fame, of the *Hispanic Business Magazine*, alongside his wife, Norma. In 2018, the AHAA, to signal that it was more than just Hispanic languages, re-branded itself as the Culture Marketing Council: The Voice of Hispanic Marketing.

By then the "Hispanic market" was seen as "Hispanic markets," plural, representing multiple cultures. In 1990, Hispanics/Latinos made up just under 9 percent of the US population. By 2019, it was 18.3 percent, and the Census Bureau projected that by 2060 they would reach 28.6 percent. This is a diverse and growing population.

THE RAINBOW CONNECTION

Other populations experiencing rapid, late integration into advertising were the gay and transgender (LGBTQ+) consumers. For millennia there was no acknowledgment that a gay or "queer" market existed. Putting our finger on when it started to change is impossible.

A major reason is because ads including queer appeals generally were "gay vague," meaning subject to multiple interpretations. Some advertisers recognized this was a viable, even valuable, market, but in early times advertisers feared backlash from customers who were homosexual aversive.

FIGURE 16.16.   A Rutland Stove Lining trade card, circa 1880–1900.

Some early depictions in ads perhaps didn't need to be so vague, because most of society pretended LGBTQ+ citizens didn't exist. Figure 16.16 is a trade card from around 1880 to 1900, which today seems clearly lesbian-oriented, or perhaps these were assumed to be simply affectionate children.

During World War II, ads for Cannon Towels depicted soldiers in towels (or less) romping together (Figure 16.17). These almost certainly were of gay interest, but it was impossible to tell the advertiser's purpose. For those not in the military, the assumption likely was that soldiers, with no women around, had no need for modesty. Most examples of this sort tend to be more clearly gay interest than gay targeting, so they might be unintentional.

The first gay magazine was *Der Eigene*, in 1892. We don't know when the first ad sold for this or later gay periodicals, but the earliest ads in gay publications were for gay organizations and an occasional gay-owned business. The first mainstream brand in a gay publication was Absolut vodka in 1981, when an ad appeared in *The Advocate*, a leading gay magazine. Since gay bars were places for LGBTQ+ people to openly gather, alcohol brands were naturals for this market.

Other brands followed over the next decade. By the early 1990s, clothiers ventured into the closet. Calvin Klein, Banana Republic, and the Gap offered ads sending "gay friendly" signals, and the Netherlands targeted gay travelers. Tobacco and music companies also targeted them (Swisher 1993). Of course, ads could target this audience without gay themes, just by running an ad in media they used.

Television commercials with openly gay characters took longer. The Ikea brand gets credit for running the first such commercial, in 1994. Ikea's stores ended up experiencing boycotts and bomb threats as a result (O'Neill 2014). IKEA's commercial depicted a gay couple as having a more highly developed sense of style, helping cement a stereotype that could appeal to the gay community, but also to many straight consumers (Dahl 2014).

Some "underground" gay brands developed. Subaru became the unofficial "official car of lesbians." Through research, it recognized that single women were buying the car and then figured out they were lesbians. This began without Subaru's push, but it seemed like an opportunity. As the company tested ads, it was clear that more overt pitches were not liked by gays as well as "winks and nudges." So in the 1990s the brand began portraying women shoppers with license plates like "Xena LVR," referring to the *Xena: Warrior Princess* television show, or "P-TOWN," implying Provincetown, Massachusetts, a well-recognized gay vacation spot. It also included taglines with double meanings, such as "Get Out. And Stay

Illustration as described by the Army Medico

Did you ever have to put a net across your bathtub — and share it with a crocodile? Sometimes, according to this medical corps captain, you have to do that for a bath — in the South Pacific Islands. Since "crocks" have finicky palates, with a marked partiality for legs, the kids put two nets across a stream and weight them down. Thereafter the "crocks" are on the outside — looking in!

You might not enjoy the bathing facilities of our boys in the service, but you'd heartily approve of their towels. For in many of their service packs are those same husky, durable Cannons you're so proud to use in your own home. . . . You know how welcome a bath and a good towel are after a trying day. You can imagine how welcome to our men after long stints of marching or combat!

They need them more than we do. That's why there are fewer towels for us. That's why, too, it's important that we take good care of those we have.

Millions of Cannon Towels
are now going to the Armed Forces. So you may find a smaller selection in the stores — fewer styles and a limited variety of colors. But the durable Cannon quality, the hardy quality that will see you through, remains the same. When the war is over, Cannon will again present the newest styles in the most charming colors.

FOR VICTORY—BUY U. S. WAR BONDS!

HOW TO MAKE YOUR TOWELS
LAST LONGER AND STAY
"DURABLE FOR THE DURATION"

Launder before they become too soiled
Fluff-dry terry towels — never iron
If loops are snagged — cut off, never pull
Mend selvage and other breaks immediately
Buy good-quality towels — always the best economy

TRADE MARK
CANNON

Cannon Towels

CANNON SHEETS   CANNON HOSIERY

XR

FIGURE 16.17.   A 1943 advertisement by Cannon Towels.

Out" (Mayyasi & Priceonomics 2016). Without making obvious gay appeals, this car company staked its position as car-of-choice for lesbians.

There were many events affecting the move toward normalization. Of course LGBTQ+ discrimination has always existed, and laws were written to advance that discrimination. Only in the late twentieth century were some of those laws overturned, protecting these citizens.

Kathy Kozachenko, a lesbian, was the first openly LGBTQ+ person to win elected office, in 1974, when she became a city council member in Ann Arbor, Michigan. And the first television show with an openly gay character was *Soap* in 1977, bringing a gay person into people's houses every week. Artist Gilbert Baker first used a rainbow flag, the "Pride Flag," as a symbol of the gay community in 1978. A National March on Washington for Lesbian and Gay Rights was held in 1979, placing those suppressed rights in the public eye.

Billy Jean King, a professional tennis player, was publicly outed as a lesbian in 1981. It caused her to lose all of her advertising endorsements in twenty-four hours—about $2 million per year.

Then acquired immunodeficiency syndrome (AIDS) took root, initially dubbed "the gay disease," with religious fundamentalists suggesting it was God's punishment for gay lifestyles. As the disease spread to heterosexuals, the injustice of placing blame on gays became even more apparent.

Elisabeth Glaser, wife of actor Paul Michael Glaser, contracted HIV in 1981 through a blood transfusion, unknowingly passing it to their children. Ryan White was thirteen when diagnosed in 1984, also getting it through contaminated blood. He was kicked out of school, from fear the disease was contagious. These victims weren't gay, but HIV and AIDS still were perceived as coming from the gay community.

In 1985, actor Rock Hudson was the first really famous person to acknowledge contracting the disease. This drove home to heterosexuals that AIDS could affect their lives. As the AIDS crisis grew, a Second National March on Washington for Lesbian and Gay Rights was held in 1987.

Then, in 1991, basketball star Magic Johnson—a popular, athletic heterosexual—announced he had HIV, which could lead to AIDS, as he retired from professional sports. Johnson became an advocate for AIDS prevention. His condition made it clear the LGBTQ+ community had been treated unfairly.

Another well-loved celebrity had an impact when in 1997 she "came out" as lesbian: Ellen DeGeneres. About forty-two million viewers saw it live. Her action was condemned by some. DeGeneres was a talented comedian but was blackballed from TV for a few years. She recovered, eventually becoming a leading US talk show host, starting in 2003. Millions of people grew to love and accept her, so advertisers followed.

Advertisers weren't reacting to social change but merely recognized gay and lesbian society had more disposable income because they generally had no kids, so no college funds, no diapers, no other expenses associated with parenthood. Their discretionary funds made them a desirable target. So by 2000 even the conservative *Wall Street Journal* ran an ad for the Gay Financial Network, targeting the gay market.

There were many court cases in this story, but the most notable was *U.S. v. Windsor* (2013), overturning the Defense of Marriage Act, which prohibited federal recognition of same-sex marriages. It protected gay marriage, guaranteeing legal rights to gay families.

By 2019, television's Hallmark Channel was lambasted on social media and boycotted, not for running a gay ad, but for pulling ads that contained same-sex couples (Duffy 2019). That same year Kellogg produced a special LGBTQ+-themed cereal called All Together (Figure 16.18). This idea, for a cereal eaten by children, would have been unthinkable a few years earlier.

By the 2020 Super Bowl, this market was front and center. At least six commercials in that prime-time program had known gay actors, including Ellen DeGeneres (Baume 2020). Rather than fear of association, advertisers now welcomed LGBTQ+ celebrities as brand ambassadors during the most expensive advertising venue on earth!

FIGURE 16.18. Kellogg's All Together cereal from 2019.

A simple study by Sender (2017) counted the gay-focused articles in advertising trade publications over a few decades. Results appear in Figure 16.19. The first article was in 1975; the numbers exploded in the 1990s, and then dropped off. The 2010s only included the first

seven years or so, but professional interest in this topic clearly peaked in the 1990s. The declining numbers likely reflect some normalization of the topic, making it no longer newsworthy.

Unlike other groups discussed here, agencies run by or specializing in LBGTQ+ are nearly impossible to track. Unlike those other groups, this one usually couldn't be identified on sight. And this community already had a large presence in advertising, likely reaching back to the nineteenth

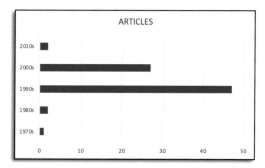

FIGURE 16.19. Number of articles about the gay market appearing in advertising trade publications, by decade.

century. But as advertisers began wanting to reach them, agencies figured it out, and some gained a reputation for understanding this community.

One New York agency with such a reputation was Mulryan/Nash, founded in 1983. By the twenty-first century, it was considered a specialist in this market. But several agencies now openly claimed special knowledge in this area. Large agencies also were helping clients reach LGBTQ+ consumers, but the Ogilvy & Mather Group UK created a special unit for this in 2015: Ogilvy Pride. As a part of Ogilvy's network, this created an LGBTQ+ agency with instant worldwide presence. The gay community was now an influential demographic market for advertising.

ADVERTISING, LIKE A GIRL

Women made strides in the 1800s, both in society and in advertising (Chapter 8). They obtained the right to vote in Canada in 1917, in England and Germany in 1918, and in the United States in 1920. Some countries were much later. But as consumers (and in other ways) women ruled. In the late 1800s they made 90 percent of purchases (Fox 1984). Advertisers couldn't ignore them. Newspapers and magazines focused tremendous efforts on appealing to women, for that very reason (Presbrey 1929).

Agencies opened more hiring opportunities for women, thinking women might understand other women. J. Walter Thompson (JWT) was the first major agency to embrace them in any meaningful way (Editors of Advertising Age 1976). Recall Helen Lansdowne, whom Stanley Resor brought to JWT in 1908 as the first female advertising copywriter at a major agency. Ruth Waldo was hired in 1915; by 1922 she headed JWT's London office copy department, and in 1930 she supervised copy for the entire multinational agency. In 1944, she became vice president. Waldo and Lansdowne opened doors, both within JWT and across the industry. The executive dining room at JWT was men-only until Lansdowne (Resor) and Waldo were permitted to bring in women executives *once a week*, with men being barred from entry that day (Fox 1984). Women weren't allowed in the executive washroom, though.

Erma Perham Proetz, from a small agency in St. Louis, Gardner Advertising, also was a copywriter. She is remembered for her work for PET Evaporated Milk, winning the prestigious Harvard Advertising Awards for distinguished individual advertisements in 1924 and 1925, and Harvard's even more prestigious Edward W. Bok award in 1927. She became executive vice president of Gardner Advertising, and in 1935 she was named among the top sixteen outstanding women in America by *Fortune* magazine. Posthumously, in 1952, she was the first woman inducted into the Advertising Hall of Fame.

By the 1920s, women found placement in agencies beyond copywriting. They became secretaries, media space buyers, account executives, and even production managers (Nevett 1982). In 1926, Nedda McGrath became the first woman art director employed by a major ad agency, Blackman Advertising. But a 1931 survey of ad personnel found that 97 percent of those responding were men (Pope 1983).

Women began to organize. The Association of Advertising Women was formed in London in 1910, the Women's Publicity Club of Boston in 1911, and the League of Advertising Women of New York in 1912. Clubs arose in St. Louis (1916), Chicago (1917), and London (1923). Note that the majority of this was during the suffrage movement's most active years, leading to their voting rights.

World War II was a contributor to women's advancement in advertising, and as household income generators. As during World War I, women filled jobs vacated by men. For the United States this war was twice as long, so women settled into those jobs. Artist J. Howard Miller used a woman model when he producing a poster headed "We Can Do It" in 1943 (Figure 16.20) to motivate Westinghouse factory workers. That image survived, and because the name "Rosie the Riveter" was used in a song during the war, as well as by Norman Rockwell for a *Saturday Evening Post* cover, Miller's poster became Rosie. It was iconic of women's abilities, as realized during the war.

Women were, indeed, empowered, and many found they enjoyed the independence of being wage earners. But sexist advertisements continued. A 1951 Van Heusen necktie ad depicted a woman on her knees serving a man breakfast in bed with the headline "show her it's a man's world" (Figure 16.21). Volkswagen ran an ad with a damaged car and the heading "Sooner or later, your wife will drive home one of the best reasons for owning a Volkswagen."

In the profession women still lagged far behind men, but there were moves toward inclusion. This was evident even in novels targeted at teenage girls. *Patsy Breaks into Advertising* (1939) and *Patsy Succeeds in Advertising* (1944), by Evalyn Grumbine, and *Nathalie Enters Advertising* (1939), by Dorothy Dwight Hutchison, are examples. The Patsy books were part of the Dodd Mead Career Books collection, aimed at promoting careers in advertising for women. The second Patsy book's foreword says:

> Advertising is rapidly becoming a woman's world. Accelerated by the pressures of a wartime economy, a trend that began shortly after the first World War, is bringing women into positions of influence and importance in the advertising field. (Grumbine 1944)

The Nathalie book is dedicated "To Helen Lansdowne Resor who 'practically invented' women in advertising" (Hutchison 1939).

In 1960, McCann Erickson "seemed the most enlightened place for women," but only six out of one hundred vice presidents were women. Leo Burnett had forty-five vice presidents, and zero were women (Fox 1984).

FIGURE 16.20. J. Howard Miller's 1943 poster that later came to be known as "Rosie the Riveter."

FIGURE 16.21.
1951 Van Heusen ad.

One woman making a mark before, during, and after the war was Bernice Fitz-Gibbon. One path into the ad industry was through department stores and specialty stores. In 1931, over 44 percent of such stores in New York, and 27 percent elsewhere, had women as ad managers (Fox 1984). Fitz-Gibbon worked for the R. H. Macy department store's ad department for a dozen years beginning in the 1920s, moved to Wanamaker's department store as publicity director, and in 1940 went to Gimbel Brothers department store. In 1954, she opened an agency, Bernice Fitz-Gibbon, Inc. Across those years she made quite a reputation, revolutionizing retailing and, as a copywriter, creating memorable ads. The slogan "Nobody, but nobody, undersells Gimbels" was a cornerstone of its advertising for years. But perhaps the most influential aspect of her career was the number of women she taught to write copy.

Overlapping with Fitz-Gibbon was Phyllis Robinson. She had gone to work for Grey Advertising in 1947 as, yes, another copywriter, the year Bill Bernbach was elevated to creative

You don't have to be Jewish

to love Levy's
real Jewish Rye

FIGURE 16.22.   Levy's ad from a campaign that began in 1961.

director at Grey. When Bernbach left with James Doyle, joining Max Dane, to start Doyle Dane Bernbach (DDB), they took Robinson and art director Bob Gage with them. Bernbach is credited with planting seeds for the creative revolution, but Robinson was a starter plant he carried from Grey. She became VP in 1956 and created her own amazing campaigns. Levy's Rye Bread's "You don't have to be Jewish" is one (Figure 16.22), though this copy also is credited to Judy Protas, another female DDB copywriter (see Elliott 2011 and Fox 2014, both from the *New York Times*). Either way, it was created by a talented adwoman.

As both Robinson and Fitz-Gibbon were winding down in the early 1960s, Mary Wells (Lawrence) was gaining fame. It turns out Wells had been trained by Phyllis Robinson. Like Fitz-Gibbon, Wells cut her teeth in department stores. But she soon went into agencies as a copywriter and in 1966 founded the Wells Rich Green agency, serving as president and then CEO. Her fame came from numerous famous campaigns for Braniff, Alka-Seltzer, Midas, Bic, and more.

Shirley Polykoff, the queen of the double entendre, also deserves mention. Again, she was a talented copywriter. Her ad writing career began in the 1920s as a teenager at *Harper's Bazaar* magazine. She went on to work for Foote, Cone & Belding (FCB), and in 1955 it won the Clairol account, putting Polykoff on it. Her fame began with a slogan: "Does she . . . or doesn't she?" The double meaning became a part of popular culture, cementing the Clairol name in women's minds. Another catchy line she wrote: "Is it true blondes have more fun?" In 1968, she was elevated to FCB's Creative Board chairman and vice president. In 1973, she left FCB and formed an agency.

Charlotte Beers—*not* a copywriter—distinguished herself by becoming the first female senior vice president at J. Walter Thompson, in 1973, where Ruth Waldo was VP nearly three decades earlier. Beers served as CEO of Tatham-Laird & Kudner in 1982, and then CEO and chairman of Ogilvy & Mather Worldwide from 1992 to 1997. In 1999, she was recruited back to JWT as CEO. She left two years later, becoming undersecretary for public diplomacy and public affairs in the US State Department from 2001 to 2003. She was the first woman to chair the American Association of Advertising Agencies, in 1988.

Behind Beers came Shelly Lazarus. She joined Ogilvy & Mather in 1971, becoming president of Ogilvy & Mather Direct in 1981, and president of O&M New York in 1991. In 1994, she became president of Ogilvy's North American operations, and then chairman and CEO of Ogilvy & Mather Worldwide when Beers left. O&M became the first major advertising agency to have two successive female CEOs. Lazarus left the CEO position in 2008, and resigned the chairman role in 2012.

By the twenty-first century, the ad industry's glass ceiling had shattered. The same might be said of women consumers. There still remained sexist appeals, of course, but more campaigns were showing respect for women. In 2004, Dove's "Campaign for Real Beauty" abandoned the perfect, retouched models used in most ads depicting or targeted at women, instead using a range of women who proudly displayed imperfections they might have (e.g., heavier weight, birthmarks, etc.). It was about embracing those things making each woman unique. The campaign was criticized, but it won closets full of awards and was hailed as promoting mental health in women by not holding up unrealistic images that provoke insecurities (Neff 2014).

Another campaign was "#LikeAGirl," for Always sanitary pads, in 2015. It took a disparaging phrase, "like a girl," and asked, "What does it mean to do things like a girl?" Adult women and men acted out what they thought when hearing phrases like "run like a girl." The results didn't make girls look good. When young children were asked the same thing, their responses were quite the opposite. It then asked, "When did doing something 'like a girl' become an insult?" Again, it was about how society undermines women's confidence. This campaign affected the social meaning of that phrase.

Unlike in the past, advertising finally promoted strong and positive images of women. And all the women mentioned above taught this industry the meaning of "make advertising like a girl."

THAT'S ENTERTAINMENT!

Advertising's impact on culture goes beyond specific groups. Advertising touches everyone, and is both a reflection and a change agent of society. That influence is found in entertainment of all types.

Charles Dickens, for one, mentioned advertisements in his writing. I already mentioned *The Critic*, a play from 1779, though it was more about public relations than advertising per se. By the 1900s, advertising was in every aspect of entertainment.

A play opening on Broadway in 1914 was *It Pays to Advertise*, by Roi Cooper Megrue. The plot wasn't complimentary to this industry, but it was popular and became a silent film in

1919. A version with sound appeared in 1931. These were the first and second commercial movies about the ad industry. The female lead in 1931 was played by Carole Lombard, who soon was the highest-paid actor in Hollywood. She married another star who also became huge, Clark Gable (see below).

The play was revived as late as 2002 and 2009. Just four years after the original, in 1918, another play appeared—*Nothing But Lies*, by Aaron Hoffman, which "depicted admen as liars and crooks who sold junk with the help of a corrupt politician" (Fox 1984). It wasn't as popular as Megrue's, but other plays appeared with advertising as a central character.

FIGURE 16.23. A major motion picture about the ad business, from 1947.

Those plays came from books. As the movie industry developed, motion pictures likewise sprang from books. *The Hucksters*, by Frederic Wakeman, became a play in 1947, starring, coincidentally, Clark Gable (Figure 16.23). It was about an ad agency and its biggest client, and became a box office hit. Like the earlier plays, the film wasn't especially flattering to the industry, but it wasn't as critical as the book from which it came. As a side note, it's generally believed the character portraying the agency head was fashioned after a real-life agency head: Emerson Foote of the Foote, Cone & Belding agency.

Advertising played big and small roles in films. The year after *The Hucksters*, a movie starring famed actor Cary Grant was *Mr. Blandings Builds His Dream House*. The plot was about an advertising executive's disastrous and expensive effort to restore a house. Interestingly, Grant again played an ad executive in 1959 in Alfred Hitchcock's *North by Northwest*. Once again his profession was more backdrop than centerpiece of the story. But in one line Grant's character says, "In the world of advertising there's no such thing as a lie. There's only the expedient exaggeration" (Tungate 2007). Sadly, again, it was a slap at advertising.

These weren't the only major films portraying the advertising industry. In 1957's *Will Success Spoil Rock Hunter?*, Tony Randall played an advertising copywriter. *Lover Come Back*, with Rock Hudson and Doris Day, in 1961, was about an ad executive needing to come up with a product *after* he made it popular.

In 1990 came *Crazy People*, starring Dudley Moore and Daryl Hannah, two A-list actors. In the story, it's believed an ad exec has cracked from pressure, given his crazy ads, so he's sent to a mental health facility. But the ads are incredibly effective, and soon he's recruiting other residents of the facility to help develop unusual advertising solutions. The crazy people, it turns out, are exceptionally good advertising creatives. Duh!

Years later, in 2000, Mel Gibson starred as an ad exec in *What Women Want*. He discovers he can read women's minds, which allows him to develop ads addressing precisely what women want.

Another novel worth mentioning is Dorothy L. Sayers' *Murder Must Advertise* in 1933, about a murder in an ad agency. Sayers herself was an ad copywriter. In the novel she quotes a slogan she actually developed for a client. The book never became a movie, but it was adapted to television in 1973 for a miniseries.

Books involving advertising weren't all novels. In 1957, Vance Packard published *The Hidden Persauders*. He argued the ad industry was using lessons from psychology to manipulate shoppers without their knowing it. Conspiracy theories sell well, and it was a best seller that still was reprinted in the twenty-first century.

The year 1958 brought another best seller about advertising: Martin Mayer's *Madison Avenue, U.S.A.* Mayer's book pointed out that Madison Avenue, New York, agencies handled half of all the advertising money in the United States. This was a nonfiction explanation of the ad industry.

Wilson Bryan Key told readers in 1973 that the ad industry uses subliminal appeals to manipulate buyers, in *Subliminal Seduction*. Another story of conspiracy in the ad world, it was another best seller.

As television became the medium of choice, the ad industry was part of its stories, too. A notable one was *Bewitched* (1964–1972). In it a human man, Darrin, is married to a witch, Samantha, and a recurring part of the show is Darrin's job as an adman.

From 1980 to 1982 was *Bosom Buddies*, about two young New York City admen posing as women to obtain cheap rent. Then there was *Thirtysomething* (1987–1991), about two men who open their own ad agency.

One series about the advertising industry was a drama set in the 1960s, called *Mad Men*, an abbreviation of "Madison Avenue Men" (2007–2015). It was a soap opera–type story about workers in a New York advertising agency. The male lead was Don Draper, played by Jon Hamm. The name was pulled from famed adman Draper Daniels. This show developed a cult-like following. A 2009 Nielsen list of TV shows that were time-shifted (recorded to watch later) placed *Mad Men* second among all shows. The March 26–April 2 issue of *Newsweek* magazine put the show on its cover. Don Draper became a household name.

There are other forms of entertainment. For example, the card game *Cards Against Humanity* became popular, with "expansion packs" available to purchase, increasing the options in the game. An entrepreneur, Craig Small, devised his own expansion pack: *Advertising Against Humanity* (Figure 16.24). Since the ad industry seems almost universally disliked, this made sense.

FIGURE 16.24.   A *Cards Against Humanity* game expansion pack from 2014.

That wasn't the first advertising-related game. Aside from computer games, mentioned in Chapter 15, there were board games. *Advert*easing: *The Game of Slogans, Commercials and Jingles* came in 1989, as did a children's version, *Advert*easing *Junior* (Figure 16.25). *Advert*easing *II* followed in 1991, and *Commercial Breaks* in 1992. *Ad Liners*, all

FIGURE 16.25. *Adver*teasing *Junior*, from 1989, a game for children.

about slogans, also was introduced in 1989. *Ad Mania: The Game of Advertising Trivia!* arrived in 1997. *AdVersity: The Game of Crazy Mixed-Up Ads* was spawned in 2003. Let's face it, it would never have been possible to sell any of these if advertising weren't a large piece of contemporary culture.

I once tried making a list of all movies and television shows with advertising characters or plots. The list became so long I finally quit. So I've only provided a few big ones. There likewise are more books than I could list. But clearly advertising is a pervasive cultural force.

Aside from ad themes in entertainment, advertising is what you might call a "stand-alone" cultural experience. It has been displayed and appreciated as art. In 1900, the International Advertisers' Exhibition, a gallery of ad posters, was at the Crystal Palace in Hyde Park, London. A reviewer commented, "Amongst other things it proved that advertising, so far from being a necessary evil, may be a source of very genuine delight" (Hiatt 1900). Another showing of posters before that was at Niagra Hall in London, but that one apparently was less impressive.

Another exhibition was in the Netherlands in 1909. And in 1912 one exhibition organized by *Advertising World* magazine was at Horticultural Hall in Westminster, and another was

FIGURE 16.26. The first musical focused on advertising, in 2019, was performed only once.

in Munich, though its focus was on advertising stamps (*reklame-marken*) as art. Another International Advertising Exhibition was at White City, London, in 1920. The Art Director's Club of New York began sponsoring an Annual Exhibition of Advertising and Editorial Art in 1921.

A truly unique cultural experience was the world's first musical about advertising. It was called *Skittles Commercial: The Broadway Musical*, in 2019 (Figure 16.26), and was created by the Skittles candy's parent company, Mars, Inc., and the DDB ad agency. The lead was a well-known actor, Michael C. Hall. It was performed just once, at the Town Hall on New York's 43rd Street, on Super Bowl Sunday, before the game. It was only forty-five minutes long and wasn't televised. The intent was to stand out from brands pouring millions of dollars into Super Bowl ads by doing, essentially, counterprogramming. Proceeds went to charity. One song performed was "Advertising Ruins Everything." The show was declared one of the most successful ad campaigns associated with that year's Super Bowl (Diaz 2019).

CONSUMER DIRECTORS

While advertising definitely affects society, society also changes advertising. As styles change, ads must adapt. Popular songs frequently end up in ads. Even typographic fonts change, and ads reflect that. But the twenty-first century introduced a new impact on advertising: user-generated content (UGC).

Video once was a pricey venture for individuals. The cameras were bulky, not very high quality, and they required film. Sound on consumer-grade cameras was suboptimal. But digital video brought costs down and quality up, at affordable costs. And then there was YouTube, beginning in 2005, offering a venue for personal videos. The advertising world changed.

In fall 2006, Frito-Lay announced its "Crash the Super Bowl" contest, challenging consumers to create thirty-second commercials for Doritos tortilla chips, promising the best would be broadcast during the 2007 Super Bowl. It was a risky strategy, but 1,065 consumer-created ads were submitted. This was, in effect, a form of crowdsourcing. One ad, "Live the Flavor," was selected as the first user-generated commercial aired during the Super Bowl. Amazingly, of all ads during that game, it was ranked #4 on *USA Today*'s Ad Meter poll. A second one, "Check Out Girl," was run later in the game. This tactic was viewed by some as the future of the industry (O'Hern 2013).

Doritos continued sponsoring this contest in future years, and over the next decade it ran twenty-one user-created ads. In both 2009 and 2012, the winning ads ranked #1 on the Ad Meter poll. The filmmakers were awarded $1 million for their contribution. But on a show where the cost to run an ad was $3 million and $3.8 million, respectively, the award wasn't excessive, especially when it succeeded. In 2012, Chevy Camaro also had a UGC ad in the game (Krashinsky 2012). A 2013 Doritos ad cost $300 to make, and ranked #4 on the Ad Meter (Schultz 2016).

And Doritos didn't give up the idea. It ended its "Crash the Super Bowl" contest in 2016 but began a "Legion of the Bold" venture, inviting consumers to submit content for other company promotions (Schultz 2016). The success of these nonprofessional, very low-cost commercials sparked the imagination of other advertisers. By 2009, advertisers like Wilkinson Sword, McDonald's, MasterCard, Westpac, T-Mobile, and Sony Ericsson had joined the UGC fad.

Doritos wasn't the first with user-generated content. In 2006, Chevrolet created a website displaying a Tahoe SUV commercial, letting users write their own text. That effort, though, wasn't so successful. Some consumers wrote text criticizing the vehicle (Krashinsky 2012). It made clear the need for advertisers to approve the work before anyone sees it, as was done with agencies. But even that wasn't the earliest UGC advertising.

Recall that in 1932—about seventy-five years before Doritos—Burma-Shave created a contest where consumers wrote serial-sign jingles, and received fifty-thousand-plus entries (Chapter 13). This was like the Doritos contest, but with wooden signs. Oh, and the prize was $100 instead of $1 million. Even so, the first UGC likely was a friend or neighbor making a sign for someone's stand or booth in an ancient marketplace.

By 2020, the idea of user-generated advertising was no longer unique, but its popularity had lost that initial sparkle. Consumers as advertising creators no longer were seen as the industry's future, except in the areas of social media and online product reviews. Pro-brand consumer reviews and fan pages were now embraced as another form of UGC, and one that was here to stay.

ADVERTISING LIBERATES ANOTHER NATION . . . BRIEFLY

A famous name in the twentieth century, mentioned earlier, was Howard Gossage. There is a story about a Gossage exploit that is worth recording as a notable episode in advertising history. Some stories just need to be told.

There's a small Caribbean island called Anguilla. It's not quite four miles wide and ten miles long. On a good day it might be thirty-five square miles total. In 1967, its population was just over six thousand.

It was a British territory, and Britain on February 27, 1967, merged it with some nearby islands, creating an "independent federation." The problem was that Anguillans were now being governed by a dictator from a neighboring island, and they weren't happy. In fact, they'd been unhappy with leadership for some time. It wasn't British rule that they hated, but rather the control by another island. On May 29, they revolted. On July 11, they adopted a declaration of independence. So what does this have to do with advertising?

Scott Newhall was editor of the *San Francisco Chronicle* and owner/editor of the *Newhall Signal* newspaper. Scott was a character known for using various escapades to promote newspapers, being in constant competition with William Randolph Hearst's *Examiner*. Scott learned of Anguilla's problem and witnessed the Anguillan revolution, so he plotted to be a part of it. Recall the counterstamped coins used for advertising just prior to the Civil War?

Well, Newhall decided to reapply that technique, counterstamping coins to commemorate Anguilla's situation. He counterstamped 11,600 silver dollar–sized coins from Peru, Mexico, Panama, and Yemen, in the *Chronicle* building's basement. They were silver, because silver was being pulled out of circulation. Hence the "Anguilla Liberty Dollar" was born (Figure 16.27). The idea was to sell the dollars, raising money for the new country. Only two thousand to three thousand Liberty coins ended up in circulation, and Newhall got stuck with suitcases full of defaced coins. He claimed he sold them for enough to cover his costs. But the Anguillans took the idea and issued a series of commemorative coins from 1968 to 1970.

FIGURE 16.27. The Anguilla Liberty Dollar, created from a 1953 Mexican silver five-peso coin.

Newhall also got Howard Gossage involved. This was quintessential Gossage. The two of them set out to help liberate Anguilla from neighboring islands and get it back under direct British rule. They designed a new Anguillan flag, with mermaids against a field of blue. They brought the provisional Anguillan government to San Francisco, borrowed the mayor's car, and put those flags on it. They drove around holding press conferences. The *Chronicle*, of course, covered it with a series of stories.

Gossage's team created an ad that ran in the *New York Times*, as a response to an editorial that appeared in the *Times*. Gossage called it "The Anguilla White Paper" (Figure 16.28). The headline read, "Is it 'silly' that Anguilla does not want to become a nation of bus boys?"

(The Anguilla White Paper)

Is it "silly" that Anguilla does not want to become a nation of bus boys?

THE NEW YORK TIMES, in its editorial of August 7, described the Republic of Anguilla's desperate efforts to remain independent as "touching and silly."

With a pat on the head, the Times advised us to return to the awkward Federation of St. Kitts-Nevis-Anguilla, itself newly formed, from which we had withdrawn shortly after its arbitrary inception on February 27.

We say "arbitrary" because, as you can see from the map, Anguilla does not, even geographically, have much in common with the other two islands. St. Kitts and Nevis are right next door to one another and share a common one-crop, sugar cane, economy dominated by huge, foreign land holdings. Anguilla's land is owned by the islanders themselves; each family has its own little plot and lives off it. Why, then, did Britain lump us in with the other two islands? Because we were their last odd-parcel of real estate in the Caribbean; it's probably that simple. (The Times disregarded these basics, if it ever knew them.)

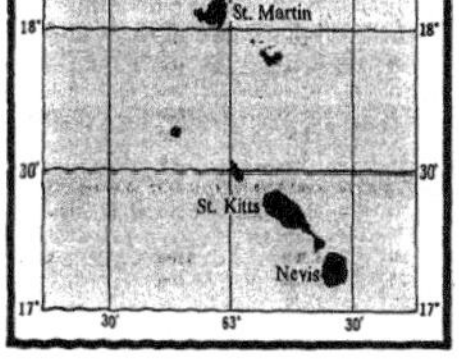

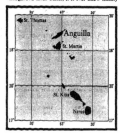

The Times then dismissed our aspirations to independence by pointing out that, "Anguilla has an area of only 35 square miles and a population of 6000. Its people subsist on agriculture and fishing and *lack such modern amenities as telephones.*" (Italics ours.)

This is a terrible indictment in New York eyes, we suppose, but do you know what one Anguillian does when he wants to telephone another Anguillian? He walks up the road and talks to him. Primitive as this arrangement is, it is hardly grounds for justifying the Times' conclusion that Anguilla cannot hope to go it alone.

The fact is that we *have* gone it alone economically, socially, and politically for centuries. The British have neither bothered us, nor bothered about us. We have never been exploited, possibly because there has been nothing much to exploit.

UGLY DUCKLING

To understand this, you must know that Anguilla is referred to in guidebooks as "the ugly duckling of the Caribbean." Objectively that may be so, though to us Anguilla is beautiful because it is our homeland.

There is not enough water on the island for major crop cultivation, nor is it a "tropical paradise"; it is not the prettiest island in the West Indies. The highest point on Anguilla is but 200-and-some-odd feet. There used to be a lot of trees we are told, but these were burned for charcoal long ago. So we must bring in wood to build Anguilla's famous knife-like schooners and sloops.

OLDER THAN U.S.

Anguilla has been left to herself, with generations of the same people, since the 17th century. We are, therefore, a very old nation by any standards. It can even be argued that, as a distinct nation with a stable people, we are older than the United States.

Anguilla is only "new" in the sense that the New York Times had never heard of us before, nor have we had to assert ourselves recently. The last time we were threatened was 250 years ago when the French attempted an invasion with 600 men. They were thrown back by 60 of us, men whose names nearly all Anguillians still bear in direct descent.

There is also this, and it is all-important: Anguilla has proved its self-reliance. It can feed itself, and does. How else do you suppose it could have withstood a blockade—the impounding of our funds, and even our mail—plus the threat of siege by the St. Kitts Government for more than three months now?

"ERRATIC PROCEDURE"

Back to the Times editorial, there is more than a suggestion that Anguillians, though enthusiastic for freedom, are also undisciplined, unrealistic, and given to "erratic procedure." In a word: natives.

We would point out that, whatever the British failed to do on Anguilla, they did give us 300 years of grounding in democratic institutions; and they did establish schools: Anguilla's literacy rate is over 70%, by far the highest in these islands

Which brings us to the Times's unfounded assertion that "there is no truly representative government to speak for the island." That is quite untrue. Anguilla is ruled by a duly elected Council. The premise for this statement was the supposition that Mr. Peter Adams, who has served as a member of the Council, "had a mandate to negotiate for Anguilla" with the British. This is not true either.

Mr. Adams was in the United States seeking help and recognition for us when he, already at the point of exhaustion, enplaned in the middle of the night for Barbados to meet with Great Britain's Minister for Commonwealth Affairs, Lord Shepherd. He flew there from San Francisco arriving after 15 hours of hard travel, with no luggage—only the clothes on his back.

UNREMITTING PRESSURE

It is impossible to know the pressures that were subsequently exerted on this man whom we know to be ordinarily unswerving and extraordinarily dedicated. But after a week, virtually incommunicado toward the end, he submitted to the following demand (in writing) by Lord Shepherd:

> "If you now reject the settlement which we regard as being very reasonable, I must say, in all seriousness, that the British Government cannot continue to countenance the present situation in Anguilla, which constitutes a threat to the stability of the whole Caribbean.
>
> "I shall therefore have to consult with the other Caribbean Governments as to the steps which shall have to be taken to deal with this serious situation."

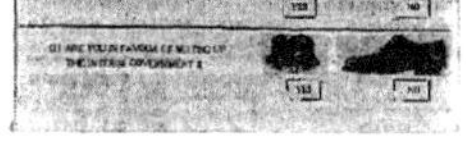

This "serious situation" was simply that Anguilla, after withdrawing from the embryo Federation in May, had, on July 11, held a plebiscite by secret ballot (above) to confirm its independence beyond question. To insure complete accuracy and believability to the world, this election was supervised, and the ballot count confirmed, by outsiders; correspondents, chiefly.

The returns were embarrassingly lopsided: 1813 For independence, 5 Against. It is therefore utterly impossible that Mr. Adams carried with him what the Times calls "a mandate to negotiate"; i.e., to give up.

BRITISH THREAT NOT EMPTY

Why did he succumb? Well, the British threat of force has seldom been an empty one. Also recall that the St. Kitts government's Prime Minister Bradshaw had, in addition to blocking our mail and our money, threatened—and continues to threaten—our small island with armed force; with no success thus far, though it has meant manning our beaches all night every night for months.

Meanwhile, a British frigate with a force of Royal Marines aboard, lies off our shores. One imagines that the least civil disturbance on Anguilla would serve as a pretext for landing these imposing troops. There is small likelihood of an *internally* induced incident of any kind.

To resume, the Barbados Agreement was immediately declared invalid by the Island Council and by the people themselves in mass meeting. A provisional head of state, Mr. Ronald Webster, was immediately acclaimed pending regular election.

One last insight into why the unfortunate and unauthorized Barbados Agreement calling for Anguilla's return to the St. Kitts-Nevis Federation was signed at all: We do not mean to suggest that melancholy measures were applied to gain assent, but the might and authority of Great Britain—especially when embodied in one who is a high British official *and* a Lord—is not easily ignored after centuries of respect.

WHY WANT US NOW?

It occurs to us that one question may remain in American minds. If Anguilla is as we say it is, why would St. Kitts-Nevis, or the British for that matter, wish to bother with us now? Well, we *are* somewhat of an affront to what they would regard as fitting and proper; and we are a maddening challenge to Prime Minister Bradshaw's authority over his own troubled domain. The fact that unreachable Anguilla is not troubled by St. Kitts's inherited economic and political ills likely does nothing to allay his discontent; that is only human nature.

But there is another reason, quite new, for finding Anguilla desirable. Anguilla, though unassuming, does have an extremely pleasant climate, cool and dry...and magnificent, untouched beaches. We are "developable."

We could settle our financial distress today were we willing to sign any of the numerous offers we have received from land and resort developers. One company dangled $1,000,000 cash for gambling concessions. We turned it down flatly, despite the anguished realization that this amount of money would underwrite our development for years.

EVEN ONE GREAT HOTEL

Why did we turn these offers down? Because even one magnificent, Hiltonesque hotel on an island of 6000 people, *4000 of whom are youngsters,* would turn us into a nation of bus boys, waiters, and servants.

There is nothing wrong with service or hard physical work, you understand, but a whole *nation* of servants is unthinkable. In five years—or perhaps less—Anguillians would become as sullen, malcontent, and rootless as the rest of the Caribbean; or Harlem, as far as that goes.

Though we haven't mentioned it before, we are a nation of what you would call "Negroes." To us, we are simply Anguillians, because nobody has ever brought the subject up, and that's the way we intend to keep it. But you do see what we mean, don't you? Even one fine hotel and we would become "natives."

HOW LONG CAN WE RESIST?

That brings us up to now. As of this writing the British have not landed troops nor are we given to despair. We still hope for recognition from the United States, from the United Nations, from Great Britain, or from anyone. But if no one chooses to recognize us we shall continue, as we always have, to go it alone.

How long can we hold out? Indefinitely—even without recognition—but we can use temporary financial aid in the meantime.

Our needs are ridiculously small by any standards but our own. For example: our entire island budget—including schools (for those 4000 children)—comes to only $25,000 per month. All our island funds to the amount of $250,000 U.S. are impounded in St. Kitts, yet we have managed.

We have eased the currency shortage somewhat by the issuance of emergency coinage. These "Anguilla Liberty Dollars" are overstamped South American silver dollars, for the most part (see next column).

These coins are being redeemed by friends of Anguilla abroad, and we are putting into circulation the money they fetch.

...TO SURVIVE NOW

It is a little embarrassing for our government to ask you for financial aid on the basis of the unique collateral we have presented here. However, we have no doubt that we will survive this crisis—and do it without selling ourselves out—if we have enough money to survive *now.* We must seek assistance from individuals.

To show our gratitude, we should like to give you something in return, if only to prove that Anguilla is really here and thinking of you even as you think of us.

First off (to disprove the Times's allegation that we don't really have a "representative government"), we had better send you an autographed picture of the Island Council, a facsimile of the original handwritten version of our national anthem, and a small Anguillian flag (a replica of the one now flying over the airstrip). If you wish to help us with as much as $25.00, we'll also send you one of the Anguilla Liberty Dollars.

Those sending $100 or more will become Honorary Citizens of Anguilla. They will receive a document in the form of an Anguillian passport, identical to that which we are issuing to Anguillians, except that it will have an Anguillian Dollar inlaid as shown in the picture. While Americans should not expect to use this passport for foreign travel, it will be good for entering Anguilla. In fact, *only* holders of this passport will be able to visit Anguilla as guests. Why?

In the first place, we have only 30 guest rooms on the entire island at the moment, with no plans to expand. We would not think it either good or polite that so many visitors should be on the island at once that they couldn't at least have lunch with the President. (Besides, since we have such a small population, any more than a very few guests would automatically become "tourists"; we wouldn't want that, and neither would you.)

> HOW TO SEND CONTRIBUTIONS TO ANGUILLA
>
> *Since we are cut off from direct postal service—and to give you assurance that your money is safe—an account is being established at the Chase Manhattan Bank on nearby St. Thomas, U.S. Virgin Islands. So please make out your check to : THE ANGUILLA TRUST FUND. And address the letter to: The Anguilla Trust Fund, Chase Manhattan Bank, St. Thomas, U.S. Virgin Islands.*

Thank you for your kind attention during all these troubled weeks, and for hearing us out now, and for your generosity. We won't forget it, or you.

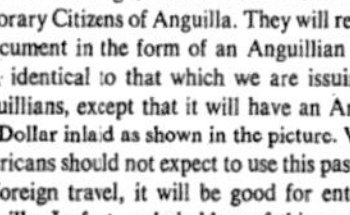

Ronald Webster
Chairman, The Anguilla Island Council

FIGURE 16.28. Gossage's "Anguilla White Paper," published August 14, 1967.

It protested real estate developers putting up hotels, forcing citizens into lives of cleaning rooms and busing tables. The ad ran on August 14, 1967, seeking money to support this new nation and offering "honorary citizenship" for $100, implying a cheap way to obtain dual citizenship. At that time the ad noted there were just thirty guest rooms on the island. It received significant international attention, including attracting developers, giving them the idea to build hotels there.

On February 6, 1969, the "Republic of Anguilla" issued a constitution. Newhall and Gossage's efforts had borne fruit, and Anguilla was a true nation—for about six weeks.

On March 18, 1969, the British mustered a strike force of paratroopers and London bobbies, invading the island in a predawn landing the world press derided as the "Bay of Piglets." They reestablished control of the island, which is what Anguillans actually wanted. But the invasion created a PR nightmare for the United Kingdom, since the British justified it with claims about gangster elements in Anguilla that were pure bunkum.

Bruce Bendinger, a devotee of Gossage, explains that when the Anguillan revolutionary leader, Ronald Webster, was taken on his US press tour, he stayed in a nice hotel. Per Bendinger, "He discovered room service lamb chops. He ordered them and ordered them and ordered them. As he wiped his greasy fingers, he observed that maybe it wouldn't be so bad to have some hotels and bus boys, and the idea of an independent Anguilla left with the room service dishes." By 2016, the Anguilla Four Seasons Resort alone had 181 guest accommodations. As of 2019, there were at least forty-seven hotels on that tiny island, and the population now was more than fourteen thousand.

Advertising (and public relations) played a vital role in Anguilla's becoming a nation, and also in its returning to the status of British colony, which ultimately was the goal of its people. On top of that, advertising helps keep those hotels in business, driving the island's economy.

A CAUSE OF ADVERTISING

There is one topic not yet addressed, and in reality the history of it is anything but clear. However, its relevance and importance to understanding advertising's impact on our culture is tremendous. I'm talking about cause-related advertising. It also is known as issue advertising, and overlaps greatly with nonprofit advertising. Basically this is advertising not for commercial profit, but for some (at least in someone's mind) greater social purpose.

Causes have been promoted forever, and commercial advertisers have supported advertising for causes across much of that. Ads raising money for the fight against cancer or multiple sclerosis or poverty all are cause ads. Some causes are political issues, too, such as ads directed at gaining public support for gun control laws.

The suffrage movement, around 1900, had women carrying signs calling for the right to vote. They were advertising for a cause, and one about which they desperately cared. The time donated by agencies for the Committee on Public Information in World War I and the War Advertising Council in World War II went toward causes like conservation, supporting soldiers, and working hard to supply troops (Chapter 9). I mentioned the LiveStrong promotional rubber bracelet (Chapter 13). That was for a charity, so it was cause advertising. The Anguilla advertising discussed above really was a cause for Gossage and Newhall. They weren't in it to make money. A 2013 ad by Volkswagen, promoting the "don't text and drive" cause, can be seen in Figure 16.29. The point is that this has a history too intertwined with other advertising to trace, but it certainly is ever present in our culture.

CONCLUSION

Advertising has been both cause and consequence of social change. Never was it more obvious than since the start of the twentieth century. That, of course, is both a positive and a negative. It is a powerful tool of change, and like any tool, it can be misused. And at times it has been.

FIGURE 16.29. Text: I'll be there in a wh (autofill: while, wheelchair). Cause: Please don't text and drive. Sponsor: Volkswagen.

17

2020 and Beyond

Quarantine has me realizing why my dog gets so excited about something moving outside and going for walks and car rides. I just barked at a squirrel.

—*Anonymous, 2020*

The year 2020 completes this story. It turns out, however, that year was like no other. The first couple of months seemed quite normal, other than it being a US election year. Enter COVID-19, the pandemic. Suddenly, nearly everyone was ordered to stay at home for months, wear masks, and stay at least six feet from anything resembling a human.

The so-called Spanish Flu of 1918–1920 killed 50-plus million (675,000 in the United States). That pandemic had enormous tragic impact, but its effects on advertising are difficult to tease apart from the effects of World War I. While some ads at that time mentioned the flu, most advertising seems to have ignored it. The COVID-19 story was different. There is no doubt this virus was a watershed event for this industry.

This time a significant portion of commercial advertising put the virus front and center (Figures 17.1 and 17.2), and many ads from government and nonprofit agencies encouraged use of masks, social distancing, staying home, or proper methods of hand washing. Others thanked nurses, doctors, and other "front line" workers and "first responders" who put themselves at great risk (Figure 17.3).

FIGURE 17.1. Social distancing was a recurring theme during the pandemic.

FIGURE 17.2.   Coke's version of a social distancing ad.

As of this writing, the virus continues to plague every corner of the planet, so its final impacts on advertising are a matter of speculation. Therefore, it seemed wise to ask someone who has observed the industry from the inside, over many decades, to reflect on this last chapter of our 300,000-year journey.

Keith Reinhard, a giant of twentieth-century advertising, retired as chairman of DDB Worldwide in 2006. But he has continued living up to his role as chairman emeritus, never entirely retired. Over the years he has proved himself a visionary with a firm grasp on the field's direction, so I asked whether he would contribute insights regarding what this virus meant for advertising. He graciously provided the following perspective on what it meant in 2020, and what he sees coming around the corner.

FIGURE 17.3.   This type of "thank you" billboard became commonplace during the pandemic.

OBSERVATIONS ABOUT ADVERTISING AMID A PANDEMIC

Keith Reinhard, June 2020

Advertising executives described the 2020 coronavirus pandemic as a "seismic shock," unlike anything they'd ever seen. COVID-19 had an immediate impact on the industry as clients slashed budgets, which in turn forced agencies to dramatically reduce staff along with eliminating all nonessential costs like award ceremonies and industry conferences. In just one example of serious ad spending cuts, pre-pandemic projections included $373 million budgeted for sports advertising, opportunities that were wiped out in one fell swoop by the sudden cancellation of all sporting events.

It's always been true that advertising is among the first things cut by companies looking to preserve cash in times of crisis. But the COVID-19 crisis was more serious, and spending cuts were widespread across all media. In the March–April period of 2020, ad spending on television was off by 41 percent, digital was down 38 percent, and print media saw a 43 percent reduction. So the coronavirus pandemic had an immediate shrinking effect on the advertising industry, in terms of both dollars spent and numbers of people employed.

It also changed how advertising was made, as ad makers were now forced to work from home, meeting virtually via Zoom and similar platforms to devise strategies, hatch ideas, and execute them remotely. It's not that advertising people were unfamiliar with working from remote locations, but being forced to work exclusively from home eliminated the important collaboration of creative minds huddling together to spark ideas spontaneously, bounce them off each other, and then collectively build on them. Advertising has always been a team sport, and great ideas are best developed when a talented group of like-minded problem solvers can work in close proximity to each other.

In addition, the pandemic changed the look of television advertising. Given travel bans and cost cutting, the "Hollywood" era of advertising ended abruptly. No more production trips with teams traveling to distant locations to spend days filming a TV commercial. Instead, homebound viewers watched look-alike television commercials that used stock footage and flashed photos of satisfied consumers or heroic first responders. Advertisers tried to quickly adjust their messages to the pandemic concerns of consumers. Social media was flooded with offers of fashionable face masks. Tylenol, heavily prescribed for reducing fever, which is one of the symptoms of COVID-19, simply urged viewers to stay safe, stay well, and stay home. Papa John's promised that no one would touch your pizza, and car insurance companies offered to reduce premiums for policyholders whose cars were quarantined along with them.

While overall spending was down, some product categories (such as food delivery services) dramatically increased their advertising to an audience forced to stay home. Language courses like Duolingo and Babbel upped their ad spending 148 percent and 50 percent, respectively, during the height of the pandemic. At the same time, brands with no direct relation to the pandemic aired hollow claims that "We're all in this together." But many of those advertisers wanted assurance from media suppliers that their messages would be suitably distanced from any grim reports about the virus.

The virus caused us to reevaluate our values and priorities. Among other things, the accumulation of stuff became less important. It will be interesting to see whether the long-predicted age of postmaterialism might actually materialize. Daily reports of deaths from the pandemic called attention to systemic inequities in our society. People of color were disproportionately affected by COVID-19, and hundreds of marginalized kids who were now expected to be schooled from home had no computers or tablets or even access to the internet, a cruel result of the continuing rich-poor tech divide.

The trend for advertisers to be held accountable for the stands they take or don't take on social issues was accelerated by the pandemic. Even before COVID-19, a 2018 survey by Sprout Social reported that two-thirds of consumers believe it's important for brands to take public stands on social and political issues. And a 2017 Edelman study found that, even then, more than half of the respondents believed that brands have more power to solve social issues than the government.

A company's position on social issues is important not only for consumers but also for its workforce. In one pre-pandemic survey of employees from various companies, 92 percent said that "it's very important that my CEO speak out on one or more of these issues: training for jobs of the future, ethical use of tech, automation's impact on jobs, income inequality, diversity, climate change, or immigration." But when a company takes a stand, it must be sure to align its actions with its statements. And care must be taken to avoid costly missteps like the 2017 Kendall Jenner ad that tried to co-opt the imagery of protest movements to sell Pepsi.

Post-COVID, the advertising industry will restructure and reform itself as it always has in response to changing influences and client needs. Some agencies will disappear; new ones claiming a revolutionary model will form and declare that all legacy agencies are dinosaurs. In turn, strong legacy agencies will find ways to become nimbler and may even find ways to regain access to the C-suite in client companies. Some advertisers will bring more work in-house, others will ask for bespoke agencies, smart clients will still prefer a strong partnership with an agency of choice, and others will choose to work with a roster of agencies. As to which approach is best, the metric should not be which is more "efficient" (aka cheaper), but rather which structure and arrangement results in the most effective work.

Some agencies have declared that they will continue to ask their staffers to work from home exclusively, claiming this is the way of the future. Most agencies, however, will understand that collaboration and personal interaction are essential to the creative process, and, as they work to creatively reconfigure their offices to allow for social distancing, it will be interesting to see how they revise, or even reverse, the decades-old trend toward ever more open spaces. A physical place—how it looks and feels—is a key element of an agency's culture, which, in turn, is key to an agency's success.

Digital advertising will increase, as will ads on social media and podcasts, but television will continue to be the best way to reach a mass audience. For a while the commercials will be limited to stock footage, scampering type, still photos, computer-created graphics, and animation. At some point, instead of generating more of those forgettable flashing images, an advertiser and its agency will break the pattern with a return to storytelling and start a whole "new" trend. On digital platforms, influencers will continue to recommend products, just as celebrities have always been paid to sell things.

Branded content, which has been around since the beginning of advertising (think about the medicine shows of the nineteenth century), will continue, and sports sponsorship will return big-time when the pandemic lets the games begin. So-called native advertising will go the way of the old advertorials, because any attempt to deceive consumers breaches the integrity of the advertised brand, as well as that of the media vehicle that agrees to disguise an ad as news or editorial content.

The creative and media functions should never have been separated, and the pre-pandemic trend to reintegrate the two will continue, perhaps accelerated by a desire for simplification of the whole process. Advertisers will decide that just because there are myriad channels available through which to reach consumers, they don't need to be on all of them all the time. And maybe that will finally lead to the needed tearing down of silos of "digital" and "traditional."

Amid all the changes, "the fundamental things apply as time goes by," to quote the famous song from the classic movie *Casablanca*. A kiss is still a kiss, a sigh is still a sigh, and human nature doesn't change over time. Our obsessive drives to survive, to succeed, to belong and to be loved, to take care of our own—those passions have been heightened by the pandemic, and advertisers and their agencies who are sensitive to those basic needs will create brands to meet them, an act that will always require advertising.

Creativity will remain the most powerful force in business, and instead of changing campaigns with every change of a CMO, advertisers will rediscover the importance of consistently projecting a clear sense of purpose and doing so with a distinctive brand voice. Along the way, we'll learn the difference between an algorithm and a true insight into human nature and the important difference between big data and a big idea.

Finally, given the more socially conscious post-pandemic consumers, those who work in advertising will have a special responsibility. As Bill Bernbach famously said, "All of us who professionally use the mass media are the shapers of society. We can vulgarize that society. We can brutalize it. Or we can help lift it onto a higher level."

I have no doubt that advertising will rise to meet that challenge.

Conclusion

Advertising is as far-reaching a discipline as just about any, aside from perhaps politics. It reaches into every corner of our lives, and looking back through its history shows it was a big part of our parents' lives, our grandparents' lives, and so on. At the same time, there is little doubt that in the most recent century it has found ways to flow into nooks and crannies never before saturated with it. And it is pretty evident, too, that what once was simple enough for anyone to do has grown far more complex. Advertising still can be done by a vendor at a farmers' market, but what never would have been imagined before the late twentieth century is the possibility of that same vendor, working out of his/her garage, conducting intercontinental commerce over a worldwide network. Nor could computer database management or programmatic media buying have been imagined at that time. The world and the world of advertising are forever changed. And those changes will only continue. This history is a backdrop to what is coming.

Covering this much history means, above all, that I have favored breadth over depth. Entire books have been written about topics I cover in a page or less. That is simply a choice I had to make. But the thing I most regret omitting is people. There have been so many people in this industry who, frankly, deserve more discussion than I gave them, and so many more whom I didn't even mention. It is people who make history, so I am barely mentioning the makers. I hope their works will intrigue you enough to dig deeper into the people behind those works.

I also barely skimmed the surface of the context of each topic. For example, there's an intriguing little book by a former ad exec that opens with a description of his office at Boase Massimi Pollitt (BMP) in 1974:

> Photocopiers and pocket calculators were still recent inventions. We didn't, of course, have mobile phones, personal computers, email, the web. TV commercials, which had only been in colour for a couple of years, were shot on 35 mm stock which had to be viewed on the massive double head projector in the room called The Cinema. Artwork was pasted up in the studio with a lot of cow gum. Presentations required several hundredweight of 20×30 polyboard which had to be sent out to a studio forty-eight hours ahead of the meeting. (Feldwick 2015)

This beautifully sketches a wealth of detail about agency life at that time. Any ad practitioner looking at this today can immediately spot so many ways life differed back then, and it adds color to our understanding of the efforts behind the advertisements produced at that time. And there is so much more, even from that single year, that could be added to our vision of the time. Then multiply that by the thousands of years described in this book. (I just didn't think my publisher would give me that much leeway in the page count for this book.)

In addition, topics were omitted, either intentionally or through oversight. I would imagine you might find something missing that you hoped would be here. While I wanted to cover absolutely every conceivable topic from the field's history, lines had to be drawn somewhere. You might not agree with where I drew them, but my decisions were driven in large part—surprise, surprise—by what interested me. And really, I chose to cover several issues because they were ignored by other historical accounts. The truth is, though, if I had the time and the pages to write more, I could and would.

I promise this: If enough people read this book that I'm able to write an update, I will try to include more. Hopefully, by then some readers will have sent me some suggestions of what they found lacking, helping me to fill some holes. I did purposely choose to write this topic by topic, rather than as a single continuous story, so that it would be easily extensible.

My purpose in writing this was five-fold. First, most histories put too little attention on what happened pre-1800. They tend to act as though advertising really was invented in the nineteenth century, and I wanted you to know more about what happened before that. Second, those accounts focused so much on newspaper, radio, and television that they tended to ignore so many other media used through the ages. I especially wanted my students to know there was more to the story. Third, they tended to be written in a form that made it hard to look up specific topics, or to follow the development of a specific topic, such as children's advertising. That meant the topic-focused approach was needed. Fourth, historical accounts are outdated the moment they are completed, and so much has occurred in recent years that had yet to be put into the context of an ad history, I felt it was past time to do so. And, finally, I wanted pictures, as I mentioned in the introduction. Most historical treatments include only a handful of pictures, unless they cover just a few years. My idea was that this should be more like a museum, where seeing is believing, Seeing can provide a better understanding, too. Even if you had heard there were slavery ads in past centuries, seeing the real thing can help you envision what newspaper readers of that time experienced. This was important to me.

I also should mention that I found, and still find, some historical treatments to be, well, not as reader-friendly as they might be. That's a challenge, of course, when you're not writing a murder mystery or a love story, but I have tried to make this fairly readable. I hope you agree. Please feel free to let me know what you think.

By the time you read this, of course, it will be out of date. But the nice thing about history is that it doesn't change (though some interpretations might). I've tried my best to cover the first 300,000 years. I'll let someone else write about the next 300,000, but I think it will need more pages.

Notes

CHAPTER 1. ADVERTISING ARCHAEOLOGY: WHERE TO BEGIN?

1. My description is based on modern sciences. If you believe the earth is only six thousand years old, of course, advertising plays a much grander role in history.

2. Special thanks to Pierre-Jean Texier for providing a photograph of part of his discovery for inclusion in this book.

3. This quote, from 2014, no longer appears on the bank's site at https://www.nbbmuseum.be.

4. Special thanks to Dr. Almásy for all the effort put into researching this claim.

CHAPTER 2. FROM LATE BCE TO EARLY CE

1. An immense "thank you" is owed to the Louvre in Paris, for providing access to this artifact, and especially to Sophie Padel-Imbaud, curator, who gave generously of her time and expertise as I researched this item.

2. Special thanks to Dr. Qingjiang Yao for suggesting this addition.

3. This sign can be found at the Museo Archeologico Nazionale di Napoli.

4. This sign, too, can be found at the Museo Archeologico Nazionale di Napoli.

5. Special thanks to Dr. Qingjiang Yao, yet again, for calling my attention to this.

CHAPTER 3. THE DARK AGES OF ADVERTISING

1. This is from folio 8r, from MS. e. Mus. 198*. The other pieces are in folios 5r, 6r, and 7r. Special thanks to the staff of Oxford's Bodleian Library for their wonderful assistance in identifying and photographing this section.

CHAPTER 4. EMERGING FROM THE DARK

1. Also, various sources identify different dates and uses for terms. For consistency, I rely primarily on Merriam-Webster's wonderful "Time Traveler" word database.

2. Nathaniel Butter published the *Weekly Newes* and Thomas Archer published *A continuation of the weekely newes*. They were business partners who became competitors (Shaaber 1932).

3. Prior to the nineteenth century, the "long s," which resembles an "f" today, was a common lowercase "s" in newsprint.

4. *The Tatler* also invented the concept of "frequency rate," a discount for running an ad multiple times.

5. An ad did precede this one in Franklin's magazine, but it was Franklin's own ad soliciting advertisers, so it was not a "paid" ad.

6. Jean d'Arras (1491). *De schoone historie van Melusina.* Antwerp: Gheraert Leeu. There is some speculation that today's Starbuck's coffee logo mermaid is from another depiction of Melusina.

7. Price (1895) provides far more detail than I can include here about some old London signs.

8. This entire catalog is available on Google Books.

9. https://founders.archives.gov/documents/Franklin/01-02-02-0114.

10. For those unfamiliar with old British currency (and it can be rather confusing), 2 farthings = 1 halfpenny, 2 halfpennies (or halfpence) = 1 penny, 240 pennies = 1 pound. The farthing and halfpenny are now obsolete, and today there are 100 pennies to a pound.

11. Full text can be found at https://quod.lib.umich.edu/e/eebo2/A54214.0001.001/1:1?rgn=div1;view=fulltext.

12. A complete set of these cards is in the collection of the New York Public Library.

CHAPTER 5. SOME SEVENTEENTH- AND EIGHTEENTH-CENTURY ADVERTISEMENTS

1. A "mountebank" is a charlatan or swindler.

2. The three samples are omitted here, for brevity.

CHAPTER 6. THE RESULT OF REVOLUTIONS

1. They didn't start at that time, since the white rabbit character was used in China around 1200 CE.

CHAPTER 7. NINETEENTH-CENTURY METHODS AND MEDIA

1. One mention suggests Charles F. Scripps preceded Tayler by three years, but this claim remains unsupported.

2. It is complicated by the fact that today Warwick Court is north of Newgate Street, across from Chancery Lane, while it appears the Warwick Court of 1786 was in a location that today is called Warwick Square. A City of London building stands on that spot in 2019. To confuse it further, today that is across the street from a courthouse called, yes, Warwick Court.

3. Schuwer (1966) suggests that the first newspaper to do this was *La Presse,* in France, and implies it was decades earlier, but I have not been able to verify this claim.

4. From the US Postal Service creed.

5. The *New York Times,* front page, January 26, 1913.

6. Some stamps had a slightly different message, "Use Pears Soap." One scholar has labeled those as fakes (Wiseman 1984).

7. Several sources claim this, but without details. There was no good way to print a photo in a newspaper then, so it is unclear how Cornelius accomplished this feat. It wasn't impossible, but I have not found definitive proof.

8. Robertson claims this ad is at the Southern Historical Collection, University of North Carolina at Chapel Hill.

9. In "The Dancing Academy," Dickens describes "an animated sandwich composed of a boy between two boards."

10. One ad history book was earlier, by Larwood & Hotten, but it focused on signboards alone. The version I cite here is 1875, but their book originally was 1866, before Sampson.

CHAPTER 9. THE TWENTIETH-CENTURY ADVERTISING EXPLOSION AND BEYOND

1. While there is a difference between circulation, subscriptions, and paid subscriptions, most newspaper industry statistics are sloppy about those distinctions. Consequently, I don't dwell on it, either.

CHAPTER 10. INDUSTRY PEOPLE, AGENCIES, AND CHANGES

1. New Zealanders attended a conference in Australia in 1920.

CHAPTER 11. THE SCIENCE OF ADVERTISING

1. "Basic" was a computer language used at the time.

CHAPTER 12. CRITICISM, LAW, AND POLICY

1. For more background on this Act, see discussion of the Copeland Bill in Chapter 9.

2. *The New York Times Advertising Acceptability Manual*, 2015, appears at https://nytco-assets.nytimes .com/m/ADVERTISING-ACCEPTABILITY-2015.pdf.

3. The ABC Television Network Advertising Standards and Guidelines, 2016, is at https://abcallaccess .com/app/uploads/2017/01/Advertising-Guidelines-2016.pdf.

CHAPTER 14. NEWEST MEDIA AND METHODS

1. Again, most of these dates are found in *Merriam-Webster*'s "Time Traveler" database.

2. In Great Britain, it wasn't until 1919 that their equivalent, the National Association of British Display Men, was formed.

CHAPTER 15. LIVING IN A VIRTUAL WORLD

1. I don't distinguish between social media and social networks (Edosomwan et al. 2011). My meaning is an online location for making, maintaining, or facilitating social relationships.

2. The 2009 Family Smoking Prevention and Tobacco Control Act ended this.

3. Where.com applied for this patent five years earlier, but it wasn't granted until 2010.

4. It used the form of text messaging called Short Message Service (SMS).

CHAPTER 16. ADS AND CULTURE

1. Ries (2015) argues that a slogan positions a brand, but a tagline seldom does. I disagree, but these two terms are used interchangeably by most practitioners. Taglines tend to be at the end of the ad, but slogans can be as well. A strapline is really just another name for a tagline. Slogan tends to be a broader, more inclusive term, so I'll use that.

2. The Howdy Doody puppet on this button was the original. A dispute with the puppet designer resulted in a new, less creepy design. Unveiled in June 1948, the new puppet was used for many years.

Bibliography

44 Liquormart v. Rhode Island, 517 U.S. 484 (1996).

Ahmed, Mukhtar (2014). Ancient Pakistan: An Archaeological History, Volume IV. *Harappan Civilization, Theoretical and the Abstract*. Foursome Group.

Ainsworth, William Harrison (1856). *New Monthly Magazine*, vol. 107. London: Chapman & Hall.

Akerman, John Yonge (1849). *Tradesmen's Tokens, Current in London and Its Vicinity Between the Years 1648 and 1672*. London: John Russell Smith.

Akst, Jef (2013). The Elixir Tragedy, 1937. *The Scientist*, May 31, accessed at https://www.the-scientist.com/foundations/the-elixir-tragedy-1937-39231.

Albarda, Maarten (2018). The End of 15% Agency Commission? *MediaPost*, September 21, accessed at https://www.mediapost.com/publications/article/325449/the-end-of-15-agency-commission.html.

Albarran, Alan B. (2009). *The Handbook of Spanish Language Media*. New York, NY: Routledge.

Amos, J. (2012). Red Dot Becomes "Oldest Cave Art." BBC News, June 15, accessed at http://www.bbc.com/news/science-environment-18449711.

Anonymous (1901). The First Full-Page Ad. *The Fourth Estate*, No. 360, January 19, p. 7.

Anonymous (1909). Artemas Ward Leaves Sapolio Company. *Retail Grocers Advocate*, May 21, pp. 10–11.

Anonymous (1914). *Advertising and Postal Publicity: Library of Business Practice, Vol. III*. London: Shaw Publishing.

Anonymous (1935). Ancient Egyptian Message Found on Temple Wall. *Popular Science*, October, p. 37.

Anonymous (2001). Archaeologists Find World's Earliest Paper Package Ads. *People's Daily*, July 24, accessed at http://en.people.cn/200107/24/eng20010724_75682.html.

Anonymous (2007). Getting the Message, at Last. *The Economist*, December 13, accessed at https://www.economist.com/node/10286400/print?story_id=10286400.

Anonymous (2016). A Brief History of the Sign Industry. Accessed at https://www.linkedin.com/pulse/brief-history-sign-industry-dps-world-digital-printing-and-signage/.

Appel, Marsha (2017a). Defining Moments in Agency History | Evolution of Media Unbundling. American Association of Advertising Agencies. Accessed at https://www.aaaa.org/evolution-media-unbundling/.

Appel, Marsha (2017b). Defining Moments in Agency History | Agencies Join the Ticker Tape Parade. American Association of Advertising Agencies. Accessed at https://www.aaaa.org/agencies-join-ticker-tape-parade/.

Appel, Marsha (2017c). Defining Moments in Agency History | Madison Avenue: Place or Mindset? American Association of Advertising Agencies. Accessed at https://www.aaaa.org/madison-avenue-place-or-mindset/.

Applegate, Edd (1998). *Personalities and Products: A Historical Perspective on Advertising in America*. Westport, CT: Greenwood Press.

Applegate, Edd (2012). *The Rise of Advertising in the United States: A History of Innovation to 1960*. Lanham, MD: Scarecrow Press.

Aransiola, Adebayo (2017). History of Advertising in Nigeria Since 1960 Till Date. *Introduction to Advertising*. Accessed at https://samleadek.wordpress.com/tag/introduction-to-advertising/.

Astor, Maggie (2017). Dove Drops an Ad Accused of Racism. *New York Times*, October 8, p. B2.

Atkinson, Claire (2016). NYers Could Soon Make Bank Just by Wrapping Their Cars in Ads. *New York Post*, January 29, accessed at https://nypost.com/2016/01/29/nyers-could-soon-make-bank-just-by-wrapping -their-cars-in-ads/.

Baglee, Christopher, & Andrew Morley (1988). *Street Jewellery: A History of Enamel Advertising Signs*. London: New Cavendish Books.

Barklow, E. J. (1922). History of Calendar Advertising. *Associated Advertising*, April, pp. 32, 35.

Barnes, Trevor J. (2013). Big Data, Little History. *Dialogues in Human Geography*, 3(3), pp. 297–302.

Barrès-Baker, M. C. (2006). An Introduction to the Early History of Newspaper Advertising. Brent Museum and Archive occasional publications, No. 2.

Barsanti, Sam (2016). The USSR's First TV Commercial Was a Socialist Take on Wet Hot American Summer. *A.V. Club*, August 17, accessed at https://news.avclub.com/the-ussr-s-first-tv-commercial-was-a -socialist-take-on-1798250746.

Bates, Charles Austin. *Short Talks on Advertising*. New York, NY: Charles Austin Bates Press, 1898.

Bates v. State Bar of Arizona, 433 U.S. 350 (1977).

Baume, Matt (2020). This Year's Superbowl Ads Are Making History for LGBTQ+ Inclusivity. *Them*, January 31, accessed at https://www.them.us/story/superbowl-2020-lgbtq-ads.

Beard, Fred K. (2005). One Hundred Years of Humor in American Advertising. *Journal of Macromarketing*, 25(1), pp. 54–65.

Beard, Fred K. (2017). The Ancient History of Advertising: Insights and Implications for Practitioners. *Journal of Advertising Research*, September, pp. 239–44.

Beare, Margaret E. (2012). *Encyclopedia of Transnational Crime and Justice*. Thousand Oaks, CA: Sage.

Bekiempis, Victoria (2019). New Knees and Tourist Selfies: OJ Simpson on Life Post-Prison in Las Vegas. *The Guardian*, June 10, accessed at https://www.theguardian.com/us-news/2019/jun/10/oj-simpson-says -post-prison-life-playing-golf-in-las-vegas-is-fine.

Bennett, Peter D., ed. (1995). *AMA Dictionary of Marketing Terms*, 2d ed. Lincolnwood, IL: NTC Business Books.

Bigelow v. Virginia, 421 U.S. 809 (1975).

Blake, Eli W. (1860). In B. Silliman, B. Silliman Jr., and James D. Dana, *American Journal of Science and Arts* (aka the *Silliman Journal*), 30, November.

Blancou, J. (2001). A History of the Traceability of Animals and Animal Products. *Scientific and Technical Review*, 20(2), pp. 420–25.

Boardman, John (2003). "Reading" Greek Vases? *Oxford Journal of Archaeology*, 22(1), pp. 109–14.

Bodel, John P. (1983). *Roman Brick Stamps in the Kelsey Museum*. Ann Arbor, MI: University of Michigan Press.

Bond, Jonathan, & Richard Kirshenbaum (1998). *Under the Radar: Talking to Today's Cynical Consumer*. New York, NY: John Wiley & Sons.

Bond, Sarah W. (2016). *Trade & Taboo: Disreputable Professions in the Roman Mediterranean*. Ann Arbor, MI: University of Michigan Press.

Borrell Associates (2015). *The Changing Face of Co-Op Programs: A White Paper*. Sponsored by Netsertive, August, Williamsburg, VA.

Bosarge, Alexandra B. (2015). *The Impact of the Civil Rights Movement on the Advertising Industry.* Honors Thesis, Paper 326, University of Southern Mississippi.

Bouchoux, Deborah E. (2009). *Intellectual Property: The Law of Trademarks, Copyrights, Patents and Trade Secrets.* Clifton Park, NY: Delmar Cengage Learning.

Bourbon, Fabio, ed. (2001). *Lost Civilizations: Rediscovering the Great Cultures of the Past.* Vercelli, Italy: White Star.

Braine, Theresa (2019). Grocery Owner Charged with Skimming More Than $300G in Coupons. *New York Daily News*, February 13, accessed at https://www.nydailynews.com/news/national/ny-news-pittsburgh -coupons-embezzle-theft-grocery-20190213-story.html.

Britnell, R. H. (2001). Specialization of Work in England, 1100-1300. *The Economic History Review*, 54(1), pp. 1–16.

Browne, Ray B., & Lawrence A. Kreiser Jr. (2003). *The Civil War and Reconstruction.* Westport, CT: Greenwood Press.

Brownlee, John (2006). A Brief History of Smell-O-Vision. *Wired*, December 7, accessed at https://www .wired.com/2006/12/a-brief-history-2-2/.

Bruce, Bill (2009). SunnyD Creates A Peel 'n' Taste Sensory Experience. *Foodbev Media*, August 3, accessed at https://www.foodbev.com/news/sunny-ds-peel-n-taste-sensory-experience/.

Brumfield, Dale M. (2019). The Blessings of Radium Water Made His Head Disintegrate. *Medium*, March 15, accessed at https://medium.com/lessons-from-history/the-blessings-of-radium-water-made-his-head -disintegrate-3ac052cb8620.

Bryson, Steve, David Kenwright, Michael Cox, David Ellsworth, & Robert Haimes (1999). Visually Exploring Gigabyte Data Sets in Real Time. *Communications of the ACM* 42(8), pp. 83–90.

Bunting, Henry S. (1925). *Specialty Advertising—The New Way to Build Business.* Waukegan, IL: Novelty News Press.

Calkins, Earnest Elmo, & Ralph Holden (1912). *Modern Advertising.* New York, NY: D. Appleton and Company.

Cameron, Glen T., Kuen-Hee Ju-Pak, & Bong-Hyun Kim (1996). Advertorials in Magazines: Current Use and Compliance with Industry Guidelines. *Journalism & Mass Communication Quarterly*, 73(3), pp. 722–33.

Carson, Gerald (1961). *One for a Man, Two for a Horse.* New York, NY: Bramhall House.

Cartwright, Mark (2018). Medieval Heraldry. *Ancient History Encyclopedia*, May 22, accessed at https:// www.ancient.eu/Medieval_Heraldry/.

Case, Andrew N. (2015). "The Solid Gold Mailbox": Direct Mail and the Changing Nature of Buying and Selling in the Postwar United States. *History of Retailing and Consumption*, 1(1), pp. 28–46.

Casey, Thom (2013). The History of Advertising Signs: Petroglyphs to Present Day. *Tex Visions*, September 30, accessed at https://www.texvisions.com/history-of-advertising-signs.

Central Hudson Gas and Electric v. Public Service Commission of New York, 447 U.S. 557 (1980).

Chamberlain, Henry (1770). *A New and Compleat History and Survey of the Cities of London and Westminster, The Borough of Southwark, and Parts adjacent; From the Earliest Accounts, to the Beginning of the Year 1770.* London: J. Cooke.

Chappell, Bill (2015). Jared Fogle Sentenced to 15 Years in Prison for Sex with Minors, Child Pornography. NPR, November 19, accessed at https://www.npr.org/sections/thetwo-way/2015/11/19/456622271/jared -fogle-to-learn-sentence-for-sex-with-minors-child-pornography.

Christopher, Maurine (1963). Desegregate Ads, TV, Lever Tells Agencies. *Advertising Age*, 34(33), August 12, p. 1.

Chrystal, Paul (2016). *In Bed with the Ancient Greeks.* Stroud, Gloucestershire, England: Amberley.

Church, Alfred John (1886). *The Story of Carthage*. New York, NY: Putnam's Sons.

City of Ladue v. Gilleo, 114 S.Ct. 2038 (1994).

Clark, Eric (1988). *The Want Makers: Inside the World of Advertising*. New York, NY: Penguin Books.

Clarke, D. H. "Nobby" (1983). This Is Not Yachting. *Cruising World*, May, pp. 93–95.

Clarke, George T. (1970). *Transit Advertising*. New York, NY: Transit Advertising Association.

Coen, Robert J. (2009). Coen Structured Advertising Expenditure dataset v.1.15. Accessed at https://docs .google.com/spreadsheets/d/1gUKzS-AKs8dqCntYJs0ot3Rmgr1KWeUHEFmYuo5F3W8/edit#gid=0.

Cohen, Jennie (2012). A Brief History of Bloodletting. *History*, May 30, accessed at https://www.history .com/news/a-brief-history-of-bloodletting.

Cone, Fairfax M. (1969). *With All Its Faults: A Candid Account of Forty Years in Advertising*. Boston, MA: Little, Brown.

Cook, Karla (2016). A Brief History of Online Advertising. *HubSpot*, accessed at https://blog.hubspot.com /marketing/history-of-online-advertising.

Cooley, Alison E., & M. G. L. Cooley (2004). *Pompeii and Herculaneum: A Sourcebook*. New York, NY: Routledge.

Coolsen, Frank G. (1947). Pioneers in the Development of Advertising. *Journal of Marketing*, 12(1), pp. 80–86.

Cox, Jim (2008). *Sold on Radio: Advertisers in the Golden Age of Broadcasting*. Jefferson, NC: McFarland.

Craddock, Ashley (1997). Spamming Lawyer Disbarred. *Wired*, July 10, accessed at https://web.archive.org /web/20041231030825/http://www.wired.com/news/politics/0%2C1283%2C5060%2C00.html.

Cramer, Maria (2020). Johnson & Johnson Says It Will Stop Selling Skin-Whitening Products. *New York Times*, June 20, p. A18.

Crane, Ben (n.d.). A Brief History of Trade Cards. Accessed at http://www.tradecards.com/articles/history /history.html.

Crawford, Robert (2008). Advertising. *The Dictionary of Sydney*. Accessed at https://dictionaryofsydney.org /entry/advertising#ref-uuid=2723d092-b638-85e0-d7c2-60cc007e8b9d.

Cruikshank, Jeffrey L., & Arthur W. Schultz (2010). *The Man Who Sold America: The Amazing (But True!) Story of Albert D. Lasker and the Creation of the Advertising Century*. Boston, MA: Harvard Business Review Press.

Curran, Catharine M., & Jef I. Richards (2000). The Regulation of Children's Advertising in the U.S. *International Journal of Advertising & Marketing to Children*, 2(2), pp. 139–54.

Curran, Catharine M., & Jef I. Richards (2004). The Complex Web of Regulation in the US: The Case of Privacy. *International Journal of Electronic Business*, 2(2), pp. 205–26.

Curran-Kelly, Catharine, and John P. Workman (2007). "It's Not My Father's University": Balancing the Role of Markets, Educational Institutions, and Society's Interests in Education. Unpublished manuscript, University of Massachusetts-Dartmouth.

Curth, Louise Hill (2006). *From Physick to Pharmacology: Five Hundred Years of British Drug Retailing*. Burlington, VT: Ashgate.

Cutlip, Scott M., & Brent Baker (2012). A Brief History of Public Relations: The Unseen Power. In Caywood, Clarke L., *The Handbook of Strategic Public Relations and Integrated Marketing Communications*, 2nd ed. New York, NY: McGraw-Hill.

Czinkota, Michael R. et al. (2000). *Marketing: Best Practices*. Orlando, FL: Dryden Press.

Dahl, Stephan (2014). The Rise of Pride Marketing and the Curse of "Pink Washing." *The Conversation*, August 26, accessed at https://theconversation.com/the-rise-of-pride-marketing-and-the-curse-of-pink -washing-30925.

Davies, Anjuli, Soyoung Kim, & Leila Abboud (2014). Battle for Control Destroyed $35-billion Omnicom-Publicis Merger. *Reuters*, May 8, accessed at https://www.reuters.com/article/us-omnicom-group-publicis

-groupe/battle-for-control-destroyed-35-billion-omnicom-publicis-merger-idUSBREA4713R20140509
?feedType=RSS&feedName=businessNews.

Dedovic, Milica (2019). Blockchain: The Hero Digital Advertising Truly Needs? *Business 2 Community*,
September 2, accessed at https://www.business2community.com/online-marketing/blockchain-the-hero
-digital-advertising-truly-needs-02235427.

Di Palma, Salvatore (2015). *The History of Marks from Antiquity to the Middle Ages*. Paris: Société des
Ecrivains.

Diaz, Ann-Christine (2019). Best of 2019: Skittles' Broadway Musical was a Big F.U. to Advertising (and Also
an Ad). *Advertising Age*, January 28, accessed at https://adage.com/creativity/work/best-2019-skittles
-broadway-musical-was-big-fu-advertising-and-also-ad/970156.

Donohue, Julie (2006). A History of Drug Advertising: The Evolving Roles of Consumers and Consumer
Protection. *Milbank Quarterly*, 84(4), pp. 659–99.

Doyle, Charles (2011). *Oxford Dictionary of Marketing: The One-Stop Guide for Marketeers*. New York, NY:
Oxford University Press.

Duffy, Clare (2019). Hallmark Channel Faces Backlash after It Pulled Ads Featuring Same-Sex Couples.
CNN, December 15, accessed at https://www.cnn.com/2019/12/15/business/hallmark-same-sex-adver
tisement-backlash/index.html.

Duhigg, Charles (2012). How Companies Learn Your Secrets. *New York Times Magazine*, February 16, accessed
at https://www.nytimes.com/2012/02/19/magazine/shopping-habits.html?_r=1&hp=&pagewanted=all.

Dukesmith, Frank Hutchinson, Adrian W. McCoy, Worthington C. Holman, & F. H. Hamilton (1904).
Three Natural Fields of Salesmanship. *Salesmanship*, 2(1).

Dunn, Andrew (2019). Pharma DTC Spending Outpaces Rest of Medical Marketing, JAMA study finds.
BioPharmaDive, January 7, accessed at https://www.biopharmadive.com/news/pharma-dtc-spending
-outpaces-rest-of-medical-marketing-jama-study-finds/545441/.

Dvorkin, Lewis (2015). Inside Forbes: The Next Step in Our BrandVoice Native Ad Platform. *Forbes*, February 17, accessed at https://www.forbes.com/sites/lewisdvorkin/2015/02/17/inside-forbes-the-next-step
-in-our-brandvoice-native-ad-platform/#54960d4c422a.

Dvorsky, George (2018). Humans Didn't Evolve from a Single Ancestral Population. *Gizmodo*, accessed at
https://gizmodo.com/humans-didn-t-evolve-from-a-single-ancestral-population-1827483838.

Dyer, George L. (1905). What a Man Has Done—Being a Brief Sketch of the Career of Ralph Tilton, Advertising Manager of the Butterick Trio—His Ideas, Beliefs, and Achievements. *Profitable Advertising*,
15, pp. 264–67.

Dynel, Marta (2011). *The Pragmatics of Humour across Discourse Domains*. Philadelphia-Amsterdam: John
Benjamins.

Eckhardt, Giana M., & Anders Bengtsson (2010). A Brief History of Branding in China. *Journal of Macromarketing*, 30(3), pp. 210–21.

Eckhardt, Hella (2018). The Archaeology of Roman Literacy. A talk to the Berkshire Archaeological Society on January 20, as reported by Janet Sharpe, accessed at http://www.berksarch.co.uk/index.php/the
-archaeology-of-roman-literature/.

Editors of Advertising Age (1976). *How It Was in Advertising: 1776–1976*. Chicago, IL: Crain Books.

Editors (2016). The World's Oldest Writing. *Archaeology*, May/June, accessed at https://www.archaeology
.org/issues/213-1605/features/4326-cuneiform-the-world-s-oldest-writing.

Edosomwan, Simeon, Sitalaskshmi Kalangot Prakasan, Doriane Kouame, Jonelle Watson, & Tom Seymour
(2011). The History of Social Media and Its Impact on Business. *Journal of Applied Management and
Entrepreneurship*, 16(3), pp. 79–91.

Edwards, Jim (2009). The Tiger Woods Sponsor Deathwatch: AT&T, Gillette, Accenture Waver; Nike Digs in Heels. *CBS News*, December 13, accessed at https://www.cbsnews.com/news/the-tiger-woods-sponsor-deathwatch-at038t-gillette-accenture-waver-nike-digs-in-heels/.

Edwards, Phil (2016). The Hidden War over Grocery Shelf Space. *Vox*, November 22, accessed at https://www.vox.com/2016/11/22/13707022/grocery-store-slotting-fees-slotting-allowances.

Eff, Elaine (2013). *The Painted Screens of Baltimore: An Urban Folk Art Revealed*. Jackson, MS: University Press of Mississippi.

Elejalde-Ruiz, Alexia (2014). For Branding, Many Places Adopt Signature Scents. *Los Angeles Times*, April 18, accessed at http://www.latimes.com/business/la-fi-scent-branding-20140419-story.html.

Ellerbach, John (2004). The Advertorial as Information Pollution. *Journal of Information Ethics*, Spring, pp. 61–75, 100.

Elliott, Blanche B. (1962). *A History of English Advertising*. London: Business Publications.

Elliott, Stuart (1991). For the Clios, a Night to Forget. *New York Times*, June 15, Sect. 1, p. 35.

Elliott, Stuart (1996). Liquor Industry Ends Its Ad Ban in Broadcasting. *New York Times*, November 8, p. A1.

Elliott, Stuart (2000). Coke to Disband In-House Agency That Handles Its Flagship Brand. *New York Times*, p. C1.

Elliott, Stuart (2004). Highlights of Advertising Week. *New York Times*, September 27, p. C12.

Elliott, Stuart (2011). Phyllis K. Robinson, a Top Copywriter, Dies at 89. *New York Times*, January 21, p. A19.

Elliott, Stuart (2012). Renaming the Circulation Overseer. *New York Times*, November 15, p. B2.

Esner, Rachel (2019). "Ateliers d'artistes" (1898): An Advertorial for the "Lady Readers" of the Figaro Illustré. *Early Popular Visual Culture*, 16(4), pp. 368–84.

Evans, Andrew (2016). Is Iceland Really Green and Greenland Really Icy? A Longstanding Rumor Claims the Names Are Bait and Switch. *National Geographic*, June 30, accessed at https://news.nationalgeographic.com/2016/06/iceland-greenland-name-swap/.

Evans, John C. (1992). *Tea in China: The History of China's National Drink*. New York: Greenwood Press.

Ewen, Cecil L'Estrange (1932). *Lotteries and Sweepstakes: An Historical, Legal, and Ethical Survey of Their Introduction, Supression, and Re-establishment in the British Isles*. London: Heath Cranton.

Falk, Dan (2012). More People Were Literate in Ancient Judah Than We Knew. *Mental Floss*, April 11, accessed at http://mentalfloss.com/article/78416/more-people-were-literate-ancient-judah-we-knew.

Febvre, Lucien, & Henri-Jean Martin (1976). *The Coming of the Book: The Impact of Printing 1450–1800*. London: New Left Books.

Feldwick, Paul (2015). *The Anatomy of Humbug: How to Think Differently About Advertising*. Leicestershire, UK: Matador.

Finet, André (1983). *Le Code de Hammurabi. Introduction, traduction et annotations*, 2nd ed. Cerf, Paris.

Fisher, David (1983). *The War Magician*. New York, NY: Coward-McCann.

Fitzharris, Lindsey (2013). The Bloody History Behind the Barber's Pole. *Huffington Post* (UK ed.), March 7, accessed at https://www.huffingtonpost.co.uk/dr-lindsey-fitzharris/the-bloody-history-behind-barbers-pole_b_3537716.html?guccounter=1&guce_referrer_us=aHR0cHM6Ly93d3cuZ29vZ2xlLmNvbS8&guce_referrer_cs=wY1WkgEg_jF9e3j0mh-ysQ.

FitzPatrick, Lauren (2008). Money Squeeze: History of Coupons. *Herald News*, May 29, accessed at https://www.heraldnews.com/x1218083753/Money-squeeze-History-of-Coupons.

Flaws, Bob (1994). *Chinese Medicinal Wines & Elixirs*. Boulder, CO: Blue Poppy Press.

Fletcher, Winston (2008). *Powers of Persuasion: The Inside Story of British Advertising 1951–2000*. New York, NY: Oxford University Press.

Foley, John P., & the Pontifical Council for Social Communications (1997). *The Catholic Church's Handbook on Ethics in Advertising*. February 22, Vatican City.

Foltz, Kim (1990). THE MEDIA BUSINESS: ADVERTISING; Scali Quits Volvo Account, Citing Faked Commercial. *New York Times*, November 14, p. D1.

Foote, Emerson (2014). *The Lost Diary of a Real Mad Man: Tales of Advertising & Mental Health.*, J. I. Richards and B. I. Ross, eds. Pittsboro, NC: American Academy of Advertising.

Foster, Patrick (2011). BBC Apologises for Screening First Advert. *The Telegraph*, July 23, accessed at https://www.telegraph.co.uk/culture/tvandradio/8654970/BBC-apologises-for-screening-first-advert.html.

Foster, G. Allen (1967). *Advertising: Ancient Market Place to Television*. New York, NY: Criterion Books.

Fox, Margalit (2014). Judy Protas, Writer of Slogan for Levy's Real Jewish Rye, Dies at 91. *New York Times*, January 11, p. A22.

Fox, Stephen (1984). *The Mirror Makers: A History of American Advertising and Its Creators*. New York, NY: William Morrow.

Frank, E. H. (1919). Aeroplane Industry in the First Stage of its Advertising Evolution. *Printers' Ink*, 108(4), July 24, pp. 77–80.

Fredericks, Steven J. (2007). *StrADegy: Advertising in the Digital Age*. New York, NY: TNS Media Intelligence.

Frucci, Adam (2010). The Steak-Scented Billboard: Advertising's Stinking Future. *Gizmodo*, June 2, accessed at https://gizmodo.com/the-steak-scented-billboard-advertisings-stinking-futu-5553576.

Fryxell, David A. (2012). History Matters: Mail-order Catalogues. *Family Tree Magazine*, September, accessed at https://www.familytreemagazine.com/premium/history-matters-mail-order-catalogues/.

FTC v. Gratz, 253 U.S. 421 (1920).

FTC v. Raladam, 283 U.S. 643 (1931).

Gale Group (2000). Advertising Industry. *Gale Encyclopedia of U.S. Economic History*. Available at http://shora.tabriz.ir/Uploads/83/cms/user/File/657/E_Book/Economics/GALE.pdf.

Gallo, Max (1972). *The Poster in History*. Rockville, MD: American Heritage Publishing.

Gandhi, Lakshmi (2013). A History of "Snake Oil Salesmen." NPR, August 26, accessed at https://www.npr.org/sections/codeswitch/2013/08/26/215761377/a-history-of-snake-oil-salesmen.

Garber, Megan (2012). The Future of Advertising (Will Be Squirted Into Your Nostrils as You Sit on a Bus). *The Atlantic*, July 26.

Gardner, J. Starkie (1899a). Tradesmen's Signs. *British Architect: A Journal of Architecture and its Accessory Arts*, 51, pp. 429–30.

Gardner, J. Starkie (1899b). The Revival of Tradesmen's Signs. *American Architect and Building News*, pp. 65, 21–23.

Gardner, Victoria E. M. (2016). *The Business of News in England, 1760–1820*. New York, NY: Palgrave MacMillan.

Gellene, Denise (1996). Seagram Bucks Voluntary Ban on TV Advertising with Spot on Cable. *Los Angeles Times*, May 1, accessed at https://www.latimes.com/archives/la-xpm-1996-05-01-fi-64710-story.html.

Gersuny, Carl (1974). Occupations, Occupational Surnames and the Development of Society. *Journal of Popular Culture*, 8(1), pp. 99–106.

Gianatasio, David (2013). Refreshing as Fanta itself: The Latest in Edible Advertising. *Adweek*, February 26, accessed at https://www.adweek.com/creativity/fanta-flavored-print-ad-probably-not-quite-tasty-or-refreshing-fanta-itself-147567/.

Glanton, Dahleen (2005). Coupon Clippers Clean Up. *Chicago Tribune*, May 8, accessed at https://www.chicagotribune.com/news/ct-xpm-2005-05-08-0505080303-story.html.

Godwin, R. Kenneth (1988). *One Billion Dollars of Influence: The Direct Marketing of Politics*. Chatham, NJ: Chatham House.

Gormley, Myra Vanderpool (1987). Many Surnames Built on Occupations. *Los Angeles Times*, September 4, accessed at http://articles.latimes.com/1987-09-04/news/vw-3882_1_american-surnames.

Granville, Kevin (2018). Facebook and Cambridge Analytica: What You Need to Know as Fallout Widens. *New York Times*, March 19, accessed at https://www.nytimes.com/2018/03/19/technology/facebook-cam bridge-analytica-explained.html.

Greenstone, Gerry (2010). The History of Bloodletting. *British Columbia Medical Journal*, 52(1), pp. 12–14.

Griswold v. Connecticut, 381 U.S. 479 (1965).

Groark, Virginia (2000). James D. Powell, 92, Started Black Ad Agency. *Chicago Tribune*, April 14, accessed at https://www.chicagotribune.com/news/ct-xpm-2000-04-14-0004140131-story.html.

Gross, Michelle L. (2010). Advergames and the Effects of Game-Product Congruity. *Computers in Human Behavior*, 26, pp. 1259–65.

Grumbine, E. Evalyn (1939). *Patsy Breaks into Advertising*. New York, NY: Dodd, Mead & Company.

Grumbine, E. Evalyn (1944). *Patsy Succeeds in Advertising*. New York, NY: Dodd, Mead & Company.

Guasco, Michael (2017). The Misguided Focus on 1619 as the Beginning of Slavery in the U.S. Damages Our Understanding of American History. *Smithsonian Magazine*, September 13, accessed at https://www .smithsonianmag.com/history/misguided-focus-1619-beginning-slavery-us-damages-our-understand ing-american-history-180964873/.

Gudis, Catherine (2004). *Buyways: Billboards, Automobiles, and the American Landscape*. New York, NY: Routledge.

Gupta, Seema (2009). *Branding and Advertising*. New Delhi, India: Global India Publications.

Guth, David W., & Charles Marsh (2003). *Public Relations: A Values-Driven Approach*. Upper Saddle River, NJ: Pearson Education.

Hagist, Don N. (2016). *Wives, Slaves, and Servant Girls: Advertisements for Female Runaways in American Newspapers, 1770–1783*. Yardley, PA: Westholme.

Haines, Michael R. (1994). The Population of the United States, 1790–1920 (Historical Paper #56). *NBER Working Paper Series on Historical Factors in Long Run Growth*, June, National Bureau of Economic Research.

Hall, S. Roland (1926). *Theory and Advertising of Advertising*. New York, NY: McGraw-Hill.

Halldin, Olof (2013). *The History of Posters*. National Library of Sweden. Accessed at http://www.kb.se /Docs/collections/history-posters.pdf.

Hammer, Joshua (2015). Finally, the Beauty of France's Chauvet Cave Makes Its Grand Public Debut. *Smithsonian Magazine*, April, accessed at https://www.smithsonianmag.com/history/france-chauvet -cave-makes-grand-debut-180954582/.

Handley, Lucy (2017). Maltesers Uses "Chocolate" Braille on UK Billboard Advertising. CNBC, January 5, accessed at https://www.cnbc.com/2017/01/05/maltesers-uses-chocolate-braille-on-uk-billboard-adver tising.html.

Hastak, Manoj, & Mary J. Culnan (2010). *Online Behavioral Advertising "Icon" Study*. A Report of the Future of Privacy Forum, January 25, accessed at https://fpf.org/wp-content/uploads/2016/06/Ad_Icon_Study.pdf.

Hausknecht, Douglas R., J. G. B. Wilkinson, & George E. Prough (1991). Advertorials: Effective? Deceptive? Or Tempest in a Teapot? *Akron Business and Economic Review*, 22(4), pp. 41–52.

Haveman, Heather A. (2015). *Magazines and the Making of America: Modernization, Community, and Print Culture, 1741–1860*. Princeton, NJ: Princeton University Press.

Hays, Kali (2020). Coronavirus Poised to Be Worse for Advertising, Media Than Last Recession. *WWD*, April 13, accessed at https://wwd.com/business-news/media/coronavirus-business-impact-advertising -media-recession-1203559395/.

Heal, Ambrose (1968). *London Tradesmen's Cards of the XVIII Century: An Account of Their Origin and Use*. New York, NY: Dover.

Hendon, Donald W., & William F. Muhs (1985). Origin and Early Development of Outdoor Advertising in the United States. In *Historical Perspective in Consumer Research: National and International Perspective*, Jagdish N. Sheth and Chin Tiong Tan, eds. Singapore: Association for Consumer Research, pp. 309–13.

Henshilwood, Christopher S., Francesco d'Errico, Karen L. van Niekerk, Laure Dayet, Alain Queffelec, & Luca Pollarolo (2018). *Nature*, September 12, accessed at https://doi.org/10.1038/s41586-018-0514-3.

Herpel, George L., & Steve Slack (1983). *Specialty Advertising: New Dimensions in Creative Marketing*. Irving, TX: Specialty Advertising Association International.

Herzberg, Oscar (1897). The Evolution of Newspaper Advertising. *McBride's Magazine*, 60, pp. 107–12.

Hettinger, Herman S. (1933). *A Decade of Radio Advertising*. Chicago, IL: University of Chicago Press.

Hiatt, Charles (1900). The Posters at the Advertisers' Exhibition. *The Poster*, 4, June, pp. 143–51.

Hicks, Gary (2012). *The First Adman: Thomas Bish and the Birth of Modern Advertising*. Brighton, UK: Victorian Secrets Limited.

Hinckley, David (2017). Showbiz Scandals: The TV Quiz Show and Radio Payola Controversies. *New York Daily News*, August 14, accessed at https://www.nydailynews.com/new-york/showbiz-scandals-tv-quiz -show-radio-payola-controversies-article-1.808513.

Hind, James Fox (1958). The History of Transportation Advertising, 1850–1956, and A Study of Its Importance in Knoxville, Tennessee. Master's Thesis, University of Tennessee. Available at https://trace.tennes see.edu/utk_gradthes/1749/.

H. M. (1961). The Drug Hearings: To No One's Surprise, Kefauver and the AMA Do Not Agree on What Should Be Done. *Science (New Series)*, 134(3472), July 14, pp. 89–90.

Holiday, Steven (2019). *Jack and Jill* Be Nimble: A Historical Analysis of an "Adless" Children's Magazine. *Journal of Advertising*, 47(4), pp. 412–28.

Hong, Ge. Biographies of the Devine Immortals (also known as Shenxian Zhuan), 317–18. Available in Robert F Campany. (2002). *To Live as Long as Heaven and Earth: A Translation and Study of Ge Hong's Traditions of Devine Transcendents*. Berkeley, CA: University of California Press.

Horovitz, Bruce (1987). Women Will Model Bras in TV Ads as Decades-Old Taboo Falls. *Los Angeles Times*, April 21, accessed at https://www.latimes.com/archives/la-xpm-1987-04-21-fi-341-story.html.

Hsu, Tiffany (2018). Racial Slur Leads to Papa John's Founder Quitting Chairman Post. *New York Times*, July 11, accessed at https://www.nytimes.com/2018/07/11/business/papa-johns-racial-slur.html.

Hsu, Tiffany (2019). Ad Giant Wins Over Disney with Big Data Pitch. *New York Times*, October 16, p. 3.

Hsu, Tiffany (2020). "A Seismic Shock": Jittery Companies Pull Back on Ads During Pandemic. *New York Times*, April 4, pg. B1.

Hubbard, Rita C. (1993). Shock Advertising: The Benetton Case. *Studies in Popular Culture*, 16(1), pp. 39–51.

Huhtamo, Erkki (2010). The Sky Is (Not) the Limit: Envisioning the Ultimate Public Media Display. *Journal of Visual Culture*, 8(3), pp. 329–48.

Hutchinson, Lydia (2015). Alan Freed and the Radio Payola Scandal. *Performing Songwriter Magazine*, August 20, accessed at http://performingsongwriter.com/alan-freed-payola-scandal/.

Hutchison, Dorothy Dwight (1939). *Nathalie Enters Advertising*. Boston, MA: Little, Brown.

Jackson, Nicholas (2011). Infographic: The History of Video Advertising on YouTube. *The Atlantic*, August 3, accessed at https://www.theatlantic.com/technology/archive/2011/08/infographic-the-history-of -video-advertising-on-youtube/242836/.

Jenkins, Robert C. (1886). *Heraldry, English and Foreign*. London: Kegan Paul, Trench & Co.

Johnson, Ben (n.d.). Pub Signs of Britain. Historic UK: History and Heritage Accommodation Guide. Accessed at https://www.historic-uk.com/CultureUK/Pub-Signs-of-Britain/.

Johnson, Bradley (2020). Ad Business Cut 36,400 Jobs in April. *AdAge*, May 8, accessed at https://adage.com/article/datacenter/ad-business-cut-36400-jobs-april/2255426.

Johnson, David (2005). Trademarks—A History of a Billion-Dollar Business. *Infoplease*, accessed at https://www.infoplease.com/trademarks-history.

Johnson, Marguerite (2017). The Grim Reality of the Brothels of Pompeii. *The Conversation*, December 12, accessed at https://theconversation.com/the-grim-reality-of-the-brothels-of-pompeii-88853.

Johnson, Samuel (1759). No. 40. The Art of Advertising Exemplified. *The Idler*, January 20, accessed at http://www.johnsonessays.com/the-idler/no-40-art-of-advertising/.

Jones, Duane (1955). *Ads, Women and Boxtops*. Pleasantville, NY: Printers' Ink Books.

Jones, John Philip (1999). *The Advertising Business*. Thousand Oaks, CA: Sage.

Jones, Mary Gardiner (1991). Privacy: A Significant Marketing Issue for the 1990s. *Journal of Public Policy & Marketing*, 10(1), pp. 133–48.

Kahl, William (1961). Five Centuries of Printing in London. A Review Article. *Business History Review*, 35(3), pp. 445–56.

Kak, Subhash C. (1989). Indus Writing. *Mankind Quarterly*, 30(1), pp. 113–18.

Kaput, Mike (2020). AI for Advertising: Everything You Need to Know. *Marketing Artificial Intelligence Institute*, January 8, accessed at https://www.marketingaiinstitute.com/blog/ai-in-advertising.

Kazmi, S. H. H., & Satish K. Batra (2009). *Advertising and Sales Promotion*, 3rd ed. New Delhi: Excel Books.

Keltie, John Scott (1870). *The Works of Daniel Defoe*. Edinburgh: William P. Nimmo.

Kenner, H. J. (1936). *The Fight for Truth in Advertising*. New York, NY: Round Table Press.

Keppie, Lawrence (1991). *Understanding Roman Inscriptions*. Baltimore, MD: Johns Hopkins University Press.

Kern-Foxworth, Marilyn (1994). *Aunt Jemima, Uncle Ben, and Rastus: Blacks in Advertising, Yesterday, Today, and Tomorrow*. Westport, CT: Praeger.

Kerr, G., & J. I. Richards (2020). Redefining Advertising in Research and Practice. *International Journal of Advertising*, DOI: 10.1080/02650487.2020.1769407.

Kesslen, Ben (2020). Aunt Jemima Brand to change name, remove Image That Quaker Says Is "Based on a Racial Stereotype." *NBC News*, June 17, accessed at https://www.nbcnews.com/news/us-news/aunt-jemima-brand-will-change-name-remove-image-quaker-says-n1231260.

Khan, S. U., & O. Mufti (2007). The Hot History and Cold Future of Brands. *Journal of Managerial Sciencie*s, 1(1), pp. 25–87.

Kielbowicz, Richard B. (1993). Origins of the Junk-Mail Controversy: A Media Battle over Advertising and Postal Policy. *Journal of Policy History*, 5(2), pp. 248–72.

Kietzmann, Jan, Jeannette Paschen, & Emily Treen (2018). Artificial Intelligence in Advertising: How Marketers Can Leverage Artificial Intelligence Along the Consumer Journey. *Journal of Advertising Research*, September, pp. 263–67.

Kim, Bong-Hyun, Yorgo Pasadeos, & Arnold Barban (2001). Deceptive Effectiveness of Labeled and Unlabeled Advertorial Formats. *Mass Communication & Society*, 4(3), pp. 265–81.

King, Andy, & David Simpkin (2012). *England and Scotland at War, c. 1296–c.1513*. Boston, MA: Brill.

Klaffke, Pamela (2003). *Spree: A Cultural History of Shopping*. Vancouver, BC: Arsenal Pulp Press.

Kleinfield, N. R. (1991). Targeting the Grocery Shopper. *New York Times*, May 26, Sect. 3, p. 1.

Koren, Marina (2019). A Soda Company's Long Obsession with Outer Space. *The Atlantic*, April 19, accessed at https://www.theatlantic.com/science/archive/2019/04/pepsi-advertisement-space/587608/.

Krashinsky, Susan (2012). Advertising's Newest Ploy? Get Consumers to Make Your Ads. *Globe and Mail*, February 10, p. B6.

Kreshel, Peggy J. (1990). John B. Watson at J. Walter Thompson: The Legitimation of "Science" in Advertising. *Journal of Advertising*, 19(2), pp. 49–59.

Krismann, Carol H. (2005). *Encyclopedia of American Women in Business: From Colonial Times to the Present*. Westport, CT: Greenwood Press.

Kuenstler, Walt (2012). *Myth, Magic, and Marketing: An Irreverent History of Branding from the Acropolis to the Apple Store*. Havertown, PA: Zolexa.

Laible, Myron (1997). Changeable Message Signs: A Technology Whose Time Has Come. *Journal of Public Policy & Marketing*, 16(1), pp. 173–76.

Laird, Pamela Walker (2001). *Advertising Progress: American Business and the Rise of Consumer Marketing*. Baltimore, MD: Johns Hopkins University Press.

Lamb, Charles (1879). *The Complete Works of Charles Lamb: Containing His Letters, Essays, Poems, Etc.* Philadelphia, PA: William T. Amies.

Lant, Karla, & Kelly Morr (2017). The History of Logos. *99designs*. Accessed at https://99designs.com/blog/design-history-movements/the-history-of-logos/.

Larwood, Jacob, and John Camden Hotten (1875). *The History of Signboards, From the Earliest Times to the Present Day*, 8th ed. London: Chatto and Windus, Piccadilly.

Lasker, Albert D., & Robert C. Worstell (2014). *The Untold Story of Advertising*. Columbia, MO: Midwest Journal Press.

Lazzaro, Sage (2017). Archaeologists Just Discovered Some of the Earliest Egyptian Hieroglyphics. *New York Observer*, June 22, accessed at http://ezproxy.msu.edu.proxy2.cl.msu.edu/login?url=https://search-proquest-com.proxy2.cl.msu.edu/docview/1912587538?accountid=12598.

Leeds, Jeff, & Louise Story (2005). Radio Payoffs Are Described as Sony Settles. *New York Times*, July 26, p. A1.

Leighton, Richard J. (1973). Consumer Protection Agency Proposals: The Origin of the Species. *Administrative Law Review*, 25(3), pp. 269–312.

Lewis, Al (2016). "Payola" May Explain Celine Dion. *Denver Post*, May 8, accessed at https://www.denverpost.com/2005/07/25/payola-may-explain-celine-dion/.

Lewis, Paul (1909). Farm Journals Were First in Protecting Subscribers: The Movement to Safeguard Readers Against Fraudulent Advertising Started Many Years Ago with the Big Farm Papers. *Printers' Ink*, March 31, p. 28.

Li, Hongmei (2017). Advertising in China. *Post Series*, 16(1), chapter 3.

Liao, W. K. (1959). *The Complete Works of Han Fei Tzu*, Capt. XXXIV, Outer Songeries of Sayings, The Upper Right Series. Translated by W. K. Liao, accessed at http://www.xinfajia.net/8348.html.

Linmark Associates, Inc. v. Township of Willingboro, 431 U.S. 85 (1977).

Lois, George, with Bill Pitts (1991). *What's the Big Idea? How to Win with Outrageous Ideas (That Sell!)* New York, NY: Doubleday.

Lowinger, Pat (2017). Of Gods, Kings and Men: The Coinage of Antiochus IV. Accessed at https://discoveringancienthistory.wordpress.com/2017/12/16/of-gods-kings-and-men-the-coinage-of-antiochus-iv/.

Lucas, Christopher J. (1994). *American Higher Education: A History*. New York, NY: St. Martin's Press.

MacRury, Ian (2009). *Advertising*. New York, NY: Routledge.

Magnet, Myron (2010). How American Press Freedom Began on Wall Street. *City Journal*, Autumn, accessed at https://www.city-journal.org/html/how-american-press-freedom-began-wall-street-13336.html.

Mahoney, John (2015). A Complete Taxonomy of Internet Chum. *The Awl*, June 4, accessed at https://www.theawl.com/2015/06/a-complete-taxonomy-of-internet-chum/.

Mansoor, Sanya (2020). Starbucks Says It Will "Pause Advertising" on Social Media to "Stop the Spread of Hate Speech." *Time*, June 28, accessed at https://time.com/5860928/starbucks-pause-social-media-advertising-stop-hate-for-profit/.

Marchand, Roland (1985). *Advertising the American Dream: Making Way for Modernity, 1920–1940*. Berkeley, CA: University of California Press.

Marchini, Lucia (2018). New Finds from Pompeii. *Current World Archaeology*, 90, July 19, accessed at https://www.world-archaeology.com/features/new-finds-from-pompeii/.

Marheshwari, Sapna (2020). Sephora Signs "15 Percent Pledge" to Carry More Black-Owned Brands. *New York Times*, June 11, p. B6.

Marshall, Aarian (2016). So Digital Billboard Ads Change with the Speed of Traffic Now. *Wired*, July 29, accessed at https://www.wired.com/2016/07/digital-billboard-ads-change-speed-traffic-now/.

Martins, Chris (2013). The App That Kinda-Sorta Plays Vinyl Through Your Phone. *Spin*, June 20, accessed at https://www.spin.com/2013/06/vinyl-playing-app-digital-promo-kontor-records/.

Mason, Nicholas (2013). *Literary Advertising and the Shaping of British Romanticism*. Baltimore, MD: Johns Hopkins University Press.

Maysh, Jeff (2018). How an Ex-Cop Rigged McDonald's Monopoly Game and Stole Millions. *Daily Beast*, July 28, accessed at https://www.thedailybeast.com/how-an-ex-cop-rigged-mcdonalds-monopoly-game -and-stole-millions.

Mayyasi, Alex, & Priceonomics (2016). How Subarus Came to Be Seen as Cars for Lesbians. *The Atlantic*, June 22, accessed at https://www.theatlantic.com/business/archive/2016/06/how-subarus-came-to-be -seen-as-cars-for-lesbians/488042/.

McChesney, Kathleen (1982). Coupon Fraud: Profiting from "Cents-Off" Coupons. *FBI Law Enforcement Bulletin*, May, Federal Bureau of Investigation.

McCluskey, Megan (2018). 81-Year-Old Town Crier Is Everyone's Favorite New Royal Baby Meme. *Time*, April 23, accessed at http://time.com/5250510/town-crier-announces-royal-baby-memes-reactions/.

McDonough, John, & Karen Egolf (2002). *The Advertising Age Encyclopedia of Advertising*. Chicago, IL: Fitzroy Dearborn.

McGowan, Molly K. (2010). The Unexplored New Medium: Recent Trends in Podcast Advertising. *Elon Journal of Undergraduate Research in Communications*, 1(2), Fall, pp. 97–111.

McLaren, Carrie, & Rick Prelinger (1998). The Convergence of Music and Advertising. *Stay Free!*, 15, Fall.

McLellan, Dennis (2009). Marilyn Chambers Dies at 56; '70s Porn Star and Ivory Snow Model. *Los Angeles Times*, April 14, accessed at https://www.latimes.com/local/obituaries/la-me-marilyn-chambers14 -2009apr14-story.html.

Mencken, H. L. (1948). American Street Names. *American Speech*, 23(2), pp. 81–88.

Mendle, Michael (1995). De Facto Freedom, De Facto Authority: Press and Parliament, 1640–1643. *Historical Journal*, 38(2), pp. 307–32.

Metromedia, Inc. v. City of San Diego, 453 U.S. 490 (1981).

Meyers, Cynthia B. (2011). The Problems with Sponsorship in US Broadcasting, 1930s–1950s: Perspectives from the Advertising Industry. *Historical Journal of Film, Radio and Television*, 31(3), September, pp. 355–72.

Mierau, Christina (2000). *Accept No Substitutes! The History of American Advertising*. Minneapolis, MN: Lerner.

Miller, John C. (1936). *Sam Adams: Pioneer in Propaganda*. Palo Alto, CA: Stanford University Press.

Miracle, Gordon E. (1977). An Historical Analysis to Explain the Evolution of Advertising Agency Services. *Journal of Advertising*, 6(3), p. 24.

Mogel, Leonard (1993). *Making It in Advertising: An Insider's Guide to Career Opportunities*. New York, NY: Macmillan.

Montgomery, Joel (2014). Is Your Brand Selling A Lie? Values-Based Business, December 19, accessed at http://joelrmontgomery.com/category/values-based-business/.

Moore, Karl, & Susan Reid (2008). The Birth of Brand: 4,000 Years of Branding History. *Business History* 4(4).

Moss, Janice Ward (2003). *The History and Advancement of African Americans in the Advertising Industry, 1895–1999*. Lewiston, NY: Edwin Mellen Press.

Moulding, John (2019). Marketers Need TV to Scale Audience-Based Buying, so Broadcasters Must Become Data-Enabled. *Videonet*, January 18, accessed at https://www.v-net.tv/2019/01/18/marketers-need-tv-to -scale-audience-based-buying-so-broadcasters-must-become-data-enabled/.

Mull, Marison (1988). Pepsi Ads to Run on Soviet TV. *Los Angeles Times*, May 6, accessed at https://www .latimes.com/archives/la-xpm-1988-05-06-ca-2868-story.html.

Mullman, Jeremy, & Natalie Zmuda (2009). Coke Pushes Pay-for-Performance Model Urges Industry to Let Shops Profit Only if They Hit Established Targets. *Advertising Age*, April 27, accessed at http://adage .com/article?article_id=136266.

Murchison, Claudius Temple (1919). Resale Price Maintenance. *Studies in History, Economics and Public Law*, 82(1). New York, NY: Columbia University Press.

Murray, William D. (1994). Hertz Says No to O.J. *United Press International*, June 17, accessed at https:// www.upi.com/Archives/1994/06/17/Hertz-says-no-to-OJ/7893771825600/.

Myers, Jack (1993). *Ad Bashing: Surviving the Attacks on Advertising*. Parsippany, NJ: American Media Council.

Myers, Kenneth H. (1960). ABC and SRDS: The Evolution of Two Specialized Advertising Services. *Business History Review*, 34(3), pp. 302–26.

Neff, Jack (2013). Incentives Rise in Agency Compensation Deals, ANA Finds. *Advertising Age*, May 9, accessed at http://adage.com/article/news/incentives-rise-agency-deals-ana-finds/241365/?utm _source=daily_email&utm_medium=newsletter&utm_campaign=adage&ttl=1368700767.

Neff, Jack (2014). Ten Years In, Dove's "Real Beauty" Seems to Be Aging Well. *Advertising Age*, January 22, accessed at https://adage.com/article/news/ten-years-dove-s-real-beauty-aging/291216.

Nelson, Raphael (1941). *Cries and Criers of Old London*. London: Collins.

Nevett, T. R. (1982). *Advertising in Britain: A History*. London: Heinemann.

Newell, Jay, Charles T. Salmon, & Susan Chang (2006). The Hidden History of Product Placement. *Journal of Broadcasting & Electronic Media*, 50(4), pp. 575–94.

Newitz, Annalee (2014). A History of Clickbait: The First 100 Years. *Gizmodo*, February 25, accessed at https://io9.gizmodo.com/a-history-of-clickbait-the-first-100-years-1530683235.

Newman, Daniel (2015). Research Shows Millennials Don't Respond to Ads. *Forbes*, April 28, accessed at https://www.forbes.com/sites/danielnewman/2015/04/28/research-shows-millennials-dont-respond-to -ads/#6a17344b5dcb.

Newman, Lily Hay (2016). America's First TV Ad Cost $9 for 9 Seconds. *Slate*, July 1, accessed at https:// slate.com/business/2016/07/the-first-legal-tv-commercial-aired-on-july-1-1941-for-bulova-watch-co -watch-it.html.

New York Times v. Sullivan, 376 U.S. 254 (1964).

Nicolaides, Becky M. (2006). Radio Electioneering in the American Presidential Campaigns of 1932 and 1936. *Historical Journal of Film, Radio and Television*, 8(2), pp. 115–38.

Norman, Philip (1893). *London Signs and Inscriptions*. London: Elliot Stock.

Norris, James D. (1990). *Advertising and the Transformation of American Society, 1865–1920*. Westport, CT: Greenwood Press.

O'Barr, William M. (2007). Advertising in China. *Advertising & Society Review*, 8(3).

O'Barr, William M. (2008). Children and Advertising. *Advertising & Society Review*, 9(4).

Oberoi, Ankit (2013). The History of Online Advertising. *adpushup*, July 3, accessed at https://www.ad pushup.com/blog/the-history-of-online-advertising/.

O'Boyle, Edward J., & Lyndon E. Dawson Jr. (1992). The American Marketing Association Code of Ethics: Instructions for Marketers. *Journal of Business Ethics*, 11(12), pp. 921–32.

O'Connor, Thomas S. (2012). Intellectual Property in the Managerial Portfolio: Its Creation, Development, and Protection. New York, NY: Business Expert Press.

O'Guinn, Thomas C., Chris T. Allen, & Richard J. Semenik (2000). *Advertising*, 2nd ed. Cincinnati, OH: South-Western College Publishing.

O'Hern, Matthew S. (2013). The Empowered Customer: User-Generated Content and the Future of Marketing. *Global Economics and Management Review*, 18(1), pp. 22–30.

Ohralik v. Ohio State Bar Association, 436 U.S. 447 (1978).

Oklahoma Broadcasters Association v. Crisp, 636 F. Supp. 978 (1985).

O'Neill, Patrick (2014). 20 Years Before It Was Cool to Cast Gay Couples, Ikea Made This Pioneering Ad. *Adweek*, October 30, accessed at https://www.adweek.com/creativity/20-years-it-was-cool-cast-gay-couples-ikea-made-pioneering-ad-161054/.

Oppenheim, A. Leo (1967). *Letters from Mesopotamia: Official, Business, and Private Letters on Clay Tablets from Two Millenia*. Chicago, IL: University of Chicago Press.

O'Reilly, Lara (2015). The Inventor of Adblock Tells Us He Wrote the Code as a "Procrastination Project" at University—and He's Never Made Money from It. *Business Insider*, July 14, accessed at https://www.businessinsider.com/interview-with-the-inventor-of-the-ad-blocker-henrik-aasted-srensen-2015-7.

Oremus, Will (2013). Google's Big Break. *Slate*, October 13, accessed at https://slate.com/business/2013/10/googles-big-break-how-bill-gross-goto-com-inspired-the-adwords-business-model.html.

Oswald, John Clyde (1917). *Benjamin Franklin, Printer*. Garden City, NY: Doubleday, Page & Company.

O'Toole, John (1981). *The Trouble with Advertising*. New York, NY: Chelsea House.

Page, Edward T. (1904). *Fowler's Publicity, Volume II*. London: Publicity Publishing Company.

Pappas, Stephanie (2013). Pompeii "Wall Posts" Reveal Ancient Social Networks. *LiveScience*, accessed at https://www.livescience.com/26164-pompeii-wall-graffiti-social-networks.html.

Parry, Sara, Rosalind Jones, Philip Stern, & Matthew Robinson (2013). "Shockvertising": An Exploratory Investigation into Attitudinal Variations and Emotional Reactions to Shock Advertising. *Journal of Consumer Behaviour*, 12(2), pp. 112–21.

Parsons, Patrick R. (1996). Two tales of a city: John Walson, Sr., Mahanoy city, and the "founding" of cable TV. *Journal of Broadcasting & Electronic Media*, 40(3), pp. 354–65.

Perelló-Oliver, Salvador, & Clara Muela-Molina (2019). The Use of Radio Advertorials in Spanish Radio Stations. *Palabra-Clave*, 22(3), pp. 1–25.

Pertschuk, Michael (1982). *Revolt Against Regulation: The Rise and Pause of the Consumer Movement*. Berkeley, CA: University of California Press.

Peterson, Tim (2015). See the First 360-Degree Video Ads on Facebook. *AdAge*, November 12, accessed at https://adage.com/article/digital/360-degree-video-ads-facebook/301314.

Petrie, W. M. Flinders (1900). *The Royal Tombs of the Earliest Dynasties, Part 1*. London, England: Egypt Exploration Fund.

Pettengill & Co. (1897). *Pettengill & Co.'s Newspaper Directory*, 5th ed. Boston, MA: F. E. Bacon & Co.

Petty, Ross D. (2013). From Puffery to Penalties: A Historical Analysis of US Masked Marketing Public Policy Concerns. *Journal of Historical Research in Marketing*, 5(1), pp. 10–26.

Petty, Ross D. (2016). A History of Brand Identity Protection and Brand Marketing. In *The Routledge Companion to Marketing History*, D. G. Brian Jones and Mark Tadajewski, eds. New York, NY: Routledge.

Petty, Ross D. (2018). The US Battle Against Brand Marketing: Circa 1930–1980. *Journal of Historical Research in Marketing*, 10(1), pp. 60–85, https://doi.org/10.1108/JHRM-03-2017-0008.

Pfizer, Inc., 81 F.T.C. 23 (1972).

Pike, A. W. G., D. L. Hoffman, M. Garcia-Diez, P. Pettitt, J. Alcolea, R. DeBalbin, C. Gonzalez-Sainz, C. de las Heras, J. A. Lasheras, R. Montes, & J. Zilhao (2012). U.Series Dating of Paleolithic Art in 11 Caves in Spain. *Science*, 336, issue 6087, pp. 1409–13.

Pittsburgh Press v. Human Relations Commission of Pittsburgh, 413 U.S. 376 (1972).

Pollay, Richard W. (1985). The Subsiding Sizzle: A Descriptive History of Print Advertising, 1900–1980. *Journal of Marketing*, 49(3), pp. 24–37.

Pomranz, Mike (2018). This Tiny Record Player Plays Oreo Cookies . . . Kinda. *Food & Wine*, November 19, accessed at https://www.foodandwine.com/news/oreo-cookie-record-player.

Pongsapitaksanti, Piya (2010). A Comparison of Thai and Japanese Advertising Industries. *Japanese Studies Journal*, accessed at https://www.tci-thaijo.org/index.php/japanese/article/view/51804/42924.

Pop, Madalina Ruxandra (2018). A Study of Personal Advertisements in Romania. *Journal of Romanian Literary Studies*, 13, pp. 834–46.

Pope, Daniel (1983). *The Making of Modern Advertising*. New York, NY: Basic Books.

Posadas de Puerto Rico v. Tourism Company, 478 U.S. 328 (1986).

Post Office Department (1912). *Report of the Third Assistant Postmaster General*. December 1, Washington, DC: Government Printing Office.

Potts, Daniel Thomas (2018). Personal email to the author.

Potts, Daniel T. (1981). The Potter's Marks of Tepe Yahya. *Paléorient*, 7(1), pp. 107–22.

Presbrey, Frank (1929). *The History and Development of Advertising*. Garden City, NY: Doubleday, Doran & Company.

Preston, Ivan L. (1975). *The Great American Blow-Up: Puffery in Advertising and Selling*. Madison, WI: University of Wisconsin Press.

Price, F. G. Hilton (1895). The Signs of Old Fleet Street to the End of the Eighteenth Century. *Archaeological Journal*, 52, pp. 348–91.

Printers' Ink (1938). *Printers' Ink: A Journal for Advertisers—50 Years*. New York, NY: Printers' Ink Publishing Company.

Putnam, George Haven (1898). *Books and Their Makers in the Middle Ages*. New York, NY: Knickerbocker Press.

Random House (1997). *Webster's College Dictionary*. New York, NY: Random House.

Ranly, Donald P. (1976). Action for Children's Television, Freedom of Information Report No. 364. Freedom of Information Center, Columbia, Missouri.

Raymond, Joad (1996). *The Invention of the Newspaper: English Newsbooks 1641–1649*. London: Oxford University Press.

Reed v. Town of Gilbert, 576 U.S. ___ (2015).

Reed, Christopher (1999). The Damn'd South Sea. *Harvard Magazine*, May–June.

Reese, William J. (2000). "Public Schools and the Elusive Search for the Common Good." In *Reconstructing the Common Good in Education: Coping with Intractable Dilemmas*, Larry and Dorothy Shipps Cuban, eds. Stanford: Stanford University Press.

Reyes, David (1998). Latino Leader Calls for Taco Bell Boycott. *Los Angeles Times*, July 14, accessed at http://articles.latimes.com/1998/jul/14/business/fi-3450.

Richards, Jef I. (1987). Clearing the Air About Cigarettes: Will Advertisers' Rights Go Up in Smoke? *Pacific Law Journal*, 19, pp. 1–70.

Richards, Jef I. (1990). *Deceptive Advertising: Behavioral Study of a Legal Concept*. Hillsdale, NJ: Lawrence Erlbaum Associates.

Richards, Jef I. (1991). FTC or NAAG: Who Will Win the Territorial Battle? *Journal of Public Policy and Marketing*, 10(1), pp. 118–32.

Richards, Jef I. (1996). Politicizing Cigarette Advertising. *Catholic University Law Review*, 45(4), pp. 1147–212.

Richards, Jef I. (1997). Is 44 Liquormart a Turning Point? *Journal of Public Policy and Marketing*, 16(1), pp. 156–62.

Richards, Jef I., & Catharine M. Curran (2002). Oracles on "Advertising": Searching for a Definition. *Journal of Advertising*, 31(2), Summer, pp 63–77.

Richards, Jef I., and Laleah Fernandez (2014). Private Information in the Age of Online Behavioral Advertising. Presented at the Australian Association of Social Marketing 2014 International Social Marketing Conference, Melbourne, Australia, July 17.

Richards, Jef I., and Billy I. Ross (2014). *Advertising Education Around the World*. Pittsboro, NC: American Academy of Advertising.

Richards, Jef I., Ellen A. Wartella, Cynthia Morton, & Lisa Thompson (1998). The Growing Commercialization of Schools: Issues and Practices. *ANNALS of the American Academy of Political and Social Science*, 557, pp. 148–63.

Richards, Jef I., & Richard Zakia (1981). Pictures: An Advertiser's Expressway Through FTC Regulation. *Georgia Law Review*, 16, pp. 77–134.

Rickards, Maurice (1971). *The Rise and Fall of the Poster*. New York, NY: McGraw-Hill.

Ries, Laura (2015). Slogans vs. Taglines: What Is Your Brand's Battlecry? *AdAge*, November 11, accessed at https://adage.com/article/cmo-strategy/slogans-taglines-brand-s-battlecry/301217.

Riggs, Tom (2015). *Gale Encyclopedia of U.S. Economic History*. Farmington Hills, MI: Gale Group.

Rivers, Hugh W. (1929). *Ancient Advertising and Publicity*. Chicago, IL: Kroch's.

Rivkin, Steve, & Fraser Sutherland (2004). *The Making of a Name: The Inside Story of the Brands We Buy*. New York, NY: Oxford University Press.

Robb, John, Ernestine S. Elster, Eugenia Isetti, Christopher J. Knüsel, Mary Anne Tafuri, & Antonella Traverso (2015). Cleaning the dead: Neolithic ritual processing of human bone at Scaloria Cave, Italy. *Antiquity*, 89(343), pp. 39–54.

Robertson, Kellie, & Michael Uebel (2004). *The Middle Ages at Work*. New York, NY: Palgrave MacMillan.

Robertson, Patrick (2011). *Robertson's Book of Firsts: Who Did What for the First Time*. New York, NY: Bloomsbury.

Rokicki, John (1987). Advertising in the Roman Empire. *Whole Earth Review*, 54, pp. 84–87.

Roling, R. W. (2011). *Advertising Amsterdam: The Rise and Growth of an International Advertising Industry*. Amsterdam: Universiteit van Amsterdam.

Roman, Kenneth (2009). *The King of Madison Avenue: David Ogilvy and the Making of Modern Advertising*. New York, NY: St. Martin's Press.

Roser, Max, & Esteban Ortiz-Ospina (2018). Literacy. OurWorldInData.org, accessed at https://ourworldindata.org/literacy.

Ross, Billy I., & Jef I. Richards (2008). *A Century of Advertising Education*. Beachwood, OH: American Academy of Advertising.

Rotfeld, Herbert J. (2001). *Adventures in Misplaced Marketing*. Westport, CT: Quorum Books.

Rothenberg, Randall (1989). Madison Ave. Quits Madison Ave. *New York Times*, February 2, p. D1.

Rothenberg, Randall (1990). Y.&R. Pleads Guilty in Bribe Case. *New York Times*, February 10, Sect. 1, p. 33.

Rowell, George Presbury (1906). *Forty Years an Advertising Agent, 1865–1905*. New York, NY: Printers Ink Publications.

Rowse, Edward J., & Louis J. Fish (1943). *Fundamentals of Advertising (War Department Education Manual—EM 730)*. Madison, WI: South-Western Publishing Company.

Rowsome, Frank (1959). *They Laughed When I Sat Down*. New York, NY: Bonanza Books.

Rowsome, Frank (1965). *The Verse by the Side of the Road: The Story of the Burma-Shave Signs and Jingles with All 600 of the Roadside Rhymes*. New York, NY: Penguin Books.

Russell, C. P. (1921). How to Write a Sales-Making Letter. *Printers' Ink*, June 2, pp. 49–56.

Russell, Thomas H. (1937). *Advertising Methods and Mediums*. England: Oxford Institute.

Russell, Karen Miller, & Carl O. Bishop (2009). Understanding Ivy Lee's Declaration of Principles: U.S. Newspaper and Magazine Coverage of Publicity and Press Agentry, 1865–1904. *Public Relations Review*, 35, pp. 91–101.

Sale, Jonathan (2002). The first colour advert. *The Guardian*, October 6, accessed at https://www.theguardian.com/media/2002/oct/07/mondaymediasection2.

Sales, José Das Candeias (2012). The Smiting of the Enemies Scenes in the Mortuary Temple of Ramses III at Medinet Habu. *Journal of Oriental and Ancient History* 1, pp. 85–116.

Sampson, Henry (1874). *History of Advertising from the Earliest Times*. London: Chatto and Windus, Piccadilly.

Samuel, Lawrence R. (2001). *Brought to You By: Postwar Television Advertising and the American Dream*. Austin, TX: University of Texas Press.

Samuel, Lawrence R. (2012). Thinking Smaller: Bill Bernbach and the Creative Revolution. *Advertising & Society Review*, 13(3), accessed at https://muse.jhu.edu/article/491080.

Sandage, Charles H. (1998). *Advertising as a Social Force*. Champaign, IL: Stipes.

Sawyer, Samuel (1900). *Secrets of the Mail-Order Trade*. New York, NY: Sawyer Publishing Company.

Schmeisser, Elmar, Kimberly A. Pollard, and Tomasz Letowski (2013). *Olfaction Warfare: Odor as Sword and Shield*. Army Research Laboratory, March, ARL-SR-0258, accessed at http://www.arl.army.mil/arlreports/2013/ARL-SR-0258.pdf.

Schoettle, Anthony (2007). Billboards Enter Digital Era: High-Tech Signs Are Big Business Nationally, but Regulations Prevent Their Use in Indianapolis. *Indianapolis Business Journal*, 28(36), p. A3.

Schonfeld, Erick (2010). Where Is Awarded the "Mother of All Geofencing Patents." *TechCrunch*, December 22, accessed at https://techcrunch.com/2010/12/21/where-geofencing-patent/.

Schroeder, Lauryn (2015). Almost 200 Banner Planes Have Crashed. *San Diego Union-Tribune*, August 9, accessed at https://www.sandiegouniontribune.com/news/data-watch/sdut-banner-planes-2015aug09-story.html.

Schultz, E. J. (2012). Hard Time: Liquor Advertising Pours into TV. *Ad Age*, May 14, accessed at https://adage.com/article/news/hard-time-liquor-advertising-pours-tv/234733.

Schultz, E. J. (2016). The Final "Crash": How Doritos' "Crash the Super Bowl" contest changed advertising and what's next for the snack brand. *Advertising Age*, 87(1), January 11, p. 21.

Schuwer, Philippe (1966). *History of Advertising*. London: Leisure Arts.

Schwab, Frank (2016). Hertz Made Advertising History with O.J. Simpson's Airport Runs. *Yahoo! Sports*, June 13, accessed at https://ca.sports.yahoo.com/blogs/nfl-shutdown-corner/hertz-made-advertising-history-with-o-j--simpson-s-airport-runs-140015008.html.

Schwartz, Barry (2010). Google AdSense Using Search History in Contextual Matching. *Search Engine Land*, February 11, accessed at https://searchengineland.com/google-adsense-using-search-history-in-contextual-matching-35955.

Scott, Carole E. (2000). The History of the Radio Industry in the United States to 1940. Economic History Association, in *Infrastructure and Services, A Historiographical and Bibliographical Guide*, by David O. Whitten and Bessie E. Whitten, pp. 55–101. https://eh.net/encyclopedia/the-history-of-the-radio-industry-in-the-united-states-to-1940/.

Scott, Dylan (2015). The Untold Story of TV's First Prescription Drug Ad. *Stat*, December 11, accessed at https://www.statnews.com/2015/12/11/untold-story-tvs-first-prescription-drug-ad/.

Scott, James (1895). Shopkeepers' Advertising Novelties. *Strand Magazine*, 10, November, pp. 505–11.

Scott, Walter Dill (1902). The Psychological Value of the Return Coupon. *Mahin's Magazine*, July, pp. 14–18.

Seidel, K. H., Edmund E. Kelly, & James B. Lowery (1958). *Essentials of Outdoor Advertising*. New York, NY: Association of National Advertisers.

Seitel, Fraser P. (2004). *The Practice of Public Relations*, 9th ed. Upper Saddle River, NJ: Pearson Education.

Sender, Katherine (2017). The Gay Market Is Dead, Long Live the Gay Market. *Advertising & Society Quarterly*, 18(4), accessed at https://muse.jhu.edu/article/684249.

Sessions, Ralph (1996/97). The Image Business: Shop and Cigar Store Figures in America. *Folk Art*, 21, Winter, pp. 54–60.

Shaaber, Matthias A. (1932). The History of the First English Newspaper. *Studies in Philology* 29(4), pp. 551–87.

Sharma, Neelam (2004). Oldest Harappan signboard at Kutch township. *Times of India*, February 19, accessed at https://timesofindia.indiatimes.com/city/chandigarh/Oldest-Harappan-signboard-at-Kutch-township/articleshow/505144.cms.

Sheasby, Geoff (2014). Pocklington Town Criers—A History. *Pocklington Post*, May 23, accessed at https://www.pocklingtonpost.co.uk/news/your-article-pocklington-town-criers-a-history-1-6633996.

Sherefkin, Jack (2012). Literacy—What Is It Good For? New York Public Library. Retrieved from https://www.nypl.org/blog/2012/03/19/literacy-what-it-good-for.

Simpson, A. W. B. (1985). Quackery and Contract Law: The Case of the Carbolic Smoke Ball. *Journal of Legal Studies* 14(2), June, pp. 345–89.

Sivulka, Juliann (1998). *Soap, Sex, and Cigarettes: A Cultural History of American Advertising*. Belmont, CA: Wadsworth.

Sivulka, Juliann (2001). *Stronger Than Dirt: A Cultural History of Advertising Personal Hygiene in America, 1875 to 1940*. Amherst, NY: Humanity Books.

Sloane, Leonard (1972). Advertising: One Industry Award. *New York Times*, August 29, p. 50.

Sloane, Leonard (1990). Electronic "Coupons": Savings but No Scissors. *New York Times*, April 21, Sect. 1, p. 48.

Smith, Clayton Lindsay (1923). *The History of Trade Marks*. New York, NY: Thomas H. Stuart.

Smothers, Ronald (1992). Soldier of Fortune Magazine Held Liable for Killer's Ad. *New York Times*, August 19, p. A18.

Sobel, Russell S. (2002). Public Health and the Placebo: The Legacy of the 1906 Pure Food and Drugs Act. *Cato Journal*, 21(3), pp. 463–79.

Solomon, Stephen (1981). The Controversy over Infant Formula. *New York Times*, December 6, Sect. 6, p. 92.

Somaiya, Ravi (2015). The Times Partners With Google on Virtual Reality Project. *New York Times*, October 21, p. B4.

Spake, Deborah F., Giles D'souza, Tammy Neal Crutchfield, & Robert M. Morgan (1999). Advertising Agency Compensation: An Agency Theory Explanation. *Journal of Advertising*, 28(3), pp. 53–72.

Spring, Joel (1992). *Images of American Life: A History of Ideological Management in Schools, Movies, Radio, and Television*. Albany, NY: State University of New York Press.

Stampler, Laura (2012). The 13 Worst Celebrity Endorsement Fails. *Business Insider*, January 31, accessed at https://www.businessinsider.com/the-13-worst-celebrity-endorsement-fails-2012-1.

Starčević, Slađana (2015). The Origin and Historical Development of Branding and Advertising in the Old Civilizations of Africa, Asia and Europe. *Marketing*, 46(3), pp. 29–46.

Starch, Daniel (1914). *Advertising: Its Principles, Practice, and Technique*. Chicago, IL: Scott, Foresman and Company.

Starch, Daniel (1926). *Principles of Advertising*. New York, NY: A.W. Shaw Company.

Stead, Deborah (1997). Corporate Classrooms and Commercialism. *New York Times*, January 5, p. A4.

Stearns, Bertha-Monica (1930). The First English Periodical for Women. *Modern Philology*, 28(1), pp. 45–59.

Stein, Sadie (2009). Mad Men, Indeed: The "Real" Don Draper is Somewhat Disturbing. *Jezebel*, August 5, accessed at https://jezebel.com/mad-men-indeed-the-real-don-draper-is-somewhat-dist-5330713.

Sterchi, Karen L. (1985). Restraints on Alcoholic Beverage Advertising: A Constitutional Analysis. *Notre Dame Law Review*, 60(4), pp. 779–99.

Stole, Inger L. (2006). *Advertising on Trial: Consumer Activism and Corporate Public Relations in the 1930s.* Urbana, IL: University of Illinois Press.

Stolte, Keith M. (1997). How Early Did Anglo-American Trademark Law Begin? An Answer to Schechter's Conundrum. *Fordham Intellectual Property, Media and Entertainment Law Journal*, 8(2), pp. 505–47.

Strachan, John (2007). *Advertising and Satirical Culture in the Romantic Period.* Cambridge, UK: Cambridge University Press.

Struck, Peter (2010). Greatest of All Time: Lifestyles of the Rich and Famous Roman Athletes. *Lapham's Quarterly*, August 2.

Stump, Scott (2013). Cheerios Ad with Mixed-Race Family Draws racist Responses. *Today*, June 3, accessed at https://www.today.com/news/cheerios-ad-mixed-race-family-draws-racist-responses-6C10169988.

S.U.N.Y. v. Fox, 492 U.S. 469 (1989).

Swisher, Kara (1993). Targeting the Gay Market. *Washington Post*, April 25, accessed at https://www.washingtonpost.com/archive/business/1993/04/25/targeting-the-gay-market/439a211e-ddf4-4a8e-8dac-85af9ac3ffe5/.

Taggart, David Richard (1977). The Traditional Ban on Advertising by Attorneys and the Expanding Scope of the First Amendment. *Louisiana Law Review*, 38(1), pp. 258–78.

Tantner, Anton (2009). Addressing the Houses: The Introduction of House Numbering in Europe. *Histoire & Mesure*, 24(2), pp. 7–30.

Taylor, Charles R. (1997). A Technology Whose Time Has Come or the Same Old Litter on a Stick? An Analysis of Changeable Message Billboards. *Journal of Public Policy & Marketing*, 16(1), pp. 179–86.

Taylor, Charles R., Thomas A. Claus, & Susan L. Claus (2005). *On-Premise Signs as Storefront Marketing Devices and Systems.* South Bend, IN: Signage Foundation.

Taylor, Sol (2006). Coins Used for Advertising. *The Signal*, July 22. Available at https://scvhistory.com/scvhistory/signal/coins/sg072206-coins.htm.

Tedlow, Richard S., & Geoffrey G. Jones (1993). *The Rise and Fall of Mass Marketing.* New York, NY: Routledge.

Texier, Pierre-Jean, Guillaume Porraz, John Parkington, Jean-Philippe Rigaud, Cedric Poggenpoel, Christopher Miller, Chantal Tribolo, Caroline Cartwright, Aude Coudenneau, Richard Klein, Teresa Steele, and Christine Verna (2010). A Howiesons Poort tradition of engraving ostrich eggshell containers dated to 60,000 years ago at Diepkloof Rock Shelter, South Africa. *Proceedings of the National Academy of Sciences*, April 6, 107(14), pp. 6180–85.

Thompson, Susan (2004). *The Penny Press: The Origins of the Modern News Media, 1833–1861.* Newport, AL: Vision Press.

Tipper, Harry, & George Burton Hotchkiss (1914). *Advertising: A Practical Presentation of the Principles Underlying the Planning of Successful Advertising Campaigns and the Preparation of Advertising Copy, Modern Business Volume IV*. New York, NY: Alexander Hamilton Institute.

Tracy, Marc (2020a). Subscriptions to the *Times* Top 5 Million as Ads Decline. *New York Times*, February 7, p. B3.

Tracy, Marc (2020b). The *New York Times* Tops 6 Million Subscribers as Ad Revenue Plummets. *New York Times*, May 6, accessed at https://www.nytimes.com/2020/05/06/business/media/new-york-times-earnings-subscriptions-coronavirus.html.

Treichler, Paula A. (2014). "When Pirates Feast . . . Who Pays?" Condoms, Advertising, and the Visibility Paradox, 1920s and 1930s. *Journal of Bioethical Inquiry*, 11, pp. 479–505.

Trout, Jack (2008). *In Search of the Obvious: The Antidote for Today's Marketing Mess.* Hoboken, NJ: John Wiley & Sons.

Troxell, Hyla A. (1997). *Studies in the Macedonian Coinage of Alexander the Great* (digital edition), *Numismatic Studies*, 21. New York: American Numismatic Society, accessed at http://numismatics.org/digital library/ark:/53695/nnan174624.

Tsoi, Grace (2016). Wang Hong: China's online stars making real cash. *BBC News*, August 1, accessed at https://www.bbc.com/news/world-asia-china-36802769.

Tungate, Mark (2007). *Adland: A Global History of Advertising*. London and Philadelphia: Kogan Page.

Turcotte, Samuel (1995). *Gimme a Bud! The Feature Film Product Placement Industry*. Master's thesis, University of Texas–Austin.

Turner, E. S. (1953). *The Shocking History of Advertising*. New York, NY: Ballantine Books.

Tuttle, Brad (2010). The History of Coupons. *Time*, April 6, accessed at https://business.time.com/2010/04/06/the-history-of-coupons/.

Twitchell, James B. (1996). *Adcult USA*. New York: Columbia University Press.

Ukers, William Harrison (1922). *All About Coffee*. New York, NY: Tea & Coffee Trade Journal Co.

US Senate (1963). First Session on Competitive and Antitrust Aspects of Joint Advertising Programs by Retailers, and the Nature and Purpose of Advertising Allowances Given to Retailers by Manufacturers and Wholesalers. *Hearing Before the Select Committee on Small Business*, September 11.

U.S. v. Andreadis, 366 F.2d 423 (2d Cir. 1966).

U.S. v. Edge Broadcasting, 509 U.S. 418 (1993).

U.S. v. Johnson, 221 U.S. 488 (1911).

U.S. v. Windsor, 570 U.S. 744 (2013).

Valentine v. Chrestensen, 316 U.S. 52 (1942).

Van Dijk, Stephen Joseph Peter (1956). An advertisement sheet of an early fourteenth-century writing master at Oxford. *Scriptorium*, 10(1), pp. 47–64.

VanHooker, Brian (2015). 9 Spokespeople Who Fell From Grace. *Men's Health*, July 12, accessed at https://www.menshealth.com/trending-news/g19547318/spokespeople-who-fell-from-grace/?slide=9.

Vespe, Frank (1997). High-Tech Billboards: The Same Old Litter on a Stick. *Journal of Public Policy & Marketing*, 16(1), pp. 176–79.

Villeneuve, Suzanne Natascha (2008). Looking at caves from the bottom-up: a visual and contextual analysis of four Paleolithic painted caves in Southwest France (Dordogne). Master of Arts Thesis, Department of Anthropology, University of Victoria.

Virginia Board of Pharmacy v. Virginia Citizens' Consumer Council, 425 U.S. 748 (1976).

Vivian, Herbert (1902). The Hoardings of the Air. *Strand Magazine*, May, p. 507.

Wagner, Charles L. H. (1954). *The Story of Signs: An Outline History of the Sign Arts from Earliest Recorded Times to the Present "Atomic Age."* Boston, MA: Arthur MacGibbon.

Walker, Andrew (2001). *Aspects of Lincoln: Discovering Local History*. South Yorkshire, UK: Wharncliffe.

Wallace-Hadrill, Andrew (1986). Image and Authority in the Coinage of Augustus. *Journal of Roman Studies*, 76, pp. 66–87.

Waller, David S. (2012). "Truth in Advertising": The Beginning of Advertising Ethics in Australia. *Journal of Mass Media Ethics*, 27, pp. 46–56.

Walsh, Claire (1995). Shop Design and the Display of Goods in Eighteenth-Century London. *Journal of Design History*, 8(3), pp. 157–76.

Walsh, Patrick (2014). *The South Sea Bubble and Ireland: Money, Banking and Investment, 1690–1721*. Woodbridge, UK: Boydell Press.

Wang, Amy B. (2017). Nivea's "White Is Purity" Ad Campaign Didn't End Well. *Washington Post*, April 5, accessed at https://www.washingtonpost.com/news/business/wp/2017/04/05/niveas-white-is-purity-ad-campaign-didnt-end-well/.

Wang, Cynthia (2010). Hanes Suspends Charlie Sheen Commercials. *People*, January 6, accessed at https://people.com/crime/hanes-suspends-charlie-sheen-commercials/.

Warner, Melanie (2005). Addenda; Former Ogilvy Executives Sentenced for Overbilling. *New York Times*, July 15, p. C5.

Watson, Burton (1964). *Han Fei Tzu: Basic Writings*. Translated by Burton Watson. New York, NY: Columbia University Press.

Waugh, Alec (1950). *The Lipton Story: A Centennial Biography*. London: Bloomsbury.

Wengrow, David (2008). Prehistories of Commodity Branding. *Current Anthropology*, 49(1), pp. 7–34.

West, Christopher J. (1999). *Marketing Research*. London: MacMillan Press.

Wheeler, H. (1946). *The Miracle of Man*. London: Longacre.

White, Hooper (1995). Thanks, from Bing. *50 Years of TV Advertising, Advertising Age*, Spring, p. 16.

Whiting, J. R. S. (1971). *Trade Tokens: A Social and Economic History*. Great Britain: David & Charles.

Willard, Frances E., Helen M. Winslow, & Sallie Joy White (1897). *Occupations for Women: A Book of Practical Suggestions for the Material Advancement, the Mental and Physical Development, and the Moral and Spiritual Uplift of Women*. Cooper Union, NY: Success Company.

Willard, J., William Tailer, John Clark, & Anna Janney de Armond (1938). Andrew Bradford. *Pennsylvania Magazine of History and Biography*, 62(4), pp. 463–87.

Williamson, Gillian (2016). *British Masculinity in the Gentleman's Magazine, 1731 to 1815*. London: Palgrave Macmillan.

Willoughby, Martin (1992). *A History of Postcards*. London: Bracken Books.

Wiseman, W. A. (1984). *Great Britain: The De La Rue Years, 1878–1910 (Vol. 1)*. London: Bridger and Kay.

Wolpert, Stanley (2000). *A New History of India*, 6th ed. Oxford: Oxford University Press.

Wong, Steven (2018). More Brands Are Turning to In-Game Advertising. *a.list*, September 7, accessed at https://www.alistdaily.com/entertainment/more-brands-are-turning-to-in-game-advertising/.

Wood, James Playsted (1958). *The Story of Advertising*. New York, NY: Ronald Press.

World Association of News Publishers (2015). WorldPressTrends. Accessed at https://www.wan-ifra.org/sites/default/files/field_message_file/250515%20WPT%202015%20Final.pdf.

Yagos, Alberto (2017). When Were Street Names and Numbers First Used, as We Know Them Today? How Were Places Labeled Before? *Quora*, accessed at https://www.quora.com/When-were-street-names-and-numbers-first-used-as-we-know-them-today-How-were-places-labeled-before.

Yakabuski, Konrad (2013). Big Data Should Inspire Humility, Not Hype. *Globe and Mail*, March 4, p. A11.

Ye, Fan (c. 445). *The Book of the Later Han* (also known as Hou Hanshu).

Zanot, Eric J. (1979). The National Advertising Review Board, 1971–1976. *Journalism Monographs*, 59.

Zauderer v. Office of Disc. Counsel, 471 U.S. 626 (1985).

Ziaukas, Tim (2007). E. H. Heinrichs: Profile of a Founding Practitioner. *American Journalism*, 24(2), pp. 35–59.

Zmuda, Natalie (2008). Taste Strips Give Ads a New Flavor. *Advertising Age*, June 2, accessed at https://adage.com/article/news/taste-strips-give-ads-a-flavor/127453/.

Zuckerman, Ethan (2014). The Internet's Original Sin. *The Atlantic*, August 14, accessed at http://www.theatlantic.com/technology/archive/2014/08/advertising-is-the-internets-original-sin/376041/?single_page=true.

Index

Page references for figures are italicized.